Peasants and Proletarians

Peasants and Proletarians

The Struggles
of Third World Workers

Edited by Robin Cohen,
Peter C.W. Gutkind, and Phyllis Brazier

Monthly Review Press
New York and London

Library of Congress Cataloging in Publication Data
Main entry under title:

Peasants and proletarians.

    Bibliography: p. 483.
    1. Underdeveloped areas—Labor and laboring classes—
Addresses, essays, lectures. 2. Underdeveloped areas—
Trade-unions—Addresses, essays, lectures. 3. Under-
developed areas—Peasantry—Addresses, essays, lectures.
I. Cohen, Robin. II. Gutkind, Peter Claus Wolfgang.
III. Brazier, Phyllis.
HD8943.P42   331'.09172'4   79-10020
ISBN 0-85345-421-3
ISBN 0-85345-505-8 pbk.

Monthly Review Press
62 West 14th Street, New York, N.Y. 10011
47 Red Lion Street, London WC1R 4PF

Manufactured in the United States of America

10 9 8 7 6 5 4 3 2 1

Contents

Preface and Acknowledgments

This book originated from discussions between P.C.W.G. and R.C. several years ago. The project we set ourselves then, and which in various ways, scholarly and practical, we are still working on now, was to establish a corpus of shared knowledge and understanding between scholars and activists interested in the study of workers in Africa, Asia, and Latin America, and between workers from the three continents in the advanced capitalist countries and their metropolitan counterparts. This reader is one of the major outcomes of our concern. It establishes a larger canvas for the study and comparison of workers throughout the world than any other volume we are familiar with. The list of references collected under "Further Reading" draws the attention of our readers to the hundreds of detailed monographs and studies of workers in individual countries conducted by many authors.

The twenty-one selections we have collected here represent but a fragment of this wider literature. We have selected items, first, on the basis of their scholarly importance, second, to provide a rough balance between the continents, third, on their political relevance, and finally, on their closeness to the themes that are identified in the five parts of the volume. Each part is provided with a separate editorial comment, while we have tried to identify more general issues in the introduction that opens the volume.

The collection of material for this book has been attended by many difficulties. We were fortunate in that through the good offices of Shirley Joshi of the Birmingham Polytechnic, P.B. was able to join us on a research placement to Birmingham University. There she undertook much of the preliminary work of compiling the bibliography, contacting authors, and securing permissions from publishers. The Faculty of Commerce and Social Science of Birmingham University provided some modest assistance for the large amount of photocopying of otherwise unobtainable items for inclusion in the book or bibliography. But the reader soon ran into a more serious problem—the scattering of the editors. P.B. left Britain for India and Pakistan, while R.C. departed for the Caribbean. To add to the difficulties of communication, P.C.W.G. had to periodically abandon his academic base in Montreal for examination duties and research in Africa. That the book didn't flounder at this point is because of three reasons.

First, several of our authors gave us some useful support.

Carmen Deere soon provided a revised article and intervened to secure copyright permissions from the Union of Radical Political Economists; Josh DeWind answered a last-minute request to reprint an article promptly and efficiently; Ken Post showed his characteristic generosity in allowing his articles to be used free of charge; Helen Safa tried (though failed) to persuade her publishers to allow a gratis reprinting, while Francisco Zapata gave us a first translation of his own article.

Second, we have to thank our publishers, Judy Ruben, Susan Lowes, and Jules Geller of Monthly Review Press, for their good-will. Jules Geller in particular was asked both to show open-handedness in respect of copyright payments and the patience of Job in respect of the completed manuscript.

Finally, we are in the debt of Selina Cohen who shared in the translation of an article, typed and retyped several articles and editorial contributions, tracked down elusive authors and publishers, and generally provided large doses of enthusiasm and experience to help bring the manuscript to its final shape.

—R.C., P.C.W.G., and P.B.

Introduction

Although this book was not intended as a memorial volume, it comes as something of a surprise to realize that in a few years' time, in 1983 to be precise, it will be the hundredth anniversary of Karl Marx's death. One is jarred because many of Marx's views seem to be both startlingly relevant and even contemporaneous. In his name great states like the USSR and the People's Republic of China have forged their ideologies and now confront their adversaries. National liberation movements in Vietnam, Cambodia, Cuba, Mozambique, Guinea-Bissau, Angola, and currently in Zimbabwe—their fighters carrying guns in one hand and Marxist texts in the other—are defeating the forces of high-technology imperialism, unyielding colonialism, and antediluvian racism. In the advanced capitalist countries Marx's ghost, long thought laid to rest, once again wafted down the streets of Paris in 1968, loomed over the public squares of Madrid, Lisbon, and Rome, and, even now, haunts (intermittently to be sure) the corridors of power and the groves of academe in Washington and London, Paris and California. Are we in the seventies in the midst of one of those crises Marx had held to be endemic to the capitalist mode of production? Will the capitalist machine, overhauled and burnished by Keynes, Roosevelt, and Marshall, be able to absorb the demands of blacks, students, women, and the unemployed through the now-traditional mixture of welfare benefits, cooptation, and cultural hegemony (via the media, the educational system, and the general process of political socialization)?

In some ways the prognosis for the advanced capitalist countries looks good. Their worldwide pretensions have been trimmed and deflated to be sure—France by Algeria, Britain by Suez, the United States by the extraordinary steadfastness of the Vietnamese people. But Western European economies have begun a shaky recovery from the oil, commodity, and monetary crises of the early 1970s. And, more importantly, the working classes in the metropoles (with some notable exceptions in Japan, France, and Italy) appear to be quiescent, if not totally supine, in the face of levels of unemployment, redundancy, and recession (this time combined with inflation) unknown since the 1930s.

Once again left-wing theorists must confront the question of the direction of the revolutionary impulse. Is it, one must ask, by now clear that revolution can only be exported from the periphery into the center? But in what senses can a socialist revolution in a peripheral state succeed while its trade is still embedded in a world market, predominantly controlled by the Western consumer nations? Is one to abandon the metropolitan working class as hopelessly enmeshed in the nexus of embourgeoisement, consumerism, and their parochial, national forms of consciousness? What forms of international and inter-racial working-class action can be realistically expected? These questions are bluntly put because it is our belief that they haven't been firmly enough addressed, let alone answered. While Marx has now secured a new, even a fashionable, reputation in the fields of philosophy, economics, social theory, and aesthetics, somehow he still appears passé, even ridiculous, in his ringing declarations about the workers of the world. Let us for a moment recall the familiar end of the 1848 Manifesto by Marx and Engels:

> Let the ruling classes tremble at a communist revolution. The proletarians have nothing to lose but their chains. They have a world to win.
> *Workingmen of all countries, unite!*

Now this, it may seem, is the stuff for May Day rallies, conferences in Havana, or bedroom posters for Western middle-class children playing ego games with their respectable parents. Or can Marx's rhetoric be dismissed so easily? The fact is that there has been little systematic attempt to examine the shape and characteristics of the working class (indeed, is it one working class or many?) on a worldwide scale. Certainly it is time for a reassessment, for a debunking of myths, for a sharing and pooling of empirical information about workers in all countries, and for the beginning of at least some theoretical speculations. But before examining the nature of workers in the Third World, the forms of consciousness that they express, and the forms of action they are able to undertake to pursue their class interests, it is necessary to challenge certain conventional wisdoms and old assumptions.

Two Current Misconceptions

The first, and perhaps most widely held, misapprehension is that there are few, if any, workers in Africa, Asia, and Latin America. Even thoughtful observers tend to think of the people as "primitive," as primarily rural, as peasants leading their daily lives in much the same manner as they did generations ago.

Prevailing opinion holds to the view that the poor nations are poor because their citizens lack the will to be modern, that they do not embrace the idea of progress, and that they lack the kind of initiative which has made the wealthy nations powerful. Because these nations are not competitive within the modern world economic and political order, their fate is clear: they are destined to supply the industrial world with the agricultural and mineral resources which they have, but often do not control, and which the rich world needs to maintain and increase its own standard of life. It is certainly the case that to obtain these resources Western nations embarked on colonial conquests and put into force a hegemony through which they exercised control over a great part of the world. It was this hegemony, now converted into the contemporary neocolonial relationship, which not only progressively incorporated non-Western nations into the evolving capitalist system but also created a system of stratification on the international level.

But essential to our understanding of the economic, political, and social structures of the poor nations are not only the macro processes of colonialism and imperialism but also the recognition of the uneven penetration of capitalism into the Third World. It is to this process that we must attribute the virtual destruction of the "natural economy" of the preindustrial order, the development of unequal exchange relations, and the siphoning off of the surplus created by local efforts—all of which, with the help of local compradores, contributed to the accumulation of European capital. Equally consequential has been the effect of these developments on the creation of a new social order internal to Third-World countries, the rise of a labor force to produce the wealth, and the subordination of the (new) workers, both rural and urban, to the particular organizational structure and mode of production of mercantile, colonial, and now postcolonial capitalism.

It is true, of course, that the absolute numbers of wage and salaried workers drawn directly into capitalist production in the periphery usually comprise a considerably smaller proportion of the national population compared with that involved in the advanced capitalist countries. So much can be gleaned at a glance from any copy of the *Yearbook of Labor Statistics* issued by the International Labor Office. One must be careful, however, not to miss a recent trend in the diffusion of capitalist industrial enterprises to the peripheral zones, initially in import-substitution industries and more lately (a trend pioneered in Hong Kong, Taiwan, and South Korea) in export-oriented manufacturing. Though it is also clear that "the unemployment problem" is not going to be solved by the instant recipe of export manufacturing now being paraded about the "development" agencies, there is little doubt that we are in the midst of a substantial relocation of industries on a worldwide scale, a trend being orchestrated and led by transnational companies. The working class in the Third World, as normally defined, is thus small, but growing at a significant rate. However, in our view it is not necessary to adopt a restrictive definition of "a working class" in order to understand how surplus value is expropriated in Third-World societies. For *this* is the critical definitional question, not whether workers in the Third World meet some arbitrary criteria drawn up by international bureaucrats in Geneva. As soon as we pose the question in this way, we are drawn to examine the whole spectrum of underclasses drawn into relations of capitalist production, distribution, and exchange. The peasantry is rarely solely engaged in subsistence production; more frequently the products of their labors are specialized and traded via a host of middlemen to local, regional, and international world markets. Moreover, the land is deserted in favor of contract, seasonal, or temporary wage labor. The collapse of subsistence economies in the face of capitalist penetration has led to the growth of a large group of workers who are ambiguously and simultaneously "semiproletarians" and "semipeasants." Women in the rural areas are either engaged both in household and petty commodity production, thus lowering the cost of the reproduction of labor power (see Deere, part 2), or enter directly into manufacturing production, at least for some period of their lives (see Safa, part 5). Large numbers of agricultural or rural proletarians, whose social characteristics have often escaped formalized definition (see Mintz and Post, part 2), act as a concealed source of cheap labor power. The same is true of the so-called unemployed, marginalized segment of the labor force of the burgeoning Third-World cities, whose economic role is better characterized in terms of Marx's "latent," "floating," and "stagnant" sections of the relative surplus population.

A second misconception which we wish to draw attention to, and which is often shared by left-wing theorists, is that revolutions in the Third World are "peasant revolutions." Such a simplification stems from many sources: From the writings (and more often the commentaries on the writings) of practicing revolutionaries themselves—including Mao, Che Guevara, Cabral, and Fanon. From certain widely accepted academic interpretations, particularly those proffered by Barrington Moore and Eric Wolf.[1] And, of course, from the assumption already discussed, that workers are an insignificant social force in Third-World countries. On closer examination, the image of solely peasant-based revolutions fails to convince. Even within the selection of readings presented here, both Post and Mintz show the salience of the political role of urban and rural proletarians in the Caribbean (Post and Mintz, part 2), while Chesneaux describes the growth of revolutionary consciousness among the Shanghai workers (Chesneaux, part 1). Confronting the thesis even more decisively is Clegg's strong attack on Fanon's "peasant interpretation" of the Algerian revolution (Clegg, part 3). Lest we be misunderstood, we do not argue that it is necessary to replace one (newer) orthodoxy with the rigid adherence to an older model of the exclusive authenticity of a proletarian struggle. On the contrary, as reflected in the title of the volume, we see the dominant form of successful political struggle as a constellation of class forces, an alliance and combination of peasants and workers (rural and urban) often cemented together by revolutionary intellectuals and an appropriate revolutionary ideology and organization. At a theoretical level the notion of class alliance is closely argued in a second article by Post, who talks in terms of "a complex articulation among potentially revolutionary classes and strata" (Post, part 3). Perhaps the most satisfying general formulation is that provided by Petras:

> It appears that in most of the socialist revolutions the original impetus, organization, leadership, and ideology of the revolutionary struggle *began* precisely in the more "advanced" sectors of the peripheral economy: in Russia the Petrograd proletariat led by the Bolshevik party; in China in the coastal cities; in Cuba in Havana. In all cases, however, the *success* of the revolution which began in the advanced enclaves depended on joining efforts with the bulk of the social forces (peasants) located in the "backward" areas of the economy.[2]

The Class Structure and Class Consciousness

Certain analytical consequences flow from the widening of our conception of the social forces in play. We must start by re-establishing the utility and relevance of class analysis to the examination of the material conditions, and the economic and political processes, which have stratified societies through time, changed the structure of power and controls, and shaped the patterning of authority and ideology at the corporate level, i.e., at the level of government and state. Conceptually and empirically, class analysis is further rooted in (a) the study of modes of production, (b) the analysis of productive forces, (c) the figuration of relations of production, and (d) in dialectical analysis, i.e., the antagonistic relations contained in the above. While not every author whose work is included in this volume expresses a formal adherence to such a model, it nonetheless underlies the selection of all the articles, which we see, in one form or another, as contributing to the evolution of such a perspective. In particular, the articles document the increasing complexity of the internal stratification of the various countries from which studies have been taken, the attempts to forge alliances and linkages between class forces, and, above all, the ways in which colonial and postcolonial labor has asserted itself in the struggles against the oppression and brutality it has had to face—and continues to meet.

Critical to the formation of the class structure in the Third World is an understanding of the penetration of merchant capitalism and its more recent transformation into industrial capital; of the change from circulation of commodities and services to production on a mass scale; of the transformation from control of the means of distribution and exchange to control of the means of production; and finally of the switch from the appropriation of surplus product to the expropriation of surplus value.

Urban workers in the Third World—as well as their compatriots in the rural areas, the poor peasantry, the landless, and the agricultural wage workers—may all be considered as part of a huge army of labor at the beck and call of an internally entrenched managerial and bureaucratic class, which, in turn, is subject to tight external control and manipulation by the industrialized, rich Western nations. One major problem raised in all the selections is whether we can justifiably, and in fact, view Third-World labor as a true working class, a proletariat, or whether we must assign weight to such categories as subproletariat, rural proletariat, or lumpen. Coupled to this issue of conceptualization and definition, which remains controversial, is the question of how class conscious the workers are, and whether they recognize the dialectic of the class struggle. Do they comprise a true class revealing consistently, or situationally, an *an sich* or a *für sich* syndrome?[3]

The essential issue is not whether there is a proletariat in the low-income countries, because where there is capitalism of any variety, there is some form of proletariat, but rather how contemporary classes have come into being in the complex setting of multiple ethnic and linguistic communities, and how workers in the Third World reveal their class position and class and political consciousness. In some cases we need a historian's skill to identify the origins of class consciousness. Chesneaux, for example, considers much older guild traditions in China as influencing the expression of working-class consciousness (Chesneaux, part 1). Others point to the consciousness and organizational efforts of the peasantry, from whom urban workers, as migrants, were drawn. Hopkins, likewise, takes us back to the late nineteenth century, casting his analysis in a general debate, critical to an understanding of colonial labor, of wage policy and the labor supply, a topic also treated extensively by Deere and Barrera (Hopkins, part 1; Deere, part 2; Barrera, part 4).

As Hopkins argues, the strikes manifested at the early stages of industrialization should not be treated as novel and sudden outbursts of workers' discontent. Rather their roots are anchored in the structure of internal slavery. Angell not only takes us back to an attempt at organizing a National Chilean Workers' Movement in 1893 but, in his effort to expose the early history of unionization, also places these efforts squarely in the history of resistance, brotherhoods, and mutualist societies. Much the same story is told by Clark of Mexico, where the struggles by workers culminated in the establishment of a Department of Labor in 1911 against formidable opposition from, among many, the Catholic Church, which used its tremendous hold over the minds of the people to try to prevent the emergence of any theories which might upset the traditional status of the "lower classes" (Angell, part 1; Clark, part 1). The Mexican case illustrates how a class structure evolved as a result of the country's long and agonizing domination by external capital, despite the events commencing with the 1910 revolution and the failure of the Diaz government to understand the significance of labor unrest.

The transition from peasant to urban worker provides the dominant linkage between precapitalist modes of production and the capitalist mode. But there is no simple transition, as Mintz forcibly argues. He points instead to the internal differentiation of the peasantry under the special conditions and structures operating under peripheral capitalism. This issue is also joined by Deere in her concentration on women in agricultural production (Deere, part 2). However, both peasants and urban workers operate within the matrix of the capitalist modes of production and their accompanying changes in technology, which, as much as anything else, contribute to a clearly defined class structure dominated by managers and owners. In his discussion Mintz raises the proposition, also implied in other selections more directly concerned with urban workers, that class consciousness . . . does not assume certain forms *until* individuals see themselves as defenseless, and thus *individual,* because they have become disengaged from those traditional protections of community, kinship, and personal association that typify an earlier stage of economic history.[4]

While Mintz appears reluctant to come down fully on the side of Marxist class analysis, DeWind has no such problem in his more direct examination of the transition from peasant to miner in Peru (DeWind, part 2). This reveals the declining connection of the latter with the former and a dependency on "the market for consumption goods." He points to the enormous impact which mechanization has had on the structure of the labor force, the creation of a "free labor market" for the skilled workers, and the way in which the mining companies hire outside building and maintenance contractors whose workers are paid far less than the mine laborer, thus reducing their overall labor costs. Like others, DeWind raises the question of whether the "present-day miners should be considered a proletariat in the classical Marxist sense." His answer is explicit, yet offered with some reservations:

The miners are proletarians in that they sell their labor power for wages in order to gain a livelihood, but the term cannot be applied yet to all miners without some qualification. The proletariat socio-economic status of many miners is modified by their access to land, technical skills, and money—each of which can be used to get out of the mines, and return to agriculture or engage in some petty-bourgeois economic activity.[5]

One reason for these aspirations, which are probably widespread among urban workers in the Third World, is the fact that it becomes more difficult year by year for these workers, particularly the unskilled, to live on their earnings, even after wages are raised. Urban workers have developed a high degree of dependency on the capitalist consumer market for their most basic needs. This may well explain why the class struggle appears to take the form of reformism, and often operates within an existing system of economic and political power.

This brings us to a major issue, the distinction, posed by Post, between rebellion and revolution: the intensity of the commitment of workers, both rural and urban, on the one hand to class struggle and a major and radical transformation, or, on the other, to reliance on reformism, patron-client networks, economism, and a consumption orientation. Post concludes that the events of May-June 1938 in Jamaica "were rebellions rather than revolutions," an observation based on the fact that the strikers and demonstrators were demanding only those things which they believed the existing system to be capable of giving them— "higher wages, more work, and more land" (Post, part 2).

Is this generally applicable to most workers' demands in the Third World today and in the recent past? Clearly not, since all we need to consider are the events which have taken place in Angola, Algeria, Mozambique, China, Cuba, Vietnam, and North Korea. To those we must add the workers' support given to the nationalist struggles in India and Africa, which culminated in the overthrow of colonialism. We must also take into account the enormous obstacles, both economic and political, which peasants and urbanites face when they are confronted by all the power available to repressive and racist governments—as our selection dealing with the Durban strikes in South Africa in 1973 so clearly illustrates (Institute for Industrial Education, part 5).

While the thrust and objectives behind strike actions may well be contained by the power available to the state, the state almost invariably treats them as a threat to its authority, i.e., as containing the potential for a revolutionary transformation. This view seems surely to have been in the mind of Governor Henry McCallum in Lagos in 1897, and certainly prevailed in Mexico from 1910 onward. Thus, the distinction between rebellion and revolution hinges as much on the reaction by the state as on the consciousness, motivations, and organizational skills of the workers themselves. This reformulation seems to be supportable in light of the articles by Ramaswamy (India) and Kearney (Sri Lanka). The former draws our attention to the intensity of party commitment among the rank and file, while Kearney analyzes the importance of the political strike. It is also clear that an initial objective, to work within an oppressive structure, can easily transform itself as a basic challenge to it. Worker consciousness is not, of course, homogeneous and without its negative features, as we learn from Ramaswamy. However, Indian trade unions are truly organizations of workers which certainly can and do pose a threat (as they have done repeatedly) to the capitalist state, even when, as is often the case, trade-union unity is brittle. But as Kearney points out, the political strike can be a double-edged weapon which the state can use in an attempt to separate the populace from the workers (Ramaswamy, part 3; Kearney, part 3).

We can turn now to the consideration of the workers' role in two, at least formally constituted, socialist states, Allende's Chile and Algeria. The case of Algeria merits special consideration if only because workers seemed poised at one juncture to transcend defensive struggles and take command of their own work places.

But "self-management" did not meet with much success, primarily because the Algerian revolution was never fully consummated. The workers were unable and unwilling to respond to the new policy, while the administrative cadre was composed of backward-looking lower-middle-class elements, "the petty bourgeoisie of the colonial period." No genuine socialist structure evolved. Workers were expected to show a higher level of socialist consciousness than that which prevailed among the power holders of the Algerian state, and to grasp the meaning and content of class conflict. Instead, all they could hope to respond to was the ever more intense struggle for personal and family survival, a demand which Clegg suggests limited their political and class outlook. To the workers, the state became just another employer and their consciousness ultimately became directed toward a recognition of the power of the state and its bureaucracy (Clegg, part 3). The story Zapata unfolds in the case of the Chuquicamata miners of Chile is, in a sense, also one of disappointed hopes, though this time shared mainly by the politicians of the Unidad Popular, the coalition of left-wing parties that Allende headed. Lacking a secure organizational base themselves, the politicians attributed an unrealistic degree of confidence to the support the miners were supposedly giving them. The miners were not, however, ready to lend their unqualified support, largely, Zapata suggests, because they saw their interests (economic *and* political) in coalescing behind their relatively strongly organized unions, rather than in acting in some vanguardist role for a party whose trajectory was at least uncertain and confused, even when its policies were generally well intentioned (Zapata, part 5).

Peace, by contrast, takes us firmly back to the world of the capitalist postcolonial state in his study of class consciousness among factory workers in Ikeja, Nigeria. He suggests that these workers have a "cognitive map" of their position and that they were "vitally concerned about the success of negotiations with management," whether they were conducted at the national or factory level, and that the workers were "firm in supporting their leaders." Yet Peace, too, is compelled to observe that many factory workers see their actions "as a variant on the normal process of accommodation to the social order" even in a "highly structured conflict situation," i.e., strikes (Peace, part 5). Evidently the workers at Ikeja could and did show solidarity, as did the workers in Durban, despite repeated attempts to divide them, to threaten them, or to bring out the police to harass and injure them. In both contexts, as elsewhere, the workers acted in terms of their own perceived interests, rather than as passive agents in some preordained revolutionary purpose. Despite their subordinate status, and the determination with which they are exploited, workers' solidarity and action, even when not continuous, can be viewed as more than labor protest, more than rebellion, and as mounting a concerted action toward the kind of objectives which can only be achieved through the transformation of the systems which oppress them. That they do not leap instantly into revolution is perhaps a function of the great risks they are expected to take and which few can afford.

A similar theme of survival in the face of crushing adversity is outlined by Safa in her discussion of Puerto Rican women workers. Consciousness, in her formulation, is doubly constrained by class oppression at the work place and sexual repression at home (Safa, part 5). Still it is difficult to imagine more difficult conditions than those confronting the black workers of South Africa. Yet despite the state's notorious brutality and the forces of white racism (often most virulent in white workers), Durban workers staged successful and heroic strikes at enormous risks to themselves. These strikes revealed a particular looseness of structure, a deliberate "protective ambiguity," illustrated by the strikers' refusal to organize themselves under a common banner of leadership. Indeed, the initiative was firmly in the hands of nonunionized African workers, yet the result was "a sense of solidarity and potential power." This alleged "ambiguity," which the workers created, helped them to rise to a greater political and class consciousness, a greater recognition that class consciousness and class struggle are the means of solving those problems which spring from economic deprivation. Their actions revealed the kind of consciousness, an identification with class, which the individual senses when the potential of revolutionary action is the only alternative left. South African workers are probably closer to such action than is generally recognized. In the face of their oppression, what other alternatives are in the long run open to them?

While the colonial governments were forever debating wage and labor policy, African workers also revealed their own perceptions of the work place and employment policies designed to incorporate them into modes of production in which they were forced to become partners in their own exploitation. The colonial masters were never able to make up their minds whether they wanted a stable or fluid labor force, although in the end they generally came down on the side of the pernicious migrant labor system. They feared stabilization, except for the most essential and skilled workers, because they feared the "urban mob."[6]

The African workers' responses to colonial labor policies and conditions revealed a bitter resistance even, as van Onselen points out in his contribution, in the absence of workers' or political organizations (van Onselen, part 1). Workers often withheld their labor, deserted in large numbers, sabotaged equipment; in short, they resisted incorporation which they recognized was not on their terms. In doing so they showed a "self-awareness of their position as exploited workers," which escalated in relation to the intensity of the rapidly developing capital-intensive industry (of mining). But despite their resistance, a story which van Onselen has told in even more fascinating detail elsewhere,[7] they also paid a price, their progressive detachment from their natal communities and all that this implied. The migrant workers of Southern Africa continue to pay the heaviest price of all.

What our selections, from a wide range of colonial and post-colonial capitalist states, have indicated is an enormous range of structures, responses, and adaptations as well as ambiguity, of thrusts which have meant a leap forward, and those which have failed. What is clear is that workers laid down that essential infrastructure for capitalist development which made it possible for the Western nations to obtain the important resources they required. Workers built the roads, the railways and harbors; they provided the miners, the dockworkers, and the railway workers, the public works' laborers and the messengers and cleaners. In doing so they moved from slave and forced labor to so-called free labor. There they became subject to the vagaries of colonial labor policies, the market, and the capitalist labor process, all manipulated to their disadvantage.

The twin processes of peasantization and proletarianization have created too some highly visible casualties—the urban poor, the casual workers, and the petty entrepreneurs, who occupy a particular and highly exposed position in the peripheral economies. They hover constantly between capitalist and noncapitalist modes of production. In this very "murky" sector of the economy the costs of production and reproduction of labor are absorbed in the noncapitalist sector, thus allowing capital to extract a significant portion of its surplus from the frantic efforts of the poor to survive. While the processes of peasantization and proletarianization each have their distinct characteristics, they come together in a unity formed by the class position in which peasants and urban workers find themselves. The class identity of peasants and urbanites may differ in time and situationally. Class identity and various other forms of identity, ethnicity-language-religion-sex, are not necessarily mutually exclusive and incompatible.

Class identity allows workers to fight "against the system," while other forms of adherence may result in divisiveness and fights "within the system." Yet although each situation must be evaluated in terms of the particular historical situation confronting particular workers and peasants, one cannot escape a more general sense of resistance and struggle, a common crucible in which class identity and class awareness are activated and become gelled.

The Possibilities for Internationalism

It is necessary now to turn from a review of the forms of class solidarity and consciousness among workers within Third-World societies to a brief consideration of the conditions confronting migrant and Third-World laborers within metropolitan societies. This, of course, is the other face of the internationalization of capitalist production—the export of capital from the metropoles paralleling, to some degree at least, the import of labor power from the peripheral zones of the capitalist system. This phenomenon is not new, of course. The Irish, as Marx and Engels observed, provided the depressed, politically defenseless colonial labor of the English industrial revolution: the navvies who stood with their ankles in the mud of the railway tracks, roads, and construction sites. Again, before the war (in 1936 to be exact) there were 2.2 million foreign workers in France, the majority of them from French colonial areas. But the pace and volume of immigration to Europe have increased dramatically since World War II, and migrants now form an increasing proportion of the adult work force. According to a recent estimate, in Britain and Germany one in seven manual workers is an immigrant, while in France, Switzerland, and Belgium about 25 percent of the industrial labor force are foreigners.[8] In 1972 there were 4 million foreign workers in France alone. Castells, who reviews the European situation (though concentrating on France), concludes that immigrant labor is a "fundamental element in the economic structure of European capitalism" and that capital can act toward immigrants as though the labor movement did not exist, a circumstance produced by their mobility and, hence, their "limited capacity for organization and struggle and very great vulnerability to repression." He writes:

> The advantage of immigrant labor for capital stems precisely from the specificity of its inferior position in the class struggle, which derives from the legal-political status of immigrants. From the *point*

of view of capital this status can be modified in minor ways, but not transformed, because it is the source of the basic structural role of immigration.[9]

Barerra calls our attention to Chicano and black workers in a major U.S. multinational corporation, analyzing their role in the context of racial inequality and colonial labor theory. His conclusions are basically similar to those drawn by Castells. Minority workers, he shows, fill the least desirable jobs, and such workers, as do many in the Third World, serve as a reserve army of labor—a vast reserve resulting from the busts and booms, the dislocations and fundamental contradictions in monopoly capitalism, stemming both from the periodic economic crises in the industrialized world and the unevenness of capitalist penetration of the Third World (Castells, part 4; Barrera, part 4). It is as if the grim hand of colonial underdevelopment has reached out toward the heart of the metropolis. How else is one to comprehend the desolate, incongruous figures that Adams depicts in her study of the Senegalese workers in Paris or the desperate search for work that drives West Indian laborers to cut cane in the sugarcane fields of Florida (Adams, part 4; DeWind, Seidl, and Shenk, part 4)?

However, a critique of migrant labor cannot, as Castells argues, stop at the level of a moral indictment. For as capitalism has decomposed and fractured the working class into national, occupational, and racial segments, it has also opened out possibilities for cooperation and class solidarity among workers long separated by historical forces beyond their control or comprehension. Immigrants' struggles for political rights, for consideration of their human dignity, for their rights to join and participate in trade unions are therefore part and parcel of a wider struggle against capitalism. So far, to be realistic, it is evident that many metropolitan workers have reacted defensively to the internationalization of capitalist production. Many U.S. workers have only stirred out of their customary national torpor to protest at the export of "American" jobs abroad, while a significant number of their British counterparts have fallen an easy victim to the appeals of racist demagogues. Are we to witness the collapse of proletarian internationalism upon the shoals of racism, as we once, in 1914, witnessed its collapse to the ideologies of jingoism and nationalism? Or are metropolitan workers going to establish bonds of solidarity with migrants at home and their brothers abroad, so as to match the flexibility and adaptability of transnational capital? To this question we can still pose no definitive answer. But we can at least share with our contributors, and hopefully our readers, our conviction that the peasants and workers of the Third World have "stood up" to the forces that oppress them and in so doing have shown the way to their fellow workers in the metropole.

Notes

1. B. Moore, *Social Origins of Dictatorship and Democracy* (Boston: Beacon, 1966); and E. Wolf, *Peasant Wars of the Twentieth Century* (New York: Harper & Row, 1969).
2. J. F. Petras, "New Perspectives on Imperialism and Social Classes in the Periphery," *Journal of Contemporary Asia* 5, no. 3 (1975): 307.
3. For some contending positions, see R. Cohen and D. Michael, "The Revolutionary Potential of the African Lumpenproletariat: A Sceptical View," *Bulletin of the Institute of Development Studies* 5, nos. 2-3 (October 1973); N. Levine, "The Revolutionary Non-Potential of the 'Lumpen': Essence or Technical Deficiency?" ibid., pp. 43–52; R. Kaplinsky, "Myths about the 'Revolutionary Proletariat' in Developing Countries," ibid. 3, no. 4 (August 1971): 15–21; H. Wolpe, "Some Problems Concerning Revolutionary Consciousness," in *The Socialist Register 1970,* ed. R. Miliband and J. Saville (London: Merlin Press, 1970), pp. 251–81.
4. S. W. Mintz, part 2 below, p. 187.
5. J. DeWind, part 2 below, p. 167.
6. P. C. W. Gutkind, *The Emergent African Urban Proletariat,* McGill University Centre for Developing Area Studies, Occasional Paper Series, no. 8 (Montreal, 1974).
7. C. van Onselen, *Chibaro: African Mine Labour in Southern Rhodesia, 1900-1933* (London: Pluto Press, 1976).
8. J. Berger and J. Mohr, *A Seventh Man* (New York: Viking Press, 1975), p. 12.
9. M. Castells, part 4 below, p. 364.

Part 1

Early Forms of Resistance

As a world system, capitalism penetrated most areas of Africa, Latin America, and Asia from the sixteenth century onward. At first, the penetration was confined to trade in commodities and the plunder of precious metals (a contribution vital to the accumulation of European capital). Because exploration and "discovery" were carried out under the aegis of merchant capital, often backed by the monarchies of Europe, there was little incentive to move beyond commerce to industry. The forms of production found in the periphery were left undisturbed, or destroyed in the stampede for loot. Even in the new metropole of Spain, development was retarded. Three centuries of exacting tribute, then mining gold and silver from New Spain (Mexico), did not shake the largely ossified social structure, and Spain failed to seize the opportunity for industrialization that its commanding commercial role made possible. Other bourgeoisies in England and France were not so slow-witted or, what would be more accurate, were in a better position to challenge the reactionary forces of the clergy, monarchy, and feudal aristocracy. The profits of the slave trade and the more general expansion of merchant capital were put to work in the sugar plantations of the Caribbean and later, to even greater effect, in the factories of the core countries themselves.

Within the periphery, the implantation of capitalist social relations was neither a smooth nor a simple process. The very presence of Europeans produced a massive dislocation of economic activities in the hinterland. Whole populations were wiped out (in the Pacific, the Canaries, the Caribbean) or suffered catastrophic population declines (Mexico, Brazil, Peru, Australia) due to European diseases, military brutality, or simply being worked to death. Those that took their place from the best available labor reservoir, western Africa, were set to work, formally under a slave mode of production, but in practice under an order that was established to serve a world market and embodied relations of production (in the allocation of tasks, the supervisory functions, etc.) that were closer to a capitalist mode of production. Though this thesis is, no doubt, a controversial one, it leads to the argument that the Third World's first "proletariat" was nurtured in the plantation economies of Brazil, the Caribbean islands, and the American South. Certainly it is to the peculiar mix of slave and capitalist mode that we must look to find the origins of the distinctive "rural proletariat" described by both Post and Mintz in the second part of this volume.

But we are more immediately concerned in part 1 of the book with the emergence of a proletariat working directly for wages in the capitalist periphery. The origins of such a proletariat show considerable diversity. In some areas technological requirements determined that a stable labor force be created (e.g., with the spread of the patio process, invented in 1557, deep mining for silver, involving a continuous labor process, became possible). Again, when the booty and tribute were exhausted, as in Mexico, it was necessary to deploy manpower on more long-term tasks—clearing land, growing commercial crops like tobacco, working on the haciendas, and so on. Where merchant capital was still predominant and profitable, an infrastructure needed to be built to facilitate and expedite trade. The Shanghai docks (where Chesneaux's article in this section is set) were built on the profits of the opium trade by generations of Chinese laborers. Finally, where colonialism obtained, the colonial powers became fundamentally involved in laying the infrastructure for capitalist development (principally roads, railways, and ports) or providing the political and administrative framework in which foreign-owned mines and plantations could flourish. At first "forced," "compulsory," "political," or "repartimento" labor was used, but the scale and continuous nature of the public works undertaken demanded a stabilized proletariat.

Part 1 of this volume is concerned with the responses of new workers in the periphery to their involvement in a capitalist labor process. While, with Marx, one can agree that such a process is intrinsically and endemically exploitative, the extent of the withdrawal of labor and the violent and often dramatic confrontations with which workers all over the world responded to the conditions that oppressed them have not always been fully appreciated. In the opening article from Chile, Angell shows how the great massacres of the Chilean working class around the turn of the century led first to organized and spontaneous mass assemblies, and then to a spate of organizational endeavors. These varied from "mutualist societies" (self-help groups, mainly among artisans) to resistance societies (important among anarchist-influenced workers), and mancomunales ("brotherhoods," mainly found among the miners and dockers). This flowering of organizations culminated in a nationally organized revolutionary federation of unions, founded as early as 1917.

Almost at the other end of the organizational spectrum, though describing events over the same period, is van Onselen's study of miners in Southern Rhodesia. There, in the closed, brutalizing world of the mining compound, miners were unable to create associations or organizations like trade unions. Yet, so the author forcibly argues, "from the very earliest years of capital-intensive industry, Africans had a well-developed and demonstrable self-awareness of their position as exploited workers." The author shows how protest and class consciousness is to be found in the nooks and crannies of everyday life. Withholding labor and mass desertions became important forms of combination, while the company managers were constrained to try to prosecute workers for "crimes," such as refusing to work, carelessness in handling tools, destroying property, and "impertinence."

The other selection from Africa, by Hopkins, is concerned not with the workers in an extractive industry, but with the proletariat created in Lagos, Nigeria, by the colonial administration itself. The strike the author describes, when three thousand laborers in the Public Works Department came out on strike in 1897, represents a significant "rescue from historical obscurity." It puts an end to the conventional wisdom that class organization and action by the African proletariat have barely begun. Where, unlike in the supervised "total institutions" of the mining compound, it was possible to organize, African workers did so at a very early stage, in this case successfully challenging the British colonial authorities.

The events that Clark describes in Mexico took place some years later, in 1906 and 1907, and involved strikes in the mines at Cananea (where twenty workers were killed by men acting for the U.S. company) and in the textile mills of Puebla and Veracruz. Though Clark's account is marred by her occasional U.S.-centrisms and her tendency to overemphasize the role of intellectuals in the labor movement, her book from which we take our extract, first published in 1934, has stood for many years as a useful and sympathetic account of the origins of the Mexican labor movement.

In the final selection in part 1 we turn to Shanghai, where Chesneaux describes an extraordinarily complex picture. Here, the labor movement stood at the center of a coalition of class forces (including the indigenous bourgeoisie, the students, and the petty bourgeoisie), all of whom opposed the depredation of British and Japanese firms. The richness of Chesneaux's wider study of the 1919-1927 period, the only Western account of the Chinese labor movement of major scholarly importance, can but be glimpsed in the extract we are able to reprint. But even this extract raises fundamental questions concerning the balance and alliance of class forces and the role of the dockworkers (with whom Mao, of course, first worked) in establishing the preconditions for the revolutionary upsurge of the Chinese peasantry.

The Origins of the Chilean Labor Movement

Alan Angell

[The Chilean working class was first organized mainly through mutualist societies, though eventually a revolutionary federation of unions, the Federación Obrera de Chile (FOCh) was formed in 1917. To understand the high level of organization present in Chile, it is necessary to begin the narrative in the 1880s.[1]—Eds.]

The War of the Pacific (1879-1883) and its aftermath had effected considerable changes in the society and economy. Whereas in 1880 in the northern provinces on Antofagasta and Tarapacá there were only 2,848 workers in the nitrate industry, by 1890 this number had increased to 13,060, with a corresponding increase in employment in related port and transport work. By then in the country as a whole the number employed in the nonrural manual labor force had risen by almost 50 percent in a decade, to 150,000 workers.[2] Though money wages were rising in the period 1890-1914, given the rate of inflation it has been estimated that real wages overall were falling.[3] A rapidly depreciating currency was a spur to working-class protest at this time, and one of the first minor working-class parties formed was a party advocating a convertible currency.

The end of the nineteenth century and the beginning of the twentieth witnessed the great massacres of Chilean working-class history: the first general strike of the nitrate workers in Iquique in July 1890, which spread to Valparaíso and was severely repressed by the army; the merchant marine strike in Valparaíso in mid-1903 that started the fight for an eight-hour day and resulted in some forty workers losing their lives; the "red week" in Santiago in October 1905 when many workers were killed in protests against the rising cost of living; the railway workers' strike in 1906 in Antofagasta; and, the most infamous of all, the massacre when between one thousand and three thousand nitrate workers were mown down by the army in a school yard in Iquique in 1907 while protesting against conditions in the mines and the policies of mass dismissals at the onset of recessions in the industry.[4] Estimates of dead and wounded are of course very uncertain, but the pattern

Extracted from Alan Angell, *Politics and the Labor Movement in Chile* (New York and London: Oxford University Press for the Royal Institute of International Affairs, 1972), with the permission of the publisher.

of action seems clear. Worsening conditions brought about mass protest, which provoked quick, brutal army and state repression. The causes of the protests were very similar: intolerance on the part of employers; the "truck system" of payment which meant further abuses by company shops; bias of the authorities favoring employers; appalling working conditions that endangered life.[5] The demands made were often very similar and seem quite modest by present standards: payment in legal tender; freedom to buy from noncompany shops; the right to meet and to form associations; no illegal deductions from salaries; safer working conditions.

The workers' short-term response to oppression and exploitation was unorganized and spontaneous. They seemed to think that a mass assembly would by sheer numbers draw attention to their demands; this and the occasional act of violence exhausted their tactics. Thus, after a massacre in 1908 a labor newspaper berated the working class for its stupidity, lack of purpose, and reliance on violence as its only method.[6]

There were two long-term responses to these working conditions; one was to establish and support a number of reformist and revolutionary political parties; the other was to form unions. There were three sorts of unions—the mutualist societies, important in the artisanal sectors; the "resistance societies" or "unions for the protection of labor," important for the anarchist-influenced workers; and the *mancomunales,* or "brotherhoods," predominant among the northern miners and port workers.

The Mutualist Societies

Mutualist societies started very early in the history of Chilean working-class organization. By 1870, thirteen had been recognized by the government; by 1880, thirty-nine; and by 1924 there were six hundred, with ninety thousand members, apart from those societies that had not sought local recognition.[7]

Their aims were mutual cooperation among members and the provision of a rudimentary social security system that neither state nor employer was likely to provide. Though at first they included only artisans, they seem later to have been organized among other workers. Their relationship with trade unionism was ambivalent. By the educational services they provided and the experience of organization, they trained leaders of more "typical" unions. They themselves under pressure of events could act like unions, but their stated aim was cooperation, not conflict, with employer and state. In their first national congress in 1901 they excluded the resistance societies from membership, and it seems that the congress was held with government support and protection. By this action they made clear their desire to break from the radical working-class groups that had been associated with them, and confirmed the artisanal and cooperative character of the movement. They were linked with the Democratic party rather than with any of the socialist groups, preferring to work inside the law, and susceptible to clerical influences which held that the mutualist societies were the Christian solution to working-class problems. Though the later growth of the societies took place rather separately from the unions, early on at least the two were interconnected. Mutualist societies demonstrated the possibility of organization, they spread ideas, they showed that cooperation could bring benefits, but their organization was intended to serve purposes outside the work place, for their aim was to establish the social position of their members.[8] Unlike the northern working class, they had enjoyed the support and inspiration of middle-class liberals like Santiago Arcos and Francisco Bilboa, who were influenced by mid-nineteenth century European ideas.

Mutualism was not a prehistory of the labor movement. As long as there was a numerous artisanal sector in Chile, the mutualist societies continued, especially until the state began to fulfill some of the basic social security functions originally performed by them. That they influenced the union movement seems to be indicated by the fact that the FOCh started as a mutualist society. At the political level it has been suggested that the society members, lacking a firm socialist ideology, could easily be incorporated into populist movements, such as that of Alessandri in 1920, whose program contained many promises central to the mutualist movement.[9]

The Resistance Societies

Resistance societies and unions for the protection of labor were more common among the industrial and port workers than among the miners. They were not so important or numerous as the *mancomunales* in the north. Rather than the influence of Proudhon brought by Bilboa and Arcos, their intellectual antecedents lay more in the diffusion of anarchist and socialist ideas from Argentina.[10] They concentrated their activities at the level of the work place, not outside it, and fought for the eight-hour day, salary increases, and better conditions. Though anarchists were represented among them, there were also more moderate sectors linked to the Democratic party. The resistance societies were concentrated geographically in the central zone of the country, especially in Santiago and Valparaíso, though there were some in the north until they were generally replaced there by the *mancomunales*. They were based in such industrial activities—often of an artisanal or near-artisanal character—as printing, shoemaking, transport, and carpentry. Among this group also fall the unions for the protection of labor, as they were then called. These were distinct from the anarchist groups, which generally used the name of resistance societies, but the distinctions were far from clear and there was much overlapping. By the end of the nineteenth century, one estimate is that there were thirty unions of this type, of which ten called themselves resistance societies. They were active among port workers, who in 1893, with a nucleus of Valparaíso anarchists, made the first attempt in Chile to organize a national (later intended to be continental) federation, the South American General Federation of Unions for the Protection of Labor; but it collapsed in the year of its creation.

The resistance societies declined with the decline of anarchism, and they tended to be replaced either by a more professional nonpolitical type of unionism on mutual lines or by politicized, Marxist unions. Very often their existence was fleeting, called into being by a protest and disappearing shortly after, and they tended to decline in importance as industry developed larger and more modern units.

The Mancomunales

The core of Chilean unionism lay in the *mancomunales*, or "brotherhoods," though their development must not be isolated from the mutualist and resistance societies which influenced their growth. If the brotherhoods bore traces of both these forms of worker unions, their role in the economy, social composition, geographical isolation, and conditions of work made them distinctive.

The labor force grew rapidly in the north following the War of the Pacific. Whereas in 1884, 5,505 workers were employed in the nitrate industry, 19,345 were employed in 1896 and 48,476 in 1912. Most of them came from the southern and central zones, though a considerable number of foreign laborers, especially Peruvians, Bolivians, and Chinese, were employed.[11] Peruvians and Bolivians constituted close to a third of the total population of Tarapacá in 1907. The foreign capitalists who controlled nitrate production preferred foreign laborers, alleging that they gave far less trouble than the Chileans. But there does not seem to have been much racial tension between the different groups of workers; in the protests and uprisings in that area the great stress was on wages and living and working conditions, and the solutions proposed by the workers did not refer to the problem of foreign labor.[12]

The labor force seems constantly to have been shifting from one nitrate mine to another, which made working-class organization difficult. Partly this was a search for better conditions, but mostly it was a consequence of the fluctuating employment between times of restricted production and of maximum production, caused not only by world demand but also by the ability of the producers to form combines to limit production and force up prices. Thus, in 1884 employment fell by half, and the employers were often readier to dismiss their Chilean workers first; in 1896 in the course of two months alone some six thousand workers were dismissed.[13]

The Congressional Commission of Inquiry in 1904, reflecting the values of Catholic paternalism, reported that low wages were not the main cause of misery, for they found wages on average high enough to purchase the necessities of life. They also felt that the dangers of work and the issue of abuses by company shops had been overrated (though worker protests at the time place these high on their list of complaints). They did, however, point to genuine enough grievances. Apart from work, there was little to do in the nitrate pampa; laborers lived completely abandoned by employers, state, and church, often without their families. The fact that owners and managers were largely foreigners caused grave social tensions. The commission also found that nearly all the judges in the area were either employees of the companies or received payment from them.

The situation of the nitrate workers is typical of the one-industry town noted for its bad labor-relations system. On the one hand there was a relatively homogeneous labor force, or at least one with similar labor conditions; on the other, an intransigent employers' group, foreign in nationality, out of sympathy with the workers they employed, and backed up by state and army.

The Chilean mining labor force mostly came from rural areas; its value systems derived from the traditional rural social structure, and required time and upheaval to convert into union militancy; it was not, as in Argentina, already anarchist or socialist, willing to challenge the state on arrival from Europe. The Chilean working class was hardly accepted or represented in the social and political system, but until the growth of FOCh it was too weak to try to undermine or even reform that system.

The homogeneity of the mining labor force made it a fairly solid social group, with its own culture and class consciousness, even if still affected by its rural background. Despite the fewer European immigrants, the influence of European ideas helped to lead the early unions toward radicalism. There were divisions among the workers; the more advanced and more politicized tried to improve conditions by organizing and by conflict with employer and state; the less advanced, who were a powerful restraining force, tended to demand benefits from employer and state, to alternate between passivity and protest, and thus to suffer exploitation and repression. Both groups were nevertheless bound together and relatively isolated from the other sectors of society. In this working-class attitude, opposition to the foreign capitalist played an important part, for most of the nitrate areas were controlled by British and American companies, and this tended to drive capital and labor into two clearly defined groups. As the nitrate concerns also needed to control transport, port facilities, and in fact the greater part of the economic structure of the north, the labor movement had a clear image of the extent of the power of capital. The work force was also relatively homogeneous, mostly consisting of unskilled rural migrants, possibly earning better salaries than the national average, but suffering similar deprivations and always subject to regular periods of unemployment.[14] Given the crucial importance of nitrate in the state economy, it was natural that the government should seek to maintain regular production. It therefore chose to repress labor rather than cause difficulties with the employers. Thus, while there was a continuing and strong tendency in certain sectors of the labor force to seek support and benefit from the state, the constant use of the army to put down protest, the regular use of the legal system against the workers, the abandonment of the workers by the state in all matters pertaining to living conditions were bound to impress on the workers' leaders the notion of the state as an enemy of the people and an ally of capital.

The union organization created to combat these conditions, the *mancomunales,* reflected the situation of the northern worker. The *mancomunales* were territorially based and were not organized by craft, for there were few distinctions of this sort in the labor force; they made general demands about wages and work and living conditions; they were weak and constantly subject to harassment by state and employer, which made their existence temporary and dangerous; but because they represented the demands of a majority of the labor force they were constantly reappearing.

The *mancomunales* did not preclude other forms of organization in the area. The mutualist unions were quite strong, with an estimated membership of ten thousand in 1910 in the two northern provinces.[15] There were more of them in the towns than in the mining camps. Many of them developed into *mancomunales,* while many of the *mancomunales* continued to perform mutualist functions.

In essence, the aims of the *mancomunales* were more akin to the resistance societies than to the mutualist associations, even if in many cases thay had been consciously set up in opposition to the anarchist models. They started in the ports of the nitrate areas, and also in the coal-mining districts near Concepción in the south, but soon spread to the nitrate-mining camps proper. They were basically organizations of manual workers, and it was often stipulated that members had to belong to the working class and that the leaders should be active workers. They usually began by starting a short-lived newspaper or periodical. The first *mancomunal* to be founded seems to have been the Combinación Mancomunal de Obreros in Iquique in 1901. By 1904 it had about four thousand to six thousand members, and had created in 1903 a short-lived political party. Though at least some of them seem to have had radical ideas (the *mancomunal* of Tocopilla expressed solidarity with the Russian workers in the 1905 revolution),[16] the first *mancomunal* convention passed a relatively moderate set of resolutions, most of which demanded that the state should provide services like education and request employers to improve safety standards.[17] There was a strong streak of puritanism in the *mancomunales;* they insistently demanded education for their children and themselves and the prohibition of alcoholic drinks, gambling, and prostitution. One ex-labor inspector affirms that unlike many other movements their funds were never fraudulently misused, but that almost all were spent on schools, libraries, newspapers, and mutual help during sickness.

The *mancomunales* were the expression of the social cohesion and solidarity of their members, and in this sense followed the example of the mutualist societies; but in their demands and actions they looked forward to more modern trade unionism. All the important strikes of the period in the north were their work.[18] Yet they were weak organizations, based on a relatively small part of the total working population for their regular functioning, and as such they were vulnerable. After the great period of strikes from 1905 to 1907, with subsequent prolonged unemployment, they practically disappeared. Their leaders enjoyed no immunity from dismissal and were easily singled out by the employers. Early political rivalries in the *mancomunal* movement, often between the Democratic party groups and others such as the early socialist parties, or even sections of the Radical party, were an additional source of weakness. They revived again in the later part of the second decade of this century to take part in the activities of the FOCh and the Communist party. Their role had been crucial in training leaders, in spreading ideas and organization, often through a lively press, and in preparing the way for later union developments. [Formal union organization was to gain a large boost as a consequence of a dispute in the State Railway.]

The FOCh

In 1908 the State Railway Companies, arguing financial crisis and the need for economies, reduced their workers' wages by 10 percent. A conservative lawyer helped the workers to organize, in September 1909, the Workers' Federation and to mount a successful campaign for the reinstatement of the cut. In 1911 railway workers held their first congress, where they called their union the Grand Workers' Federation of Chile. They were organized as a mutualist society of railwaymen, with a very moderate program stressing cooperation with employers and the government. Their union was incorporated as a mutualist society under the civil code.

The federation was severely criticized by Recabarren for being an instrument of the bourgeoisie to control the workers. But it did provide relatively strong organization in the days of generally weak unions. Some of its more militant sections in Valparaíso used it to launch a general strike in 1913 in protest against the decree compelling railwaymen to carry photographs as a means of identification.[19] The federation itself started to develop militant tendencies. Union organization elsewhere was in disarray. The *mancomunales* and the resistance societies were suffering from the repressions of the period. In 1917, at its second congress in Valparaíso, representatives of the *mancomunales* were allowed to participate, and it was decided to open the federation—now renamed the FOCh—to all workers. Workers from many industries and of all political persuasions were attracted; like the Partido Obrero Socialista (POS), the federation brought together initially socialists, Democratic party supporters, anarchists, and nonpolitical unionists.[20] It was far stronger in the north and south of the country than in Santiago itself, where it had little support, compared with the anarcho-syndicalists.[21]

The postwar period was one of considerable social tension and the years 1917-1920 were marked by an increasing number of strikes and of mass movements like the Asamblea Obrera de Alimentación Nacional (the Workers' Assembly for National Food Supply), formed in late 1918 to combat the high cost of food (with representatives of the FOCh, the students' federation, the POS, and the Democratic and Radical parties).

The FOCh itself began to reflect this sharpening of tensions. At its 1919 congress in Concepción it changed its structure and character. The basic organizational unit became the union, which grouped all workers of an area without distinction of function or profession. The FOCh demanded the abolition of the capitalist system and proposed that industry should be run by the unions. Recabarren estimated that just after the war it had close to sixty thousand members, but that by 1922 membership had dropped to thirty thousand because of unemployment and repression by state and employers.

The period 1920-1922 was vital in the development of the FOCh, for this was the time of the great debate over the formation of one single political party on the style of the British Labour party, and over entry into the Red International of Labor Unions (RILU). A congress in 1920, with Recabarren as chairman, considered the idea, which had the approval of FOCh's executive, of forming a mass popular political party. The congress agreed that discussions should be opened with the Partido Obrero Socialista and the Democratic party; and hoped that the 1921 FOCh congress would be able to celebrate the fusion of the three bodies. However, the Democratic party could not accept the idea of forming only one party which would not enter into alliances with any other group; but it did accept in principle the idea of cooperating with the FOCh in its fight against capitalism and of making electoral pacts with it to the exclusion of other groups (which it soon repudiated in favor of an alliance with the Radicals). At the 1921 congress, however, the FOCh resolved that, because of the reformism of the Democratic party and its collaboration with the government, it would have no further contacts with that party. This resolution was carried out by only seventy-seven votes to thirty-three, and the minority (mostly of the Democratic party) retired from the congress. The POS had also, in its 1920 congress, agreed to the formation of a united party and had participated in the fruitless negotiations with the Democratic party.[22]

The 1920 FOCh congress had also resolved that its branches should consider entry into the RILU, and at the 1921 congress this was approved by an overwhelming majority. That congress passed a radical statement of policy about the need to control the means of production, as well as the usual resolution on the need to combat vice, especially gambling and drink. The organization was again changed; the Federal Councils, which existed in most cities on a professional basis, were reorganized on an industry basis, classified in six major groups. The FOCh resolved to work with the POS for their common ends, which were to be propagated by jointly owned newspapers.

Part of the reason for the move of both party and union into the camp of international communism was the quick disappointment after Alessandri's election in 1920. The candidacy of Recabarren was little more than a gesture (and could hardly be more, considering that he was imprisoned at the time). Little attention was paid to the election in the contemporary working-class press, for workers in general did not have the right to vote. Even so, the 1920 election was the first one to engage the sympathies and interest of many members of the working class. However, a massacre of nitrate workers in San Gregorio led to disillusionment when Alessandri refused to repudiate, and, indeed, even supported, the sections of the army responsible for it. As he was blocked in congress by a conservative majority, he could do little to fulfill his electoral pledges.

If the ideological clarity and political unity produced by the entry into the RILU and the increasing identification with the Communist party—which name the POS now adopted—brought some benefits to the union movement, it had disadvantages too. The movement became more concerned with political, and less with economic, ends; and it lost supporters, like the members of the Democratic party, who did not accept its ideas. It lost unions as well, like the railwaymen in 1923, who felt that their interests did not receive enough attention in the new FOCh. The FOCh tended to concentrate its activities where the CP was also active, i.e., in the coal and nitrate sectors, to the neglect of the urban centers, so in Santiago it had scarcely one thousand members.[23] Communist historians now regard this period as one in which the wrong tactics were drawn from the right conclusions. The right conclusion was that the emancipation of the workers could only be the product of their own efforts; but the movement was far too inward-looking and far too pessimistic and mistrustful of other social groups. These tactics were not changed until the formation of the Popular Front.[24] Moreover, according to official party historians, the FOCh underestimated the staying power of capitalism and overestimated its own strength to change the system; and the virtual identification of the FOCh and the CP caused the FOCh to decline, and groups like IWW to grow. Yet party historians are too critical. The IWW, with its open membership policy and radical tactics, was attacked and destroyed. The CP and the Communist unions suffered, but survived and later continued to grow.

The FOCh probably reached its peak in 1924, before the combined effects of military intervention in politics, Ibáñez's dictatorship, and the world depression threw the whole labor movement into confusion and decline as it felt the joint impact of persecution and unemployment. The approximate size of the labor movement is shown in the table below.

Table 1
Federations and Obrero Unions, 1925

	Unions	Members
Railway Workers' Federation (affiliated directly to RILU)	30	15,000
Coal-miners' unions (in FOCh)	12	10,000
Metallurgical unions (some only in FOCh)	15	16,000
Nitrate workers' unions (in FOCh)	40	40,000
Seamen's union (divided between FOCh and IWW)	30	11,000
Rural unions (in FOCh)	10	5,000
Tram workers' unions (in FOCh)	7	5,000
Other unions in FOCh	50	60,000
Other unions not in FOCh	20	40,000
	214	204,000

Source: Poblete, *Organización sindical en Chile* (1926), annex 5. Poblete was an official at the Ministry of Labor and played an important role in drafting the labor code.

From 1924 onward the FOCh became embroiled in the turbulent politics of the time and suffered accordingly, as did most political parties and unions.[25] Recabarren's suicide in 1924 was a great blow; the establishment of legal unions drew support away from the movement, for the FOCh was ambivalent toward seeking legal status; the movement and party suffered divisions over the attitude to adopt toward Ibáñez when a Communist senator and four Communist deputies (the party had elected two senators and seven deputies in 1924) advised support for him at a time when he was persecuting many FOCh and Communist leaders.

The FOCh was active in the creation of the Social Republican Union of Chilean Wage and Salary Earners in 1925, which claimed one hundred thousand members from workers, teachers, and white-collar employees. It supported the candidacy for the presidency of far-from-Communist José Santos Salas, who gained 80,000 votes against 180,000 for the right-wing candidate. But this precursor of the Popular Front was taken over by groups seeking to build up a reformist party (though it ended by supporting Ibáñez—who later banned it), and the Communists split from the organization, taking along the FOCh.

Conclusion

By 1924 it is possible to define some general and persistent features of the labor movement. In the first place it is a highly politicized movement. Union divisions are party or ideological divisions; there is little room for the leader who advocates the complete separation of union from party or nonpolitical unionism, even though this is a theory to which many pay lip-service. The issues debated are political ones—whether there should be a revolutionary syndical movement or whether the task of the political revolution should be left to a separate political party; whether the inspiration of the unions should be Marxist, Bakuninist, or Christian (and later Trotskyist, Christian Democrat, or North American). The fact that this political debate takes place in the unions sets up a tension between inclusivity (all members of the working class including white-collar workers) and exclusivity (party faithful only), and this debate has been a continuous one. Each party believes it alone follows the correct union policy; but on the other hand members of other groups speak for larger sections of the working class.

Notes

1. The most useful publications dealing with this period are: H. Ramírez, *Historia del movimiento obrero* (Santiago: Austral, 1956); J. C. Jobet, *Recabarren: Los origenes del movimiento obrero y del socialismo chileno* (Santiago, 1955); M. Poblete, *Organización sindical en Chile* (1926); and two university theses, or *memorias,* by J. Barría, *Movimientos sociales en Chile 1900-10* and *1910-26* (Santiago, 1952 and 1960).
2. Ramírez, *Historia,* pp. 190–91.
3. Solberg, "Immigration and Social Problems in Argentina and Chile," *Hispanic American Historical Review* (May 1969).
4. G. Kaempffer, *Así sucedió* (1962); also "Masacres en la historia chilena," *Punto final,* January 2, 1968.
5. These were the grievances in the first recorded workers' strike in Chile, of a group of miners in September 1864. C. M. Ortíz and P. I. Ljubetic, "Estudio sobre el origen y desarrollo del proletariado en Chile durante el siglo XIX" (*Memoria,* Inst. Pedagógico, Universidad Chile, 1954), pp. 274–76.
6. *La voz del obrero* (Taltal), January 13, 1908, quoted by O. Millas in *Principios* (the official CP monthly), July-August 1962, p. 9.
7. Poblete, *Organización sindical,* p. 24. The first one he cites is the Society of Artisans of Valparaíso, formed in 1858, though Ramírez (*Historia,* p. 166) refers to one of the same name in Santiago in 1847.
8. A. Gurrieri and F. Zapata, *Sectores obreros y desarrollo en Chile* (1967), p. 27.
9. Ibid., p. 29; see also B. G. Burnett, *Political Groups in Chile: The Dialogue Between Order and Change* (Austin, Tex.: University of Texas Press, 1970), pp. 102–3.
10. Gurrieri, "Consideraciones sobre los sindicatos chilenos," *Aportes* (July 1968), p. 88.
11. F. Recabarren Rojas, "Historia del proletariado de Tarapacá y Antofagasta, 1884–1913" (*Memoria,* Inst. Pedagógico, Universidad Chile, 1954), p. 13. Other sectors of the economy serving the nitrate industry grew too. The numbers of Chinese laborers are not known exactly; but rather doubtful census returns for 1907 produce a figure of two thousand (ibid., p. 36).
12. At least this is categorically asserted by Elías Lafertte, for many years secretary-general of the FOCh and leader of the Chilean CP, in his *Vida de un communista* (1961), pp. 63–64. For some time Lafertte worked in the nitrate areas and claims that blame was laid on foreign capitalists, not workers. On the other hand, Kaempffer (*Así sucedió,* p. 105) claims that owners put Peruvians or Bolivians in charge of groups of Chilean workers to discharge tensions at a lower level than the management. While this undoubtedly did occur, it does not seem to have displaced economic grievances directed at the capitalists from the first attention of the workers.
13. Recabarren, "Historia del proletariado," pp. 81–91. They could either drift to the towns, or, as many did, return to rural areas in the

south and await the next demand for labor from the north. See also Ramírez, *Historia*, p. 279.

14. Gurrieri and Zapata, *Sectores obreros*, p. 20. And as the work force had few internal professional distinctions, worker demands tended to be general and applicable to all, rather than seeking differentiation and privilege for a specialized sector.

15. Recabarren, "Historia del proletariado," p. 174.

16. Ramírez, *Historia*, p. 270; and it also condemned the "authoritarian and bourgeois despotism that in all parts of the world weighs like a granite mountain on the shoulders of the workers."

17. This was held in Santiago in 1904, with fifteen organizations represented by twenty-five delegates on behalf of twenty thousand members. They asked for the abolition of whipping in the army and navy; state acquisition of public services like water and transport; free and compulsory primary education; night school for adults; hygienic housing; employers to indemnify injuries at work; and the appointment of factory inspectors (Jobet, *Recabarren*, pp. 108–9). Some resistance societies withdrew from this convention on the grounds that workers should ask nothing from the government (Barría, *Breve historia del sindicalismo chileno* [Santiago, 1967], p. 19).

18. Gurrieri and Zapata, *Sectores obreros*, p. 31. And more strikes took place in the northernmost provinces than in any other areas of Chile.

19. Barría, *Movimientos*, p. 114.

20. Lafertte, *Vida*, pp. 149–50.

21. L. Vitale, *Discursos de Clotario Blest* (1961), p. 49.

22. There is contradictory evidence on the role of Recabarren in this episode. According to Chacón, Recabarren advised against making the FOCh the basis of a political party (at the FOCh Rancagua Congress in 1920). Vitale (a Trotskyist) alleges that, on the other hand, it was Recabarren who promoted the venture, (*Discursos*, p. 56). An article in *El Siglo*, December 22, 1968 (the official CP daily), gives the impression that he changed his mind between 1920 and 1921.

23. Barría, *Movimientos*, p. 146. The then secretary-general of the FOCh, C. A. Martínez, attributed this to ideological competition and factionalism in the working class.

24. Ramírez, *Historia*, pp. 45–46. In his *Origen* he writes: "The outstanding participation of communist militants in the FOCh, and the recognized leadership of Recabarren both in the party and in the union, the fact that the FOCh had expressed its sympathies for the Russian revolution and had joined RILU, the circumstance that—from the very beginning—the party had intimate and harmonious links with the FOCh, were factors that created the impression that, for Communists and enemies of the working class alike, the party and FOCh were one and the same thing." This tended to divide the working class, on the one hand, and on the other seemed to make FOCh, which was a mass organization, the guiding force of the Communist movement, which lessened its political weight (pp. 209–20). In 1933 the Comintern's South American bureau made the same criticism.

25. Between 1925 and 1933 it was unable to hold congresses and by the latter date had been reduced to a quarter of its size, though there was a convention in 1931, basically to engage in the Stalinist–Trotskyist disputes of the time. This convention expelled the allegedly Trotskyist group of Manuel Hidalgo (which had captured the party's central committee for a time under the Ibáñez dictatorship when almost all members of the Lafertte–Contreras Labarca group were in exile or imprisoned), which favored working with the legal unions. Hidalgo's group also attacked the current Communist line on "social-fascism" (R. J. Alexander, *Communism in Latin America* [New Brunswick, N.J.: Rutgers University Press, 1957], p. 185).

The May Thirtieth Movement in Shanghai

Jean Chesneaux

The whole complex of workers', merchants', and students' strikes, of street demonstrations, press campaigns, and political moves of various kinds that took place in Shanghai (for the sake of convenience they will be termed the "May Thirtieth Movement") might be said to be the first dramatic outcome of the new balance of political forces that had begun to emerge at the end of 1923. The May Thirtieth Movement demonstrated the new possibilities that were opened up for the Nationalist movement by the alliance between the Kuomintang and the Communist party, and it was sustained by the sudden upsurge of labor activities throughout the country that had taken place at the beginning of 1925. It also gave expression to the growing antagonism felt by the national bourgeoisie, the students, and the urban petty bourgeoisie toward the Treaty Powers.

The May Thirtieth Movement was also the outcome of the local situation in Shanghai, where for the previous few weeks there had been a renewal of activities among the bourgeoisie as well as in the labor movement. The upper bourgeoisie, through the medium of the General Chamber of Commerce, had reacted vigorously against the proposed bylaws concerning an increase in wharfage dues, press control over Chinese newspapers published within Settlement territory, and other matters, all of which the municipal council of the International Settlement had announced it would put to a vote at a meeting of ratepayers. These influential bourgeois Chinese were backed in their opposition by the shop-keepers' associations (representing petty traders and craftsmen), which registered their protest by means of appeals and demonstrations.[1] The authoritarian attitude of the municipal council was thrown into relief by the measures recently taken by the Peking government, especially Peking's transfer of the arsenal installations into private hands, in what appeared to be an attempt to encourage the economic development of Shanghai in accordance with the wishes of the local bourgeoisie.[2]

Extracted from Jean Chesneaux, *The Chinese Labor Movement, 1919-1927* (Stanford, Ca.: Stanford University Press, 1968). Translated from the French by H. M. Wright. Copyright © 1968 by the Board of Trustees of the Leland Stanford Junior University and reprinted with the permission of the publishers.

As for labor agitation, it had continued almost without pause since the February strikes in the Japanese cotton mills, for in the meantime there had been a sharp fall in the value of copper currency,[3] and the wholesale price of rice had risen from 9.20-10.40 yuan (minimum and maximum) in January to 10.30-11.40 in May.[4] The West Shanghai Workers' Club, which had now become the cotton workers' union, took control of the strikes that broke out during May as a result of various incidents in several Japanese cotton mills.[5] (The club's leaders—particularly Liu Hua and Sun Liang-hui—had acquired a great deal of authority since the February strikes.) The club distributed strike certificates to individual workers, organized pickets, and made contact with the shopkeepers' associations for the purpose of creating a strike fund.[6] At the start of these strikes a worker named Ku Cheng-hung was killed by a Japanese foreman during a scuffle that ensued from a typical occurrence of *ta-ch'ang*, when gates were broken down, machinery wrecked, and so forth. This happened on May 15. The union decided to hold a memorial service in his honor on May 24, with the backing of the student associations, and some five thousand people took part. Meanwhile the cotton-mill strike continued to spread.[7] The central committee of the Communist party discussed the situation on May 28 at an emergency meeting that was made still more tense by the approaching meeting of the municipal council, arranged for June 2, at which the new bylaws would be put to a vote. The committee was disturbed also by recent news from Peking that serious incidents had occurred there in a clash between students and police.[8] After what seems to have been a very lively discussion, those in favor of adopting a bold line, led by Ts'ai Ho-sen, overcame the hesitations of Ch'en Tu-hsiu, and it was decided to hold another demonstration for the combined purpose of further commemorating Ku Cheng-hung and of stimulating an all-out fight against the Treaty Powers.[9] The workers' clubs prepared to take part in this demonstration, fixed for May 30, and made approaches to the student associations, calling upon them to "revive the spirit of May 4."[10]

The demonstration took place as planned in the afternoon of May 30, and several thousand people took part. In a clash in Nanking Road with the police of the Louza police station, the police inspector, without warning, gave the order to fire in order to free his men from the crowd, with the result that ten people were killed and over fifty injured, most of them workers.[11]

Serious incidents like this had occurred in Shanghai before, for instance during the anti-American boycott in 1905, when this same Louza police station had been besieged by the crowd and Sikh police had fired, killing three and wounding large numbers.[12] The victims of the 1905 shootings were, however, quickly forgotten. The repercussions throughout the country of the Nanking Road incident therefore gave some indication of the advance in national awareness during the intervening twenty years. Not all these repercussions can be discussed here, since the May Thirtieth Movement involved almost all social strata in the cities and affected foreign as well as internal policy. Discussion will be confined to the part played in the movement by the working class and to the new stimulus labor derived from it.

On the day after the shootings a meeting was held in the offices of the General Chamber of Commerce, in the presence of the acting president, Fang Chiao-po.[13] It was attended by about fifteen hundred persons, and chaired by a leader of the students' federation. Several of the Communist leaders of the Chapei Workers' Club spoke, as did delegates of the shopkeepers' associations. It was decided to hold a general strike of workers, students, and merchants, and to boycott the foreign banks and withdraw sums deposited in them by Chinese. The meeting also demanded that whatever those responsible for the shootings might say, compensation had to be paid to the victims and their families, and that those arrested must be released. Regarding municipal affairs, it called for the withdrawal of the three bylaws recently put before the municipal electors, Chinese control over the Shanghai police, and the removal of foreign ships from the Whangpoo.[14] Further resolutions were along the lines of proposals in the handbills distributed that morning by Liu Hua and the Chapei Workers' Club,[15] demanding the right to strike, improvement of working conditions in the cotton mills, and an end to both the ill-treatment of workers and the employment of foreigners to police them.

On June 1 all work came to a standstill in shops and teaching establishments, and the strike spread rapidly in the factories. The evening before, a new organization called the Shanghai General Union had been formed to take control of the strike. It had direct links with the Communist party, since its leaders were Li Li-san, Liu Shao-ch'i, Liu Hua, Sun Liang-hui, and the student Yang Chih-hua, who was the wife of Ch'ü Ch'iu-pai.[16] At the General Union's request, meetings of employees in the public utilities and all the big enterprises were held in order to decide upon strike action.[17] By June 4 there were seventy-four thousand strikers,[18] and by June 13 nearly one hundred sixty thousand.[19] The enterprises primarily affected were the Japanese and British firms and the municipal services. The ships in the docks were immobilized and the goods left standing; the telephones ceased to function, and foreign newspapers ceased publication; there was nothing but a skeleton staff left at the power station in the International Settlement,[20] and there were even quite a number of defections among the Sikhs of the municipal police.[21]

The foreign authorities countered with the use of force. The Volunteers were mobilized, martial law was declared, twenty-six gunboats were brought up the Whangpoo and marines were landed, and Shanghai University was closed.[22] During the first few days of June many violent incidents occurred in the center of the Settlement, and the police and the Volunteers several times opened fire on the students and workers who were distributing handbills and haranguing the crowd, with as many as sixty people killed and as many again seriously wounded.[23]

The tense situation that now existed in Shanghai merely strengthened the determination of the strikers. On June 7 an action committee was formed at the instigation of the unions, with joint participation of the Shanghai General Union, the Shanghai Students' Federation, the National Students' Federation, and the federated shopkeepers' associations.[24] The General Chamber of Commerce was approached about joining, but refused. The new organization was called the Shanghai Federation of Workers, Merchants, and Students, and its political program, consisting of seventeen points, was ratified on June 11 during a demonstration held in Chapei, in which twenty thousand took part.[25] The program, in addition to repeating the demands formulated on May 31 for the settlement of the May 30 incident and for the rights to strike and to form trade unions, went much further and included demands for changes in the status of the International Settlement. In accordance with the often expressed wishes of the local bourgeoisie, it called for the abolition of the Volunteer Corps, freedom of speech, of assembly, and of the press on settlement territory, the return of the Mixed Court to Chinese control, the right to vote for Chinese ratepayers, the withdrawal of foreign armed forces, and the abolition of extraterritoriality and consular jurisdiction.[26]

The General Union that had been formed on May 31 was in firm control of the entire Shanghai proletariat. Its headquarters were in Chapei,[27] but it established branches in the working-class areas of Pootung, Yangtzepoo, Chapei, and Hsiaoshatu[28] so as to be able to deal more efficiently with local matters and in particular with the allocation of strike duties. It encouraged the formation of unions in certain enterprises or trades, such as a union for the employees of the Chinese-owned tramway company[29] and unions for printing and postal workers. In order to counteract the propaganda in Chinese issued by the municipal council of the International Settlement,[30] it distributed a bulletin—published several times a week[31]—that provided a supplement to the *Je-hsueh jih-pao* ("Bloodshed Journal") published by the new action committee.[32] It organized pickets *(chiu-ch'a-tui)* at each of its branches and in the principal trade unions, which, although armed only with thick sticks, were given some kind of military training. These pickets kept watch over attempts to hire strike-breakers, and held any such persons in detention at branch head-quarters. They also prevented the transportation of Japanese goods and kept order at workers' meetings, especially when strike funds were being distributed.[33] Altogether, the General Union seems to have established contact with all sections of the Shanghai proletariat from the very beginning of the movement. At its headquarters in Chapei, where already in March and April the indefatigable Liu Hua and his collaborators had tried to show the workers the way forward, hundreds, and sometimes thousands, of strikers arrived to proclaim their support.[34] As the strike wore on, they queued up to show the strike certificates that had been issued to them, which entitled them to a minimum of twenty cents in silver per day.[35]

This touches upon the major problem of how the strike was financed. It is estimated to have cost over a million yuan per month;[36] in order to meet the cost, a strike fund was organized with the help of the students, and contributions were collected in the Chinese-owned factories in Shanghai (where work continued) and throughout the entire country. The extent to which the movement enjoyed popular sympathy can be measured by the millions of small coins collected for the fund.[37] Appeals for sympathy were also made to the international labor movement, and particularly to the Red International via the All-China General Union formed the month before.[38] The Red International pro-posed to the Amsterdam International that they furnish joint aid, but Amsterdam decided to confine its contribution to a commission of inquiry;[39] its affiliated organizations contributed large sums, however, especially the affiliated Soviet trade unions, which sent 400,000 rubles.[40][. . .] By June the expenses of the strike were more or less met, the Committee for Aid and Peace having con-tributed 470,000 yuan, the General Union having collected, through its own efforts, 350,000 yuan,[41] and the remainder having been advanced by the Chinese banks through the inter-vention of the chamber of commerce.[42]

There seems, however, to have been little response from the peasants of the Yangtze estuary to the Shanghai strikes, despite repeated appeals made by the unions and the Communist party for unity between workers and peasants ("of capital importance in the struggle against imperialism," according to a leaflet distributed in June).[43] At the most, attempts seem to have been made to collect provisions and spread propaganda in the villages with the help of strikers who came from the rural districts in the neighborhood of Shanghai and who had returned home at the beginning of June.[44]

Compromises and Strike Settlements

Before long, however, enthusiasm began to wane, and by the end of June cracks were appearing in the common front of those engaged in the struggle to get the settlement authorities to accept the program laid down on May 31.[. . .]

The municipal council, in order to create a rift between the Chinese industrialists and the laboring masses and thereby to consolidate its gains, then did something quite unprecedented: following a suggestion made by the manager of one of the British cotton mills a few days before, it cut off the supply of electricity to Chinese-owned factories on July 6.[45] It was solely to supply power to these factories, where the workers were not on strike, that the settlement electric power plant, where the workers had gone on strike on the first day of the movement, had been kept in operation. It was hoped that by cutting off the supply the number of people out of work would be increased, thus placing an additional strain on the financial resources of the General Union, while at the same time bringing pressure to bear on the bourgeoisie in order to discourage their furnishing further aid to the General Union. It did indeed become more and more difficult to provide for the strikers, whose numbers, although they had fallen to eighty thousand on July 1, had risen again to one hundred thousand by the end of the month,[46] and the cutting off of the supply of electric current did immediately result in the chamber of commerce's dissolving its Committee for Aid and Peace.[47] The Peking government sent another 150,000 yuan,[48] but this was not enough to cover the deficit, nor was there a sufficient return from such expedients as demanding contributions to the strike fund from Chinese newspapers as a form of fine if they had published communications from the municipal council[49] or instituting a temporary tax (by agreement with the chamber of commerce) on goods piled up in the foreign warehouses since the beginning of the strike to ensure the removal of those goods.[50] Toward the end of July it was beginning to look as though the working class was becoming dangerously isolated, with a falloff not only of contributors to the strike fund but also of political allies. Even its most ardent allies—the students—were beginning to flag, though at their seventh annual conference they had resolved not to weaken in their fight for the workers' cause but rather to continue helping the unions and spreading propaganda for the strikers.[51] The members of the shopkeepers' associations were also losing their enthusiasm, since they were financially dependent on the Chinese banks and thus affected by the bankers' policy of compromise.[52]

Difficulties were also arising with the Chinese authorities. The unstable coalition that had been established in Peking after the defeat of the Chihli faction in the fall of 1924 had at first shown sympathy toward the strike. Tuan, the head of the executive, had sent large sums of money, and had even agreed to pass on the watered-down form of the strikers' demands, sent to him by the Shanghai Chamber of Commerce, to the diplomatic corps.[53] This was a gesture he could afford to make, because, like Yü Hsia-ch'ing, he was a friend of Japan, and the moderates had seen to it that Japan was spared the worst of the attack in June in order to ensure that Great Britain bore the brunt of it. The Fengtien military authorities, who at that time administered Shanghai in the name of the Peking government, also showed tolerance in June. The strike organizations were allowed to function more or less without interference on Chinese territory, especially in Chapei,[54] even to the point where the police of the International Settlement complained about an unaccustomed lack of cooperation from the Chinese police.[55] But after the defection of the bourgeoisie in July, when the movement became more of a class struggle, there was a change of attitude. On July 8 the military commander of Shanghai issued a proclamation complaining of the "troublemakers" who claimed to be labor leaders and who disturbed public order; the proclamation went on to order compulsory registration and inspection of all unions formed since May 30 on penalty of dissolution.[56] On July 23 this stiffening of attitude became still more pronounced when the seal was put on the Seamen's Union, the unions in foreign firms, and the Federation of Workers, Merchants, and Students.[57] Yü Hsia-ch'ing, who was anxious to maintain a limited degree of cooperation with the strikers, immediately intervened to request that these organizations be reopened and the arrested leaders released.[58][. . .]

What with the withdrawal of the bourgeoisie, the hardening of

Western attitudes in the International Settlement, the disapproval of the Chinese authorities, and the attacks of the *kung-tsei,* who were trying to cash in on the weariness of the strikers, the strike leaders realized that they would have to reach a compromise. But they wanted a real compromise, not a capitulation; for after the General Union had gradually been deserted by its allies, it had done a tremendous job of organization during July and August, and had given the working masses of Shanghai a unity and a crusading spirit they had never known before. On July 28 the General Union was able to announce that 117 unions, with a combined membership of 218,000, were affiliated with it.[59][. . .] The General Union had, however, failed to gain much influence in sectors of industry that had not been directly affected by the May Thirtieth Movement, such as the Chinese-owned silk-reeling factories, the shipyards, the small Chinese-owned mechanical workshops, and the tramways in the French Concession. Its most striking successes were its innovative attempts to organize the dockers (who until then had only had their traditional *pang*), the cotton workers (who for many years had been without any proper form of organization and had instead resorted to the use of *ta-ch'ang*), and the printing workers (whose only form of organization hitherto had been demarcated trade associations.)[. . .]

The main purpose of this intensive organizing effort was to establish a firm control over the shifting and unstable Shanghai proletariat and make it capable of prolonged, sustained effort, so that it would not have to resort to occasional destructive outbursts of *ta-ch'ang* as hitherto. The General Union had several times officially condemned such outbursts. It had also attempted, in contrast to policies followed by the Federation of Labor Organizations during 1923-1924, to form unions on a mainly industrial basis so as to get rid of the demarcation problems and the regional rivalries that were precisely what the federation delighted in making use of.[. . .]

At the beginning of August, when it had become clear that the May Thirtieth Movement could no longer hope to win, the General Union made public its proposals for reaching a compromise. These included clauses for settling the strike and the incidents that gave rise to it (reinstatement of workers and strike pay amounting to one-third of the normal wage, punishment for those responsible for the Nanking Road incident, and compensation for the families of the victims), as well as demands for recognition of the unions affiliated with the General Union as representative spokesmen of the workers, a general 10 percent raise in wages to be paid only in *ta-yang,* and guarantees against ill-treatment and unjust dismissal of workers.[60] What this spelled out was that the working class, like the bourgeoisie several weeks earlier, had now abandoned the original political aims of the movement, and instead was pressing only its own economic demands. The Japanese were the first to take steps toward meeting these demands. Their consul general agreed to meet Li Li-san and other representatives of the General Union at the Foreign Affairs Office in Shanghai, in the presence of representatives of the Chinese Chamber of Commerce.[61] Agreement was soon reached concerning compensation for the family of Ku Cheng-hung, the worker whose murder had been the starting point of the whole affair, and on recognition of the unions' right to represent the workers, the prevention of ill-treatment of workers and unjust dismissals, and the payment of wages in *ta-yang* (with a further promise from the Japanese to consider a possible raise in wages).[62] Nothing was mentioned about strike pay, but the Chamber of Commerce paid out a sum of 260,000 yuan for this purpose.[63][. . .]

At the same time these negotiations were being carried out with the Japanese,[64] three big economic strikes were declared: that of the postal workers on August 17,[65] one at the Commercial Press on August 22,[66] and another at the China Bookshop on August 29.[67] Was this an adroit move on the part of the General Union to compensate for the failure to obtain the political objectives of the May Thirtieth Movement by switching the energies of the labor movement to the presentation of economic demands?[68] Or was it simply that skilled workers such as the printers and the postal workers (who in addition were still under the burden of foreign control)[69] had been sufficiently stimulated by the class struggle that had been going on in Shanghai since the beginning of June to fight for their own interests? Certainly all three strikes showed how even those sections of the Shanghai proletariat that had been most influenced by the old guild traditions had acquired a new unity and a new class consciousness since the Nanking Road incident.[. . .] At the end of August labor agitation spread to the railways in the Shanghai region. Without recourse to a strike, the railwaymen on the Shanghai-Nanking[70] and the Shanghai-Hangchow lines[71] obtained a raise in wages. But this spread of the movement that had begun on May 30 to Chinese-owned private firms and public utilities did not improve relations between the General Union and the Chinese bourgeoisie and authorities in Shanghai. After work was resumed at the electric power plant on September 8,[72] the Fengtien military authorities in Shanghai put an abrupt end to the tolerance they had been showing the labor movement since May 30. The police announced on September 19 that until the trade-union legislation promised by the Peking government was promulgated, all labor organizations were illegal; consequently, the General Union was declared to be dissolved, and a warrant was taken out for Li Li-san's arrest.[73] The main unions affiliated with the General Union—the Commercial Press unions, the cotton-mill unions, and about fifteen others—were also closed down.[74] The great strike wave had temporarily come to an end. On September 23 the Federation of Workers, Merchants, and Students, which had nominally survived the break in July between the labor movement and the bourgeoisie, was officially dissolved.[75][. . .]

Response in Other Parts of China

When news of the Nanking Road incident reached the various provinces of China during the first days in June, it started a movement of solidarity such as had never occurred before, and the movement lasted throughout the summer. I cannot attempt to give a complete account of it here, or to examine in any depth the class relations and political alliances involved. As with the Shanghai movement, discussion will be confined to the part played in it by the working class.[76]

Workers and workers' associations joined with students, merchants, and other representatives of the middle classes to support the Shanghai movement, forming in Wuhan a "Committee of Support for May 30,"[77] in Peking a "Committee of Support for the Workers, Merchants, and Students,"[78] and in Hunan a "Committee for Effacing Shame."[79] Large numbers of workers took part in the widely held demonstrations in order to assure the Shanghai strikers of the support of the rest of the country, to condemn the actions of the British police of Shanghai, and to demand justice. In Peking a big meeting, attended by over three hundred thousand people of all kinds, was held on June 10 in front of T'ien-an Gate, under the chairmanship of Li Yü-ying, an intellectual who was a member of the central committee of the Kuomintang. Many railwaymen, printers, rickshaw men, and tramway employees were present.[80] Similar meetings were held in Kirin, Mukden, and Dairen in the northeast,[81] one at Changsha in Hunan on June 6,[82] one in Tientsin on June 14,[83] one in Shameen on June 6,[84] and others in many other industrial and university centers. In Kiukiang violence broke out between the crowd and the police of the British Concession, following which the crowd, led by dockers and seamen, set fire to the Bank of Taiwan (Japanese) and attacked the offices of the shipping firms Jardine, Matheson & Company and Naigai Wata Kaisha.[85] It was mainly the students' associations that organized the collection of sub-scriptions to the fund set up throughout China for the main-tenance of the strikers and that also handled the boycott of foreign goods that had been started in the Yangtze valley; but workers too took part in both these activities. In Wuhan and Changsha the federations of labor organizations, inactive throughout 1923-1924, helped the students and the shopkeepers' associations collect funds.[86] The Chiao-Chi railwaymen formed a "Committee in Support of the Shanghai Victims," each contributing a day's wages;[87] and the Dairen printers,[88] the Ching-Han railwaymen, the workers of Harbin,[89] and many others organized collections for the fund. As usual, the rickshaw men and dockers were keen supporters of the boycott of foreign goods and nationals, for instance in Chungking, where the boycott continued until October,[90] in Nanchang,[91] and in Amoy.[92][. . .]

The movement of solidarity with the Shanghai strikers was more vigorous still in the big foreign enterprises in the interior. There the workers conducted a direct attack, both political and economic, against Japanese and British interests. During the fall of 1922 strikes had taken place there that were essentially economic in nature, even if sometimes tinged with Nationalist aims. In the summer of 1925, however, strikes were held mainly for political ends, although at the same time the workers employed by foreign firms tried to obtain a substantial improvement in their conditions of employment.

In Nanking, while the rickshaw men were refusing to trans-port British and Japanese goods and nationals, and the seamen employed by British firms were on strike, the workers in a big British powdered-egg factory, the International Export Company, went on strike on June 8, both to protest the Shanghai incident and to demand a raise in wages, guarantees for stability of employ-ment, and recognition of the union they had just formed.[93] Their demands were met, and they returned to work after being out for over a month. But at the end of June the firm, probably thinking that the slowing down of the Shanghai movement had made trouble much less likely, dismissed several hundred employees. A crowd of workers invaded the factory in retaliation and wrecked the plant and the machinery. The British gunboat *Durban* inter-vened; several people were killed and many wounded.[94][. . .]

In July the movement spread to other foreign enterprises, such as the mines of the Peking Syndicate at Kiaotso (in Honan), an industrial center that had so far been very little affected by strikes and union organization, probably because of its geographical isolation. Urged by a group of students who came to organize the workers, the miners ceased work on July 7; guards and pickets were organized, and telephone and water lines were cut off. The only thing the European staff at the mine could do was depart for Peking, leaving the miners in charge. Work was not resumed until the end of August, after substantial concessions had been granted.[95] The strikers had enjoyed the protection of the units of Feng Yü-hsiang's People's National Army that were stationed in the area.[. . .]

There were repercussions of the Shanghai incident in many other enterprises in north and central China. On the South Manchuria Railway, for instance, the leaders of a Chinese union obtained a raise in wages and the same treatment for Chinese as for Japanese workers without going on strike.[96] In the British KMA mines the workers at the Chao-ko-chuang pit made contact in August with the Shanghai General Union, the Tangshan railwaymen's union, and students' associations in the area. As a result, a union was formed which issued an inaugural manifesto[97] that was clear evidence of the influence the events in Shanghai were having and the extent to which the labor and Nationalist movements were merging all over China. It was this union that on September 13 declared another strike of the KMA miners, demanding higher wages and recognition of the union by the mine owners.[98][. . .]

However various the ways in which the working class took part in the May Thirtieth Movement, it was almost always supported by the students' organizations and by the shopkeepers. In Wuhan, Changsha, Tientsin, Tsingtao, Peking, and all the other big cities, the working class maintained a close association with these two allies in demonstrating solidarity with the Shanghai strikers, while at the same time fighting its own battles. It had also shown itself capable of winning a considerable amount of international support for the Chinese revolution. While the wave of activity that began in May 1919 had passed almost unnoticed by the rest of the world, and that of 1922 had aroused only a faint response, even among members of the extreme left in the West, the Shanghai incident and the political agitation that followed during the summer of 1925 brought expressions of sympathy from all over the world. Not only was sympathy manifested by the Comintern[99] and the Soviet Union, which sent vast sums of money as well as a trade-union delegation to China,[100] and by the Overseas Chinese (especially those in the Paris group),[101] who were very active in their support, but also campaigns in support of the Shanghai strikers were organized by workers' associations and left-wing intellectuals in the very countries—Great Britain, Japan, France —whose governments were in conflict with the Chinese Nationalist movement. Meetings of solidarity were held in Paris, London, Berlin, and Tokyo, and on June 6 an International Committee of Aid was formed in Berlin, sponsored by Henri Barbusse, Bernard Shaw, Upton Sinclair, Klara Zetkin, Auguste Forel, and other big names among the progressive intelligentsia of the West.[102]

On the other hand, throughout China, as in Shanghai, there was a noticeable lack of peasant support for the May Thirtieth Movement. In the main, and in spite of the fact that its aims were Nationalist ones, the movement was conducted by the industrial proletariat, the students, and the middle and petty bourgeoisie in the towns, and it very rarely affected the countryside. The Hunan Committee for Effacing Shame had branches in forty-six rural *hsien*, many of which were in effect small country towns;[103] and in one rural *hsien* in Honan the peasants held a meeting to condemn British and Japanese activities in China.[104] But Chinese peasants seldom came into contact with the big foreign interests in China, one of the few exceptions being Honan, where BAT agents collected tobacco crops. Of the two declared objectives of the Nationalist revolution laid down in Canton in 1924—the struggle against the Treaty Powers and the struggle against the conservatives and warlords—it was the second that had the most direct appeal for the peasants;[105] and since the May Thirtieth Movement was aimed primarily at the big foreign interests, it could not hope to gain much support from the peasants. It was only during the Northern Expedition in the following year that they entered the political arena.

The upper bourgeoisie in the interior at first gave wide support to the movement, but, as in Shanghai, it soon began to show hesitations, anxieties about the growing labor agitation, and preference for a policy of compromise. In Changsha the General Chamber of Commerce and the provincial teachers' association, with the full approval of the governor, Chao Heng-t'i, made efforts from the middle of June to curb the activities of the Committee for Effacing Shame.[106] In Wuhan the General Chamber of Commerce and the General Association of Chinese Commerce (the latter representing the compradores) urged the governor, Hsiao Yao-nan, to prevent the general strike planned for June 10.[107] In Kirin the Provincial Assembly and the Merchants' Guild got the governor there to prohibit students from collecting contributions for the Shanghai fund on the grounds that their own contributions were sufficient.[108] In Amoy, thanks to the reports of a rather vain and slow-witted British consul, we know in some detail about a deal made between him and the chamber of commerce, the president of which played a double game, informing the consulate of the strikers' intentions and complying with British directives for reducing as much as possible the effects of the boycott.[109]

Finally, to complete this brief sketch of the relation between the industrial proletariat and the other social strata in China during the May Thirtieth Movement, a word should be said about the attitude of the provincial military commanders, all of whom, with one notable exception, adopted the same policy as the commander of the Fengtien troops in the Shanghai area: after a show of tolerance, they soon reverted to the ruthless repressive methods they had begun to use in February 1923. Li Ching-lin in Tientsin and Hsiao Yao-nan in Wuhan collaborated with Western and Japanese authorities in order to repress labor agitation directed against foreign-owned industries. Chang Tsung-ch'ang, who in June had felt he must make a gesture and had sent 2,000 yuan to the Shanghai victims,[110] used force at the end of July to dissolve the organizations in Tsingtao that supported the movement. He even appropriated for his own use the contributions to the Shanghai fund they had recently collected, amounting, appropriately enough, to 2,000 yuan.[111] In Mukden, when the labor organizations there announced their intention to declare a general strike and refused to accept foreign currency and goods or to travel on foreign trains and boats, the military governor, who was a direct subordinate of Chang Tso-lin, put an immediate end to the agitation.[112]

The only area where the military authorities adopted a policy of cooperation with the labor movement, instead of repression of it, was the area under the control of the Kuominchun (the "People's National Army"). This was the name adopted by Feng Yü-hsiang's army as a mark of its sympathy with the Canton government after Feng and his army had fallen out with the Anfu and Fengtien factions, whose accomplices Feng and his troops had been in the coup d'état of November 1924.[113] When the Nanking Road incident occurred, Feng declared his sympathy with the Shanghai strikers, issued an appeal to fight against foreign aggression,[114] and published a letter addressed to "the Christians of the world," in which he condemned the behavior of the Western nations in China.[115] In Honan and Suiyuan, the areas under his control, the military government actually encouraged the development of a labor movement after May 30, instead of opposing it as the rulers of Chihli and Shantung did. In August a strike broke out at the Chengchow cotton mill, with the strikers presenting demands not only for higher wages and various forms of compensation but also for wider benefits: improved conditions for women and children, sickness benefits, and the recognition of the union and its right to control the engagement and dismissal of workers. When, probably at the instigation of the mill owner,[116] armed bands attacked the strikers and destroyed the union head-quarters, the Second Army of the Kuominchun helped the workers repulse the attacks and obtain their demands.[117][. . .]

General Union Activities after the May Thirtieth Incident

In Shanghai, no sooner had the May Thirtieth activities died down than an intensive wave of strikes began, heralded by the postal and printing workers' strikes in August. The strike wave lasted from October 1925 through the winter and the spring, and was still in full swing when the Northern Expedition set forth from Canton in July 1926.

This strike wave grew steadily in intensity throughout the period: six strikes in November 1925, ten in January 1926, twenty-one in March, twenty-five in May.[118] In June, when the price of rice suddenly shot up,[119] over a hundred enterprises were affected, many of them textile concerns, and over seventy thousand strikers were involved.[120] Although low wages and bad working conditions were the chief causes of these strikes, the part played by the Shanghai General Union, formed the day after the May 30 incident, made them very different from the spontaneous protests of the earlier period. In spite of frequent attempts to ban it,[121] the General Union managed in the main to hold together the unions that had been formed during the summer in industries, trades, and enterprises. In June 1926, just before the departure of the Northern Expedition, it claimed a membership of 210,000 —a figure which, it is true, included a number of craftsmen.[. . .]

In spite, however, of the traditional reluctance of the Shanghai proletariat to submit to strict organization, the General Union and the unions affiliated with it seem to have had considerable authority and prestige.[. . .] Prestige was regarded as important, [as] shown by the frequency with which strikers put forth demands for employers' recognition of unions,[122] for the right to collect union subscriptions,[123] for the right to hold union meetings,[124] and for the protection of union officials, including reinstatement after strikes and release from arrest.[125]

The spread of modern trade unionism does not, of course, mean that older features of the labor movement had been entirely eliminated. Provincial rivalries still arose during the 1925-1926 strike wave, and so did outbursts of *ta-ch'ang*. In June 1926 a violent brawl, in which several people were wounded, broke out in the Naigai No. 5 cotton mill between unskilled workers from the Kompo (in Kiangsu) and workers from Shantung,[126] an occurrence likely to happen in Japanese mills because Shantung men often occupied minor managerial posts, such as overseer or "number one." Again, a fight over nothing occurred in March in Chapei between several hundred Hupeh boathands and Kompo dock laborers.[127] Machine wrecking was the reply to the decision of the management of the Nanyang tobacco factory in September to install new machines that would reduce the number of workers employed,[128] and to the refusal in June of the management of the Naigai No. 4 cotton mill to comply with the Kompo workers' repeated demands for the dismissal of an overseer who was a native of Anhwei.[129] But incidents of this kind were becoming less frequent, and were officially frowned upon by the General Union, one of its leaders declaring that "destruction of the means of production is unnecessary and even dangerous."[130] The cotton-mills union did its best to calm down the conflict between the Kompo and Shantung workers in the Naigai No. 5 mill.[131] On the other hand, the General Union encouraged go-slow tactics *(tai-kung)*, a strategy the hot-headed Shanghai proletariat took some time to get used to.[132]

Faced with the powerful organizational apparatus of the General Union, the moderate associations that had been so active in 1922-1924 and the Federation of Labor Organizations they had formed, which in the spring of 1924 had made a first attempt to provide central control of the Shanghai labor movement, were now losing ground. But they still tried to put themselves forward as an alternative form of unionism.[. . .]

This attempt to take an independent left-wing stand against the General Union failed, however, to disguise the fact that all these associations were becoming more and more closely linked with the Shanghai employers. The friendly society for women employed in the silk-reeling factories, run by Mrs. Mu Chih-ying, had gained so much support since 1923 that silkworkers were prevented from taking part in the May Thirtieth Movement; and when the General Union announced in June 1926 that it proposed to form a General Silk Filatures Union, Mrs. Mu tried to get the workers under her control to go on strike to protest the "violent methods of the General Union."[. . .]

Thus, the May Thirtieth Movement brought to an end the fierce struggle to gain influence among the Shanghai proletariat that had been waged for several years between the militant Communists and the *kung-tsei* associations, the latter groups fostered by the local employers and the right wing of the Kuomintang. The *kung-tsei* had now suffered complete defeat; even their most ardent supporters realized that the Federation of Labor Organizations, owing to a lack of real working-class support, had been unable to play any part in the Nationalist strikes during the summer of 1925.[133] It had, in fact, opposed them, and had thereby lost all its influence. During these mass struggles, the entire working class had rallied to the support of the General Union, which remained in control of the economic and political struggles of the Shanghai proletariat until April 1927.

The strikes that took place toward the end of 1925 and during the first part of 1926 not only reflected the growing authority of the General Union, but were also characterized by a widening of the demands presented. In addition to the usual demand for higher wages, there were demands for the abolition of fines, the payment of bonuses when no absenteeism had occurred over a given period *(shen-kung)*, a reduction in hours, maternity leave for women, the right to take meals during working hours, and the improvement of conditions for young workers and apprentices.[134] The strikes were also directed against the counterattack that seems to have been staged at this time by both foreign and Chinese employers. The employers were encouraged to move against the workers by the tactical withdrawal of the unions after the failure to obtain the political objectives of the May Thirtieth Movement. Thus, many strikes, with the support of the General Union and the cotton-mills union,[135] stopped attempts to lay off workers, especially in the Japanese mills,[136] and got various identity checks on workers abolished.[137] Others protested the lengthening of hours,[138] the use of efficiency experts,[139] and the installation of machines for recording the rate of output.[140] Another move in the employers' counterattack was to increase the staff employed in the control and supervision of factory work, and many strikes were held to protest the brutal behavior of Chinese, Japanese, White Russian, and Sikh foremen, overseers, "number one" men, and "armed bullies"—as they were called in the English newspapers in Shanghai—engaged to keep order in the factories.[141] The workers demanded their dismissal, sometimes with success, as in January in the Japanese Toa jute factory, in March in the Naigai No. 7 cotton mill, in April in the British Lumber Import-Export Company, in May in the Japanese Kiwa cotton mill and the Swiss ABC printing works, and in June in the BAT Pootung factory, the Naigai No. 13 cotton mill, and the Jih-hua cotton mill.[142] The employers' counterattack did not succeed in breaking the strike wave. Out of the 127 disputes between October 1925 and June 1926 for which the results are known, 82 were either partially or entirely successful.[143]

During this period the same uneasy, knife-edge relations continued between the General Union and the military authorities in the Shanghai region. The Fengtien army, which had occupied the city from the beginning of 1925 and which, after showing a certain amount of tolerance at the time of the May 30 demonstrations, had banned all labor organizations in the middle of September, was evicted a few weeks later by Sun Ch'uan-fang and his army.[144] Sun was a warlord with a reputation for liberal views because of his support for the restoration of the 1912 Constitution in 1922. Formerly a follower of the Chihli faction, he now kept only a nominal allegiance to Wu P'ei-fu. After taking Shanghai, he proclaimed himself inspector general of the five southeastern provinces and clearly had every intention of working for his own ends. The leaders of the General Union, Liu Hua, Sun Liang-hui, and Hsiang Ying, thought that this might be an opportunity to gain official sanction for the unions. They offered Sun union support in his fight against his Fengtien opponents, who were still active in the Lower Yangtze region.[145] Sun seems to have been uncertain at first whether to accept this offer, and meanwhile allowed the General Union and its local branches to resume their activities more or less openly. On November 29 the General Union returned officially to its headquarters, and on December 7 it held a meeting in Chapei attended by several thousand. But on December 10 it was once again closed down,[146] Sun having in the end opted for the classic warlord policy of repression. He had got in contact with the compradore section of the big bourgeoisie in Shanghai through its most typical representative, the banker Yü Hsia-ch'ing, whose hostility towards the labor movement had steadily increased ever since May 30, while his ties with the Western authorities in Shanghai had become closer.[147] On December 17 the president of the General Union, the former printing worker Liu Hua, who had been arrested at the end of November by the police of the International Settlement, was turned over by them to Sun Ch'uan-fang's military authorities and was executed—on the insistence of Yü Hsia-ch'ing, according to a tradition in the labor movement.[148] But the Shanghai unions could no longer be broken as easily as this. Although the Chinese police continued to be hostile to the General Union, and in April arrested its new president, Wang Ching-yun, a worker in the Commercial Press and president of the union in that firm,[149] it was nevertheless still influential and active at the beginning of 1926. Its activities were semilegal rather than clandestine. In January it launched a campaign to help the unemployed,[150] and in February it issued a political manifesto urging the people of Shanghai to cooperate with the Canton government and the People's National Armies in the northwest, and calling for the convocation of a national convention.[151] Despite police prohibitions, it celebrated May Day by holding a public meeting;[152] and on May 30 it commemorated the anniversary of the Nanking Road incident at a meeting of several thousand held in Chapei and organized with the help of associations of students and shopkeepers; the Commercial Press and other Chinese-owned enterprises allowed their employees to take time off for the occasion.[153] On July 11, despite new prohibitions against its activities following its support for the strike in the Chapei silk factories at the end of June,[154] the General Union held a conference of delegates from the principal unions affiliated with it, at which a program of minimum economic demands was worked out, including demands for a minimum wage based on the price of rice, a weekly day of rest, a ten-hour day, the abolition of fines, insurance against accidents and illness, and recognition of the right to strike and the right to form trade unions.[155] When the Northern Expedition set out from Canton at the end of July 1926, the Shanghai labor movement was still as strong as ever despite the setbacks of August and September 1925. It was very soon able, in collaboration with the advancing Cantonese armies, to launch the "three armed uprisings," the last of which left the trade unions in control of Shanghai in March 1927.

Crackdowns on Labor in Large Industrial Centers

In the industrial centers in the interior, both Chinese and foreign employers began in the fall to mount an even stronger counterattack than that launched against the Shanghai labor movement. Many workers were laid off, provoking a strike in the BAT Hankow factory and one in a Japanese cotton mill in the same city in February 1926,[156] and as in Shanghai, there was a tendency to mechanize production, probably in order to reduce the risk of strikes rather than for the purely economic purpose of increasing fixed capital investment. Strikes in protest against newly installed machinery broke out in May and June at the BAT Hankow factory,[157] and in April at the Japanese hemp factory in Mukden.[158] Control over workers was tightened also, again for political reasons rather than to decrease labor turn-over in the interests of production. The Japanese enterprises in Manchuria gradually adopted the practice of taking the finger-prints of their workers, and this became general at the beginning of 1927.[159] At that former stronghold of the labor movement, the Anyuan mine, the employers' counterattack was more violent still.[160] The economic difficulties of the Hanyehping Company had steadily increased during 1925, and at the time of the May Thirtieth Movement had reached the point where wages had not been paid for four months—which explains why the miners confined themselves to organizing a Committee for Effacing Shame, rather than declaring a sympathy strike as did their comrades at Shuikowshan and other industrial centers in the region. When in September they went on strike to obtain back payment of wages, the manager called in the police and the army, and there were three deaths and forty arrests. Several thousand workers were laid off and *hsin-kung* hired to take their place.[161] The Workers' Club, which since 1922 had been the pride of the Chinese labor movement with its twelve thousand members, its seven night schools that taught around two thousand pupils, its twelve reading rooms, its women's education department, and its consumers' cooperative with a capital of 13,000 one-yuan shares, was closed down and its property dispersed or wrecked. In Changsha students demonstrated in protest, and rickshaw men and printers went on a sympathy strike (the city went for four days without newspapers), only to meet with severe repression by Chao Heng-t'i.[162]

The employers' counterattack was accompanied by a renewal of activity on the part of the *kung-tsei,* the deserters from the labor movement. In central and north China there were no organizations similar to either the Cantonese guilds or the semi-working-class associations of Shanghai for these opponents of the left-wing unions to join. All they could do was find support as best they could among a very small section of employees—on the railways, for instance—and, for the rest, obtain supporters from the lumpenproletariat. Only after the warning of the May Thirtieth Movement were efforts apparently made by Chinese and foreign employers and government authorities to create a rival force that would take determined action against the left-wing unions. It seems to have been a force of this kind that carried out an armed attack on the strikers at the Chengchow cotton mill in August 1925; and in Peking a "General Union of Changsintien" was formed, supported by elements of the right wing of the Kuomintang, which had moved further away from the left wing of the party since the summer of 1925.[163] This new organization accused the Communists of being the slaves of Russia and of betraying the workers, and also accused the Kuominchun of collaborating with the Communists.[164][. . .]

Despite the counterattack, economic strikes came thick and fast throughout the fall, winter, and spring, an added stimulus being the renewed fighting between the warlords in the north and the Yangtze valley,[165] with the usual sequel of requisitioning of labor, slowing down of business, and inflation.[166] In Chang Tso-lin's territory the feng-p'iao, which was theoretically at par with the yuan, stood at 200 to the yuan in January and 391 in May, with over 500 million in banknotes in circulation,[167] and this certainly had a good deal to do with the sudden outburst of strikes in the northeast, where hitherto the development of the labor movement had lagged behind that in other regions.[. . .]

Another area where economic strikes were frequent during this period was the secondary textile center in the Lower Yangtze region, including the cities of Chinkiang, Soochow, Hangchow, Wusih, Nantung, and Shaohing. These were all cities where, in contrast to Shanghai, the modern cotton and silk industries were direct heirs to the old craft traditions of manufacture, and where the guilds still flourished, and modern trade unionism had made scarcely any progress at all. There the wave of economic strikes that began early in 1926 seems to have been activated by the Shanghai textile unions, which had been very active since the summer of 1925, rather than to have been the result of a crisis brought about by military operations.[168]

The only area where the Chinese labor movement was free to develop was still, as in the summer of 1925, the territory controlled by the Kuominchun. After the withdrawal of the Fengtien armies in December 1925, this territory included the industrial areas of Chihli and of western Shantung in addition to the parts of Honan and the northwestern plateaus already under Feng Yü-hsiang's control.[169]

The importance of Kuominchun support for the Nationalist revolution must not, of course, be exaggerated. Feng Yü-hsiang and his generals may have been on good terms with the Nationalist government in Canton,[170] and Hsü Ch'ien, a jurist and a Christian, who was one of Feng's political advisers, may have had close ties with the left wing of the Kuomintang;[171] but, after all, the

Kuominchun was a military organization that was recruited from a rather narrow section of society and that was only gradually coming under the influence of new ideas. Although Feng seems to have had ideas of reaching a military pact with the Soviet Union even before his visit to Moscow in January 1926 and although there was close collaboration between his armies and the Communists,[172] there was never any question of a real political alliance,[173] and the Communists themselves do not ever seem to have seriously considered one or to have regarded the Kuominchun as a genuinely revolutionary force.[174]

Nevertheless, during the short period when Feng's armies were in control of the whole of north China, they gave every support to the labor movement. Unions sprang up "like bamboo shoots after the rain," as one conservative newspaper in Peking put it.[175] The Cheng-T'ai railwaymen's union was allowed to resume its activities,[176] and, thanks to a subsidy of 500 yuan granted by the Kuominchun First Army, the Ching-Feng railwaymen's union reopened its library at the Tangshan depot and renewed its social and cultural services.[177] When the Kuominchun entered Tientsin, they released the KMA union leaders who had been arrested by Li Ching-lin after the defeat of the strike in August 1925, and on January 18 the Tangshan miners' union was officially reinstated in the presence of officers of the Ninth Regiment.[178] The Kuominchun also gave permission for the re-formation of the Tientsin General Union[179] and for the creation of a General Union in Peking with which printers', merchants', and craftsmen's unions would be affiliated;[180] and it supported the Tangshan miners' strike in February, called to obtain a bonus from the British owners.[181] In exchange, the unions gave the Kuominchun active support when military operations began at the end of the winter, during which the Fengtien armies gradually reconquered the whole of Chihli. The railwaymen in particular declared their support for Feng's armies[182] and did their best to hinder the movements of enemy troops.[183][. . .]

When the Kuominchun armies were chased out of Chihli and Honan in the spring of 1926, they took refuge in Shensi and Kansu, where they adopted the same liberal attitude toward labor problems. In the enterprises in Sian, Lanchow, and other urban centers in the region, hours of work were limited to nine or ten a day, child labor was controlled, and one day or a half-day off per week was granted.[184] At the beginning of 1927 this policy was given official expression in "Provisional Labor Legislation for the Northwestern Provinces," which went so far as to accept the principle of the minimum wage under a system of factory inspection, and the possibility of collective bargaining.[185] In this remote region, however, there were no big factories, but only small textile workshops employing a few dozen workers, so only a very marginal section of the Chinese working class was affected.

It was in fact this marginal role of the Kuominchun that was its congenital weakness. No one has yet made a study of its contribution to the Chinese political scene and its unique attempt to combine Christianity and Sunyatsenism,[186] but one thing is certain: it was able to create a stable counterpart in the north to the revolutionary Canton government in the south. When the Kuomintang launched its Northern Expedition in July 1926, the industrial areas of Chihli and Honan, which could have been of both economic and strategic importance, had already been evacuated by the Kuominchun. Feng's armies were not in control there long enough to enable the labor movement to recover from the setbacks caused by the general policy of repression adopted by the warlords from 1923 on.

In Hupeh, held by the Chihli faction, and in the northeast and in Shantung, controlled by the Fengtien faction, this policy of repression had operated almost continuously since the fall of 1925, and had added to the labor movement's difficulties stemming from the counterattack of the employers and the activities of the *kung-tsei* there. It is true that the railwaymen had succeeded in carrying out the task of restoring the unions, begun in 1924-1925. When they held their third national congress in February 1926, they had unions on all of the sixteen main railways in China,[187] including the provincially owned Nanchang-Kiukiang line[188] and the Chinese Eastern Railway.[189] But all these unions were more and more reduced to operating through clandestine activities and were continually hunted down by the police of the various warlords, especially after the defeat of the Kuominchun in the spring.[190][. . .]

This "White Terror" became all the more acute when in the spring the hatred between the Fengtien and Chihli factions was suddenly ended by their coming to terms in order to consummate the defeat of the Kuominchun and prepare themselves for the threatened attack from Canton. Marshals Wu P'ei-fu (who reappeared after two years in retirement) and Chang Tso-lin solemnly agreed to forget their long-standing enmity, and declared that priority must be given to the fight against communism and the labor movement.[191] Both of them issued strict instructions that all labor activities be suppressed, especially in Peking and Tientsin.[192] Thus, the rivalries between the warlords, those so-to-speak medieval relics who dominated the Chinese political scene during the years after World War I, were abruptly terminated when they sensed the pressure of the labor movement within the Nationalist movement as a whole; and the sudden realignment of the northern warlords was certainly not unconnected with the policies of the Canton government after the May Thirtieth Movement.

Notes

1. Shanghai, Archives of the Secretariat of the Municipal Council of the International Settlement of Shanghai, *Police Daily Reports (PDR)*, May 30, 1925. It will be remembered that the bylaw on child labor came up at the same meeting of the municipal council as these other bylaws, either through inadvertence or possibly with intent, and that the failure to vote it through was largely due to the dislike that the Chinese population of the International Settlement had for the other bylaws.
2. A. Kotenev, *New Lamps for Old* (Shanghai, 1931), pp. 117–21. The Fengtien armies had been occupying the Shanghai area since January 1925.
3. It fell from 195-209 cents to the yuan in January to 226-230 cents to the yuan in May (*Chinese Economic Bulletin* [Peking], August 8, 1925).
4. *PDR*, passim. During the same period in 1923 and 1924, prices had remained almost stationary.
5. Teng Chung-hsia, *Chung-kuo chih-kung yun-tung chien-shih* [Short History of the Chinese Labor Movement] (Peking, 1949), p. 181; Kotenev *New Lamps for Old*, pp. 121ff.
6. *PDR*, May 21-23, 1925.
7. *PDR*, May 25-28, 1925.
8. The students, having been forbidden by the Minister of Education to celebrate May 7 (a "Day of National Humiliation"), proceeded to attack his house; seventeen of them were arrested and three were killed (Kotenev, *New Lamps for Old*, pp. 121ff).
9. *Hu-nan ko-ming lieh-shih-chuan* [Revolutionary Martyrs of Hunan] (Chungsha, 1952), p. 15 (biography of Ts'ai Ho-sen). Ch'en Tu-hsiu seems to have thought that no more than three to five hundred people would take part in the demonstration.
10. Committee for the Labor History of Shanghai, "Wu-sa yun-tung chung ti Shang-hai kung-jen" [The Workers of Shanghai during the May 30th Movement], mimeographed (Shanghai, 1957), p. 11.
11. A complete list of the victims was published in Hsü Shih-hua et al., *Wu-sa yun-tung* [The May 30th Movement] (Peking, 1956), p. 31; they include cotton workers, stokers, telephone workers, tramwaymen, and BAT workers. Ma Ch'ao-chün, *Chung-kuo lao-tung yuntung shih* [History of the Chinese Labor Movement], 5 vols. (Taipei, 1959), p. 387, gives a rather different account of these events, and himself assumes responsibility for the demonstration on May 30. He was in Shanghai at the time trying to gain support among the

Kuomintang right wing for the Sunyatsenist Society he and his political associates had recently founded in Canton. He claims to have arranged the demonstration in association with students' groups and people like Tu Yueh-sheng, whom he describes as a "notable" *(shen)*, although it is difficult to believe that he was unaware of the fact that Tu was head of the Green Gang and engaged in the drug traffic in the French Concession. Actually Ma Ch'ao-chün's role must have been a very minor one, and even a non-Communist account such as Chang Wei-ying's "Wu-sa yun-tung chung ch'üan-kuo jen-min fan-ti tou-cheng ti kai-k'uang" [A Sketch of the Anti-Imperialist Struggle of the People Throughout the Country During the May 30th Movement] in *Ti-i-tz'u kuo-nei ko-ming chan-cheng shih-lun-chi* [On the History of the First Revolutionary Civil War], ed. Lai Hsin-hsia (Peking, 1957), makes no mention of him.

12. Kotenev, *New Lamps for Old,* p. 132.

13. *PDR,* June 1, 1925. Yü Hsia-ch'ing, the president of the chamber, was in Peking at the time (Teng Chung-hsia, *Chien-shih,* p. 195).

14. *North China Herald (NCH),* June 6, 1925. See also *Shanghai Municipal Council Report (SMCR),* 1925, p. 67.

15. *PDR,* June 1, 1925.

16. Teng Chung-hsia, *Chien-shih,* p. 185. It had been decided at the Second National Labor Congress to form a general union in Shanghai, and preparations had already been made. On the activities of the General Union at this time, see Kartunova, *Problemy Vostokovedeniya (PV),* 1960, no. 2. This article is based on *Je-hsüeh jih-pao* [The Bloodshed Journal], published by the Workers', Merchants', and Students' Federation.

17. Examples are the meeting on June 1 of two hundred employees of the Chinese Tramways and another on June 2 of two hundred fifty telephone workers and two hundred employees of the electric power plant (*PDR,* June 2, 1925, and June 3, 1925).

18. *SMCR,* 1925, p. 68; Hsü Shih-hua, *Wu-sa yun-tung,* pp. 60–77.

19. Hsü Shih-hua, *Wu-sa yun-tung,* pp. 60–77.

20. *China Weekly Review (CWR),* July 25, 1925.

21. *SMCR,* 1925, pp. 29–31.

22. Teng Chung-hsia, *Chien-shih,* pp. 185–86. On June 6, 1,337 marines of various nationalities were landed (Shanghai Municipal Council Archives, document 4207, part I, a letter from the commander of the American flotilla in Shanghai).

23. Teng Chung-hsia, *Chien-shih,* p. 187 (according to an inquiry made by the Peking government).

24. Ibid., p. 188.

25. *PDR,* June 12, 1925.

26. Teng Chung-hsia, *Chien-shih,* pp. 197–98.

27. *PDR,* June 12, 1925.

28. "Wu-sa yun-tung chung ti Shang-hai kung-jen," p. 16.

29. *PDR,* June 10, 1925.

30. Throughout the Movement the municipal council published a large number of leaflets and pamphlets in Chinese, under the general title of "The Truth." In July, for instance, 731,000 leaflets on "The Soviet Danger," "What Is Extraterritoriality?" and "The Facts of May 30" were distributed, and over 800,000 yuan were spent on propaganda (Shanghai Municipal Council Archives, document 4207, part I).

31. Chang Ching-lu et al., *Chung-kuo hsien-tai ch'u-pan shih-liao* [Materials on Recent Chinese Publications], supplementary volume (Peking, 1957), pp. 263–64; the bulletin appeared every three or five days.

32. *Hung-ch'i p'iao-p'iao (HCPP)*, no. 8, "I Ch'iu Pai." Ch'iu Pai was the editor of this paper, of which twenty-four issues appeared in all.

33. *PDR*, June 15, 1925, June 26, 1925, and July 7, 1925. Also from information obtained in interviews with Wang Jui-an (who in 1925 was a member of the Chapei picket corps) and with Chao Chin-ying and Chao Yin-ying, who in 1925 belonged to the pickets in the BAT factory in Pootung.

34. See for instance *PDR*, June 4, 1925, which reports that on June 3 Liu Hua held four meetings of cotton workers, each attended by several hundred people; and *PDR*, June 10, 1925, which reports that 7,000 strikers registered at the Chapei center and that a meeting of 5,000 strikers was held in Yangtzepoo.

35. The dockers and coolies received twenty cents a day (*PDR*, June 26, 1925; also information obtained from the former docker Chung Sheng-fu). According to *PDR*, June 11, 1925, June 15, 1925, June 21, 1925, the Pootung and Yangtzepoo cotton workers received one yuan a day, but this seems much too high. According to Communist sources (*International Press Correspondence [IPC]*, August 25, 1925), the rates of payment were six yuan a month for coolies, eight yuan for factory workers, and twenty yuan for skilled workers.

36. *IPC*, August 6, 1925.

37. At a meeting of the Action Committee on July 15, it was announced that 165,000 yuan had been collected in ten-cent silver coins, and 93,000 yuan in copper cash (*NCH*, July 18, 1925).

38. *IPC*, June 25, 1925. See also T. Mandalyan, "Das Internationale Proletariat und die Ereignisse in China," in *Arbeiterbewegung und Revolution in China* (Berlin: Red International of Trade Unions, 1925).

39. "Amsterdam and China," *Pan-Pacific Worker (PPW)*, no. 7, October 1, 1925.

40. P'eng Ming, *Chung-Su yu-i shih* [History of Sino-Soviet Friendship] (Peking, 1957), p. 122.

41. *IPC*, August 6, 1925.

42. *PDR*, July 3, 1925.

43. Shanghai Municipal Council, *Municipal Gazette*, August 6, 1925 (the report of the commissioner of police). The leaflet was distributed in the name of the Kuomintang, but it reads as if it had been written by the Communist militants who were members of the Shanghai committee of the KMT.

44. Interviews with Chao Chin-ying and Chao Yin-ying.
45. *NCH,* July 11, 1925. It was the manager of the Arnhold & Company cotton mill who made the suggestion on June 27 (Shanghai Municipal Council Archives, document 4207, part I).
46. *Municipal Gazette,* August 6, 1925 (the report of the commissioner of police).
47. *IPC,* August 6, 1925.
48. *NCH,* July 25, 1925.
49. *PDR,* July 15, 1925.
50. *South China Morning Post (SCMP),* July 30, 1925.
51. Lo Ren-yen, *China's Revolution from the Inside* (New York, 1930), p. 90.
52. Teng Chung-hsia, *Chien-shih,* p. 200. (No actual examples are given.)
53. *China Year Book (CYB),* 1926, p. 929.
54. *PDR,* August 14, 1925.
55. *SMCR,* 1925, p. 62.
56. *NCH,* July 18, 1925; *PDR,* July 9, 1925.
57. *PDR,* July 24, 1925.
58. *PDR,* July 26, 1925 and July 28, 1925.
59. *PDR,* August 7, 1925. See Wang Ch'ing-pin et al., *Ti-i-tz'u Chung-kuo lao-tung nien-chien* [The First Chinese Labor Yearbook], vol. 2 (Peking, 1928), pp. 63–65, for a complete list of the unions, including membership figures. The same list is given in T'ang Hai, *Chung-kuo lao-tung wen-t'i* [Labor Problems in China] (Shanghai, 1926), pp. 510–20, where the names and the districts of origin of the union presidents are also given.
60. *PDR,* August 7, 1925; see also Teng Chung-hsia, *Chien-shih,* pp. 211–12.
61. *PDR,* August 12, 1925.
62. *PDR,* August 13, 1925. This agreement was made public on August 14 (*PDR,* August 16, 1925).
63. *PDR,* August 19, 1925.
64. On these negotiations, see *Die Arbeiter Chinas im Kampf gegen Imperialismus* (Berlin and Moscow, 1927), pp. 22–29.
65. *NCH,* August 22, 1925; *Hsiang-tao (HT),* August 30, 1925; T'ang Hai, *Chung-kuo lao-tung wen-t'i* [Labor Problems in China] (Shanghai, 1926), pp. 468–72. See also Chu Pang-hsing et al., *Shang-hai ch'an-yeh yü Shang-hai chih-kung* [The Industries of Shanghai and Shanghai's Workers] (Shanghai, 1939), p. 421, for the manifesto of the post office strikers.
66. T'ang Hai, *Chung-kuo lao-tung wen-t'i,* pp. 73–86. See also Chang Ching-lu et al., *Ch'u-pan shih-liao* 1: 445–46 for the manifesto of the Commercial Press strikers; also *NCH,* August 29, 1925.
67. *NCH,* September 5, 1925.
68. This is the theory propounded by C. Brandt, *Stalin's Failure in China* (Cambridge, Mass., 1958).
69. The decisions adopted at the Washington Conference were only very gradually implemented, and in 1925 a number of important posi-

tions in the Chinese postal service were still held by foreigners *(CYB,* 1925, p. 394). The postal workers' manifesto simply complained about the control exercised by "foreigners," and did not mention the word "imperialists."

70. *NCH,* September 5, 1925, September 12, 1925. A union was formed on this line as a result of this success. Hsü Hsieh-hua, *T'ieh-lu lao-kung wen-t'i* [Labor Problems on the Railways] (Peking, 1931), p. 176.

71. Teng Chung-hsia, *Chien-shih,* p. 214.

72. *NCH,* September 12, 1925. Work was resumed after there had been a well-disciplined procession conducted by the leaders of the union, arranged in agreement with the General Union, and on the understanding that the cotton-mill owners and the Chinese Chamber of Commerce would contribute 90,000 yuan toward the expenses of the strike.

73. *NCH,* September 26, 1925.

74. *NCH,* September 26, 1925 and October 3, 1925 (concerning the cotton mills), and October 17, 1925 (concerning the Commercial Press).

75. *PDR,* September 24, 1925.

76. See Hsü Shih-hua, *Wu-sa yun-tung* and *Wu-sa t'ung shih* [The Painful History of May 30] (Peking, 1925); see also Chang Wei-ying, "Wu-sa yun-tung."

77. *HT,* July 2, 1925.

78. Wang Ch'ing-pin et al., *Nien-chien* 2: 457.

79. *HT,* July 26, 1925.

80. *Politique de Pékin (PP),* June 14, 1925.

81. *Manchuria Daily News (MDN),* June 17, 1925.

82. *NCH,* June 27, 1925. According to Teng Chung-hsia, *Chien-shih,* p. 121, this meeting was held on June 2.

83. Hsü Shih-hua, *Wu-sa yun-tung,* p. 21.

84. M. Hewlett, *Forty Years in China* (London, 1943), p. 154.

85. *PP,* June 14, 1925; see also Hsü Shih-hua, *Wu-sa yun-tung,* p. 78.

86. Hsü Shih-hua, *Wu-sa yun-tung,* pp. 125 and 134.

87. *HT,* August 15, 1925.

88. *MDN,* June 17, 1925.

89. *Wu-sa t'ung-shih,* p. 50.

90. *China Weekly Review (CWR),* October 17, 1925.

91. *Wu-sa t'ung-shih,* p. 51.

92. Hewlett, *Forty Years in China,* p. 154.

93. Teng Chung-hsia, *Chien-shih,* p. 190. See also Wang Ch'ing-pin, *Nien-chien* 2: 456 (a detailed analysis of the strikers' demands).

94. *NCH,* August 8, 1925; Teng Chung-hsia, *Chien-shih,* p. 209.

95. *NCH,* August 15, 1925 (report of J. P. Kenrick, general manager of the Kiaotso mines).

96. *MDN,* June 23, 1925 and June 30, 1925.

97. Archives of the Kailan Mining Administration (KMA), dossier 14/2/21, no. 46A (report of the managing director on the September

strike), and no. 71 (manifesto and rules of the Chaokochwang union).

98. Ibid.
99. See *IPC*, June, July, and August 1925, passim.
100. See above.
101. See L. Wieger, *La Chine moderne*, 10 vols. (Hsien-hsien, 1920-1932), vol. 6, pp. 196–98.
102. *Wu-sa t'ung-shih,* p. 113ff.
103. Hü Shih-hua, *Wu-sa yun-tung*, p. 37.
104. Ibid., p. 41.
105. See for instance how the peasants took part in the fight of the Canton government against the petty warlords of Kwangtung.
106. *HT,* July 26, 1925.
107. Chang Wei-ying, "Wu-sa yun-tung," p. 86.
108. *MDN,* June 25, 1925.
109. Hewlett, *Forty Years in China,* p. 154. See also *SCMP,* July 30, 1925, on the efforts of the Amoy compradores and their staffs to hinder the boycott.
110. *NCH,* June 13, 1925.
111. *HT,* August 15, 1925.
112. *MDN,* June 17, 1925.
113. Li Chien-nung, *The Political History of China, 1840-1928,* trans. from the Chinese by Ssu-yü Teng and Jeremy Ingalls (Princeton, N.J., 1956), pp. 482–84.
114. Wieger, *La Chine moderne* 6: 205.
115. *NCH,* July 11, 1925.
116. The mill belonged to the big industrialist Mu Ou-ch'u (H. Y. Moh); the Communist paper *HT* (August 31, 1925) accused him of having arranged the attack.
117. *Hsin-wen-pao (HWP),* August 20, 1925; *I-shih-pao* [Public Welfare] (Peking), August 23, 1925; *I-shih-pao* (Tientsin) August 30, 1925.
118. According to lists in Wang Ch'ing-pin, *Nien-chien* 2: 154–282.
119. The price rose from eleven yuan the picul in spring 1925 to sixteen yuan in April 1926 and eighteen yuan in June 1926, owing to rumors of a bad harvest which reached Shanghai, and also to the warlords' taxes (*Chinese Economic Bulletin [CEB],* August 21, 1926).
120. These figures are from *HT,* July 7, 1926 (which lists thirty-five strikes, most of which affected several firms at once). The report of the commissioner of police of the International Settlement lists forty strikes for the month of June, with over fifty thousand strikers; Wang Ch'ing-pin, *Nien-chien* 2: 154–282, lists forty-nine strikes for this month.
121. See below.
122. This demand was made in the strike of the telegraphers (*NCH,* October 10, 1925), and in the one at the No. 3 mill of the Naigai Wata Kaisha (*NCH,* June 19, 1926).
123. A right demanded in the British Oriental cotton mill (*NCH,* December 19, 1925). This right was granted (*CEB,* January 23, 1926).

124. Demand made in the British Ewo cotton mill (*NCH,* December 12, 1925).
125. Demanded by the strikers at the Japanese Jih-hua cotton mill, held to protest the arrest of a worker by the Chinese police of Pootung (*NCH,* November 21, 1925), and by the Commercial Press strikers who were protesting the dismissal of the leaders of the strike in August 1925 (*NCH,* January 2, 1926).
126. *NCH,* June 26, 1926.
127. *NCH,* March 20, 1926.
128. *CEB,* October 16, 1926.
129. "Strikes in Shanghai," *Chinese Economic Monthly (CEM)* (Peking), October 1926.
130. *HT,* June 23, 1926. Already in March the General Union frowned on the use of *ta-ch'ang* by strikers in a Yangtzepoo cotton mill (*NCH,* March 13, 1926).
131. *NCH,* June 26, 1926.
132. *HT,* June 23, 1926.
133. Ma Ch'ao-chün, *Chung-kuo lao-tung yun-tung shih,* says nothing at all about any activities of the Federation during the May Thirtieth Movement; he admits (p. 486) that very few of the members were industrial workers, and that such as there were were all employed in small workshops.
134. See Wang Ch'ing-pin, *Nien-chien* 2: 154–282, for a chronology of strikes during this period.
135. *PDR,* November 1925, passim.
136. "Strikes in Shanghai," *CEM,* October 1926.
137. For instance, a system of identity discs in the Société Franco-Chinoise de Construction Métallique was protested (*CEB,* August 21, 1926). After the May Thirtieth Movement each worker in the Japanese cotton mills was compelled to wear a numbered disc and to carry identity papers with a photograph (interview with the worker Wang Jui-an). The French Tramways took the fingerprints of their workers (*NCH,* December 31, 1926).
138. This was protested in an embroidery factory in April (*CEM,* October 1926).
139. Protested in a British cotton mill in May (ibid.).
140. Protested in the Naigai cotton mill No. 3 in March (ibid.).
141. One example is the strike in the Naigai cotton mills Nos. 2 and 3 in June 1926, demanding the dismissal of four "armed bullies" recently engaged by the factory (*NCH,* June 19, 1926).
142. *CEM,* October 1926.
143. Wang Ch'ing-pin, *Nien-chien* 2: 154–282.
144. Li Chien-nung, *Political History,* p. 487.
145. *NCH,* November 7, 1925; *PDR,* October 21, 1925.
146. *PDR,* November–December 1925, passim.
147. H. Issacs, *The Tragedy of the Chinese Revolution,* rev. ed. (Stanford, Calif., 1951), pp. 78–79.
148. *Chung-kuo ko-ming lieh-shih-chuan* [Chinese Revolutionary Martyrs] (Hong Kong, 1948), pp. 189ff (biography of Liu Hua).

149. *PDR*, April 10, 1926.
150. *NCH*, January 23, 1926.
151. *NCH*, February 27, 1926.
152. *PDR*, May 3, 1926.
153. *PDR*, May 27, 1926, May 31, 1926, June 1, 1926.
154. *PDR*, June 28, 1926; *HT*, June 30, 1926.
155. Wang Ch'ing-pin, *Nien-chien* 2: 396–97.
156. *Ch'en pao (CP)*, December 12, 1925 (report of a strike against the dismissal of 100 women by the BAT); *Min-kuo jih-pao (MKJP)*, February 23, 1926 (report of a strike against the dismissal of 700 older workers in a hemp factory).
157. *HT*, August 6, 1926; *CWR*, June 12, 1926.
158. *MDN*, April 6, 1926.
159. *MDN*, March 16, 1927. (This Japanese-owned paper explicitly stated that it was a question of getting rid of workers with "unwholesome ideas.")
160. *MKJP*, September 23, 1925 and September 24, 1925; *HT*, December 3, 1925.
161. According to *HT*, 5,000 were laid off; the figure was 8,000 according to *MKJP*, September 24, 1925, and 10,000 according to *CP*, October 2, 1925.
162. *HT*, December 30, 1925; *NCH*, November 28, 1925.
163. On the split in the Kuomintang see below.
164. *Shun-t'ien shih-pao (STSP)*, December 24, 1925; *Shih-shih hsin-pao* [New Times] (Shanghai), January 3, 1926.
165. For details concerning these wars see Wieger, *La Chine moderne* 6: 33–76.
166. In Hupeh the provincial paper money depreciated rapidly during 1926, falling as low as 20 percent below nominal value; the exchange rate with the silver yuan changed from 3,000 to 11,000 paper cash (*Returns of Trade [RT]*, Shasi, 1926, p. 3).
167. *MDN*, February 23, 1926 and passim. The yuan was worth 500 feng-p'iao at the beginning of August and 850 in March 1927.
168. "Labor Conditions in Chekiang," *CEJ*, February 1927.
169. See Wieger, *La Chine moderne* 6: 58ff.
170. *PP*, January 17, 1926 (exchange of messages between Feng and the Central Executive Committee of the Kuomintang).
171. Hsü Ch'ien, surrounded by officers of the Second Kuominchun, made a speech at the funeral service held in Peking on January 27 for Kuo Sung-ling (*Japan Weekly Chronicle*, January 4, 1926), who had just been killed in battle in his abortive revolt against his chief, Chang Tso-lin; he wanted to join forces with the Kuominchun (Wieger, *La Chine moderne* 6: 64–68).
172. For example, the student Li Chih-tan was assigned by the CP to be political adviser to the Second Kuominchun (*Ko-ming lieh-shih-chuan*, p. 68).
173. *PP*, January 21, 1926 (on a circular in which the First Kuominchun denied that it was Bolshevist. "Since our country is based on

agriculture, there are neither very rich nor very poor people.").

174. *HT,* December 1925-January 1926, passim.

175. *I-shih-pao,* January 3, 1926.

176. Wang Ch'ing-pin, *Nien-chien* 2: 115.

177. *I-shih-pao,* January 19, 1926.

178. Ibid., January 26, 1926.

179. *HT,* May 1, 1926. Before the retreat of the Kuominchun, this union is said to have had fifty thousand members.

180. Wang Ch'ing-pin, *Nien-chien,* pp. 98–99; *I-shih-pao,* January 4, 1926.

181. *STSP,* February 8, 1926. On this occasion the Kuominchun called upon workers' groups in Tangshan to support the strikers "against British imperialism."

182. *CP,* December 15, 1925. In Nankow two thousand railwaymen held a meeting to express their hostility toward the Fengtien faction and their support for the Kuominchun, and they called for a national association for the abolition of the unequal treaties and the introduction of civil liberties.

183. Interview with the railwayman Li Ch'en-kang, who took part in the actions of the "special groups" of railwaymen on the Lunghai line, operating in liaison with the Kuominchun. See also Ch'üan-Kuo tsung-kung-hui, *Ko-ming chan-shih-chi ti-i ts'e* [First Collection of Biographies of Revolutionaries] (Canton, 1926), p. 34 (biography of the Communist railwayman Ma Ch'i, who collaborated with the Kuominchun on the Ching-Sui line and was killed in a battle against the Fengtien faction).

184. "Factories in Shensi and Kansu," *CEM,* November 1926. The "model cotton mill" in Sian employed 85 workers on a nine-hour day (seven hours for apprentices); the 50 workers employed by a Lanchow wool factory worked a seven-hour day, and the 125 workers in a match factory worked a nine-and-a-half-hour day. In all three cases Sunday was a day of rest.

185. J. D. H. Lamb, *Origin and Development of Social Legislation in China* (Peking, 1930), appendix; see also Wang Ch'ing-pin, *Nien-chien* 3: 191–95.

186. J. Sheridan, *Chinese Warlord: The Career of Feng Yü-hsiang* (Stanford, Calif., 1966). This study of Feng Yü-hsiang was published in 1966, after the original edition of the present work came out.

187. *HT,* February 10, 1926.

188. *I-shih-pao,* November 25, 1925.

189. *CP,* January 19, 1926. In giving this information, this conservative paper denounced the "red influence" in the C.E.R. union.

190. *PP,* May 9, 1925 (instructions given by Wu P'ei-fu to the management of the Ching-Han for the repression of union activities).

191. See for instance an interview with a representative of Wu P'ei-fu in *PP,* May 2, 1926, who said that Wu was prepared to fight to the end in order to crush Bolshevism in China, and that this was why he had formed an alliance with Marshal Chang. See also a statement made by Chang Tso-lin to foreign journalists in Mukden (*PP,* April 19,

1926), in which he declared that his sole aim was to exterminate Bolshevism, after which he would withdraw north of the Great Wall and devote himself to the reconstruction of Manchuria.

192. *PP*, May 9, 1926 (an account of large-scale arrests in Peking by order of the commander of the Fengtien garrison).

Historical Backgrounds and Beginnings
of the Mexican Labor Movement
before the Revolution of 1910

M. R. Clark

It has become fairly customary to date the organized labor movement in Mexico from the day in October 1910 when Francisco I. Madero began the revolution against Porfirio Díaz, president and dictator since 1876, and to make the development of the labor movement exactly synchronize with the revolution.[1] To a certain degree this is accurate. Nevertheless, while certainly the Mexican labor movement is almost entirely a product of the present century, its origin antedates by some years the political revolution of 1910.[. . .] In the last years of the nineteenth century Díaz turned his attention to the industrialization of the country. Foreign capital was invited into Mexico on most favorable terms, railroad construction went forward rapidly, factories sprang up in great numbers, relatively, and veritable industrial centers were created in some parts of the republic.[2] Despite all these changes taking place, every effort was made to preserve the worker in that status occupied in a nonindustrialized society. It was considered to be in the interest of the state, as well as of the landed class, that both the industrial and the agricultural workers should be kept ignorant, servile, unorganized, and not class conscious. It did not, seemingly, occur to the government that protection of the worker was either necessary or desirable. A cheap labor supply was one of the principal inducements held forth to foreign capitalists.

Trade unionism, of course, was quite unknown in Mexico in the nineteenth century. Yet the working classes, in spite of the almost insuperable difficulties that faced them, were desperately attempting to achieve some form of organization. As had been almost universally true of labor organization the world over, these early attempts took the form of mutualist societies, in reality little more than sickness and death benefit associations. In Mexico, particularly, mutualism was looked upon as the first, and for a long time, the only recourse the working people had for personal protection and for any improvement of their condition.

Extracted from Marjorie Ruth Clark, *Organized Labor in Mexico* (Chapel Hill, N.C.: University of North Carolina Press, 1934; reissued, New York: Russell & Russell, 1973).

The most important of the early attempts at organization in mutualist societies occurred among the railwaymen. In 1888 the Supreme Order of Mexican Railway Employees was formed under the leadership of Nicasio Idar, an employee in the express department of the National Railways. Idar had spent considerable time in the United States, and the methods he used show how greatly he was influenced by the unions in that country. Even the name given the Mexican organization was decidedly reminiscent of organizations in the United States. The aims of this group were strictly mutualist in character, but it was so short lived (lasting but three or four years) that it accomplished little. In 1897 the railwaymen formed a second organization, also mutualist. This, the Confederation of Railway Societies of the Mexican Republic, had a much greater effect upon the railway unions of the present. The leaders of this early organization were instrumental in forming, in 1904, the Grand League of Railway Workers, on more clearly defined trade-union lines, and the Grand League was the model for later unions.

The railway societies, however, if the most important, were not the first ones formed. A mutualist society known by the name of "Union and Concord" was formed in the Federal District as early as 1874. By 1879 there was in existence a central organization of mutualist societies, which called itself the Grand Labor Congress.[3] The shoemakers, the bakers, the pulque workers, the musicians, the mechanics, and other groups created mutual aid societies. The pulque workers showed imagination by naming their society "Divine Providence."[4] The leaders of these societies, however, were always persons closely connected with the government. The formation of these societies represented, more nearly than a bona fide movement among the workers, an attempt on the part of the government to prevent such a movement. For a long time Mexican workers were convinced that when they had formed a mutualist society, even under official control, they had found the only possible solution to their problems.

By the beginning of the twentieth century there were evidences of a change in this situation. Socialist doctrines had begun to filter into the country; Mexico was growing increasingly weary of Díaz and his dictatorship. A very small group of intellectuals, made up of probably not more than a hundred people in the whole of the republic, was trying to spread new social doctrines among the masses.

[. . .] About the same time that attempts were being made to better the condition of the workers in Yucatán, in Mexico City the brothers Ricardo and Enrique Flores Magón were the center of an anti-Díaz, anarchist group whose members devoted their efforts about equally to the promulgation of anarchist doctrines and to a fight against the dictatorship.[. . .]

In Guadalajara a third nucleus of labor organization was led by Ramón Morales, Roque Estrada, Juan I. Martínez, José María Loreto, Primitivo R. Valencia, and others. This group also published a newspaper, *El obrero socialista,* and their purpose, more definitely than that of the other groups, was concentrated on the formation of trade unions. The Guadalajara leaders emphatically denied any relationship with the Flores Magón group, saying that they believed only in trade unionism.[5]

As industrialization of the country proceeded, the cost of living rose rapidly, while wages, generally speaking, remained almost stationary.[6] The already miserable standard of living became still lower. Increases in prices for a few of the standard foods of the working classes are shown in Table 1.

Table 1
(Prices in pesos)[7]

	1792	1891	1908
Rice, 100 kilos	7.60	12.87	13.32
Sugar, 100 kilos	30.40	17.43	23.00
Flour, 100 kilos	2.71	10.87	21.89
Maize, hectoliter	1.75	2.50	4.89
Wheat, 100 kilos	1.80	5.09	10.17
Beans, 100 kilos	1.63	6.61	10.84
Chile, 100 kilos	26.08	27.13	57.94

Average money wage per day for agricultural laborers has been generally estimated at 25.5 centavos in 1793, 36 centavos in 1891, and 42.5 centavos in 1908. As one author expressed this discrepancy between the rise of prices and the rise of wages,

> it resulted, then, that the laborer of the viceregal epoch, with the product of two hundred and fifty days of work could buy 35.7 hectoliters of maize; in 1891 he could buy 42.5 hectoliters, and in 1908 only 23.51 hectoliters. In 1792 he could buy 23 measures of flour, of 100 kilos each; in 1891, he could buy only 9.71 measures, and in 1908, only 5.25.[8]

These figures, either of commodity prices or of wages, are not to be taken as more than indicative of the trend during this period. Statistics in Mexico are far from complete or accurate. It must also be noted that the wage of agricultural laborers paid in money or in tokens has never been all that the worker received. Laborers usually received some kind of shelter and an allowance of corn or beans, or both, and in addition the right to cultivate a small patch of land for their own use. The figures do show, however, a steadily increasing pressure upon the lower classes, which in itself was sufficient to cause the growing discontent that made itself apparent in the first ten years of the twentieth century. Added to this discontent, the gradual infiltration of revolutionary doctrines caused sporadic attempts on the part of the working classes to improve their lot.

But any such attempts were strictly prohibited by law. The Constitution of 1857, far from recognizing the rights of the working class, was a stronghold against any legal agitation for the betterment of the workers' economic condition. The Penal Code of the Federal District, which became effective in 1872, provided that

> from eight days to three months' imprisonment and a fine of from 25 to 500 pesos, or only one of these punishments, will be imposed upon anyone who creates a tumult or riot or uses any other mode of physical or moral force with the object of increasing or decreasing the salaries or wages of the workers or to impede the free exercise of industry or labor.

This code remained on the statute books of the Federal District until 1927, and many states had much the same provisions. After the beginning of the revolution in 1910, however, such articles remained law on paper only.

In December 1904 a request of clerks in certain stores in Mexico City that the stores should be closed for a few hours on Sunday afternoons so alarmed and enraged many proprietors that meetings were called in which it was proposed to "throw into the street" all those clerks who had signed petitions for the closing. A society was formed to decide what the proprietors must do in view of this unprecedented "initiative" on the part of their employees.[9] A few months later the workers of Guadalajara, under the leadership of Ramón Morales, declared a strike. It was the announced purpose of the Guadalajara group to foment at least one strike each year, until the condition of the working classes should receive attention. The two strikes of outstanding importance in the prerevolutionary period of the Mexican labor movement occurred in 1906 and 1907, one in the mines of Cananea in the state of Sonora, the other in the textile mills of the Orizaba region in the state of Veracruz.

The strike in the mines of Cananea took place in June 1906. It was ostensibly a strike for higher wages for the Mexican workers, who claimed they were discriminated against in comparison with Americans employed in the mines. This was only part of the story, however. In Cananea there was a liberal club which was affiliated with the party headed by Ricardo Flores Magón. This club was very active in preparing and distributing strike propaganda. The manifestos issued to arouse the workers included also demands for representative government and for the withdrawal of Díaz from the presidency.[10] The Western Federation of Miners was also active in stirring up the Mexicans.[11] This strike, the first of importance in Mexican labor history, was accompanied by bloodshed and violence. Buildings were burned, stores sacked, and fights between the strikers and the company men resulted in more than twenty killed and as many wounded. The government sent federal troops to restore order, and some American miners were hurried across the border to help quell the "outbreak," in which it was alleged American women and children were at the mercy of Mexican miners. The company and the government were successful, and the strikers were forced to return to work under the same conditions as before the conflict began. The leaders who had not been killed in the fighting, or who were unable to escape, were imprisoned. Some of them were still confined in the prison of San Juan de Ulúa, a fortress on a tiny island in the harbor of Veracruz, when Díaz was overthrown years later.

In spite of the failure of this strike, the next year witnessed an even more violent outbreak on the part of the workers. The textile industry in 1907 was the most highly developed industry in Mexico, but working conditions were very bad. And so in July 1906 there had been formed among the textile workers the first real trade union of Mexico. It was called the Grand Circle of Free Workers, and it adopted principles that were outlined in a manifesto issued by the Flores Magón group in St. Louis, Missouri, on July 1, 1906. These principles the Grand Circle translated as, "War to the death to the tyrant who sells us, to the merchant who robs us, and to the employer who exploits us; war without quarter . . . by reason or by force,"[12] though this was much more radical than the original manifesto. So ready were the workers for revolt that within a very short time the Grand Circle could boast of branch organizations in the states of Jalisco, Oaxaca, Tlascala, Mexico, the Federal District, Querétaro, and Hidalgo, in addition to Puebla and Veracruz, the two states in which the movement began. The assertion is now made that at the time of the strike the Grand Circle had ninety-nine branches.

At the end of 1906 the textile manufacturers in Puebla and Tlascala issued new regulations with which the workers were not in accord. In December, therefore, a strike was declared in various textile factories in the two states, and it rapidly spread to the neighboring state of Veracruz, where it assumed much more serious proportions. Some of the leaders of the Guadalajara movement were in Veracruz at the time and had a part in fomenting the strike.

President Díaz was asked by the employers to act as arbiter and he conceded to the striking workers permission to send representatives to lay their claims before him. On January 5, 1907, the president gave his decision, after granting hearings to the workers' delegates as well as to those of the employers. This in itself was unprecedented: it was unquestionably the first time that labor in Mexico had been permitted to express its demands. However, the judgment rendered by Díaz was on almost every count unfavorable to the workers.[13] Wages were still subject to fines, although the fines were to be used in the establishment of funds for widows and orphans, where before they had reverted to the employers; each worker was required to have a book in which the employers were to enter all the worker's faults and good qualities, and without the presentation of this book no worker could be hired; children under seven were prohibited from working in textile factories except upon permission of their parents, and then they might work part time only; any publications the workers might wish to distribute must be supervised by persons named by the political chief of the district; and strikes were prohibited. The twelve-hour day was established, and employers were urged, but not ordered, to equalize wages on the basis of the highest wages paid in each industrial district. Most of these provisions had been included in the regulations issued by the textile employers a few months earlier, and they were the immediate cause of the strike. It is also noted that before the president's decision was made public, federal troops were installed in the various strike centers.

The workers in the Orizaba textile district in the state of Veracruz refused to accept the dictates of the president. In this district are located the largest textile factories of the country, including those of Río Blanco, Santa Rosa, and Nogales. The workers, in an attempt to get food, attacked the company stores. When they met with resistance, they set fire to buildings, whereupon the federal troops that had been installed there, under the command of Rosalino Martínez, proceeded immediately to the suppression of the strikers' demonstrations. Most of the actual fighting took place at the factory of Río Blanco, and there was considerable loss of life. The actual number of workers who lost their lives in these encounters has never been determined, but estimates range from twenty or twenty-five to several hundred. And in Mexican labor history January 7, 1907, has become a symbol of martyrdom to the labor cause.

The prompt and drastic action of the federal government, together with the rigid supervision to which the workers were subjected, utterly destroyed the Grand Circle of Free Workers. It never showed signs of life after the Río Blanco debacle. Nevertheless, the following year (1908) the indefatigable leaders attempted another strike, this time on the railways of Aguascalientes. The Grand League of Railway Workers was apparently strongly organized, and it was the members of this organization who were to strike. But the strike never took place. Díaz threatened to mobilize the railway workers if they attempted it, and interest in politics was becoming so great as to overshadow any interest the workers might have in striking. President Díaz had just given his famous Creelman interview, in which he stated that he was ready to retire from the presidency and "would welcome the emergence of an opposition party as proof of Mexico's ability to develop a true democracy." This statement was taken seriously, and it aroused tremendous interest in political action. Among the working classes political organizations sprang up with much the same rapidity which, later, labor unions were to show. Madero's book, *The Presidential Succession in 1910,* published in the same year, added tremendously to the excitement. Several of the newly formed parties included in their programs demands for social and economic reform, including the breakup of the great landed estates, the regulation of the right to strike, and general protection of the workers. Practically every group of workers organized, whether it professed political aims or not, formulated a petition to President Díaz to renounce his office. All the interest of the working classes centered, at the moment, on political change.

It seems incredible, in the light of later events, that the Díaz government failed utterly to realize the significance of the strikes of Cananea and Río Blanco and of the continually growing organization and restlessness of the mass of the people. It was quite satisfied to arrest or exile the leaders of the workers' groups, establish martial law when a strike actually occurred, break up the incipient labor organizations, and impose its will by force. Meanwhile, political and economic dissatisfaction was rapidly bringing on the revolution of 1910, which, political in its inception, soon made social reform its chief issue, but which had only vague and conflicting ideas as to the direction such social reform should take.[. . .] So when Madero entered Mexico City in triumph, he was given a welcome by the working classes such as had never been given before, spontaneously, to anyone. They thronged the streets, wild with excitement and joy, convinced that he had brought them victory in their own fight against poverty and oppression.

The Right to Organize

At once there began what amounted to a riot of labor organization. Political clubs formed in the period of agitation against Díaz disappeared, while unions of workers emerged. At last, it seemed, all need for secrecy or caution in labor organization was removed. The law against such organization, to be sure, remained unchanged, but the Madero government interposed no obstacles, and this right to open formation of unions was, to the workers, the visible symbol of the change which had occurred. Every kind of social theory the Mexican workers had ever heard of was embraced. Some of the unions formed were mutualist in character, as this was the type which was most familiar; others professed syndicalist or socialist or anarchist or communist doctrines. In every case, however, the newly created organizations were without definite aims and without any clear understanding of the place they should fill in the life of the worker.

So there developed a period of experimentation in labor organization and of preparation for the creation of more enduring groups. Leaders were wholly untrained, and the masses of the workers were entirely undisciplined. It was a period of blind drawing together, and the organizations created proved to be of such a loose and casual character that definite action was impossible. There were many strikes, but they were almost always the result of purely local conditions, and if they resulted in gains at all, such gains affected only small and isolated groups; they had little effect on the working class as a whole.

In Mexico City, particularly, organization progressed rapidly. On May 2, 1911, the Typographical Confederation of Mexico was formed under the leadership of Amadeo Ferrés, a Spaniard; it became the nucleus of the first fighting organization in Mexico after the short-lived and unfortunate Grand Circle of Workers of 1906 and the Grand League of Railway Workers of 1908. The Typographical Confederation later became known as the National Confederation of Graphic Arts, one of the powerful labor groups of the country. A few months after the formation of the Typographical Confederation, a newspaper was launched (*El tipógrafo mexicano*). This confederation has been especially important in Mexican labor history, since in it some of the future labor leaders, among them Ezequiel Salcedo, Eduardo Moneda, Rafael Quintero, and Alfredo Pérez Medina, gained their first experience.

Other groups soon followed the example of the typographical workers, and among the unions formed were those of the stonemasons, the shoemakers, the tailors, and the bakers. A second Spaniard, Juan Francisco Moncaleano, was especially active in the organization of the stonemasons' union. At the same time new mutualist societies appeared among the carpenters, the railwaymen, the musicians, and many other groups.[14] Some of these organizations never functioned, and most of them failed entirely to live up to the grandiloquence of their names or the hopes of their founders.

[. . .] By the time Madero was forced out of the presidency, some of the tendencies which were later to become characteristic of the Mexican labor movement had clearly emerged. One of these was the tendency of the unions to lean upon the government. Did the workers want a meeting place? They went to the government. Did they need money? They asked a government official for it, and very often got it. Were they involved in a conflict with employers? Again a government official was selected to act as arbiter. Along with this dependence on official support went an individualism among labor leaders which made cooperation among the various workers' groups impossible. The tendency of the masses to follow persons and not convictions was evident in the earliest organizations, and this in large measure prevented the development of any real class consciousness among the Mexican working classes.

Another marked tendency of the labor unions was the desire to protect their interests through legislation. Proposals for all sorts of labor laws were prepared, but before any of them became enacted into laws Mexican labor passed through many years of struggle.

Notes

1. Francisco I. Madero issued his Plan of San Luis Potosí from San Antonio, Texas, on October 5, 1910.

2. The cotton-textile industry was the first to be developed to any considerable extent. By 1910 there were 135 factories, employing 33,000 workers. For a discussion of the industrialization of the country, see Herbert Ingram Priestley, *The Mexican Nation: A History* (New York: Macmillan Co., 1930), pp. 391–92.

3. Mexico, Archivo de la Secretaría de Industria, Comercio y Trabajo, *Convención radical*, August 24, 1887, Exp. 30-3-10-11.

4. Mexican workers have always been very fond of giving their unions names which seem strange to foreigners. Many unions are called "Martyrs of Chicago," "Martyrs of the 7th of January," "Martyrs of Work," "Sacco and Vanzetti," "Faith and Work," "The Avengers," "The Weapon of Destruction," and so on.

5. *El obrero socialista*, March 21, 1906.

6. Jesús Silva Herzog, in "El salario de nuestros campesinos," *La antorcha*, July 4, 1925, p. 10, says that from 1810-1910 the wages of agricultural workers remained stationary, while the price of the staple articles in their diet increased 300 percent.

7. *Estadística nacional*, May 31, 1925, pp. 15–19.

8. Toribio Esquivel Obregón, *La influencia de España y los Estados Unidos sobre México* (Madrid: Casa Editorial Culleja, 1918), p. 343.

9. *El diario del hogar*, December 18, 1905.

10. Report of Rafael Izabal, governor of Sonora, to the Minister of the Interior, published in *Diario oficial*, June 28, 1906, pp. 801–8.

11. It was not until some years later that the claim was made that the Western Federation of Miners brought about the Cananea strike as the first step in their campaign to organize all the mine workers of Mexico. John Murray, *Schoolmaster Gun in Mexico*, pp. 16–19.

12. Pánfilo Méndez, in *Pro paria*, January 7, 1927.

13. *El imparcial*, January 5, 1907.

14. Mexico, Archivo de la Secretaría de Industria, Comercio y Trabajo, *El intransigente*, May 20, 1912, Exp. 32-3-2-6.

The Lagos Strike of 1897:
An Exploration in Nigerian Labor History

A.G. Hopkins

[. . .] The main purpose of this article is to draw attention to labor history as an important subject of research in African studies by examining some of the problems which arose in southwest Nigeria during a time of rapid economic change at the close of the nineteenth century. The article will first reconstruct the history of a strike which occurred in Lagos in 1897. This strike, which has not been investigated previously, was the first major labor protest of the colonial period; as such, it deserves to be rescued from obscurity. The second part of the article will concentrate on an analysis of some of the wider issues which the strike illustrates, and from which it derives its significance. These are four in number; first, the problem of the supply of labor to wage-earning employment during a period of transition from slave to free labor; second, the nature of government policy regarding labor matters; third, the question of the standard of living of the workers of Lagos; and, finally, the problem of the organization of labor and of the political implications of the rise of an urban labor force.

The Strike

[. . .] As a commercial rather than an industrial center, Lagos did not at first require a large body of permanent, full-time laborers. But in the 1890s, after the expansion of British rule into the hinterland, the demand for labor in Lagos increased rapidly as a result of the inauguration of a program of large-scale public works. For reasons which will be considered in the second part of this article, this demand did not meet with an adequate response from the sources of supply, and the outcome was that the government, which was the largest single employer, was faced with an

This article is reprinted from *Past and Present: A Journal of Historical Studies*, no. 35 (December 1966), with the permission of The Past and Present Society and the author. Copyright © 1966 by The Past and Present Society, Corpus Christi College, Oxford, England.

acute shortage of labor. This, in brief, was the situation when Henry McCallum, the new governor of Lagos, first took up his appointment in April 1897. McCallum was a soldier and engineer by training who had served the empire for over twenty years in the Far East before coming to West Africa. He was an energetic administrator, but his energy sprang in part from a conviction that he knew the answers to problems which, as subsequent events showed, he had failed to study fully. On arriving in Lagos, McCallum quickly made up his mind that a number of far-reaching economic and administrative reforms were needed, and he made it plain that the new broom would not sweep old and dusty problems under the carpet. In a private letter sent shortly before the strike to a senior civil servant in the Colonial Office, McCallum wrote:

> I have been brought up in a different school to my predecessors and have been accustomed to see the paramount authority of government maintained pretty severely against a riotous mob & I am prepared for a row here, which one sees *must* come.[1]

The Colonial Office, while approving of the new governor's enthusiasm, was nevertheless a little nervous of where it might lead him, for it was suspected that his prescription for West African ills was based on a diagnosis of Far Eastern ailments.[2] Such reservations were justified, for McCallum's kill-or-cure policy was very largely responsible for provoking the strike of 1897.

McCallum approached the labor problem from two directions. The first approach involved the adoption of a low-wage policy. He expressed his unequivocal support for such a policy in a letter to the governor of the Gold Coast toward the end of April.

> What is distressing me (& it is a subject we can well work on together) is the high price of labour when taken into consideration with what we get for it. When we know the conditions of life here a uniform sum of 1s. 3d. per diem including subsistence is downright absurd, 9d. would be too high for the ordinary nigger if we are ever to develop our Colonies agriculturally and allow their products to compete with those produced in other parts of the world.[3]

Two months later McCallum wrote another revealing letter, which is also worth quoting on the subject of wage rates. This was a private letter to Shelford, the consulting engineer appointed by the Crown Agents to build the Lagos railway.

> I am now engaged, in working with the Chamber of Commerce in bringing about a reduction of local labor which is absurdly high especially for mechanics and artisans. It wd. pay us well at present

rates to import the industrious and shifty Chinaman. We shall probably have a strike when a general reduction of labour is brought about; that will not last long—an African worships his stomach and will be back again to work before many days. Prices will then go down all round and you should make savings in the Estimates.[4]

The assumptions lurking behind these two statements will be examined fully in the second part of this article. All that need be said at present is that McCallum's low-wage policy was based on three main supports: first, the subjective, racist argument that the Negro (who, it will be remembered, ranked below the yellow races in the hierarchy invented by social Darwinians) did not merit a wage of nine pence a day; second, the fear that high wages in the public sector would bid up the cost of agricultural labor and thus increase the selling price of export crops; and, third, that the government could use its quasi-monopolistic powers in the urban labor market to cut wages and still be in a position to attract an adequate number of laborers. This point was further strengthened by the argument that African workers had specific and limited wants and that by reducing wages the supply of labor would be increased, since workers would have to remain in employment longer in order to reach their set targets. With these advantages in mind, McCallum deliberately set out to provoke a strike, smash it, and then dictate terms of employment to the workers.

The governor's second line of attack was to attempt to raise the productivity of the existing labor force. Shortly after his arrival in Lagos he ordered a general tightening of discipline in the Public Works Department (PWD). Early in July this step led to unrest among the laborers, some of whom had been fined for failing to obey the instructions of their European foremen. McCallum also introduced a system by which each worker had to keep a record of work completed and the time spent performing it. This, too, in the words of the *Lagos Standard* caused "no little commotion among the easy-going and happy fraternity of workmen in the PWD. . . ."[5] In his zeal for reform, the governor even designed a special bucket, which was supposed to represent a true measure of what each man should be able to carry! The issue which finally provoked the strike was McCallum's decision to alter the hours of work in the PWD in an attempt to reduce the incidence of sickness and death among foremen and laborers. At the beginning of August he suggested to the acting senior medical officer that the widespread ill health among employees might have been the result of beginning work too early in the day, "before there is time for the malaria which has been given out from the soil during the night to be dissipated by the morning sun."[6] The medical officer agreed that a change in the hours of work was worth trying as an experiment. (At that time, it should be remembered, Ross had still to make his famous discovery of the true cause of malaria.) The existing hours of work were 6 A.M. to 11 A.M., and 1 P.M. to 5 P.M. Nine hours daily manual labor in tropical conditions was a considerable burden, but McCallum does not seem to have considered the possibility that the length of the working day itself might have been at least partly responsible for the high rate of sickness and absenteeism. Instead he decided to alter the morning shift so that work began at 7 A.M. and continued until 12 A.M. The effect of the change was that work started one hour later in the morning, thus allowing a break of only one hour in the middle of the day. The workers immediately protested against the alteration, arguing that they would have to work longer during the period when the sun was at its height, and that they would have only one hour for taking their midday meal and resting. This period, they claimed, was inadequate, because many of them had to walk to their homes, while the remainder had to buy and cook their own food.

McCallum ignored their protests. The result was that on Monday, August 9, virtually all the artisans and laborers of the PWD struck work. The total number of workers involved approached three thousand, so there can be no doubt that the strike was a massive demonstration against the governor's labor policy.[7] McCallum instructed the director of works to deal firmly with the situation. Accordingly, the strikers were informed that unless they returned to work immediately they would be locked out and their places taken by recruits from the hinterland of Lagos and from the Gold Coast. This threat evidently failed to impress the strikers, for they realized, if the governor did not, that there was no prospect of attracting replacements at the wage rates ruling in Lagos. The precise timing of the strike was particularly unfortunate from the governor's point of view. On Tuesday, the day after the strike had broken out, the police force mutinied in protest against a reorganization of duty arrangements—yet another of McCallum's reforms. The mutiny was quelled, mainly by bluff, but the men were still "sullen and insubordinate,"[8] and the governor began to feel some anxiety lest he should prove incapable of controlling the forces he had unleashed. But this was not the limit of his problems. Not only did McCallum lack the police to deal with the strikers, he also lacked sufficient troops to deal with the police, for he had loaned the greater part of his military force to the governor of the Gold Coast. Having provoked a strike, McCallum found that he was unable to coerce the strikers and instead was forced to come to terms with them. Talks were held between the two parties on Wednesday, and a settlement was reached on the same day. The settlement was concerned mainly to resolve the dispute over the hours of work, for there was no question of there being any reduction in the wage rate, as McCallum had originally hoped. It was agreed that work was to begin at 7 A.M., as the governor had requested, but there was to be a break of one and a half hours in the middle of the day, so that the working day was cut from nine to eight and a half hours. The outcome must be counted a victory for the strikers, who returned to work on Thursday "quite contented," and conveyed to the governor their satisfaction with the new arrangements.[9] Thus ended the Lagos strike of 1897.

The Transition from Slave to Free Labor

An attempt will be made now to link the events of August 1897 to some wider issues by broadening the analysis and examining, in turn, the four topics listed at the beginning of this article. The problem of the transition from slave to free labor forms an appropriate starting point because it raises the fundamental question of the factors influencing the supply of labor to wage-earning employment, and this, as has been shown, was a matter which greatly concerned Governor McCallum. Although the export of slaves from Lagos ceased in 1861, the institution of domestic slavery was not abolished, and internal trade in slaves continued to flourish. Indeed, it is one of the ironies of West African history that the rise of "legitimate commerce," the trade which was intended to supplant the sale of slaves, should have helped to perpetuate internal slavery during the second half of the nineteenth century. Labor, instead of being exported, was used more intensively than ever before in the collection, preparation, and transportation of the new export crops. It was not until the close of the century, with the expansion of British power into the hinterland of Lagos, that internal slavery began to be undermined. The significance of the economic and social revolution arising out of the disintegration of this institution should hardly require comment, yet the subject is one which has scarcely even been noticed, let alone investigated.[10]

Nineteenth-century observers tended to apply the term "slavery" indiscriminately to all sections of the dependent labor force, thereby creating the impression that there was one rigidly defined and wholly unprivileged group whose sole concern was to perform all the menial tasks of the community. This view oversimplifies what now appears to have been a more complex situation. In reality, slaves constituted only part of the total labor force, which also included serfs and free workers. Moreover, the dividing lines between the slaves, the serfs, and the free were blurred and indistinct. A slave might suffer certain legal disabilities, but it was possible, if not uncommon, for that person to attain an economic position which was far superior to that of many serfs and free workers, the majority of whom were occupied in fairly humble work in agriculture and trade. In some cases the very dependence of a slave might assist elevation to a position of authority and prestige, where the slave might become a slave owner and perhaps even surpass the power of the master.[11] Thus slaves, as well as the serfs and the free, were well represented in all the main occupations: in agriculture, trade, transport, domestic service, and the army. The prospect of upward mobility must have acted as an important safety valve, helping to preserve the existing social structure by giving it a flexible quality. Insofar as the slave population was integrated into the community, the institution of domestic slavery may be viewed as being consistent with a functionalist model of precolonial society.

The numerical and economic significance of the various groups which made up the labor force is hard to assess, but the evidence suggests that slave and serf labor played a vital part in the production and exchange of export crops. In 1873 Administrator Pope Hennessey claimed that "the whole of the produce shipped from Lagos is the result of the slave labor," and he went on to note that "thousands" of slaves from the interior were to be seen in Lagos every day, bringing their masters' produce to market.[12]

Information respecting the various regions in the hinterland would seem to substantiate the administrator's view, providing the term "slavery" is interpreted rather more widely to refer to serf as well as to slave labor. The economy of Ibadan, for example, was dominated at the close of the nineteenth century by about one hundred ruling chieftancy houses, which between them employed a very large number of slaves in agriculture and in the army. In Badagri, too, the chiefs held slaves and used them mainly in the production of foodstuffs and export crops. In Abeokuta there were men who, in the 1880s, owned as many as four hundred slaves each, and employed them to produce and transport export crops. In Ijebu Ode production also depended on slave labor, though in this case at least the slaves were allowed to work for themselves as well as for their masters. They were employed by their masters from 6 A.M. to 2 P.M., and could then use the rest of the day as they liked. They were permitted to work their own farms and could redeem themselves, buy slaves of their own, and attain any rank except that of Awujale (king).[13] In Lagos itself the dominant occupation was trade, and most traders were slaves whose business activities were directed by their masters. The position of such slaves was described in 1881 by Brimah Apatira, who was a prominent trader and slave owner.

> The boys live with their masters in the house, receiving food, clothing, and being treated as one of the family. But no wages are paid. If they need money they are dashed some. If they conduct themselves well the master gets them wives and gives them money to start for themselves. The boys work for their masters & go to market for them. If they don't behave they are sent away with nothing.[14]

Clearly, this was a state of dependency which could be interpreted to mean either the full exploitation of the slave as a unit of production or the operation of a more lenient system of apprenticeship. However, in drawing attention to the variety and flexibility of slavery as an institution, care must be taken not to obliterate the essential features of the labor force as it existed toward the close of the nineteenth century. In Lagos and its hinterland, production and exchange depended not only on a multiplicity of small producers, who used mainly family labor but also on a relatively small number of important entrepreneurs, who controlled a large labor force consisting mainly of slaves and serfs. While it was possible for some slaves and serfs to improve their position in society, the great majority remained bound to their employers by a contract which had not been negotiated freely, and which benefited the masters to the extent that they were unwilling to encourage the development of a competitive labor market.

The expansion of British power into the hinterland of Lagos in the 1890s brought about a shift in political power which greatly weakened the hold of the indigenous ruling class over its dependent labor force. By 1892 slave traders in the interior had realized that a movement inland was imminent, and slave clearance sales became common, prices in some cases dropping by as much as half. After the success of the British expedition against the Ijebu in 1892 the pace of change quickened. In certain instances the power of a wealthy man was destroyed almost overnight. Thus fell Jasimi, the Balogun (military commander) of Ikorodu, who for many years had been a figure of great influence in a town which itself was of considerable commercial and strategic importance.

> In the twelve months immediately succeeding the Jebu expedition [reported Acting-Governor Denton] a great change arose as over 400 of this chief's slaves, whose average value at that time was £10 to £12, ran away and never returned. He thus lost at least £4,000 and is in consequence a poor man now. This speaks for itself and I think explains the dread with which rich natives in the Interior view our advance into the country.[15]

By 1895 it was reported that labor was very scarce in Abeokuta because the slaves were "running away in great numbers."[16] In the following year the authorities at Ijebu Ode informed the governor of Lagos that "there was not a slave left in the place . . ."[17] and their disappearance was said to have "greatly impoverished" the chiefs and elders of the town.[18] By 1898 the *Lagos Annual Report* could claim, in its inimitable prose, that "the sale of slaves in the interior has almost entirely been put a stop to. . . ." A further step was taken in 1901 when an ordinance was passed which conferred free status on all children born in the Lagos protectorate after April 1 of that year. Two years later an official of the Lagos administration recorded that "slavery as an institution is now in this territory in a state of decrepitude," though it was not until 1916 that it was abolished formally throughout Nigeria.[19]

This outline of the disintegration of the precolonial labor force can now be related more closely to the problems raised by the strike of 1897. Precisely at a time when Governor McCallum was complaining of a labor shortage, a social revolution was taking place which opened up the possibility of increasing both the mobility of labor and also the number of laborers in the free labor market. At first sight it would appear reasonable to expect that Lagos, far from being short of laborers, would have been flooded by unskilled workers searching for jobs. Clearly, this was not the case. The escape of slaves and the sudden downfall of some large slave owners were obvious signs of rapid change. Yet they were not inconsistent with a marked element of continuity. What, then, did the slaves do with their newfound freedom?

The broad answer to this question seems to be fairly clear: some slaves escaped, but the majority stayed where they were and continued to work in agriculture. The evidence indicates that those who ran away from their masters were those who felt that they had no stake at all in the local community. For example, those who fled to the Eastern District of the colony of Lagos during the latter part of 1892 were mainly Hausa slaves who came from northern Nigeria. Similarly, those who left Abeokuta were also nearly all Hausa slaves, who in all probability occupied a very unprivileged position as aliens among the Egba. Most journeyed north to their homeland, though some remained in the locality, where they formed bands of marauders and for a while lived by preying on the country which had oppressed them. As for Jasimi, the Balogun, many of his slaves were probably reluctant warriors who were only too anxious to escape from the army. On the whole, the transition from slavery to freedom was accomplished relatively smoothly. As early as 1896 the governor of Lagos reported that the inhabitants of the state of Ibadan had taken the change in their stride. "It has surprised me not a little," he wrote, "to see how well they have settled down to the new régime and how steadily they have taken to commerce and agriculture in place of the lawless methods which found favour with them in the past."[20] Information relating to Abeokuta, Badagri, and Iseyin serves to confirm this view. In 1903 MacGregor, who had replaced McCallum as governor, commented that "the position of the slave was among the Yorubas so tolerable that very few of them have fled to Lagos to claim liberty."

There were two main reasons for this pronounced element of continuity. In the first place, as has been shown, the conditions of slavery in Yorubaland were very flexible, and the life of a slave was often very similar to that of a free person. Second, and more important, the economic development of Nigeria during the colonial period did not involve the creation of a landless proletariat in response to the demands of new urban industries. On the contrary, growth was based on the expansion of agriculture in a situation where there was a favorable ratio between population and land. The freed slaves stayed in agriculture, colonized virgin land, and by the labor-intensive application of traditional techniques brought about a massive increase in the volume of export crops placed on the market. However, it would be a mistake to think that the revolution was superficial merely because it was silent. The traditional rulers were no longer able to command labor on the same terms as in the precolonial era, and the slaves and serfs began to assert their right to deploy their labor as they chose. The large holdings worked by slave labor, which had been a common feature of the Lagos hinterland in the second half of the nineteenth century, were replaced by numerous small farms worked by a new generation of free people, and it seems likely that the slaves of the late nineteenth century became the independent cocoa farmers of the early colonial period. At least part of the explanation of why Governor McCallum faced a shortage of labor in 1897 should now be clear. The collapse of slavery, far from forcing labor off the land, made agriculture a more attractive occupation than it had been previously. Land was abundant, and a boom in rubber exports between 1895 and 1899 meant that the returns were considerable. Consequently, the supply price of labor to permanent, nonagricultural employment was high—too high for McCallum, even though he was anxious to secure more laborers. The Chinese laborer, on the other hand, was an "industrious and shifty" worker at a low wage rate precisely because he had no alternative occupation. This was one of the cardinal facts that McCallum overlooked in his analysis of the labor situation.

Government Policy Toward Labor

It is now appropriate to examine the second question noted at the beginning of this article, namely the policy of the government on labor matters. As the government was by far the largest single employer in Lagos, it was in a position to exert a considerable influence on the labor market. What, then, was the attitude of the administration toward a situation in which the disintegration of the old, dependent labor force had not led automatically to the appearance of the required number of urban workers? Paradoxically, the measures adopted by the administration, far from solving the problem of the shortage and the high cost of urban labor, helped to perpetuate it. The principal aim of British policy was to create the political conditions most favorable to the development of an export economy; there was no desire to see the Pax Britannica inaugurate a social revolution. Thus, the Lagos administration sought to delay the emergence of a free labor market because it was afraid that the abolition of slavery would dislocate production. "I much fear," commented Acting Governor Denton in 1898, "that as they [the slaves] can find the means of subsistence ready to hand without work they will cease to do anything in the way of cultivating the land as soon as the restrictions of domestic slavery are removed."[21] Total and immediate abolition of domestic slavery was in any case ruled out on purely financial grounds, as the government could not afford to pay compensation to the slave owners. Moreover, the British were anxious to maintain the authority of the indigenous ruling classes, since they were destined to become the political and administrative agents of the colonial regime. Hence a British compromise was reached:

"trading in slaves, which means raiding for them, must of course be put a stop to with a strong hand but domestic slavery is quite another matter. . . ."[22] This policy caused some heart-searching among the custodians of the humanitarian conscience in the Colonial Office, but it was agreed eventually to support it on the grounds that evolution was always preferable to revolution. Of course, the Lagos administration was unable to dictate the pace of social change, and, as has been shown, the institution of slavery was fast being undermined by the turn of the century. However, the important point in the present context is that government policy was not directed toward encouraging mobility of labor; the administration needed urban laborers, but it did not intend to acquire them at the risk of widespread social upheaval. Some attempt was made to increase the size of the labor force by making use of compulsory labor and by restricting the migration of workers, at least to non-British territories, but these measures met with little success because the Colonial Office took care to prevent local officials from carrying ideas of this kind too far.

The Lagos administration also sought to influence the supply of labor through its wages policy, which was based on a belief in the value of maintaining low rates of pay. This policy was not simply an eccentricity which found brief expression during McCallum's short stay in Lagos; it was a commonplace among entrepreneurs during the early phase of the industrial revolution in England,[23] and it was widely applied to underdeveloped areas during the colonial period in the twentieth century. In 1905 the Colonial Office laid down for southern Nigeria the principle that ". . . every effort will be made to keep the rates of wages as low as possible."[24] Similarly, Lord Lugard, reflecting in 1922 on his long experience in Africa, stated: "It is an economic disadvantage to any country if the wage rate for unskilled labour is unduly high, for it arrests development." Granted that the wants of the African worker were both limited and inflexible, it followed that "the higher the wages in such a case the less the work. . . ."[25] The attractiveness of a low-wage policy is easy to understand. In the first place, it has to be admitted that racial prejudice played a part in holding wages down. There were those who believed that the "ordinary nigger" simply was not worth nine pence a day. The first sin, that of being a member of an embryonic proletariat, was compounded by a second, that of being black; a man like McCallum found it hard to forgive both transgressions. Second, a low-wage policy won support because it kept down costs; whatever the possible long-term advantages of paying high wages, they were unable to compete with the immediate and constant short-term needs for administrative economies. Apart from the anxiety about increasing the operating costs of government departments, such as the PWD, there was also a fear that high wages in the public sector would bid up the price of agricultural labor and thus increase the cost of putting produce on the world market. This argument was greatly exaggerated. It was based on the false assumption that urban wages had to be kept more or less at parity with agricultural wages, and made no allowance for the fact that a laborer coming to the town had involved himself in certain real and opportunity costs which justified the maintenance of a differential between the two sectors. It failed also to appreciate that a small increase in this differential would have improved the supply of labor without having a catastrophic effect on farm costs, since the number of additional laborers required by the government was very small in comparison with the size of the total labor force. Finally, a low-wage policy was attractive because it was held to increase, or at least to maintain, the volume of labor on offer. This view was based on the assumption that African wage earners had specific and limited wants and that they would work just long enough to obtain sufficient money to reach their targets. Once these targets were achieved, it was argued, African workers would prefer to hold their labor in reserve in the form of leisure. From the notion of the target worker is derived the concept of the backward-bending supply curve of labor, which expresses the idea that as wages rise, so the volume of labor on offer tends to diminish. Clearly, if the wants of the African worker were limited and the number of wage earners remained constant, then the supply curve of labor would quickly become regressive, as Lugard suggested it would. In these circumstances any increase in wages would mean merely that less hours were worked because targets could be reached more quickly. On the other hand, a cut in wages would increase the supply of labor because targets could be attained only by working longer hours.

The question arises now as to how far the government's analysis was an accurate assessment of labor-supply conditions in the Lagos area. In the long run, it is true, the number of laborers increased. In 1881 the census recorded that there were 2,357 laborers in Lagos, which was equivalent to 9 percent of the total occupied population; thirty years later, in 1911, the number had reached 6,388, or 13.7 percent of the total occupied population.[26] That there should have been some increase is not inconsistent with the argument that the wage rate was too low to attract sufficient workers, because there were many other factors which in the long term influenced the supply of labor. In the case of

Lagos it seems likely that a large part of the increase can be accounted for by a rise in the number of migrant laborers following the improvement of transport facilities after the turn of the century. Nevertheless, demand continued to exceed supply. In 1903 the government admitted that labor was still very scarce in Lagos, and in 1909 the Colonial Office even gave serious consideration to the possibility of importing Indian labor into West Africa. In the short run at least, the failure of the government to attract the required number of laborers was the result primarily of its low-wage policy. In theory, it could be argued that the shortage persisted because McCallum had failed in his attempt to reduce wages, thus enabling wage earners to reach their targets more easily. In practice, the evidence suggests that the real reason why labor remained in short supply was because wages were too low. Precisely at the time when the administration was complaining about the scarcity of labor, large numbers of unskilled workers were leaving Lagos in search of higher wages. Between June 1900 and January 1902 approximately sixty-five hundred laborers left Lagos to work on the Sekondi railway and in the gold mines of the Gold Coast, where the rate of pay was higher than in Nigeria. This example shows that ordinary, unskilled laborers had more flexible targets and were more responsive to monetary incentives than the administration supposed. Of course there were individual cases which served to confirm the government's view of the motivation of workers in Lagos, but there can be no doubt that the aggregate supply curve of labor was more positively sloped than the official mind was prepared to admit. It is clear that it was not wants that were limited so much as the means of satisfying them. No wonder that Lagos was unable to attract a sufficient body of permanent wage earners when potential recruits could earn more by taking employment elsewhere.

The Standard of Living of Lagos Workers

Discussion of the wage rate leads to the third problem noted at the beginning of this article, that of the standard of living of the workers of Lagos. Unfortunately, this important topic can be touched on only briefly as insufficient information is available at present to sustain a detailed analysis. The laborers of Lagos were a minority group in a predominantly commercial community. They were also the lowest-paid section of that community, receiving a wage of about nine pence a day. The rate varied between extremes of 6d. and 1s.3d., but these figures were exceptional, and 9d. remained the most usual wage for unskilled labor throughout the period 1880 to 1910, in spite of persistent efforts by the administration to reduce it. Food prices also remained remarkably steady during the same period. Indeed, a rough comparison between the years 1880-1885 and the years 1905-1910 shows that if anything the cost of the main items of food was slightly lower during the latter period.[27] Of course, these figures of income and expenditure are of very limited value. On the one hand, some permanent laborers, and nearly all migrant workers, had other sources of income which cannot be assessed. On the other hand, they also had additional items of expenditure besides food, the chief of which was probably the cost of accommodation. If there are indications that farm incomes were rising during the first decade of the twentieth century, there is evidence as well that rents in Lagos were also increasing. Nevertheless, two very tentative conclusions may be hazarded. In the first place, it seems unlikely that the strike of 1897 represented a reaction by the workers to either a gradual or a sudden downturn in their standard of living; their principal concern was to maintain their existing conditions in the face of an aggressive act by the governor. Second, it seems possible that in 1897 unskilled wage earners in Lagos were better off than they were forty years later in 1937. It was not until the latter year that the wage rate was raised from nine pence to one shilling, and by that date there is clear evidence that the cost of living was greatly in excess of what it had been at the close of the nineteenth century.

The Political Implications of the Strike

The fourth and final topic which requires examination concerns the political implications of the strike. As well as being a struggle between employers and employees, the demonstration which occurred in 1897 could easily have developed into a conflict between rulers and ruled. In the first place, the strike involved a large number of men and received solid support. Second, it coincided with a mutiny in the police force. Third, the governor had scarcely any troops in Lagos to deal with the situation. Fourth, a few days before the strike began there had been a public demonstration against the proposed introduction of municipal rating, and the atmosphere was still highly charged with anti-government sentiment. It seems clear that the governor and his small administration could have been overturned without difficulty. Yet the occasion did not become a major trial of strength for British rule in Nigeria. McCallum bluffed and compromised; the crisis passed, and the whole matter was quickly forgotten. The quiescent nature of this outcome is worthy of analysis, for it provides a valuable insight into the relationship between economic problems and political activity during the early part of the colonial period.

The solidarity of the strike and the conduct of the strikers indicate the presence of both leaders and organization. But if this was the case, and unfortunately there is insufficient material to confirm the suggestion, it seems likely that the leaders and their organization arose with the strike and disappeared soon after it had been settled. Certainly, there is little evidence to show that the unskilled workers of Lagos had a permanent trade union at this early date. A few trade unions had appeared before 1897,[28] and more sprang up shortly after the turn of the century, but on the whole they catered to the artisan and professional classes and were careful to remain at some distance from the ordinary, unskilled workers. The Lagos laborers were a small group, but because they contained many migrant and temporary workers in their ranks they were poorly organized and tended to fragment. For these reasons they also lacked political consciousness; it is most unlikely, for example, that the strike leaders attempted to establish contact with any of the recognized political figures in Lagos. The laborers' demands were purely of an industrial nature. Once McCallum had shown that he was prepared to give ground on the issue of the hours of work, the strikers were satisfied. Insofar as the strike of 1897 set a pattern for the early years of the colonial period, it was a pattern of occasional and spontaneous protests arising out of local and often temporary grievances. These grievances were mainly economic, but frequently they were also the product of racial conflict.

The limited aims of the workers were matched by the narrow outlook of political leaders in Lagos. Their attitude toward discontent among the unskilled wage earners can be seen in the Lagos press, which was owned, written, and read by the educated African elite, whose main spokesmen are counted now among the founders of Nigerian nationalism. In commenting on the strike, the *Lagos Standard* inclined cautiously to the view that, on this occasion, the workers had justice on their side. But this did not imply any permanent commitment to the labor cause, and the paper made it clear that it frowned on "extreme" measures such as strike action.[29] A more radical newspaper, the *Lagos Weekly Record,* made the following comment about the strike:

> Strikes are unknown in this part of the world, and it is infinitely more to the advantage of the Colony that this condition of things should be preserved, than that the people should be driven into learning how to combine for their own protection and interest.[30]

The leading African businessmen were also opposed to the strike. Indeed, the issue even brought about a split between African and European merchants in the chamber of commerce, not because the Africans were anxious to demonstrate their support for the strikers, but because they felt slighted by McCallum's failure to warn them, as he had warned the Europeans, of the danger of riots and disturbances in the town. The African merchants expressed their sentiments by sending the governor a loyal address to show that they, too, were faithful supporters of his adminstration.[31] The gulf between the elite and the workers is well illustrated by an interview between John Burns, the British labor leader, and Henry Carr, a highly educated African and senior civil servant in Lagos. In 1897, shortly before the strike took place, Carr called to see Burns at his London home. Burns questioned him eagerly in order to find out whether the educated African was "using his opportunities for uplifting his less favoured countrymen or whether he held aloof with disdain from them," and he suggested that Carr should devote some of his time and considerable ability to writing on the subject of the African working man. Carr never took up this suggestion; he abhorred the ignorant populace, and it is unlikely that the welfare of the African laborer was a subject which disturbed his mind for long. In common with the great majority of political and business leaders in Lagos, he could see no future in arousing the aspirations of the nascent proletariat. Even Macaulay, the acknowledged leader of the "agitators," disapproved of strike action and took care not to become too closely involved with the urban workers, lest he should encourage the growth of a power which could not be confined within the limits of his own political program and organization. The early nationalists were cautious and moderate men, whose limited aims centered mainly on constitutional reforms and the improvement of the position of the educated elite. It was not until the close of the interwar period that politics in Nigeria took a more radical turn. On the one hand, the 1930s saw the development of several militant unions with articulate spokesmen of their own. On the other hand, there was also the appearance of a new generation of nationalist leaders, headed by men like Azikiwe and Enahoro, who succeeded in changing the nature of opposition politics in the colonial context so that they came to reflect the economic problems which faced African farmers, traders, and urban workers. They united the economic with the political struggle; and it was this alliance which made possible the successful Nigerian general strike of 1945 and which contributed to the strength of the nationalist movement after World War II.

Conclusion

This article has attempted to focus attention on some of the important problems relating to the development of urban wage labor in southwest Nigeria during the early part of the colonial period. Accordingly, the conclusion contains as many questions as it does answers. In the first place, it should be clear that there is room for further work on the size, the composition, and the nature of the ties of dependency which characterized the precolonial labor force. What kind of distinctions can be drawn between slaves and serfs, and are such terms permissible in the African context? What were the conditions on which unfree laborers could become free, and just how free were the free? How swift was the transition to a free labor force at the beginning of the colonial period? What steps did the slaves and serfs take to assert their independence, and what effect did their emancipation have on their former masters? Second, there are a number of issues concerning government policy which at present remain unresolved. Its wage policy has been analyzed here, but there were other economic and noneconomic determinants of the labor supply which the colonial administration may have considered at a later date.[32] How was it, for example, that officials could regard the urban labor force as being unresponsive to wage incentives, and at the same time place their faith in the development of West Africa through peasant cash cropping? Third, the question of the standard of living of urban wage earners needs exploring further. What was the trend of real incomes during the colonial period, and what light (if any) does it throw on the controversy over the gains and losses of colonialism? Finally, more work needs to be carried out on the history of trade unions in Nigeria, and on the relationship between organized labor and the nationalist movement. What were the stages by which the "semiproletariat" became involved in politics, first backing those who led the opposition to colonial rule, and then supporting those who began to criticize the federal government after independence?

Until these and other questions have been answered, the final remarks of this article must be treated more as speculations than as definitive statements. It would appear that during the pre-colonial period production and exchange in Lagos and its hinterland depended to a large extent on a labor force of slaves and serfs. The advent of colonial rule greatly weakened the ties which bound these dependent laborers; by ending slave raiding and by assuming responsibility for law and order, the British deprived the indigenous rulers of some of their most important functions, and thus undermined their control over both slaves and serfs. This development, in conjunction with the stimulus provided by new opportunities, particularly in the production of rubber and cocoa, encouraged the labor force to assert its independence. In some cases slaves ran away from their masters as soon as they could, but on the whole the transition was relatively smooth because it occurred in a situation where land was abundant and trade was expanding rapidly. In these circumstances, manual labor in Lagos was not an attractive occupation, at least on the terms of employment imposed by the colonial administration. Government policy was characterized by an authoritarian attitude toward labor problems and by a firm belief in the value of maintaining low wages. The evidence indicates that this approach was very largely misconceived and that the problem of the shortage of laborers in Lagos could have been overcome if the administration had been prepared to offer an inducement in the form of higher wages. It was Governor McCallum's heavy-handed attempt to implement this misguided policy that was responsible for provoking the strike of 1897. The strike can best be seen as a successful defensive action on the part of the wage earners, whose principal aim was to prevent the governor from altering the status quo. The strikers stood alone; they received no encouragement from the educated elite, who were not prepared to support popular demonstrations on issues which did not fit in with their own narrow interests. The strike was quickly settled and soon forgotten. Nevertheless, it was a significant event, for it was one of the earliest and most widely spread protests of the urban wage-labor force, and it can be interpreted without exaggeration as marking the beginning of the development of a new sector of the economy. The pattern of economic growth during the greater part of the colonial period did not lead to any very rapid expansion of the urban labor force. But in more recent years some attempts have been made to diversify the economy by establishing manufacturing industries. This departure suggests that the urban labor force will become increasingly important in the future, both in the economy and in politics. This point was underlined by the general strike of 1964, in which the Joint Action Committee of labor leaders, backed by over five hundred thousand workers, successfully defied the federal government. The events of 1964 showed that class consciousness had developed rapidly. As one strike leader put it: "Although the cause of the strike was based on economic demands, yet in its development it has raised possible political action which, with a developed Marxist-Leninist party, could have led to a proletarian revolution."[33] If this is indeed the shape of things to come, then the strike of 1897 may be seen eventually, not as an isolated event which left only a temporary mark on Nigerian history, but as the starting point of a process of development which is now about to enter its most interesting phase.

Notes

1. McCallum to Antrobus, August 5, 1897, C.S.O. 8/5/9.
2. Minute by Mercer, June 10, 1897, on McCallum to Chamberlain, May 12, 1897, C.O. 147/113.
3. McCallum to Maxwell, April 25, 1897, C.S.O. 8/5/9.
4. McCallum to Shelford, June 11, 1897, C.S.O. 8/5/9.
5. *Lagos Standard,* July 21, 1897.
6. McCallum to Chamberlain, August 16, 1897, C.O. 147/116.
7. The figure of three thousand is an estimate based on information contained in Denton to Chamberlain, June 4, 1898, C.O. 147/133; and Denton to Chamberlain, August 3, 1898, C.O. 147/134.
8. McCallum to Chamberlain, August 16, 1897, C.O. 147/116.
9. Ibid.
10. For some interesting exceptions to this generalization, see the following: M. G. Smith, "Slavery and Emancipation in Two Societies," *Social and Economic Studies,* 3 (1954); W. R. G. Horton, "The Ohu System of Slavery in a Northern Ibo Village-Group," *Africa* 24 (1954); C. C. Newbury, "An Early Enquiry into Slavery and Captivity in Dahomey," *Zaire* 14 (1960); Jean Sûret-Canale, *Afrique noire occidentale et centrale, l'ère coloniale 1900-1945* (Paris, 1964), pp. 81–89.
11. T. J. Hutchinson, "The Social and Domestic Slavery of Western Africa, and its Evil Influence on Commercial Progress," *Journal of the Society of Arts* 23 (1875), pp. 315–16.
12. J. Pope-Hennessy, "On the British Settlements in Western Africa," *Journal of the Society of Arts* 21 (1873), p. 443.
13. Evidence of J. A. O. Payne enclosed in Denton to Chamberlain, June 4, 1898, C.O. 147/133. It is only fair to point out that Payne's sympathies lay with the masters rather than with the slaves. The

evidence given by James Johnson (enclosed in the same dispatch) confirms Payne's account at most points, but claims that slaves could *not* purchase their freedom.

14. Evidence in Omotosho *v.* Sedu Olowu, July 13, 1881, Civil 3, Supreme Court Records, Lagos.
15. Denton to Chamberlain, August 3, 1898, C.O. 147/134.
16. Denton to Chamberlain, November 5, 1895, C.O. 147/100.
17. Carter to Chamberlain, January 9, 1896, C.O. 147/104.
18. Evidence of J. A. O. Payne, enc. in Denton to Chamberlain, June 4, 1898, C.O. 147/133.
19. A. McPhee, *The Economic Revolution in British West Africa* (London, 1926), p. 257.
20. Carter to Chamberlain, January 9, 1896, C.O. 147/104.
21. Denton to Chamberlain, August 3, 1898, C.O. 147/143.
22. Denton to Chamberlain, April 10, 1897, C.O. 147/113.
23. E. J. Hobsbawm, *Labouring Men* (London, 1964), pp. 352–58.
24. C.O. to British Cotton Growing Association, January 31, 1905, C.O. 147/173.
25. F. D. Lugard, *The Dual Mandate in British Tropical Africa* (London, 1922), pp. 404, 405.
26. A. G. Hopkins, "An Economic History of Lagos, 1880–1914" (Ph.D. thesis, London University, 1964), pp. 25, 418.
27. *Lagos Blue Books,* 1880–1905; *Southern Nigeria Blue Books,* 1906–1910.
28. A "Mechanics Mutual Aid Provident and Mutual Improvement Association" was formed in 1883 with J. S. Leigh as its first president (*Lagos Times,* August 8, 1883). There were also a number of craft unions of the type described by P. C. Lloyd in his article, "Craft Organisation in Yoruba Towns," *Africa* 23 (1953).
29. *Lagos Standard,* August 11, 1897.
30. *Lagos Weekly Record,* September 25, 1897.
31. McCallum to Chamberlain, August 29, 1897, C.O. 147/116.
32. One of the earliest attempts to do so was Major G. St. J. Orde-Browne's book *The African Labourer* (London: Frank Cass & Co., 1967).
33. I. Davies, *African Trade Unions* (Harmondsworth, Eng.: Penguin Books, 1966), pp. 143–47.

Worker Consciousness in Black Miners:
Southern Rhodesia, 1900-1920

Charles van Onselen

It has become axiomatic for historians of Southern Rhodesia to accept the relatively late emergence of organized African protest in the industrial setting as being indicative of stunted political consciousness. Writing of the 1920s and 1930s, Gann and Gelfand suggest that "the country's unskilled hands on the whole remained inefficient, unreliable, poorly paid and yet without much political consciousness."[1] Hooker is even more specific in his suggestion that Africans were "slow to think themselves into the industrial context of Southern Rhodesia."[2] And in a more recent study it is suggested that the 1927 strike at the Shamva mine was "the first industrial action ever seen in the country."[3] Only Terence Ranger's stimulating study of the "African Voice" attempts a more systematic historical probing for the basis of such observations. But even Ranger doubts the existence of worker consciousness in the first two decades of this century: "At the beginning of the 1920s, . . . there were few evidences of any effective articulation of the hopes, fears and grievances of the workers."[4]

All of these observations seem to be underpinned by a common assumption—that the political consciousness of black workers should be assessed largely through the presence or absence of associations and organizations which manifestly articulate worker interests. If this assumption is accepted, then the assessment of these historians is, in large measure, correct. It was not until well into the 1920s that the Industrial and Commercial Workers' Union (ICU) of Clements Kadalie became part of the Rhodesian political scene and addressed itself specifically to black workers. Later still were the appeals of the more broadly based African National Congress for the identification of Africans with *Zhuwawo* —the "ordinary laborer."[5] Measured in these terms, worker consciousness was not a marked feature of early Rhodesian history.

This assumption, however, has created problems for social scientists and historians alike. The most obvious problem has been the need to explain the apparent absence of worker consciousness among Africans in the three decades of their industrial experience prior to 1920.[. . .] By a more detailed consideration

Extracted from Charles van Onselen, "Worker Consciousness in Black Miners: Southern Rhodesia 1900-1920," *Journal of African History* 14, no. 2 (1973): 237-55.

of African experiences in a specific industry it is intended to demonstrate that the "absence" of worker consciousness is more apparent than real. First, it will be suggested that from the very earliest days of capital-intensive industry Africans had a well-developed and demonstrable self-awareness of their position as exploited workers. Second, it will be suggested that it is inadequate to gauge this worker consciousness through the relative absence of overt industrial action aimed at securing improvements through readily identifiable organizations with articulate leadership. Rather, it should be sought in workers' strategy in the context of the overall functioning of the political economy and in day-to-day responses in the work situation. If this can be shown, it will be clear that later organizations like the dance societies, Watch Tower, and the ICU should not be seen as the first evidence of worker consciousness.

The Rhodesian Mines

As it is the largest employer and premier industry of the country, it is appropriate to illustrate this from the experiences of Africans in the mining industry. Capital-intensive gold mining in Rhodesia developed from two mines opened in 1893 to the point where, in 1920, there were 295 producers, including eight "large" mines. This expansion was paralleled by the growth in demand for cheap African labor. The black labor force of over seventeen thousand in 1906 had expanded to thirty-six thousand by 1920.

This expansion and consolidation of the Rhodesian gold-mining industry was not, however, the uninterrupted and unqualified success of the Witwatersrand gold mines of South Africa. The early progress of the industry was halted by the African revolt of 1896-1897, and it was only after the turn of the century that there was extended progress. There were also problems of a more lasting nature. In Rhodesia, as in South Africa, the ore bodies were of an exceptionally low grade. But in Rhodesia this problem was complicated by the fact that the ore was not contained in a reasonably continuous reef. In most parts of Rhodesia there were fluctuations in the profitability of ore within even a single mining property.[6]

These geological realities shaped the organization of the Rhodesian mining industry. Unlike the Rand, the Rhodesian mines were spread over a wide area and operated on a much smaller scale. The average output of a "large" Rhodesian mine was only one-tenth of that of a Witwatersrand mine. It was only within the constraints of these factors that Rhodesian mines were profitable, and the industry had to organize accordingly. Mines had to limit managerial overheads and operate with the minimum of expensive plant and machinery. Within this context the "small worker" became a characteristic and important part of the industry.

Operating within these profitability constraints also led to the curtailing of direct and indirect expenditure on African labor. Direct expenditure on wages was minimized through coordinated employer action which attempted to ensure a uniformly low wage structure.[7] Low wages were justified on the grounds that in the mine compounds African workers also received food and accommodation. In theory, the minimization of indirect expenditure on food and accommodation was more difficult to achieve because of the existence of protective labor legislation. In practice, however, the British South Africa Company, acting as company-government—part shareholder, part legislator—was reluctant fully to implement labor legislation which ensured minimum standards of food and housing. These inadequacies in wages, food, and accommodation manifested themselves in the conditions in the mine compounds.

Conditions in the compounds were appalling, and it is only with a wide stretch of the imagination that we can accept Lewis Gann's comparison of the position of mine workers with that of domestic servants in England.[8] It was precisely because of inadequate food and housing that the majority of fatalities among black miners in Rhodesia occurred. This is clear from the fact that in the twenty years under review, two thousand black workers died from accidents, but in the same twenty-year period over eighteen thousand workers died in the compounds from diseases.[9] Unhygienic compounds inhabited by successive generations of migrant laborers and the lack of adequate change-house facilities ensured that pneumonia was the major killer. Prior to 1911, it alone had accounted for twenty-five hundred lives. Crowded compounds were particularly vulnerable to epidemics, and in 1918, the year of the Spanish flu, 7 percent of all black workers died. Other diseases reflect the inadequacy of compound food. It was not simply the case that "many men reported sick with scurvy," as Gann suggests;[10] up to 1920—excluding the first three years up to 1903 when registration of deaths in compounds was not a legal requirement—at least five hundred fifty workers had died of the disease.[11] Further, it is exceptionally misleading to assert that from 1907 "the Government . . . enforced the proper feeding and housing of African miners."[12] In 1908 at a "low estimate" there were 207 deaths directly attributable to scurvy,[13] though there were some improvements in the first twenty years of this century.[. . .]

In these circumstances, for an African mine worker the choice of employer or employment center was, in many cases, a life-and-death decision. Within the premier industry of the colony the day-to-day working conditions must have been so disagreeable for migrant workers that the thought of a better tomorrow in the peasant community, or the intervention of an industrial inspector, must have been a small consolation. What was more pertinent was the development of an efficient system of intelligence, which enabled workers to make critical assessments of wages and working conditions in different parts of the labor market. It is within the context of this system of market intelligence that we have to seek for indications of worker consciousness and try to understand labor strategies.

For Africans living in the area between the Limpopo and the Zambezi this can best be seen in their total avoidance of the Rhodesian mines. The 1910-1911 Native Affairs Committee noted that in many instances African families would sell stock to meet tax obligations rather than allow kin to seek employment in the mines.[14] Shona communities in particular sold grain to meet their legal obligations, and so avoided mine labor. It was not until well into the 1920s that Rhodesian Africans were sufficiently proletarianized for them to form a majority of black mine employees.[15] While this widespread avoidance no doubt reflects labor conditions and wage prospects in the industry as a whole, it seems difficult to draw specific conclusions about "worker consciousness" at this level of abstraction. The picture emerges with greater clarity, however, when the fate of individual mines is considered.

The Bonsor Mine

The Bonsor was one of the first large mines to come into production after the revolt, and it started production in November 1898 with a crushing capacity of forty stamps. In common with other mines of the period, its compound consisted of African huts, constructed by the laborers who first arrived and inhabited by successive generations of workers. The lack of change-house facilities coupled with an unhygienic compound did not hamper initial operations during the warm summer months. But with the onset of colder weather, which the night shift in particular felt, problems appeared. During four weeks in June 1899, twenty-one workers died of pneumonia. The situation was serious enough to warrant a visit from the chief native commissioner, who instructed the manager to supervise the erection of a new compound.[16] Conveniently forgetting the issue of compound accommodation, the company explained to the London shareholders that "the natives are very careless of chills and every possible precaution was taken and everything tried to make them wear blankets, but they would not do so."[17] Since they were expected to purchase such blankets for themselves out of a cash wage of thirty-three shillings to fifty-five shillings, the reluctance of the workers is hardly incomprehensible. In any event, the abnormal death rate at the Bonsor that June heralded the start of "labor troubles" for the management.

Within a matter of days, word was spread on the labor grapevine that the mine was "bewitched."[18] In a fascinating way a "traditional" belief of peasant society was now extended to operate in the industrial setting and to protect prospective workers from exploitation. Over the following weeks this belief spread so rapidly that in a period of two months not a single African applied for work at the Bonsor, and the mine was forced to close for a short period. This "boycott by bewitchment" forced the management to turn to foreign black labor.

In October 1900 an attempt was made to procure labor from the Butterworth District in the Transkei. With the Rand gold mines closed during the South African war, it was hoped to recruit five hundred workers for the Bonsor mine. Only three hundred were recruited, but on their arrival in Rhodesia they demanded higher wages than were being offered. Rhodesian wage rates must have been a considerable shock to workers familiar with the relatively liberal South African rates. It was probably for this reason that these laborers were "unsatisfactory," and that they were passed on to the Tebekwe mine, where they were reported to have caused "disaffection" among local workers.[19] Thus, the first attempt to get foreign labor failed. The Bonsor was saved from closing down yet again by making use of Shangaan laborers from Portuguese East Africa who also could not sell their labor on the Rand during the war.

It was still necessary for the Bonsor to augment its labor supply with further outside labor, and this time the management turned to the north, to Barotseland. This attempt, too, was unsuccessful. When the 159 workers from across the Zambezi learned they were bound for the Bonsor, all but 7 deserted.[20] It seems unlikely that local witchcraft beliefs alone produced this result. What started as "boycott by bewitchment" for local labor may already have become simply "boycott" for long-distance migrant laborers.

Matters did not improve at the Bonsor during the remainder of 1900, when the mine was rocked by a series of explosions which resulted in further loss of life and an official inquiry. The cause of the explosions was difficult to determine, but the inquiry exonerated the mine management. At least one leading mine engineer of the day, however, was of the opinion that "the explosions were caused through malice."[21] Whether the cause of the explosions was industrial sabotage or not, it certainly did not increase the popularity of the mine, and the labor "shortage" now became acute.

Recruitment under false pretenses was resorted to in 1901. Five hundred workers were especially recruited in rural areas, and the name of their destination carefully kept from them. During an overnight stop, however, somebody bungled, and the workers were "injudiciously told their destination"; by morning all five hundred had deserted.[22]

By now the situation was desperate, and while the Selukwe mine, a mere four miles away, worked through most of 1901, the Bonsor stood idle for nine months for want of labor. In 1902 the mine resumed production, but in September there was a further setback when nine African workers were killed in an accident. Events were reaching a climax, and Leyson, the manager, wrote to his London head office:

> On no less than three occasions has it seemed probable that sufficient labor was coming forward . . . but these schemes, like those that had gone before, failed absolutely at the last moment. . . . It is with great regret that I have recommended the closing down of this mine.[23]

It is possible that it was not simply want of labor that closed the Bonsor mine. Like most mines in Rhodesia at the time, it was badly overcapitalized and did not yield sufficient profit.[24] Nevertheless, there is little doubt that an effective boycott of the mine by African workers contributed to its demise.

The Ayrshire Mine

The case of the Ayrshire mine hinges around wage policy rather than health, and is perhaps even more instructive. The year 1903 was a particularly bad one for peasants in many parts of Rhodesia.

Faced with a severe drought, many must have been forced to consider a spell of work on the mines to raise the cash that would normally have come from the sale of grain. Unlike the rains, the administration's tax demands did not fail to materialize, and peasants made their way to the mines in considerable numbers. In these circumstances, mine managers soon found that they could lower wages by a substantial margin.

The Ayrshire mine, astride the labor routes to the south, was well sited to exploit the situation. Not only could it rely on a stream of migrant workers making their way south to the mines of Matabeleland and South Africa, but, situated in the heart of a badly affected drought area, it could also expect an abundant supply of labor from local sources. So favorable was the situation for exploitation by management that a point was reached where it was reported that many workers were being employed for food only.[25]

As the year progressed, however, this position produced changes in the composition of the labor force. The mine became increasingly reliant on "passers-by"—migrants who, for want of savings or food on the journey south, were forced to take employment at the Ayrshire. As this process got more firmly established, the percentage of local labor decreased, and by the time that the season changed in August the management was uttering the familiar cry of "labor shortage." In that month the chief secretary in the Salisbury administration, H. H. Castens, in a letter to the high commissioner in Pretoria, pointed out what he considered to be the perversity of the local laborers:

> Within the district [in] which is situated the Ayrshire mine, 12,000 Mashona natives are said to be in want of food. The mine is 400 boys short of its complement, and has only six Mashonas working on it.[26]

Out of a labor force of over three hundred, only six—or a little more than 1 percent—were drawn from the adjacent area, in spite of severe drought.

For the administration and the management this was yet a further illustration of what was considered to be Shona perversity and laziness—something that was proverbial in mining circles. The fact of the matter was very different, for in two other Mashonaland mines to the east of Ayrshire Shona laborers were working in considerable numbers. At the Penhalonga mine they formed 30 percent of the labor force out of a complement of 550, and at the Rezende mine 41 percent of a force of 523 laborers. Both of these mines held out better working conditions, and operated with less exploitative wage policies. This demonstrates a highly selective withholding of labor, despite the added pressure occasioned by the drought. That the percentage of Shona labor could fluctuate on Mashonaland mines from 1 percent at the Ayrshire to 41 percent at the Rezende seems to show both the strength and spread of worker consciousness.

Desertion as Protest

[. . .] Rhodesia, in common with other settler societies, possessed a web of coercive labor legislation designed to regulate the mobility of labor and stabilize employment under contract. The legislation was in force from the earliest years, and two ordinances in particular were central. First, the Rhodesian administration took over the harsh Cape Master and Servants Law, which made it a criminal offense to break a labor contract; and second, for the benefit of the mining industry in particular, the Rhodesia Chamber of Mines drafted a pass law, which limited the mobility of labor and facilitated the tracing of deserters.[27] How was worker consciousness manifested in relation to this web of legislation?

For many years the most obvious, the most widespread, and the most successful African response to this legislation was to ignore it and desert. T. O. Ranger has pointed to desertion as an index of discontent, and suggested that before World War I "the characteristic expression of discontent . . . was desertion rather than combination."[28] This suggestion, however, unintentionally conceals the rationality which underlies the majority of desertions. A systematic probe of the causes of desertion makes it apparent that desertion *was,* in many cases, a form of combination—and in some cases an extremely effective form. Ignoring for present purposes those cases in which desertions were prompted by the grievances of an individual worker, one can find three sets of causes which demonstrate desertion as a form of combination and as a manifestation of worker consciousness.

Desertion was in the first instance an African reflex reaction to a system of forced labor. This was particularly marked in the first three years of the period under review, when forced labor was widely resorted to. In many cases, workers were "recruited" in rural areas by agents of the Labour Board and forwarded under escort to the mines. Frequently, both agents and escorts were armed, and this must have done much to assist in the flow of labor to the mines. That much of the labor was, to put it mildly, "reluctant" is evident from the fact that of 8,429 workers "engaged" by the board between October 1900 and March 1901 no fewer than 2,160 deserted.[29] Since the mines had to pay capitation fees to the board for labor procured in this manner, they complained bitterly about the rate of desertion. In 1902, for example, the manager of the Surprise mine, in a letter to the Labour Board enclosing a detailed schedule, pointed out that

> of the total boys dispatched from Bulawayo, 22.8% deserted before reaching the mine. Of those who duly arrived, 66.6% deserted before working an average of 14 days. Of the small balance left, 40% are in hospital sick.[30]

Africans simply waited for the first opportunity to desert and avoid forced labor. Opportunity presented itself in different ways, either on the way to the mine or within the compound. T. C. Blundel, the compound manager at the Globe and Phoenix mine, apparently did not understand what was happening in the rural areas, for he was puzzled by the reports on desertion of laborers forwarded by Native Commissioner Taylor:

> Since Mr. Taylor recalled his head police boy Semunto . . . a large number of the boys supplied by him have deserted, although none of them have made complaints to me as Compound Manager. They were all under contract for three months; most of them cleared after working a few days only, not even completing a month's work.[31]

It would seem that opportunity for these particular workers presented itself the moment coercion was removed.

The second set of causes underlying the decision to desert relates to work conditions. The reasons for these poor conditions have already been recounted, and need not be elaborated here. It is sufficient to note that sudden and violent fluctuations in the death rate, coupled with managerial indifference, could induce desertions so promptly and on such a scale that there can be little doubt that they represented a form of combination. Another illustration from the Ayrshire mine shows this clearly. Between August and November 1904 the mine employed, on average, thirteen hundred workers. During these four months there was a considerable increase in the death rate, and forty-three workers died from pneumonia. At the end of October two hundred workers left the mine, and the following month saw a further three hundred desert.[32]

Desertions due to an increase in the death rate do not reflect simply a state of blind panic among black workers. It is significant that they left the Ayrshire *after* the end of the month, i.e., after payday. Other instances show that where the manager or staff showed concern about the welfare of black workers, the rate of desertion was significantly lower.

When the industry was paralyzed by the Spanish flu epidemic of 1918, many Africans deserted from unpopular employers: they had more than sufficient cause to desert, for in crowded compounds 7 percent of all black workers died.[33] But even in these circumstances, this was not the blind panic implied by Gann and Gelfand;[34] for example, at the Falcon mine seven hundred fifty workers took the opportunity to desert, but at the Cam and Motor mine, where the management made considerable efforts on behalf of the workers, fewer than ten deserted.[35] Even in the midst of crisis, there is striking rationality in the response of African labor.

If these desertion rates can be largely attributed to the system of forced labor or bad working conditions, another consideration can be derived from a more lasting feature of the political economy. In many cases the reasons for desertion can be traced to the systematic and conscious attempts of workers to reach a market where their labor would fetch the highest price—a worker strategy directly opposed to the purpose of the legislation mentioned above.

Such desertion patterns can best be understood when it is appreciated that the Rhodesian mining industry operated within the context of a southern African economic system. The center of this economic system and the most lucrative labor market for African workers from central Africa was the Witwatersrand industrial complex. Individual state economies within its orbit all had to compete, in varying degrees, with the Rand for their African labor resources. For most of the contiguous states it was a fact of economic life that most Africans would sell their labor in the Witwatersrand complex.

Rhodesia, however, differed qualitatively from most of these adjacent states. Not only did it have a sizable and well-established population of settlers who were anxious for their own economic advancement, but it also had its own mining industry, which was in the unenviable position of having to compete with the Rand mines for its African labor supply. To make matters worse, the bulk of the mines were situated in the southern half of the colony, in Matabeleland, very close to the direct labor-catchment area of the Rand.

These disadvantages were partly offset by some compensating geographical factors, the most important being that labor from

Nyasaland, Portuguese East Africa, and Northern Rhodesia had to make the long journey to Witwatersrand through Southern Rhodesia. Thus, whatever the economic circumstances of Rhodesia, there would always be a certain number of migrants passing through on their way to the Rand.

Thus, in order to be able to sell its services at the highest price, labor from the territories to the north of Rhodesia, as well as from within the territory itself, had to journey hundreds of miles to the Rand. In general, the object of the migrant worker was to get as far south as possible. His ability to sell his labor in the highest market was directly proportional to the amount of savings (in the form of food and cash) which he could muster at the outset of the journey. The more money and food he commanded, the further south he could travel. The further south he could travel, the larger the wage packet he was likely to receive.

In this respect, the bargaining power of the worker in the labor market depended on the extent of his initial savings. Those migrants who possessed neither food nor cash were forced to accept the "facilities" (food and escorts) provided by the Rhodesian Native Labour Bureau (RNLB). In return for this assistance, the workers had to sign long-term contracts at low wages and were drafted to the most unpopular Rhodesian mines that were suffering from "labor shortages." Many of these RNLB laborers used the system for their own ends by simply making use of the facilities for the duration of the journey, and then deserting at the earliest opportunity to continue the journey south.

Understandably, however, the majority of workers attempted to avoid the RNLB agents and make their way south independently. But because of the limited amount of savings they possessed, they were forced to break their journeys south and take temporary employment in order to accumulate further food and cash. In some cases, workers would offer their services to African farmers in return for food only. More frequently, at the point where the labor routes entered Rhodesia, they would accept employment from white farmers, accumulate savings, and head for the next employment center to the south. Mashonaland farmers and mine owners were aware of the fact that they had an assured supply of passing migrant labor and lowered their wages accordingly. These lower wage rates on Mashonaland mines resulted in consistently higher desertion rates than those found in Matebeleland mines.[36] Having deserted from Mashonaland mines, many workers would make their way south to the Matabeleland mines, where the process would repeat itself as workers left for the Witwatersrand.

This process, and the "stop-go" labor route, were so well known to workers that individual mines were chosen for their suitability as desertion points. The Jessie mine in the remote southern Gwanda district is perhaps the best illustration of this. Along with other mines in the dry Gwanda district, far from fresh produce markets, the Jessie had an extremely high incidence of scurvy among its labor force. Despite the bad diet, the manager was able to point to the fact that the mine had never suffered from a labor shortage.[37] This apparent paradox is easily explicable: the Jessie was the last stop of laborers in Rhodesia before they deserted and made their way to South Africa. For many years this "drainage" from mines in the Gwanda district, like the Jessie, was accepted. By 1927, however, when Rhodesia had to compete not only with the Rand but also with the Copperbelt for its labor supplies, this systematic desertion could no longer be tolerated. In that year, the prime minister gave the Native Affairs Department explicit instructions to exercise the greatest possible care before issuing passes for work in the Gwanda district.[38]

Hopefully it has been demonstrated that besides individual grievance as a cause for desertion there were more deep-seated rational and structural reasons for African desertion. Desertion was, in the bulk of cases, a conscious rejection of bad working conditions or an attempt to reach the best labor market in a system of coercive labor legislation. In these terms desertion emerges as one of the clearest expressions of worker consciousness.

The Compound System

Up to this point, broad patterns of worker response (withholding labor or desertion) within the mining industry have been singled out. The similarities of these responses lie in the fact that they demonstrate large-scale expressions of discontent. The control of expressions of discontent on this wide and diffuse level were dependent on the size, strength, and efficiency of the state's coercive capacity. As mine managers were fond of pointing out, the ability to enforce pass laws, for example, depended on the size of the police force in the mining districts.[39] In a territory controlled by a company-government, there was a constant desire to reduce administrative expenditure, and there were considerable reductions in the size of the police force during the period under review. It is largely for this reason that control of desertion or of the withholding of labor could never be complete.

Workers could, however, be more readily controlled and disciplined on individual mines through the use of the compound system. Within the confines of barrack-like accommodation, surrounded in some cases by barbed-wire fences, a quasi-military system of labor discipline operated. Large numbers of black workers were controlled, marshaled, and disciplined through the agency of black compound police, suitably armed with *sjamboks* (leather whips). Underground control was effected through black *capitãos*, or "boss boys," who were in turn under the supervision of white miners.

The close supervision and discipline ensured through these more highly paid black intermediaries militated against more direct expressions of discontent. Given this repressive control of labor, one must seek the expression of worker discontent in the nooks and crannies of the day-to-day work situation. In many ways the situation closely parallels that of a slave plantation, and the techniques of resistance that slaves developed:

> Side by side with ordinary loafing and mindless labor went deliberate wastefulness, slowdowns, feigned illnesses, self-inflicted injuries, and the well known abuse of livestock and equipment.[40]

At least one of these techniques formed a central and continuous problem for mine managers. "Loafing" constituted such a central part of mine labor that methods of coping with it had to be entrenched in the system. The most important of these was the "ticket system." Workers contracted for the completion of a certain number of "tickets," rather than for a specified period of time. At the end of each shift worked, the laborer's ticket had to be signed by the person in charge at the time. If the black miner's work had not been satisfactorily performed, the ticket was not marked, or was simply marked "loafer." Tickets marked in this manner were not considered as having contributed to the contract. Since no cash wages were paid on an unsigned ticket, the system was obviously open to considerable abuse, and in many cases the "ticket system" was used to reduce the wage bill rather than to discipline reluctant workers. In any event, the ticket system did not eradicate the problem. In evidence to the South African Native Affairs Commission of 1903-1905, the Rhodesian Chamber of Mines complained that

> from the majority of natives of the town to obtain a good day's work is an impossibility. By a system of passive resistance they are able to defeat the objects of a master who deserves value for his money.[41]

This situation did not improve, and a few years later the size of the problem became apparent. Thus, the Selukwe District Mine Managers' Association, addressing itself to the Chamber of Mines, complained that

> the daily average of loafers reaches as high as 20 per cent. That is to say that employers have to keep 20 per cent. more boys on their books than are required for the proper working of their mines.[42]

By prodding the Chamber of Mines, the Selukwe managers were, in the long run, hoping to get government action in the matter.

Indirectly, the state did respond to these problems on the mines after the Native Affairs Committee of Enquiry in 1910-1911. In 1912 the Native Labour Regulations came into force, and it became possible to prosecute black workers for obvious forms of resistance. A list of the more "common charges" brought against the workers is revealing. Workers were charged who "refused or neglected to do work," showed "gross carelessness in handling tools," were "impertinent" and "willfully destroyed compound huts and other property."[43] The possibilities for legal action created by the 1912 ordinance were not widely resorted to by mine managers. Managers found that successful prosecutions were not only hard to come by, but extremely time-consuming, and prosecutions declined in the following years.

While prosecutions declined, however, the techniques continued to play an important part in worker strategy—sometimes with serious consequences for management. During 1918, for example, when coal from the Wankie Colliery was required not only for central African industry but also for ships of the British Navy requiring fuel at Beira, there was such a successful slowdown by black workers with grievances that the administrator was forced to recommend that the manager be "relieved from supervision of native labour."[44] Though less dramatic, these forms of resistance leave little doubt about the existence of worker consciousness.

The strategies still do not give us a clear insight, however, into the sophistication of the perception of the African laborers. It seems legitimate to ask to what extent the category of "African worker" is in the mind of the present analyst rather than that of the "workers"? To what extent is it justified to talk of "African workers" as a class in what was obviously a multiethnic and multilinguistic compound setting?

It is certainly true that one of the most outstanding characteristics of the African labor force was its multiethnic composition, and ethnicity clearly played an important part in worker interaction. The problem is that consideration of ethnicity as the only factor has led to the overstatement of its importance in defining worker interaction. Thus, for example, one sociologist suggests of labor centers in South Central Africa that

> ethnicity became a category of interaction defining appropriate modes of behaviour between people in situations where the transitory nature of social contacts entailed only superficial relationships.[45]

This observation does not seem to fit the case of workers in the major industry of South Central Africa—at least not in the present formulation. There are several reasons for this, two of which should be noted here.

First, it underestimates the impact of the shared work experience within the context of compound discipline. Workers who are collectively housed, fed, worked, and paid in a relatively closed environment have substantial interests in common for most of their working day. Second, not all contracts were short term. Certainly the mines had large numbers of short-term workers, but there was also a well-established core of black workers, whom the chief native commissioner termed "continual workers."[46] Thus, while black workers had many interests in common, there were also significant differences between them other than simply "ethnic" ones. This is best illustrated by examining the employees of the Rhodesian Native Labour Bureau.

The Rhodesian Native Labour Bureau and the Labor Market

As pointed out earlier, RNLB employees were often drawn from the ranks of poorer peasants—for example, those with insufficient savings to get to the mines independently or those who came from far afield. As such, these workers and others, who in the early years were simply commandeered, were forced to contract themselves for lengthy periods. Mine managers, on payment of a capitation fee to the RNLB, secured their services for periods ranging from nine to twelve months. This capitation fee did not arise in the case of short-term independent laborers, and mine owners were naturally anxious to recoup it in any way possible. In practice the outlay of capitation fees was recouped by keeping RNLB workers on the lowest wage rate for their entire contract. In fact, RNLB employees formed a pool of cheap labor which acted as insurance for the mining industry against wage demands by other black workers. The bargaining power of the "voluntary" or "independent" workers was limited because of the presence of RNLB workers.

From this it can be understood why it was that RNLB workers occupied the lowest social and economic rung in the compound hierarchy, and why, for quite different reasons, managers and fellow black workers perceived them in very different ways. The unfortunate status of the RNLB workers was apparent from the earliest days of the industry, and by 1910 it also became apparent to the manager of the bureau who

> regretted to report the complaint of natives on long service that many employers treated them differently to independent natives, apparently with a view to making the Bureau unpopular amongst recruits. The differences in treatment consist not only in paying Bureau natives a lower rate of wages, but also in using opprobrious terms and epithets in connection with these natives, for the purpose of making them a cause of ridicule to "independent boys."[47]

Thus, managers and miners used the RNLB employees as scapegoats to divert worker hostility and divide the black labor force. In many cases the diversion of this aggression was only too successful, and the term which black workers applied to RNLB workers reveals that they were more than capable of interacting on a basis other than ethnicity. *Chibaro*—"slave," or "forced labor"—the term used to refer to RNLB labor throughout central Africa, reflects not only on RNLB recruiting tactics but also on the social and economic status of these workers.

The fact that African workers were aware of stratification within their ranks did not preclude the possibility of their cooperating in order to achieve economic objectives for all workers. Illustrations of this reveal that worker consciousness was capable of embracing all workers within an exploited situation.

In keeping with the mainstream interpretation of Rhodesian history, which suggests the slow evolution of political consciousness of African workers, it has often been suggested that there was no industrial action before 1918.[48] In fact, the period before 1918 saw at least two strikes by African mine workers in Rhodesia. To understand their background and causation, it is again necessary to see the Rhodesian mining industry within the context of the southern African economic system.

Between 1899 and 1902 many workers in southern Africa could not work on the Witwatersrand because of the South African war and had to consider working on the Rhodesian mines. To the delight of the mine managers, skilled Shangaan workers from Mozambique came to work on the Rhodesian mines in considerable numbers. For once, the southward flow of labor was stemmed, and there were even workers from

Bechuanaland, Basutoland, and the Transkei who worked on Rhodesian mines.

This temporary situation changed some of the labor patterns in the southern Africa regional economy. But, while these changes were welcomed in Rhodesia, they did not meet with the same favorable reception in Mozambique and the Transvaal. The Transvaal mines did not want their labor supplies permanently threatened by Rhodesia, and the Mozambique administration resented the higher wages of Rhodesian mines, which pushed up wages within their own territory.[49]

During 1901 discussions were held between all three parties over future labor allocations from Mozambique. Anxious to lower the wage bill of the Rhodesian mines (especially in the favorable circumstances of increased supply) and to accommodate the other two parties, late in 1901 the labor board in Rhodesia generally reduced African wages.[50] No sooner had this reduction been effected at the Camperdown mine, however, then "all the natives struck work on account of the reduction of wages and refused to start again until the Manager promised to pay the ordinary rates."[51]

The composition of the African work force on the Camperdown mine is not known, but it is possible that there was a significant proportion of foreign workers from South Africa involved in the strike. It will be remembered too that workers imported from the Transkei caused "disaffection" at the Tebekwe mine (see above). Other indications, however, show that local laborers were equally sensitive to the wage reductions made on the Matabeleland mines in October and November 1901. The reduction brought about such a dramatic fall in the labor supply that early in 1902 the old wage rates had to be restored.[52]

These events show that African mine workers had considerable insight into conditions of supply and demand, and the effect that it had on wage rates. It is bizarre to suggest, as a 1906 government commission did, that

> one of the chief causes of the shortage of labour is the failure on the part of the native to understand the state of the labour market—i.e. the law of supply and demand.[53]

The problem was not that the "native" did not understand the law of supply and demand, but that he understood its functioning only too well. The chief native commissioner should have been aware of this, since his attention had been drawn to it by individual African workers. At an *indaba* at Mpateni in 1899, one Mahlabatsha had pointed out to him that "they did not get so much pay when they went out to work at the call of the government as when they went out independently,"[54] and at another *indaba* in the same year one Mpome had told him that "in Belingwe, they had never received full wages, especially when they turned out in large gangs as they had lately."[55] A clearer understanding of supply, demand, and wage rates could hardly be expected.[56]

The fact that it was not simply wage rates, but wage rates within the southern Africa economic system that influenced mine workers is clearly evident from the second strike that we will consider. In mid-1904 the Witwatersrand Native Labour Association (WNLA) recuited five thousand workers in Nyasaland for work in the Witwatersrand mines. The first of these workers were taken to the east coast, whence they went by ship to Delagoa Bay and later by train to Johannesburg.[57] This was a very roundabout route, and subsequent "batches" of WNLA laborers were made to follow an overland route through Rhodesia. The lengthy overland marches necessitated stops in Rhodesia, and it would seem that laborers were sometimes housed in Rhodesian compounds overnight. These occasions must have given black miners the opportunity to discuss and compare conditions of employment in the respective territories.

It quickly became clear to Rhodesian workers that their wages did not compare favorably with those that were being offered to WNLA recruits. In 1906 passing WNLA recruits gave such a glowing account to Rhodesian workers of their employment prospects in South Africa that "they caused a mutiny in the compound of a large mine."[58] This strike obviously made a deep impression on the mind of the mine owner, Col. Raleigh Grey. In the same year Grey was made a member of the "Native Labour Enquiry Committee," and thus it is not surprising to find in the report of that committee the view that

> the practice of bringing gangs of laborers recruited by the Witwatersrand Native Labour Association in Northern Zambesia and territories lying to the north, through Rhodesia, is detrimental to Rhodesian industries, and is calculated to spread discontent among natives of Southern Rhodesia.[59]

This is yet a further indication of a well-developed worker consciousness, not in a vague, ill-defined way, but in such a way that it required mine owners to take notice.

Conclusion

A systematic probe of the response of African workers within the context of a specific industry suggests that there was a well-developed worker consciousness from the very earliest days of the mining industry. In settler-dominated economies with repressive labor legislation, it is, in the first instance, to the less dramatic underlying worker responses that we have to turn in looking for this consciousness. Important as they were, the activities of the dance societies, the Watch Tower Society, and the ICU do not represent the first signs of its development. Rather, they are simply a later and more articulate expression of discontent that was present throughout the history of the mining industry in Rhodesia.

Notes

1. L. H. Gann and M. Gelfand, *Huggins of Rhodesia: The Man and His Country* (London: Allen & Unwin, 1964), p. 76.
2. J. R. Hooker, "The African Worker in Southern Rhodesia: Black Aspirations in a White Economy," *Race* 6 (October 1964): 142.
3. E. Mlambo, *Rhodesia: The Struggle for a Birthright* (London: C. Hurst & Co., 1972), p. 186.
4. T. O. Ranger, *The African Voice in Southern Rhodesia, 1898-1930* (London: Heinemann Educational, 1970), p. 141.
5. N. Shamuyarira, *Crisis in Rhodesia* (London: A. Deutsch, 1965), p. 51.
6. Rhodesia, *Report of the Commission of Enquiry into the Mining Industry of Southern Rhodesia* (1945), p. 3.
7. A number of attempts were made to reduce African wages. The most important of these were made in 1898, 1901, and 1906. See, for example, *Rhodesia Chamber of Mines Annual Report* (1906), p. 28.
8. L. H. Gann, *A History of Southern Rhodesia: Early Days to 1934* (London: Chatto & Windus, 1965), p. 173.
9. Based on calculation derived from data in Rhodesia, *Reports on the Public Health* covering the period 1911 to 1920.
10. Gann, *History of Southern Rhodesia*, p. 180.
11. Figure based on data in Rhodesia, *Reports on the Public Health* and other sources.
12. Gann, *History of Southern Rhodesia*, p. 180.
13. Rhodesia, *Report of the Committee appointed to enquire into the prevalence and prevention of Scurvy and Pneumonia amongst Native labourers* (1910), p. 1.
14. Rhodesia, *Report of the Native Affairs Committee of Enquiry* (1910-1911), p. 6.
15. For an excellent account of this process of proletarianization in Rhodesia, see G. Arrighi, "Labour Supplies in Historical Perspective: A Study of the Proletarianisation of the African Peasantry in Rhodesia," *Journal of Development Studies* 6, no. 3 (1971): 197–234.
16. *Rhodesia*, no. 171 (February 16, 1901), p. 92.
17. Ibid., no. 170 (February 9, 1901), p. 82.
18. Rhodesia, *Report on the Administration of Rhodesia* (1898–1900), p. 27.
19. *Rhodesia Chamber of Mines Annual Report* (1901), p. 35.

20. British South Africa Company, "Minutes," October 11, 1900, annexure 19 (C.O. 417/311), Public Records Office, London.

21. *The Labour Problem in Rhodesia* (Bulawayo, 1901), p. 20.

22. *Chinese Question in Rhodesia* (Bulawayo, 1901), p. 6.

23. British South Africa Co., *Mining in Rhodesia* (London, 1902), p. 49.

24. For a general statement on the overcapitalized state of the industry, see H. M. Hole, *Old Rhodesian Days* (London, 1928), p. 40. For low productivity at the Bonsor mine, see *Rhodesia* 6, no. 145 (August 18, 1900), p. 611.

25. British South Africa Co., "Minutes," November 4, 1903, annexure 18 (C.O. 417/387).

26. British South Africa Co., "Minutes," October 29, 1903, annexure 1 (C.O. 417/387).

27. *Rhodesia Chamber of Mines Annual Report* (1901), p. 19.

28. Ranger, *African Voice*, p. 141.

29. *Rhodesia Chamber of Mines Annual Report* (1902), p. 64.

30. Ibid.

31. Ibid., p. 73.

32. Ibid. (1908), p. 58.

33. Great Britain, Colonial Office, "Memorandum. Labour and Mortality Returns, October 1918," (C.O. 417/628).

34. Gann and Gelfand, *Huggins*, p. 50, suggest that "Many Africans seized with panic, fled from the European settlements and died miserably along the roadside or on the veld."

35. *The Rhodesia Herald,* November 8, 1918.

36. Rhodesian Native Labour Bureau, *Proceedings at the Annual and Quarterly General Meeting* (May 26, 1910), p. 10.

37. *Rhodesia* 7, no. 159 (November 24, 1900), p. 810.

38. Southern Rhodesia, *Debates in the Legislative Assembly*, 6, 2, col. 57.

39. *Rhodesia Chamber of Mines Annual Report* (1909), p. 65.

40. Eugene D. Genovese, *The Political Economy of Slavery* (New York: Pantheon Books, 1967), p. 74.

41. *Rhodesia Chamber of Mines Annual Report* (1905), p. 55.

42. Ibid. (1909), p. 65.

43. *Report on the Public Health* (1912), p. 32.

44. British South Africa Co., telegram: Chaplin to BSA Co. Board, August 24, 1918 (C.O. 417/613).

45. J. C. Mitchell, "Race, Class and Status in South Central Africa," in *Social Stratification in Africa*, ed. A. Tuden and L. Plotnicov (New York: The Free Press, 1970), p. 325.

46. In 1909 it was estimated that there were 4,000 such workers out of 32,000 that were fully proletarianized. See British South Africa Company, *Directors' Report and Accounts for the year ending 31st March 1909*, p. 40.

47. Rhodesian Native Labour Bureau, *Proceedings at the Half Yearly and Quarterly General Meeting* (December 8, 1910), p. 13.

48. See, for example, Mlambo, *Struggle for a Birthright*, p. 186 or Ranger, *African Voice*, p. 141.

49. See J. M. Mackenzie, "African Labour in South Central Africa 1890–1914" (Ph.D. diss., University of British Columbia, 1969), p. 315.
50. Ibid.
51. British South Africa Company, *Reports on the Administration of Rhodesia 1900-2*, p. 175.
52. Ibid.
53. *Report of the Native Labour Enquiry Committee* (1906), p. 5.
54. Rhodesia, *Correspondence Relating to the Regulation and Supply of Labour in Southern Rhodesia* (1902), p. 11.
55. Ibid., p. 15.
56. This type of evidence continues to be rejected or ignored by social scientists. For example, "wages were not an effective incentive and general wage increases would not have improved the supply of labour; they might have depressed it." G. Kay, *Rhodesia: A Human Geography* (London: University of London Press, 1970), p. 55.
57. M. Gelfand, "Migration of African Labourers in Rhodesia and Nyasaland 1809–1914," *The Central African Journal of Medicine* 7, no. 8 (August 1961): 298.
58. British South Africa Co., telegram: Milton to High Commissioner, January 17, 1908 (C.O. 417/461).
59. *Report of the Native Labour Enquiry Committee* (1906), p. 4.

Part 2

Workers on the Land

The commercialization of agricultural production, consequent upon the worldwide expansion of capitalism from the sixteenth century onward, led to a variety of labor practices in the countryside of the capitalist periphery. At one end of the spectrum, a full-fledged rural proletariat, working wholly for wages, emerged in several countries. At the other end, it was quite possible to establish highly successful commercial agriculture on the basis of slave labor, i.e., where only the initial cost of the labor power and the costs of the reproduction of the labor power were met by the owner-employer. But both plantation slavery and rural proletarianization have this in common: the laborer is detached, usually violently, from earlier forms of family and household production.

The violent rupture of household production, though occurring in a significant number of countries, is not as widespread as the more common form of capitalist-oriented agricultural production, i.e., where two or more modes of production overlap. Here, rural producers and laborers may be working partly on their own account and partly for wages. They may equally be producing a combination of goods, some for household consumption, some for sale in a local market, and some for export. The selections in part 2 of this volume both discuss the forms of rural work and provide some case studies of the consequences of this "combined and uneven development."

The opening selection by Deere is of fundamental importance in understanding how women become part and parcel of capitalist expansion in the periphery, not by direct expropriation of their surplus generated by production, but rather through their increased involvement in subsistence production. Of course, as she points out, women in the periphery also play a central role in the sphere of circulation and in petty commodity production. But the major thrust of her argument is that rural women, by growing food, tending animals, and engaging in domestic work, allow the capitalist to buy the labor power of "semiproletarian" male workers for less than a subsistence familial wage. Thus, by absorbing some of the costs of production and the reproduction of labor power in the noncapitalist mode, the employer can extract an increased rate of surplus value within the capitalist mode. The initially attractive analogy between the peasant unit in the periphery and the household in advanced capitalist societies is drawn, though finally rejected by the author.

While Deere's tableau is widely drawn, DeWind focuses on a segment of the labor force in one country, the mine workers of the Peruvian Andes.

129

Though initially concerned with a more contemporary event—a succession of strikes during the 1969-1971 period—DeWind is soon pulled into a discussion of the relationship between the commercialization of agriculture and the supply of laborers to the mines. At the turn of the century temporary unskilled labor was drawn off the land through the enganche system (where peasants would pay off large debts through wage labor in the mines). The issuing of tokens, only redeemable at the mercantil ("company store") was used to tie a generally reluctant proletariat to the apron strings of the company. The intimate connection between the state of the peasant economy and the extent of proletarianization is demonstrated by the fact that a stabilized proletariat emerged only in the 1940s with the collapse of the rural economy (the fiesta providing one source of instant emiseration) and the shift to the planting of commercial crops. In an interesting twist to the normal pattern, the Cerro de Pasco Corporation, the principal mining company, purchased large acreages of land and subsidized the reproduction costs of its labor power through its ownership of the haciendas.

Sydney Mintz's article on the rural proletariat provides a fascinating extension of his earlier, and well-known, work on Puerto Rico, a retrospective review of the state of the literature, and a substantive contribution to the discussion of rural proletarianization in its own right. In his article Mintz directs his attention to four major issues. First, he creates a typology of a rural proletariat, particularly in colonial or neocolonial societies. Second, he looks more sharply at the social differentiation within peasant communities and shows how a wage-labor group is often concealed within such general rubrics as a "peasantry." Third, he considers how a process of proletarianization occurs. Finally, he tackles the thorny problem of rural proletarian consciousness, the manifestation of which, so one might expect, differs in several fundamental respects from that of the "classical" urban industrial proletariat formed in the factories of Europe.

But while Mintz provides some interesting theoretical and comparative views on rural proletarian consciousness, Post's detailed study of the labor rebellion of 1938 in Jamaica presents the issue in a sharper focus. The events he describes involved a wide range of workers—sugarcane workers, dockers, and public employees, ex-servicemen settled on land grants, as well as banana workers— each group having, to some degree at least, separate motives and interests for joining the strikes and protests in 1938. But it is in the case of the banana workers, whom Post singles out for special attention, that the possibilities of rural proletarian consciousness are graphically polarized. On the one hand, the aims of the men "included higher wages and more regular work." In this case, the completion of the process of proletarianization was taken as given—the workers, like their counterparts in Europe or America, wanted simply to reduce their rate of exploitation. On the other hand, Post argues that "it is not primarily as wage workers that the banana plantation workers must be seen but as peasant farmers . . . it was [the] hunger for land . . . which was the main motive force of the strikers." In this statement we see the second possibility of rural proletarian consciousness emerge—the promotion of agrarian goals through industrial means—thereby reducing the workers' rate of exploitation by the workers' total denial of their labor power to the capitalist. The wider, and possibly revolutionary, nature of this second form of consciousness for other societies remains to be explored.

Rural Women's Subsistence Production in the Capitalist Periphery

Carmen Diana Deere

Introduction

Women's economic participation in the periphery of the world capitalist system, just as within center economies, has been conditioned by the requirements of capital accumulation. But to the extent that capitalist expansion engenders a process of underdevelopment in the periphery, the economic participation of women in the Third World differs significantly from women's economic participation within the center of the world capitalist system.

Whereas capitalist development in center economies has often increased women's participation in the wage-labor force, and hence, in the capitalist production process, capitalist expansion on the periphery has often intensified women's economic participation in noncapitalist modes of production. This is not to imply that female labor force participation is unimportant in the periphery.[1] Rather, the majority of women in the Third World are rural women, and women's economic participation is particularly notable in rural areas where women participate in subsistence agricultural production as well as in petty commodity production and circulation. Thus, to analyze the significance of women's economic participation within the periphery, as well as to understand the significance of women's work for the development of female social status, requires a theoretical framework based on the articulation,[2] or interconnection, between modes of production within a given social formation.

The primary objective of this paper is to develop a theoretical framework for the analysis of rural women's contribution to capital accumulation. My principal hypothesis is that family structure and the attendant division of labor by sex are key to the extraction of surplus from noncapitalist modes of production. In particular, the division of labor by sex characterized by female production of subsistence foodstuffs and male semi-

Reprinted from *The Review of Radical Political Economics* 8, no. 1 (Spring 1976), with the permission of the Union for Radical Political Economics. Copyright © 1976 *Review of Radical Political Economics*.

proletarianization allows the payment by capital of a male wage rate insufficient for familial maintenance and reproduction.[3] The articulation between modes of production, based on the familial division of labor by sex, thus allows the wage to be less than the cost of production and reproduction of labor power. This inequality is then reflected in a low value of labor power within the periphery, which either enhances peripheral capital accumulation or is transferred to the center via unequal exchange, financial imperialism, or other forms of surplus extraction.

The organization of the paper is as follows. In the first section the relevant cross-cultural data on women's agricultural participation is reviewed. The theoretical framework is then developed in the second section. It is argued that women's production of foodstuffs within the noncapitalist mode of production lowers the value of labor power indirectly, enhancing relative surplus value for capital accumulation. Since the household in advanced capitalism is so often compared with the peasant productive unit, the third section contrasts the functions of these forms of production and reproduction of labor power in terms of their contribution to capital accumulation in the center and periphery. The concluding section considers why this particular division of labor by sex has ensued in the periphery, with women's subsistence production maintaining the low-cost, male, rural labor reserve.

Women's Agricultural Participation in the Third World

In this section I argue that women's agricultural participation reflects the conditions that serve to maintain the cheapest labor force for capitalist expansion and accumulation. For once Latin America, Africa, and Asia came into contact with the world market economy, and were later transformed into the periphery of the world capitalist system,[4] women's production of subsistence foodstuffs or actual labor force participation has served as a force for the maintenance of low wages.

Boserup's comparison of women's agricultural participation in Africa and Asia illustrates how the division of labor by sex may contribute toward the maintenance of the cheapest labor force for the export economy, given the ecological and demographic conditions influencing the type of cultivation.[5] Typical of much of precolonial Africa were the female farming systems based on shifting cultivation. Colonial plantations and other export industries were able to recruit only male workers and to pay them a wage insufficient to provide for the workers' families, for the women and children remained in the villages. Women's subsistence agricultural production continued to support the family, as well as the men, during periods of unemployment or sickness.

In Asia, on the other hand, where agriculture was characterized by an irrigated, labor-intensive system, male labor could not be recruited without providing for the women and children, since the predominant type of cultivation required full familial participation. For the Asian plantations to assure themselves of a sufficient labor supply, whole families had to be recruited; the most efficacious means of keeping the effective wage rate low was to put the whole family to work. Boserup thus concludes that in the Asian as well as the African case the plantation avoided paying a "family wage" to the male by relying on women's agricultural participation either as direct producers or as semiproletarians.

Van Allen's analysis of the effect of modernization on African women also suggests how the development of Africa's export economy has depended on the labor of rural women.[6] The export industries have been able to maintain low wages, and hence high profits, because of women's contribution to the family's subsistence from agricultural production. She notes that the profits extracted from Africa

> would not be possible except for the unpaid labor of the wives of their African workers, who feed, clothe and care for themselves and their children at no cost whatsoever to the companies. Far from being a drag on the modern sector, then, as it is sometimes claimed, the modern sector is dependent for its profits on the free labor done by women.[7]

African women have generally remained in the villages while their men have migrated, but where provision is made for a worker to have his family with him—such as in the Zambian copper mines—subsistence land plots are provided to the women so that they may produce the foodstuffs to maintain the workers and children. There too, the wage is kept low by the possibility that the woman can provide at least a portion of the family's subsistence requirements.

Caulfield points out that this manner of keeping labor costs below the level required to support whole families is also found on West Indian plantations.[8] There, plantation owners recruit whole families for work on the plantations, using the wage labor of women and children only during the peak agricultural periods and relying on women's subsistence production of foodstuffs to feed the families from small land parcels which are provided to them. The male wage is thus held to an absolute minimum.

Latin American peasant societies are typically depicted as male farming systems; men are considered the primary agriculturalists, although it is increasingly recognized that women are often active participants in agricultural activities.[9] But the division of labor by sex in agriculture is rarely static; rather, women's involvement in agricultural production activities is responsive to changing socio-economic conditions. In the Andean case, for example, the division of labor by sex in agriculture appears to be changing in response to rural poverty; women's participation in agricultural production is increasing, particularly among the poorer strata of the peasantry. Peasant women are becoming the principal agriculturalists when the men migrate to the mines, plantations, and urban centers in search of wage income.[10]

In sum, women's agricultural participation cross-culturally takes a variety of forms—from full proletarianization, to a temporary labor reserve responsive to agriculture's seasonal demand for labor, to subsistence producers on plantations, haciendas, or independent land parcels. What is apparent is that women's agricultural participation does reflect the immediate conditions that maintain the cheapest labor force for capital accumulation based on the particular requirements for labor.

But it should be made clear that the agricultural division of labor by sex is not just responsive to the capitalist's desire to maintain low wages; rather, intrafamilial labor deployment is responsive to the need to attain subsistence in the face of rural poverty. And what is rural poverty but a reflection of the overall pattern of peripheral capitalist development—the growing lack of access to the means of production of subsistence, which forces the peasantry into wage labor, yet the inability of dependent capitalist industrialization to fully absorb the available labor supply. The division of labor by sex reflects a familial reproduction strategy to these overall socioeconomic constraints.

The theoretical framework to follow highlights one particular pattern of the sexual division of labor—that which corresponds to male semiproletarianization and female production of subsistence foodstuffs. While this particular division of labor by sex is not a necessary outcome of the pattern of peripheral capitalist development, it does appear to be most prevalent in the periphery. It also provides us with a clear example of the significance of the articulation between modes of production in peripheral social formations.

The Value of Labor Power and the
Articulation Between Modes of Production

Once the capitalist mode of production is dominant within a social formation, if the articulation between modes of production is to affect capital acumulation, it must do so by increasing the mass surplus value. For capital accumulation is predicated on the extraction of surplus labor time from workers, which, within capitalist relations of production,[11] takes the form of the mass of surplus value (equivalent to the rate of surplus value times the employment base).

The rate of surplus value (or the rate of exploitation) may be increased either absolutely or relatively by capital. Absolute surplus value is increased by lengthening the working day, a direct increase in the surplus labor time which is appropriated by capital. Relative surplus value is increased by lowering the value of labor power, either through a reduction of the real wage or an increase in the intensity of the labor process.

As with other commodities, the value of labor power is determined by the socially necessary labor time embodied in its production; this amounts to the socially necessary labor time expended on the production of the commodities that constitute the worker's means of subsistence.[12] The commodities that make up the wage-good bundle are a function of the moral-historical determination of the subsistence wage; i.e., the class struggle over the functional distribution of income.[13]

If all of the goods and services required for the production and reproduction of labor power were produced within capitalist relations of production and if labor power were paid at its value, the wage, then, would be equivalent to the value of the worker's means of subsistence. But at any given historically defined level of subsistence consumption, not all of the goods and services required for the production and reproduction of labor power need be produced under capitalist relations of production; the bundle of commodities purchased with the wage is not necessarily equal to the worker's means of subsistence. However, since only commodities reflect socially necessary labor or abstract labor based on the average social conditions of production, the value of labor power only refers to the value of the bundle of commodities that can be purchased with the wage.[14]

Other labor, external to the capitalist production process, may be required to produce additional goods and services required for subsistence; other labor may also be required to transform the commodities purchased with the wage into use values. As long as a portion of the goods and services required to maintain and reproduce labor power are produced external to capitalist relations of production, the necessary labor time embodied in the mass of wage-good commodities—or the value of labor power to capital—is reduced.

Now, the necessary labor time encompassed in the value of labor power is not only a function of the size of the wage-good bundle but also a function of the productivity of the wage-good industry and, consequently, the productivity of all those industries serving the wage-good industry directly or indirectly. Productivity increases are realized either as an increase in the relative rate of surplus value or as an increase in the moral-historical element of the wage-good bundle, depending on the class struggle.

Due to the rapid development of the productive forces within advanced capitalism, the focus of the class struggle in center economics has been upon the distribution of productivity gains between labor and capital. In contrast, in peripheral economies surplus population with respect to the available employment opportunities has ensured that labor's wage be maintained at subsistence; the focus of the class struggle has thus been upon the composition of the wage-good bundle in terms of the physiological subsistence requirements of the working class. For capitalists need not concern themselves with the reproduction of the class of laborers if workers or their families have access to the means of production of subsistence to partially cover their subsistence requirements. And if a noncapitalist mode of production can provide at least a portion of the goods and services required for the maintenance and reproduction of labor power for the labor market, as well as store the seasonally fluctuating labor reserve, the necessary labor time required for the production and reproduction of labor power for capitalist expansion and accumulation is reduced. The productive efforts of the noncapitalist mode thus indirectly contribute to the generation of a larger mass of surplus value within capitalist units of production than would otherwise be the case if the value of labor power reflected the actual costs of production and reproduction of labor power.

Some Refinements

Thus far I am assuming that the value of labor power refers to the value of the means of subsistence required by workers *and* their families.[15] Therefore, the inequality of the wage to the costs of production and reproduction of labor power is based on a lower value of labor power than that required for full familial reproduction. But is there any scientific reason to suppose that the wage should be sufficient in magnitude to provide for the subsistence requirements of a whole family?

For an "individual wage" to ensure the daily maintenance and generational reproduction of the labor force, either (1) sufficient employment has to be available to employ all adult family members at a wage sufficient to cover the full costs of their maintenance as well as of generational reproduction; or (2) the family must have access to the means of production of subsistence. If sufficient employment is not forthcoming from the pattern of industrialization (depending on the particular historical process, reflecting either the substitution of capital for labor in the productive process, the capital-intensiveness of industrialization, or the low level of accumulation) or if the family does not have access to the means of production of subsistence, then a "family wage" is required if the population is to reproduce in a normal and healthy manner.[16]

If the wage is sufficient to maintain the wage worker but not to assure the reproduction of the wage worker, then the moral-historical component of the wage would appear to be absent, for the generation reproduction of the working class must depend on the productive efforts of a noncapitalist mode of production with access to the means of production of subsistence. Certainly the value of labor power to capital is reduced in the short run, since the necessary labor time embodied in the wage-good bundle is minimized.

If the wage is less than that required to maintain the wage worker so that familial labor power must be expended in the production of the means of subsistence to reproduce the worker's daily expenditure of labor power, then, clearly, this would define the concept of the superexploitation of familial labor. Here, the moral-historical element of the wage is negative, for the wage is insufficient to provide the commodities for even the physiological subsistence of the wage worker. In this situation women's labor within the noncapitalist mode accounts for the reproduction of future generations of workers as well as for the reproduction of the labor power expended on a daily basis in the capitalist production process.

But what is unique to this interface between modes of production within the periphery? For common to all modes of production within capitalist social formations is the possibility for the exploitation of labor. Exploitation, rigorously defined, exists if the total labor hours worked exceed the necessary labor hours required to produce and reproduce the worker's means of subsistence, i.e., if surplus labor hours are performed and appropriated.

Within most noncapitalist modes of production, the basic unit of production is the family. Production and consumption of the means of subsistence are not divorced from each other, and thus the reproduction of labor power is embedded within the unit of social production. The major implication of this unity of functions is that the division of labor by sex does not limit the extraction of surplus labor time, under the various forms of appropriation, to only one member of the family. For example, under servile relations of production the peasant family acquires access to the usufruct of land through the payment of rent in labor services or in kind to the landlord. Although a division of tasks between men and women or adults and children may take place between the field work performed for the landlord and that required for the family's subsistence production, or in domestic work for the landlord and that for the family's maintenance, the surplus labor time which is appropriated by the landlord is undifferentiable.

Among petty commodity producers other mechanisms of surplus extraction may be more important: merchant, commercial, and financial capital may all play a role in assuring that the petty-commodity-producing sector engages only in simple reproduction. But here, too, the family is still the principal unit subject to exploitation, and the unity between production of the commodities which constitute the family's means of subsistence and the reproduction and maintenance of labor power makes the division of labor by sex superfluous as a mechanism of surplus extraction.

If the peasant family must participate in the labor market to assure its full reproduction, then this unity is broken as the noncapitalist unit is integrated into the capitalist mode of production. Semiproletarianization requires that the family still be in possession of the means of production from which to obtain some portion of subsistence; thus, production of the means of subsistence is still tied to the reproduction of labor power. But the sale of labor power at a wage insufficient to cover at least the worker's subsistence means that the reproduction and maintenance of labor power only results from the superexploitation of familial labor on the unit of subsistence production. Here, then, the division of labor is key in the extraction of surplus: the women and children are mobilized to produce the means of subsistence for the production and reproduction of labor power for the labor market.

The articulation between modes of production in this case assures that the surplus labor time which is appropriated indirectly from the noncapitalist mode is realized as surplus value by capitalist units of production. Women's labor within the noncapitalist mode reduces the value of labor power to capital, thus the rate of surplus value is increased and capital accumulation enhanced.

The Peasant Unit and the Household in Advanced Capitalism

In both center and periphery the economic participation of women may increase the mass of surplus value generated for capital accumulation directly or indirectly. Women's labor force participation increases the number of proletarians subject to direct exploitation by capital. Indirectly, women's labor in noncapitalist units of production may affect the rate of surplus value through the lowering of the value of labor power. In this section I argue that, while women's work may appear to have similar functions for capital accumulation in both center and periphery, the qualitative as well as quantitative dimensions of the significance of women's work for capital accumulation differ between center and periphery.

In the earlier discussion of the costs of production and reproduction of labor power it was noted that other labor, external to the capitalist production process, is usually required within capitalist social formations to transform the commodities purchased with the wage into use values and to produce additional goods and services required for subsistence. We have seen that within the periphery additional goods and services for the production and reproduction of labor power are produced by rural women within noncapitalist modes of production which serve to lower the value of labor power for peripheral capital accumulation.

But does women's labor within the household in center economies serve a similar function for capital accumulation within the advanced capitalist mode of production? Additional labor, external to the capitalist production process, is expended within the household in the transformation of commodities into use values. For if all of the goods and services required for the maintenance and reproduction of labor power were to be purchased as commodities, the magnitude of the wage would presumably have to be increased or the standard of living of the working class reduced.[17] Thus, domestic labor also enhances capital accumulation in that the necessary labor time within the wage-good industry is reduced by the payment by capitalists of wages unequal to the actual costs of production and reproduction of labor power. Hence, the value of labor power to capital is lowered, and, correspondingly, the relative rate of surplus value is increased through the productive efforts of women in the household.

The domestic unit in advanced capitalism and the peasant unit in the periphery thus appear to perform a similar function for capital accumulation in reducing the value of labor power; however, the quantitative aspect as well as the qualitative dynamic of this function in the center and in the periphery must be distinguished. First, the domestic unit within advanced capitalism is divorced from both the means of production of subsistence and from the means of exchange;[18] the reproduction of the domestic unit is dependent upon the redistribution of the wage, as is its production of use values for the maintenance of labor power.[19] The semiproletarianized peasant unit in the periphery does possess the means of production of subsistence; there, the production of subsistence foodstuffs is an independent source of use-value production which is not dependent on the wage. The essential difference between the two units in terms of the production and reproduction of labor power is that the domestic unit in advanced capitalist countries stretches the wage through the transformation of commodities into use values, thereby maintaining the worker's standard of living above what it would otherwise be; the peasant unit in the periphery produces the goods and services which are purchased with the wage in the center.

Second, the household in the center and the peasant productive unit in the periphery perform different functions in the dynamic of capital accumulation. In center economies labor incomes serve to increase the size of the domestic market; thus, it is not surprising that the expansion of the market size has been closely geared to the increased commoditization of the goods and services formerly produced within the domestic unit. In fact, women's economic functionality within the household has evolved historically from that of being a producer of goods and services to being the transformer of commodities into use values to being a proletarian within the reserve army of labor. Women in center economies are increasingly drawn into wage employment, and the increased demand for female labor has simultaneously expanded the commodity market for the use values formerly produced within the household.[20] And as many socialist feminists point out, although the forces for complete socialization (or commoditization) of the household are strong within center economies—tied to the expansion of the market size and the demand for female labor—these forces clash with the ideological foundations of the patriarchal family, leading to contradictory pressures for both the preservation and extinction of the bourgeois family.[21]

In the periphery the expansion of the domestic market as an impetus to capital accumulation has been minimal because of the structural composition of the export and industrial enclaves. With little incentive for the increased commoditization of the household, let alone a demand for female labor within the enclave's productive structure, women have been relegated to the maintenance and reproduction of the low-cost rural labor reserve. For the logic to the preservation of a noncapitalist mode of production alongside capitalist development is geared to ensure the reproduction of a future class of wage workers, and to provide the means to store the seasonally fluctuating temporary labor reserve.

In summary, within center economies the essential nexus in women's economic functionality rotates between stretching the wage through the production of use values, to the increasing proletarianization that accompanies capital accumulation and the increased commoditization of the household. The total absence of these factors within the periphery ensures that women's economic functionality in the rural areas centers on the maintenance of a low value of labor power through their production of subsistence foodstuffs for the production and reproduction of labor power.

Concluding Comments

I have argued that the agricultural division of labor in the periphery—with male semiproletarians and female agriculturalists—contributes to the maintenance of a low value of labor power for peripheral capital accumulation through the production of subsistence foodstuffs by the noncapitalist mode of production for the reproduction and maintenance of the labor force. But why should this particular division of labor by sex result in the periphery?

If a significant wage differential exists between men's and women's reward from employment, or if local prejudice discriminates against women's labor force participation, the ensuing allocation of familial tasks within the peasant unit might reflect this economic reality. But for the division of labor to be determined endogenously to the peasant family, generational reproduction must be taken into account as the only element which confers an absolute comparative advantage to one sex in the allocation of tasks.

If the individually rational response to rural poverty is to have as large a family as possible (for more children provide more agricultural help, increase the family's ability to engage in alternative income-generating activities, and assure social security to the parents in old age),[22] then a primary consideration in the familial allocation of tasks is that women's economic activities be compatible with the requirements of biological reproduction. Rather than residing in tremendous differences in physical requirements between work performed in or outside the subsistence unit, I suggest that it is the qualitative nature of proletarianization—loss of control over the production process, rigid schedules, hierarchical organization—which most distinguishes the employment alternatives. The nature of agricultural activities on the subsistence production unit—which does allow the producer to be in control of the productive process, working at one's own pace while attending to other tasks—is more compatible with women's biological reproduction requirements if having as many children as possible is viewed by the family as an economic necessity.

The differences in the work experiences of men and women have significant implications for the respective statuses of the sexes as well as for the development of their political consciousness. Women's increased participation in subsistence agricultural activities, including agricultural decision-making as well as participation in community affairs, would seemingly increase women's self-esteem. But women's increased economic role is not a sufficient condition for the development of women's status.[23] And in the particular case of women's economic participation in the noncapitalist mode as the man is semiproletarianized, contradictory forces operate to perpetuate women's subjugation. The fact that women's participation is in the subordinate mode, while men participate in the dominant capitalist mode of production, has important repercussions for the aspirations and the values which tend to depreciate women's work in the "traditional" mode of production.

But perhaps more important, the differences in men's and women's work experiences may have different consequences for the development of class consciousness. The male semiproletarian, by partaking in capitalist social production, is brought into direct struggle with capital, not as an individual, but as a member of an incipient class. The woman agriculturalist, in contrast, must rely on her own self-sufficiency; it is not surprising that a significant number of peasant leaders in land seizures from Zambia to Peru have been peasant women defending their direct material interest: access to land.

Notes

1. A good framework for the analysis of women's labor force participation in the periphery is provided by Marianne Schmink, "Dependent Development and the Division of Labor by Sex: Venezuela," *Latin American Perspectives* 4, nos. 1 and 2 (Winter and Spring 1977): 153–79. Also see Heleieth Saffioti, *Women in Class Society* (New York: Monthly Review Press, 1978) for an analysis of women's role in the reserve army of labor in the periphery.

2. A primary characteristic of peripheral social formations is the maintenance of precapitalist modes of production alongside the dominant capitalist mode, as well as the creation of other non-capitalist modes by the very process of capitalist expansion. Although capitalist development does not necessarily require the perpetuation of noncapitalist modes of production, the uneven and distorted nature of capitalist expansion in the periphery has functioned to assure that the reproduction of noncapitalist modes is subservient to the interests of the dominant mode. The historically determined relationship which serves the process of capital accumulation in the periphery is characterized by the concept of the articulation between modes of production. The applicability of utilizing the theoretical construct of mode of production as a general concept has been raised in a recent work on modes of production by B. Hindess and P. Hirst, *Pre-Capitalist Modes of Production* (London: Routledge & Kegan Paul, 1975). Possibly, a more correct formulation would be in terms of noncapitalist "forms" of production which are articulated within a social formation dominated by the capitalist mode of production. The terminology of mode of production has been retained herein to maintain consistency with the earlier version of this article.

3. For the sake of consistency and to assure the generality of the analysis for the periphery as a whole, I have chosen to call the peasant productive unit characterized by labor market participation (semi-proletarianization) a part of a noncapitalist mode of production, rather than a precapitalist mode. By a noncapitalist mode of production I refer to the fact that the peasant unit possesses the means of production of subsistence; although the individual peasant may participate temporarily in capitalist relations of production, access to the means of production of subsistence assures that the peasant unit is not dependent on the wage for the full production and reproduction of familial labor power.

Within certain social formations this noncapitalist mode of subsistence production is certainly of precapitalist origin. In other historical circumstances this form of subsistence production is the direct product of the introduction of capitalism in agriculture, resulting from a parceling of haciendas, for example. What stands out in the dynamic context is how the units of subsistence production which must participate in the labor market are the result of the process of capitalist expansion into the rural areas and, hence, may be viewed as a low-cost labor reserve created by the requirements of capitalist development. In this regard, also see Claude Meillassoux, "From Reproduction to Production," *Economy and Society* 1 (1972): 93–105.

4. This transformation was characterized by the imposition, primarily through free trade, of an international division of labor, whereby the periphery specialized in the production of primary materials for export to the center economies in return for the import of manufactured goods. See Franz Hinkelammert, *Dialéctica del desarrollo desigual* (Santiago de Chile: CEREN, 1972).

5. Ester Boserup, *Woman's Role in Economic Development* (London: George Allen and Unwin, 1970), pp. 76–78.

6. Judith Van Allen, "Women in Africa: Modernization Means More Dependency," *The Center Magazine* 12, no. 3 (May-June 1974): 60–67.

7. Ibid., p. 6.

8. Mina Davis Caulfield, "Imperialism, the Family, and Cultures of Resistance," *Socialist Revolution*, no. 20 (October 1974): 67–85.

9. In *Woman's Role in Economic Development*, chapter 1, comparison of census data regarding women's agricultural participation in Latin America, Africa, and Asia has done much to obscure the active role that Latin American peasant women actually play in agriculture. Peasant women in Latin America are active participants in such agricultural tasks as planting, weeding, harvesting, and threshing. In certain areas women control agricultural inputs such as seed selection and fertilizer collection. Women, with the aid of children, are often charged with tending the livestock and other farm animals; most generally, the women process the agricultural products for home use as well as for market exchange. See Lourdes Carpio, "La mujer campesina: una alarmante postergación," *Educación* 1, no. 3 (November 1970): 9–17, on peasant women's agricultural participation in Peru; Julia Elena Fortun, "La mujer aymara en Bolivia," *America indígena* 23, no. 3 (July 1972): 935–48, on their participation in Bolivia; and Lourdes Arizpe, "Mujer campesina, mujer indígena," mimeographed (Colegio de Mexico, March 1975), on rural women's participation in Mexico.

10. The need for active female participation in agriculture as men migrate seasonally to seek wage income, in the Peruvian case, is noted by Carpio, "La mujer campesina," and by C. D. Deere, "Changing Social Relations of Production and Peruvian Peasant Women's Work," *Latin American Perspectives* 4, nos. 1 and 2 (Winter and Spring 1977): 48–69. Violeta Sara Lafosse notes that some 21 percent of the women in the Peruvian Sierra are agriculturalists on their own account, with their partners deriving wage income from outside employment, "La ley de reforma agrarian (no. 17710) y sus implicaciones en la

estructura familial," *Serie Documentos de Trabajo,* no. 3 (Lima: Pontificia Universidad Católica, November 1969).

But why the need for wage income? In much of Latin America the concentration of landholdings by a rural elite, combined with demographic growth, has led to severe land fragmentation evidenced in the prevalence of the minifundio, defined as land units too small to employ all family members or to provide full subsistence for all family members. Thus, the possibility of outside employment—semiproletarianization—becomes necessary for the family's survival. This structural characteristic implies that the minifundio, rather than being isolated bastions of "traditional agriculture," are integrated into the wider economy; instead of being integrated through the product market, these units of subsistence production are integrated into the labor market. For a full treatment of this phenomenon in the context of rural poverty, see Alain de Janvry, "The Political Economy of Rural Development in Latin America: An Interpretation," *American Journal of Agricultural Economics* 57, no. 3 (August 1975): 490–99.

11. Capitalist relations of production are characterized by the sale of labor power by the owner of labor power, the worker, to the capitalist, who owns the means of production. Hence, the worker loses possession and property of the means of production of subsistence and is dependent on the wage. Surplus value is created in the capitalist production process, since the value labor creates (embodied in commodities) is greater than the value of labor power (embodied in the commodities which constitute the worker's means of subsistence).

12. Karl Marx, *Capital,* vol. 1 (New York: International Publishers, 1967), pp. 170–71.

13. Marx's concept of the value of labor power, insofar as it is reducible to a more or less definite quantity of consumption items, did not imply that the wage would fall or always equilibrate at a purely physical-biological minimum of consumption required for existence. He noted that the "means of subsistence that are physically indispensable" would constitute the minimum level of the value of labor power. In addition, historical and moral elements play a decisive role in determining what the average quantity of the means of subsistence necessary to maintain the worker would be in any given country, at any given period. Ibid., p. 171.

14. Here I am following the more orthodox interpretation of value theory as applied to the production and reproduction of labor power as proposed by Jean Gardiner, "Women's Domestic Labour," *New Left Review,* no. 89 (January-February 1975): 47–58. Labor external to the capitalist production process does not enter into the necessary labor time encompassed in the value of labor power (although many more labor hours may be required to produce and reproduce labor power than if such labor were performed under capitalist relations of production), since such labor is not socially necessary labor. See Marx, *Capital,* vol. 1, p. 39.

15. Marx was fairly explicit: "The value of labor power was determined,

not only by the labor time necessary to maintain the individual adult laborer, but also by that necessary to maintain his family." Ibid., p. 395. See Lise Vogel's "The Earthly Family," *Radical America* 7, nos. 4-5 (Fall 1973): 9–50, for a discussion of the implications of this assumption.

16. See Jane Humphries' analysis of how the family wage in center economies was the result of the class struggle and constituted a victory for the working class, "The Working Class Family, Women's Liberation and Class Struggle: The Implications of 19th Century British History," *Review of Radical Political Economics* 9, no. 3 (1977).

17. Jean Gardiner in "Women's Domestic Labour" discusses this point in detail.

18. Wally Secombe, "The Housewife and Her Labour under Capitalism," *New Left Review*, no. 83 (January-February 1974): 3–24, points this out.

19. The dependence of the domestic unit in advanced capitalism on the wage and, hence, on the capitalist mode of production for its own reproduction has led some theorists to designate the capitalist domestic unit a client mode of production to the dominant capitalist mode of production. See John Harrison, "The Political Economy of Housework," *Bulletin of the Conference of Socialist Economists* (Winter 1973). The relevance of considering the household a mode of production in its own right is questioned by Jean Gardiner, Susan Himmelweit, and Maureen Mackintosh in "Women's Domestic Labour," *Bulletin of the Conference of Socialist Economists* (March 1975).

20. See Nancy Hartsock's "Women and Economics: A Theoretical Appraisal," mimeographed (Baltimore: Department of Political Science, Johns Hopkins University, 1975).

21. See ibid.; Gardiner, "Women's Domestic Labour"; and Margaret Coulson, Branka Magas, and Hilary Wainwright, "The Housewife and Her Labour under Capitalism—A Critique," *New Left Review*, no. 89 (January-February 1975): 59–71.

22. Mahmood Mamdani, *The Myth of Population Control* (New York: Monthly Review Press, 1972), has an excellent discussion of the rationale for large families in the face of rural poverty.

23. See, for example, Peggy Sanday's article, "Toward a Theory of the Status of Women," *American Anthropologist* 75 (1973): 1682-1700, on the correlation between women's involvement in agricultural production and the development of female status.

From Peasants to Miners:
The Background to Strikes
in the Mines of Peru

Josh DeWind

A strike wave swept through the mining camps of the Peruvian Andes from the beginning of 1969 through 1971.[1] There had been occasional strikes by mine workers in the past, but never before had the strikes been so frequent and rarely so militant. The mines of the Cerro de Pasco Corporation were affected most. During this period the corporation's loss of production days was more than three times greater than that of the entire previous decade. The long strikes included *marchas de sacrificio* on the capital, violent confrontations with the police, kidnappings, and killings.

The Cerro de Pasco Corporation was a wholly owned subsidiary of the Cerro Corporation, whose main offices are in New York City. The company was formed in 1902 as the Cerro de Pasco Mining Company with a capital of $10 million obtained from prominent North American businessmen and financiers. Over the next seventy years the company (with several changes in its name) bought and developed foreign- and Peruvian-owned mines, acquired the largest and one of the most efficient haciendas in the country, built its own railroads, constructed one of the largest and most complex smelting and refining plants in the world, and dominated the mining industry in the mineral-rich central region of Peru. At the time of the recent strikes the Cerro de Pasco Corporation was the largest private employer in the country. Its operations required over fourteen thousand miners. As one of the most important companies in Peru, the Cerro de Pasco Corporation had always enjoyed considerable political influence.

Traditionally the Peruvian government had cooperated with the company in controlling, and at times in repressing, the unions. In October 1968 the military took over the government and adopted a friendlier attitude toward the miners. Not only were strikes permitted to continue for as long as a month or more, but also, as final arbitrator of labor disputes, the government

Reprinted from *Science & Society* 39, no. 1 (Spring 1975), with the permission of the publishers.

granted the miners improvements in working and living conditions and unprecedented wage increases.

The military had come to power through a bloodless coup d'état and immediately began a series of socially progressive programs, including extensive agrarian and educational reforms. Although there was little resistance, there also was practically no popular support. The poor and middle classes of both urban and rural areas greeted the new laws with apathy and suspicion. They doubted whether the military *gobierno de decretos* ("government of decrees") had either the inherent interest or the resources to carry out significant reforms. The government tried to convince the public of the earnestness of its populist intentions by making generous strike settlements for the miners at the expense of the foreign-owned mining companies.

In the fall of 1971 the federation of the fourteen unions representing the miners, the railroad workers, and the smelters of the Cerro de Pasco Corporation went on strike. The unions' demands for wages and improved living conditions were greater than ever before. For the first time a political demand was added: the nationalization of the three largest mining companies in Peru, which were all owned by North Americans.

The call for nationalization of the mines was advanced by leftist union leaders and political organizers without very much debate in the miners' assemblies in each camp. Daily conversations with the miners and union leaders over a period of more than a year revealed that in principle most miners supported the idea of nationalization, but they were concerned about the practical effects nationalization might have on their everyday lives. They believed that if the government were to become the owner, it would be more difficult to obtain wage raises. They felt that while Americans were the owners, the miners were bound to win something from almost every strike, since government arbitration inevitably imposed a compromise solution. With the government as owner, however, a strike for wages could also be interpreted as an attack on the state and thus could be politically dangerous. Futhermore, the miners tended to prefer foreign bosses, who, they felt, were fairer than the Peruvian engineers in their work relations and technically better prepared to operate the mines. They feared that a government administration would be corrupt and inefficient.

Despite the recognized lack of enthusiastic mass support for nationalization, the leftist leaders decided to push forward with the new demand, intending to turn the strike into a political education for the miners. The leftists believed that the government's reforms and liberality in settling previous strikes was deceiving the miners with false ideas about whose interests the government ultimately represented. One of the decreed but still unimplemented reforms was the gradual institutionalization of worker participation in the ownership and administration of the mining companies through a new legal entity, the *Comunidad Minera* ("Mining Community"). The leftists saw co-ownership as a myth designed to obscure the conflict of class interests of the mine workers and the foreign mine owners. They believed that the government would reject the demand for nationalization and would thereby reveal to the miners its true political objective: a renegotiation of the terms of Peru's economic dependency on foreign capital.

In its defense against the strike the Cerro de Pasco Corporation ignored the call for nationalization and argued only against the economic demands. It claimed to be operating the mines at a loss due to the recent series of strikes and, consequently, to be financially unable to meet the unions' *pliego de reclamas* ("petition of demands"). The company called on the government to postpone any renegotiation of the annual labor contract for two more years, when, they predicted, they would be solvent again.

While arguments on both sides were being considered by the Ministry of Labor arbitrators in Lima, the conflict between the workers and the company erupted into violence in the Cobriza mine. A minor provocation by the company began a chain of events which ended with the hospitalization of one of the miners and the mine's superintendent. Two company officials were taken hostage. They would be held in the union hall, said the secretary general of the union, until the demands of the strike had been met.

The government's response was determined by its policy for economic development, which was to make mining the basis for the industrialization of the country. More than one-half of Peru's foreign exchange came from the taxation of mineral exports. In addition, Peru had at least five rich but unexploited copper deposits which could be brought into production. The government had decided on the path of foreign financing for the projects; to implement it, the government had to maintain a favorable investment climate.

In the view of the government, nationalization of the Cerro de Pasco Corporation was not, ultimately, out of the realm of consideration. However, repatriation of ownership had to proceed in a way that would not scare off foreign investors. The government was therefore reluctant to make any unilateral move that would lead to the nationalization of the mines, and it definitely did not want the issue forced on it by the miners. Indeed, the generals were so cautious that they waited until December 1971, when the Cerro de Pasco Corporation took the initiative and proposed selling its holdings to the government. Then it took two years of secret negotiations before the Peruvian military announced that it would nationalize the mines, agreeing to pay the Cerro Corporation $75 million to $87 million. By following this slow procedure and agreeing to pay substantial indemnification for the nationalized companies, the military government was successful in opening up foreign capital for the development of the mining industry.[2]

Aside from the question of nationalization, constant labor unrest was a serious obstacle to attracting foreign capital. The military believed that it would not be able to interest foreign investors in Peruvian mines if the frequent strikes by the miners went unchecked.

In view of the economic and political priorities necessitated by its development plans, the government decided to end the strike. It suspended all constitutional guarantees in Peru's central region and imposed martial law. On November 10 a special antiguerrilla force disguised as construction workers, entered the Cobriza camp. They broke into the union hall and freed the hostages. In the process they killed at least five miners, including the secretary general of the union. In the following days the government arrested and imprisoned leftists and union leaders in all the camps and over one hundred twenty miners in Cobriza. The strike wave was over.

Why the Miners Struck

The government and the company explained the numerous strikes primarily in political terms. President Juan Velasco Alvarado and officials of the Ministry of the Interior accused left-wing agitators of promoting the strikes to create political chaos which would topple the government. Company officials agreed that left-wing agitators were to blame, but tended to see themselves as the major target. These interpretations did not explain why so many of the miners had supported the strikes. In Cobriza one of the administrators claimed unconvincingly that the union leaders had coerced the miners into joining the strikes with kangaroo trials and threats of beatings or killing the *amarillos* (those who did not support the strike). Whatever the explanation, the government and the company agreed that the time had come to control the miners with a stronger hand.

To understand the strike wave it is necessary to probe a little deeper. To be sure, the leftists and union leaders encouraged and led the miners into making militant economic and political demands, but they did not create the basic motivation. What made the miners willing and even anxious to engage in the long and difficult strikes was fundamental. Mining production had become highly mechanized since the 1930s. This change gradually formed a new labor system which created new economic and social problems. The need to solve these problems motivated the miners.

The mining system introduced by the Cerro de Pasco Company at the beginning of the century required a large and unskilled labor force. Peasants were recruited to serve as miners on a part-time basis. These peasant-miners maintained ties to their communities and depended on their own agricultural production for a livelihood, even when they were receiving wages in the mines.

By 1935 the corporation had acquired and was operating all but one of the mines it would ever own in Peru. Increments in production time were obtained primarily through mechanization. The introduction of advanced machinery created a need for a skilled and full-time labor force. After World War II increasing land pressure and the commercialization of the peasant economy made full-time laborers available for the mines in large numbers. Separated from their communities and fields, full-time miners could not rely on agricultural production for any substantial portion of their livelihood. They depended entirely on full participation in the commercial market. As the percentage of full-time miners in the labor force increased, so did the need for higher wages and better living conditions in the mine camps.

Throughout the 1960s strikes became more frequent, but they were controlled and repressed by both the company and the government through such techniques as manipulating and buying off the union leaders or sending in troops. The most severe strike repression occurred in 1963 when troops occupied the smelter town, La Oroya, and union leaders were imprisoned.[3] The strike wave of 1969 to 1971 was primarily an expression of the growing economic and social aspects of the miners' needs, which had been largely ignored or repressed. The history of mine mechanization and the transformation of the labor system show that the basic cause of labor unrest was the relations of production within the mining industry itself.

The Mechanization of Mining

The fabulously rich gold and silver deposits of Peru were the Spaniards' major objective in the conquest and colonization of the Incas. Although the mining industry declined during most of the century following independence from Spain, the extraction of precious metals was continued by English and Peruvian miners. With the depletion of the richest silver deposits and the rise of large-scale industry in the United States and Europe, the focus of mining in Peru shifted from precious to industrial metals: copper, lead, zinc, and iron. Although silver and, to a lesser extent, gold were still mined, industrial metals became the mainstay of the industry.

With the diversification at the end of the nineteenth century of the types of metals produced, the technological problems of mining and metallurgy became more complicated. In general the richest and most easily treated ores were mined first. The remaining ores, being deeper in the ground, were harder to extract. They were also chemically more complex and more difficult to reduce. Having a lower percentage of metal content, a larger quantity of ore had to be processed to maintain the same level of production.

The traditional Peruvian mining methods were not adequate under these conditions. The extractive system was labor-intensive, based on hand tools, and the metallurgical processes were based on amalgamation, a process which had not been fundamentally improved in over three hundred years.

The industrialization of the mines in Peru began in 1902 with the formation of the North American company that became the Cerro de Pasco Corporation. The introduction of advanced technology (the combustion engine, electricity, and compressed air) raised the productivity of the mines. The hand drill and hammer were replaced by hardened drills, some with diamond tips, driven by compressed air. Less dangerous and more powerful explosives replaced dynamite. In underground mines the workers no longer carried ore from the face to the surface in leather sacks or wheelbarrows, but in machine-loaded gondolas on rails pulled by electric engines.

The shift from a labor-intensive to a capital-intensive mining system was gradual and cumulative, some of the most important steps in mechanization taking place only after 1950. The most mechanized mines are in Cerro de Pasco and Cobriza. The Cerro de Pasco mine has been worked by the open-pit method since 1956. In this system ore is taken out of a large open-air pit by huge earth-moving machines and gigantic trucks loaded by power shovels. In 1967 a relatively new extractive system called "trackless mining" was introduced in Cobriza, described by the company as the most highly mechanized underground mining technique in Latin America. The trackless mining system replaced underground rails and trains with diesel-powered loaders and trucks which drive into the mine. This system gives a speed and mobility in working different parts of the mine which are not possible with the cumbersome and slow train and rail system. Also found in Cobriza is the raise-boring machine, a sort of drill operated by only two men, which can cut connecting shafts between levels of a mine. This machine can do in three weeks what the older system of drilling and blasting required eight months to do.[. . .]

The gradual increase in mechanization created the need for a highly skilled labor force. At first unskilled laborers working under the direction of a technician or engineer were used. But mechanization reduced the need for unskilled workers and increased the need for mechanics, electricians, welders, and other workers who could understand the basic principles of the combustion engine, electric circuitry, and metallurgy. The mechanization of the different parts of the productive process took place over an extended period, but the need for skilled laborers became most acute after the construction of the complex metallurgical processing plants in La Oroya in 1922 and the installation of concentration mills in the mines in the late 1930s and early 1940s.[4][. . .]

The Transformation of the Labor System

At the beginning of the century it was difficult for mine companies to find workers. Most of the labor force was tied to agriculture, either in small villages *(comunidades)* or on large haciendas. Village agriculture depended upon both communal labor *(minga)* and reciprocal labor exchanged by individuals *(aine)*. A *comunero* tempted to go to the mines had to fight social pressure to fulfill his labor obligations in the village. Because of his absence he would also face the possibility of losing the commitment of others to help him after he returned. On the haciendas the laborers were usually granted access to agricultural land and pastures only in return for working for the *hacendado*, and if they went to the mines, they risked losing their lands. The *hacendados* tried to keep their laborers, using persuasion or, if necessary, force. In spite of these obstacles, the mining companies were able to obtain the laborers they needed with a system of debt labor, the *enganche* system.

During the first few decades of its operations the Cerro de Pasco Corporation, like other mining companies, recruited large numbers of laborers by commissioning labor recruiters, called *enganchedores*, to supply a certain number of workers. The *enganchedor* attracted workers in the countryside by offering them large sums of money, which had to be repaid by working in the mines. The debt owed the *enganchedor*, plus the fee which the company had promised him, was discounted from the miners' wages. After working long enough to pay off their debts, the miners could return to their villages.[5]

A major drawback to this system for the mining companies was the extent to which the supply of laborers depended on the agricultural cycle. Most of the workers were peasants, who would contract for labor only when they were free from agricultural labor, especially after the harvest. Hildebrando Castro Pozo described the mass migration to the mines at this time of year:

> Entire communities would enlist and march to the large centers of work, leaving only the old men and a few boys to prepare the fields for planting ... the *enganche* agents double, and many times triple the number of railroad passengers who travel at their employers' expense.[6]

Most of the *enganche* contracts were calculated to expire before the next harvest because most miners would abandon the mines to return to their fields even if their debts were not totally repaid. During the harvest, mining operations had to be slowed down and at times temporarily suspended.[7]

One of the reasons why temporary and unskilled labor was acceptable to the mining companies was that it was cheap. Since the miners got their major livelihood from their agricultural produce, their wages could be set at an extremely low level. Furthermore, a large percentage of the wages paid the miners was taken back at the company store.

The method of paying wages first used by the Cerro de Pasco Corporation virtually forced the miners to spend what they earned at the company store, known as the *mercantil*. The company paid the miners in cash only once a month. During the interim period miners were issued metal coins at the end of every day's work. To get credited for work, these coins had to be exchanged for a piece of cardboard the following morning (a way of ensuring daily attendance at work). The cardboard could, in turn, be exchanged immediately for a bond which was good for making purchases at the *mercantil,* or it could be exchanged at the end of the month for cash wages. If the miner needed to buy goods during the month, he had no choice but to make his purchase at the *mercantil,* since the bonds were not valid anywhere else. After repaying the original loan and the recruitment fee owed the *enganchedor,* the miners found they had new debts to the *mercantil,* which had to be worked off in the mines.[8]

The miners' debts were often inflated by two types of unequal exchange which forced them to stay in the mines longer. First, the advances given by the *enganchedor* were, in part or in whole, in the form of overpriced goods rather than money. Second, the articles for sale in the *mercantil* were priced higher than in other stores.

This state of indebtedness, in some cases, continued indefinitely and kept the workers in the mines for years. If a miner became incapacitated or died, his debt could be passed on to his children. If the miner attempted to escape without paying off his debt, he could be forced to work in the mines for even longer. On being returned to the mine, he was fined an amount equal to 70 percent of the original loan.[9]

To get themselves out of debt, many miners brought animals and food with them to the camps. The mine companies welcomed the miners' living off of their agricultural production because it enabled them to keep wages low.

As mechanization increased in the mines, the company sought more highly skilled and more permanent laborers. To attract competent workers the company offered 25-50 percent higher wages than the temporary *enganchados* received.[10] In the late 1930s increasing numbers of peasants began to come to the mines without the coercion of the *enganche* system as a result of the transformations taking place in the peasant economy as well as of the prospect of higher wages.

Mine Labor and the Commercialization of Agriculture

The susceptibility of peasants to the *enganche* system stemmed from the increasing inability of the peasant agricultural economy to sustain people on the land. One of the major strains on the peasant economy came from the division of lands into *minifundios.* This division was due to centuries of encroachments on communal lands by outsiders, to increasing population, and to the Spanish-derived system of partible inheritance.[11] By the end of the nineteenth century land pressure had begun to force peasants to expand their participation in the commercial market. The need for money to purchase consumption goods led the peasants to accept onerous loans from the *enganchedores*. The ties of peasants to the market were not, however, purely a result of land pressure.

The traditional closed, corporate peasant community had never been entirely shut off from the outside economy, nor had it ever been entirely self-sufficient.[12] One of its central institutions, the *fiesta* system, had originally been imposed by the Spaniards during the colonial period. In the *fiesta* system, sponsorship of a celebration of one of the village saints often overtaxed the resources of the *mayordomo* responsible. He was forced to seek help through other means, such as a loan from an *enganchedor*. These loans were, of course, paid back by working in the mines. The sponsors of *fiestas* became known as easy marks for the *enganchedores*.[13]

The large-scale recruitment of peasants by the *enganchedores* in the first few decades of the twentieth century set in motion a process by which the migration to the mines became self-perpetuating. Wage labor in the mines on the part of some village members increased the need for money in the villages, and forced additional community members to go to work in the mines for wages. By the early 1940s the *enganche* system became less important in recruiting laborers because of the commercialization of the peasant economy. Reciprocal labor in the fields *(aine)* gave way to wage labor; subsistence agriculture became increasingly supplanted by the planting of commercial crops; and artisan goods were replaced by manufactures.[14]

The departure of some members of a community for the mines meant that they could not fulfill their reciprocal labor obligations to other members. The people with whom they had been exchanging work had to find a new source of laborers, often being forced to hire *peones* from outside the community. Peasants who kept their fields in production while away at the mines usually entered into a contract of *al partir* with a relative or neighbor. In this arrangement the miner provided the land and seeds, while the person staying in the village recruited and paid laborers and supervised the work. The miner and the villager divided the produce equally. The money to pay the laborers came either from working in the mines or from selling part of the crop to local merchants prior to the harvest. Should the crop fail (a common occurrence in the *sierra* due to hail storms, drought, and plant diseases), the villager would end up in debt to the local merchant. Since these local merchants acted as agents for *enganchedores,* they would often force the peasants to work in the mines to repay the debts.[. . .]

As year-round mine labor kept most peasants from engaging in agricultural production or obtaining any significant sustenance from their villages, the company had to pay higher wages to full-time miners than they did to the part-time *enganchedos.* Even so, a miner could not maintain a family without some additional income. Rather than raise wages still further, the Cerro de Pasco Corporation purchased extensive pasture lands and devised a new relationship of support between the miners and the agricultural sector. The miners were now tied, not to the peasant villages, but to the large haciendas of the *sierra.*

The process by which the Cerro de Pasco Corporation became the owner of the largest latifundia in Peru provoked considerable conflict. The controversy began in 1922, when the large smelter in La Oroya began operations. The smoke from the smelter contained destructive amounts of arsenic, lead, and sulfer dioxide. These chemicals poisoned animals and destroyed crops as far away as forty kilometers. The owners of the affected haciendas and community lands complained and threatened to sue for damages. The company responded by buying up the hacienda lands and livestock. Since communal lands legally could not be sold, the company finally agreed to pay the communities indemnification after a long series of battles in the courts. Small indemnification payments are still being made to some communities.

Critics of the company charged that, on the basis of its own previous smelter operations in Peru and from the experience of other smelteries in the United States, the company must have known of the danger from the smoke well in advance. The company could have installed a Cotrell plant, which would have removed most of the noxious elements. The reason for the company's lack of precautions, they asserted, was that it had planned all along to buy up the haciendas; it used the smoke to discourage other buyers and to get a cheap price. It was further charged that by destroying the crops in the surrounding communities, the company had planned to create an ample labor supply.[15][. . .] In buying the haciendas instead of installing the Cotrell plant, the company was making a good long-term investment. It became owner of some of the best pasture lands in the central region, knowing that when it became advantageous to begin adequate smoke control, the haciendas could be put back into profitable operation.

By 1926 the company had bought close to thirty haciendas covering 270,000 hectares, or 1,057 square miles (nearly the size

of the state of Rhode Island). Apparently the harmful effects of
the smoke on livestock were quickly reduced. The gravity system
eliminated the lead and, in the course of time, the animals
developed some immunity to the arsenic. The company soon
began to expand its herds of sheep and cattle. In 1930, when the
economic depression drove the company to cut back on the
salaries of white-collar workers, it opened a modern meat shop to
supply them with low-cost meat and dairy products. In 1941 an
adequate Cotrell plant, which removed more than 90 percent of
the noxious elements from the smoke, was finally installed.
Helped by modern veterinary practice, herd control, and careful
cross-breeding which produced a new type of sheep far superior
to the native *chuscos,* the haciendas began to supply enough meat
and milk for all the miners.

Meanwhile, the pressure for higher wages was mounting. As
the effects of the depression wore off, the company resumed
operation, opening new mines and plants, diversifying its products, and, especially, enlarging lead and zinc production. Despite
the expansion, mechanization allowed the company to keep the
number of workers at about the same level as before the depression. The difference was that more miners were working on a
full-time basis and were becoming increasingly skilled on the job.
To attract and keep workers, the company now offered wages up
to twelve times higher than those paid in 1917. Another reason
for the higher wages was pressure from the workers' unions,
which were officially recognized in the 1940s.

The sale of meat from the haciendas contributed toward
cutting labor costs. The company was able to supply meat considerably below the market price. It is difficult to calculate the
savings in wages made by the company, but an indication of their
magnitude can be derived from company statistics. From 1960
through 1965 the company sold an average of 1.11 million kilos
of meat to its employees every year. Assuming the price averaged
about five soles below the market price, as one company administrator claimed, the company's employees saved 5.55 million soles
(equal to approximately $220,000) annually. Another way of
looking at this figure is as an almost 3 percent reduction in labor
costs. Even though the company was selling its meat below the
market price, the haciendas still earned an average profit of 6.20
million soles (approximately $250,000) during the same period.[16]

The profits made on the hacienda operations resulted from
efficient production methods, the export of wool, and extremely
low wages as compared with those paid the miners. In 1966, for
example, when the average basic wage for the miners was seventy

soles, the basic wage paid to the shepherds was only forty-one soles. One reason why the hacienda workers were able to endure such low wages was that, like the miners recruited in the *enganche* system, they supported themselves with agricultural production on garden plots permitted them by the company.[17]

Under the *enganche* system the miners had been dependent on agricultural production for their livelihood, and the company had profited from this dependency by being able to keep wages low. After 1940 miners stayed on the job full time more than they had in the past, and they gradually broke their ties with the peasant economy. Although the company had been forced to raise wages somewhat, it managed to maintain the workers' dependency on agriculture by transferring it, at no cost to itself, to the commercialized sector. This profitable relationship between the mines and the haciendas lasted until 1969, when the government nationalized the haciendas and converted them into a cooperative, the Sociedad Agricola de Interés Social "Tupac Amaru." In order to satisfy the demands of the middle class in Lima during a meat shortage and to raise the profits of the SAIS "Tupac Amaru" so that it could pay for the nationalized lands, the meat was sold on the open market at double the previous price.

A Free Labor Market

In the two and a half decades after World War II the difficulty of recruiting labor disappeared. The stream of migrants from rural areas grew tremendously. More laborers sought employment in the mines than the Cerro de Pasco Corporation could hire. Those who could not find work in the *sierra* migrated to urban areas and filled the *barriadas* of Lima and other cities. A competitive free labor market was created. Laborers who could no longer depend upon agriculture were forced to work for wages.

The company took advantage of the surplus of laborers to create a skilled labor force. Since it could employ only some of the job applicants, it began to set selective criteria, which were not only technical but also cultural, medical, and political.

The most important requirement was the ability not only to speak Spanish but also to be able to read and write to some extent. At times this requirement was only imperfectly fulfilled, but eventually almost all the miners were able to read company work bulletins, safety regulations, romance comic books, and newspapers.

Medical criteria were the strictest, primarily for economic

reasons. Labor laws and the *convenio colectivo* (the labor contract signed with the unions) required the company to provide the workers extensive free medical care. Each worker had to pass a medical examination before being hired. Anyone who needed dental work, who showed a serious lung ailment in an X-ray (silicosis from previous work in the mines and tuberculosis are common in the *sierra)*, or who had a physical handicap was not hired. Most of the rejected applicants were turned down for medical reasons.

Political requirements were numerous; they included (1) clearance by the PIP (equivalent to the FBI) to show lack of a criminal record; (2) presentation of identity cards given by the state for tax and social security purposes; (3) proof of military service to show that the applicant was over twenty years old and would not be conscripted from the job; (4) a check against the company "black list," which included a large number of known political agitators, militant unionists, thieves, and people the company considered to be social or disciplinary problems.[18]

A free labor market enabled the company to select workers with basic skills, but not necessarily with the specialized skills which the company needed. Many of the jobs in the mines required knowledge or experience in mechanics, carpentry, electricity, and so on beyond what most applicants had. The company met this problem in two ways: first, it developed a training program to prepare workers for specific jobs; second, it began to hire *contratistas,* or outside companies, with already skilled workers.[. . .]

The hiring of *contratistas* began for reasons of economy. For short-term jobs which required skilled laborers or equipment that would be used only briefly, it was cheaper to hire a specialist rather than to buy special machinery and train new laborers. In Cobriza the Utah Construction Company (a North American firm employing Peruvians) was hired to erect the concentration plant, workshops, and housing. One of the advantages in contracting another company to do this construction lay in the reduction of labor costs. Although the construction workers and miners received equal wages, Utah was able to fire its workers whenever it was convenient. Peruvian labor law prohibits permanent employers like mining companies from firing workers without just cause, the conditions for which are strictly defined in the law. If the Cerro de Pasco Corporation had used its own construction workers, it would have been forced to keep the workers on the payroll after the project was finished. Because of the short-term nature of their work, companies like Utah were exempt from this law.

In some cases it was cheaper to hire *contratistas* because they paid their laborers much less than the mine company paid. In Cobriza, for example, two *contratistas* from a nearby village were hired for ground maintenance. At the time (1971) the lowest wage paid by the Cerro de Pasco Corporation was 150 soles, while the men under the *contratistas* got only 70 soles. Other savings for the company resulted from not having to provide housing, tools, hospital care, or schooling, and not having to contend with the union when it decided to lay off some of the workers. One of the reasons the Cerro de Pasco Corporation paid wages so much higher than other companies was because of the unions.

Successful unionization seems to have been related to the emergence of a full-time labor force. Attempts to unionize the mines began as early as 1918, but they had little effect until 1929, when members of the Communist party led a strike in Morococha. On the basis of this success, unions sprang up in other mines, and the Communist unionists called for the formation of a national federation of miners. The organization was not strong enough to survive government repression the following year, when the union leaders were arrested, and many workers were massacred by government troops in Malpaso, the site of the company's first hydroelectric plant.

The unions were not strong enough to assert themselves until after World War II. By this time the percentage of full-time workers in the mines had grown, and the need for unionization was stronger than in the past, when there had been a high rate of turnover due to the workers' reliance on agricultural production. In 1945 the first miners' unions won recognition from both the government and the company, and other unions were formed in the following years. As the miners found themselves increasingly cut off from agriculture, the question of wage levels and living and working conditions in the mines became crucial. These issues were debated annually in the negotiations for a collective labor contract between the unions and the company.[19]

After the unions were legally recognized, they represented a labor force which had been markedly transformed in the half century since the Cerro de Pasco first began. Recruitment by *enganche* and debt labor had been replaced by a competitive labor market. Mine laborers were no longer peasants who migrated to and from the mines to make up for what they could not produce in their fields for themselves. They were full-time miners, whose livelihood depended on wages and commercial consumption.

The Problems of Wage Labor

Full-time work in the mines and severance of ties with peasant agriculture transformed the domestic economy of the miner and his family. The nuclear family tended to replace the extended family as an economic unit as it became increasingly dependent on the miner's wages for a livelihood. In 1970 this adjustment was still an ongoing process.

The company's interest in promoting this process was both economic and political. It wanted a sedentary labor force which would build up skills and a tradition in mining. For many years the company had played what it considered an overly paternal role, providing the miners with services ranging from medicine and housing to soccer uniforms and movies. Not only had it borne the expense of these services but, company officials felt, it also had received criticism rather than praise for its contributions. The company believed that if the workers would settle permanently in the mines and assume responsibility for personal services, the company would be saved both expense and criticism.

The company began by selling houses to the workers. When the project was inaugurated, only 40 percent of the miners in the Cerro de Pasco mine lived in company housing; the rest lived in rented quarters in the old city. To make room for expanding its open-pit operations, the company bought up and leveled the houses in the old city. Displaced miners and townspeople were relocated in houses built by the company in a new city. They could not rent these houses, but were forced to buy them on a rent-purchase basis. After this part of the project got under way, the company presented plans to the government to build a similar urban complex between the La Oroya smelter and the Morococha mine. The company's intention was to shift to the workers the responsibility for maintaining and improving housing, thereby lowering its costs and evading union demands for expensive improvements.

Regardless of who owned the houses, the company wanted the workers to adjust to mining-camp life. It recognized some of the practical and cultural problems in such a transformation from a rural to a basically urban way of life, and it hired social workers to see that the transition was made as smooth as possible. The social workers performed three major functions. First, they helped the miners and their families solve some very real problems which resulted from their having to learn a new life-style (with films and group discussions on hygiene, infectious diseases, the uses of modern bathrooms, etc.). Second, they tried to inculcate their own middle-class values in the workers. They demanded that the miners' homes always be "presentable." At the same time they denigrated rural living habits, criticizing visits by members of miners' extended families as a "moral problem." Finally, they served as watchdogs for the company's interests. They policed the company-owned houses to make sure they were properly maintained and used only by the people designated by the company.[20]

The social workers evaluated the miners' homes monthly and gave courses to help the families "improve" their place in a ranking system which they established. Because the men were away at work, the main burden of a family's adaptation to camp life was placed on the women, for whom the most important problem was to make ends meet on a miner's wages. The courses were aimed at practical problems. Women had to cope with a new variety of industrially produced foods (noodles, instant coffee, jello, bleached flour, canned fruit, etc.), and they had to learn not only how to prepare them (on a kerosene stove) but also what combinations provided a nutritious diet. Clothing worn in the mine camps was mostly store-bought. In the sewing courses the social workers taught the women how to make similar clothes by hand and thereby save money. The social workers also made house visits to teach women how to furnish and keep their homes. Their suggestions ranged from the "proper" way to arrange calendar pictures on the wall to admonitions against the "unsanitary" storing of vegetables in the wet, cool shower stalls, a practice begun in Cobriza because refrigerators were too expensive to buy.

The counseling of the social workers was for the most part related to the problem of how to spend money judiciously. One of the major familial conflicts was over the division and allocation of a miner's wages—the obligations of a father in supporting his children, the rights of a woman to share her husband's earnings or to determine how they should be spent, and so on.[. . .]

In the end the social-work program backfired against the company. Its purpose was aptly described by one of the North American administrators in Cerro de Pasco:

> The point is to keep the women happy. Otherwise on some rainy day they'll corner their husbands and take their complaints out on them. Then the husbands will go get drunk and when they get together like that they go on strike and blame everything on the company.

But rather than make the women happy, the social-work program humiliated them by making them feel as though their rural way of life was inferior. Then it frustrated them by teaching them to want and need more than they could afford to buy. Anger was directed at the company because it set wages at levels which would not support the standard of living it taught the women to aspire to. Added to this indignity and frustration was the knowledge that the company was pressing them to change their lives out of its own self-interest. It was the increasing pressure on the women and their resulting frustration and anger that motivated the formation of the *Comités de Damas* (organizations which paralleled the men's unions). It is no surprise that in many strikes the women were more militant and aggressive than the men.

In the process of establishing a permanent supply of skilled laborers with no support from peasant agriculture and entirely dependent on mining wages, the company forced miners to depend entirely on the market for consumption goods. The more the miners conformed to the company's ideal of an adjusted family life, the more their needs for market consumption expanded. At the same time the company's attempt to make workers self-reliant by cutting back on "paternalistic" services added to the expenses which had to be covered by a miner's wages. The government exacerbated the problem by nationalizing the company's haciendas, thereby forcing the miners to spend almost twice as much money on meat in the open market.

Each time the workers went out on strike between 1969 and 1971 they complained that it was more difficult to live on their wages than it had been in the past. The company tried to discredit this claim by pointing out that wages had risen more than the cost of living over the previous fifteen years. Although the company's contention may have been correct, its argument failed to take into account the fact that the workers had become increasingly dependent on market consumption and needed to buy more from the market than ever before. Ironically, the company's attempt to create a stable, economically independent, and well-adjusted labor force had only increased the difficulties and frustrations of living on wages and the market, and had done more to provoke strikes and political criticism than to create labor peace.

Proletarianization and Class Conflict

The transformation of the mine labor force from part-time peasant-miners into a body of skilled, full-time wage laborers suggests that the present-day miners should be considered a proletariat in the Marxist sense. The miners are proletarian in that they sell their labor power for wages in order to gain a livelihood, but the term cannot be applied yet to all the miners without some qualification. The proletarian socioeconomic status of many miners is modified by their access to land, technical skills, and money—each of which can be used to get out of the mines, and return to agriculture or engage in some other petty-bourgeois economic activity.

Almost all the laborers who come to the mines still own or have access to land. Most have only small plots of land, which provide a form of temporary economic security in case of illness, accident, or loss of job. A smaller number of miners, however, have more substantial holdings, which can become the basis for an agricultural life to return to after leaving the mines. On their return they use whatever savings and separation pay they may have as capital investment in new land, animals, tools, or whatever else is necessary to begin commercial farming.

Some miners who do not return to agriculture take up a trade. On the basis of skills learned in the mines and with their cash savings, they open their own carpentry, mechanic, or welding shops in urban areas. Others enter commerce. They open small stores in cities, towns, or their own villages, or they buy a truck and hire themselves out as *transportistas*. Often they are able to use their contacts in the mines and win a contract to haul ore and supplies for the company. Some miners become traveling merchants and go from mine camp to mine camp selling manufactured goods.[21]

Workers taking employment in the mines often arrive with the intention of engaging in wage labor only temporarily, as a stepping stone to some other economic activity. Many of these workers leave the mines after a short period of time, perhaps only a few years. As a result, the average rate of labor turnover for the Cerro de Pasco Corporation has been high—20 percent in 1969.[22] This figure suggests that miners can be categorized loosely into two groups. For the first group mine labor is a relatively short-term means to an end, which is some form of self-employment. Because their livelihood is only temporarily based on wage labor, they can be said to be only partially or only temporarily proletarianized. For the second and larger group of miners, however, wage labor is a more permanent way of life. They stay in the mines for long periods of time, an average of ten years or more. They become the most skilled workers and occupy the highest-paid positions. Their livelihood depends upon their wages, and for most of them leaving the mines or changing their socioeconomic status remains only a possibility for the distant future. This group can more justly be called proletarian.

The proportion of miners who are permanent, or proletarianized, has been growing since the 1930s—a result, as we have seen, of mechanization in the mines and commercialization of the peasant economy. Corporation statistics indicate that this trend has continued into recent years. The annual rate of labor turnover declined from 30 percent in 1958 to 20 percent in 1969, showing greater stability in the labor force.[23] The present ratio of permanent miners to short-term miners has probably increased because of the special laws governing peasant communities decreed in February 1970. Articles 23 and 29 of this law require that all *comuneros* establish permanent residence in their communities and that they earn their living primarily from agricultural labor. They are not permitted to have other major sources of income, such as mine labor. If a community's land is not sufficient to support all of its members, the government is obliged by Article 126 of the Agrarian Reform Law to give the *comuneros* more land so that they will no longer need to work in the mines. Having a permanent residence outside the community is grounds for losing the rights of a *comunero,* including access to land.[24] As these laws are applied, miners will have to choose between returning to their villages (as many did when the law was announced) or losing their lands. Since there is not enough agricultural land available in the *sierra* to provide each rural family with landholdings of the size stipulated as necessary according to the Agrarian Reform Law, there is bound to be an increase in the number of landless workers competing for permanent employment in the mines.[25]

An increase in the number of permanent, proletarianized laborers will intensify the miners' demands for better living and working conditions in the camps. Laborers who in the past expected to be in the mines for only a few years accepted rundown, single-room habitations to live in because they believed the situation to be only temporary. Their intention was to escape these conditions as quickly as possible rather than to improve them. As a larger number of permanent miners settle in the mines, they will demand adequate housing. Further, as they adapt to the life of the camps (a process described earlier), their needs for consumption goods will grow, and this will inevitably be expressed in demands for higher wages.

Full-time miners are likely to be more willing to engage in strikes to obtain the living conditions and wages they need. Miners with plans to leave the mines within a few years calculate the possible benefits of strikes differently from those who foresee a long future as miners. Temporary miners can gain very little or nothing from a long strike, which may win only a moderate wage increase. For a worker who knows he will remain a miner for many years the calculation includes future, as well as immediate, gains. The losses incurred during a strike can be more than repaid, if not in the next year, then over the years which follow.

After Nationalization

Having nationalized the Cerro de Pasco Corporation and entered into the mining industry as an entrepreneur, the Peruvian government has taken on the responsibility of responding to the growing needs and demands of the miners. Much as nationalization may aid the Peruvian economy in general by increasing the inflow of dollars from minerals sold abroad, these benefits will be felt only indirectly, if at all, by the miners. Nationalization replaces foreign ownership with state ownership without changing the economic and social conditions in the mines. For the miners the same problems, demands, and conflicts continue. It is the government's belief that class conflict between the laborers and the owners can be avoided, but the programs which it has proposed are not likely to accomplish this end.

The *Comunidad Minera* and the *Comunidad de Compensación Minera* were established by the government with the primary purpose of eliminating class conflict between the miners and the owners by giving the miners a vested interest in the profitable operation of the mining companies. The *Comunidad Minera* was designed to create co-ownership by awarding the miners 6 percent of the annual net income *(renta neta),* which must be reinvested in the company until it reaches a value equal to 50 percent of the company's capital shares *(capital social).*[26] Co-ownership was an unlikely prospect even when the Cerro de Pasco Corporation owned the mines. In 1969 the net profits of the corporation were approximately $9.4 million, and the capital shares were valued at approximately $40 million.[27] Assuming that the corporation would have maintained the same high rate of profitability in the future, it would have taken the miners at least thirty-five years to acquire one-half of the capital shares. Following nationalization even this hope of co-ownership becomes more remote. According to the General Mining Law, Article 286, workers in the mines belonging to the public sector or involving partial state ownership will be issued bonds from either the mining companies or from the Corporation Financiera de Desarrollo (COFIDE) rather than being permitted to obtain shares of the company.

In addition to projecting co-ownership, the mining law states that the workers are to receive 4 percent of the annual net income as cash benefits. These monetary payments will not, however, substantially alter the miners' present income. Dividing 4 percent of the 1969 profits among 15,000 of the corporation's workers yields an average of less than a week's wages for each miner. This amount is about the same as that which miners received under the old profit-sharing plan which the new law abolished. Although the *Comunidad Minera* and the *Comunidad de Compensación Minera* may be transformed in the future to adapt to the special situation of the nationalized mines, as the present law now stands the miners are not likely to have any more interest in the profitable operation of the mining companies than they had in the past.

The government has long recognized the need for more and better houses for the miners, and during the nationalization negotiations it sharply criticized the Cerro de Pasco Corporation for failing to build them. Following nationalization, the government has indicated that it will undertake large-scale construction of new homes. Even if the government does provide the long overdue and badly needed housing, this improvement in the miners' standard of living will not decrease their need for wage increases. We have already seen that adaptation to a modern way of life in the mine camps tends to create demands for greater commercial consumption. The problem is that to live in new and larger homes the miners will have to spend more money. Rather than disappearing, the conflict between miners and the state as owner could even increase. Not only are the laborers' demands likely to grow, but also the government is going to feel great pressure to resist any increase in labor costs.

The mining industry is a keystone in the government's program for industrialization and economic development. General Jorge Fernández Maldonado, minister of energy and mines, has gone so far as to claim that the entire success of the Peruvian revolution depends upon the performance of his sector of the economy (which includes petroleum).[28] The large-scale expansion of the mining industry is to be financed by international loans totaling hundreds of millions of dollars. The government and private companies contract the loans, and they assume the responsibility for their repayment, but ultimately it is the miners who will have to pay off the interest and the principal. The government has appealed to the miners' patriotism, calling on them to tighten their belts and accept self-discipline at a time when their consumption needs are growing. So far, however, the government has obtained from the miners neither substantial support for its nationalist philosophy nor cooperation in its programs. Labor discontent continues in the mines of the ex-Cerro de Pasco Corporation, now called Centromín. If the military generals cannot persuade the miners to accept voluntarily the discipline and sacrifices which they think are necessary, their past record indicates that they will not hesitate to impose their will with armed force.

Notes

1. Most of the material for this article was gathered in Peru from July 1970 to December 1971. The research was financed by the Doherty Charitable Foundation at Princeton University and the Department of Anthropology of Columbia University.
2. *Latin America Economic Report (Andean Times)*, March 1, 1974, pp. 33–34.
3. Genaro Ledesma Izquieta, *Complot* (Lima, 1964).
4. *Andean Air Mail and Peruvian Times* (Lima), December 11, 1970, pp. 22–23.
5. Alberto Noriega, "El enganche en la minería del Perú," *Boletin de minas, industrias, y construcciones*, ser. 2, vol. 3, nos. 4–6 (Lima, 1911), pp. 43–46; and Hildebrando Castro Pozo, *Nuestra comunidad indigena* (Lima: Editorial "El Lucera"), pp. 117–24.
6. Castro Pozo, *Nuestra comunidad*, pp. 101–2. (My translation.)
7. Ibid., pp. 97–98.
8. Dora Mayer de Zulem, *The Conduct of the Cerro de Pasco Mining Company* (Lima, 1913), pp. 8–11; and Moisés Poblete Truncoso, *Condiciones de vida y de trabajo de la población indígena del Perú* (Geneva, 1938), pp. 145–46.
9. Julian Laite, "Industrialization and Land Tenure in the Peruvian Andes," mimeographed (Manchester, Eng.: Department of Sociology, University of Manchester, 1971); Noriega, "El enganche," pp. 51–53; and de Zulem, *Cerro de Pasco Mining Company*, p. 11.
10. Castro Pozo, *Nuestra comunidad*, p. 120n.
11. Thomas R. Ford, *Man and Land in Peru* (Gainesville, Fla.: University of Florida Press, 1955), pp. 42–52, 66–67, 97.
12. Eric R. Wolf, "Types of Latin American Peasantry: A Preliminary Discussion," *American Anthropologist* 57 (1955): 465–71.
13. Marvin Harris, *Patterns of Race in the Americas* (New York: W. W. Norton & Co., 1964), pp. 25–36.
14. The commercial transfer of land titles, as described by Laite, "Industrialization and Land Tenure," was also increased by emigration to the mines.
15. CIDA, *Perú—Tenencia de la tierra y desarrollo socio-ecónomico del sector*

agrícola (Washington, D.C., 1966), cited in Sven Lindquist, *The Shadow: Latin America Faces the Seventies* (London, 1972), pp. 220–22.

16. These figures are based on Cerro de Pasco Corporation, *Annual Report* (Lima, 1969).

17. A similar relationship between a hacienda and a mining company was established by the Northern Peru Mining Corporation, a wholly owned subsidiary of the American Smelting and Refining Company (ASARCO), based in New York. How the mining company used the hacienda to provide supplies and labor for the mines is described by Solomon Miller, "Hacienda to Plantation in Northern Peru: The Process of Proletarianization of a Tenant Farmer Society," in *Contemporary Change in Traditional Society,* vol. 3, ed. Julian Steward (Urbana, Ill.: University of Illinois Press, 1967), pp. 135–225.

18. These selective criteria created a fairly homogeneous labor force, which was not present in less mechanized mines. In Huancavelica, Henri Favre found that skilled and unskilled work was performed by distinct sociocultural groups: *cholos,* who tend to be fully integrated into the commercial market, and *indígenas,* who tend to maintain ties with more traditional peasant communities. See Henri Favre, "Algunos problemas referentes a la industria minera de Huancavelica," *Cuadernos de antropología* 3, no. 8 (1965): 20.

19. For a more complete history of the miners' unions, see Ricardo Martínez de la Torre, *Apuntes para una interpretación marxista de la historia social del Perú,* vol. 4 (Lima, 1949), pp. 5–137; and Denis Sulmont and Roelfin Haak, "El movimiento obrero minero peruano," mimeographed (Lima: Taller Urbano Industrial, Universidad Católica, 1971).

20. Cerro de Pasco Corp., *Annual Report* (1969).

21. Richard N. Adams observed in Muquiyauyo that temporary mine labor provided some of the owners of small plots of land with enough supplemental income to continue traditional subsistence agriculture. Mine labor led others into nonagricultural trades. See Richard N. Adams, *A Community in the Andes: Problems and Progress in Muquiyauyo* (Seattle: University of Washington Press, 1959), pp. 93–98.

22. Cerro de Pasco Corp., *Annual Report* (1969).

23. Ibid.

24. Peru, *Estatuto de comunidades campesinos,* Decreto Supremo no. 37-70-A (1970); and *Texto único de la ley de reforma agraria,* Decreto Supremo no. 265-70-AG (1970).

25. *Andean Air Mail and Peruvian Times* (Lima), August 24, 1973, pp. 3–4.

26. Peru, *Ley general de minería,* Decreto Ley no. 18880 (1970).

27. Peru, Ministerio de Energia y Minas, *Declaración anual de la Cerro de Pasco Corporation* (1969).

28. *Latin America* (London), April 20, 1973, p. 125.

The Rural Proletariat and the
Problem of the Rural Proletarian Consciousness

Sidney W. Mintz

Introduction

This paper consists of five parts.[1][. . .]

The first part aims at defining and describing the rural proletariat—a typological category that has received relatively little attention in the literature of the social sciences, in spite of its importance—particularly in colonial and neocolonial societies. Field data from sugarcane-producing communities in Puerto Rico are provided to exemplify rural proletarians as a group.

The second part deals with so-called peasant communities, in order to call attention to the common presence of landless wage-earning individuals within them. Such individuals not only deviate from the stereotype of peasant folk, but may contribute to the viability of the peasant adaptation, even though they themselves are not "average peasants." The "concealment" of such apparently atypical individuals within peasant communities is discussed.

The third part of the paper deals with the process of proletarianization: how a rural proletariat forms; how the process may be analyzed into different aspects; and the special significance of a rural proletariat that emerges in the form of homogeneous wage-earning communities, rather than irregularly, and within peasant communities.

The fourth part deals with class consciousness, particularly rural proletarian class consciousness; while the fifth and concluding part aims at summarizing the paper's principal points.[. . .]

The Rural Proletariat

The terms "proletariat" and "proletarian" had been developed to describe populations very different from those one finds associated with large-scale agricultural estates in the plantation areas of the New World, and elsewhere in the world outside

Extracted from *Journal of Peasant Studies* 1, no. 3 (1974): 291-325, with permission of the publishers and the author.

Europe. It may even be supposed by some that the term "rural proletariat" is inherently contradictory. But Marx and those who read him carefully were fully aware of the presence of groups of agricultural wage laborers, and recognized that such populations were neither peasantries on the one hand, nor urban folk on the other. Thus, for instance, Lenin's discussion of "the toiling peasantry" accounts not only for the "genuine" (that is, urban or industrial) proletariat, but also specifies distinctions among rural classes, whom he describes as "the small peasantry," the "semi-proletarian," or "parcelized" peasant, and *"the agricultural proletariat* [emphasis added], wage workers (by the year, season, or day) who obtain their livelihood by working for wages in capitalist agricultural enterprises."[2][. . .] In 1951, when I attempted to describe "the rural proletariat" in Puerto Rico, it was plain that neither the terminology nor the criteria of the type were in any significant sense original. But Caribbean plantations had not much been studied by sociologists or anthropologists before 1948.[. . .] Hence, the writer attempted to develop a typological formulation for rural proletariats, and the following purposes of such an undertaking seemed promising: (1) to separate the concept of the modern wage worker from an exclusively urban context; (2) to raise questions about what "urban" means, once the characteristics of a rural proletariat could be enumerated; (3) to relate the emergence of a rural proletariat to previous ways of exploiting labor in use within the area, so that a region such as the Caribbean might be contrasted in these terms with non-colonial situations, and with those nearer to the core of European capitalism; and (4) to raise the question of rural proletarian consciousness, in the light of the colonial (plantation, mine, oil well, etc.) experience.

The minimal characteristics of a rural proletariat, as set forth in an early paper, were tied to the character of plantation communities, the rural proletarian groupings with which the writer was personally familiar:

> In these communities the vast majority of people is landless, propertyless (in the sense of *productive* property), wage-earning, store-buying (the stores [in this case] being a chain owned by the corporation with few competitors), corporately employed, and standing in like relationship to the main source of employment. These rural proletarian communities might also be considered class isolates, in the sense that economic alternatives to wage labor in the sugar-cane industry, other than via migration to the United States mainland, are very scarce. The working people not only stand in like relationship to the productive apparatus but are also

interacting in reciprocal social relationships with each other and
subordinate social relationships to members of higher classes (such
as managers).[3]

Among other things, it was intended to set this type in an evolutionary context, the type itself corresponding to a particular stage
in the development of overseas agricultural capitalism, emerging
out of a less developed and more "traditional" past. In the
Caribbean region, this earlier stage, too, presumably had its
predecessor, as represented commonly by a slave labor force.

A rural proletariat is endowed with some of its social characteristics by virtue of the demands made upon it by the plantation
system. This part of the argument is straightforward, even simplistic. Plantation enterprises are, though rural, in some aspects
industrial in character. They impose certain features of life-style
upon their laboring populations without regard to the antecedent
cultures of the working people; rural proletarians thus come to
behave sociologically in ways associated with such economic
characteristics as wage labor, dependence on imported goods,
lack of productive property (especially land), and so on. Of
course, these features do not necessarily communicate their
effects directly, and the antecedent behavioral and attitudinal
patterns of rural proletarians surely play a part in the eventual
shape of their life as wage earners. But the nature of productive
relations is critical in determining the character of rural proletarians as a class; and the behavior that accompanies their class
position is in some measure informed by that position.[. . .]

The argument, as developed so far, conceives of the rural
proletariat as a class because of its economic position and character;
as we shall see, in many rural communities all or nearly all of the
inhabitants stand in very similar relationships to the means of
production, and, in this regard at least, communities seem very
homogeneous. But even in cases where a rural proletarian community may appear to consist entirely of landless, wage-earning,
store-buying, and corporately employed agricultural workers,
many of its members may come from families that are or were
landholders or sharecroppers or both, while others may combine
their wage-earning activities with other adaptations of a "peasant-
like" kind. Moreover, rural proletarian communities often coexist
with other communities composed largely or wholly of peasants.
In the Caribbean region, these adaptations appear to be mutually
reinforcing in some ways, and conflictive in others, such that the
characteristics of either "sector"—that is, rural proletarian *versus*
peasant—can only be wholly understood if the other is taken into
account. Thus, the present writer has suggested that we view

rural proletarians and peasants as usually forming conjunctive (but also competing) sectors of the same society, at least for the region under discussion. The relationship of these sectors to each other may be very complex, sometimes because a substantial proportion of the population oscillates between these adaptations, sometimes because tenancy arrangements of various kinds predominate over these types, sometimes because yet other types are to be found in one system.[4]

But where land ownership is vested in one family or corporation, where production is intended primarily for a national or international market, where wages and salaries are standardized, worker-owner relationships impersonal, and productive activity outside the enterprise by those who work its lands minimal, the contrast of the rural proletarian community with other sorts of rural settlements is very sharp; and here one thinks of the plantation system and its satellite villages as prototypical. In these cases, too, there may be some cloaking of economic linkages by various means; but the counterpositions of owner and worker, capitalist and rural proletarian, landed and landless is unmistakable.

The writer wishes to glance briefly here at the small communities in which he worked in 1948-1949. The reason for doing so is to be able to suggest that the conceptualization of a rural proletariat, at least with regard to plantation communities, can arise out of the study of specific populations and their life-ways. The communities the writer knows best—and they are no longer what they were twenty-five years ago—here serve only as illustrations. In this rather arid, southeastern coastal region of Puerto Rico, composed mainly of alluvial fans and floodplains extending northward from the sea, people were grouped physically in three kinds of hamlet or village, outside the municipal seats and the sugar factories. The first and most visible kind of village consisted of shacks strung along the main roads, sometimes two or three deep, but just as commonly one row of shacks only, on each shoulder of the road. These shacks were interspersed at rare intervals with small stores—groceries and bars, mostly— but usually each store was also partly a residence. One could not guess beforehand what kind of domestic group occupied one such shack or house; we might expect it to consist of a nuclear family, with its own or adopted children, and possibly a grandparent. (In Puerto Rico, in fact, one or another spouse—usually the father—may be absent; the presence of a grandparent is rare; the children may in part be adopted, and some may be half-siblings on either the father's or the mother's side.) These line-villages or *Strassendörfer* were one of the three types of "community" one could make out in the plantation regions of Puerto Rico at the time.

A second such type, perhaps the most interesting since all or nearly all such groupings are gone in Puerto Rico, consisted of the more orderly and uniform shacks built to plantation specifications on plantation land, usually adjoining the central place *(plaza)* of the "farm," or *colonia.* Such *colonias* were sometimes very large— commonly, a few thousand acres—being nothing more nor less, in fact, than ancient haciendas that had lost all of their former character except as landholdings when assimilated into the enormous corporate North American "land-and-factory combines."[5] These *colonias* were "company-towns" much like those around the mills, but they lacked both the concentrations of skilled personnel (factory workers, managerial staff, etc.) and facilities (theaters, churches, school, pharmacy, and the like) typical of the mill complexes. The new corporate arrangements, launched mostly soon after the U.S. invasion and seizure of Puerto Rico, involved the purchase (or sometimes the rental) of such estates intact, commonly allowing everything—old-fashioned sugar mill, subsistence plots, distillery, etc.—to fall into disuse except the cane land itself. The work force, if resident, would be provided by some arrangement with housing of a kind; if nonresident, it would be settled in such housing. But all else that might have given to the hacienda its prior estate-like or manor-like qualities would disappear. It was within these internal settlements that corporate power was wielded with the greatest authority and, often enough, ruthlessness.[6]

The residential composition of these shacks on privately owned land would be determined (or limited, at least nominally) by the managing authority. Such populations were obviously subject to greater controls than were those of the other aggregates being discussed here (which were on land owned by the resident or house-owner, or on government land), and changes in household membership—the addition of an outsider, of persons who were not employees of the corporate landowner, etc.—could be subject to arbitrary decision by higher authority.

Finally, there were the tiny communities that grew, almost as if by spontaneous generation, along the government-owned littoral. Often their inhabitants were migrants from the highlands who had come seeking casual wage labor, and then—for one reason or another—had decided to stay. Here, as in the line-villages (but not in the company towns), one might find tiny bars, shops, and the like. Here, too, the domestic arrangements might be expected to be somewhat more variable, more open to change than in the case of the shacks on estate land.

In all of these three communities, the majority of adult males, and many females, were cane workers. Such work was seasonal for most people, beginning around Christmas and continuing until midsummer; it included planting, cultivating, irrigating, cutting, and loading the sugarcane. Some specialists in irrigation, rail crews, machinists, and a few others had year-round work. Moreover, the percentages of cane workers varied from one community to the next. Everyone who lived on company land—the so-called *agregados*—was a cane worker; but some of those self-dubbed *independizados* who lived along the beach were fishermen, or had part-time activities of other kinds, while some of the *independizados* along the road were storekeepers, taxi-drivers, or did other things for a living. All three communities appeared to have been fairly stable in population; though by the late 1940s, people were beginning to emigrate to the mainland United States in large numbers.

The *agregados* on company land and the *independizados* along the highway were privately a bit contemptuous of the beach-dwellers, many of whom were fairly recent migrants from the highlands. The beach-dwellers were less sophisticated, were happy to do cane-cutting (which lowlanders disdain and avoid, when possible), tried to grow tiny plots of root foods, put up little fences around their shacks, and—the epitome of their backwardness—married their own cousins. Even in racial (phenotypic) terms, there were some differences among these communities: there were relatively fewer dark-complexioned persons in the beach population, relatively more along the road and at the *colonia*. And while standpipes, electricity, and stores were readily available along the road and on the plantation, such services were absent or very limited at the beach. Hence, it would be somewhat inaccurate to describe these communities as completely alike, even though all three seemed to the writer to be correctly described as "rural proletarian" settlements at the time.[7][. . .]

All of these communities participated in, and were deeply affected by, the general changes that marked the history of the *barrio* ("county") and the emergence of a clear-cut rural proletariat after 1899. At the same time, the distinctions setting one settlement apart from another also demonstrate the variability obtaining among members of the same class. Thus, for instance, the beach-dwellers, many of whom were migrants (or the children of migrants) from the highlands, were often part-time fishermen; they tried to cultivate tiny plots of food crops; and they differed otherwise from their neighbors on the road and in the *colonias*. They liked to cut cane, whereas most typical coastal dwellers did not; and they would often compete for incentive payments for cane-cutting, which most coastal people disdained or actively disliked. While many of them had lived locally for decades, and some had been born there, they were still looked upon as unsophisticated and rather "hickish" by others, because—among other things—they responded to the demands of the plantation regimen more unquestioningly. Their willingness to marry their own cousins was regarded as particularly ludicrous by coastal people, though this criticism was never phrased in religious terms. Old-time coastal dwellers, both black and white, also joked about the highlanders' fear of black people, whom the highlanders were said to consider sorcerers and hence dangerous.

Another difference had to do with attitudes toward the sugar-workers' union, and the willingness of individuals to support the union, participate in strikes, and relate broad-based political action to their personal life-chances. While it is true that the *colonia* dwellers were particularly liable to retaliation for supporting the union, there were some antiunion persons in all three communities, as well as many enthusiasts. Other differences related to job skills (though not necessarily to pay or privilege), religious persuasion and fervency, manipulation of ritual co-parenthood *(compadrazgo)* for personal security, and so on.

In sum, the class position (or productive relations) of these rural proletarians did not impart a sufficiently firm homogeneity to the persons involved to allow the observer to ignore intragroup or individual differences of many kinds. It is in connection with this admittedly obvious social fact that the subsequent argument concerning class consciousness, and particularly proletarian class consciousness, may be advanced: class membership influences but does not wholly determine such consciousness. And yet, from the perspective of the core features of the rural proletarian category, the people in these three hamlets showed considerable uniformity. Taken together, they contrasted sharply with the agricultural populations described, for instance, by Eric Wolf for a highland Puerto Rican community,[8] even though that community contained many people who were comparably landless (though not usually equally dependent on wage labor, store-buying, etc.). Several points may be made in passing in this connection. First, we need note again that, so far as wage labor for the plantations is concerned, the peasant communities of the highlands and the plantations of the coast were to some degree interdependent. We are dealing, as in most Caribbean cases, with a society and an economy made up of different sectors, none of which is fully interpretable without reference to the others.

Second, these communities represent different kinds and degrees of fit with the economy at large, though capitalistic modes of production prevail overall. Third, we can derive some sense of the processes of proletarianization—here, of rural populations— by viewing the ways in which nonproletarians become assimilated to large-scale agricultural production of a capitalist kind, in this situation. In discovering the ways that this assimilation occurs, we may also help to reveal the similarities and differences between the processes Marx described for industrial capitalism in the European heartland, and those that occurred, and continue to occur, in the agricultural capitalism of the colonial and neocolonial world.

The Heterogeneity of "Peasant Communities"

It is with the process of proletarianization and its significance for class consciousness that the balance of this paper is mainly concerned. But before turning to those questions, it may be useful to comment on those qualities of so-called peasant communities which make so striking their contrast with rural proletarian settlements of the kind we have been describing. This paper is not concerned with the peasantry as such, but a major risk of typological exercises is the tendency to see different "types" or categories primarily in terms of their differences, without noticing that their nature as separate categories often depends to some extent on the particular ways in which they intermesh socially and economically. Hence, there may be some justification for this digression.

To do so, however, we need not repeat the various definitions scholars have advanced for the peasantry, from Kroeber and Redfield to Wolf and Shanin.[9] Suffice it to accept for present purposes Wolf's conception of rural landholders who produce both subsistence and commodities for sale, who are part of a larger social system, and upon whom others of greater power exercise an exaction of productivity in one or another form, which Wolf subsumes under the term "rent."[10] There are tens or scores of thousands of rural agricultural communities in the world today—so-called peasant communities—where a large fraction or a majority of the inhabitants fit this description. But such communities almost always also include some or many landless workers—Lenin's "agricultural proletariat" or "semiproletarians"— whose sustenance depends at least in part upon the sale (or less commonly on the barter) of their labor. It is far from clear how the presence of such persons, sometimes in large numbers, affects the specification of a "peasant" community; and in certain cases, the difficulty may be compounded if the thoroughgoing "peasant" quality of the community is dependent precisely on the presence (that is, the labor power) of these landless individuals. Such persons may hardly be visible figuratively and literally in local affairs; in fact, the greater their alienation from the "typically peasant" pattern, the less visible they may be. But there are other aspects of the relationship between landless and landed that complicate our difficulties in understanding the sociology of such communities. In many situations, the landless laborers may be concealed, so to speak, by the nature of their ties to others and to the means of production, and by the particular character of life in these small agricultural settlements, where some self-sustaining peasant landholders live. This "concealment," if one may continue to use that word, originates in several different factors. First of all, the landless may be the kinsmen of the landholders, and may even occupy the same household or compound. Second, such kin relationships, if they do exist, will probably color other ties between landholders and the landless. Third, the exchange of goods and services between landed and landless (perhaps particularly if they are kinsmen) may not involve cash payment. This, like the kinship upon which it may be predicated, makes less simple and obvious the economic ties, since they are embedded in many-sided relationships of other kinds. Fourth, the agricultural services rendered by the landless may differ according to whether the object of their labor on the land of others is to produce goods for consumption or for outside sale. Finally, where land is held in units by kin collectives, households, nuclear families, and so on, rather than in large estates, one would not normally expect to find a wholly uniform landholding group or class, in terms of the quantity or quality of land, or of the purposes for which such land is worked. Thus, differences of various kinds between the land-rich and the land-poor, for instance, may be at least as important for our understanding of rural sociology and the nature of class consciousness as those between the land-poor and the landless.

This digression upon the presence of landless wage earners within peasant communities had as its objective to point up the "concealment" of nonpeasant aggregates or groups within the infrastructure of peasant society. That these are communities in which many or most inhabitants are landholders is the principal economic fact by which the landlessness of some part of the population is cloaked or disguised. If we turn back now to communities in which land is largely or entirely held by a single family or corporation, this disguise nearly vanishes, and the landlessness of the rural population becomes the most important fact in describing it economically.

In a lengthy paper I outlined the history of the *barrio* in which the three villages described earlier were found, beginning with the slave plantations of the nineteenth century and passing through a "family-type hacienda" stage before the North American invasion brought new capital, new technology, and vast new markets to the sugarcane industry of the south. Both in that paper and in the life-history of a local worker, the writer sought to document the ways in which local working people were brought into the modern world, so to speak—clumsily and ruthlessly, but effectively, nonetheless.[11] For present purposes, the process might be said to have had four interlocking aspects: (1) the rationalization of production, as part of an intensification of the capitalist mode of production; (2) working-class consolidation, as traditional differences based on differential skills, personal relationships, and a more elaborate social hierarchy crumbled; (3) the growth of awareness of class membership—ignoring for the moment the term "proletarian consciousness"—as an accompaniment to the firmer emergence of the class itself; and (4) most paradoxically, it might seem, the growth of individualization, as the creation of qualitatively different capitalist enterprises affected the nature of all pre-existing local social groupings. A discussion of these four aspects of the proletarianization process constitutes the next part of this paper.

Proletarianization

After 1899 North American control of Puerto Rico facilitated the creation of large, modern plantation enterprises, qualitatively different in scale from the family-owned haciendas of the preceding century. The distinguishing mark of these enterprises was the amount of capital their creation required. By 1899 a mill that could produce 5,000 tons of crude sugar annually required an investment of $500,000.[12] Between 1909 and 1919, the period of florescence of the North American plantation system in Puerto Rico, there was a shift both in the level of investment in mills (Table 1) and from individual to corporate ownership (Table 2). During the same time, the number of mills owned by individuals decreased from fifty-one to twelve, while the number owned by corporations increased from twenty-three to thirty-three.

Table 1

	1909	1919
Less than $5,000	48	0
$5,000 to $20,000	12	8
$20,000 to $100,000	8	5
$100,000 to $500,000	37	10
$500,000 to $1,000,000	—	14
More than $1,000,000	3	18

Table 2

	Individual ownership	Corporate ownership	Other
1909	$1,328,809	$13,129,453	$6,111,086
1919	$3,333,521	$45,925,205	$7,153,206

Source for Tables 1 and 2: F. A. Lopez Dominguez, "Origen y desarollo de la industria del azucar de Puerto Rico," *Revista de agricultura de Puerto Rico* 19 (1927).

But the construction and corporate ownership of mills cannot guarantee success unless control over land is also assured. Between 1909 and 1919 the number of plantations increased from 6,816 to 8,839; the total acreage in cane from 145,433 cuerdas to 227,815 cuerdas (a *cuerda* is slightly less than one acre), and the percentage of all arable land in cane from 9.3 percent to 17.5 percent. Not all such land was acquired in freehold by the plantation enterprises; much of it was rented, or its crop was secured by contractual arrangements with owner-producers *(colonos)*. Such arrangements did, however, assure the mill owners that the flow of sugarcane to the factories would be adequate and uninterrupted. It would be fair to say that in many municipalities, particularly in the south where alluvial coastlands were especially fitted for irrigation and cane production, single corporations created effective land monopolies. Thus, for instance, in Santa Isabel, the municipality in which the three proletarian communities discussed earlier are located, the spread of sugarcane cultivation took the form shown in Table 3.

Table 3

	1897	1910	1940
Number of farms	141	77	16
Cuerdas in cane	1,328	3,071	6,031
Cuerdas in other crops	193	169	under 25

Of the sixteen farms reporting in 1940, seven were owned and six managed, two were operated by tenants and one by a part-owner. The average size of the seven owned farms was 5.9 cuerdas; that of the six managed farms was 3,731.8 cuerdas; managed farms controlled 99.6 percent of the cultivated land (much of the acreage was in pasture for plantation oxen).[13]

I coined the term "corporate land-and-factory combine" to describe enterprises of this kind, since that term denotes the organization (though not the scale) of modern cane-sugar plantations: corporate ownership and combined, centralized control of both land and factory. Obviously, if markets are assured, the remaining imponderable is labor. In the case of Puerto Rico's south coast, that labor was drawn both from the pre-existing hacienda populations of the region and from other regions. Such labor was either left within the shells of the former haciendas or allowed to collect in the communities on the margins of plantation land, as previously described. A major feature of this process was the concentration of people and of land in larger enterprises than has been typical of the past. "On the present area of the estate of one of the largest American companies," a Department of Commerce report for 1917 asserts, "there were formerly 31 mills. The cane now grown on this area is ground by one factory." This lateral integration of the labor force was accompanied by an increasing standardization of production, with the creation of an elaborate managerial hierarchy to get the job done. The tiny hacienda estates of the past, now *colonias,* became cogs in the great wheel of combine production; their work forces became productive parts of the whole, rather than the integers they had been under the hacienda system of the past. All of these changes combined to make the new enterprises qualitatively different from those which had preceded them.

An inevitable consequence of these steps toward the rationalization of production was the growth of a newly defined sugarcane working class. This is by no means to say that no such class had existed before; but its character was noticeably changed after 1899. The North American invasion led not only to heavy investment and the institution of a new kind of enterprise, but also to the introduction of better means of transport and communication, greater geographical mobility on the part of the laboring population, and new bases for social assortment and interaction among working people. The ties to the old haciendas, and to particular *hacendados,* bosses, and owners withered. Work-gang and labor-recruiter practices, with several varieties of foreman-middleman supplying crew labor at cut prices to estate managers, caused considerable abuse in the early decades after 1899, but also reassorted and homogenized the work force, without reference to older ties and personal associations. The process was accelerated by the sale of hacienda lands and the emigration of the landowning class, many of the members of which had previously resided on their haciendas and had maintained personal associations with their resident laborers. It was also hastened by the decline in the economic value of older skills tied to the operation of local haciendas and to more traditional ways of working the land and producing sugar. The greater the rationalization of production, and the faster the replacement of labor-intensive and poorly capitalized agriculture with new systems, the more complete the depersonalization and homogenization of the labor force itself. Inevitably, workers came to see themselves as undifferentiated in terms of their fates, more and more dependent on enterprises to which they could build no personal attachments.

These changes, in turn, led working people to look to themselves, rather than to those more powerful than they, for the solution of their problems. In the choice of godparents for their children, assistance with tasks they could not carry out themselves, and help of all kinds, they turned to other workers, rather than to the *hacendados,* foremen, and *gente importante* ("influential people") upon whom they might have been able to rely in the past. Their class membership, as such, may have become no different; but the existence of that class itself was now unmitigated by other aspects of the social environment. The reader will of course notice that the changes involved all had the effect of stripping from the landless worker's social ambiance those elements which go to make up the "concealment" of landlessness in so-called peasant communities, even though in this case we are dealing with a population most of whose members had been landless for generations. The key to this picture is not, then, landlessness as such, but landlessness in the context of rapidly expanding capitalist enterprise, and the crystallization of a land-less class within proletarian communities.

Finally, and in delicate integration with these other processes, the spread of the new plantation system effected a new kind of individualization among these rural proletarians. Individualiza-tion, in the sense in which the term is used here, bears a significant relationship to Marx's concept of the objectification of labor and the alienation of the laborer, as experienced by individual workers, and the significance of these processes as they effect the emergence both of class and of class consciousness. Marx's use of the term "social class" was invariably collective: "When Marx described the proletariat as a revolutionary class, he did not wish to say that each and every proletarian was a revolutionary, but that the proletariat as a whole had this characteristic."[14] What is meant by "individu-alization" is that the objectification of labor and the alienation of the laborer enable individuals to objectify themselves, particularly as regards the traditional social forms, which, until the advent of modern factory-style capitalism, interfered with precisely this kind of self-objectification.

In describing such a process for a single person, by means of the life-history of a resident of the Puerto Rican plantation communities studied, I suggested that "the individual is gradually torn loose from the old personal security networks and eventually may come to see himself alone and to think of his fate as most comprehensible in terms of his own acts."[15] But it would be erroneous to translate this assertion into a conceptual restraint upon the idea of class membership. Rather, it is meant to suggest that *proletarian* class membership carries with it a consciousness of individuality within the class, as well as the consciousness of the existence of the class itself.

There is, in the writer's view, no contradiction here. Members of a rural proletarian class who are conscious of their class mem-bership will recognize the need to act collectively in their own interest, even if they do not or cannot discover the most appro-priate means for acting: "the working class, like the peasantry, consists almost by definition of people who cannot make things happen except collectively, though, *unlike peasants,* their experi-ence of labour demonstrates every day that they must act collec-tively or not at all."[16] Moreover, whether their consciousness of class membership will be transformed into political response is not a question always answerable affirmatively.[17] The aim here is to suggest that individualization is a vital aspect of proletarianiza-tion, so far as our understanding of class consciousness is con-cerned, and is *in the service of that consciousness,* even if it appears not to be. Of the history of proletarianization of plantation communities, the writer has noted that "people were simultaneously reorienting themselves to deal with some of their problems on an institutionalized and mass basis, through political parties and labor unions. [But] the increase of a sense of identity with people of one's class or region need not contradict or rule out the possibility of a heightened feeling of aloneness and individuality."[18]

One is tempted to press this assertion slightly further. To what extent can it be contended that class consciousness—at least when dealing with populations of the sort described here—does not assume certain forms *until* individuals see themselves as defenseless, and thus *individual,* because they have become disengaged from those traditional protections of community, kinship, and personal association that typify an earlier stage of economic history?

Rural Proletarian Class Consciousness

Arguments about Latin American rural sociology, with particular reference to the etiology of revolution, have been concerned not only with the differentiation of rural groupings but also with the significance of such groupings in political terms. It has sometimes been contended that Marxist theory ordains no revolutionary role for the peasantry. Whatever the merits of that contention—and it is doubtful that Marx himself would have advanced it as a universal "law"—it certainly cannot be tested without a careful specification of who and what "peasants" are, economically and socially. Moreover, if some consensus as to the nature of the peasantry were attained, wider questions would naturally arise, having to do with the character of peasantries outside the European heartland. Wolf's study of peasant revolutions conceptualizes the peasantry as a revolutionary force, and does so in the context of the expansion of world capitalism, transforming both the economic relations and the awareness of peasant peoples, rather than moving them from one sociological category (e.g., "the peasantry") to another (e.g., "the rural proletariat"). But he also deals with societies such as Cuba where, he points out, whole sectors of the rural population cannot defensibly be described as "peasants," unless that word is to be stripped of all analytical meaning. In these cases, and particularly where a population justifiably defined as a peasantry is a numerical minority, the relationship between economic function and political response becomes a critical question for the analyst.[19]

Put very crudely, a political analysis of rural sectors requires a firm understanding of rural class structure. That understanding is basic if rural groups (or classes) are to be conceptualized in terms of their relationships to the means of production, and if their political consciousness is hypothesized to arise from (or to be, in any less deterministic sense, informed by) such relationships. Only in this way—unless one chooses to reject any linkage between class structure and politics—will it be possible for the serious student to escape from the verbal trap in which adjectives from the "hard" sciences ("inert," "volatile," "labile," etc.) are substituted for on-the-ground understanding of rural political behavior.

The four aspects of the proletarianization process described in the preceding section are intended to clarify how class identity of a certain kind increases under specific conditions. Most of the people subjected to this process had long been landless coastal dwellers, others were smallholders, or the children of smallholders, who emigrated to the coast in search of work or cash. Between 1899, when the economic transformation of Puerto Rico's south coast began, and the mid-twentieth century, large masses of such persons were proletarianized, and the term here refers primarily to their understanding of their situation and of their commonality with each other, rather than to the economic changes which the writer believes to have underlain these attitudinal shifts.

It would be possible, of course, to describe proletarianization in other ways—to reduce it, for instance, to a formula of the sort employed by Robert Redfield in his study of Yucatán.[20] But as the writer has suggested in an earlier paper,[21] Redfield ignored the henequen haciendas of Yucatán as a basic dimension of Yucatecan rural life, choosing instead to extend his continuum for a small "tribal" village to the capital city of Merida, thus phrasing change in terms of a rural-urban dimension, rather than some other. For rural proletarians, however, the continuum is not from "folk" to "urban," so much as from one stage of capitalism to another. And while Redfield found homogeneity in the countryside and heterogeneity in the city, a contrast of peasantry and rural proletariat (as in the Puerto Rican case) suggests that it is the peasants who are heterogeneous and the proletarians who are homogenized. In fact, the development of rural capitalist enterprise on a plantation basis in many Latin American countries leads one to believe that plantation communities there may be more "urban" in some ways than the cities themselves, since the cities of the colonial world are often mere adjuncts to foreign capitalist agriculture, rather than dominating the hinterland in the European mode. The basic distinction, that is, may not be along any continuum from the rural to the urban, so much as along that continuum provided by the intensification of a particular mode of economic organization—in this case, overseas capitalist estate agriculture. The following discussion of class consciousness—here, of rural proletarian class consciousness—proceeds with these assertions in mind.

The three stages in the history of proletarianization of the Puerto Rican population with which the writer has been dealing were significantly different from each other. During the first (pre-1873) stage the sugar industry of the south coast had developed rapidly, on a base of slave and forced (but technically free) labor. During the second stage the scale of enterprise did not change, but the labor force, still resident in the haciendas themselves, was free in fact. After 1899 the family-type haciendas of the second stage were assimilated in their entirety, as we have seen, into enormous modern corporate combines, controlling both land and mills.

The pre-Emancipation haciendas, dependent as they were on unfree labor, were one example of a special stage in the history of New World agricultural capitalism. Their slaves and forced laborers were only rarely able to fight back against the system that bound them; and 1873 brought an end to both slavery and forced-labor legislation. The successors of the slaves and forced laborers, the free but politically powerless plantation laborers of the late nineteenth century, were in certain ways less clearly defined in class terms than had been the slaves. The chasm between slave and free had been bridged (or better, perhaps, mitigated) by Emancipation, while the hacienda capitalism of the late nineteenth century was less intense than the slave-based capitalism that had preceded it.

It was only with the advent of North American capital, destroying the pseudomanorial character of the family-type haciendas, erasing class distinctions among laborers, undermining the system of payment in the form of noncash perquisites and the pattern of paternalist favoritism, standardizing wages and hours, eliminating nonplantation sources of income and of subsistence, and aggregating sources of separate hacienda units into vast, undifferentiated estates, that the proletarianization process we have described could unfold clearly and firmly. Such a process, of course, relates closely to the concept of class consciousness, as commonly applied to an industrial proletariat. But here we deal with a proletariat of a different kind, and it must be kept in mind that the class consciousness of a rural plantation proletariat, of the sort depicted here, may differ significantly from that of the classic example, associated with the rise of the factory system in Western Europe.

It is not only that the processes involved must be distinguished as occurring in industry on the one hand and agriculture on the other. Nor is it enough to emphasize that one case involves the European mainland and the others—for the most part—the non-Western world outside. Nor is the difference adequately handled even if we add to these other distinctions the need, fully recognized by the Marxists, to view the different sectors of a single society as conjunctive and interdependent in our analysis of class consciousness. There is yet another very important distinction, difficult to handle in view of the confusion over "rural" and "urban," but essential to our treatment nonetheless: the notion of *community*. The writer has described very briefly the landless wage earners of three neighboring Puerto Rican villages and the differing attitudes the people there have about each other, even though they clearly share their rural proletarian status. Since these villages are small and near each other, people in them are in fairly frequent interaction, and there is a noticeable responsiveness to community norms in many regards. These circumstances affect the ways in which people change their behavior, carry out social (and antisocial) acts, and evaluate each other's opinions about the world in which they live.

The writer cannot make comparisons of these communities with other rural proletarian communities elsewhere, in these terms. He can only claim that the "urban" qualities of plantation life, hinged as they are to the intensification of agricultural exploitation, the depersonalization of relationships between workers and managers, the piecework and task-splitting of daily labor, and all the rest, are pitted against pre-existing values and beliefs of members of the working class that find their principal basis for perpetuation in the quality of community itself.[. . .]

The preceding argument has to do with the emergence of class consciousness—here, of rural proletarian class consciousness. The emergence of such consciousness presumably reflects some transformation of a class's view of itself and of its political stakes:

> Economic conditions had first transformed the mass of the people of the country into workers. The domination of capital had created for this mass a common situation, common interests. This mass is thus already *a class as against capital,* but not yet *for itself.* In the struggle, of which we have noted only a few phases, this mass becomes united, and *constitutes itself as a class for itself.* The interests it

defends become class interests. But the struggle of class against class is a political struggle.[22]

This citation from Marx, however, gives no hint why a class which can be defined objectively may exhibit variations in the consciousness of its members, variations which are not simply products (mirror images) of its objective, class-in-itself characteristics. Members of the same class may differ widely in their particular attitudes. Moreover, the specific conditions under which such persons live—the quality of the community in which they function —may affect their variable class awareness or consciousness. Even the extent to which such conditions are analytically independent of class position, or of the concept of class itself, is not entirely clear. All of which we may be certain is that the gap between class membership and class consciousness, if we mean by the latter the ideology of a "class-for-itself," may be a wide one. That this subject matter remains highly controversial, even among Marxists, is very clear.

There is no doubt that Marx himself, in discussing proletarian consciousness, had in mind a conception of such consciousness— of a class "for itself"—that would perceive revolution as the only sure test of the legitimacy of the distribution of power.[23] One need not, of course, agree with this view. But Mészáros, among others, has argued convincingly that this stress on a revolutionary role is in no important sense contradictory to the view of a Marxist such as Gramsci, who stressed the need for political organization of the working class, if it is to achieve political objectives.[24] What is finally at stake, says Mészáros, quoting Marx while interpreting him, is not "how to obtain 'a better wage for the slave,' nor indeed that of a change in the tone of voice—carefully filtered by 'human engineering'—which transmits the dictates of commodity production to the workers, but a *radical restructuring* of the established order of society."[25]

The argument devolves upon those points in history when proletariats have responded politically by questioning and attacking the established order, rather than by organizing to reform it. To put it otherwise, it is important to understand how populations come to the recognition that their felt oppression is not merely a matter of *poor* times, but of *evil* times—when, in short, they question the *legitimacy* of an existing allocation of power, rather than the terms of that allocation. For if it is not the degree of oppression that matters, but the right not to be oppressed, then the class consciousness of the oppressed has, it seems, changed radically. But the writer has sought to suggest that, if this be the test of class *consciousness,* we shall need to know a great deal more about the factors which mediate between class identity and a revolutionary response before the concept of a class-for-itself can acquire analytical significance.

It is also at this point that simple comparisons of categories within a typology, without reference to the environing conditions within which national classes form and the intricate relationships between different classes in the same society, can prove most misleading.[26] Knight, writing of sugarcane workers in Colombia, has suggested that we can usefully view rural proletariats as "an extension of the national proletariat into the fields."[27] But in many Latin American societies the rural proletariat constitutes the largest and most substantial proletarian group of all. To label it "an extension" in cases where an urban industrial proletariat is little developed or entirely lacking entails risks, as Knight would no doubt agree. Part of the peculiar nature of Caribbean rural proletariats is precisely that they did not take shape simply as an accompaniment to industrial growth in the colony, nor only in response to such growth, but *in the absence* of developments typical of the history of Western Europe in its own heartlands. That is, the history of classes in the colonies is a colonial history, even when such classes formed under pressures originating in the metropolis. Such an assertion, of course, does not explain why colonial class structures (and the particular class groupings that compose them) are different from the metropolitan cases; but it does suggest that we show care in drawing analogies.[28]

Moreover, the colonial context sets the terms by which different classes are interrelated and the extent to which class interests may conflict or overlap. The ties between peasantries and proletariats; the presence of groups, sometimes numerous, that alternate between a peasant and a proletarian adaptation; the presence or absence of significant ethnic differences within a proletarian class; these and numerous other specific features may affect the ways one class may (or may not) be defined in contrast to another. Accordingly, any uncritical transfer of analytic categories developed to describe Western European history to cases of the Caribbean kind may vitiate the analysis itself.[. . .]

Caribbean plantation proletariats represent a particular series of stages in the evolution of capitalist enterprise in the colonies. Unlike the peasantries discussed by Wolf,[29] who became revolutionary under the impact of significantly different forms of overseas capitalism, Caribbean plantation proletariats are the endpoint in lengthy processes of disenfranchisement, beginning in many instances with enslavement and transportation, and finally achieving clear proletarian status as free but landless wage

earners employed *en masse* by modern corporate enterprises.
That the historical experiences of such groups are very remote
from those of the industrial proletariats of the European heartland is obvious. That this class consciousness should both share
some features with that of industrial proletariats and differ in
other features should occasion no surprise.

But when reverting to the question of rural proletarian consciousness among Caribbean peoples, an apparent contradiction
emerges. It is the peasant sectors of Caribbean societies that have
often been viewed as possessing and even sometimes exercising
the revolutionary potential Marx attributes to the industrial
proletariat; and while rural proletarian sectors in the Antilles have
repeatedly demonstrated their capacities for political response
and political action, only rarely have they shown their proletarian
consciousness as a revolutionary force. How contrary this may
seem, in the light of the imputed Marxist view of the politically
inactive peasantry on the one hand and of the (industrial) proletariat as the vanguard of the revolution on the other, is clear.

In the Cuban case, Draper's research led him to conclude that
the revolution was firmly middle class, so far as the origins of its
first leaders are concerned, and this conclusion seems correct,
though he is probably on much weaker ground in discounting the
eventual mass support of other sectors.[30] Are there reasons for
claiming that the Cuban rural proletariat, rather than becoming a
vanguard, was only an accompaniment to a revolution led by
middle-class professionals and students and supported by some
variety or varieties of peasantry? If so, then rural proletarian
consciousness is certainly of a different order from the consciousness of the industrial proletariat as Marx and others portrayed it.
It cannot be expected, of course, that the class consciousness of
rural proletarian peoples in countries such as Cuba would have
evolved in a fashion indistinguishable from that of industrial
proletariats in Europe itself. Political organization among rural
proletariats of the sort considered here is often achieved through
unions, linked in many cases to local political parties, and devoted
to the realization of certain demands in the sphere of wages,
job security, unemployment insurance, medical and educational
services, and the like. State ownership of the means of production
—the plantation lands and mills—may not even arise as an issue
for the workers; the legitimacy of the system may never be thrown
into question. But this will not mean that such rural proletariats
lack class consciousness, that their experiences are not in certain
fundamental ways parallel to those of industrial proletariats or—
most importantly—that they are incapable of forging links with

other classes in a revolutionary situation. In fact, the labor history of countries such as Bolivia, Peru, Guyana, and Cuba strongly suggests that the forging of such links between rural proletariats and peasantries may be vital to a political future—even if rural proletariats do not play a vanguard role.

Accurate and adequate typologies of rural classes—and of the variety of constellations of such classes in particular societies—may prove to be a precondition for analyzing effectively the way in which different classes in the same society are able to unite their differing consciousness in supporting a common political program. Whether that program is aimed at testing the legitimacy of an existing distribution of power or at changing the terms will presumably depend upon specific local conditions that cannot yet be generalized effectively by theorists.

The writer does not profess to stand the theory of the proletariat on its head. In fact, the major purpose here has been to suggest substantial analogies between the Marxist theory of proletarian consciousness, as applied to the industrial wage-earning classes of Europe, and varieties of rural and colonial counterparts in the rest of the world.[. . .]

Conclusions

In some instances, a readiness to view the countryside as populated by a homogeneous "peasantry" has misled observers. Often the predominant rural population is landless, wage-earning, store-buying, and corporately employed—a proletariat, in short, but a rural proletariat. Study of rural proletarian communities suggests that their inhabitants may have a sturdy awareness of their class membership, but this is not to say that this awareness is equally shared or that it leads to a predictable homogeneity in political (or other) attitudes.

Peasant communities, in contrast, may include in their membership some or many persons who are landless and even wage-earning; but their proletarian status is cloaked by the many relationships they have with the landed. On these grounds, and on others, peasant communities may be economically much more heterogeneous than rural proletarian communities; but the landless within peasant communities are not so likely to develop the consciousness of class membership common to those who live in rural proletarian communities.

The rural proletarian communities described in this paper serve as useful examples of the process of proletarianization, accelerated and dramatized by qualitative changes in the scale of agro-industry and the organization of enterprise. Proletarianization is described here in terms of four major aspects: rationalization of production; consolidation of class membership; the growth of an accompanying consciousness of such membership; and the individualization of the working class. Such individualization is projected hypothetically as a precondition for working-class consciousness, since it involves the destruction of those very links among persons that "conceal the individual from himself" in peasant communities.

Awareness of membership in the rural proletarian class, and rural proletarian class consciousness, may be somewhat different phenomena, however. If such consciousness is to be defined by the workers' assertion that the system under which they live is illegitimate, then rural proletarian class consciousness has only rarely manifested itself as such. In fact, the history of rural proletariats more commonly reveals a readiness to work for reform within an existing system of power. What does appear to be the case is that, under revolutionary conditions, rural proletarians sometimes build coalitions with members of other classes (including segments of the peasantry) in achieving a common political objective, as may have been the case in Cuba and, more problematically, in Bolivia and Guatemala. Our understanding of how these coalitions are built remains fragmentary and inconclusive, however.

The course of the argument has purported to suggest both important similarities and equally important differences between the history of industrial proletariats in the West and that of rural proletariats in the colonial and neocolonial regions. The aim of the paper has not been to provide a definitive picture of the rural proletariat and its characteristics so much as to call for more care in the construction of typologies to describe and analyze the rural sociology of the wider world.

Notes

1. For reasons of space, it was necessary to exclude an earlier part of this article. It examined how conceptual confusions between "peasant" and "proletarian" in Cuba led to serious misunderstandings of the roles of different classes in the making of the Cuban revolution. [Eds.]
2. V. Bystryansky and M. Mishan, eds., *The Theory of the Proletarian Revolution* (New York: International Publishers, 1936), pp. 41–43.
3. Sidney W. Mintz, "The Folk-Urban Continuum and the Rural Proletarian Community," *American Journal of Sociology* 34 (1953): 139–40.

4. See Sidney W. Mintz, "Petits cultivateurs et prolétaires ruraux dans la région des Caraïbes," *Les problèmes agraires des Ameriques Latines* (Paris: Colloques Internationaux de CNRS, 1967), pp. 93–100; Sidney W. Mintz, "A Note on the Definition of Peasantries," *Journal of Peasant Studies* 1, no. 1 (October 1973): 91–106; and Sidney W. Mintz, "The Plantation as a Socio-cultural Type," Document no. 3, *Seminar on Plantation Systems of the New World* (Washington, D.C.: Pan-American Union, 1957), pp. 1–12, esp. p. 2.

5. Sidney W. Mintz, "Cañamelar: The Contemporary Culture of a Rural Puerto Rican Proletariat (Ph.D. diss., Columbia University, 1951).

6. Sidney W. Mintz, *Worker in the Cane* (New Haven: Yale University Press, 1960).

7. Mintz, *Cañamelar;* Sidney W. Mintz, "The Culture History of a Puerto Rican Sugar-Cane Plantation, 1876-1949," *The Hispanic American Historical Review* 33, no. 2: 224–51; Mintz, "Folk-Urban Continuum"; Sidney W. Mintz, "Cañamelar: The Sub-culture of a Rural Plantation Proletarian," in *The People of Puerto Rico,* by J. H. Steward et al. (Urbana, Ill.: University of Illinois Press, 1956), pp. 314–417.

8. Eric Wolf, *Culture Change and Culture Stability in a Puerto Rican Coffee Growing Community* (Ph.D. diss., Columbia University, 1951); and Eric Wolf, "San José: Subcultures of a 'Traditional' Coffee Municipality," in *People of Puerto Rico,* Steward et al., pp. 171–264.

9. Mintz, "Definition of Peasantries."

10. Eric Wolf, *Peasants* (Englewood Cliffs, N.J.: Prentice-Hall, 1966), p. 10; and Eric Wolf, "Reply to Dalton," *Current Anthropology* 13, nos. 3–4 (1972): 411.

11. Mintz, "Culture History"; and Mintz, *Worker in the Cane.*

12. W. D. Davis, *Civil Affairs of Puerto Rico, 1899* (Washington, D.C.: Government Printing Office, 1900), pp. 37–38.

13. Henry K. Carroll, *Report on the Island of Puerto Rico* (Washington, D.C.: Government Printing Office, 1900), p. 118; U.S. Bureau of the Census, *Thirteenth Census of the United States* (Washington, D.C.: Government Printing Office, 1910); and the U.S. Bureau of the Census, *Sixteenth Census of the United States* (Washington, D.C.: Government Printing Office, 1943).

14. Z. A. Jordan, ed., *Karl Marx: Economy, Social Class and Revolution* (London: Michael Joseph, 1971), p. 23.

15. Mintz, *Worker in the Cane,* p. 261.

16. Eric Hobsbawm, "Class Consciousness in History" in *Aspects of History and Class Consciousness,* ed. I Mészáros (London: Routledge & Kegan Paul, 1971), p. 14.

17. This treatment does considerable injustice to the Marxist theory of class, as well as to the concept of class consciousness; but considerations of space prevent an adequate discussion here. Cf., for instance, Mészáros, ed., *Aspects of History and Class Consciousness* and Jordan, ed., *Karl Marx,* pp. 21–30.

18. Mintz, *Worker in the Cane,* p. 262.

19. Eric Wolf, *Peasant Wars in the Twentieth Century* (New York: Harper &

Row, 1969), pp. 257 and 299; and Sidney W. Mintz, Foreword to *Sugar and Society in the Caribbean*, by R. Guerra y Sánchez (New Haven: Yale University Press, 1964).

20. Robert Redfield, *The Folk Culture of Yucatan* (Chicago: University of Chicago Press, 1960).

21. Mintz, "Folk-Urban Continuum."

22. Karl Marx, *The Poverty of Philosophy* (New York: International Publishers, 1963), p. 173.

23. Karl Marx, *The Eighteenth Brumaire of Louis Napoleon* (New York: International Publishers, 1963), pp. 123–24 and 173–75.

24. Antonio Gramsci, *The Modern Prince and Other Writings* (London: Lawrence & Wishart, 1957), pp. 172–73.

25. Mészáros, ed., *Aspects of History and Class Consciousness*, p. 98.

26. Thomas C. Greaves, "The Andean Rural Proletarians," *Anthropological Quarterly* 45, no. 2 (1972).

27. Rolf Knight, "Sugar Plantations and Labour Patterns in the Canca Valley," *University of Toronto Anthropological Series*, no. 12 (1972), p. 185.

28. The history of the Caribbean region also makes clear that the processes involved are not necessarily unilinear or irreversible. Peasants may become proletarians; but nonpeasants of different kinds may also become peasants. Thus, for instance, the decline of Jamaican plantation slavery and the growth of the Jamaican peasantry occurred at the same time that Puerto Rico's peasantry was disappearing under the brunt of a rapid expansion of plantations and the spread of forced labor. See Sidney W. Mintz, "Labor and Sugar in Puerto Rico and in Jamaica 1800-1850," *Comparative Studies in Society and History* 1, no. 3 (1959): 273–81.

29. Wolf, *Peasant Wars*.

30. Theodore Draper, *Castro's Revolution: Myths and Realities* (New York: Frederick A. Praeger, 1962).

The Politics of Protest in Jamaica, 1938:
Some Problems of Analysis and Conceptualization

K. W. J. Post

The events of May and June 1938 in Jamaica have taken on a legendary aspect; to many contemporary radicals they seem to represent the counterpart of 1905 in Russia: at first an assurance that 1917 must follow and then a source of alarm that the final revolution is taking so long to come. It seems opportune, therefore, at this time to try to establish what actually did happen in 1938, and from there proceed to elucidate what we can about the conditions which gave rise to the particular events, and to see them in relation to what has happened since. Two points should be made immediately about this essay. First, it will deal only with 1938 and will not touch subsequent events; questions of length and the state of my own knowledge make this restriction necessary.[1] Second, as its title is meant to suggest, this essay is only a preliminary exploration of data and hypotheses; it will undoubtedly raise more questions than it answers.

I will begin, therefore, by discussing what actually took place. This will lead to an attempted analysis of the groups involved in these events. Then I will follow with an examination of the factor of leadership in 1938. By that stage we should be far enough advanced to look at some of the broader problems of the analysis of economic and political structures, whose basic contradictions produced the phenomena with which we began our study. Last, as a way of pulling the threads together, we can consider the question, "1938, rebellion or revolution?"

What Happened in Jamaica in May and June 1938?

This was the first question I asked myself in beginning work on this problem. It seems an obvious one, but it should be pointed out that, with only one exception, the frequent invocations of 1938 have not been supported by attempts to answer it. The exception is O. W. Phelps, and, as I will attempt to show shortly,

Reprinted from *Social and Economic Studies* 18, no. 4 (1969): 374-90, with the permission of the author and publisher.

his emphases give a wrong overall impression.[2] What I have done is to collect accounts of events given in the contemporary newspapers (primarily the *Daily Gleaner* and *Jamaica Standard*) and the official reports of the disturbances.[3] I have as yet interviewed few surviving participants, but would in any case expect such material to be more important in interpreting the data than in establishing what actually happened. The first, indispensable research step was thus to build a day-by-day account of what happened. From this point hypotheses could begin to suggest themselves. Space does not permit the reproduction of such an account here. What may be done, however, is to attempt a number of generalizations about crucial features of the events.

Viewed in a West Indian perspective, of course, May-June 1938 in Jamaica, was only part of a series of similar disturbances which had shaken the British West Indies since 1935 and was to continue after Jamaica's events. In general, the problems of Jamaica were the problems of all, as the report of the Moyne Commission gives gloomy witness.[4] But it may be argued that the Jamaican disturbances had qualities of their own which distinguished that territory from the others. The outbreak in Jamaica was more widespread than the others, even taking account of the greater size of the island. The riots in Barbados in April 1937 did spread beyond Bridgetown, but the capital was the main scene of events. Similarly, Port of Spain was affected by the troubles of June 1937, as were other parts of Trinidad, but the southern oilfields provided the real center of gravity. In Jamaica scarcely a parish remained without serious riots, strikes, and demonstrations, though the bulk of the most serious trouble was in the east and the northeast, and the most disturbed area of all (with the exception of Kingston) was eastern St. Mary. The Jamaican events were not only more widespread than elsewhere but also more prolonged. The Frome outbreak from April 29 to May 2 was a prologue to a major drama which began on May 21 with a dockers' strike in Kingston and petered out on July 10 with minor incidents in both the east and the west of the island. During that three weeks the whole colonial system was under the severest pressure, and it can be argued that not until June 5 did the administration really show signs of being able to handle the situation other than by brute force.

This last point is an important one. In face of official rationalizations, it is necessary to emphasize the seriousness of the threat which the events of 1938 constituted to the established order. The official report stressed the absence of violence:

> In reviewing these disturbances, we are struck by the remarkably small number of casualties, considering how prolonged and wide-

> spread was the disorder. It is a tribute alike to the good temper
> of the labouring classes of Jamaica and to the forbearance and
> humanity of those whose duty it was to preserve order.[5]

The last point is open to the gravest doubt. Two labor leaders,
S. Kerr Coombs and H. C. Buchanan, were jailed for six months
for exposing the brutality of the police in St. James, and the much
more "respectable" *Jamaica Standard* also questioned the activities
of special constables in Montego Bay.[6] The report itself describes
the case of Edgar Daley, who on refusing to give up his stick to a
policeman when the crowd he was leading was halted, and
throwing the policeman to the ground when he tried to take the
stick, was bayoneted and had his back broken with rifle butts.[7] As
to the "good temper of the labouring classes," it is necessary to
remember how essential this view is to the colonial myth: the
masses must be seen as simple, happy people, either misled by
agitators or (in the more "liberal" version, which prevailed in the
official reports) with genuine grievances but expressing them in
the wrong way because of ignorance and the lack of proper
leadership. What these good-tempered people were in fact doing
was blocking roads, cutting telephone wires, breaking down
bridges, burning cane, destroying banana trees, and on several
occasions, ambushing armed police with nothing but sticks and
stones. Given arms, ideology, and different leaders, the story
might have been quite a different one; it is instructive to remember
that only five years before communist-inspired peasants had set
up their own independent soviets.

A further point which must be emphasized is the extent of
the disturbances in the rural areas. References to the events
of 1938 tend to dwell on what happened in Kingston. Thus,
Len S. Nembhard, for example, makes no reference to any other
events.[8] Phelps, in the essay already cited, devotes three and a half
pages of his account of 1938 to Kingston and one and a half to the
rest of the island.[9] Thus, even the best account so far tends to
portray Kingston as the center of gravity. There is no gainsaying
that events there were very important. With an estimated ten
thousand people taking part at the peak of the strikes and
demonstrations there, and given that the city was the center of
administration and commerce, it could not be otherwise. But the
dockers' strike, the focus of the events in Kingston, was over
by May 28, and essential services had been restored before that;
the city was in fact paralyzed for only two days. The dockers
and other strikers had shown a willingness to negotiate from
the beginning, though they refused to listen to Manley while
Bustamante was in jail. Above all, perhaps, the presence of

N. W. Manley and Alexander Bustamante in the city and their willingness to act as negotiators (on which more later) gave the authorities an opportunity, which they took, of bringing the situation rapidly under control. In the rural areas there were direct assaults upon the representatives of authority, a much more direct confrontation between the demonstrators and the agents of repression, and events were far more prolonged. When Manley and Bustamante extended their mediatory efforts beyond Kingston there is evidence that on occasion they were not heeded. What is certain is that rural discontent was only pacified by a promise made first by the acting governor on June 5 (Sir Edward Denham had died on the second) that £500,000 (in later versions £650,000) would be spent on the purchase of land for settlement by peasant farmers. The implications of this bring us to the next section of the paper.

Who Were the Demonstrators?

There is at first glance a blanket answer to this question— virtually everyone who was a wage laborer or unemployed or for some other reason regarded himself or herself as a sufferer. This is, however, far too simplistic. For example, it raises without answering the very complex question of consciousness—why did some people identify themselves as sufferers and others not? Why did shop assistants and clerks, often as miserably paid and generally abused as other wage earners, persist in regarding themselves as "middle class" (or at least aspirants thereto) and thus separate from the demonstrators? This is one of the problems which is worth raising here, but which I cannot yet answer, while space forbids further speculation.[10] What it may serve to do, nevertheless, is to remind us of the need for careful delineation of the separate groups involved in protest in 1938. Attention may be drawn to six of these.

1. *The workers at the Frome sugar estate.* As already noted, events at Frome served as a prologue to the main drama, though unrest continued there through May. This was a somewhat exceptional case, with special local causes for discontent as a result of the activities of the West Indies Sugar Company in developing its new estates. With a labor force of only about seven hundred involved, the Frome workers are to be distinguished as a special separate interest, mainly because they gave the "cue" to the rest.

2. *The dockers and other public and private employees in Kingston.* Again this group is singled out mainly because of Kingston's general importance, its large concentration of wage workers and unemployed, and because events there do form a distinct constellation with its own dynamic. In other respects the interests of, say, dockers or Public Works Department laborers in the corporate area did not differ from those elsewhere.

3. *Public Works Department laborers.* These seem to have been a radical force throughout the island. Since about the middle of April the government had been trying to relieve unemployment by expanding this labor force and setting them to work on roads and railways and the new airfield at Palisadoes. A very similar case was that of laborers employed by the parochial boards.

4. *Ex-servicemen who had been settled on government land grants.* This is a group on which more research must be done, but there is some indication that this was a militant group in Manchester, where there were two large schemes of this kind. There were other such settlers in St. Thomas, Clarendon, St. Ann, Westmoreland, and Hanover. It would appear that inadequate provision for further assistance through agricultural extension services to these men, once settled, and lack of capital had resulted in hardship.

5. *Cane workers.* These were an important disaffected group; serious strikes and disturbances occurred on at least fourteen of the thirty-four big estates. However, in assessing their role two problems arise. First, what happened on the other twenty estates, where (as far as I can gather) there were no major disturbances? Further research may reveal differences between estates which help to explain this distinction.[11] The second problem arises from a lack of knowledge of the exact structure of sugar estates in 1938, so it is impossible to know what kind of workers were most militant there—for example, field or factory workers. (At Frome the most militant were not cane workers at all, but construction workers who were building the new factory.) A further complication is that a number of estates combined sugar with bananas, or cattle, or both. In these cases the actual sugar workers might not have been the most militant. One further point is that in some ways the actions of the sugar workers could be contained by the management and the administration. There are indications that early in the disturbances the workers were often willing to negotiate, with the absence of a formal union structure proving to be a handicap. It seems particularly significant that at Frome, where A. G. S. Coombs, president of the Jamaica Workers' and Tradesmen's Union, did intervene, discussions between workers and management took place. Even the widespread burning of cane

is inconclusive; it may have been intended to hit the owners where it hurt most—their profits—but it should also be remembered that burned cane can be saved if cut within twenty-four hours; burnings may therefore have been attempts to force management to settle quickly.

6. *Banana workers*. In my view, based on the number and intensity of incidents in 1938, these were the most important single group involved. In areas of banana cultivation, especially St. Mary and Portland, we find the greatest militancy and intransigence. Roadblocks, bridge-breaking, and wire-cutting were most evident there. The majority of direct confrontations with the police were in the banana areas, and in consequence (with the exception of the first Frome affair) so were most of the major shooting incidents. Banana workers were responsible for the physical attacks on important individuals, and, on a few occasions, for besieging others in their homes. I suggest that this adds up to an attempt to force concessions from the system by doing actual damage to it in a more serious way than anywhere else on the island.

If banana workers were the most militant in 1938, we must look more closely at who they were. Hard data is tantalizingly scarce, and it must be admitted that my views at this stage tend to be based on deduction rather than induction. One category of banana worker is immediately discernible, however—the dock-workers and boatmen who loaded at the ports like Montego Bay (and Kingston, where the dockers' strike started among banana loaders). Yet these were not the most militant; they were prepared from the start to negotiate for higher wages, and A. G. S. Coombs secured these for them at Montego Bay after five days of strikes and demonstrations. It was the banana plantation workers in the hinterland who were the intransigents, bringing the whole industry to a halt by rolling strikes, which would start on one plantation and then spread for miles as the workers marched from plantation to plantation, bringing out the rest. Following this would come the actions described above, and also the temporary occupation of small country towns like Islington, where the most serious shooting took place on June 3.

What were the aims of these men? Certainly they included higher wages and more regular work. At least two developments of the 1930s must have affected the position of the plantation workers adversely. First, the loss of banana-growing acreage through Panama disease had been severe; by late 1936 (the latest date for which figures are available) nearly twelve thousand acres had gone out of use in St. Mary and at least twelve thousand in

Portland.[12] Second, it had been the policy of the banana companies to close down most of the banana ports and concentrate activities on a few of them. This would have affected the dockers and boatmen most immediately, but also the workers inland, whose services would have been an obvious target for economy on the part of growers now having to meet greater transport costs.

Nevertheless, I would argue that it is not primarily as wage workers that the banana plantation workers must be seen, but as peasant farmers. What little evidence I have suggests that those working as carriers were either supplementing incomes derived from growing bananas on small holdings themselves, or else wished to get some land in order to become growers. I would argue that this hunger for land—either to add to an existing plot or to turn a landless laborer into a proprietor—was the main motive force of the strikers in the banana areas. Three pieces of data seem relevant here. First, in one of the general reports on the West Indies which resulted from the wave of disturbances, Major G. St. J. Orde Browne remarked on the tendency to what he termed "agricultural gambling":

> There is a noticeable tendency in certain islands for land development to be taken up by people who only intend to produce an exportable article, and who will thus be rendered destitute by its failure; bananas are often selected, in the hope that disease will be absent for a sufficient number of seasons to make quick profits possible, though eventual disaster lies ahead.[13]

With this we may link, in the Jamaican context, the policy of the foreign banana companies (and, to a lesser extent, the local Banana Producers' Association) during the 1930s of increasing their purchases from small producers.[14] Obviously the knowledge that the major buyers were making more contracts with small growers would encourage the tendency to "agricultural gambling" in bananas. Money could be made by the little growers, the peasant farmers, if only they could get some land. In 1938 the major demand of the Jamaican banana carrier was the archetypal peasant demand—more land. Our third datum bears this out. The strikers in St. Mary refused to go back to work after Manley and Bustamante addressed them at Port Maria and Annotto Bay on May 31. They refused to go back when wages in the parish were raised on June 2; indeed, the biggest single disturbance occurred on the following day. It was only after the announcement of the new land-settlement scheme on June 5 that they began to listen to the government and then gradually to return to work.

The Anonymous Sufferer

We have now seen something of the major groups involved in the mass uprising of 1938. Some of the problems of hypothesis formation and data collection have also been illustrated. Nevertheless, it is worth dwelling on such problems a little longer. Nineteen thirty-eight was a mass movement; for the first time since 1865 the people forced the powers-that-be to listen to them, and this time to respond, not only repress. Yet history is made by the masses, not written by them. Even to a sympathetic middle-class figure like E. S. Barrington Williams, the demonstrators were, in retrospect, "marching mobs of irresponsibles," "lawless bands . . . driving terror into the hearts of law-abiding citizens."[15] In other contexts a few Marxist historians like George Rudé and Eric Hobsbawm have made the sufferer heard.[16] But in Jamaica in 1938 the voice of the sufferer remains almost completely silent. Occasionally something comes through—the words of Edgar Daley, quoted in note 7, or some of the strikers' songs.[17] Two contemporary weeklies, the *Jamaica Labour Weekly* and *Plain Talk*, are invaluable in bringing us closer to the masses. But it is extremely difficult to glean anything about their aims, except for what may be arrived at by the sort of process we have already followed. It is even more difficult to discover what sort of organizational forms came spontaneously into being, or what grass-roots leaders emerged. Sometimes a genuine worker appears, like Daley or W. Williams of the Kingston dockers. Sometimes the strikers sought an educated person to speak for them—a local pharmacist at Raheen Sugar Estate, for example, and a Baptist clergyman at Seville in St. Ann. But it is difficult to learn anything of the process of selection of the leaders and the nature of such leadership. The leaders whom we know were self-appointed and not of the masses—N. W. Manley and Alexander Bustamante.

A Note Concerning Heroes and Crowds

A full study of the role of Manley and Bustamante is not possible here. However, some of its aspects must be understood if we are to appreciate how the system survived its crisis in 1938. Significantly, almost as soon as the general disturbances broke out, the *Jamaica Standard*, in Jamaican conditions at that time the voice of "enlightened capitalism," called for "a man of high calibre, with no desire for personal aggrandizement, willing to come forward and take up this heavy burden of leadership."[18] Bustamante had already associated himself with the aspirations of the poor, but this had earned him arrest and imprisonment on May 24. Now Manley stepped forward to fill the breach, to the great relief of the middle class.[19] His mission, as he conceived it, was to work with the new Conciliation Board, made up of colonial officials, politicians, and businessmen, to express the views and demands of labor. On May 26, however, he was rebuffed by the dockers, who would not agree to return to work until Bustamante was released; as their leader, Williams, put it, "Now that we have seen that Jehovah has put this great knowledge in our heads today we are not going to let one another down."[20] On the twenty-eighth, Bustamante was released on Manley's surety. The governor's dislike of "agitators" was not proof against his realization that Manley needed Bustamante's help to get things under control. Bustamante immediately proved his worth; released just after noon, he had by nightfall persuaded the dockers to resume work.

From our point of view, the crucial question is the nature of the relationship of Manley and Bustamante with the masses. Were they Weberian charismatic leaders? Or were they perhaps playing A. W. Singham's conjectured role of the hero to the Jamaican crowd?[21] On the surface, either of these might seem more true of Bustamante than of Manley; the latter, former Rhodes scholar, eminent barrister, was not the sort of leader of whom crowds would sing, as they did later of his cousin, "We will follow Bustamante till we die." If we accept (as I do) Harold Wolpe's point that Weber's concept of charismatic authority is ambiguous because it leaves us uncertain as to whether that authority is based on pre-existing values or creates new ones, we come nearer to the heart of the matter.[22] Agreeing again with Wolpe that the general drift of Weber is to suggest that charismatic authority creates values rather than exploits them, then Manley's position was not a charismatic one. It depended rather upon the acceptance by the masses of the already existing values of the class structure, the acceptance of a hierarchy of classes, which gave a middle-class figure like Manley the right to claim superior wisdom and the ability to put the case of the masses better than they could: "My head is wiser than yours tonight," as he put it in a speech to strikers at Highgate, appealing for "faith, hope and trust in the people who are trying to help you."[23] Or, as Bustamante said of Manley to another crowd at Annotto Bay: "He had nothing to gain by helping them save the pleasure of knowing that he had helped to make them happy."[24]

The important point about Bustamante in terms of the values

that he put before his followers is that his position was identical with that of Manley. He too was not charismatic, if by that we mean a value-creating figure. In his speeches he skillfully associated himself with Manley as a person who came from a higher social level, and who, at great personal cost, was seeking to help the sufferer. Once again, he was dependent upon the acceptance by the masses of the existing values of the class structure. His view of his relationship with his followers is tellingly revealed in a single sentence: "The day you have leaders, the police will not have to come out, for you will all be at your homes while I am with the employers adjusting matters on your behalf."[25]

If Bustamante was no Weberian charismatic figure, neither was he Singham's hero. He himself had not risen from the crowd. Indeed, as indicated above, his whole strategy was to suggest the opposite. Nor was he, like the hero, challenging the legitimacy of the colonial system. Again, he certainly did not "threaten to upset the whole system of social relations within the colony."[26] Quite the contrary, his whole message was that labor's problems must be solved within the existing class system and colonial economic and political structures. Bustamante's supreme ability as a leader was that he could manipulate accepted values, which had not been rejected by the masses, despite their discontents, in favor of some new consciousness of their own. Bustamante, Manley, and the masses (the crucial factor) all subscribed to the views of A. G. S. Coombs: "Leaders are what the labourers want. Good leaders, Temperate Speeches, work within the bounds of British Principles and Policies, with grim determination you must win."[27] As might be supposed, Coombs was at this time playing exactly the same role as Bustamante and Manley. Indeed, in terms of 1938, his activities have suffered an undeserved eclipse; it was Coombs and his associates in the Workers' and Tradesmen's Union who were responsible for the work of mediation in the west and center of the island.

In terms of Singham's analysis, it might be argued that Bustamante and Manley conform to his type of the "middle-class hero," "claiming that he has sacrificed his career for the sake of helping the people."[28] As it stands at the moment, however, the concept cannot take us any further in our analysis, in part because of its own ambiguity.[29] More particularly, if Singham intends the middle-class hero to be seen as opposed to the colonial system, as he apparently does, then neither Manley nor Bustamante can be regarded as falling within this category in mid-1938, though Manley's views were changed by his experiences then. Perhaps we might rather speak of another type of leader, "the colonial hero as mediator." A hero to the masses because he acts as their spokesman to the authorities in a situation in which they can imagine no other form of communication, he is also a hero to the powers-that-be: as the official report on the disturbances said of Manley, "He appreciated that what was desired could only be obtained by constitutional means and that if the disturbances were to continue, the chief sufferers would be the labouring classes themselves."[30]

Problems of Economic Structural Analysis

Up to this point we have raised a number of related problems in terms of various aspects of the events of May and June 1938 and put forward some hypotheses. It would be extremely satisfying if we could now bring all these elements together and relate them by showing their dialectical relationship with total economic and political structures. This, unfortunately, I am not in a position to do. It would require an act of historical re-creation, the delineation of the total position thirty years ago, for which I do not at present possess the data. (Indeed, I am rather doubtful whether sufficient data exist to answer all the questions we would need to ask for a complete picture.) Nevertheless, what we might do is to raise some of the major problems and indicate some of the main areas in which much more data need to be acquired if we are fully to understand the Jamaican colonial system in 1938 and the crisis which it underwent.

1. *The peasant farmer.* It should already be evident that analysis at this level is essential for an understanding of 1938 and beyond. Not only have the rural areas been insufficiently emphasized in previous descriptions and analyses of events but we have to remember also that the migrants who went abroad and returned, and the people who moved into the corporate area looking for work, were for the most part from those areas.[31] In 1938 the Jamaican economy was completely based upon agriculture; there was no bauxite industry and little tourism (Sir Edward Denham was noted for trying to promote this). This makes it more than ever essential to analyze the class structure of rural Jamaica. Orde Browne in his report distinguishes four types of peasant farmer in the West Indies: the estate laborer who had only a small vegetable garden; the wage laborer who possessed his own plot of land, though this was too small to provide anything but a site for his house and some food; "the wage-earning laborer who is also part peasant proprietor," with two to three acres (three acres

seem to have been enough to provide a reasonable return from bananas); and the peasant proprietor working full time on his land and raising food and export crops.[32] This would be a useful point at which to begin to look at matters such as numbers of farmers in each group, sizes of holdings, and types of land tenure. This last subject is of particular potential importance because of the possible significance of government land-settlement schemes, involving, for example, nearly six thousand acres in Clarendon and over three thousand in Manchester in 1938.[33] Also in terms of land tenure, the whole phenomenon of squatting on land without legal rights deserves attention. I have already suggested certain categories of peasant farmers in the banana areas who seem to have been most involved in radical action in 1938; what evidence I have reveals no direct connection between land-settlement schemes (except ex-soldiers in Manchester) or squatting and the disturbances.

In terms of the structure of rural Jamaica, special attention also needs to be paid to the various structural segments. It is probably impossible to generalize fruitfully for the whole agricultural population. Thus, we need to look at the structure of banana growing separately from cane. For the latter, it would be interesting to know something about the relations between independent cane farmers and the big estates. Were the cane farmers, for example, active in the 1938 disturbances? On the surface it does not seem so, but, if not, were they merely passive, or did they perhaps supply special constables to the government? I have already raised the problem of possible differential reactions on the estates themselves. Then there are coconut plantation workers, who featured strongly in the disturbances; growers of pimento, which had been badly hit by disease; and coffee-growing workers, who do not seem to have been involved in the disturbances.

2. *The plantocracy.* All the discussion so far has been in terms of who rioted, not who was rioted against. It is abundantly clear that the colonial administration and expatriate business were not the only targets; indeed, I would argue that they were not even the prime targets. In bananas the expatriate companies had reduced their role as growers (as opposed to buyers) by 1938. The United Fruit Company had pulled out of Portland and Clarendon and confined its activities as a grower virtually to St. Thomas and St. Catherine, often reducing the size of its plantations there. We have already noted the tendency to replace this source of supply by buying from the smaller growers. What is significant, however, is that the buying was done through a network of agents who were

often growers themselves, with plantation owners like F. H. and H. G. DeLisser, A. D. Goffe, and Isachar Magnus among the most important agents. Eighteen of the sixty-two agents in 1935 were receiving £2,000 or more a year, and two over £10,000, from their purchasing alone, while the cost of wharf labor was static or actually declining.[34] Reading between the lines of the report on bananas of 1936, it is obvious that the whole agency system was a source of great discontent.[35] Significantly, DeLisser, Goffe, and Magnus figure largely among the names of prime targets for strikes in 1938. From the example of data on the ownership and control patterns in this one structural segment of the economy, it is to be hoped that it can be seen in general how important is this question of the role of the Jamaican plantocracy and their relations with foreign enterprise.

Also of great importance is the relationship between Jamaican and expatriate economic interests and the colonial administration. One aspect of this can be seen in the personnel of the new conciliation board to deal with labor disputes—the island treasurer, a retired attorney general, a retired assistant colonial secretary, the mayor of Kingston, a former general manager of the Jamaica division of the United Fruit Company, the member of the Legislative Council for Manchester, who was a big citrus and banana planter at Christiana, and H. P. Jacobs, at that time news editor of the *Standard* (presumably to act as a "liberal" element). On the other hand, we must be sensitive to possible clashes of interest, as in the hint conveyed by the *Gleaner*, writing about Denham after his death: "Some public utterances of his have been definitely socialistic."[36] It is evident that in the last few years before the uprising the administration was becoming alarmed about the situation, and was belatedly endeavoring to collect information and pass remedial legislation. It is equally obvious that it had neither the tools nor the necessary support from the rich to be effective.

Problems of Political Structural Analysis

At this point it seems apt to pass on to the political structure, since the problems of analysis of economic and political control are so closely interwoven. It seems hardly necessary to point out that in 1938 it was the classical British colonial pattern which prevailed politically, with the substantial power formally in the hands of the governor and his administrative subordinates, and the only element of "popular" participation the tiny part of the population qualified to vote in local and Legislative Council elections. On the other hand, our understanding of political power in Jamaica in 1938 (and beyond) cannot be complete unless we take into account the parish level. Increasingly I am of the opinion that the introduction of Crown Colony government from 1865 only grafted a new set of central institutions, political relationships, and sources of power onto the old power structure, which remained virtually intact in the parishes. At that level the plantocracy still controlled major segments of the economy, through land ownership and through their ability to control new institutions developing since 1865, like banana-buying agencies and agricultural credit banks. Through the parochial boards and the office of Custos Rotulorum they were able to control the parishes politically, and they could manipulate the legal system by filling the posts of local justices of the peace. Last, they had a link to the center through the parish member of the Legislative Council. Thus any full understanding of the events of 1938 must involve analyses of parish power structures, and, at least in those parishes in the north and east where the peasant-farmer element was a major factor in the uprising, it will be found that action was usually directed against those who played large parts both in the economic and political structures of districts and parishes.

Two other dimensions of political activity in Jamaica in 1938 require further investigation. One of these is the question of organization at the grass-roots level. The masses were not necessarily the amorphous lump which the name seems to suggest. The 1930s witnessed the emergence of numerous organizations, in which it would seem that returning migrants from the United States, Cuba, and Central America often played an important leadership role. Some of them are fairly well known already, like the National Reform Association and the Federation of Citizens' Associations. These were, however, middle-class organizations. We need to know far more about other groups like the Workers' and Tradesmen's Union, the Universal Negro Improvement Association (which founded a new division, Harmony, in May 1938), the Jamaica Protective Association, the Jamaica Labour party (formed in April 1937 and thus antedating Bustamante's by six years), the Artisan's Federated Union, the Social Reconstruction League, and the Jamaica Permanent Development Convention, to name only some of those which I have come across in my research. It is evident that many such groups were formed by elements like shopkeepers and small contractors, and were concerned with economic "self-help" and mutual protection against big business. Nevertheless, even these were much closer to the masses than anything that had gone before (with Bogle and Bedward as exceptions, insofar as they had permanent organizations). Nor is it a necessary detraction from their significance that their membership was obviously small in most cases. Their emergence in the 1930s is a sign that at some lower levels of the class hierarchy a consciousness was beginning to emerge which could only in the end find itself opposed to existing power structures. This organizational activity was the first sign of a praxis—a testing of emerging consciousness against objective reality through action—which was to have important future repercussions.

All of this activity, however, was urban in nature. Whatever new consciousness may have begun to develop in the towns, there is little sign of new organizational developments in the rural areas. Yet there was one important exception, and further research may show it not to have been unique. Apparently, early in 1938 Robert E. Rumble founded the Poor Man's Improvement Land Settlement and Labour Association in Upper Clarendon. This seems to have been a squatters' organization, and it became involved in court cases regarding tenants at Trout Hall and Cocoa Walk. In a petition to the governor dated April 23, 1938, it claimed eight hundred members.[37] Ideologically it was comparatively advanced, since Rumble drew his views on land, rent, and taxes from the writings of Henry George, and was in touch with the Henry George Foundation in London. Such an organization is obviously of great significance, and it is extremely interesting that it seems to have played no significant part in the May-June disturbances, something which, if true, will require explanation.[38]

The other political dimension at the mass level which needs further study is the influence of the Garveyite movement after the departure of the founder from Jamaica in 1935. Garvey himself had in his last years in the island been turning his attention more specifically than before to problems of poverty and unemployment and trade-union organization.[39] Nevertheless, the development of Garveyism after 1935 is ambivalent. On the one hand, in terms of those who remained linked with the formal UNIA structure, it tended increasingly to express the aspirations of the petty bourgeoisie and the less successful of the black bourgeoisie, whose concern was with such forms of economic organization as banks and loan societies, which would provide capital and enhance their business competitiveness. Thus, already by 1938 Garveyites were prominent in groups like the Protective League and the Permanent Development Convention. It is significant in this respect that there was a noticeable influx of leading

UNIA members into the PNP (People's National Party) after September 1938.

On the other hand, Garveyism in the broadest ideological sense, with its emphasis on blackness, Africa, and Ethiopia, had its effect on the sufferers. For the reasons discussed in an earlier section, it is at this level that it is most difficult to obtain information, but one can at least cite the most obvious example, the Ras Tafari movement, which owed its origins, in part at least, to a feedback from Garveyism in Central America and the United States.[40] By March 1938 Ras Tafari was becoming significant enough to provoke a judge's remark on "the undoubted nuisance the Ras Tafari people were becoming," and in the same month there were police raids on cult members in different parts of the island.[41] Though at present I know of only one instance of explicit Rastafarian (or Rastafarian-type) participation in the events of May-June 1938, this aspect of the consciousness of the masses requires very careful study.

1938, Rebellion or Revolution?

If we are to conclude this discussion by asking whether the events of 1938 constituted a rebellion or a revolution, some consideration of terms is necessary. I would distinguish a rebellion from a revolution along two main lines. First, rebels accept the prevailing social values, particularly those concerning the class system. What they are seeking to do, in fact, is to restore those values—or, more accurately, an idealized version of them— maintaining that they have been flouted. Revolutionaries, on the other hand, assert against existing values a counterconsciousness with values of its own. Second, rebels do not seek major structural change; they desire either minor adjustments, or else that the system should work in the idealized fashion which its own ideology (values) suggests that it should. (The rebels may, of course, be seeking both things.) Revolutionaries believe that their ultimate aims in terms of their new values can only be achieved if existing structures are destroyed and rebuilt. A further rider might be added to these distinctions. It follows from the whole question of consciousness that the aims of revolutionaries are likely to be far more clearly articulated than those of rebels.

Seen in this light, there can be little doubt that the events of May-June 1938 in Jamaica were rebellious rather than revolutionary. From the discussion above, we can see that the strikers and demonstrators were demanding only those things which they believed the existing system to be capable of giving them—higher wages, more work, and more land. In objective terms the system was in fact capable of raising wages, and did so, for dockers and banana and sugar workers. We must have grave doubts, however, whether the system of 1938 was objectively capable of providing more work or substantially increasing the amount of land in the hands of peasant farmers. More especially, in the latter case, it may be doubted whether the existing system was capable of providing the whole range of structural features, particularly credit and marketing facilities, which would have been needed to establish peasant farming as the dominant sector of the economy— a step that would have been the only permanent solution to the unemployment problem. Certainly, although we cannot go into the matter here, the next few years saw the failure of the much-trumpeted "New Deal" in land settlement first announced on June 5. Thus, what the rebels *believed* the system capable of granting them, it in fact substantially could not; this is the basic contradiction in the whole situation.

Thus, while the situation in Jamaica in 1938 was, in terms of the conscious aims of the masses, only a rebellion, its dialectic was that of a revolution. The system could only have met the demands of the masses if there had been major structural change, in other words, revolution; the sufferers were revolutionary in spite of themselves. Two essential prerequisites were missing from the situation if revolution was in fact to come about—a new consciousness on the part of the sufferers which they could oppose to existing values and an organization to lead them.

We have seen enough by now to know that such a consciousness did not exist. The proliferation of organizations in the 1930s suggests that, given a suitable praxis, one might have emerged, as it did in Cuba, but 1938 was far too soon. (The process took thirty years in Cuba.) If anything, the masses at that stage tended to eschew political consciousness and take refuge in the millennial dreams of Ras Tafari or the mysteries of Pocomania. That is, if they were sufficiently alienated to wish to take refuge at all; the role of Manley and Bustamante amply demonstrates that many, if not most, were still prepared to accept the existing social structure and trust the words of their "betters"—"My head is wiser than yours tonight." Similarly, the role of the two middle-class leaders and A. G. S. Coombs illuminates the converse absence of any even potentially revolutionary leaders. Despite the gloomy muttering of the wealthy that Cuban communists, "or certain persons here receiving emoluments from the communist party in Cuba," were responsible for Frome and other strikes, only a literal handful of people on the island regarded themselves as Marxists, and they were not organized.[42]

In 1938, then, the politics of protest was rebellious, but not yet revolutionary. If praxis were ever to make it such, much depended upon the policy adopted by the colonial administration and by the upper and middle classes. Force was of course part of this policy, with the police backed up by six platoons of the Sherwood Foresters and nearly five thousand armed special constables, and two cruisers of the Royal Navy standing offshore. Concessions were another part—the appointment of the conciliation board, its work in persuading employers to grant wage increases, finally the announcement of the "New Deal" in land. The plantocracy, obviously alarmed by events, concurred in all this, at least in public; no major reactionary voice was heard. Instinctively planto-crats and administrators realized the line to take—separate the "workers" from the "hooligans" and grant limited concessions to one while suppressing the other. Thus, the resident magistrate of St. Catherine made this perfectly plain in the course of charging a group of alleged rioters. Recognizing that men had a right to expect work, if available (an important reservation), and "a fair living wage," he reminded the "working class" that

> everything is being done for you by those that are to do so, in a dispassionate manner. Those people will understand that when I say that the present deliberations must be done with perfect quiet. The only thing to be done at the moment is to leave the matter to those who are working on your behalf.

On the other hand,

> all hooliganism and ruffianism will be suppressed and I want the hooligans and roughs to know that the honest workers and citizens have a feeling of hatred for them in their hearts. The Law protects the lives and properties of all citizens, and it protects them to such an extent that it goes the length of making provisions whereby killing could be done whilst one's life or one's property was in danger.

Having thus reminded "honest citizens" that violence used to defend the system had the sanction of the state, the magistrate adjured his listeners to "Go away and take to heart what I have said."[43]

Putting this line into practice, the powers-that-be turned to Coombs, Manley, and—after initial hesitation—Bustamante. With this was initiated the whole policy of building a "legitimate" labor movement, which the few existing labor leaders, the emerging middle-class leaders, and the government all now felt to be essential. Thus the "politics of protest" was met with the "politics of control." The foundation of the Bustamante Industrial Trade Union, then of the PNP, as another "legitimate" way of expressing demands, and then of the Trade Union Congress began the whole process of development of modern Jamaican politics. That, however, takes us far beyond the scope of this paper, which has sought merely to show some of the methodological problems involved in the analysis of the events of May and June 1938 and some of the implications of those events.

Notes

1. Ultimately, a discussion of 1938 will form a chapter of my much longer study, "The Politics of Protest in Jamaica, 1938-62."

2. O. W. Phelps, "Rise of the Labour Movement in Jamaica," *Social and Economic Studies* 9, no. 4: especially pp. 422–35.

3. *Report (with Appendices) of the Commission appointed to enquire into the Disturbances which occurred on Frome Estate in Westmoreland on 2nd May, 1938* (Kingston: Government Printing Office, 1938); and *Report (with Appendices) of the Commission appointed to enquire into the Disturbances which occurred in Jamaica Between the 23rd May, and the 8th June, 1938* (Kingston: Government Printing Office, 1938).

4. *West India Royal Commission Report,* Cmd. 6607 (London: H.M.S.O., 1945).

5. *Report of the Disturbances in Jamaica,* p. 2.

6. "Resentment Is Hiding Under Montego Bay's Peaceful Face," *Jamaica Standard,* June 18, 1938, p. 4.

7. His actual words, given in the report, are worth recording, since the voice of the sufferer is rarely heard: "He said 'No, not a rass. You have you gun. I have my stick.'" (*Report of the Disturbances in Jamaica,* p. 14.)

8. Len S. Nembhard, *Jamaica: The Awakening* (Kingston, 1943), p. 13.

9. Phelps, "Rise of the Labour Movement."

10. There was, indeed, a whole phenomenon of "middle-class backlash" in 1938, as a result of attempts to meet labor's demands. As early as May 28, letters and articles began to appear in the press, typified by Esther Chapman's plea for "the uncomplaining, unstriking mass known as the middle classes, who find it difficult to maintain the respectability and refinement which their upbringing imposes and their employment demands upon narrow means." "This class," she went on, "must not be forgotten." ("A Plea for Sanity," *Daily Gleaner,* June 2, 1938, p. 7.) I am inclined to link the emergence of the People's National Party in September with this "backlash."

11. A hypothesis worth testing, which suggests itself on a preliminary survey, is that strikes and other action were by no means solely, and possibly not even primarily, directed against foreign-owned estates.

At least nine of the fourteen worst-hit estates belonged to Jamaicans, including such well-known names as Lindo, Charley, and Farquharson. This is consonant with certain questions concerning the structure of the Jamaican economy in 1938, which will be discussed later in this paper.

12. See *The Report of the Jamaica Banana Commission 1936* (Kingston: Government Printing Office, 1936), table on p. 83. In order to give some perspective on these losses, it might be useful to note that in 1933-1934 the total acreage under bananas in St. Mary had been 22,710.

13. *Labour Conditions in the West Indies,* Cmd. 6070 (London: H.M.S.O., 1939), p. 33.

14. The changing pattern can be seen in the table on p. 9 of the *Report of the Jamaica Banana Commission.*

15. E. S. Barrington Williams, *Progress of a People* (Kingston, n.d.), p. 43. Williams played an important part, as secretary of the Social Reconstruction League, in holding public meetings in Kingston and giving a platform to Bustamante.

16. See, for example, Rude's *The Crowd in the French Revolution* and Hobsbawms' *Primitive Rebels.*

17. Such as "For We Are Jolly Good Strikers" (to be sung to the tune of "For He's a Jolly Good Fellow") and "White Man Ha' de Money, Black Man Ha' de Labor" (apparently to the tune of "John Brown's Body").

18. Editorial, May 25, 1938, p. 6.

19. See, for example, the *Standard* editorial on May 28, and, on the same p. 6, the column by "Sinbad" and letter from P. M. Sherlock, then headmaster of Wolmer's Boys' School.

20. *Daily Gleaner,* May 27, 1938, p. 18.

21. A. W. Singham, *The Hero and the Crowd in a Colonial Polity* (New Haven: Yale University Press, 1968).

22. "A Critical Analysis of Some Aspects of Charisma," *The Sociological Review* 16, no. 3, New Series (November 1968); see especially pp. 306–12.

23. *Daily Gleaner,* June 4, 1938, p. 19.

24. *Jamaica Standard,* June 6, 1938, p. 4.

25. *Gleaner,* June 4, 1938, p. 19.

26. Singham, *The Hero and the Crowd,* p. 323.

27. *Jamaica Standard,* June 2, 1938, letter on p. 5.

28. Singham, *The Hero and the Crowd,* p. 152.

29. Thus, it seems to be suggested in different places that this kind of hero is socially from the middle class, but a hero to the *masses* (pp. 152 and 315), and that he is a middle-class figure who is a hero of the *middle class* (pp. 259–60). Singham may, however, intend him to be both.

30. *Report of the Disturbances in Jamaica,* p. 3.

31. Or were they? Some work on migration in Africa seems to suggest a pattern of moving indirectly from rural areas into large towns via

smaller ones. And did people migrate abroad directly from the rural areas, or after a period of trying their luck in Kingston?

32. *Labour Conditions in the West Indies,* pp. 32–33.

33. There were twenty-one land-settlement schemes in mid-1938, and thirteen more with plots not yet allocated. See Appendices 13 and 63, *Minutes of the Legislative Council of Jamaica for the Year 1938* (Kingston: Government Printer, 1940).

34. See tables on pp. 77 and 79 of the *Report of the Jamaica Banana Commission.*

35. The key paragraph is in Appendix F, p. 75: "The present agency system allows one agent to control large areas of country and large quantities of bananas. The disadvantages of this system are two-fold. Firstly, an agent cannot keep in contact with large numbers of contractors and consequently tends to allow direct control to rest in the hands of a less responsible sub-agent. Secondly, the knowledge that one man is controlling and drawing commission on a large number of bananas has a bad psychological effect on the mind of the small grower."

36. *Daily Gleaner,* June 3, 1938, p. 1.

37. *Plain Talk,* April 30, 1938, p. 7.

38. While writing the first draft of this paper, I learned that Mr. Rumble is still alive, but I was unable to interview him before leaving Jamaica.

39. See Richard Hart, "The Life and Resurrection of Marcus Garvey," *Race* 9, no. 2 (October 1967): 226.

40. See M. G. Smith, Roy Augier, and Rex Nettleford, *The Ras Tafari Movement in Kingston, Jamaica* (Kingston: Institute of Social and Economic Research, U.W.I., 1960), pp. 8–10.

41. See reports in the *Jamaica Standard,* March 15, 1938, pp. 3 and 4; and March 16, 1938, p. 4.

42. See the *Daily Gleaner,* May 23, 1938, p. 11.

43. The speech is reported in the *Daily Gleaner,* June 2, 1938, which endorsed the magistrate's "good counsel."

Part 3

Strategies of Working-Class Action

The apparent differences in living standards between urban (industrial, commercial, and public) employees and the peasantry of the Third World have often led commentators to conceive urban workers as a "labor aristocracy"—severed from the conditions of poverty that oppress the people of the countryside. Such a theory, which in fact is an extension of Lenin's conception of the metropolitan labor aristocracy nurtured by imperialism into the Third World, at the very least holds that the political struggles of urban workers can be held distinct from those of the peasantry.

Yet one should be wary of accepting such a distinction too readily. As has been shown in earlier parts of this book, the categories "worker" and "peasant" are by no means easy to separate, and, even where a clear distinction exists, the ties of religion, kinship, environment, and so on often produce a blending of the social circumstances of these two groups. There are certainly particular countries, particular unions, and particular circumstances where workers, in an attempt to secure better wages and conditions, identify "upwardly" to patrons and politicians who are seen as providers and gatekeepers of resources, both economic and political. This attempt by workers to secure a foothold in the conventional political forums of political parties, parliaments, and other institutions is considered here as one of the possible strategies of action available to the working class. The article by Ramaswamy on the case of Indian trade unions exemplifies the interpenetration of party politics and trade unionism. Ramaswamy's study, based on fieldwork between 1963 and 1970 among the textile workers of Tamilnadu, is directed principally to examining the extent and intensity of workers' political commitment as well as the form in which this is expressed. In fact, the form seems very much dictated by the limitations of the parliamentary system itself. On the one hand, as the parliamentary struggle evolves, parties twist and turn to appeal to their electoral constituencies, among whom urban workers are an important element—in themselves and as leaders of public opinion. On the other hand, unions in this situation either tie themselves to the apron strings of a single political party—in this case the Praja Socialist party—or trade their influence and favor between several parties. The net result is hardly spectacular or revolutionary—the unions fragment, while their capacity for independent political action is vitiated and emasculated in the attempt to secure marginal political advantages.

The "parliamentary road" seems in most cases to offer little to the mass of workers, even where a parliament continues to survive, which, of course, is increasingly rare in Third-World countries. A second strategy of working-class action is to use their own primary form of influence—the withdrawal of their labor power in a strike. Kearney's article deals directly with the political impact of strikes in Sri Lanka ("Ceylon," at the time of his writing). He trisects the strikes he is concerned with into those that are overtly and solely political, those that combine industrial and political demands, and those which are primarily industrial but involve the prestige and interest of the government and therefore have necessary political implications. While obviously these distinctions are not watertight, the author does provide a number of examples drawn from the course of Sri Lanka's recent trade-union history which validate his general classification. Kearney also mentions the interesting form of protest, used also in other parts of Asia, of the "hartal," in which shops are shut and black flags are flown from the window, usually in a short-term protest against a particular piece of government legislation. Insofar as workers participate or act as community leaders in such events, they can be seen as representing a generalized popular reaction, rather like the reactions of Parisians to the occupying German army or like the Palestinians protesting the Israeli occupation of the West Bank. But Kearney, of course, deals with more conventionally defined strikes, including several strikes in which an initially economistic demand became politicized by the government. As the government is often the major employer in Third-World countries, its prestige can be affected both in terms of its perceived managerial capacity and, more generally, of its political legitimacy.

Strikes and support for political parties are limited forms of working-class action compared with the idea of workers seizing control of the means of production and running the show for themselves. In the selection from Algeria, Clegg documents the brief period when autogestion—*workers' self-management—seemed possible. Clegg argues that though workers seized* part *of the control over the means of production during the height of the revolutionary thrust in Algeria (1962), they lost their control to the party and administrative bureaucracy, which came to look increasingly like a "new bourgeoisie." The rapid loss of control by the workers to the petty bourgeoisie of the colonial period, i.e., the managers of the post-colonial period, is explained by three principal arguments: (1) the origins of the* comités de gestion *as an emergency measure adopted by workers when the former owners abandoned their enterprise (i.e., the origins of the program were defensive, not positive); (2) the limited horizons of the workers, derived from their immediate material needs; and (3) the continuing global dominance of neoimperialism. In developing these arguments, Clegg has opened up a major (and as yet not seriously debated) encounter with "Fanonism." The Algerian struggle was anticolonial, not anticapitalist; it was for independence, not for socialism. Clegg argues that to see the struggle against colonialism as itself revolutionary is a profound error perpetrated by Fanon and his followers. Clegg then makes a statement which will, no doubt, surprise those who had accepted a Fanonist view of the Algerian struggle: "Neither the peasantry nor the truly 'wretched'—the subproletariat—can be said to have played an objectively revolutionary role in Algeria." While this assertion separates the social categories we have earlier argued are difficult to sever, Clegg's emphasis does offer an explanation as to why the revolutionary possibilities of Algerian society have been absorbed so easily by the intendants of the postcolonial state.*

Clegg's study of autogestion, *together with Chesneaux's study of the Chinese labor movement (extracted in part 1 of this volume), provides the empirical referent for Post's more theoretical approach to the question of a worker-peasant alliance, the fourth and final strategy of working-class action considered here. The possibilities and limitations of a worker-peasant alliance are perhaps the major questions confronting revolutionary strategy in the Third World today. Post, however, probably exaggerates the extent to which left-wing Third-World theorists accept this proposition. We have little doubt that there are still some nineteenth-century Marxists who would have us sacrifice all other social classes on the altar of the industrial working class; equally there are (perhaps many more) dogmatic Fanonists, Narodniks, and Guevarists who would have us believe in the exclusive revolutionary authenticity of the peasantry. But let us take these positions as unconvincing and consider the construction of a worker-peasant alliance. As Post points out, this question has to be addressed at different levels. At the level of ideas and organization certainly, but also at the base levels—the penetration, articulation, and disarticulation of modes of production. It is at the substructural level that we see the complex lines of class formation and class identity occurring—the agricultural worker, seasonal and permanent, the peasant engaged in petty commodity production, and so on. In other words, in underdeveloped capitalist societies a worker-peasant alliance should not be read as a formal contract between two distinct identities, but more precisely as a combination and interpenetration of these two entities such that a mutual political interest is often paralleled by a common oppressive situation.*

Finally, it is necessary to emphasize that engaging in party politics, undertaking strike actions, creating thrusts toward workers' self-management, and moving toward worker-peasant alliances do not exhaust the possible range of working-class strategies. Linking with a populist party like that of Perón brought some immediate benefits to the workers of Argentina, while in many countries workers and union leaders have attempted (usually without success) to launch a political party directly answerable to the rank and file. Space forbids the inclusion of readings on these and other forms of working-class struggle.

Workers and Managers in Algeria

Ian Clegg

The class struggle for political and economic control of independent Algeria and other structural factors formed the context within which *autogestion* ("self-management") emerged and which eventually molded its defeat. The colonial prehistory, the fight for independence, the revolution of 1962, the economic and social structures all deeply affected the modes of political and economic organization. The eventual political victory of the new bourgeoisie reflected a pre-established hegemony over the means of production. Though part of the means of production was seized by the workers in 1962, they lost this control to the "new bourgeoisie." The *décrets de mars* that handed over the supervision of *autogestion* to an unreconstituted administration clearly allowed this bureaucracy to control the economic activities of the *comités de gestion*. Equally, the decrees enabled them to practice widespread manipulation and intervention in the composition of the *comités* and their day-to-day functioning.

The de facto administrative control of the machinery of *autogestion,* the failure of the revolution to extend any further than a change in the direct management of production, the restriction of the principles of *autogestion* to the point of production, all explain, on an external level, the eventual defeat of the revolution. What they do not explain is why many *comités de gestion* and their workers accepted this counterrevolution; how in face of the gains of 1962-1963 it was possible for the new bourgeoisie to impose its control so rapidly. To understand this we have to look at the way *autogestion* operated within the majority of the enterprises under self-management; in other words, how the component parts of the system—director, *comité de gestion,* and workers—grasped the concept of self-management. It is here that we come face-to-face with the question of the extent and nature of the consciousness of the Algerian working class. A large part of the success or failure of the Algerian revolution depended, in the last analysis, on the ability of the working class to grasp the political implications of *autogestion.*

Extracted from Ian Clegg, *Workers' Self-Management in Algeria* (London: Allen Lane; and New York: Monthly Review Press, 1971). Copyright © 1971 by Ian Clegg, and reprinted with permission.

The Director and the Comité de Gestion

Any discussion of the role of management in workers' self-management involves the identification of two main groups: the nonelected director and administrative staff, and the elected management committee. The relative powers of these groups to affect decisions depends to a large extent on the relation between the state and the enterprise. In the Yugoslav experience of self-management the influence of the director was at its highest when state controls over the enterprise were greatest. The slackening of state controls led to the erosion of directorial power and the appearance of a "factory bureaucracy." Although the managerial powers of this bureaucracy are similar to those of the director, its composition is heterogeneous. The exact composition of this group has to be related to the social, political, and economic structures of the country concerned.

In Algeria, although the *décrets de mars* created the post of director, the number of people trained in the appropriate technical skills was extremely low. The organization of the FLN was too fragmented, its ideological content too eclectic to create a homogeneous body of loyal cadres as had been possible for the Communist party in Yugoslavia. In this situation the government could not always rely on the director to represent the interests of the state. The administration had to evolve other means of control over the economic and political actions of the concerns under *autogestion*. As I have already described, the two major means used in this process were electoral manipulation and strict economic control.

Economic independence was effectively reduced by the administrative control of sales, profits, and credit. The overt success of the directors and the administratively manipulated *comités* was less apparent in containing *autogestion*, economically or politically. The way in which these two elements succeeded in deforming the original concept of *autogestion* lay less in the fact that they were a transmission belt for state policy than in the class values they possessed and developed. In other words, it is necessary to identify subjective expressions of class interest rather than develop a conscious exposition of an objective political policy.

The administrative cadres of independent Algeria were largely composed of lower-middle-class elements or, more correctly, the petty bourgeoisie of the colonial period. Apart from a small minority of genuine revolutionary militants this was the only class with sufficient opportunity and educational background for it to become upwardly mobile. Those who became directors in nationalized enterprises, whether state-run or self-managed, formed part of this social group.[. . .]

The absence of ideological commitment, the stresses of mobility and the lack of any immediate conscious class orientation created an anomic situation for the majority of the administrative cadres. In the absence of any ethical code or explicit class structure with which to identify, the new bureaucrats sought, not unnaturally, satisfaction in material terms. The only life-style which they could emulate was that of the *pieds-noirs*. In view of the early strict "official" morality on salary differentials, the only access to material enrichment was through corruption. Corruption, in the sense of the appropriation of social property for personal ends, became an accepted mode of material advancement within the administration.

The effect of this type of corruption on *comités de gestion* is shown by the following instances. The iron-mining complex of Zaccar, Miliana, was placed under *autogestion* in July 1963. The first director was imprisoned after selling the complex products for his own profit. The second director hired his own friends as the administrative staff. He kept the profits made by an eighty-hectare farm attached to the complex for his own use. He used the repair shops to repair private cars and again took the proceeds. Finally, he sold machinery, destined for the complex, to private industry, again taking the profits.[1] Another case concerns the *Société d'Entreprise de Routes en Algérie,* controlling four concerns in Algiers and two in Oran. The European owners left in 1963 and, after six months' stoppage, during which the army tried to take over the road-mending machinery, a government *commissaire* was appointed. The *commissaire* dismissed many of the original workers, even framing some of them for theft. In 1965 he disappeared, and the workers set up a *comité de gestion*. They found that there were only 560 dinars left in the firm's account and that the *commissaire* had drawn out 140,000 dinars before fleeing the country.[2][. . .]

Corruption was not usually as flagrant as this. It was mostly confined to petty embezzlement. In recent years it has become less frequent. The administration, initially in an anomic situation extremely conducive to deviation, became consolidated as a class. It came to possess a value system and ideology that confirmed individual members in their status as part of a hegemonic class, which had begun to establish its own system of rewards. There is a growing identification with the technocratic ideas expressed by the group in power, even though financial rewards, now officially condoned, are still important. The growing homogeneity in terms of values and consciousness has created a greater coherence in the activities of the state organs and their subordinate administrators. Bureaucrats have moved from utilizing the situation for their own immediate personal ends to using it for class ends.

The role of the director within the enterprise is intimately related to the composition and attitudes of the *comité de gestion* and its president. The vagueness of the original decrees created an implicit jurisdictional conflict between director and *comité*. Within this arena of possible conflict the ability of the director to impose either his own or the state's goals lies in several factors. The strength of his position rests on his connections with the administration (party and state), his technical knowledge, and the relative inability of the workers to assert their formal rights because of illiteracy, lack of technical expertise, or a low level of political training.

Except in the larger enterprises in industry, the factor of the director's technical competence did not play a large part in enabling him to dominate *comités de gestion*. The lack of trained technical or managerial cadres often meant that directors were less competent to take decisions on production than the more experienced workers. A far more important factor was the workers' own uncertainty as to their rights. There was no really effective campaign to explain the *décrets de mars*, and the overwhelming level of illiteracy meant that few workers could read the published texts. As Juliette Minces points out, although the press in the early days was in the hands of left-wing elements supporting *autogestion*, few could read it, and most people relied instead on the radio, which did not display the same enthusiasm.[3] In agriculture, the director, or *chargé de gestion*, was often the only literate member of the concern and was thus usually called upon to explain the decrees. In the large towns, the Union Générale des Travailleurs Algériens (UGTA) made great efforts to create a clear awareness of the content and meaning of the decrees and kept a close watch on the activities of directors.

Despite the opportunites, the directors in *autogestion* played a relatively minor role in deforming the original purposes of the decrees. Certainly they were able to manipulate the activities of many *comités*, but the state's success in containing *autogestion* lay largely in the external controls. Much more serious for the future of self-management as a mode of political or economic organization in countries like Algeria are the attitudes among the workers themselves.

Technically, the *comité de gestion* is responsible to the *assemblée des travailleurs* which elects it. But even disregarding the fact that many *comités* were appointed by the local administration, the form of the original decrees gave the *comité* the means of asserting its independence. The *assemblée* was not allowed to make and pass amendments or counterproposals to those elaborated by the *comité*. These had to be sent to the *comité*, which only had to send them back for a vote by the *assemblée* if it thought fit. The length of time formally needed to re-elect a *comité*—three years—also contributed to its relative immunity. But these purely technical considerations, allowing the *comité* a large measure of independence from its electorate, had only a marginal effect in the development of some *comités* into a "factory bureaucracy."

The emergence of authoritarian and undemocratic tendencies within the internal organs of *autogestion* was rooted in the political and social conditions at the time of their formation. The widespread manipulation of the original elections meant that many *comité* members were chosen in view of their relations with the local administration, the FLN, the army, or the supervisory organs. As we have seen, since this time there has been no general renewal of the *comités*. Not only did many *comité* members owe their position to these external groups but they also derived power and prestige from them. The resulting evolution in the attitudes and actions of such *comité* members was described rather simplistically by Juliette Minces: "The local administration named the management in *autogestion,* many of whom, in consequence, take themselves for the new owners."[4] But the process whereby *comités* or their presidents objectively participated in the deformation and containment of *autogestion* is not so straightforward. They have rarely consciously subscribed to the class ideology of the new bourgeoisie.[. . .]

In the outlying rural areas the *comité* members who exerted personal or autocratic control over their enterprises were often fulfilling a traditional role in Muslim rural society. The remains of the indigenous local leadership, in the shape of the *caïds,* was annexed by French colonialism as part of its system of local political control. The *caïds,* chosen and suitably rewarded for their loyalty to colonialism, dispensed patronage, adjudicated in disputes, and acted as informers for the state. In view of their close identification with colonialism, many of the *caïds* were killed during the war or at independence, while others were imprisoned or fled to avoid retribution. But as independence failed to bring any alternative system of local government or any widespread change in social structure, their political and social role was filled by others. When the UGTA stated, "The presidents of *comités de gestion* are often just new *caïds,*" it was accurately describing not only their mode of action but also the social role they fulfilled.[5]

The so-called new feudalism of the *comités* was, in part, merely the expression of one of the few forms of social solidarity to survive colonialism. In the absence of other social links, such as class, and in the absence of any clearly based ideology, the concepts of cooperation inherent in *autogestion* were often, in the outlying rural areas, translated into traditional forms of social solidarity. The nepotism prevalent among some rural *comités*, and bitterly denounced at several congresses, was the expression of the normal values of traditional society.[. . .] The workers' acceptance of the authority wielded by *comités* or their presidents is similarly rooted in the norms of traditional society. In the past it had been customary for men of local eminence, such as the *caïds*, to establish their position through the distribution of favors like employment. In accepting the personal autocracy of some presidents, the workers were expressing a sense of reciprocal obligation.

The close identification between the *comité* and the organizational chain of command reinforced these traditional obligations. Very often the president, whether a political appointee or not, was the foreman or senior Muslim worker under the colonial management, while the *comité* members were the most senior or most experienced workers. At times this identification between the *comité* and the hierarchy of production management was total.

The strength of this duplication of authority roles rests on the workers' acceptance of a status hierarchy internalized before independence. This hierarchy was compounded both of the ascribed status of traditional society and the achieved status of industrial society. The ability of *comité* members to capitalize on the accepted norms of authority roles in two cultures rendered their position doubly strong. Only the internalization of a third ideology, such as that contained in *autogestion,* which challenged the value system of the other cultures, could render the workers conceptually capable of challenging the authority of the *comité.*

In the large estates of the coastal areas and the industrial units under *autogestion* the autocratic and illegal behavior of some presidents and their *comités* must be ascribed to different causes. The breakdown of the structure and values of traditional society in these areas made it impossible for *comité* members to fulfill traditional authority roles based on ascribed status. When not political, their authority was based on their role in the organization of production. The attitudes of some presidents and the extent to which they misused their positions were severely criticized at the 1964 conference of the socialist industrial sector.

> There are still the remnants of neo-colonialism in their heads. They
> waste the property of the people. They have the same disdain for
> the workers as the old owners. They make fat provision for them-
> selves. They give themselves apartments and take other privileges
> without justification. They drive round in Peugeot 404s [the local
> prestige car].

These criticisms are similar to those leveled at state-appointed
directors and, in fact, the position and attitudes of a number of
presidents and *comité* members were similar to those of directors.

Comité members in industry, like those in agriculture, were
often the foremen and senior workers under the previous colonial
management. Their delegated authority as members of a *comité*
thus coincided with their organizational authority based on
achieved status. One of the clearest examples of this coincidence
was in COGEHORE, the *comité de gestion* managing hotels and
restaurants in the Algiers area.[. . .] Here the manager of each
unit was also the unit's representative on the *conseil des travailleurs*.
Besides this duplication of functions, the *comité* collectively or the
president individually was often filling the organizational role
of the director because of the shortage of trained cadres for
that position. Many *comité* members had achieved a position of
authority with no well-defined social value system. Unlike those in
the outlying rural areas, they were unable to cloak their newfound authority in the values of traditional society. The absence
of a generalized socialist "culture" meant that there were few who
had internalized the values implicit in such a culture. A large
number of *comité* members were thus unable to achieve any
gratification from the roles prescribed for them in the ideal type
of *autogestion* as laid down in the *décrets de mars*. In this situation
they turned to the other value system most available to them—
that of the previous *pied-noir* management.

The failure of many *comités* to fulfill the role allotted them in the
original decrees must be seen in the light of cultural as well
as political and economic factors. Strict financial control and
electoral manipulation were definite political decisions aimed at
reducing the independence of the *comités*. The authoritarian,
nepotistic, and corrupt nature of some *comités* was not the result of
any overt manipulation by the administration. It was the product
of the social and cultural superstructures of the pre-existing
colonial society. These, whether based on the traditional rural
economy or colonial capitalism, were carried over into post-
colonial Algeria, because the fact of independence itself was not
enough to change the prevailing systems of values. The partial
imposition of a socialist economic organization, whatever its

form, does not imply a de facto modification of cultural norms. Only those who had implicitly internalized the concepts involved in *autogestion* were fully capable of identifying with its norms.

The Workers

The formation of *comités de gestion* and the elaboration of *autogestion* in Algeria created a radical departure from the pre-existing capitalist mode of organization of the means of production. In assessing the role of the workers, as distinct from the *comités*, in this process the key question is whether in fact they grasped it as a radical departure. Workers' attitude to self-management, in any form, is determined by the cultural values of their society and class. This attitude is essentially circumscribed by the worker's subjective relationship to the means of production and, consequently, work itself. In order to assess the ability or desire of workers to participate in management, the role played by work in their lives must be gauged.

The means of production and work may be grasped by the worker in different ways. Work may be a means of providing the income necessary to satisfy material or status needs. It may provide a source of intrinsic satisfaction in the process of the job itself or in the status connected with it. Alternatively, workers may see their own relationship to the means of production within the totality of economic, political, and social organization. In other words, workers may be conscious of the social context of their individual relationships to the means of production. All of these determining attitudes are to be found among workers in the industrialized West.

In a society such as Algeria, where unemployment or underemployment is the norm, work takes on a meaning that is radically different from that in advanced industrial countries. "In such a context, competition for a job is the foremost form of the struggle for existence; a struggle which, for some, begins each morning in anxiety and uncertainty."[6][. . .] In 1960, 88.6 percent of all permanent workers when faced with low wages chose to raise them by maximization of effort rather than fighting for higher wages for the same amount of work. It was only among the better educated, more skilled, and consequently higher paid workers that any form of trade-union consciousness appeared. Only these workers had the conceptual ability to grasp the economic system as a rational entity that could be acted on rather than the operation of a capricious fate that had to be accepted.

The struggle for employment and material survival, and the relative inability to grasp the economic system as a social totality are both crucial in their effect on the worker's attitude to self-management. *Autogestion,* whether conceived of as a form of production management or as the basis of a socialist organization of economy and society, is not confined to the provision of employment and wages. It demands that the new managers, the workers, should be aware of a whole complex of economic and social problems. It implies not only that they are capable of solving these problems but also that they actively desire to do so. Self-management, if it is not to be an empty formalism, demands a high level of class consciousness, an ability to grasp the meaning and content of class conflict. In Algeria the majority of workers were, and still are, deeply immersed in an everyday struggle for material survival where the next job or the next wage packet becomes the limit of their horizon. Their attitude to self-management is radically circumscribed by this context. The life situation and belief system of the vast majority of Algerians are inimical to the development of that form of consciousness implied by self-management.

We have already seen how the occupation of factories and farms in 1962 was spurred on by basic economic necessity. Despite the attempts by the UGTA, and some FLN militants, to give a political content to these actions, the majority of workers were impelled to form *comités de gestion* by the demands of material survival, rather than by a coherent revolutionary consciousness. In the breakdown of normal social structures following independence the workers recreated a classic socialist form of organization because at that juncture it was the only form open to them. The absence of a state, or an entrepreneurial bourgeoisie, left them face-to-face with the problem of organizing their own survival. They were driven by material necessity to give actuality to their objective situation as the negation of capitalism. But it was not a conscious seizure of the means of production by a class fully aware that it was engaged in a class struggle.

The authors of the *décrets de mars* and the *Charte d'Alger* conceived of a system whose success depended on the existence of a working class with a sufficient degree of consciousness to grasp the revolutionary content of *autogestion.* The demand, so often voiced by the Harbi group, the Parti de la Révolution Socialiste (PRS), and other left-wing groups, for an avant-garde party represented their fears that the workers had not developed a sufficient level of consciousness to combat the bureaucratic tendencies of the state. Orthodox socialists like Boumaza criticized what they termed the *ouvrierist* tendencies of the workers. "The great difficulty in *autogestion*, an essentially evolutionary formula, is to find the right mean between the anarchic, *ouvrierist* tendency at the base and the centralizing, bureaucratic, *étatiste* current at the top."[7] Foreign observers also noted the existence of this *ouvrierist* attitude among the workers. "In practice it happens that the *comité de gestion* appears to face the director or supervisory organ as an organized trade union, more ready to obtain particular advantages than to improve production."[8] This identification of the workers' attitudes, which provided yet another rationalization for imposing greater central control, is too simplistic.

The struggle for material survival was, for many workers, of greater importance than fulfilling the wider economic role allotted them by the *décrets de mars*. They tended to visualize their job in an instrumental fashion, according to the equation: work equals money and security. *Autogestion* as a mode of organization capable of solving the political and economic problems of a revolutionary society was not only a concept foreign to their experience but was felt as marginal to their immediate needs. This basic concern with survival in the immediate present is clearly reflected in the statements of two workers from farms where no wages had been paid for two and a half months in September 1965. One worker from the Domaine Hassamène said: "My children have only maize to eat, they have not tasted this season's fruits . . . every new day is a burden for us; how can we work on empty stomachs?" The other, from the Domaine Amirouche, complained: "We have lived like wolves for seventy-five days . . . we are in a situation of misery without escape. Everywhere we are ignored; for them we don't exist; they want to take the fruits of our work without repaying the producer."[9]

The workers did not form *comités de gestion* in 1962 and thus implicitly seize control of the means of production for purely political reasons. They did so because not to work meant to starve and because elimination of the capitalist owner would mean higher wages. This material and instrumental involvement of workers in the *comités* was explicitly recognized by the *décrets de mars* in their recommendations for the distribution of profits. The workers were given a direct economic incentive to participate in the management of their factories and farms. Yet, apart from Ben Bella's formal distribution of profits in 1964, these incentives failed to materialize. Thus, one of the main motives for involvement in *autogestion* was never satisfied. Particularly in agriculture, with fixed wages and no profit sharing, there is not much to show that anything has changed since colonialism. As the president of a self-managed farm said to me in 1965: "In this situation, how can we persuade the worker that he is no longer working for a capitalist exploiter?"

It is not surprising that, with their basic economic needs remaining unsatisfied, the workers should experience disillusion. The imposition of strict financial control by the administration served to channel the hostility and despair of the workers. For them the state clearly had taken on the role of the ex-owners, and they responded accordingly. "Their attitude remains the attitude of paid employees, all the more clearly manifested as they feel the state's supervision as if it were the authority of a private owner. It is the state that pays them, so it is to the state that wage claims are made."[10] With the imposition of state control on the *comités de gestion* the workers had no alternative but to treat the state as if it were an employer.

Continuing economic deprivation has provoked various reactions among workers in self-management. In 1964 the director of COTEINTAL, a self-managed cooperative laundry, had to call the police to stop the workers forcibly redistributing their own profits. In agriculture a common means of increasing wages has been for *comités de gestion* to sell produce on the black market. The more conscious translated their continuing deprivation and despair into a clear hostility toward the state, as was witnessed in the barrage of denunciations at every congress. In 1965 a worker in a self-managed transport concern noted: "The revolution pulled up a few big trees and let lots of little ones grow instead. At least the *colons* put something back. The new rulers just consume and do not reinvest."

Conditions of material insecurity and the absence of any well-defined national ideology of socialism act, at times, as a positive disincentive to become involved in *autogestion*. This can be seen in a simple and direct way in agriculture. Tractor drivers get paid twelve dinars a day, the other workers get seven and a half dinars a day. Many tractor drivers, who are usually the more skilled workers, refused to become members of *comités de gestion* because this would have meant accepting a wage cut of four and a half dinars a day.[11] At COBISCAL, another business concern, the workers refused to elect a new *comité* or share the responsibilities of management. They wanted to keep the same president because under him they made good wages and felt secure. As one of the workers said: "Wages are more important to us than politics or management." The director of another, state-owned, firm felt that workers preferred a private owner because they could demand wage increases without worrying about profitability.

The criteria by which many Algerian workers judge management are economic rather than ideological. Yet this involvement with material self-interest is not in itself evidence of a hostility to self-management or even an incapacity to take responsibilities within it. The concern with wages and security of employment creates an ideology which judges an economic and social system by its material results. The extreme exploitation of the colonial system led to the struggle for independence and the formation of *comités de gestion* in the attempt to construct a freer and more materially secure future. By these acts the Algerian workers showed themselves capable of grasping the possibility of creating their own future. Despite continuing economic deprivation, they remain prepared to work for this future. "We have our responsibilities to our families, but we must learn to take them on in other areas if we are to make Algeria a better place to live in," said a worker at the Société Algérienne des Boissons in July 1967.

The revolution contained in the formation of *comités de gestion* created a heightening of consciousness among the workers. The "anarchic, *ouvrierist* tendency of the base" criticized by orthodox socialists represented a consciousness that workers have a right to the "fruits" of their labor. It represented a clear consciousness that the economic system is not the result of blind fate but something that can be acted on. In assuming *ouvrierist* positions vis-à-vis the state, the workers were not rejecting the chance to control their own future through *autogestion*. Chaliand claims that the absence of a true revolutionary socialist avant-garde led the workers to draw the maximum immediate profit from the situation.[12] But this avant-gardist formulation is not clear enough. The imposition of state control over the *comités* through electoral manipulation and economic mechanisms meant that, even though formally involved in self-management, the workers were not in fact in control of their individual or class futures. For many workers their consciousness lay in the recognition of the bureaucracy in the party and state as part of a class that was preventing them from achieving the material benefits of their labor and disposing of them as they themselves saw fit.

The years following independence witnessed the development of a class consciousness among industrial and agricultural workers. To most, the fight against the settlers had been against colonialism rather than against capitalism, for independence rather than for socialism. After 1962 little changed for the peasants, the vast rural and urban subproletariat, and many of the lower paid workers in private industry. They remained immured in a world of unending struggle for daily survival. For the workers on the larger agricultural estates and in the socialist sector of industry, the dispossession of the *colons*, the formation of *comités de gestion*, the *décrets de mars*, the *Charte d'Alger* created a vision of socialism—a vision that was every day controverted by continuing poverty, by bureaucratic control, by cynical manipulation and corruption. The *ouvrierist* response to this situation, the demand for immediate benefits, was objectively the individual and collective expression of an implicit class conflict. To many of the workers the state had merely replaced the *colon* bourgeoisie. For the more politically aware, grouped around the UGTA, the situation was one of explicit struggle against a bureaucratic form of socialism in which *autogestion* assumed the role of an ideal of economic and political liberation.

The division between the proletariat and the mass of the Algerian population lies at the point where the involvement with survival leads to the assumption that the present and future may be acted upon. The consciousness of the possibilities of action as a means of solving economic deprivation is the beginning of a class consciousness. This consciousness becomes explicit when the individual is brought to identify as a member of a class. Classically, in Algeria it was the experience of revolution allied to economic deprivation that created the rudiments of this consciousness. Its development was partial and hesitant. In the early years the official position that there were no classes in Algeria, and the socialist language used by the state, obscured the realities of the situation. It was only after 1965 that the bourgeois class composition and ideology of the state and party became increasingly clear through their political and economic policies. The establishment of bourgeois hegemony found only a minority of the working class, itself a minority among the mass of the population, fully conscious and prepared to oppose the new elite openly.

Wider Considerations

In just over five years the Algerian revolution has been recuperated, institutionalized, and then emasculated by a new bourgeois elite firmly entrenched in the state and party. The *comités de gestion* had been suppressed or existed in name only. *Autogestion*, once so proudly proclaimed as Algeria's contribution to the construction of revolutionary societies in the Third World, had given way to a banal state capitalism. The original leaders, of whatever political complexion, had been replaced by previously unknown careerists and bureaucrats. Abroad, the revolution that had fired so many failed to live up to their expectations and their attention drifted to other areas of struggle, spectacularized in their turn by the media. Algeria became yet another revolutionary failure.[. . .] At this point the Algerian experience must be re-inserted into certain wider historical and analytical processes. We are faced not just with the specific problems of Algeria but also with the continuing dilemma of revolutionary authenticity in relatively underdeveloped societies and ultimately with the basis of authority in any revolutionary society.

The immediate misconception that must be corrected is that of the nature of the Algerian revolution. Many saw the violent resistance to colonialism and the ultimate achievement of independence as revolution. This is a profound error, which can only lead to a misunderstanding of the subsequent events. What began in 1954, with the formation of the FLN and the declaration of armed struggle, was not revolution; it was the development of the fight for national independence to an intense and violent plane. To term the struggle against colonialism revolution is to mistake the nature and aspirations of this struggle. It is to confuse the identity of revolution as a class struggle aimed at the overthrow of pre-existing social, political, and economic structures with an attempt to replace them with structures more closely related to specifically national aspirations. Although a small section of the FLN in 1954 was influenced by socialist ideas, the aims of the majority were circumscribed by nationalism; their aspirations were rooted in traditional Arab, Berber, and Islamic culture. Algerian nationalism reflected the social and cultural Manichaeism forced on the country by a specific colonial enterprise. The appeal of the FLN for the masses was its aim to restore a historical, cultural, social, and political entity that had been destroyed with the defeat of Abdel Kader.

The extreme violence of the struggle gave expression to the violence already implicit in the relations between colonizer and colonized: a violence that was itself a product of the process and mode of colonization. It is this violence that largely created the myth of the revolutionary nature of the fight for independence. Fanonism, in particular, was responsible for the widespread misconceptions over the nature of the struggle. As we have seen, the struggle was seized in racial and cultural terms: the two communities, Muslim and European, faced each other as more or less homogeneous blocs. Apart from a few exceptions, class alliances between the communities did not exist; and where they had existed the war served to sever them almost completely. This gave rise to the attempted elision of a national with a class struggle through the identification of the European settlers as the oppressors and the indigenous population as the oppressed. Such reductionism had widespread appeal because of its apparent simplicity. But, despite the political and economic hegemony of the *pieds-noirs,* it is not possible to describe the war as a class war because of the existence of parallel class structures in the two communities. Although the settler proletariat was distinguished from the Muslim proletariat by its social and economic privileges, objectively they were in a similar relationship to both colonial and metropolitan capitalism.

Certainly the war contained overtones of a class struggle as a rising of the underprivileged and dispossessed. Mass support for the FLN in the early days came extensively from the traditional rural areas, and its leaders were at pains to describe their struggle as peasant-based. It was in the countryside, with its consciousness of a past destroyed by colonialism, rather than in the towns that the FLN based both its military and political organizations. Despite this emphasis on the peasantry, dictated by tactical as well as ideological considerations, the struggle was national in orientation and extent. Members of all indigenous classes were fired by and, in varying degrees, took part in the revolt against colonialism. In seeking to overthrow French colonial hegemony, the FLN was demanding the re-establishment of an Algerian national identity. Until the Tripoli meeting of the Conseil National de la Révolution Algérienne (CNRA) in May 1962 there had been no official expression of a socialist conception of the future, and even then it had a national rather than a class definition. The continued refusal of the FLN to accept the existence of classes in post-independence Algeria is a clear witness of an inability to define the social and economic contradictions existing within the indigenous population.

If the achievement of independence was not, of itself, a revolution, the occupation of the means of production by the workers and the formation of *comités de gestion* can be said to constitute the revolutionary aftermath of independence. It was the establishment of workers' management of the ex-*colon* industrial, commercial, and agricultural concerns that formed the revolutionary nature of independent Algeria. It was the proletariat rather than the peasantry who broke through the specifically national identifications of race and culture to develop a class action. The class nature of this action raises the question of the situation and nature of revolutionary consciousness both in Algeria and in similar societies.

Since the Russian revolution confused the identification of the revolutionary overthrow of capitalism as developing in advanced industrial societies, the left has been embroiled in controversy over the nature of revolution in nonindustrialized countries. The classic, Europo-centric, Marxist thesis has been felt to be contradicted by a series of apparently successful peasant-based revolutions in largely nonindustrial societies. This has given rise to an attempted redefinition of the exact class situation of revolutionary consciousness. While not producing a complete answer to this question the Algerian experience is of great relevance.

Fallacies of Fanonism

The rejection or amplification of the classic definition of the proletariat as the sole negation of capitalism has been undertaken where there is a vast peasant majority or where the working class appears to be increasingly incorporated within capitalism. In nonindustrialized societies this has led to the identification of a revolutionary consciousness among the peasantry, stemming from their participation in wars of national liberation and, to a lesser extent, class wars against a national bourgeoisie. The Fanonist ideology, as expressed in *The Wretched of the Earth*, identified the most dispossessed as the most revolutionary. Fanon, like Marcuse,[13] appeared to be able, at one stroke, to cut through the problem of the continuing absence of revolution in advanced industrial societies. By opposing the industrialized and colonizing to the underdeveloped and colonized, the class struggle assumed global proportions. The working class of the West became the bourgeoisie of the dispossessed of the Third World. The appeal of this Manichaean division lay in its simplicity. For the "wretched" it subsumed all local contradictions within a global contradiction; it removed the necessity for any critical analysis. For the intellectuals of Europe and the United States its attraction lay in the way in which it played on the guilt mechanisms of liberalism. The sordid abasement of Sartre in his introduction to *The Wretched of the Earth* has been paralleled by the stampede of American intellectuals to prostrate themselves at the altar of black power.

In discussing the value systems and consciousness of the peasantry, subproletariat, and working class of Algeria, I have attempted, in this specific case, to unmask the absurdity of this type of reductionism. Neither the peasantry nor the truly "wretched" —the subproletariat—can be said to have played any objectively revolutionary role in Algeria. The involvement of the population of the traditional rural areas in the independence struggle must be clearly separated from their passivity in face of its revolutionary aftermath. The peasants were fighting for what they regarded as their inheritance: a heritage firmly rooted in the Arab, Berber, and Islamic past. Their consciousness was rooted in the values and traditions of this past, and their aim was its re-creation. Revolution, as a concept, is alien to the peasant consciousness, while the peasants' relationship to the environment remains one of passive endurance rather than active transformation.

The true disinherited mass of Algeria, as in the rest of the Third World, is the rural and urban subproletariat. They exist in a half world that is neither the traditional nor the modern. They are denied the uneasy security either of the traditional values of rural society or of employment in the industrial economy. This mass, spawned by demographic growth, changes in agricultural methods, by industrialization, war, and poverty, is involved in a desperate daily struggle for existence. For Fanon and for Marcuse it is this desperation and hopelessness which should drive the masses to revolt. Yet, as I have described earlier, it is this very desperation and extreme deculturation which deprives them of the ability to act on the external in a conscious manner. Subjectively, the subproletariat is not conscious of itself as a social organization: its total deprivation of social or economic self-identity makes of it a series.

Fanon, in particular, is at pains to emphasize the effect that participation in revolt has on the development of consciousness. For him, this experience breaks the chains of the psychological and social alienation forged by colonialism: the catharsis of violence liberates the individual and the society from the passivity engendered by the death of traditional cultural and social relationships. In *L'an V de la révolution algérienne* he prophesies that the participation of Algerian women in the struggle against colonialism foreshadows their liberation from traditional male dominance. The fact that this liberation was not achieved after independence is symptomatic of the underlying fallacies of Fanonism. Neither the peasantry nor the subproletariat played any other than a purely negative role in the events after independence. Involvement in the revolt against the French did not transform their consciousness. Fanonism, with its abstract Manichaean division of the world, is pure ideology. It lacks a critical and dialectical analysis of the process of the formation of consciousness.

As ideology, Fanonism must be placed in a different context from the purely tactical or strategic identification of rural areas as a suitable operational base for guerrilla activity. The FLN in Algeria eventually achieved independence, not because the peasantry emerged as a successful revolutionary class but because France could only hold the countryside by an unacceptable expenditure of effort. Depending on their physical nature, rural areas can provide a suitable base for guerrilla activity. This does not mean that the rural population is involved as a conscious revolutionary force. As we have seen, the nature of their involvement is clearly dependent on the nature of the struggle. In Algeria the peasantry was deeply immersed in the attainment of national liberation because it promised a re-creation of a glorious past to which all their values were intimately related.

The desperation that drove the Algerian industrial and agricultural working class to seize the means of production must be qualitatively separated from that of the peasantry and subproletariat. The motivation of the workers in occupying and managing the *colon* farms and factories was extensively based on the purely immediate necessities of material survival. Despite the fact that they shared the same desperation as the mass of the population, the workers reacted to this situation in an objectively revolutionary way. It cannot, however, be described as a conscious assumption of the historically revolutionary role of the proletariat. This fallacious interpretation led many to misconstrue the primitive nature of the seizure of the means of production as a sophisticated and mature revolt against capitalism.

It is in the objective relationship of the Algerian working class to the means of production that the key to their action lies. Unlike the peasantry and subproletariat, its relationship to the means of production was social rather than familial or individual. The social basis of the peasant economy is defined by a restricting relationship that pre-exists and encompasses the means of production—the extended family. Thus, although the peasant economy is apparently cooperative, the social relationships associated with it are not class-based. An industrial mode of production, despite the separation it engenders between individual workers, objectively creates an identity that transcends the boundaries of traditional relationships. The seizure of the means of production by the Algerian workers represented the subsuming of a series of individual motivations under a solidaristic, class action.

The contradictions of the Algerian revolution lay in the fact that the uprising was not a conscious praxis. It was the practice of revolution with no concomitant theory. The class initiative of the workers must be considered in relation to their relative lack of revolutionary consciousness. Although able to embark on a class solution to their common desperation, they were not, at that point, capable of fully apprehending the meaning of their action. They were accustomed to using the self-definitional concepts of race and culture and not of class. The rapid imposition of bureaucratic controls on the *comités de gestion* and the development of an authoritarian state apparatus stem from the inability of the Algerian working class to grasp the immediate necessity of extending their revolutionary initiative further than the point of production. By the time this became apparent they had lost the initiative.

Besides the absence of a hegemonic consciousness, the Algerian working class was deeply inhibited by the contradictory nature of the party and state. For the mass of Algerians, the FLN and the state under Ben Bella were cloaked in the mystique of the struggle for independence. They were vested with the authority and authenticity of success in the fight against colonialism. The Algerian working class found extreme difficulty in separating the nature of the FLN and its leaders during the war from their role after independence. The majority failed to see the full implications of their own actions: that the formation of the *comités de gestion* implicitly challenged the authority of the party and state. The tensions implicit in the tripartite division of workers' councils, party, and state in any revolutionary society were immeasurably increased in Algeria by the simple fact that the party and state were not products of the revolution.

Apart from some UGTA officials and some FLN militants, the Algerian nationalist movement was singularly unprepared to deal with the question of the country's future. During the war the heterogeneity of the FLN made agreement on anything outside the achievement of independence almost impossible. Despite its wide popular support, the FLN was never more than a loosely coordinated front for a wide assortment of political tendencies and personalities. It was not a socialist or a revolutionary party. Once independence was achieved, it fell apart into a whole series of competing factions. The extent of its irrelevance to the immediate problems of Algeria was revealed during the summer of 1962. While the political and military leaders of the front were engaged in near civil war, the working class was objectively turning independence into revolution. On his victory in September 1962, Ben Bella was forced to acknowledge that in many respects the Tripoli Program had already been surpassed in reality.

Many observers of and participants in the Algerian experience have located the failure of the revolution in the absence of an avant-garde capable of creating a theory and unifying this with the actions of the working class in a revolutionary praxis. The structure, function, and policies of the FLN in 1962 quite clearly defined it as other than an avant-garde party. After the factionalism of the summer it was patched up to represent more or less the same tendencies as before. In fact, at that point no such avant-garde existed as a coherent force. Its elements were located in several centers: in the UGTA, in Boudiaf's PRS, the Parti Communiste Algérien (PCA), and in the FLN itself. Apart from the leaders of the UGTA, few of these potential elements had played any real part in the formation of the *comités de gestion*. The conditions of the war had in any case separated them from contact with the working class. Essentially they were split between those who saw that the front had become outmoded with independence and those who wished to use its national status as a vehicle. The banning of the PRS and the PCA and the defeat of the UGTA leadership in January 1963 effectively removed the immediate possibility of developing a legal political avant-garde outside the FLN. The establishment of the FLN as the single, official, authentic, national party faced the avant-garde with the dilemma of opposition or entrism. Many, most notably the Harbi group, chose entrism.

The revolution at this point was incomplete. A sizable proportion of the means of production had been seized by the workers, but the state and party remained outside their control. This contradiction between the economic and the political manifested the underlying contradictions of the revolution. The *décrets de mars* and the *Charte d'Alger* were at once and the same time the measure and the success of entrism. The avant-garde within the FLN could produce programs and legislation, but they were utterly incapable of carrying these through into practice. They did not control the party or the state and had no mass base among the working class or peasantry. As the counterrevolution gathered strength, they were swept aside, and only their texts remained as a memorial.

The public image of the Algerian revolution, created by the institution of *autogestion*, the *décrets de mars*, the *Charte d'Alger*, and a revolutionary foreign policy, masked the deeper realities of the unfinished nature of the class struggle. The Trotskyist-influenced avant-garde's attempt to create the revolutionary tripartism of councils, party, and state was meaningless as long as the party and state remained in the hands of a bureaucracy not only totally separated from the working class but also having different class origins. The lack of critical analysis of the modes of class formation stems, once again, from Fanonist-inspired simplifications. During the war the internal class contradictions of the indigenous society were largely subsumed under the wider definitions of race and culture. To a large extent the only social formations recognized as separate from the mass of Algerians were the remnants of the tribal-feudal leadership and the Francophile bourgeoisie. Through the identification of independence with revolution it followed theoretically that these feudal and bourgeois elements had been largely dispossessed and had become peripheral to Algerian social reality. The *Charte d'Alger* recognized the existence of social divisions within Algerian society but did not use the term *class* to characterize them. The bourgeoisie, the petty bourgeoisie, and the bureaucracy are all defined as strata *(couches)* and not as classes.

This failure to identify the class characteristics, not only of the bourgeoisie but also of the new national bureaucracy, underlines the absolute necessity of rejecting the Manichaean vision of a global class struggle. It meant that the avant-garde within the FLN were unable to define the contradictions between the *comités de gestion* and the administration as part of an internal Algerian class struggle. In subordinating the *comités* to the administration, the avant-garde placed the whole revolution in jeopardy. The vision of the avant-garde was obscured by two analytical mystifications. First, they tended to accept the definition of the indigenous population as an undifferentiated mass in terms of its opposition to colonialism. Second, and more erroneously, they equated the seizure of the point of production with the seizure of the state. In their analysis the fact that the means of production were largely in the hands of the workers prohibited the development of a national middle class. They were able to identify the emergence of a bureaucracy in Russia with interests opposed to the working class. But their answer to this problem lay in *autogestion,* which, of itself, would remove the separation between the managers and the managed.

It is essential to the understanding of the failure of the Algerian revolution to realize that the bureaucracy acted as a class. It was sharply differentiated from the peasantry and the working class, and more narrowly from the classical bourgeoisie, by the nature of its consciousness and by its relationship to the means of economic and political power. Although under *autogestion* the working class formally controlled the means of production, it did not control the relations of production. The administration, through its control of the mechanisms of finance and marketing, was in fact able to determine the economic life of each enterprise. With the development of the *sociétés nationales* this control became total. The bureaucracy rapidly developed a hegemonic consciousness and within five years had carried through a successful counterrevolution.

The Algerian revolution was unfinished in the sense that the working class never seized the state and that the party was an appendage of this state. Not only did the entrist tactics of a section of the avant-garde fail to push the revolution any further than the workers had already objectively achieved in 1962; it also made the task of the counterrevolution immeasurably easier by handing the gains of the workers over to the state.

In respect of this analysis it is possible to identify three stages of class struggle in excolonial territories. The first, the struggle for national liberation, precedes the real development of class antagonisms. It is only after independence that the existence of contradictions over and above those of colonialism becomes explicit. The second is the conflict between the national bourgeoisie and the mass of the population ending in the seizure of the means of production. The third is the conflict between the working class (and peasantry) and the state and party bureaucracy, ending in the seizure of the state. The specific conditions of colonialism in Algeria made the near temporal elision of these first two stages possible; the third stage was not achieved. The seizure of the state does not depend on the existence of an avant-garde, either pursuing entrist tactics or as a party in its own right; it rests on the development of a hegemonic consciousness by the proletariat. Anything short of the full, conscious seizure of the mechanisms of the state and the economy by the proletariat leads to the development of a bureaucratic bourgeois elite within the state. In this situation both classic socialism and self-management can only represent both a recuperation of the class struggle and a mystifying obscuring of its very existence.

Conclusions

In the Third World the economic situation of most countries and of their working class and peasantry is deeply antagonistic to the development of a full revolutionary consciousness and to its realization. The problem is situated around two major factors: the global economic dominance of neoimperialism and the low level of material security of the mass of the population.[. . .]

The global dominance of neoimperialism and the historical situation of the majority of the underdeveloped territories as part of this system create a series of problems. Given that most of such countries are oriented toward the production of raw materials rather than either capital or consumer goods, any attempt to lessen this subordinate position entails the development of a comprehensive industrial infrastructure. Apart from large political and economic units, such as Russia and China, such an attempt is economic lunacy. National economic self-sufficiency and the concept of the siege economy are deeply reactionary in terms of the international division of labor made possible by advanced technology. A possible solution to the dilemma has been seen to lie in the formation of more comprehensive trade blocs in competition with neoimperialism. However, this meets with the obstacle that the economies of the potential members of such a bloc are not complementary.

The political effect of economic subordination is seen to entail neoimperialist support for either a national entrepreneurial bourgeoisie or, in its absence, a bureaucratic bourgeois elite, whether in civil or military form. It does not necessarily mean opposition to forms of state ownership and control of the means of production where this does not conflict with the interests of advanced monopoly capitalism. In fact the relationship can act as a positive incentive to the development of such forms of economic organization. The national need to avoid blatant neoimperialist exploitation makes the creation of a unified form of economic organization a positive necessity. Although cloaked in the language of socialism, the development of such forms is more likely to be an expression of nationalism. Politically and socially, this economic centralism accelerates the development of a heterogeneous coalition of petty bourgeois and bourgeois elements into a fully fledged class. Thus, in the absence of a successfully concluded revolution, any attempt to reduce global contradictions by creating unified forms of economic organization leads to the intensification of internal class contradictions.

Autogestion, as visualized by the avant-garde in Algeria, represented a revolutionary alternative to this process. Vesting control of the means of production and, after a carefully supervised period, of the state, with the workers was designed both to avoid the development of a hegemonic bureaucratic bourgeoisie and to create the conditions for economic independence. The error of the avant-garde was, as I have stressed, to misconstrue the nature of the revolution. By identifying the events of 1962-1963 as a revolution, rather than as the partial and hesitant onset of one, they

were led to simplify the class structures of Algerian society. They
also failed to appreciate the true state of the consciousness of the
working class. The institution of a unified and unifying politico-
economic structure above the point of production played directly
into the hands of a petty bourgeoisie already partially seated in
that structure. Before it had really taken place, the revolution was
institutionalized and reified into a series of symbolic forms.[. . .]

It is at this point that the relevance of *autogestion* as a form of
revolutionary organization must be called into question. In the
introduction I noted that, apart from those that were crushed by
counterrevolution, workers' councils have tended to experience
the same history. Thrown up as a basic form of political and
economic organization at particular points in a class struggle, they
have been rapidly institutionalized and emptied of anything but a
purely ritual content. Their fate has been singularly uniform,
whether within a formally socialist or capitalist society. They have
failed to create any lasting form of political or economic organization external to the point of production and have been eventually
confined to this area.[. . .]

The revolutionary nature of the class consciousness of the
Algerian workers must equally not be overstressed. The majority
did not see the formation of the *comités* as a revolutionary act.
Although this act gave witness to the emergence of a consciousness
of class identity, rather than one based on race or culture, its
nature was corporate rather than hegemonic. The occupation of
the means of production was not a direct, conscious frontal
assault on colonial capitalism; nor were the seizure of the state
and the radical transformation of all elements of Algerian society
envisaged. Despite the objectively revolutionary nature of their
action, the preoccupation of the vast majority remained the daily
struggle for material survival.

It is in this situation that *autogestion* came to form part of a
system of mystification. The creation of an official ideology of
revolution, both by the avant-garde and by the state bureaucracy,
made the rapid recuperation of the original act possible. Independence was followed by the sustained erection of a mythology
about Algeria, which asserted that class conflict, and indeed
classes as such, no longer existed; that the revolution had already
taken place; and that the conflict had taken on the dimensions
of a struggle between a unified revolutionary nation and neoimperialism. Thus, at the very moment it emerged, class conflict
was frozen by the myth of national revolutionary unity. One of
the cornerstones of this myth was *autogestion*. The *comités* became
symbols of a revolution that had already, in some mystical way,

been achieved. The few who attempted to demystify the situation were repressed in the name of national unity. Once the new ruling class had established itself, the symbolic form itself could be discarded.

Notes

1. *Révolution et travail,* no. 103 (November 1965).
2. Ibid., no. 99 (October 1965).
3. See Juliette Minces, "Self-Administration in Algeria," *International Socialist Journal,* no. 22 (August 1967).
4. Minces, "Autogestion et luttes de classe en Algérie," *Temps modernes* (June 1965): 2,210.
5. *Révolution et travail,* October 15, 1966.
6. Pierre Bourdieu, "La hantise du chômage chez l'ouvrier algérien," *Sociologie du travail,* (October-December 1962): 314.
7. Bachir Boumaza, speech, May 1963.
8. Jean Henri, "Rétrospective sur l'économie algérienne en 1963," *Confluent,* no. 39 (March 1964): 271.
9. Both quoted in *Révolution et travail,* September 17, 1965.
10. Grigori Lazavev, "Remarques sur l'autogestion agricole en Algérie," in *Institutions et développement agricole du Maghreb* (Paris, 1965), p. 27.
11. Annie Kreiger, in *Essais sur l'économie de l'Algérie nouvelle* (Paris, 1965).
12. Gérard Chaliand, *L'Algérie: est-elle socialiste?* (Paris: F. Maspero, 1964).
13. Herbert Marcuse, *One-Dimensional Man* (Boston: Beacon Press, 1964).

The Political Impact
of Strikes and Disorder
in Ceylon

Robert N. Kearney

A major political significance of trade unions stems from their capacity to exert pressure by strikes in strategic industries and to precipitate civil disorder, which may intimidate or discredit the governing politicians and produce other major political consequences. In Ceylon the strike has been viewed as a political weapon since before independence, when colonial rule prevented a fully effective political process. In 1936, within a few months of the founding of the Lanka Sama Samaja party, a strike of motor transport workers was staged by the party to protest a legislative enactment dealing with motor vehicle licensing.[1] As the colonial administration and British-owned firms were the principal employers of wage labor, strikes sometimes simultaneously involved demands for improved wages and working conditions and attempts to weaken or undermine colonial rule.[2] Strikes have continued to be used as conscious political instruments since independence, and strikes and occasional outbursts of disorder resulting from trade-union action have had important political consequences, both intended and unintended.

Some strikes have no discernible political ramifications, while others are expressly political and have slight industrial impact. There are, in addition, a considerable number of strikes which contain elements of both industrial and political conflict, either in intent or consequences, or both. Most politically significant strikes can be classified into three categories: (1) overtly political strikes, called solely and explicitly for political reasons; (2) general strikes and strikes which combine political with industrial demands and objectives; and (3) strikes which are primarily the result of industrial disputes but which involve the prestige or interests of the political government because they occur in industries operated by the state or essential to the normal life of the community.[3]

Political Protest Strikes

Exclusively political strikes are brief, generally lasting one day, and are intended as a symbolic act of protest and a means of dramatizing an issue rather than as a serious effort to topple the government. The political strike is called in protest over a specific immediate grievance or event and takes the form of a general strike of all workers in all industries who are willing to participate. Invariably, a mass rally and, unless prevented by the police, a street procession accompany the strike. The objective sought is to display the strength and determination of the participants to the government and the public and to generate popular concern with the issue. A one-day political strike in 1959, for example, was described as intended "to register a working class protest in an emphatic manner against a reactionary and anti-democratic piece of legislation."[4]

The "hartal" is closely related to, and can be considered along with, the exclusively political strike. A hartal, technically, is not limited to a strike by organized workers but involves the closing of all shops, businesses, and schools and the suspension of normal activities by all members of the community. Like the political strike, the hartal is an act of protest, and includes the flying of black flags as a sign of mourning. Hartals are called by organizations other than trade unions, generally political parties. Several hartals, for example, were called by the Federal party to protest official-language policy between 1956 and 1965. The distinction between a political strike and hartal is not always carefully maintained, and any politically motivated strike and demonstration may popularly be referred to as a hartal.

Relatively few exclusively political strikes have been staged.[5] The only one which produced profound repercussions was a hartal organized by the Marxist parties and the Federal party in 1953, attacking a cabinet decision to increase the price of subsidized rice. The forerunner of the Ceylon Workers' Congress, the Ceylon Indian Congress, called a one-day hartal in 1946 to protest legislative approval of constitutional proposals. A general strike led by the Lanka Sama Samaja party (LSSP) in March 1959 was called to protest a proposed amendment to the Public Security Act under consideration in Parliament. Trade unions associated with the Sri Lanka Freedom party (SLFP), LSSP, and Communist party called a half-day general strike and demonstration protesting the defeat in Parliament of the SLFP-LSSP coalition government late in 1964, and ordered a one-day strike and demonstration, which erupted into rioting and disorder, as a protest against official-language regulations introduced in Parliament in January 1966. As a result of the political divisions in the labor movement, political strikes frequently receive only partial support, and their impact is consequently weakened. The 1959 LSSP-led strike, for example, was considered to have achieved slight success because of the opposition of the Communist- and People's Liberation Front-controlled unions.[6] The force of the January 1966 strike was considerably reduced by the refusal of the Ceylon Mercantile Union, Ceylon Workers' Congress, Democratic Workers' Congress, and a number of other important unions to participate.

No revolutionary general strike seriously expected to overthrow the government has ever been staged, and the political and trade-union leaders of Ceylon do not look upon the unlimited revolutionary general strike as a practical weapon in present or foreseeable circumstances.[7] The hartal of 1953, later described by a CFTU [Ceylon Federation of Trade Unions] publication as "undoubtedly the highest expression of revolutionary action by the working class and people of this country,"[8] had by far the most serious political consequences of any explicitly political strike. The resignation of the prime minister, Dudley Senanayake, two months later is generally attributed to the hartal, and ramifications of the hartal were thought to have contributed to the defeat of the United National party in the 1956 election. The hartal, however, was planned for only a single day and was called off by its sponsors the following morning.[9] The 1966 political strike was described by a leading cabinet minister as "a strike which, if successful, would have meant the downfall of the Government. . . . In other words, the purpose of the strike was to bring to a standstill the whole Government machinery deliberately and designedly."[10] The strike fell far short of this result, however. It has consistently been referred to subsequently by the participating trade unionists as a "token" strike. The impact of the work stoppage seems to have been much less than that of the demonstration, which produced considerable momentary disorder in Colombo.

General Strikes and Strikes Including Political Demands

Political objectives are frequently combined with or are implicit in other objectives, particularly in general strikes or strikes by government employees. General strikes almost invariably include explicit or implicit political demands and generate important political ramifications. Although the principal immediate objective of a general strike may be related to wage or trade-union issues, the strike nonetheless is likely to challenge a major policy or position of the government. As LSSP leader N. M. Perera observed, "Every general strike must be a political strike. The moment you have a general strike, you knock against the Government and the Government machinery comes into play. Even a trade strike must be a political strike in the end."[11]

The general strikes of 1946 and 1947, which were spearheaded by public employees, developed into direct clashes between the government and the strikers. The strike in October 1946 began in the government-operated railroads and spread to other public employees, mostly laborers. Port workers, municipal employees, and workers in a number of private firms also came out on strike a short time later. The striking public servants demanded the right to form trade unions, which was then denied them, and wage increases. The strike ended after a little more than a week with the promise of some concessions.[12]

The issue of trade-union rights for public servants flared up again in the general strike of May-June 1947. The 1947 strike commenced among Colombo municipal employees and spread to several private-sector industries. Along with wage demands were included demands for constitutional reform, the nationalization of the tea and rubber industries, and several other demands of a political nature.[13] At the end of May the strikers were joined by a large number of public servants, principally clerical employees. The public servants' strike followed the dismissal of several public servants for convening a mass rally demanding trade-union rights for public servants, which was addressed by politicians in violation of public service regulations. The strikers demanded the reinstatement of the dismissed public servants and the grant of the right to form trade unions. The strike met with the determined opposition of the government and collapsed on June 19 without winning any of its objectives. Many public servants were dismissed or disciplined for participating in the strike.[14] The following year, however, the Trade Unions Ordinance was amended to allow the formation of unions by public servants.

A one-day general strike was called in January 1962 by the unions aligned with the Marxist parties in support of striking port workers. The objective of the general strike was to force the withdrawal from the port of military personnel who were maintaining harbor operations during the port workers' strike. The port strike, which involved seventeen thousand workers and was then in its third week, closely followed a transport workers' strike and coincided with strikes by bank clerks and employees of a petroleum distribution company. Immediately preceding the general strike, the prime minister had firmly declared that the port workers' demand for a monthly wage could not be granted and that troops would not be withdrawn from the port until the strike ended.[15] Leaders of the general strike asserted that its objective was not to undermine the government, but to defend trade unionism by opposing the use of troops to replace strikers.[16] The strike was, however, intended to force a reversal of a major policy decision on the government. Prime Minister Sirimavo Bandaranaike charged that there was "no doubt what so ever that the strike of the 5th January had political objectives."[17] The government refused to alter its position, and the port strike was abandoned after fifty-one days as a sign of solidarity with the government when a plot by military and police officers to overthrow the government was uncovered at the end of January.[18] Although leaders of the 1962 general strike denied it had political aims, a trade-union journal subsequently claimed it "demonstrated to the present anti-working class Government in a most convincing manner the fighting spirit of the workers."[19]

In addition to general strikes, other strikes sometimes are called on a combination of demands, some of which have clear political implications. After a large number of public servants and employees of public corporations were penalized for participation in the January 1966 political strike called by the SLFP-Marxist coalition, a demand that the punishments be revoked became a standard item in lists of demands formulated by the procoalition unions. The National government regarded the political strike as a direct political challenge on an issue with little relevance to trade unionism and took an uncompromising stand on the punishments imposed on strikers, who had defied public service regulations by participating in a political strike. During 1968 several public servants' organizations, led by the Government Clerical Service Union, joined in a "consultive committee," which drafted two demands, calling for a salary increase for all public servants' grades and the withdrawal of punishments against those who participated in the January 1966 strike.[20]

A strike on the two demands was launched in late November 1968 by the unions associated in the consultative committee, coinciding with a strike for pay increases by a front of postal workers' unions. Within a few days, the strikers were joined by the three procoalition federations of public servants' unions, the Public Service Workers' Trade Union Federation, the Government Workers' Trade Union Federation, and the Sri Lanka Nidahas Rajaya Seva Vurthiya Samithi Sammelanaya, which claimed a combined membership of two hundred thousand public servants. On the eve of the federations' entry into the strike, a large number of government departments were declared essential services under the Public Security Act, subjecting strikers to loss of employment and possible criminal prosecution. The postal workers pulled out of the strike after four days, but the contest was continued by the remaining unions although about eleven thousand strikers in the departments designated as essential services were declared to have vacated their posts. Leaders of the three coalition parties met twice with the prime minister on behalf of the strikers. Eventually, strikers were told that those who lost their jobs for disregarding the essential services order would be re-employed and a salaries commission would look into wage demands, and the strike was ended after twenty-five days without achieving either of its original objectives.[21] The contest led the Government Clerical Service Union to conclude that public servants agitating for demands were to "be faced with the might of the Government and all its oppressive machinery."[22]

Political Implications of Industrial Disputes

Strikes often are called as a result of industrial disputes and have no discernible political objectives, but nonetheless develop political overtones because they come to involve the prestige or challenge policies of the government. This is often the case with strikes in government-operated industries. The dispute producing the strike may be an uncomplicated question of wages or working conditions, but because the political government takes a stand on the issue the strike assumes a political dimension. At the time of the 1963 Ceylon Transport Board strike, an unofficial LSSP publication commented editorially that "in the context of a wage-freeze every wage demand acquires political flavour."[23]

The 1958 strike of public servants, called primarily on a wage issue, led to the declaration of a state of emergency and the assignment of troops to patrol the streets. The emergency and troop call-up produced a threat of a general strike by the major public- and private-sector labor organizations to protest the government's action.[24] Strikes in the major public corporations between 1961 and 1964, precipitated by disciplinary questions and wage demands, were regarded by the SLFP government as challenges to its authority and in some cases as politically motivated. A transport strike late in 1961 prompted the minister of labor to assert, "We cannot hold the public to ransom nor can we try to cripple the day-to-day working of the Government because some trade unionists, inspired by their political gurus, want to embarrass the Government at whatever cost."[25] The government's response probably heightened the political significance of the strikes. It is unlikely, however, that strikes in major state-operated industries essential to the normal life of the community, led by trade unions associated with opposition political parties, can be insulated from political implications.

Collective bargaining on issues of wages and conditions of employment is often suggested as an alternative to political involvement by trade unions. Collective bargaining rests on the ability of the union to use strikes or other forms of coercion to force the employer to concede demands. So long as collective bargaining is directed against fairly numerous private employers, the implicit threat of coercion does not seem directed against the community or the government, and therefore appears to be nonpolitical. However, in Ceylon, and in many other developing countries, the government increasingly is becoming the major employer of industrial labor. Trade unions representing public employees can scarcely engage in collective bargaining without threatening or applying coercive pressure against the government. Conflicts between trade unions and the government need not become partisan contests, but the collision between trade unions and the machinery of government is likely to be seen by the political parties as an opportunity to discredit or harass the governing party. Trade unions representing public employees are very likely to view control of the government by one party as favorable and another as hostile to their aims. Thus, the result of the government's increasing economic role and the growing bargaining power of trade unions may be to thrust trade unions more firmly into the political arena.

The Political Impact of Strikes

The political consequences of strikes, whether in pursuit of political objectives or not, have become so great that strikes and labor strife are viewed as among the most serious threats facing the political party in power. A Communist leader underlined the potential consequences of united action by trade unions when, after the one-day general strike on January 5, 1962, he warned the government:

I ask my hon. Friends opposite, please do not fail to take note of the lessons of the January 5th strike. About a million workers took part in that strike. Do you think all your army, all your police force and all your pioneer corps can deal with such a situation if it continues for more than one day?[26]

The SLFP decision in 1964 to form a coalition government with the LSSP was motivated, at least in part, by the need to contain mounting trade-union militancy. When asked if the coalition was formed to stem growing labor strife, Prime Minister Sirimavo Bandaranaike responded, "We have brought into the Government a party which plays a dominant role among the urban working class. . . . Without the working class lending their [sic] full support I just cannot see how enterprises like the CTB [Ceylon Transport Board] or the Port Cargo Corporation can operate effectively."[27]

The political impact of a strike may be quite different from its economic impact. Some strikes have considerably more political significance than others, irrespective of their duration or the number of strikes involved. Generally, strikes which are apparent and disruptive in Colombo, or which dislocate the island's railroad or bus transport or block the port, through which vital imports of food and other essentials flow, have a great and immediate political impact. Transportation, especially buses, the popular mass transportation in Ceylon, is a particularly important target for general strikes because of its high visibility and its tendency to magnify the effectiveness of the strike by preventing many non-strikers from reaching work. It is said that on the day of a general strike many workers first determine whether or not the buses are running, as a guide to whether the strike is a success or failure, before deciding whether or not they will attempt to appear for work.

A strike of a single day which halts public transportation through much of the island and closes workshops, port facilities, and government offices in Colombo will almost certainly have important political ramifications, although its economic consequences may be slight. Strikes on the estates, on the other hand, are much less visible and disruptive to the normal life of the community and consequently have minimal immediate political reverberations, although their economic consequences for the nation may be much more severe. An estate strike called by the Democratic Workers' Congress in 1966, for example, was claimed to have cost the country nearly 240 million rupees in desperately needed foreign exchange and, hence, to have been extremely costly to the economy.[28] The strike continued for forty-five days, however, with slight political consequences. Strikes with the least political significance are those against private employers not prominently identified with the political party in power and not involving a particularly sensitive industry. The Ceylon Bank Employees' Union's long and bitter strikes against foreign-owned commercial banks, for example, produced only minor political reverberations, although they were among the most sharply contested strikes in the history of Ceylonese trade unionism.

Strikes led by politicians opposed to the party in power are much more likely to develop political significance than strikes called by unions sympathetic with, or at least not hostile toward, the existing political government. Thus, an LSSP leader, Bernard Soysa, complained that during strikes by LSSP-controlled trade unions in 1957-1958

> the Government party and Hon. Ministers . . . [went] through the country stating, "This diabolical Lanka Sama Samaja Party is trying to overthrow the Government by means of these strikes." That, however, has not been said when the Government Party-organized trade unions launched strikes. . . . When . . . [a union sponsored by the governing party] also launched a strike in certain sectors, when an Hon. Minister led the strike, then, apparently, the Government was not in danger.[29]

The National government in power after 1965 repeatedly warned that the opposition parties were attempting to organize strikes to weaken or discredit the government, but treated with tolerant forbearance a grueling forty-two-day strike in the sensitive Colombo harbor called in 1968 by the Ceylon Mercantile Union, which, although not aligned with the government, was harshly critical of the SLFP-Marxist opposition.

The National government, opposed by parties with strong labor support, displayed serious concern with the potential political impact of strikes from its inception. In a brief message on becoming prime minister in March 1965 Dudley Senanayake appealed to "the employees in both the public and private sectors not to be misled by those who may seek to nullify the people's verdict by undemocratic means."[30] The January 8, 1966, political strike represented the first major challenge to the National government by the procoalition trade unions, and severe action was taken against strikers in the public service and public corporations. Prior to the strike, the Treasury circulated a warning that, since the strike was called on a political issue, disciplinary action would be taken against any public servant or employee of a public corporation who participated in the strike.[31] Striking public servants were fined a week's pay and a sizable number of strike leaders, including the officers of most participating unions, were suspended from duty pending dismissal proceedings.[32] In some public corporations wholesale dismissals occurred, allegedly in order to provide employment for political supporters of the parties in power. More than three thousand employees of the Ceylon Transport Board were said to have been dismissed, although about three-quarters of them were later rehired with a loss of seniority.[33] Several heads of major public servants' unions who had been released for full-time trade-union work and consequently had not absented themselves from duty were charged with circulating leaflets urging other public servants to strike on a political issue, in violation of public service regulations.[34]

The government's strong reaction to the strike seems to have intimidated the procoalition unions and considerably reduced their militancy and daring, at least temporarily. Many private employers reportedly were encouraged by the government's stand to toughen their attitude toward trade unions. Although strikes on industrial issues were launched by the Ceylon Mercantile Union and Democratic Workers' Congress, neither of which supported the coalition or joined in the 1966 political strike, it was not until the end of 1968 that procoalition unions mounted a major strike.

Trade Unions and Civil Disorder

In some cases it is not the economic losses or disruption of normal activities produced by work stoppages but the eruption of civil disorder which produces the major political impact of trade-union action. In virtually all circumstances, the incumbent holders of governmental power wish to maintain order and view an outbreak of disorder as a threat to their authority and power.[35] Trade unions are not solely, or even primarily, responsible for serious disorders. The communal riots of 1958, which were unrelated to trade unions or labor issues, constituted the most violent and sanguinary outbreak of disorder in modern times.[36] Ceylonese trade unions apparently seldom seek to create disorder, and union-promoted violence or disorder has not become a major facet of politics or collective bargaining.[37] Nonetheless, the capacity of trade unions to create disorder—whether in pursuit of political or economic objectives—contributes to the coercive effect and heightens the political significance of trade-union action.

Political and general strikes commonly involve processions and rallies in addition to work stoppages. Not infrequently, demonstrations lead to some disturbances, often involving a few stone-throwing and window-smashing incidents. Sometimes clashes occur between demonstrators and police or troops, and in a few instances demonstrators have been fired upon by police. Serious outbursts of violence involving deaths and extensive destruction have been surprisingly few in Ceylon, relative to other countries in the region. Incidents connected with the 1947 general strike, the 1965 May Day rallies, and the 1966 political strike resulted in one fatality each. The most serious eruption of violence and destruction occurred in connection with the 1953 hartal.

The 1953 Hartal

The hartal on August 12, 1953, was called to protest a decision by the United National party government to abolish a consumer subsidy on rice, which produced a rise in the price of rice from 0.25 rupee to 0.70 rupee a measure. The hartal not only closed business places and government offices but also produced widespread riots and disorders and extensive damage to transportation and communications facilities throughout the southwest corner of the island. Railroad tracks were blocked by trees and boulders, telephone lines were cut, and vehicles and buildings were set afire. A state of emergency was declared, and at least ten persons died in clashes between police and rioters.[38] Property damage was estimated at 3,500,000 rupees (nearly $750,000).[39] Damage to railroad facilites alone amounted to approximately 450,000 rupees (nearly $100,000), and normal service was not resumed for a week.[40] The specter of the hartal has probably haunted many subsequent governments. In 1966, in an announcement of a reduction in the ration of subsidized rice—the issue which touched off the 1953 hartal—Prime Minister Dudley Senanayake warned against challenging the decision by creating "civil commotion."[41]

The Disorders of 1965 and 1966

Within a year of the 1965 election two outbreaks of disorder, both involving trade unions, occurred in Colombo. The first confrontation, between the newly formed National government and the SLFP-Marxist coalition, occurred on May Day, a month after the election. The May Day incidents resulted in the death of one participant in a procession moving toward the scene of the coalition-sponsored rally and some destruction of property. The disturbances, although not of great magnitude, were the subject of a report made on orders of the government by a senior public servant. The report said of the May Day observances:

> The evidence indicates that all parties made a special effort to display their strength on this occasion. . . . Colombo was to be the rallying point of large numbers of persons from many areas of the Island. . . . The only conclusion that could be drawn was that May Day, 1965, became an occasion for a matching of political strengths in Colombo. . . . The National Government feeder processions and main procession were an expression of triumph and jubilation at its [the government party's] victory at the General Election. The characteristic feature of the coalition organisation seemed to be aimed at demonstrating their feelings of frustration, envy, and disappointment at their failure at the General Elections.[42]

M. G. Mendis, general secretary of the CFTU and a Communist party leader, described the occasion in these words:

> May Day 1965 provided the opportunity not only to celebrate the traditional Workers' holiday but also to stage the first mass demonstration against the newly formed Hath Howla [i.e., seven-part coalition, a term of derision applied to the National government by its opponents]. Our Federation joined with all the other leading trade union centres and progressive political parties to organise what was undoubtedly the biggest May Day rally ever seen in Ceylon. This mammoth May Day rally and procession proved to be such a challenge to the reactionary forces that they made a feeble effort to disrupt it by staging a provocation in which one worker who took part in the procession was killed, the first such incident to mar May Day which had been peacefully celebrated by workers in Ceylon for the last 33 years.[43]

The second and more serious disturbance accompanied the political strike and demonstration called by the opposition parties on January 8, 1966. Since formation of the National government, which included the Federal party and Tamil Congress representing the Ceylon Tamil minority, the opposition had charged that the government was planning to alter the official-language policy to undermine the position of Sinhalese as the only official language. When an announcement was made that regulations providing for the use of the Tamil language for certain public purposes would be presented to Parliament on January 8, a huge protest rally was held on January 5, at which plans were announced for a general strike and demonstration on the day the language regulations were to be debated. Demonstrators were to mass at various points and converge on the Parliament building. The government issued orders that demonstrations were not to be allowed in the vicinity of the Parliament building, and army and naval personnel were called out to assist police in maintaining order.[44]

Because of the opposition of the CMU, CFTU, and other labor organizations, the strike appears to have been less widely supported than several previous general strikes, but at least twenty thousand public servants were conceded to have participated,[45] along with employees of many private enterprises. Black flags appeared throughout the city, and huge crowds began assembling for the demonstration early in the morning, eventually totaling more than fifteen thousand. By midday a group of demonstrators had collected across from the Parliament building, were driven away by police, and reassembled in front of the prime minister's residence a short distance away. Later, a procession estimated to include eight thousand to ten thousand demonstrators, led by Buddhist *bhikkhus,* began to march toward the Parliament building. The procession was finally broken up and the demonstrators dispersed by police and military personnel using batons, tear gas, and rifles.[46] Rioting broke out, and extensive damage was done to vehicles and buildings for several blocks adjacent to the major clash between police and demonstrators. In the firing and rioting, one man, a *bhikkhu,* was killed, and at least ninety-one persons were injured.[47] A committee investigating police arrangements for the strike and demonstration summarized the later stages of the disturbances as follows:

(16) Between 1.30 and 1.45 p.m. Police resorted to firing tear gas and baton-charging to disperse the crowd at Kollupitiya. This was followed by stone-throwing and damage to property. . . .

(17) At 2.15 p.m. information was received that persons dispersed by Police at Kollupitiya were on the railway tracks between Kollupitiya and Slave Island and were attacking passing trains;

(18) At 2.20 p.m. . . . [a police officer] reported that the same persons who had been dispersed were attacking houses and shops along Galle Road and that trouble would spread immediately to other parts of the city;

(19) At 2.45 p.m. the C.I.D. reported that drivers and conductors of the C.T.B. [Ceylon Transport Board] were deserting their buses and refusing to take the vehicles out unless armed

escorts were provided as the buses were attacked and some of them had been injured;

(20) Between 2.00 p.m. and 3.30 p.m. Police Headquarters had received numerous reports from all parts of the city that the crowds that were dispersed at Kollupitiya were resorting to stone-throwing and violence;

(21) Between 1.45 p.m. and 3.00 p.m. . . . [a police party] had resorted to firing on four occasions at Kollupitiya junction, Kollupitiya railway station and along Galle Road towards Bambalapitiya;

(22) Finally, the death of a Buddhist priest as a result of gun shot injuries was known . . . [to police officials] sometime after 2.00 p.m.[48]

With the outbreak of rioting, a state of emergency was declared, and the prime minister, reflecting the almost inevitable concern of governmental authorities with spreading disorder, told the House of Representatives:

> This Government is responsible for the safety of the subjects, for the preservation of law and order. . . . And if it is necessary to shoot to preserve law and order we will shoot. Am I just to stand by when people are being attacked, when stones are being thrown at trains, when bus drivers are pulled out and hammered for driving their buses?[49]

While the capacity to strike, and to precipitate disorder, has given labor organizations a highly significant element of political power, resort to "direct action" in serious political confrontations runs the twin risks of failing to be effective and creating an adverse public reaction against the unions and their associated parties. The entire labor movement is seldom united on action with political ramifications, and strikes often lack sufficient backing by organized labor and the public to generate effective coercive pressure. Furthermore, trade unions represent only a small fraction of the society, and their efforts to use coercion frequently appear to the public to be contrary to the wider interests of the community. When Prime Minister Senanayake was denounced by the opposition parties for his determined stand against the 1968 public servants' strike, he threatened to call an election on the issue, claiming his actions were supported by public opinion.[50] A government confronted with strikes or disorder faces the danger of appearing either irresolute or repressive, but may also appear in the role of defender of the basic interests of the community as a whole.

Notes

1. *The C.F.T.U. and the Working-Class Movement* (Colombo: Ceylon Federation of Trade Unions, 1966), p. 10. Strikes in the early 1940s were attributed by Samasamajists to the inadequacies of the colonial legislature as a channel for realizing objectives. "The Real Situation in Ceylon," *Fourth International* 3 (October 1942): 301–2 (reprinted from *Samasamajist,* June 10, 1942).

2. The general strike of 1947 is thought by many to have hastened the grant of independence, which came in February 1948. Keuneman, for example, claimed that despite its failure to win immediate demands, the strike "nevertheless played a decisive part in the struggle for independence." Pieter Keuneman, *Twenty Years of the Ceylon Communist Party* (Colombo: Communist Party, 1963), p. 9.

3. In his well-known study, K.G.J.C. Knowles has categorized "consciously" political strikes as (1) revolutionary general strikes, (2) strikes having political objectives and intended to force action on the government, and (3) strikes having industrial objectives, but timed according to political considerations. He has also cited "unconsciously" political strikes as those called for industrial reasons but requiring government action or those which because of their impact are liable to lead to government action. K.G.J.C. Knowles, *Strikes—A Study in Industrial Conflict* (Oxford: Basil Blackwell, 1952), p. 292.

4. Leslie Goonewardene, *A Short History of the Lanka Sama Samaja Party* (Colombo: Lanka Sama Samaja Party, 1960), p. 61.

5. Excluded from consideration here are a few hartals which did not involve significant participation by trade unions and organized workers.

6. Goonewardene, *History of the Lanka Sama Samaja Party,* pp. 60–61.

7. Reported in interviews conducted by the author in 1965 and 1967.

8. *The History of 25 Years of Proud Service to the Working Class by the Ceylon Trade Union Federation* (Colombo: Ceylon Trade Union Federation, 1965), p. 17.

9. Goonewardene, *History of the Lanka Sama Samaja Party,* p. 45.

10. Ceylon, House of Representatives, *Parliamentary Debates (Hansard),* vol. 65, col. 613 (March 11, 1966).

11. Ibid., vol. 15, col. 2496 (September 1, 1953).

12. *Administration Report of the Commissioner of Labour for 1946* (Colombo: Government Press, 1947), p. 14; Goonewardene, *History of the Lanka Sama Samaja Party,* pp. 28–30.

13. *Memorandum by the Chief Secretary on Trade Unionism among Public Servants in Ceylon,* Sessional Paper VI—1947 (Colombo: Government Press, 1947), p. 8.

14. *Administration Report of the Commissioner of Labour for 1947* (Colombo: Government Press, 1948), pp. 26–27; *First and Second Interim Reports of the Strike Committee,* Sessional Paper XIV—1947 (Colombo: Government Press, 1947).

15. *Ceylon Observer,* December 29, 1961, p. 8.

16. Ibid., December 29, 1961, p. 1; and January 4, 1962, p. 7.

17. Ibid., January 8, 1962, p. 3.
18. The developments surrounding the attempted coup d'état are described in Robert N. Kearney, "The New Political Crises of Ceylon," *Asian Survey* 2 (June 1962): 19–27.
19. *Bank Worker,* March 1963, p. 2.
20. *Red Tape,* July 1968, pp. 1–3.
21. *Ceylon Daily News,* December 1, 2, 6, and 22, 1968.
22. *Red Tape,* June, 1969, p. 8.
23. "Editorial Notes," *Young Socialist* (Colombo), no. 9 (1963): 182.
24. Public Service Workers' Trade Union Federation, *Fifth Congress Report—From 1965 to 1967* (Colombo: Public Service Workers' Trade Union Federation, 1967), pp. 9–10; Goonewardene, *History of the Lanka Sama Samaja Party,* p. 59.
25. *Ceylon Observer,* December 12, 1961, p. 1.
26. House, *Debates,* vol. 46, col. 931 (January 25, 1962).
27. *Ceylon News,* September 24, 1964, p. 6.
28. *Ceylon Daily News,* August 28, 1967, p. 1.
29. House, *Debates,* vol. 34, cols. 736–37 (February 12, 1959).
30. *Ceylon Today,* 14 (March-April 1965): 3.
31. *Ceylon Daily News,* January 8, 1966, p. 1.
32. Government Clerical Service Union, *45th Annual Report and Statement of Accounts, 1965-1966* (Colombo: Government Clerical Service Union, 1966), pp. 35–36. An opposition leader claimed nearly forty thousand public employees were fined for participating in the strike. House, *Debates,* vol. 65, col. 589 (March 11, 1966).
33. Based on the author's interviews with trade-union officers and leaders of government and opposition political parties during 1967.
34. See *Nation* (Colombo), June 22, 1967, p. 12. Charges were brought under rule 261 of the public service regulations, which prohibits public servants from "disseminating political publications." *The Ceylon Government Manual of Procedure,* 4th ed. (Colombo: Government Press, 1957, with correction slips through no. 26, dated April 19, 1967), p. 44.
35. It is conceivable that some individuals or groups holding governmental power might accept or even encourage disorder and destruction directed toward certain groups—perhaps foreign business or other interests—against whom the governmental authorities themselves fear to move. However, such cases are, in all likelihood, highly exceptional and do not appear relevant to contemporary Ceylon. The holders of governmental power normally are able or expect to achieve their objectives by use of the machinery of the state, and would view unauthorized violence as tending to discredit their rule and bring into question their capacity to hold and exercise power.
36. One commentator, however, claimed that labor strife helped to create a climate of disorder and an appearance of governmental paralysis preceding the riots. Tarzie Vittachi, *Emergency '58: The Story of the Ceylon Race Riots* (London: Andre Deutsch, 1958), pp. 29–32, 104.

37. In a stimulating study, James L. Payne has argued that labor organizations in Peru have utilized their capacity to threaten or create violence to coerce the political executive and win demands they could not obtain through applying economic pressure on employers, due to their weak economic bargaining position. James L. Payne, *Labor and Politics in Peru* (New Haven and London: Yale University Press, 1965). The situation in Ceylon is dissimilar in several ways, primarily because, in the absence of a tradition of military overthrows, the government is less insecure. Also, many labor organizations have had relative success in collective bargaining, and the nature of the political and economic systems may make it more difficult for the government to impose settlements in many instances. Despite a lesser magnitude and role, however, the coercive power of potential disorder is apparent in union relations with the government in Ceylon as well.

38. The sponsors of the hartal claim that twelve lives were lost as a result of firing by police.

39. Administration Report of the Government Agent, Western Province, for 1953, in *Administration Reports of the Government Agents and Assistant Government Agents for 1953* (Colombo: Government Press, 1954), pp. 4–5.

40. *Administration Report of the General Manager, Ceylon Government Railway, for 1953* (Colombo: Government Press, 1954), p. 20.

41. *Ceylon Today* 15 (December 1966): 2.

42. Ceylon, House of Representatives, *Report on the Incidents in Colombo on 1st May, 1965,* Parliamentary Series no. 6 of the Sixth Parliament, First Session, 1965-66 (Colombo: Government Press, 1966), p. 10.

43. M. G. Mendis, *Ceylon Federation of Trade Unions: Report of the General Secretary to the 17th Sessions* (Colombo: Ceylon Federation of Trade Unions, 1966), p. 5.

44. *Report of the Special Committee Appointed to Inquire into and Report on the Police Arrangements on the 8th January, 1966, in Connection with the Motion in the House of Representatives on the Regulations under the Tamil Language (Special Provisions) Act,* Sessional Paper V—1966 (Colombo: Government Press, 1966), pp. 2–6, 14–15.

45. House, *Debates,* vol. 64, col. 1066 (January 26, 1966). Opposition leaders claim that at least twice that number of public servants participated in the strike.

46. *Report of the Special Committee on the 8th January 1966,* pp. 25–28.

47. *Ceylon Daily News,* January 9, 1966, p. 1.

48. *Report of the Special Committee on the 8th January 1966,* p. 29.

49. House, *Debates,* vol. 64, col. 165 (January 8, 1966).

50. Ibid., vol. 83, cols. 390–91, 396 (December 7, 1968).

The Alliance of Peasants and Workers: Some Problems Concerning the Articulation of Classes (Algeria and China)

K. W. J. Post

Introduction

Marxist writers have customarily regarded socialist revolutions as involving worker-peasant alliances, although in recent years emphasis has tended to be placed on the peasant half, and this emphasis has also spread to non-Marxist analysts. This paper seeks to establish some of the basic theoretical questions which Marxists will have to answer in order to explore more fully the problematic of such a class alliance. In doing so it draws on the historical examples of Algeria and China.

The problematic is viewed as basically that of the differing nature of the articulation of industrial capitalism with precapitalist modes of production, distribution, and exchange to produce the "underdeveloped capitalism" which has characterized much of the world. The process of articulation has involved other processes of "disarticulation" of existing social formations and their "rearticulation," and has produced complex patterns of class formation. In the perspective of worker-peasant alliances, what seems most significant is the extent to which an agricultural proletariat develops in conjunction on the one hand with the poor peasants and on the other with the nonagricultural working class. Also of great importance is the emergence of an urban "lumpen-petty bourgeoisie" and its relations with both peasants and workers.

The Problematic

For those concerned with the successful completion of a socialist revolution in a country characterized by underdeveloped capitalism—one, that is, which combines precapitalist and capitalist modes of production—the problem of the relations between two

First published as a working paper (no. 8, August 1975) issued by the Centre for Developing-Area Studies, McGill University, Montreal. Reprinted with permission of the author.

major subordinate classes, peasants and wage workers, must be central.[1] From the perspective of the Marxist left in particular it involves a debate concerning the source of the main revolutionary thrust. It does not seem too great a simplification to say that Marx and Engels looked to the industrial proletariat, Lenin to a revolutionary alliance, with the peasants in a subordinate position, and Mao (at least after 1927) to the peasants.[2] The last position has been taken even further by Marxists like Régis Debray, who scorned the cities as sources of corruption for revolutionaries, by Frantz Fanon and his disciples, strongly influenced by Marxism, who looked to a revolution of the peasants and urban lumpenproletariat, not to the working class proper, and by bourgeois scholars like Eric Wolf, who by a feat of intellectual prestidigitation lumps the Mexican, Russian, Chinese, Vietnamese, Algerian, and Cuban experiences together as "peasant wars."[3] From a different perspective, the analytical work of so careful and progressive a scholar as Jean Chesneaux illustrates the problem further. In one book he shows how the failure of the Chinese labor movement to build effective links with the poor and middle peasants in the period 1919-1927 played a major part in the defeat of the first revolutionary wave.[4] In another his verdict on the total Chinese revolutionary process is that

> the essential ingredients of the modern Chinese revolution—ideas, men and structures—had been initially the product not of the countryside but of the industrial towns, though these new revolutionary forces had themselves only been transformed and adapted as a result of the defeat of the urban revolution in 1927. Implanted in the countryside from then onwards, they allowed the peasant movement to merge with the modern Chinese revolution and provided it with a mass base and a new vigour.
>
> The peasant movement, as an essential part of the Communist revolution after 1927, was not the result of internal and spontaneous evolution of the peasantry itself. The study of twentieth-century China does not confirm the theory of Frantz Fanon and his followers that the peasantry is a kind of inherently revolutionary class. The peasants have not acted as an independent historical force. In the last analysis, political hegemony has continued to belong to those forces in the historical process which have succeeded in setting the peasantry in motion; that is to say, the Communist movement with its proletarian roots and proletarian ideology, with its party and army—the instruments of modern revolutionary struggle.[5]

It is evident that the analysis of the relations between peasants and workers in revolutionary situations involves complex questions on a number of different levels. Chesneaux makes his comments primarily upon the "superstructural" level of ideas and organization, but there is also a more fundamental one of the organization and social relations of different modes of production and the articulation among them. This paper seeks to introduce a number of theoretical questions relating to the above-mentioned analysis at both levels, but more particularly to the latter.

Some Necessary Concepts

At the risk of appearing too abstract, it is necessary to establish an understanding concerning certain concepts which will recur throughout this paper. Historical data will be derived from the cases of two social formations, Algeria and China in the nineteenth and twentieth centuries, but for purposes of theorizing we must note that any social formation is based upon specific modes of production, exchange, and distribution. These modes constitute the economic practice of that formation, the ways in which it produces and reproduces the material necessities for its existence. A mode of production has two aspects (as, in fact, do the other two closely related modes): an organizational one, determining the way in which its elements are brought together to form forces of production, and its derived *social* relations of production, which are the basis of the class structure of the given social formation.[6] Organizationally, a mode of production brings together labor power and the means of production, and to do so involves organizers and direct producers. Sometimes these roles are combined in the same person, in some forms of peasant agriculture, for example, or in petty-bourgeois trade and handicrafts. Larger-scale production involves a separation of roles and the introduction of a third, the non-laborer who either extends the organizer's capacity to organize (the feudal bailiff or capitalist industrial manager) or supplies the organizer with special knowledge (agronomists, chemists, company lawyers).[7] When it is noted that any actual social formation is based upon more than one mode of production, it can readily be seen that these organizational aspects and their expression in social relations provide the foundation for a multiple class structure. Thus capitalist formations—in one variation the concern of this paper—even in their most developed form contain petty-bourgeois small-scale producers of precapitalist origin as well as the three typical classes of capitalism itself—capitalist organizers, the directly producing proletariat, and middle-class managers, shop assistants, and so on, who do not produce directly.[8]

At the beginning of this paper it was noted that its concern was with the underdeveloped, dependent variation of capitalism and that a very important structural feature of such a capitalism is its combination of both capitalist and precapitalist modes of production, distribution, and exchange. This concern raises in its most complex form the questions of how such modes are actually joined together in a given social formation, and beyond that of what their relations are with the cognitive and political practices whose organizational structures provide the "superstructure" on the economic "substructure."[9] I will refer to this multiple joining together as "articulation," but the word is used in a double sense, since the process of joining the structures of a social formation involves two concurrent activities. In articulating, the parts not only join together but also give expression to one another and thus might be said to develop one another.[10] Articulated entities are therefore conditions for one another's existence, and hence from articulation stems contradiction, since the moments of contradiction are both conditions of one another's existence *and* obstacles to the simultaneous development of each.

Further theoretical discussion at this highly general level is precluded by space.[11] In particular, although it is central to any analysis based on dialectical materialism, the question of contradiction cannot be pursued further. Nevertheless, another point must be made about the articulation of a total social formation, which involves the structures of cognitive and political, as well as economic, practice and therefore enters directly into any discussion of workers' and peasants' revolutions. Let it be noted, therefore, that although the modes of production, exchange, and distribution are the primary determinants of class structure and human action, classes can only be fully formed and action embarked upon because economic structures are articulated with others and receive their full expression through them. Thus, the ruling class may be that which controls the dominant mode of production, and the state may be its instrument, but it is only because it can use the state to coordinate all aspects of its power that it can fully control the processes of economic practice.

Disarticulation, Rearticulation, and Class Formation

Although articulation among different modes of production is the most important determinant of the nature of any given social formation, historically this articulation has occurred in very different circumstances. Broadly, it may be said that the nature of the articulation has been governed by the relative weight of the contradictions internal to the given social formation and those external to it, that is, those resulting from its articulation with other formations. No historical formation has ever developed (or been underdeveloped in the sense of note 1 above) without the intervention of external forces; the role of imperialism in Britain's primitive accumulation and in determining the final articulation of its capitalism proves that beyond doubt. But the balance lies in the extent to which the dominant classes of a social formation retain control of its labor power and means of production, hence of the organization of its economic practice. From this proposition the hypotheses follow, first, that some formations may develop primarily through their internal articulations and contradictions (although these will mediate, and thus be mediated by, external ones). Second, it may be suggested that we may be able to differentiate along these lines among forms of imperialism and colonialism and their effects upon articulation and class struggle.

In order to do this systematically, however, it is necessary to introduce concepts of disarticulation and rearticulation as counterparts to articulation. Thus, a formation may be disarticulated when the relations of its constituent parts are severed and thus cease to be effective conditions of one another's existence. As a sequel, those parts, already changed by the process of disarticulation and with the addition of others, are rearticulated to form another formation.[12] In terms of the question of internal and external contradictions just discussed, it should be clear that disarticulation and rearticulation may receive their main impulses in different cases from either inside or outside the given social formation. It should also be obvious that not only the organization of the modes of economic practice will be affected, but also their social relations; in other words, a new class structure will begin to emerge.

What are some of the most important forces of disarticulation and rearticulation which can be seen at work in our chosen historical examples?[13] In the case of direct colonial conquest, the destruction of property and killing of people may well be the first act of disarticulation; if the population of Algeria indeed fell from nearly 6 million in 1830 to 2.5 million in 1852, it was a catastrophic blow to the present-conquest social formation.[14] Internal civil war and rebellion, and also natural disasters such as floods, may well play a similar role; the suppression of the Taiping and Nien rebellions in nineteenth-century China cost millions of lives. (China's total population was big enough, however, to permit resettlement from other areas.) Direct colonial rule enabled other destructive forces to be brought to bear. In Algeria the seizure of *beylik* and *habus* lands and the decimation of recalcitrant tribes was one element. With the creation of the colonial state at the political level legislation was another; thus, the *zaouiya* charity system to sustain the poor could be destroyed, and, even more important, French concepts of private property in land introduced. The colonial beneficiaries of these moves saw quite clearly how such disarticulation of a precapitalist mode of production could lead to a rearticulation on capitalist lines: as the newspaper *L'Indépendant* put it in April 1861, "Thanks to the constitution of property which proceeds from this, the greater part of Algerian territory passes immediately from the condition of dead value to the state of real value."[15]

The rearticulation took place in two stages, however, and not immediately on the basis of a capitalist mode of production. Large-scale settlement on the land by French and other European immigrants (344,000 already by 1876) was at first organized on the basis of small peasant farms, based mainly on family labor and with a typically petty-bourgeois combination of organizational and laboring roles. Around 1880 another element entered the rearticulation—the founding of new capitalist enterprises in agriculture, vineyards—in other words, elements of organization, capital, and technology not previously significant in the articulation of the new colonial mode of production were introduced. The vine came to dominate the Algerian economy; in the fifty years after 1900 the area devoted to it doubled, and in only five years (1927-1932) in the main vineyard region 173,013 hectares were brought under the new crop, while the wheat-growing area diminished by 79,608 hectares.[16]

China, of course, escaped the element of direct colonial rule, and the disarticulation of its economic base was slower and less extreme in consequence. The most important element was one which was also present, but less decisive, in Algeria. Speaking of China after the final collapse of the empire in 1911, Wolf notes that

> to some extent . . . population pressure, failure in water control, political fragmentation, depletion of good reserves . . . had made their appearance before in the course of Chinese history. The twentieth century, however, proved distinctive in facilitating the diffusion of private entrepreneurial capitalism into the rural areas of China and in governing specifically Chinese reactions to this spread.[17]

This diffusion had been occurring at least since the Treaty of

Nanking (1842) and the establishment of the Treaty Ports. It has led to the depreciation of copper coinage relative to silver (especially important since copper was the currency of the peasant economy), the driving out of business of precapitalist forms of river and canal transport, and, above all, the decline of village crafts, an extremely important part of peasant enterprise. Thus, Chinese scholars were able to write of a later period that "China is gradually being reduced to an agrarian country, pure and simple; and an agrarian China is inevitably a starving China."[18] Entrepreneurial capitalism penetrates precapitalist economies first by linking their modes of exchange with its own; in so doing it both disarticulates them from their modes of production, by destroying village crafts by competition, then rearticulates the modes of exchange into new market systems dependent on imported goods. Once the penetrated economy is thus incorporated into an extremely oriented capitalist cycle of production and reproduction, it is possible to introduce capitalist organization into the mode of production itself. In China this process was slower and more uneven than in a colonial possession like Algeria; data with which to measure it are scarce, but it is indicative that in 1918 foreign-owned (therefore capitalist) mines produced 8.6 million tons of China's coal, and Chinese capitalists, 2.5 million tons, but 7.3 million tons were still produced by small-scale, precapitalist enterprises.[19]

So far our discussion of disarticulation and rearticulation has been directed toward the organizational aspects of economic practice. It is necessary now to broaden it into the realm of the social relations of production, and to speak of class formation. It was suggested earlier that we can distinguish between social formations in which the major forces of change have come from outside and those which have been rearticulated primarily by internal contradictions by focusing on the ability of their ruling classes to adjust to the processes of change. Clearly in the Algerian case the preconquest ruling classes (or class, if we distinguish Turkish officials and landholders from tribal leaders) was very seriously weakened by the measures adopted by French colonialism. The creation of a settler economy based mainly upon viticulture entirely changed the shape of the class structure. Two main trends may be discerned. First, there was a shift in the settler class system associated with the move toward capitalist organization on a large scale after 1880; by the mid-1950s only 4 percent of the settlers held land, so the overwhelming majority were now urban capitalists, running petty-bourgeois enterprises or else employed in middle-class or skilled working-class occupations. Of the twenty-two thousand who held land, 30 percent controlled 85 percent of the total area; the settler ruling class was thus the constellation of big growers, merchants, and financiers who dominated agriculture (60 percent of Algeria's gross agricultural revenue came from settler farming).[20]

On the part of the Arabs and Berbers, the existence in the mid-1950s of some five hundred landholders with more than five hundred hectares each represented only a feeble and distorted survival of the old ruling class and its adaptation to capitalism. The vast majority of the approximately six hundred thirty thousand Muslims who held land were subject to severe pressures—rapid population growth, insufficient land (an average of 11 hectares each, compared with 124 for each settler), poor soil, inadequate access to credit and other facilities, inability to move into export agriculture, and so on.[21] Three courses were open to peasants who lost their land entirely or could not live from what they held. They might emigrate to France and join the most depressed stratum of the working class there (some six hundred thousand had done so by the mid-1950s). They might try their luck in the urban areas of their own country, finding unskilled work if it was good, scarcely surviving from day to day if they remained unemployed or joined the lowest stratum of the petty bourgeoisie as street hawker, shoeshiner, or whatever. Or they might try to find work on one of the capitalist farms, though the vineyards needed only fifty workdays per laborer per year and wheat farms, ten.[22]

In Algeria the rearticulation around a capitalist mode of production which was a product of settler colonialism created a new European ruling class to which the wealthy Muslims were only an adjunct. In China the old ruling class survived the less extensive rearticulation. On the one hand the landlords were disarticulated at the political level from the state by the collapse of the ancient imperial bureaucracy, which they had overlapped and interpenetrated.[23] On the other they were rearticulated into the spreading capitalist organization of production and exchange by broadening their activities and working with foreign capital, and again with the state through the warlords or the Kuomintang. As Wolf puts it:

> It was through a new symbiosis between landlords, officials, soldiers, and merchants—achieved on the local or regional level in the twenties and thirties—that potentially capitalizable wealth was mobilized in the countryside and combined with capital imported from the eastern seaboard.[24]

The long-suffering peasant, squeezed even more in the 1920s and 1930s by rising rents and taxes, on occasion saw the nature of the new ruling class equally clearly—"Never forget the hundred-headed landlords; militarist, money-lender, magistrate, tax-collector, police-chief, *min-t'uan* ("private militia") leader, chamber of commerce and Kuomintang masters, dog-men all!"[25]

The Articulation of Workers and Peasants at the Economic Level

It is time to focus on the formation of classes specifically at the level of the two most exploited, workers and peasants. Some clarification is necessary here. "Worker" as used in this paper means a capitalist wage worker, in industry, construction, transport, mining, or agriculture, selling labor power and producing surplus value.[26] Peasant production is essentially petty bourgeois and precapitalist. Peasants combine in their persons both the organization of production and direct labor; they have some sort of control over both their own labor power and land and other means of production, even when directed by a landlord as to what to plant and when they might work their own land. They do not sell their labor power. For me, agricultural wage laborers as such are not peasants, although obviously peasants may move into capitalist wage labor and out again, a point to which we must return.[27] The distinction is also very important in explaining the internal differentiation of a peasantry into poor, middle, and rich strata. The first are those who are pushed into a sale of part of their labor power, and thus articulate to some extent with the capitalist mode of production. Rich peasants are articulated in another way, directing their production toward the capitalist market and buying labor power; if they commit themselves entirely to that market and limit themselves personally to an organizing role—or even employ a manager—then they are making the transition to becoming capitalist farmers.[28]

Our focus, then, is the articulation between peasants of precapitalist origins and capitalist wage workers. Thus, the alliance between peasants and workers in an underdeveloped capitalist social formation is an alliance between elements of modes of production of different historical origins (which explains in general terms the contradictions which often arise within such an alliance). Peasants are of course articulated with other producers also in a purely precapitalist formation. As already noted, peasant production itself involves craft work by certain families or members of families—the latter a particularly close form of articulation of different kinds of production. The existence of urban settlements in precapitalist social formations also implies variations in the organization of production and some specifically urban enterprises and occupations with which the rural population is nevertheless articulated. In precolonial Algeria, for example, migrants from some Kabylie villages were linked with certain urban occupations (porters, water-carriers, food and charcoal sellers, bath attendants). In the Chinese case Chesneaux relates the recruitment of the new capitalist industrial labor force to pre-capitalist organizational forms which might bring peasants into urban occupations, labor contracting, and the guild and appren-ticeship systems.[29]

The disarticulation and rearticulation consequent upon the encroachment of capitalism link peasants with towns in other ways. Most important, those peasants who are squeezed out of the rural areas create in the urban complex new phenomena, which are partly a new working class, partly not. This duality must be recognized if we are to understand the articulation at economic and other levels between peasants and workers. On the one hand, new urban enterprises—and for that matter nonagricultural enterprises in rural areas—recruit their wage labor from the precapitalist urban poor but particularly from the dispossessed peasants. Those employed are the working class proper, along with its reserve army of temporarily unemployed, often very numerous. On the other hand, many of the temporarily unem-ployed will be eking out a living in occupations which are organized on petty-bourgeois lines, street hawkers, shoe-cleaners, and the like, and beyond that there will be many who have given up hope of wage employment (or never wanted it) and are now permanently within this lowest stratum of the petty bourgeoisie. Such a stratum may be very closely articulated with the working class proper, but it is not structurally part of it, and it is evading the issue to give it such labels as "subproletariat."[30] This whole growing urban petty bourgeoisie with which the peasantry is being rearticulated is in fact a complex phenomenon, with its own internal divisions. Pierre Bourdieu, for example, in a very interesting essay on this phenomenon in Algeria, sees that stratum as divided into those small trading and craft enterprises which are survivals from precapitalist modes (such as charcoal-sellers or embroiderers) and those which arise in association with capitalism (petrol-sellers, say, or mechanics).[31] The former seem much to outnumber the latter, and it may be suggested that peasants newly arrived in towns find it much easier to find a place in them. On the other hand Bourdieu suggests a threefold stratification into those of the urban petty bourgeoisie who are "on the frontier of capitalist enterprise" (like some at least of our rich peasants mentioned above), those who make an adequate living but have no capital for expansion, and those who cannot even make an adequate living.[32] Obviously the "lowest stratum of the petty bourgeoisie" discerned above would be identified with Bourdieu's third stratum. All three, however, represent a class which is a focus of articulation for the dispossessed peasants' alternative to the urban working class, and that articulation may the more easily be achieved because the organization of nonagricultural economic practice at that level has much in common with that of peasant cultivation.[33]

The rearticulation of capitalist and precapitalist modes of production into a new underdeveloped capitalist social formation thus pushes peasants who cannot survive purely as such into two forms of nonagricultural employment, wage labor and petty-bourgeois enterprise. It may also push them into seeking work for wages in agriculture, the importance of which for a worker-peasant alliance must be emphasized, because this division of the working class into agricultural and industrial may facilitate the link at ideological and organizational levels. What should be stressed at this point in the discussion are the diverse factors affecting the articulation at the economic level. Thus, the relative size of the nonagricultural working class will affect its capacity to absorb squeezed-out peasants, as will various aspects of its organization—for example, the relative need for skilled, as opposed to unskilled, labor. Similarly important are the size and organization of agricultural wage labor, the latter element being significant in terms of such matters as the permanent or seasonal need for labor. All these factors will affect another, what may be termed the mobility existing between the peasantry and the working class, that is, the capacity of individuals to rotate from one to another over greater or longer periods. This mobility may cover a whole spectrum of situations, from the poor peasant who alternates work on his own plot with unskilled wage labor on an estate within the same week to the one who leaves the rural area completely and becomes a skilled worker in a large factory.

Data from Algeria and China will illustrate some aspects of the foregoing discussion. Table 1 gives a partial perspective on the employment situation in Algeria in the mid-1950s.

From this it can readily be seen that the six hundred thousand or so landholding peasants were under extreme pressure to find wage employment or other sources of income, but that this was not readily available. A very large proportion had been driven to seek some amount of supplementary seasonal work as agricultural

Table 1
The Structure of Muslim Employment in Algeria

Manufacturing and service labor	333,000
Urban unemployed	150,000
Landholders	630,000
Permanent agricultural labor	108,000
Seasonal agricultural labor	434,000
"Completely or almost completely unemployed in agriculture"	370,000
"Family help . . . practically without employment"	480,000

Sources: Ian Clegg, *Workers' Self-Management in Algeria* (New York: Monthly Review Press), p. 30; and Tami Tidafi, *L'agriculture algérienne et ses perspectives de developpement* (Paris: Maspero, 1969), pp. 29 and 40–41.
Note: "Casual laborers" and those "almost completely unemployed" may overlap, and 960,000 women are not included.

wage laborers. Unfortunately, the way in which data are given in censuses and other surveys does not permit any quantification of the strata of the urban petty bourgeoisie into which rural migrants were likely to move. The structure of urban wage employment requires further comment.[34] The inclusion of "services" makes the total of 330,000 rather larger than the working class as I have defined it, but taking this unavoidably as our basic figure, it must be noted, first, that there were also 239,000 Europeans in this category. Settler colonialism and the changing class structure of the European population thus segmented the Algerian working class, and this racial division was reinforced by the fact that most skilled jobs were held by Europeans, concentrated in engineering, food-processing, textiles, and paper. With some three hundred fifty thousand jobs classified as regular sources of employment and over two hundred thousand as irregular, it is obvious that most of the former would be held by Europeans. A second important feature of the Algerian working class on the eve of the revolution was the effect upon it of the organization of production into units of various sizes. Some twenty-eight thousand artisan workshops (out of one hundred fifty-five thousand such petty-bourgeois enterprises) employed a few men each. Approximately sixteen hundred capitalist companies (out of ninety-six hundred) employed more than half the industrial work force. There was thus both concentration and dispersal, but with the bigger companies employing on the average relatively few workers by developed capitalist standards, and those disproportionately European. The Muslim working class thus tended to be unskilled, dispersed in small units, and subject to irregular employment.

Despite the admirable work of Chesneaux, less data are available for pre-1949 China. However, two comparative generalizations may be made. The best available estimate of the size of the Chinese working class around 1919 is 1,489,000, with 655,000 (44 percent) in foreign enterprises and 834,000 (56 percent and probably an underestimate) in those of Chinese capitalists.[35] Although Chesneaux emphasizes the particular importance of the foreign firms because of their technological advancement, predominance in heavy industry, and geographical concentration, we should note in general that the pattern of Chinese development had produced a significant industrial stratum in the Chinese capitalist class, consonant with our earlier characterization of its relatively advanced formation. There was, then, a real indigenous enemy for the Chinese working class. The other general point to note is that what evidence exists suggests that the agrarian working class—permanent and casual wage labor—was completely insignificant; available estimates indicate that only about 20 percent of agricultural labor was done by hired hands.[36]

The Articulation of Workers and Peasants at the Political Level

At this stage in the discussion we should be in a position to move to the level of political practice—the production and reproduction of class power—and more specifically to its revolutionary variant, when the ability of a ruling class to reproduce its power breaks down. This involves complex questions which cannot be touched here, such as the nature of the existing "power bloc" of dominant classes and its articulation with the state apparatus.[37] Here the field must be confined to a few aspects of the possible articulations between peasants and workers in revolutionary situations.

Thus, by that articulation I do not merely mean the provision of leadership for peasant movements. Certainly both peasant rebellions in precapitalist formations and peasant upsurges in underdeveloped capitalist ones would be likely to draw on leaders from other classes.[38] The importance of urban-rural links in that respect is also undeniable; as Wolf notes of Algeria:

> Reformist Islam provided the cultural form for the construction of
> a new network of social relations between clusters of middle

peasants in the countryside and the sons of the urban elite of the hinterland towns. The city-ward migration of the Algerian peasantry —more especially that of the Kabyles—not only brought them into contact with industrial and urban patterns of life, but produced a professional class in the course of that migratory experience. Once again networks were forged which linked clusters of peasants in the countryside with spokesmen and representatives in the cities.[39]

As is clear from this quotation, at the level of leadership the resources which the peasantry draws from the towns are usually not from the working class but from the lower ranks of the middle class—teachers, clerks, and the like. This paper is concerned with workers and peasants at the level of the rank and file, and with the relative weight of their classes in the mass thrust which carries a revolution forward.

In that respect two general questions—or rather, the answers to them—seem to be decisive. First, to what extent do the rhythms (or cycles) of political protest by workers and peasants coincide? Second, given that there is such a coincidence, what articulations exist on the fundamental economic level to ensure common action?

It should be apparent that the reactions of a precapitalist peasantry, articulated primarily at the level of exchange with capitalism but also providing some labor power for its mode of production, would be likely to follow a different rhythm from those of a working class which is the basic capitalist producer. Where the direct articulation between the two exploited classes remains weak, this difference is likely to remain. Thus, despite the immediate peasant origins and continuing rural links of the majority of Chinese workers in the period 1919-1927, Chesneaux has commented that

in 1919 the impoverished Chinese peasant was still expressing his resentment and his will to resist in traditional ways: and, for reasons that are not fully understood, peasant resistance was far less effective than it had been during the unrest that swept the country-side between 1850 and 1870. It did not reach Taiping heights until 1925-27; and even then the peasants did not display the capacity for political struggle that was later so notable.[40]

As noted in the beginning of this paper, the working-class movement led by the Chinese Communist party failed to intervene decisively in 1925-1927 to break this rhythm and create a double revolutionary thrust. After the failure of 1927, indeed, the party was pushed out to the most marginal (Wolf's "free") peasants, marginal in the sense of isolation from major urban centers and absence of significant articulation with the capitalist elements of the economy, which remained the domain of the Kuomintang bourgeoisie and foreigners. This separation follows from the nature of the disarticulation and rearticulation of China's socio-economic structures since the second quarter of the nineteenth century, discussed earlier, which concentrated capitalist forms in urban areas and the hinterland open to the coast, and left intact (though more or less eroded) vast parts of the peasant precapitalist mode of production. It was only the changes created by the Japanese invasion and, even more important, the growing crisis of China's underdeveloped capitalism after 1945 which permitted the Communist party to return to the cities.[41]

Algeria provides an interesting comparison. There the armed struggle against French rule began in the rural areas in 1954 and grew there, but in 1956-1957 and at the end of 1960 the FLN was able to launch major activity including mass demonstrations—in Algiers in face of increasing repression in the hinterland. It is obviously important in terms of the articulation of the peasantry and working class that this repression caused a wave of migration to the bigger towns; the population of Algiers doubled in 1959-1960 (from 293,000 to 588,000). It is most misleading to see the Algerian revolution, as Wolf does, as a "peasant war" and to look to middle peasants as the crucial group. This ignores three important factors. First, before the revolution there was a thirty-year history of working-class struggle about which we need to know much more, beginning with the activities of the Etoile Nord Africaine among the Muslim migrants in France.[42] Already by 1936-1937 the Syndicat National des Instituteurs was attempting to organize a union among agricultural laborers.[43] In February 1956 working-class struggle culminated organizationally in the formation of the Union Générale des Travailleurs Algériens (UGTA).

A second mistake is to confuse the revolutionary movement as a totality with its military activity alone. Obviously the areas which French security regarded as "rotten" or "heavily contaminated" would be the mountainous ones, inhabited by poor peasants, which were least accessible.[44] But this is to accept the authorities' own estimate of their capacity to patrol, arrest, and torture. The turning point of the revolution was probably not a military event at all, but the demonstrations by the Muslim working class and petty bourgeoisie in answer to General de Gaulle's visit to Algiers in December 1960. When in August 1962 the Muslim working class of Algiers under the leadership of the UGTA demonstrated against the feuding FLN leadership with the cry of "Sba'a snine, barakat!" ("Seven years [of war], this is enough!"), final proof was given of its maturity and high level of consciousness.

Third, it seems much more true to say that the main thrust of the revolution was generated by the articulation and interplay between workers and peasants than to look simplistically to the latter—or even just one stratum of them—alone. As Launay puts it, "If the understanding of a Revolution necessitates a dialectical spirit and method, the Algerian revolution is a characteristic example of it."[45] The data collected by the author makes it apparent that not only the urban working class but also the rural working class, which was most closely articulated with the poor peasants, was vital.[46] Thus, although Launay stresses the initiative of "the relatively well-off peasants and the inhabitants of small towns, small traders or small entrepreneurs, or teachers who visited the rural areas," it is also clear that from the beginning estate laborers went on strike or deserted, and Launay also notes that it was the "best workers" who often guided the freedom fighters in their attacks on estates and who destroyed equipment.[47] More than this, Launay notes a very important change of emphasis in the course of the struggle:

> Once the first stimulus was given, the mass of small indebted proletarianised peasants and that of the agricultural day-labourers and unemployed responded to it even beyond what the leaders foresaw . . . and progressively, with most of the F.L.N. cadres dead or on the run, this proletariat and subproletariat provided the new cadres in action in 1959-1960.[48]

In speaking of a revolutionary "dialectic" governed by the articulation of peasants and workers, I have left aside the question of the role of the urban unemployed and the semiemployed, the impoverished petty bourgeoisie discussed earlier as a typical class feature of underdeveloped capitalism. Yet, if only in face of Frantz Fanon's belief that it was the peasantry and "lumpen-proletariat" which formed the muscle of the revolution, the discussion cannot be left without some reference to that third element. The problem is lack of evidence. Amar Ouzegane speaks of the "subproletariat" of Algiers as the recruiting-ground for urban cadres.[49] On the other hand, he describes some members of this group as working with the French against their own people; the basis for such a distinction is not clear but seems to be that between professional criminals and the rest.[50] It must have been the case that both combatants and many demonstrators in Algiers and other towns were drawn from what might perhaps better be called a "lumpen–petty bourgeoisie" than some kind of proletariat, since its main distinguishing feature is that its members are *not* employed in wage labor. Nevertheless, given its self-employment, concern with small property, and small-scale organizational units, it seems doubtful that such a stratum of a larger class (the wealthier members of which provide the model for its aspirations) would respond *collectively* to a socialist revolutionary message.

A return to our starting point, the concern with *socialist* revolutions, raises problems of class consciousness which cannot now be taken up. If Ian Clegg's hypothesis is correct, for example, and the Algerian peasants fought for "the memory of Abdel Kader's Algeria," while it was the workers who pushed forward self-management in 1962, then obviously in the immediate post-revolutionary situation there was a gulf between the two classes at the ideological level, and we would have to pursue the question of their structural articulation further to account for this rift.[51] Hopefully what this paper has done is to raise three theoretical and analytical issues. First, in the most general terms, we have to come to grips with the various ways in which underdeveloped capitalist formations have been created under the pressures of different forms of imperialism. Second, we need to see the relations between classes as they emerge in such formations as complex articulations determined by the combination of precapitalist and capitalist economic modes. Third, if we are concerned with revolution we must not force different formations into some simplistic mold, but recognize that complex articulation among potentially revolutionary classes and strata produces a complex interplay of action and reaction.

Notes

1. The term "underdeveloped capitalism" requires further explanation. Historically it refers here to all those countries which have been incorporated into the international capitalist economy by the imperialist expansion (not necessarily in its colonial variant) of such powers as Britain, France, the United States, and Japan. This incorporation was a complex process, involving other capitalist countries like the Netherlands which failed to become major powers and also semicapitalist tsarist Russia. In its early stages it also involved the imperialism of essentially precapitalist powers, Spain and Portugal, which in time saw their colonies contributing to the capitalist development of other European states rather than to their own. Two general conclusions may, however, be derived. The underdevelopment of the so-called Third World is directly related in a causal sense to the development of the major and minor capitalist industrial

countries, and the main structural feature of the former, with very few exceptions (Argentina, for example), is the combination of modes of production referred to above.

2. More specifically, of course, Lenin and Mao were concerned with the poor and middle-class peasants in Russia and China. Marx and Engels have of course been labeled "antipeasant" by critics, notably David Mitrany in his *Marx Against the Peasant,* which is too great an oversimplification. The founders of Marxism recognized the revolutionary potential of the peasantry in such countries as Ireland, India, and Algeria, but denied their capacity for an independent building of socialism; see, for example, Engels' letter to Kautsky, September 12, 1882.

3. See Eric Wolf, *Peasant Wars of the Twentieth Century* (New York: Harper & Row, 1969).

4. Jean Chesneaux, *The Chinese Labor Movement, 1919-1927* (Stanford: Stanford University Press, 1968).

5. Jean Chesneaux, *Peasant Revolts in China 1840-1949* (London: Thames and Hudson, 1973), pp. 152–53.

6. My discussion here owes much to Etienne Balibar, "The Basic Concepts of Historical Materialism," in *Reading Capital,* by Louis Althusser and Etienne Balibar (London: New Left Books, 1970).

7. The extension of capacity to organize may in fact be *qualitatively* related to *skills* (managers and bailiffs) or *quantitatively* to *scale* (clerks, shop assistants).

8. Many Marxists, including Lenin, have grouped the last element with the small-scale producers as a "petty bourgeoisie." This seems to me to be misleading, since the determinant relation of each to the means of production is quite different; the petty bourgeoisie proper owns means of production, the middle class sells its labor power, to that extent, at least, resembling the proletariat.

9. I define cognitive practice as the production and reproduction of the perception of material reality, and political practice as the production and reproduction of class power. It should be noted that my categorization of practices differs from that of Althusser and Balibar.

10. The verb "to articulate" has both meanings in English and French, and so is particularly useful when applied to a simultaneous double process. Althusser and Balibar employ the term, but apparently without recognizing this duality, and Pierre-Philippe Rey makes it central to his analysis, though again he fails to distinguish clearly between the two aspects of articulation. (See his *Colonialisme, néo-colonialisme et transition au capitalisme* [Paris: Maspero, 1971]; and "Sur l'articulation des modes de production," in *Les alliances des classes* [Paris: Maspero, 1973].)

11. My forthcoming study of the Jamaican labor rebellion of 1938, which has as one of its central concerns the relations between workers and peasants, treats these theoretical questions and other related ones extensively. It is entitled *Arise Ye Starvelings! The Jamaican Labor Rebellion of 1938 and Its Aftermath* (The Hague: Mouton, 1978).

12. It may be noted incidentally that the same thing happens during a revolutionary transformation.

13. Algeria and China are, of course, very different and do not cover the totality of possible factors. The preliminary nature of this entire discussion should now be apparent.

14. Figures given in Roger Murray and Tom Wengraf (actually Murray), "The Algerian Revolution—I," *New Left Review* 22 (December 1963): 23.

15. Wolf, *Peasant Wars*, p. 213, citing André Nouschi, *Enquête sur le niveau de vie des populations rurales Constantinoises de la conquête jusqu'en 1919* (Paris: Presses Universitaires de France, 1961), p. 282. For summary discussions of French land policy see Wolf, *Peasant Wars*, pp. 212–14; and Tami Tidafi, *L'agriculture algérienne et ses perspectives de développement* (Paris: Maspero, 1969), pp. 23–24.

16. Wolf, *Peasant Wars*, p. 223; and Michel Launay, *Paysans algériens* (Paris: Editions du Seuil, 1963), p. 18, citing the unpublished third volume of H. Isnard, *La vigne en Algérie*.

17. Wolf, *Peasant Wars*, p. 128. In view of the frequency with which I cite Wolf's work, previous criticism of him in this paper should be clarified. The individual essays and conclusion in this book contain much that is perceptive and valuable; this paper is largely based on an attempt to rework his data. The problem lies in Wolf's attempt to unify his six cases as "peasant wars," which forces them into a common pattern which obfuscates and ultimately mystifies. Wolf also tries too hard to ascribe a decisive role to "middle" peasants and those whom he calls "free"—"not constrained by any power domain" (p. 292), a point to which I shall return.

18. Fei Hsiao-tung and Chang Chih-I, *Earthbound China* (Chicago: University of Chicago Press, 1945), p. 305.

19. Chesneaux, *The Chinese Labor Movement*, p. 12.

20. Wolf, *Peasant Wars*, p. 224; and Ian Clegg, *Workers' Self-Management in Algeria* (New York: Monthly Review Press, 1971), p. 29, citing P. Hernandez, "Ceux qui étaient les pieds-noirs," *La Nef* 12–13 (October 1962–January 1963).

21. Data from Tidafi, *L'agriculture algérienne*, pp. 40–41; and Launay, *Paysans algériens*, p. 62.

22. See Wolf, *Peasant Wars*, pp. 230–31. On Muslim agriculture see also Murray, "Algerian Revolution," pp. 39–40.

23. The bureaucrats had been largely recruited from the landowning class and had often been landowners themselves. For summary discussions of this phenomenon see Wolf, *Peasant Wars*, pp. 102–5; and Barrington Moore, Jr., *Social Origins of Dictatorship and Democracy* (Boston: Beacon Press, 1966), pp. 162–74.

24. Wolf, *Peasant Wars*, p. 132.

25. Peasant song from Fukien province, c. 1929, quoted in Chesneaux, *Peasant Revolts*, p. 111.

26. This sentence conceals a number of problems which cannot be discussed here. Broadly speaking, I do not take all wage employees to be workers (Marx would have said proletarians, but to distinguish

underdeveloped capitalist situations from those he studied I avoid the term). Workers are the direct producers discerned above, those who directly produce use value in commodity form, transport commodities, and (adding categories to those listed above) store and maintain them. Clerks and shop assistants, for example, may help to realize a surplus value, but they play no active role in creating or maintaining use value and are thus "non-laborers"—middle class.

27. One of the major problems in Wolf's book is his uncertainty over the identification of rural wage laborers as peasants. His tendency to so identify them seriously distorts his analyses of Cuba and Algeria.

28. They also probably abandon the use of family labor, the crucial factor for middle peasants, who in a sense are the least articulated into capitalism. This last point (formulated differently) is Wolf's main reason for treating the middle peasants as crucial in a "peasant war"; Wolf, *Peasant Wars,* pp. 291–92.

29. Chesneaux, *Chinese Labor Movement,* pp. 54–61, 113–17, and 118–19.

30. See Pierre Bourdieu's second part, "Etude sociologique," in Bourdieu, Alain Darbel, Jean-Paul Rivet, and Claude Seibel, *Travail et travailleurs en Algérie* (Paris and The Hague: Mouton, 1963), p. 385. Bourdieu places three groups in his subproletariat, the unemployed and casual laborers, petty traders and artisans, and the employees of petty-bourgeois enterprises. He notes that the distinction is artificial because the three groups are "in fact interchangeable." Much more important, I think, is that the three are not of the same class, having different relations to the means of production, while the second is in no strict sense "proletarian."

31. Ibid., pt. 2, appendix 10, "Les artisans en Algérie," passim.

32. Ibid., pp. 530–31.

33. In combining organization and laboring roles in the same individual, for example, and in dependence upon family labor power. On this point see Bourdieu et al., *Travail et travailleurs,* p. 553. If there is any sense in speaking of the "peasantization" of cities, this phenomenon would provide an economic base for such analysis.

34. My discussion is based on data in Clegg, *Workers' Self-Management,* pp. 86–87.

35. Chesneaux, *Chinese Labor Movement,* pp. 42–43.

36. See Wolf, *Peasant Wars,* pp. 134–35.

37. The term is, of course, Nicos Poulantzas' and used by him in looking at developed capitalist formations. I have found it useful in analyzing underdeveloped formations also.

38. For precapitalist China, see Chesneaux, *Peasant Revolts,* p. 16.

39. Wolf, *Peasant Wars,* p. 234.

40. Chesneaux, *Chinese Labor Movement,* p. 15.

41. Though it had never entirely left them. One of our problems is that we know very little about the party's activity among the working class, albeit clandestine, after 1927. I hope that it is obvious that I regard Wolf's "free" peasants, outside the "power domain," as decisive

only in saving the Communist party after 1927, not in the whole revolution.

42. For the early history of the Etoile, see Amar Ouzegane, *Le meilleur combat* (Paris: Julliard, 1962), pp. 177–78 and 181; its first branch in Algeria itself was formed in 1934, according to the same source. In this context it is worth noting Bourdieu's remark, "Algeria is a society which has its proletariat in France." Bourdieu et al., *Travail et travailleurs*, p. 386, note 1.

43. See Launay, *Paysans algériens*, pp. 140–41.

44. See the map of the situation in 1957 in Pierre Bourdieu, *The Algerians*, rev. ed. (Boston: Beacon Press, 1962), pp. 166–67.

45. Launay, *Paysans algériens*, p. 177.

46. It could be argued that generalizations should not be made from the region—Oranie—studied by Launay, where about 40 percent of the wine production took place and which therefore had a large agricultural working class. If this is true, then the representative character of Oranie's middle peasants (Wolf's main supporting evidence) must also be questioned.

47. Launay, *Paysans algériens*, pp. 176–82, passim.

48. Ibid., p. 177.

49. Ouzegane, *Le meilleur combat*, pp. 251–54.

50. Ibid., pp. 252–53. See also Chesneaux, *Chinese Labor Movement*, pp. 363–64 and 369–70, for the counterrevolutionary activities of the Shanghai "Green Gang" in March-April 1927.

51. Clegg, *Workers' Self-Management*.

Politics and Organized Labor in India

E. A. Ramaswamy

Trade unions in India, although not formally committed to any political party, are steeped in party politics. The political involvement of trade unions is widely attributed to the partisan links of the leaders of organized labor. It is indeed argued that, but for these leaders, organized labor might be free from the domination of political parties, and a unified labor movement might emerge.[1] Implicit in these writings is the assumption that the rank-and-file members have no stake in party politics. One of the few explicit statements on the extent of rank-and-file interest in politics is that by Agarwal:

> Union leaders set up rival unions and union centres or defect from one party to another along with their union following. In doing this, they never consult or seek approval of the constituent members. The latter naturally feel little interested in the ideological predilections or shifting political loyalties of their leaders. They often feel bewildered or even confused at the political acrobatics of their leaders.[2]

Agarwal's position truly reflects present thinking on the subject.

We may ask what evidence there is that politics is thrust on an unwilling, if not hostile, rank and file by motivated outside leaders. Scholars propounding this view base their argument mostly on historical evidence. Almost every discussion of the problem goes back to the earliest beginnings of organized labor in this country to show that the first unions were not organizations *of* workers, but organizations *for* workers run by political leaders and social workers. This is followed by a discussion of the policies of the four major national federations of unions and how they have been influenced over the years by the different political parties. Finally, it is shown that the splits and mergers in the labor movement since the earliest days of unionism have been occasioned by corresponding splits and mergers between political parties. From this the conclusion is drawn that political parties

Reprinted from *Asian Survey* 13, no. 10: 914-28, with permission of the Regents of the University of California. Copyright © 1973 The Regents of The University of California. The author wishes to thank Professor M. N. Srinivas for supervising this research and Dr. B. S. Baviskar for his criticism on an earlier draft of the paper.

have a stranglehold over trade unions. Trade unions, then, are politically involved because the political parties and partisan trade-union leaders want them to be.

This conclusion is supported by some widely held notions regarding the general makeup of factory workers in India. The most important among these notions, such as the illiteracy, rural background, and low-caste origin of the workers, have been summed up by Sharma.[3] To this we may add a few more concepts which relate to the role of industrial workers as trade unionists. It is argued that the workers' loyalty is to individual leaders, no doubt motivated by their belief in the leaders' ability to deliver the goods, rather than to a trade union. The leaders themselves, with some notable exceptions, are primarily politicians with only a peripheral interest in organized labor. The leaders use their worker-following as a lever for their own career advancement, and can carry their following from one union and party to another. It is claimed that the workers, who cannot comprehend political ideology and have only work-related interests, allow themselves to be used by the leaders.

There is one other characteristic of the advocates of this argument which deserves attention. There is near universal interest among them in social engineering.[4] They deplore the fragmentation of organized labor and hold that only a united labor movement can cure the many ills of trade unionism in this country. If it is political affiliation which has caused this fragmentation, it deserves to be condemned. It is convenient to assume that politics is forced on workers by a motivated leadership and to rule out any political commitment on the part of the rank and file. For if the workers were politically involved, the cleavage between the unions could not be bridged by simply eliminating the partisan leaders. Trade-union unity would then just be an illusion, a bleak and difficult position to accept.

The extent of rank-and-file participation in politics merits serious examination. Apart from the implications this has for the question of working-class unity, it raises fundamental questions about the nature and extent of politicization among organized workers. I shall confine myself in this paper to a discussion of four major aspects of rank-and-file interest in party politics. I shall first discuss the extent of political commitment at the various levels of leadership and among the rank and file, and then show how this commitment is manifested and how intense it is. Finally, I shall examine the process of political socialization and the factors underlying political commitment.

I shall base this discussion on data gathered during nearly

fifteen months of intensive fieldwork between 1963-1970 among the textile workers' unions in Coimbatore, Tamilnadu. I shall in particular focus on the Coimbatore District Textile Workers' Union (TWU) affiliated to the Hind Mazdoor Sabha. The question arises as to whether this is an isolated case and hence not representative of the country as a whole. No apology is, however, necessary for a microstudy, since some of the most fundamental questions regarding trade unionism, including the ones posed in this paper, can be answered only on the basis of a number of intensive case studies which, unfortunately, are conspicuous by their absence.

The TWU was formed in 1937 by nationalist leaders. Key offices in the union are at present held by nationalist-turned-trade-union leaders who owe allegiance to the Praja Socialist Party (PSP) and hold top party offices at the state level. These leaders have obviously not emerged from the rank and file of the union. The domination of unions in India by such outsiders is well known and needs no further elaboration. What is more interesting and significant is the extent of party affiliation at the lower levels of leadership manned exclusively by workers.

Leaving aside the outsiders, we can conceive of three tiers of leadership in the TWU. The first tier is made up of positions occupied by workers in the head office of the union. The second tier is made up of the members of the District Committee, a powerful body of representatives elected by the union's branches spread all over the district. The top leaders of the TWU are elected from among the District Committee's members and are ultimately responsible to this body. The third tier is made up of the leaders of the union's units in the various mills. They occupy a crucial place in the union. They constitute the liaison between the members and the head office, handle most of the industrial disputes, recruit members for the union, and generally strive to maintain the union's image at the mill.

It is pertinent to know if workers occupying offices at these three levels have any political commitments. The leaders in the first tier are invariably members of the PSP. Frequently they hold top party offices. The second tier is once again dominated by politically committed workers. Of the fifty-four members of the District Committee of the TWU in 1963-1964, all but five were members of the PSP. Nor is this case merely with the TWU. The three other unions which also organized textile workers in the Coimbatore district were similarly dominated by politically committed workers. Thirty of the forty-five members of the District Council of the Coimbatore District Mill Workers' Union (MWU) affiliated to the All India Trade Union Congress were members of the Communist Party of India (CPI). Of the eighty-two members of the General Council of the National Textile Workers' Union (NWU) affiliated to the Indian National Trade Union Congress (INTUC), all but one were members of the Congress party. All twenty-one members of the General Council of the DMK-controlled Dravida Panchalai Thozhilalar Munnetra Sangam (DPMS) were members of the DMK. It is equally significant that none of these bodies accommodated a member from a rival political party.

Political commitment is equally pronounced among mill-level leaders. Although I have no data for all the mills in the district, interviews administered to a sample of TWU members from three mills bear this out. Initially sixty-four members (10% of the total TWU membership in these three mills) were interviewed. Struck by the extent of party affiliation among the three leaders included in this sample, the interviews were extended to the ten other TWU leaders in these mills. The results of these interviews are given in Table 1. It is evident that PSP members and sympathizers control most of the mill-level union offices.

Table 1
Party Membership and Sympathy Among TWU Members

Party membership and sympathy	Workers	Leaders	Total
PSP members	4	5	9
PSP sympathizers	18	5	23
Members of other parties	1	—	1
Sympathizers of other parties	8	—	8
Politically uncommitted	30	3	33
Total	61	13	74

It may be asked why leadership positions are dominated by politically committed workers. I shall not go into this question in detail, since this would involve a discussion of the workers' participation in union activities as well as of their attitude toward leadership positions. What is relevant here is that although ideological conformity is a prerequisite for top offices in all the four unions, there is no conscious or deliberate attempt to elbow out apolitical members from lower-level leadership. The fact of the matter is simply that most workers do not feel committed enough to the union to aspire for an office. At the lower levels union office not only carries no perquisites but also exposes leaders to the hostility of the management, rival unions, and even their own members. The politically committed worker is more willing to shoulder leadership responsibilities because of a double identification with the union. The union is necessary not merely to protect job-related interests but also to further the interests of the party to which the worker owes allegiance.[5]

The extent of political affiliation among the ordinary members is even more difficult to gauge. No exact statistics of party affiliation among TWU members can be obtained from union or party records. The TWU leaders and local PSP functionaries in charge of enrolling members and maintaining records estimate that around two thousand of the 14,796 members of the TWU in 1963-1964 were dues-paying members of the PSP. But this figure does not necessarily reflect the extent of party sympathy in the union. Many workers just do not bother to renew periodically their party membership. Nor is any systematic attempt made by the party leaders to collect their membership dues. But this makes little difference to the political sympathies of these workers. There are also workers who, dismayed by the party's performance at the polls or the bickerings among its leadership, have allowed their membership to lapse. This has especially been the case since the party's debacle in the 1962 general elections. There are also a large number of workers who would not join the party but have strong sympathies for it. They contribute to the election funds of the party, attend party rallies, and vote for its candidates in the elections. Any realistic understanding of the implications of political affiliation to the TWU has to take into account not merely the dues-paying PSP members but also the sympathizers.

Even if we discount the claims of the union and party leaders, it would be realistic to estimate that PSP members and sympathizers together account for around 20 percent of the TWU's membership. Apart from the data contained in Table 1 which support this conclusion, the only other way of checking this is to observe the purely partisan processions and rallies organized by the TWU. Local leaders concede that most of the participants in these rallies and processions are party members and sympathizers, since the rest of the union's members are unwilling to spend a rest day marching the streets and presenting petitions at the collectorate. It is also common to see most of the participants dressed in party uniforms and carrying party flags and banners. The TWU can collect between three thousand and four thousand workers for these rallies. In contrast, TWU processions organized for purely trade-union purposes are indeed massive, with over ten thousand marchers.

The conclusion to be drawn from the above discussion is that political commitment is fairly widespread in the TWU. While a large majority of the membership is clearly unidentified with any political party, the number of members who are so identified is large enough to deserve consideration. Even more crucial than their numbers is the influence they wield. They control the entire leadership of the union from the head office down to the mills, besides constituting the vocal section of the rank and file.

Most PSP sympathizers in the TWU have no deep understanding of party ideology. Even at election time, few are aware of the party's manifesto. It is vaguely known that the party stands for the poor, and the working class in particular. But for all practical purposes the party is identified with the luminaries who head it and for its better-known policies. Present and past leaders of the party, beginning with Acharya Narendra Deva down to S. M. Joshi and N. G. Goray, have become household names. There is also unquestioning support for the party's policies. One of the most striking instances of this was the conviction of many that Hindi should be the national language of the country. Coming from mill workers deep in South India, many of whom cannot read or write their own mother tongue, this indeed is evidence of the internalization of party values.

TWU members do not conceive of the union and the party as distinct entities. Nor do they think of their leaders as outsiders motivated by the desire for political gain. The union and the party are viewed as being inextricably intertwined. Even the politically uncommitted members view this relationship as given. Signs of the close relationship between the TWU and PSP are everywhere, and are unmistakable. Besides the ubiquitous party flags and pictures of prominent party leaders, one visible symbol of this relationship is the union's official mouthpiece, *Samudayam* (literally, "Society"). Although it is published only sporadically, with the issues appearing more regularly as the general elections approach, it commands a wide readership in the union. While *Samudayam* carries some union news, much of the news is about the party, including reports of the party's activities in other states, where it is more powerful. Conversation in union offices and outside mill gates during recess frequently centers around such news. The loyal members of the TWU find it difficult to reconcile themselves to the insignificance of the PSP in the politics of Tamilnadu. Their discomfiture is made more acute by the fact that they are members of the largest and most powerful union in the Coimbatore textile industry and thus can look down upon the rival unions, but their party cannot compare in power or influence with the Congress, CPI, or DMK to which their rivals owe allegiance. TWU members take solace from reading that at least elsewhere in the country there are PSP leaders who make themselves heard. It is common to hear them boast about the effectiveness of their parliamentarians in exposing the ruling Congress. Many of these episodes find their way into the speeches of mill-level leaders on purely trade-union matters at union and mill-gate meetings.

Except for conversation centering around party news, and an occasional party rally or membership drive, there is not much political activity among TWU members under normal conditions. It is when the elections approach that their political commitment manifests itself most clearly. Although the trade unions in Coimbatore enter candidates for elections to *panchayats* and municipalities, their involvement is greatest in the case of the general elections. Since 1952 the candidates of the PSP and CPI in the State Assembly constituencies in Coimbatore predominated by mill workers have been trade-union leaders. The Congress-dominated NWU has been less successful in getting party nomination for its leaders, and this has in fact been a source of friction between the union and the Tamilnadu Congress Committee. In spite of this, however, the union has generally supported Congress candidates.

TWU leaders do not contest elections merely for reasons of party policy, union interests, or personal gain. While these are no doubt important factors, there is also considerable pressure from the rank and file of the union on the party and union leadership to field candidates. For months before the poll conversation in the union centers around the elections. PSP supporters in the TWU remember the party's performance in the various constituencies of the state in all the general elections since 1952. The view is frequently expressed that the party should not withdraw from any of these constituencies. Haggling between parties over electoral alignments is keenly followed and there is great dismay if the PSP withdraws its candidate in favor of a rival in one constituency without extracting a promise of support in another.

For all this the PSP has fared miserably at the polls in Tamilnadu. The party did not win even a single seat in the Legislative Assembly in 1952 and 1962, and in 1957 the secretary of the TWU was the only PSP member in the assembly. In 1967 and 1971 the PSP won four seats in the assembly, thanks largely to its electoral alliance with the ruling DMK and some other opposition parties. This

dismal performance, however, does not dissuade the party supporters in the TWU. The argument generally advanced by them
is that, win or lose, the party would have to contest the elections if
it is to have any chance of retaining its identity and preserving
whatever little following it has. Winning is important, but fear of
losing is not considered sufficient reason for not contesting.
Further, it is only by contesting and winning a fair proportion of
the vote that the party will be able to claim a constituency in future
electoral alliances among political parties. The electoral allies of
the PSP allotted the party four constituencies in the 1967 and 1971
elections, despite the fact that it had not won a single seat in 1962,
because the PSP had contested from these constituencies all along
and thereby proved that it had some following. Contesting the
elections is, then, important for the survival of the party.

Trade-union members are deeply involved in the election
campaigns of their leaders, from fund raising to soliciting votes.
Electioneering is expensive, and trade-union leaders in Coimbatore are not particularly wealthy. Neither they nor their unions
have the resources to finance a campaign. This is one of the reasons
why the Congress has generally chosen well-to-do peasants rather
than NWU leaders to contest from working-class constituencies.
Trade-union leaders rely greatly on donations from their members and mill owners to finance their campaigns.

The mechanics of raising funds from the members have been
streamlined over the past several years. About two months before
the poll, the mill-level leaders of the union set a target depending
on the size of the union's following in the mill. Since it is not easy
to persuade the members to part with cash, they are asked to give
in writing that they are willing to have a specified sum deducted
from their wages as a contribution toward the election fund. The
amount is then collected by the leaders from the mills in one lump
sum. There are, of course, unionists who do not contribute to the
fund, but a large number do. A powerful union like the TWU can
easily raise upward of 30,000 rupees from the members, a not
inconsiderable sum.

The members of the union, with the exception of the few who
are in open sympathy with a rival party, are expected to vote for
the leader or the candidate supported by the union. Party members and sympathizers among the rank and file, and even some
apolitical members active in union affairs, are expected to canvass
for the leader. This canvassing takes place at two distinct levels.
The more visible part of the campaign is made up of public
meetings, rallies, street corner meetings, and the myriad chores
connected with electioneering, such as plastering walls with elec-

tion appeals, distributing handbills, and issuing identity slips to the voters. These activities are organized by the party supporters under the direction of local PSP functionaries, themselves TWU members. It is believed that this kind of campaigning is essential to create a favorable image of the candidate among the electorate. The voters do not take seriously the candidate who does not make himself heard.

There is another, more personal, dimension to campaigning. The high politics of public meetings is not sufficient to win votes. The voters are believed to commit themselves finally to a candidate only when appealed to in an idiom they understand. The voters are approached either personally or through influential individuals who are believed to control their votes and are appealed to on the basis of caste, kinship, factional, local, regional, linguistic, and similar other ties. This campaign is managed completely by the union activists. In the 1967 and 1971 elections more than a hundred TWU members absented from work for a week before the poll to personally contact voters over whom they had influence. The union arranged for their leave but did not make good the wages lost or pay for their expenses.

It may be argued that unionists have been coerced into raising election funds and campaigning for their leaders. To counter this argument, I shall try to show the depth of intensity of the political commitment of some sections of the rank and file by briefly tracing the career of a former secretary of the TWU, one of the most influential leaders ever in the Coimbatore textile industry.

This leader was an active nationalist in the early forties, and was imprisoned for life by the British for his part in terrorist activities. With independence, he was released from prison and once again became active in party politics. He left the Congress in 1948 along with the Congress Socialists to form the Socialist party. Around this time he took over as secretary of the TWU. He later went over to the PSP and had become president of its state unit by the mid-fifties. Being a persuasive speaker and skilled negotiator, he made a name for himself and his union. He built up the TWU into a formidable force and earned for it the reputation of being a militant and uncompromising union. He was at the pinnacle of his career in 1963 when the TWU celebrated its silver jubilee with great fanfare. Soon after the silver jubilee rumors began circulating that the secretary was considering going over to the Congress. Earlier there had been a move at the national level by Asoka Mehta, then chairman of the PSP, to merge the party with the Congress. Being an ardent follower of Mehta, the secretary seriously considered this possibility. He argued that socialist forces in the country would be strengthened by a merger between the Congress and the PSP. The rank and file, nurtured by this very man on anti-Congress propaganda for over two decades, rose up in revolt. A deep cleavage developed in the TWU. The entire leadership of the TWU, with the exception of a vice-president, lined up with the secretary, and the vocal sections of the membership, led by the District Committee members and mill-level leaders, opposed him. I should add here that the merger between the Congress and the PSP also implied a possible merger of the TWU with the Congress-controlled union, a position totally repugnant to the TWU members.

Sensing the opposition to the merger proposal, the secretary suggested that the TWU should delink from the PSP and become a nonpolitical union. In a stormy District Committee meeting he argued that he was secretary of the union because of his innate talents as a labor leader and not because he belonged to a certain political party. This touched off a furor, and the District Committee members pointed out that, while they no doubt wanted a dynamic leader to head the union, this person had also to be committed to the PSP. Soon after this the District Committee members passed no-confidence motions against the entire leadership of the union.

For some time after his expulsion from the TWU the former secretary stayed away from party politics, hoping to get back into the union. The opportunity came when there was a merger at the national level between the PSP and the Socialist party, and the Samyukta Socialist party (SSP) was born. The new leaders of the TWU joined the SSP. The former secretary also joined the SSP and was elected president of the TWU. However, there was soon a split in the SSP, and the PSP re-emerged as an independent party. The new leaders of the TWU returned to the PSP and the former secretary, who chose to remain in the SSP, was once again expelled from the union.

Frustrated in his efforts to break into the TWU, the former secretary tried a new stratagem. There had for years been a small pocket of Socialist party sympathizers among the rank and file of the TWU. These workers were tolerated in the union, as were workers sympathetic to several other parties, but they were seldom entrusted with union office and never had a dynamic leader. With the formation of the SSP and the subsequent split-off of the PSP, the former supporters of the Socialist party were now with the SSP and were happy to have the dynamic former secretary come over to their party. He built up this small but active and politically conscious segment into a faction within the TWU. Their numbers were augmented by the personal supporters of the former secretary and TWU members who were unhappy with the new leadership's handling of industrial disputes. By the summer of 1966 this faction was strong enough to field candidates for election to the District Committee of the TWU. Elections to the District Committee had seldom evoked much interest in the past but now became a trial of strength between the PSP and SSP factions. Although the SSP faction annexed a sizable number of seats, the PSP supporters retained their firm hold over the District Committee. These elections once again reiterated what had been obvious all along. It was not a mere handful of top leaders who had a vested interest in the PSP. The party had taken firm roots among the rank and file of the TWU.

The advent of the fourth general elections in 1967 provided yet another opportunity for the two factions to test their strength. The vice-president of the TWU, who was then also president of the Tamilnadu PSP, contested the Legislative Assembly seat from Singanallur, a predominantly working-class constituency. He was supported by six other opposition parties with whom the PSP had entered into an electoral alliance as part of their overall strategy to unseat the Congress from power. The former secretary, sensing that the victory of the vice-president in the election might finally eliminate him from the TWU, decided to contest from the same constituency on the SSP ticket. Long after the elections were over, SSP supporters admitted that the former secretary had not so much wanted to win as to split the votes of industrial workers who might otherwise have voted en bloc for the PSP, thus enabling the Congress candidate, who had no industrial base, to win. He, however, failed dismally in his efforts. The vice-president of the TWU won the election with a thumping majority, and the former secretary, polling a mere 5,721 votes, lost his deposit.

The success of the PSP in the fourth general elections finally extinguished all hopes of the former secretary's getting back into the TWU. He took his supporters out of the TWU and started a rival union—the United Textile Workers' Union (UTWU). Just as the PSP supporters constituted the backbone of the TWU, the SSP supporters formed the core of the new union. By 1970 this union had around three thousand members. In 1971 the former TWU secretary once again contested for election to the Legislative Assembly, but from a constituency which was completely rural and where he and his party were hardly known. SSP supporters in the UTWU were puzzled by his choice of constituency. Yet they collected 10,000 rupees for his election expenses, and an influential leader of the union collected a similar sum from the mill owners. It was evident to his campaign workers that he stood no chance of winning. Unlike in the 1967 election, he was not even trying to split votes and defeat a rival. As the poll approached, it became obvious that he was more intent on holding on to the money he had collected than on running an effective campaign. The campaign workers became bitter, and their feelings were aptly summed up by the district secretary of the SSP, a mill worker and union member:

> This man [the leader] is tight fisted. All the other candidates are going ahead with their campaign, but we do not even have enough flags and banners to display. At this rate no one will even know about our candidate. We don't even have enough money for our food. Worse still, he treats me as if I am his servant, forgetting that I am the District Secretary of our party! We are holding on to this job not for his sake, but for the sake of our party. We want to see our representatives elected to the Legislative Assembly.

The former secretary once again did miserably; it was alleged that while he had lost the election, he had more than compensated for it by pocketing much of the money intended for electioneering. There was widespread disillusionment with him after the elections. Not only had he misappropriated money but he had also lost interest in trade-union work. By 1972 he had been eased out of the office of secretary and made president, a mere figurehead. He was, however, very much in the union and will presumably continue to be in it as long as he is in the SSP.

The foregoing description of the career of the former TWU secretary affords clear evidence of the intensity of party commitment among the rank and file. Lest it be argued that the downfall of the old guard was engineered by interested politicians within the party, I should emphasize that it was the workers who rose in revolt. The District Committee voted overwhelmingly to expel the leaders, and all of its members, with the exception of the ousted leaders, were mill workers. It was clearly for political reasons that the secretary was twice expelled from the TWU. In fact, the secretary could split the TWU and start a rival union only through another politically committed group of workers. Without the backing of SSP sympathizers it would not have been possible for him to stage a comeback to trade unionism.

It is obvious that political commitment is not the exclusive preserve of outside leaders. Some sections of the rank and file are so committed to the party as to want their leaders to contest elections, and to man and finance their campaigns. In their view, it is by repeatedly contesting and bagging some votes that the party can establish itself.

The extent and intensity of political commitment among the rank and file raise the question of what sustains commitment to the party. More specifically, how are union and political loyalty related? Can political loyalty, once instilled, exist independently of trade unionism? Is party support motivated by considerations different from those which underlie union support? We can gain some idea of what lies behind political loyalty if we examine the process of political socialization and, even more important, relate political relationships between rival trade unionists to inter-union relationships.

Few workers join the TWU because they support the PSP. The relationship usually runs the other way—political loyalties arise out of prolonged union membership. There is a distinct process by which party loyalty is sought to be inculcated in the members. One source of socialization is the very acceptance of the link between the union and the party. The leaders repeatedly harp on this. Even in common parlance every union is referred to not by its name, but by the name of the party to which it owes allegiance.

TWU leaders frequently refer to the party's programs and successes even in contexts where they would seem to be of no relevance. They can deftly link the recalcitrance of a mill owner to the pressing need for unseating the Congress from power. It is argued that mill owners continue to exploit the workers even after twenty-five years of trade unionism because the Congress-controlled NWU is hand-in-glove with them. The villain of the piece, then, is not so much the mill owner, who is naturally interested in profits, but the NWU and other unions affiliated to the INTUC, which make this exploitation possible by misleading the workers. The pro-management policies of the INTUC are attributed to its links with the Congress, the party of the rich. From this it is a short hop to arguing that limited gains can be had from confrontations with the management, but that the ultimate redemption of the working class lies in a change of government. The PSP is projected as the party of the working people, which has unceasingly fought for their cause. *Samudayam,* the union's mouthpiece, and the periodic elections to *panchayats,* municipalities, the Legislative Assembly, and Lok Sabha are other important agents of political socialization.

But the rationale behind political loyalty, although never explicit, is the sense of identity and distinctiveness it imparts to every union. In other words, political loyalty is not merely an end in itself. It is an essential force making for cohesion within a union as well as dividing it from other unions. This becomes evident if we examine political relations among trade unionists.

There were four unions in the Coimbatore textile industry in 1963-1964, and the number has since risen to six. Politicians and labor leaders may repeatedly support the ideal of one union in one industry, but the divisions within organized labor and the rancor between competing unions are accepted by the average worker as part of the industrial scene. A worker's identification with any one union inevitably involves him in conflicts with the other unions. Since the politically committed workers are also the most committed unionists, they are naturally involved in these conflicts to a far greater extent than the rest of the rank and file. Union loyalty and conflict are imperceptibly carried over to the political sphere. Whatever the relation between the PSP and other political parties at the state or national level, PSP supporters in the TWU see political relationships through the looking glass of union relationships.

The TWU's chief rival is the Congress-controlled NWU. The two unions are evenly matched in several mills in terms of membership. The NWU, like several other unions affiliated to the INTUC, soft-pedals confrontations with the employers, whereas the TWU is a militant union. The TWU is particularly pinched by the fact that minor routine disputes, which its own leaders have to go to great lengths to settle, are settled with ease by NWU leaders by using personal ties with mill owners. TWU leaders accuse the NWU of being a stooge. This hostility is reflected in the relationship between the PSP and the Congress. As at the national level, PSP supporters in Coimbatore have a problem differentiating their brand of socialism from that of the Congress. In spite of this absence of ideological polarization, any cooperation with the Congress is considered impossible.

The TWU confronts the Communist-controlled MWU far less frequently, since the latter's membership, although large, is confined to a few big mills where the TWU has little following. The MWU is also a militant union like the TWU, and the Communists are believed to be easier to get along with in spite of their alleged secretiveness. Even on a personal level PSP leaders have more cordial relations with Communists than with Congressmen.

The PSP's relations with the DMK and SSP are even more illustrative of the primacy of union relationships. For a long time the TWU simply ignored the DPMS, controlled by the DMK, on account of its low membership and dismissed its leaders as overenthusiastic young men who knew nothing about trade unionism. Nor was the DMK a force to reckon with in Coimbatore. But during the 1967 general elections the PSP joined a DMK-sponsored electoral alliance and for the first time won four seats in the Legislative Assembly. The chief beneficiary of the alliance was the TWU, two of whose leaders were elected.

While the TWU leaders were happy at having been elected with DMK help, they did not want their newfound ally, which now formed the government in Madras, to throw its weight around in the mill areas of Coimbatore. Their relations became soured when local DMK leaders, heady with electoral success, began building up the DPMS. Matters came to a head when the DMK insisted on naming the prestigious Employees' State Insurance hospital in Coimbatore after its founder, C. N. Annadurai. The TWU leaders countered that Annadurai had done nothing for mill workers and demanded that the hospital be named after N. G. Ramaswamy, founder of the TWU and the doyen of trade unionism in the district. Following an industry-wide strike by the TWU to press this demand, the DMK shelved the issue. The PSP once again joined a DMK-sponsored alliance during the midterm poll in 1971, and TWU leaders retained the seats they had won earlier. But this has not dissuaded them from backing practically any agitation aimed at embarrassing the DMK. While they want the political gain accruing from DMK support, they do not want their union weakened by the ambitious DPMS.

The PSP's attitude toward the SSP also fits into the above pattern. So long as SSP supporters formed an innocuous minority within the TWU, the party was ignored. But when the former secretary crossed over to the SSP and attempted to seize the union, the PSP's relations with the SSP became strained. In fact, the new leaders of the TWU forced the SSP to form a breakaway union by refusing to enroll any worker with known SSP sympathies. Although the two socialist parties have again merged at the national level, they continue to be at dagger's point in Coimbatore.

While political loyalties are deep-seated in the TWU, the political commitment of the workers, and even of the leaders holding high offices in the party, is vitally influenced by their perception of union interests. The relationship between the union and the party is a symbiotic one. The party depends on the union for support, and this is all the more the case with the PSP, whose chief support is industrial labor. The union in turn depends on the party, not merely to espouse its cause in the legislature but also to provide it a sense of identity and exclusiveness. Although the unions have been started and politicized by partisan leaders, no matter with what motives, they have developed a logic and momentum of their own. It is not only the workers for whom this logic is of prime importance. Even the partisan leaders come under its influence. Having found their way into unionism through party politics, the outsiders themselves begin to accord primacy to union interests. This is what, for example, explains the attitude of the TWU leaders toward the DMK. Had they been concerned merely with personal political gain, or even party interests, they could have continued to curry favor with the DMK, unmindful of the latter's efforts to undermine the TWU. In a nutshell, politics is imported into the trade union by partisan leaders and instilled in the members as a concomitant of union loyalty. Political loyalty then goes back full circle to reinforce commitment to the union and set it off from competing unions.

The political commitment of the rank and file in trade unions has significant implications for trade unionism as well as party politics. As far as individual unions such as the TWU are concerned, the politically committed members are obviously a godsend. They provide the union with a nucleus of committed members who are actively involved in union affairs and assume leadership. Without such a committed membership, trade unions can never become organizations *of* workers. But viewed in the context of the labor movement as a whole, political involvement of the rank and file is clearly a divisive force. If this phenomenon is widespread, as it may well be, it follows that trade-union unity is just a mirage. It is not merely that politicians will not leave the trade unions alone. Trade unionists will not leave party politics aside either. In fact, the political loyalties of workers can outlive the leaders who in the first place instilled these in them. Of course, it is not merely the political affiliation of unions which stands in the way of working-class unity. But even if it is, a united labor movement is a distant dream. The cleavages among organized labor and the consequent multiple unionism have admittedly serious practical implications. But for too long the problem of multiple unionism has been sought to be disposed of by positing a united labor movement as the goal. Multiple unionism is here to stay, even if by some accident politically inspired outsiders lose interest in trade unions, and in any case it would be more realistic to take it as given than to wish it away.

It is widely believed that the relationship between trade unions and political parties is an asymmetrical one, with the party playing the big brother. Crouch argues that the stronger the personal following of a leader, the less dependent the leader is on the party, with the consequence of being less under its control.[6] But if this following were a politically committed one instead of being a personal one, the relationship of the leader with the party could undergo a considerable change. Rather than being concerned about being more or less dependent on the party, the leader could seek to increase personal leverage within the party and influence party decisions.

Notes

1. V. B. Karnik, *Indian Trade Unions: A Survey* (Bombay: Manaktalas, 1966), pp. 304, 313; V. V. Giri, *Labour Problems in Indian Industry* (Bombay: Asia Publishing House, 1959), p. 53; R. D. Agarwal, "Political Dimensions of Trade Unions," in *Dynamics of Labour Relations in India,* ed. R. D. Agarwal (New Delhi: Tata McGraw-Hill Publishing Co., 1972), p. 64; and R. D. Agarwal, "Problems of Unionism," in *Dynamics of Labour Relations,* p. 79.
2. Agarwal, "Political Dimensions of Trade Unions," p. 66.
3. Baldev R. Sharma, "The Industrial Worker: Some Myths and Realities," *Economic and Political Weekly* 5, no. 22 (1970): 875–78.
4. See, for instance, Giri, *Labour Problems,* pp. 9, 52; Karnik, *Indian Trade Unions,* p. 313; Agarwal, "Problems of Unionism," p. 80.
5. For a discussion of the significance of political loyalties to membership commitment in the TWU, see E. A. Ramaswamy, "Trade Unions and Politics," *Sociological Bulletin* 18, no. 2 (1969): 137–47.
6. Harold Crouch, *Trade Unions and Politics in India* (Bombay: Manaktalas, 1966), p. 282.

Part 4

Migrant Workers and Advanced Capitalism

As dependency theorists have pointed out almost ad nauseum, *the benefits of "development" redound unequally between the metropoles and satellites of the capitalist system, with the poles of growth and development tending to remain with the old metropoles at the expense of the periphery. This proposition is both well known and unexceptionable—as far as it goes. But the forms in which much dependency theory is cast, i.e., as a radical international trade theory, do not always serve to illuminate the full variety and dynamic of the ties between rich and poor countries. The search for underlying continuities in the history of metropolitan-satellite relations also often distorts the immediate short- and medium-term needs of capital within the advanced countries. The effects of the crisis of the 1970s could, for example, only be arrested or mitigated through the intensified exploitation of peripheral capitalist countries. In effect, this resulted both in the export of capital and the consequent growth of the means of production in the periphery (a tendency not dealt with here) and in the increasing import of cheap, malleable, unorganized labor from the periphery to the center.*

The articles in part 4 of this volume must be understood within this general context. The opening article, by Adams, concerns what the author concedes is a small, marginal, and incongruous group of Senegalese workers in France. Certainly the group is far less numerous than the Spaniards, Italians, Algerians, and Portuguese who provide the bulk of the immigrant labor force. But Adams' article is centered around an element in the process of migration that is often neglected, i.e., the nature of the exporting region. In this case, the Senegalese workers, the Tukulor, come predominantly from Futa Toro, once a fertile granary and now a barren wasteland, unable to support its inhabitants. Marginalized from the colonial emphasis on groundnut production, the area could not survive as a subsistence enclave within the colonial economy. But the Tukulor had nonetheless to pay their taxes and work off their land debts (once the privatization of property had been established), while Tukulor artisans could not compete against manufactured goods. Migration for cash led to a decline in food production and a reinforcement of the need to migrate—first to Dakar (where the unemployment rate rocketed from 11 percent in 1959 to 38 percent ten years later), then further afield. The ugly tentacle of colonial underdevelopment has now reached from Futa Toro to France, where the Tukulor engage in those jobs which are dirty, dangerous, exhausting, and poorly paid. They come legally and illegally, the illegal being openly tolerated by the French minister of employment, who at least is no hypocrite: "Illegal immigration," he admits, "is not without its usefulness: if international regulations were strictly enforced, we might lack manpower." A self-help organization, the Union Général des Travailleurs Sénégalais en France, despite official hostility and the difficulties of organizing such a fragmented group, has shown itself capable of formulating a program both to ameliorate conditions in France and to revitalize the Futa Toro region. Adams strongly argues even against those unions sympathetic to the Senegalese workers' plight. They are too prone, she maintains, to see the problem in terms of assimilation to the French *working class, instead of finding the solution in redeveloping the area of emigration devastated by colonial rule.*

Barrera also is concerned with "the colonial problem," but he uses this as an extended analogy to examine minority relations within the United States itself. He is, in particular, concerned with black and Chicano (Mexican-American) workers in the employ of the multinational tractor company, International Harvester. His theory of colonial labor establishes a fivefold set of hypotheses: (1) that the minority-origin workers can be predominantly confined to lower-status jobs; (2) that they can be paid less for similar jobs; (3) that colonized workers act to cushion the impact of economic crises by being readily extruded from production; (4) that they act as an industrial reserve army; and finally (5) that the existence of a colonized work force can serve to divide the working class. His detailed investigation of the labor practices of International Harvester shows that in important respects the colonial labor analogy holds true. With regard to the first factor, there is strong evidence to suggest that International Harvester uses the cover of providing equal employment opportunities as a chance to slot black and Chicano workers into the lowest-paid or lowest-status jobs. While the growth in unionization seems to have eliminated differential pay for similar jobs, some evidence is produced to show that minority workers act as a buffer group at times of crises—being disproportionately laid off compared with white workers at several of the plants considered. The use of "colonial" labor as a latent reservoir and as a means to divide the working class is also shown to be evident in the case of International Harvester. Barrera's article, by considering the sphere of production as the primary arena to observe the treatment of minorities, makes a useful contribution to the study of ethnic and race relations in the metropole, while also showing how capital's decomposition of the work force can prevent effective class action.

By far the most theoretically challenging selection is, however, Castells' consideration of immigrant workers in Europe. His starting point is not a (liberal) moral condemnation of the conditions that oppress a growing number of immigrant workers, but precisely the issue that Barrera raises more marginally—the political and social struggles of immigrant workers and their role in the class struggle of the metropolitan countries. The origin of immigration is seen in the uneven development between different sectors, regions, and countries of the capitalist system. But while Castells argues that uneven development can explain why workers emigrate, it cannot in itself explain why jobs are available to immigrants in the advanced countries, even during periods of heavy unemployment. He sees the answer in discerning the particular needs of monopoly capital at this time: the need, for example, for a young, vigorous work force whose costs of reproduction have already been met in the hinterland; the need, again, for a work force that can be superexploited because of its weak civil rights and its consequent limited capacity to engage in class struggle. As Castells graphically puts it: "A twenty-first-century capital and a nineteenth-century proletariat—such is the dream of monopoly capital in order to overcome its crises." The needs of capital to decompose the working class are so pressing that the dream has to be pursued despite the attendant contradiction engendered on another level, i.e., the presence of inflation combined with recession (so-called stagflation). Capital is aided in its task by the xenophobic and racist attitudes of indigenous metropolitan workers, which can be used to fragment workers in their common struggle against capital. Castells probes the "close but problematic" relationship between the struggles of immigrant workers and the political class struggle. He poses the provoking possibility that the present stage of the struggle against monopoly capitalism demands a multinational labor movement with a multinational leadership.

While Castells pursues his theoretical concerns on a large European canvas, DeWind, Seidl, and Shenk examine the little-known case of Caribbean agricultural laborers working on the Florida sugar estates. The current debates within the United States, following President Carter's intervention on the question of illegal aliens, only rarely encompass the case of foreign workers who enter the United States for temporary agricultural work. The H-2 program, as it is known, may well be expanded, so the authors speculate, to answer agricultural capital's continuing need for cheap agricultural laborers, while assuaging popular feeling against illegal Mexican immigration. The Caribbean workers may therefore presignify what is yet to come. There is a particularly bitter irony in the case of the Caribbean sugar workers cutting Florida cane. West Indian sugar, under severe pressure from the more mechanized Australian and Mauritian cane and European beet-sugar, survives precariously through the one "advantage" that accrues to Caribbean producers—cheap labor. Now, however, the governments of Jamaica, St. Kitts, and St. Lucia, which contract with the United States Sugar Corporation, have become direct agents in the exploitation of their own nationals against the interests of their own producers (often small farmers or nationalized estates). The arrogance of the recruiting agents of the U.S. Sugar Corporation exactly reflects the power of capital on the one hand and, on the other, the

powerlessness of West Indian governments, beset by a massive unemploy-
ment problem and fearful of civic disturbances that would displace their
insecure regimes. According to one such agent quoted by our authors:
"We'll run through 800 men a day. Three tables are set up representing
three stages of processing. . . ." At the first, weak physical "specimens" are
eliminated. Next, workers' intelligence is tested, and company agents see
whether the Caribbean workers can understand English as "we speak it,"
as one agent put it. Finally, the work record and police record are checked to
sort out troublemakers. The system is now more bureaucratized, but one
cannot help recalling the beady-eyed traders in human flesh who once
flourished under the aegis of merchant capital when the Caribbean peoples
began their first migration.

Prisoners in Exile:
Senegalese Workers in France

Adrian Adams

There are not very many Senegalese workers in France, perhaps twenty-five thousand. Add to that estimate Malians, Mauri-
tanians, and other black Africans, and the total may amount
to fifty-five thousand or so. Since the circumstances in which
they enter France preclude accurate statistics, the count rather
depends on who is doing the counting.[1] In the many recent
discussions of migrant labor in France, these workers rarely
receive much notice. There are over three million immigrant
workers in France; black Africans are usually listed under "other,"
at the foot of the page, after Spaniards, Italians, Algerians, and
Portuguese. They seem marginal; slightly more incongruous,
slightly more lost-looking, not otherwise worthy of note. It is
seldom asked why they are there.

Inquiry reveals that most black African workers in France
come from the Senegal River Valley and surrounding areas,
where about three-quarters of the population are Soninke, one-
quarter Tukulor, with some Bambara, and some Mandjak from
Casamance.[2] Most Senegalese workers in France are Tukulor
from the middle valley, from the region known as Futa Toro.
There are about four hundred thousand Tukulor in Senegal
(over one-tenth of the total population of the country), more than
two hundred thousand of whom live in Futa Toro.[3] Yet in Senegal,
too, they seem a marginal group. Life in their native region seems
as remote from the social and economic life of modern Senegal as
Futa Toro is distant from the country's present heartland. Massive
emigration from Futa Toro is often seen as the natural consequence of this taken-for-granted marginality.

My intention here is to show that these people cannot be considered marginal. The causes of Tukulor migration mirror the
contradictions of present-day Senegal. The situation of Senegalese
workers in France, and indeed of all black African workers there,
can thus be seen as the direct outcome of the relations between
France and her former African dependencies. To understand
the situation of the Senegalese workers in France—why they go

Reprinted from *Race and Class* 16, no. 2 (1974), with permission of the publishers.
A fuller discussion of Senegalese workers in France can be found in the author's *Le
long voyage des gens du Fleuve* (Paris: Maspero, 1977).

there, what happens to them—is to gain a privileged insight into the nature of that connection.

Futa Toro

Despite considerable dispersal, the greater number of Tukulor are still to be found in their homeland, Futa Toro, on the left bank of the middle reaches of the River Senegal, between Dembakane and Dagana. The name "Tukulor" is a distortion of "Tekrur," a name applied by early Arabic writers to the Islamicized regions of West Africa. The Tukulor are indeed among the first black Africans to have come into contact with Islam; there were Muslims among them, it seems, as early as the eleventh century, and they remain deeply attached to the Tijaniyya persuasion. But they themselves do not use the name "Tukulor," instead calling themselves "Haal-pularen," "those who speak pular," the language they share with the Fulani.

There has been much debate about the origins of the Tukulor people. The present consensus appears to be that they were bred of intermarriage between Fulani nomads and sedentary peoples long resident in the valley, possibly connected with the Serer or Soninke of today. The debate itself need not concern us here, but it points to one matter of present concern: that Futa Toro long enjoyed a reputation for fertility, which attracted both nomads and cultivators from other regions.

Futa Toro lies within the South-Sahel climate belt and receives scant rain. But the River Senegal, like the Nile, floods its banks yearly. This makes it possible to harvest two crops a year: the rainy-season crop of millet, grown in the highlands, and the sorghum, or large millet, grown in the alluvial floodlands during the dry season. The Tukulor have always been settled cultivators; in former times, Futa Toro was known as "the granary," and exported millet.[4]

The image of a relatively fertile Futa Toro, a magnet for people of other regions, stands in stark contrast with the present. Futa Toro no longer attracts settlers. In any given recent year up to a quarter of its own people, most of them young men, have had to leave to work elsewhere.[5] It has become a commonplace that "the main distinguishing feature of . . . the Vallée de Fleuve du Senegal, is its poverty compared with that of other parts of Senegal."[6] The former "granary" was described some twenty years ago as "so wretched a place that if it were left uninhabited for two years, one would not notice the difference, so few traces are there of human labour."[7] What has happened to bring this about? It is not that the natural potential of the valley has changed—a few years ago it was still being described as a "green ribbon," an "oasis"; some human agency must have intervened.

Tukulor migration in itself is not a phenomenon of recent origin. This has created a tendency to explain it in terms of intrinsic characteristics imputed to Tukulor society, whether nomadic atavisms derived from Fulani ancestry, Muslim proselytic fervor, overpopulation, or "feudal" inequalities. None of these provides a satisfactory explanation, for there is no single, constant migratory trend among the Tukulor. One need look no further back than the mid-nineteenth century to perceive that Futa Toro has experienced since then two quite distinct movements of population: an eastward movement, connected with Al Hadj Umar's attempt to found a Tukulor empire, which reached its peak in the late 1850s and continued until 1890, and a westward movement, which began early this century and still goes on today. The connection between the two is the consolidation of French control over Senegal and the Western Sudan, which brought the former to an end, and created the conditions which gave rise to the latter.

My theme, of course, is the latter movement of Tukulor migration, first toward the urban centers of Senegal, then to France. But it may help to clarify its causes if I allude briefly to what went before. The tautologies so common in matters of this kind, which purport to explain migration by poverty and poverty by migration, often result from an inability to bring past and future to bear upon the present.

I said earlier that the Tukulor had been in contact with Islam since the eleventh century. It was not until the eighteenth century, however, that the Muslim clerics, the ToorodBe, seized temporal power from the Denyanke dynasty of pagan Fulani. Other peoples, to the east of Futa Toro, had by then lapsed from earlier conversion to Islam. A Toorodo named Umar Tall, born in the late eighteenth century, who traveled to Mecca as a young man, received there the divine call to conduct a holy war against unbelievers and lukewarm believers. He was to "sweep the country."[8]

No doubt Umar wished Futa Toro to be the heart of this enterprise, but, like the Prophet Muhammed before him, he was not well received in his own country when he returned there in 1847. He withdrew to Futa Djalon, where a number of disciples joined him; with these troops, he then set out toward the east, to do battle with the pagan Bambara. His campaign was successful, and in 1857, after the conquest of Kaarta, he decided to return to Futa Toro to recruit more troops. On the way, however, he encountered a new obstacle. The French, who had had trading stations on the River Senegal since the seventeenth century, were seeking to consolidate their position, which involved bringing Futa Toro under their control. Umar was drawn into attacking the fort of Medine, but his siege was broken by the troops of Faidherbe, and he had to retreat. The following year, he entered Futa Toro by a different route and toured the country urging the people to migrate eastward, saying: "True friends, emigrate. This country has ceased to be yours. It is the country of the European; cohabitation with him is not suitable for you."[9] Some, it seems, replied: "Yes, but we prefer this country to others our fathers did not know." But many others heeded him. It seems that the number of those who left Futa Toro on that occasion, added to the earlier migrations, can be estimated at over fifty thousand people, or one-fifth of the population.[10] And migration to the east continued, at a lesser pace, until the final defeat of Umar's son by the French, in 1890-1891. Attempts at resistance in Futa Toro itself were then finally crushed, and many migrants were made to return there.

This grossly oversimplified account does permit some preliminary ground clearing with respect to explanations of Tukulor migration. First, it shows the irrelevance of explanations founded upon some supposed collective mentality—atavistic nomadism or the impulse to *jihad*. Al Hadj Umar's movement began as an attempt to win hegemony, spiritual and temporal, for a reformed Tukulor community; as such, it won disciples and soldiers, but also evoked substantial opposition in Futa Toro itself. It was only when the movement took the character of a national resistance, when it became clear that the French intended to isolate Futa Toro from the Tukulor-held regions to the east of the Upper Senegal, that it gained a mass following. The large-scale eastward population movements were due, not to some recurrent feature of Tukulor temperament, but to the difficult political situation of Futa Toro at that time: never to become the westernmost rim of Umar's empire, yet striving not to become the northeastern rim of the French colony of Senegal.

This is not to deny the possible influence of economic and social factors within Tukulor society. The migration of this period cannot be characterized as a flight from poverty, although the first mass departures, by jeopardizing agricultural production for the season, may have prompted others. But it seems possible that the favorable response of many young men to Umar's first recruiting drive, in contrast to the marked disinclination displayed by older and more eminent members of the community, reflected some inequality of access to wealth and power in Futa Toro. This question will recur when we consider present-day migration.

It would be unwise, however, to rely overmuch on historical continuities. At the close of the period I have briefly described, Futa Toro had undergone rapid and brutal changes. Loss of population, by emigration and the cholera epidemic of the late 1860s, had meant a series of difficult years. The country had lost all connection with the former heartland of empires, Western Sudan; and the struggle for the autonomy of Futa Toro, conducted by Abdul Bokar Kan after that separation, ended with his death in 1891, the year of the final overthrow of the Tukulor empire to the east. Futa Toro was now part of the colony of Senegal; and it is in this new context that we must now consider it.

Toward Exile

The French presence on the Senegal River has already been mentioned. Saint Louis, at the mouth of the river, was one of the earliest French settlements in Senegal, founded in the mid-seventeenth century. Trading stations were soon established along the river for the periodic collection of slaves from the left bank (until the trade was abolished) and gum arabic, used in the calico-printing industry from the Moors on the right bank. At one time there was thought of establishing French settlers in the valley, and various agricultural experiments were carried out there in the 1820s. But these projects came to nothing, and in the mid-century the gum trade entered a decline from which it never recovered.[11]

While the French were still pursuing military objectives in the interior, they needed the goodwill of Futa Toro; local leaders could exercise a certain influence by threatening mass emigration toward the east, which would have imperiled the security and grain supplies of the French. But with the final defeat of Umar's son Ahmadu there was no more counterweight to the decline of French commercial interests in the Senegal River. All hopes for the colony now moved west, and focused upon a promising new crop for export—groundnuts.

Introduced in the eighteenth century and grown on a commercial basis from the 1850s on, the groundnut proved an extremely profitable crop from the French point of view. Grown with the traditional implements and techniques of subsistence farming, it required no investment, no new relations of production. Once the initial impetus had been given, the big trading houses needed only to send intermediaries to collect the produce; they grew rich by supplying the French market with cheap table oil. Groundnut production grew rapidly, spreading south from the Kajor region to Sin-Salum and Baol, then eastward as land was exhausted and transport improved. But it did not spread to Futa Toro, remote from the groundnut-growing regions.[12] Once brought under colonial domination, Futa Toro became peripheral; while most of the people of Senegal were being drawn into the trading circuit, the Tukulor were left, it seems, to their own devices.

The question which now arises is why this relegation to peripheral status should have brought about massive emigration, rather than a continued reliance upon subsistence agriculture. Here again, explanations have been offered in terms of the immanent characteristics of Tukulor society—this time economic and social, rather than psychological: "overpopulation," or "feudal inequalities."[13] But again, these seem inadequate.

The density of poulation in Futa Toro varies between ten and twenty persons per square mile; higher, certainly, than that of surrounding regions, and for obvious reasons. But "overpopulation" is an extremely imprecise notion, unless one is referring to a maximum viable population under prevailing natural conditions. A region where fertile land is left uncultivated, which still produces a modest surplus of grain, and where nutritional standards have been found to be higher than anywhere else in Senegal,[14] would seem not to have reached that hypothetical saturation point. But, of course, one can have relative overpopulation, when prevailing social conditions are such as to deny some part of the population full access to the means of subsistence—in this case, land. It was noted above that such inequalities within traditional Tukulor society may have prompted the less favored to join Al Hadj Umar's followers. Might it not be that the highly stratified nature of the society, as expressed in the land-tenure system, denies the lower strata the possibility of subsistence farming, thus forcing them to seek work elsewhere? A convenient hypothesis; unfortunately, it doesn't work.

The system of land tenure which prevailed from the eighteenth century onward, after the consolidation of ToorodBe temporal power, was extremely complex. Roughly speaking, alluvial flood-lands not under the direct control of religious leaders were under the control of the *diom leydi,* or "masters of the land." Some of this land was worked by them as family holdings, often consisting of large domains using slave labor. The remainder, however, was worked by *diom dyengol,* or "masters of fire," who had permanent hereditary rights of cultivation there, provided they paid duty in kind to the *diom leydi* concerned. These superimposed rights involved only the nobility; "masters of the land" seem often to have been ToroodBe, who asserted their right to various tithes and duties, and "masters of fire" seem often to have been SubalBe or SeBBe, members of lesser free-born strata reputed to descend from the earliest inhabitants of Futa Toro. Artisans lived by their craft, and did not have access to land; nor did the MaccuBe or slaves, descendents of captives, who labored in the fields of noblemen.[15]

This delicate balance has been disrupted during the present century by various measures, including punitive redistribution of land, emancipation of slaves, and legislation premised upon the desirability of European concepts of land ownership. The result is that rights of cultivation have become tantamount to property rights, and traditional duties tend no longer to be paid. Thus, the "masters of the land" are now in a precarious position; unable to recuperate land over which they previously had rights, they have tended to split up family holdings and have increasingly had to rent land. Other landless groups, artisans and unemancipated slaves, can hope to pay rent in kind or service; emancipated slaves and ToroodBe must pay cash. The need to rent land also affects the "masters of fire," although to a lesser extent. Those who cannot pay rents must emigrate. Thus, the more fertile land often lies untilled, while communities rely increasingly upon the rainy-season crop: with what effects, in recent drought conditions, may be imagined.[16]

It may be seen, therefore, that although there are difficulties in access to land in Futa Toro, these must be imputed to the disruptive effects of colonial rule, rather than to the intrinsic nature of traditional Tukulor social organization. The basis of explanation has shifted from supposed immanent features, to the effects of integration within the colonial system of Senegal. It must be added that indirect effects, such as the disruption of traditional order, are of secondary importance; they reinforce a process already made inevitable by the impact of a primary effect: the need for cash. It is that, rather than lack of land per se, which causes migration.

In areas where commercial groundnut cultivation was introduced, cultivators used cash earnings to pay the tax levied by the colonial administration. It was a poll tax, of course, not a tax on income or wealth—a classic device for compelling either forced

labor or production for export. As manufactured goods supplanted local crafts, more cash was needed; cultivators produced
more groundnuts, less food for themselves. The purchase of
foodstuffs meant going into debt, and still further dependence
on cash earnings.

Emphasis on groundnut cultivation for export, rather than
on grain production for local consumption, meant that regions
like Futa Toro, remote from groundnut-growing areas, became
economically peripheral. But there is no such thing as a self-
sufficient "traditional" enclave within a colonial system; those
who did not have the opportunity of being trapped by debt on
their own land had to go where they could earn cash. They too
had taxes to pay, and they too found that local artisans were
being supplanted by manufactured goods. As they left the land,
agricultural production dwindled, and those who were left behind
sometimes had to buy food. It is this need for money, confirmed
as a primary motive by Tukulor migrant workers themselves,[17]
which compels and shapes migration. As has been said of Soninke
country, further upriver, the other main source of emigration
to France:

> Military conquest and the changed system of trade, the develop-
> ment of groundnut cultivation in the central zones of Senegal,
> brought about the final ruin and abandon of the region. Lacking this
> commercial resource, remote from areas of agricultural growth, the
> inhabitants might perhaps have been able to fall back upon sub-
> sistence farming, had they not been subject to colonial taxation. . . .
> As it was, they had nothing to export but their children.[18]

In former times there was some seasonal migration from Futa
Toro to the groundnut-producing regions, encouraged by the
colonial administration. But this prospect dwindled as the situation
of the groundnut producers themselves became increasingly
precarious. The main flow of Tukulor migration has been directed
toward the urban zones of Senegal, especially Dakar. In 1926
there were already thirty-five hundred Tukulor in Dakar, out of a
population of forty thousand for the city as a whole. By 1955
there were twenty-five thousand, 12 percent of the city's population at the time. By 1960 the number of Tukulor in Dakar was
estimated at forty thousand.[19] Without entering into the details of
the life of these migrants in Dakar, ably described by Abdoulaye
Bara Diop,[20] one can note certain features which prefigure, writ
small, some of the essential characteristics of Tukulor migration
to France. At the time of Diop's survey (1958-1959), modern
education had had little impact on Futa Toro; only 5 percent of

school-age boys were actually attending school. The Tukulor migrants in Dakar, therefore, held unskilled jobs of a menial nature; they were laborers, policemen, street vendors, shoeshine boys, or domestic servants. They rarely acquired new skills during their stay in Dakar.

Most of the migrant workers interviewed by Diop intended to spend only a few years in Dakar; only one in ten could be said to have settled there permanently. This enduring attachment to Futa Toro was reflected in the considerable sums remitted there —considerable in view of the very low wages earned. This money was generally not invested in specific projects or purchases, but served only to ensure the subsistence of families left behind.

Temporary migration, unskilled work at low wages, large sums remitted home—it is no surprise to find that Tukulor migrants in Dakar lived in conditions of extreme poverty, dependent on each other for mutual assistance. It was also becoming manifest by the late 1950s that they would have to travel still further. Sixteen percent of Diop's sample were unemployed. Between 1959 and 1969 the urban population of Senegal grew from 700,000, or 22 percent of the total population, to 1,250,000, or 32 percent of the total. Unemployment grew even faster. The growth of urban industries and services was negligible, a stagnation which can be attributed to the postindependence decline of Dakar as a center of commerce and industry.[21] While it is difficult to define unemployment in a society where underemployment is endemic, it is certain that the past fifteen years have witnessed a massive increase in the number of unemployed. In 1969 fifty thousand people were registered as unemployed in the urban areas of Senegal; the true number has been estimated at nearer ninety thousand.[22] Thus, the unemployment rate as a proportion of the urban labor force has grown from 11 percent in 1959 to 38 percent in 1969.

There are no specific figures relating to Tukulor unemployment after 1958-1959. But it is clear enough that these unskilled, illiterate workers, living precariously in the *bidonvilles* of Dakar, were among the first to have to move on.

Entering France

Before independence, river people—Tukulor and Soninke— were often employed by French shipping companies, and some of them ended up in Bordeaux or Marseilles. But it was in the late

1950s and early 1960s that the trickle of immigrants became a flow—and began to arouse attention. In considering Tukulor migration to France, one may as well begin with the official regulations designed to apply to Senegalese who go to work in France; it must be said, however, that the facts of the matter bear little resemblance to official principles.

The multilateral agreement ratified by the Mali Federation in 1960, and by Senegal in 1961, after the breakup of the Federation, provided that nationals of *Communauté* member states would have free access to the territory of other *Communauté* member states, and would enjoy there the same rights as that country's nationals, including

> the free exercise of cultural, religious, economic, professional and social activities, and private and public freedoms such as freedom of thought, of conscience, of religious belief and practice; freedom of opinion, of speech, of assembly, of association; and freedom to engage in trade-union activities.[23]

To enter France, a Senegalese worker then needed only an identity card.

In 1964, however, further regulations were felt to be necessary, given the increasing numbers of Senegalese, Malian, and Mauritanian workers entering France, and bilateral agreements were negotiated between France and each of the countries involved. The agreement between France and Senegal stipulated that Senegalese nationals wishing to work in France must be in possession of a medical certificate, delivered by the French consulate after examination by an approved medical authority, *and* of a work contract in writing, ratified by the French Ministry of Employment upon submission by the employer. In 1968 a further requirement was introduced: employers must pay for a medical examination to be carried out in France by the Office National de l'Immigration, the employment agency for immigrant workers created in 1945.[24] As one might expect, the result of these new regulations, and especially of the provision relating to work contracts, has been to ensure that most Senegalese workers have to enter France illegally.

In 1968 it was officially considered that 82 percent of all immigration to France was made up of "illegal" immigrants, who entered the country as "tourists" and subsequently regularized their situation through the Office National de l'Immigration. A French minister for employment acknowledged the situation in these terms: "Illegal immigration is not without usefulness; if international regulations were strictly enforced, we might lack manpower."[25] It is not possible, for obvious reasons, to say how many Senegalese workers enter France illegally. But if one considers that only domestic servants, brought to France by their employers, are likely to have work contracts in advance of their arrival—how many French employers would give such a contract to an unknown, unskilled African—it seems probable that most of them do. Many of these "tourists" will subsequently legalize their position after one or two years; others, turned down at the ONI medical examination, will remain in France as illegal immigrants, or *clandestins.*

How do these workers enter France? One cannot chart with great precision something which officially is not meant to exist, but a general pattern can be discerned.

Migrants from Futa Toro leave their village in groups of three or four, usually after the rainy-season crop has been harvested, and make their way to a station on the Bamako-Dakar railway line. Upon arriving in Dakar—which is increasingly a mere stage in the journey, rather than a final goal—they buy their passage with money sent from France by a relative already working there; often, they must also buy false identity cards or vaccination certificates. The ticket cannot be obtained directly from the shipping companies involved; it must be bought from an intermediary who takes a cut, often half again the cost of the fourth-class passage. It seems that the sums involved are of the order of 1,500 francs—about £150.[26]

The classic ports of disembarkation are Marseilles and, to a much lesser extent, Bordeaux. There, the "tourist" must display a return ticket. Obviously, one must assume some degree of official connivance at both ends; police and customs officials must be induced to turn a blind eye. *"C'est l'administration qui est 'clandestine.'"*[27] It would seem that this tolerance has been less freely granted of late, especially at the French end; more and more African workers have been entering France through Spain or Italy, crossing the mountains on foot or being driven across the border in cars or lorries. Those who are caught will wait and try again. Some are less fortunate: found dead of exposure in the Pyrenées or stifled to death in sealed vans.[28] Few of those who make it now stay in Marseilles; most move on to Paris, some further to Rouen or the north.

Conditions in France

Senegalese workers arriving in France are young (two-thirds of them under thirty), and they are often unable to speak French, let alone read or write it. Most of them lack any qualification relevant to an industrial society, even those who have some training rarely find work commensurate with their skills.

It usually takes them several months to find work through fellow countrymen or private agencies. The largest employer is the automobile industry; other industrial employers are foundries, the chemical industry, the textile industry. Many work for local authorities as street sweepers or dustmen, especially in Paris; some are dockers. The common denominator of all these jobs is that they are dirty, exhausting, and often dangerous; wherever they work, Africans are always given the lowest-paid jobs. At work they are vulnerable and isolated, often employed by small firms which stay afloat by paring manpower costs to the bone, using "illegal" immigrants who have no recourse against exploitation. This isolation and vulnerability is heightened by the fact that even those who have legalized their status find that their rights as workers are restricted by law. Like all other immigrants, Senegalese workers in France are not permitted to be trade-union officials; in order to be elected as delegates, or even to vote, they must have a *carte de résident privilégé*, which can only be obtained after three years' uninterrupted residence in France. Few stay much longer than that at a time.[29]

Another form of statutory inequality pertains to social security. A Senegalese worker, incapacitated by an accident at work, will cease to receive his pension if he returns home. A Senegalese worker whose family remains in Senegal (and this is almost invariably the case) has the full contribution deducted from his pay, just as a French worker does; but the family allowance his family in Senegal is paid is much less than that received by a French worker's family. At rates current in August 1971 a French worker with three children received 320 francs a month. The family of a Senegalese worker with three children received 75 francs a month. Or rather, that is the sum sent the family; those familiar with Sembène Ousmane's *Mandabi* will know that they are unlikely to receive the full amount.[30]

The difference between the worker's contribution and the allowance paid his family is meant to go to the Fonds d'Action Sociale (FAS), founded in 1959 to finance the provision of housing for immigrant workers. In fact FAS delegates this task to various private associations, subsidized by its funds. Many such associations, often run by former colonial administrators, have sprung up since 1964, when FAS, originally set up just for Algerian workers, was extended to cover all immigrant workers; the most notorious, as far as African workers are concerned, are ASSOTRAF and

SOUNDIATA. These are no charities; they make a profit from such housing as they do provide. A few *foyers*, or "hostels," have been newly built, strategically isolated from work places and population centers, but most of them have been set up in disused buildings in working-class suburbs and parts of Paris due for renovation. They are dubbed "temporary" but tend to last for years. It should not be imagined that the semiofficial nature of the enterprise involves any government control of the activities of these "housing associations"; there is no rent control, no sanitary inspection. Consider the ASSOTRAF *foyer* in Pierrefitte: 267 African workers in fifteen rooms, each paying 70 francs rent a month; hence over 18,690 francs, or more than £1,800. Damp walls, cockroaches and bedbugs, sheets and blankets never changed, and grossly inadequate sanitary facilities.[31] A typical "official" hostel. But there are worse things yet than the "official" hostels.

In 1962, out of the twenty thousand or so African workers thought to be in the Paris region, only six thousand to seven thousand were housed in the "official" hostels. Since workers from Senegal or Mali rarely live on their own, and rarely live in *bidonvilles*, as must many Algerian or Portuguese workers who have their families with them, it must be presumed that the others—and their number will have grown since 1962—live in such collective accommodation as they can find.[32]

Many private individuals have set up hostels which differ very little from the "official" ones—to the latter's discredit. Even without the FAS subsidy, this sort of thing pays. Take one case among many: the Ivry *foyer*, a disused chocolate factory owned by a couple named Morael. Between 1965 and 1969 they made 913,890 francs out of the place—about £90,000. By 1969, 541 Africans were living there in eleven rooms, each averaging about one hundred twenty square yards. There were five toilets, two drinking-water taps, and two washbasins. Each occupant paid a deposit of 150 francs and 40 francs rent per month. Strictly speaking, this was a *foyer clandestin*, but the first Africans to live there were taken there in police vans. The Moraels were not gangsters; they were respectable people with good connections. The only difference between this sort of place and those run by FAS-subsidized associations is that the residents have even less recourse against a private individual.[33]

Cases like Pierrefitte and Ivry—one could cite others—have come to public notice when the residents have organized protests against their living conditions. But many African workers live in conditions even more effectively concealed: in lofts, in cellars, in garages, among damp walls and rotting floorboards, windows boarded up against the cold and to make space for one more bed. Such places are usually owned by Frenchmen but run by a North African or black African; the owner, in case of trouble, tends to disappear.[34]

It was in such a place that five workers, four Senegalese and one Mauritanian, died in Aubervilliers in the night of January 1, 1970. Ten people were living in a room five yards square, for which they each paid seventy francs a month—about £7. The electricity had been cut off because the landlord had failed to pay the bill. It was very cold that night; they burned coal in a bucket to try and keep warm. It killed them. There was a great deal in the press about it. The authorities pointed out that there was no alternative accommodation available for such people. They did not mention the Fonds d'Action Sociale.[35] One African's comment was, "Five dead—it's terrible for the families, of course. But I can't help thinking of all those who leave home in good health and return there half dead."[36]

The medical examination carried out by the Office National de l'Immigration does not make provision for treatment; paid for by the employer, it is designed merely to test suitability for employment. It rarely diagnoses illnesses brought from Africa, which therefore remain unnoticed until they become acute—bilharzia and other intestinal parasites being the most common. The most significant factor, however, in the state of health of African workers in France, is not so much what illnesses they bring with them, but what becomes of them after their arrival. The work they do is almost invariably dangerous, dirty, and exhausting. They try to avoid the building industry because of the exposure involved, but their work in foundries and chemical works and in the automobile industry is just as dangerous in more insidious ways. Those who work as sweepers or dustmen must, of course, work outside in all weather. They often have to leave their jobs after a time—having become too weak to lift the dustbins.[37]

The living conditions I have described are not such as to preserve health or allow workers to recover from the fatigue of work. On the contrary, they favor the spread of disease, especially tuberculosis, the worst scourge of all. Black African workers are twenty to thirty times more likely to have tuberculosis than French workers in similar occupations. Malnutrition, weariness, and cold are the chief causes, compounded by the overcrowding which promotes contagion.[38] Workers sometimes conceal acute illness out of fear of losing their jobs or being declared unfit to work; during the first year of their stay, when they are especially vulnerable to tuberculosis, they have the worry of trying to repay the fellow workers who advanced the money for their trip to France, as well as sending back home the money for which they came. With average wages lower than those of any other group of workers in France, this is no light burden.[39]

Under the circumstances, solidarity becomes something more than a barrier against homesickness; it is the only available means of survival. These migrants from the Senegal River Valley differ from other immigrant groups in France in that they have sought from the beginning to re-create a form of community life; they are dependent upon each other for finding work, for shelter, for help in sickness and unemployment. It is sometimes said that temporary migrant labor is essentially conservative in outlook because of its continued reliance upon village life at home. In the present case, at least, it is life at home which depends upon these workers. Often isolated at work, they have found the courage as a collectivity to protest against the conditions imposed upon them. Of all the immigrant workers in France, they might have been thought the most vulnerable; yet they, more than others, have made themselves known.

The UGTSF

This public knowledge is largely due to the existence of the Union Générale des Travailleurs Sénégalais en France (UGTSF). Neither charitable foundation nor government watchdog, the UGTSF was founded in 1961 by a small group of Senegalese workers in France, among whom was Sally N'Dongo, its president.[40] It began as an *amicale*, "a friendly society," seeking to alleviate the worst sufferings of Senegalese workers in France—helping them to find work, attempting to set up a few hostels run by the workers themselves, organizing literacy classes, helping with administrative procedures, and returning the dead and dying to their homes. In so doing, the workers were extending and adapting the highly organized principles of solidarity governing each residential community of workers, in order to make them more effective.[41] They were obviously performing a worthy service. For three years, from 1964 to 1967, they received a small subsidy from the Senegalese government.[42]

By the mid-1960s, however, while continuing its welfare activities with unstinting energy, the UGTSF had become less deferential. It seemed increasingly obvious that the interests of the workers they defended were not the same as those of the Senegalese government and its representatives in France. The latter displayed a total lack of understanding of the reasons compelling people from Senegal to seek work in France.[43] They showed themselves to be extremely reluctant to intervene in defense of the workers, even where the most elementary rights were at stake, and regularly sided with the French authorities. Attempts were made to disrupt the UGTSF, and when these failed the subsidy was withdrawn, and no further assistance given.

This hostility is understandable. The UGTSF is not a political organization as such; it has no specific affiliations with political groups, either in Senegal or in France, and accepts help from many quarters, while relying on none. But it represents a group of Senegalese—of Africans rather, since it is now open to all black African workers in France—whose situation is such that any gesture of self-defense on their part is a potential threat to the status quo. Since they do not plan to stay in France, the workers' effort to achieve better conditions in France, however vital, does not constitute an end in itself; it leads inevitably to an effort to achieve better conditions in Africa so that exile in France may no longer be necessary. But this hope, however modestly formulated, stands little chance of fulfillment within the present policy outlook of the Senegalese government, which intensifies the difficulties described in the first part of this paper; it therefore has revolutionary implications.

During the past few years African workers have shown themselves increasingly ready to organize themselves in defense of their interests. At work, where they are often isolated, they may join a French trade union; in the *foyers*, where they are together, they have initiated protracted rent strikes, usually in protest against rent increases, coercive regulations, or threatened eviction without prospect of being rehoused.[44] On the whole these actions have not achieved their stated goal: rehousing of the community in decent conditions. More often than not, after months of tension, the Service d'Assistance Technique, a special police force designated for such operations, has broken into the buildings, interrogated residents, and arrested supposed "ringleaders," without any steps being taken against the landlords. It could scarcely be otherwise. But they have brought the Africans' case to public notice, and, more to the point, Africans have taken risks together and refused to accept their situation.

The demands formulated by the UGTSF include, of course, a total repudiation of the conditions at present encountered by African workers in France; they call for decent housing, equal rights, and so on. But these rights as workers, to be sought with the essential cooperation of French trade unions, take second place to what they demand as Africans: changes in Senegal which would enable them to work in their own country. They mention, in particular, such things as the development of agriculture in the Senegal River Valley through dam building and irrigation; the mobilizing of all citizens for collective tasks, including literacy classes; an end to fraud and corruption; and the desirability of processing raw materials locally. Modest demands.

It may be objected that it is technically impossible to irrigate the Senegal River Valley. Plans for doing so have been discussed since the 1920s, and it seems clear that the obstacle has been not technical difficulties but the absence of a political will to undertake such a project in a region defined as marginal. It is significant that economists, who accept the pre-eminence of groundnuts as a natural fact, and therefore take it for granted that the rivers of Senegal are useless, do not mention the possibility, save to acknowledge the existence of the disastrous Richard Toll scheme and the random pilot projects attempted by various government organizations on a capital-intensive basis.[45] Others have seen the problem differently. René Dumont asserts that the money wasted in the aforementioned projects could, if used for irrigation in the middle valley of the River Senegal, have "provided peasants with new activities, new sources of income, making life in their own villages possible."[46] Samir Amin is even more categorical:

> Colonization created the belief that the land of Senegal could produce nothing but groundnuts. . . . In fact, Senegal's real agricultural potential probably lies elsewhere. Three areas of the country have real agricultural potential: the River valley, the Niayes, and Lower and Central Casamance. If the thousands of millions invested in infrastructure for the groundnut basin had been invested instead to provide a proper irrigation infrastructure in these three areas, intensive cultivation and modern forms of agriculture could have been developed here.[47]

The problem is one of perspectives rather than techniques. For Senegalese workers in France to be able to return home, Futa Toro must become able to support them and their families. This implies a reversal of priorities in Senegal, such as could only be envisaged in a resolutely noncapitalist perspective. Sally N'Dongo is cautious and modest about the future. But he states his perspective clearly: action in aid of African workers in France is essential at the moment, but the main task lies elsewhere:

The problem originates in Africa, and must be solved there. We realise that only a radical transformation of economic and political structures will enable our countries to recover their economic independence, without which there can be no real independence.[48]

In Lieu of Conclusion

We are now in a position to consider labor migration from Senegal to France as a total phenomenon.

People leave Futa Toro because they have to, not because they prefer it. The disruption, without compensatory innovation, of the former mode of subsistence and the concentration of effort on the extension of groundnut production have deprived the Senegal River Valley of its potential and transformed it into a "peripheral" region. As a part of Senegal, it must acquit itself of taxes in a form designed to compel wage labor or cash cropping; and trade goods have driven out local artisanal production, reinforcing the need for money. The most active members must therefore seek work elsewhere; and their departure further weakens the productive resources of the region, endangering the lives of those who are left behind.

The work they do in exile does not equip them with any skills or resources likely to enable them to break this vicious circle. A few may acquire skills enabling them to stay afloat in an industrial society, but they do not want to stay in France. They spend a few years there, living in conditions of extreme deprivation in order to send money to keep the people at home alive. When they return home, either their health is damaged beyond repair or they find that there is nothing for it but to leave again.

The consequences of this migration, in terms of broken families, broken health, institutionalized inequality, waste and pain, remind one of the use of temporary, rightless migrant labor in South Africa. The analogy is perhaps more than a superficial one. The present position of Futa Toro is like that of the "labor reserves" of Southern Africa—more like Malawi or Lesotho than the "Bantu-stans" proper, since Futa Toro is a true homeland rather than an administrative fiction and is under the authority of a nominally independent government, mediating the supply of labor to the industrial power upon which it depends.

Labor migration is often said to constitute a problem. Problem for whom? Not for the governments of France and Senegal; for them it is more like the solution to a problem. For Senegal it is the only way acceptable to the present government of relieving the tensions which would inevitably build up if all the unemployed Senegalese remained in Dakar. It also brings in money.[49] As for France, apart from the general advantages of importing full-grown manpower, Senegalese migrant labor provides a particularly vulnerable labor force inclined to tolerate pay and working conditions well below any European norm. Also, France has a strong interest in maintaining political stability in its African dependencies. French private capital is still all-powerful in Senegal,[50] and strategic mineral resources have been discovered in neighboring states.

However, France is not South Africa, by which, in the present context, I mean nothing more complimentary than that France does not depend heavily upon African labor in particular, which, after all, represents only a small proportion of immigrant labor in France. But France does depend heavily on migrant labor in general, and as long as the relationship with a dependent Senegal seems to provide more advantages than disadvantages, it will probably continue to make use of Senegalese workers. However, the situation seems unstable and open to change in the near future.

One thing seems fairly certain: given the present economic condition of Senegal, the pressures compelling migration will not ease. They will tighten with the continuing deterioration of the market for groundnuts, until peasants in groundnut-producing areas, formerly prisoners on native soil, must in turn become prisoners in exile.[51]

What seems less certain is where they will go in future. In theory, Senegalese migrant workers could continue to enter France as at present; the restrictive new immigration regulations introduced in 1972 do not yet apply to them. But the publicity given to the more flagrant aspects of their misery in France and their growing tendency to take action in self-defense cannot have reassured the French government. The present so-called *immigration sauvage* may not be allowed to last much longer.

It is just conceivable that controls might be instituted which would make of African immigrants a distinct, statutorily inferior stratum of the labor force; importing apartheid, as it were. But it seems unlikely that French trade unions and left-wing political parties would allow such a development; and it is difficult to imagine the French government and employers going to the trouble of setting up the necessary infrastructure for such a distant and scanty supply of manpower. There are, as noted above, inchoate hints at such a solution in the present situation: attempts at building isolated hostels for African workers and the institution of a separate police force to deal with Africans. But there seems little chance of a full-blown apartheid system emerging *in France itself;* although, I repeat, there are structural similarities between Senegal in its relationship with France and the labor-reserve states of Southern Africa.

Another possibility is that African migrant labor might be redirected away from France toward, perhaps, the Ivory Coast or Gabon, or wherever French or international capital could put it to work. It is being suggested more and more frequently by the more advanced sectors of the business community that importing workers is somewhat passé; the thing to do would be to export factories to places where there is cheap labor available. The *Nouvel Observateur* recently quoted, with something like admiration, a polished version of this idea, propounded by a top French civil servant now responsible for "development" at EEC level:

> [Third World countries] have raw materials, manpower, energy, space—everything we ourselves now lack. There are now nine million foreign workers on the continent of Europe. . . . If their number continues to grow at the present rate, a catastrophe will ensue. As for raw materials and energy, they might as well be processed at their point of origin; this would reduce pollution in Europe, and would mean a substantial rise in profits.[52]

This last seems the more likely solution—and the most dangerous. The principles formulated by French trade unions—CGT and CFDT—concerning the equal rights of immigrant workers in France are entirely honorable (I am not here concerned to examine how seriously they are enacted). But it is always a question of rights *in France*, of assimilation to the *French* working class. Similarly, the Communist party urges workers' solidarity and sedate progress through proper channels *in France;* the Socialists speak of men living as brothers *in France;* and certain *gauchistes* seek to use the immigrant lumpenproletariat to spark off insurrection *in France*. The UGTSF urges Senegalese and other African workers to join one of the major trade unions and support trade-union action in their place of work. They are glad of the help they receive from numerous left-wing and antiracist organizations. But they are increasingly aware that action which confines itself to palliative measures, within an assimilationist framework totally unsuited to present realities, is not enough. They know that the only solution is change in Africa. And when they say so, the French left begins to mutter about "separatism" and "divisions within the working class."

Parties of the left in France have a bad reputation where France's colonial adventures are concerned; mesmerized by rhetoric, they have been able to imagine nothing better than assimilation. *Que c'est généreux, la France.* Unless they learn, from men like Sally N'Dongo, to see France and the French influence through African eyes, the solidarity they proffer will be worthless. And when African workers disappear from France, shifted to some remote work place nearer their deserted homelands, they will disappear from the tracts and the papers and be forgotten. The sound of distant guns will trouble no one.

Notes

1. Fifty-five thousand is the figure for black African immigrant workers cited in "Statistiques des étrangers en 1969," *Hommes et migrations documents* (May 15, 1970). In 1971 the Senegalese government estimated at twenty-five thousand the number of Senegalese workers in France (quoted in Sally N'Dongo, *La "coopération" franco-africaine* [Paris, 1972]), p. 99. Several sources suggest a higher overall figure: seventy to eighty thousand (*Fiches d'information et de formation sur l'immigration* [Paris, 1972]), p. 62; eighty thousand (Bernard Granotier, *Les travailleurs immigrés en France* [Paris, 1970]), p. 50; Jean-Pierre N'Diaye asserts that fifty to sixty thousand was a reliable estimate in 1963, but the 1969 figure is nearer to two hundred thousand or two hundred and fifty thousand (*Négriers modernes* [Paris, 1970]), p. 21. Sally N'Dongo (personal interview) gives the UGTSF estimate for Senegalese workers as twenty-seven thousand, but states that the inflated figures used by the press are extremely unreliable.

2. Souleymane Diarra, "Les travailleurs africains noirs en France," *Bulletin de L'I.F.A.N.* (T. 30, sér. B, no. 3, 1968), p. 902.

3. Valy-Charles Diarassouba, *L'évolution des structures agricoles du Sénégal* (Paris, 1968), p. 20; Yaya Wane, "Les Toucouleur du Fouta Tooro," *Initiations et études africaines* 25 (Dakar: IFAN, 1969), p. 22, n. 11.

4. Most sources allude to this reputed fertility, e.g., Abdoulaye Bara Diop, "Société toucouleur et migration," *Initiations africaines* 18 (Dakar: IFAN, 1965), p. 35; Yves Saint-Martin, *L'empire toucouleur 1848-1897* (Paris, 1970), pp. 9–10.

5. Hubert Deschamps, *Le Sénégal et la Gambie* (Paris: Presses universitaires de France, 1964), p. 36. Two recent studies of villages in Futa Toro reported that in one (Kanel) 91 men out of 179 were away in 1961, and 90 out of 150 in the other (Amadi-Ounaré). Cf. François Ravault, "Kanel: l'exode rural dans un village de la vallée du Sénégal," and Colette Le Blanc, "Un village de la vallée du Sénégal: Amadi-Ounaré," both in *Cahiers d'outremer* 17 (1964).

6. Michael Crowder, *Senegal: A Study of French Assimilation Policy*, rev. ed. (London: Methuen, 1967), p. 108.

7. Vincent Monteil, *L'Islam noir* (Paris: Editions de Seuil, 1964), p. 262.

8. On Al Hadj Umar, see Saint-Martin, *L'empire toucouleur;* B. O. Oloruntimehin, *The Segu Tukulor Empire* (London: Longman, 1972).

9. D. W. Robinson, "Abdul Bokar Kan and the History of Futa Toro" (Ph.D. diss., Columbia University, 1971), p. 88.

10. Ibid., p. 94.

11. The gum trade is documented in J. D. Hargreaves, ed., *France and West Africa* (London: Macmillan, 1969), ch. 2.

12. On the development of groundnut cultivation in Senegal, see Deschamps, *Le Sénégal et la Gambie,* pp. 73–75; Samir Amin, *Neo-colonialism in West Africa* (New York: Monthly Review Press, 1974; translation of *L'Afrique de l'Ouest Bloquée,* [Paris, 1971], pp. 3–8); Paul Pélissier, *Les paysans du Sénégal* (Saint-Yrieix: Impr. Fabrique, 1966).

13. E.g., Saint-Martin, *L'empire toucouleur,* p. 39.

14. Diarassouba, *Des structures agricoles,* pp. 152–55; Ravault, "Kanel."

15. For an account of traditional social stratification, see Wane, "Les toucouleur"; Majhemout Diop, *Histoire des classes sociales dans l'Afrique de l'Ouest, II: le Sénégal* (Paris: Maspero, 1972).

16. Changes in the system of land tenure are documented in Diarassouba, *Des structures agricoles,* pp. 54–59, 136–41; A. B. Diop, "Société toucouleur," pp. 70–71; Ravault, "Kanel."

17. A. B. Diop, "Société toucouleur," pp. 86–87; nine-tenths of his sample survey of Tukulor migrants in Dakar mentioned the need to provide money for their families, the need to buy clothing no longer made by local craftsmen, and taxes as motives for migrating. Annual cash incomes per capita in Futa Toro (according to a 1957 study) varied between 3,800 and 5,500 CFA francs (76 and 110 French new francs). It is worth noting that ToroodBe have the lowest cash income. Diarassouba, *Des structures agricoles,* p. 157.

18. Union Générale des Travailleurs Sénégalais en France (UGTSF), *Le livre des travailleurs africains en France* (Paris: UGTSF, 1970), p. 17.

19. A. B. Diop, "Société toucouleur," p. 53.

20. A. B. Diop, "Société toucouleur," in spite of its limitations, is a good introduction to the subject if complemented by the UGTSF publication cited above and by N'Dongo, *La "coopération" franco-africaine.*

21. Among the reasons for this decline: the breakup of the colonial federation of French West Africa (AOF) and subsequent failure of the attempt to create a Mali Federation after independence; the withdrawal of the old French *maisons de commerce;* and the departure of French administrative and military personnel.

22. Amin, *Neo-colonialism in West Africa,* p. 23.

23. From the full text of the agreement quoted in N'Dongo, *La "coopération" franco-africaine,* p. 23.

24. On the organization of the ONI, see *Fiches d'information et de formation sur l'immigration,* pp. 92–96.

25. J. M. Jeanneney, quoted in N'Diaye, *Négriers modernes,* p. 19.

26. UGTSF, *Des travailleurs africains,* p. 72.

27. Sally N'Dongo, in ibid., p. 74.

28. Sally N'Dongo, "Nous ne venons pas manger votre pain," *Nouvel*

Observateur, August 6-12, 1973; Jonathan Power, *The New Proletarians* (Community and Race Relations Unit [BCC] pamphlet, 1972).

29. UGTSF, *Des travailleurs africains,* pp. 24–25.

30. Ibid., p. 113; Léon Gani, *Syndicats et travailleurs immigrés* (Paris, 1972), p. 196.

31. N'Dongo, *La "coopération" franco-africaine,* p. 53. See also Stephen Castles and Godula Kosack, *Immigrant Workers and Class Structure in Western Europe* (London: Oxford University Press, 1973), pp. 255–66, for a discussion of the FAS and "official" hostels.

32. UGTSF, *Des travailleurs africains,* p. 66.

33. Castles and Kosack, *Immigrant Workers,* pp. 286–87; André Gorz and Philippe Gavi, "La bataille d'Ivry," *Les temps modernes,* March 1970.

34. Diarra, "Les travailleurs africains noirs," pp. 971–79; and UGTSF, *Des travailleurs africains,* pp. 31–43, attempt to describe conditions in these places.

35. Only twenty-one *foyers* were built or renovated by the FAS during 1964-1969 (N'Dongo, *La "coopération" franco-africaine,* p. 63).

36. UGTSF, *Des travailleurs africains,* p. 77.

37. Diarra, "Les travailleurs africains noirs," p. 961, punctiliously notes that 11.8 percent of African workers employed as dustmen left their jobs for that reason.

38. The health records of residents in the Ivry *foyer* mentioned above showed that twenty-eight residents had been hospitalized for lung diseases, many for several months (UGTSF, *Des travailleurs africains,* p. 50).

39. Average wages earned are difficult to determine, probably about six hundred francs a month. See Diarra, "Les travailleurs africains noirs," pp. 964–67; Granotier, *Les travailleurs immigrés,* p. 88

40. The UGTSF now has 6,800 members. Sally N'Dongo came to France in the 1950s as a domestic servant. He could not then speak French.

41. This organized solidarity is described by Diarra, "Les travailleurs africains noirs," pp. 980–90.

42. The subsidy amounted to 100,000 francs in all. Relations between the UGTSF and the government of Senegal are described in UGTSF, *Des travailleurs africains,* ch. 7.

43. One consul general, in a speech after the inauguration of a *foyer* in Roubaix, informed the audience that the workers who came from Senegal belonged to "a peculiar race which is fond of travelling" (UGTSF, *Des travailleurs africains,* p. 166).

44. Many of these actions involving African workers' *foyers*—Ivry, Pierre-fitte, Puteaux, Saint-Denis, Raymond-Losserand—were widely reported. Cf. my note in *Race Today* (November 1973) for the motives behind one particular case.

45. On Richard Toll, the *Organisation Autonome de la Vallée,* the *Organisation Autonome du Delta,* see Diarassouba, *Des structures agricoles,* pp. 80–83, 229–34; and René Dumont, *Paysanneries aux abois* (Paris, 1972), pp. 215–20.

46. Dumont, *Paysanneries,* p. 220.

47. Amin, *Neo-colonialism in West Africa,* pp. 14–15.

48. N'Dongo, *La "coopération" franco-africaine,* p. 102.

49. Amin, *Neo-colonialism in West Africa,* p. 164: "remittances from Senegalese workers in France (500 m. francs, according to the IBRD) seem to be considerably underestimated." Amin suggests a figure eight times higher than the 500 million CFA (or 1 million French francs) he quotes as the IBRD figure for 1964-1968; but he bases his suggestion on J. P. N'Diaye's estimate of one hundred thousand Senegalese workers in France, which seems rather high. It should be remembered that "the funds sent to families at home contribute almost nothing to the development of the country, since they are used chiefly to buy consumer goods—some not even produced in the country—rather than implements of production." (N'Dongo, *La "coopération" franco-africaine,* p. 69.)

50. Cf. Rita Cruise O'Brien, *White Society in Black Africa* (London: Faber and Faber, 1972); and N'Dongo, *La "coopération" franco-africaine,* esp. pp. 25–30, which list the numerous positions in Senegalese commerce, industry, and administration held by Henry-Charles Gallenca and Pierre Delmas.

51. The present groundnut impasse is described and explained by Amin, *Neo-colonialism in West Africa;* and Dumont, *Paysanneries.*

52. M. Claude Cheysson, in *Nouvel Observateur,* February 18-24, 1974.

Colonial Labor Theories of Inequality:
The Case of International Harvester

Mario Barrera

Introduction

That America's racial minorities occupy a position of inequality in
the social structure is not in dispute. Numerous studies have
documented the existing inequalities in wealth, political power,
educational opportunity, and other dimensions of social life. Yet
there is little agreement on the fundamental causes of these
patterns of inequality, and particularly of their persistence over
time. The current study reports on the role of minority labor in
one of America's largest corporations, International Harvester,
and interprets the pattern of inequality found there within a
framework of colonial theory.[. . .]

Colonial Labor

In this paper I am examining one particular aspect of racial
inequality in the contemporary United States, that of inequality in
the labor force. My contention is that minority workers represent
a distinct structural element in the labor force and that these
workers are treated differently from other workers in several
ways which are described below. The fundamental reason that
this happens is that it serves the interests of employers to make
differential use of minority workers. To the extent that this
situation prevails, it represents a type of colonial labor. In order
to investigate the existence of colonial labor empirically, it is
necessary to specify more concretely the particular ways in which
minority labor is used. At this time it is possible to identify five
relatively distinct ways in which minority labor is used in a colonial
manner. These are listed below, along with some quotes from
various writers who have described that particular condition.

Reprinted from *The Review of Radical Political Economics* 8, no. 2 (Summer 1976),
with permission of the Union for Radical Political Economics. Copyright © 1976
The Review of Radical Political Economics. The author wishes to acknowledge the
invaluable research assistance of Art Juján and to thank Carlos Muñoz and Tomás
Almaguer for their comments on an earlier draft of this paper.

1. *Minority workers can be restricted to or concentrated in the lower-status jobs and industries.* Basically this is doing the dirty work for the society. "When working, [minority workers] tend to be concentrated in jobs that are insecure, dirty, unskilled, and at the bottom of the hierarchy of authority where there is little possibility for advancement."[1]

> In all the developed Western capitalist states, there exists a group of workers to fill the jobs that the more politically established sectors of the working class shun. These marginal workers generally are set apart in some way so that they lack the social or the political means of defending their interests. In Western Europe usually they are noncitizens coming from either Southern Europe or Northern Africa. In England they are colored peoples coming from various parts of the Empire. In the urban centers of the United States race serves to mark black and brown workers for filling in the undesirable slots.[2]

One way in which this practice is maintained is through the tacit establishment of "job ceilings," which limit how high minority workers can rise in the occupational structure. The discussion of segmented labor markets is also relevant here.

The relegation of certain types of work to colonized labor serves the interests of employers by lowering the basis for dissatisfaction among the nonminority workers. It also serves the interests of the nonminority workers, at least in the short run, by sparing them from that work. The argument has been made that this practice harms employers by keeping talented minority workers in jobs that do not fully utilize their talents, but this would not seem to be a major drawback under conditions of a labor surplus.

2. *Wage differentials can be established for the minority workers.* This means that a minority worker will receive less pay for doing the same work. "This special exploitation of the black labor force also leads to direct economic gains for the various employers. Methodologically it is very difficult to measure exactly the extra surplus extracted due to wage discrimination, although in Chicago it has been estimated that unskilled black workers earn about 17% less on similar jobs than unskilled white workers of comparable quality."[3]

The existence of wage differentials serves the interests of employers in keeping their labor costs as low as possible.

3. *Colonized workers serve as economic buffers or "shock absorbers," cushioning the impact of economic dislocations on nonminority workers.* "Any social or economic crisis that this society produces is generally

felt most strongly and 'absorbed' by Third-World people within the United States."[4] Thus, in periods of high unemployment, minority workers can be laid off disproportionately to nonminorites. Periods of economic recession invariably hit the minority communities harder than other communities.

Maintaining a colonial buffer serves the interests of employers in that it lowers the basis for dissatisfaction among the potentially more dangerous majority workers. It also benefits the majority workers in that they are spared the full impact of the dislocations.

4. *Minority workers can serve as a special "industrial reserve army."* This minority industrial reserve army consists of workers who are often unemployed or underemployed and who can be incorporated into the labor force in times of economic expansion. They provide elasticity to the labor force, allowing employers to expand their work force without having to raise wages through competing for nonminority workers.

> The dual labor market operates to create an urban-based industrial labor reserve that provides a ready supply of workers in a period of labor shortage and can be politically isolated in times of relatively high unemployment. In a tight labor market the undesirable jobs that whites leave are filled out of this labor reserve so that in time more job categories are added to the black sector of the labor market. . . . The welfare and police costs of maintaining this labor reserve are high, but they are borne by the State as a whole and therefore do not enter into the profit calculations of individual firms.[5]

> Unemployment is intimately related to the process of capital accumulation and the associated pattern of technical change. On average, the overall rate of accumulation and the rate of growth of productivity due to technical change is such that not enough employment is being created to take up the existing slack plus the labor that is displaced by the new techniques that are being introduced. Thus, a certain amount of unemployment is continuously being reproduced as the system as a whole expands. Such unemployed labor constitutes a "reserve army" upon which the system can draw when the rate of accumulation rises above average. It is replenished when the rate of accumulation falls. The system is furthermore dependent upon the continued existence of such a reserve army. This is for the reason that it weakens the bargaining power of the workers and thereby prevents rising wages from eating into profits.[6]

The existence of the minority industrial reserve army serves the interests of employers in the ways outlined above. However, it is contrary to the interests of nonminority workers in that it weakens their bargaining power and acts as a brake on wages.

5. *The existence of a colonized work force serves to divide the workers among themselves and to prevent them from pursuing a unified class interest.* Such division has been actively fostered in the past by employers who have used black and Chicano workers as strike-breakers against nonminority workers. "Colonization as a process can be seen as a method of class subjugation in which part of the working class—black Americans, and indeed Mexican Americans, Puerto Ricans and others are separated out as a distinct group from the rest of the working class to serve the function of a pariah group creating division in the working class and perpetuating division within the working class."[7]

This division among the workers serves the interest of employers as a class and acts against the interests of workers as a class.

A review of these five aspects of colonial labor establishes that, while they operate consistently in the interest of employers of labor, they benefit nonminority workers only in a limited sense, and operate in the long run against their interests as workers.

If it can be established that colonial labor has existed and continues to exist in the United States, this will represent support for the colonial theory of minority inequality and weaken the base of the deficiency and bias theories. Such a revision in our theoretical conceptions would have important implications for our understanding of what it would take to overcome the unequal status of American minorities.

The procedure I have chosen to explore this theme is that of a case study. In the following pages I present some historical material on one of America's most important industrial corpora-tions, International Harvester, which employs both Chicano and black labor. My concern has been to determine whether colonial labor has characterized International Harvester's employment practices, and if so which elements of colonial labor have been or are the most important.

International Harvester

The origins of International Harvester can be traced to western Virginia, where in 1831 Cyrus Hall McCormick developed a horse-drawn reaper. In 1847 McCormick moved to Chicago and built his own factory. This factory, known as the McCormick Works, was to remain for many years the sole manufacturing plant of the McCormick farm equipment company. By 1902 this plant was producing over a third of the United States' harvesting machinery. In that year the McCormick company merged with the next four largest farm equipment companies to form International Harvester. This giant trust then produced 85 percent of the country's harvesting machinery. In 1914 legal action was brought against the company under the Sherman Anti-Trust Act, and it was eventually forced to break up. International Harvester Company remained in existence, and although reduced in scope it has continued as the largest company in the farm equipment industry. In recent years it has ranked among the top twenty-five corporations in the United States in volume of sales, which in 1973 amounted to over \$4 billion. Throughout its history, the McCormick family has maintained a central position in management, and the current president is a McCormick. The mainstay of the company is in its lines of farm equipment and trucks, but it also operates its own steel plant (Wisconsin Steel Division) and manufactures industrial gas turbines (Solar Division). Its main plants are in the Midwest, with some in the South. The Solar Division is located in San Diego.

Starting with twenty-three workers in 1847, McCormick employed fourteen hundred in 1884. In 1950 International Harvester had over ninety thousand workers in all its divisions and in 1970, over one hundred thousand. Within the farm equipment industry generally, approximately two-thirds of the employees are blue-collar workers, with operatives, or semiskilled workers, comprising the single largest category.[8]

Trade unionism has had a long and turbulent history at McCormick and International Harvester. The earliest unions, based on crafts, appeared in the 1860s. In the late 1880s the Knights of Labor were strongly represented at McCormick. In 1886 striking McCormick workers were involved in conflicts with other workers and the police that led directly to the famous Haymarket Square bombing and the subsequent wave of antiunion repression. Union activity at McCormick and International Harvester rose and fell, as it did in industry generally, with changes in economic and political conditions. McCormick management was virulently antiunion, and it succeeded time and time again in smashing the emerging unions. The tactics used were a skillful blend of coercion and cooptation. On the coercive side there was ample use made of blacklists, police repression, and the firing of union activists. But the company also resorted to the shrewd use of bonuses, intracompany welfare programs, and company unions as the occasion demanded. After World War I International Harvester was one of the members of the Special Conference Committee, a secret organization of ten of the largest corporations in the United States. It included Du Pont, General Electric, General Motors, Standard Oil, U.S. Rubber, Bethlehem Steel, and later AT&T and U.S. Steel. The purpose of the organization was to deal with the threat of unionism and related labor matters. In this, as in other ways, International Harvester proved itself to be a highly class-conscious corporation.[9]

International Harvester was successful in delaying the recognition of unions until 1941, several years after most of America's large industrial concerns. After the war there was a struggle for union dominance between the left-influenced Farm Equipment Workers and the United Automobile Workers, with the initially stronger Farm Equipment Workers losing out during the McCarthy era in the early 1950s. Since that time the UAW has been the largest union among International Harvester workers.

International Harvester and McCormick also have a long history of ethnic diversity in their work force. During the nineteenth and early twentieth centuries the succession of ethnic workers included Irish, Scandinavians, Germans, and Poles. World War I, however, signaled the end of large-scale European migration, and the entrance of black and Chicano workers in significant numbers into the International Harvester labor force. This trend was reinforced by the stringent postwar restrictions on immigration. Whereas blacks had established a presence in Chicago industry earlier in the century, World War I marked a sharp rise in their level of industrial employment. For Chicanos, World War I marks their entry into the Chicago labor market.

It is important to keep in mind that even before this period the management of large industrial concerns was highly conscious of the ethnicity of its workers. During the nineteenth century International Harvester had pursued a deliberate policy of encouraging ethnic diversity in its workers as a means of keeping them weak and divided. According to Robert Ozanne, "Harvester experience showed that the cohesiveness of nationality groups worked against the company in strike situations."[10] In 1916 labor strife prompted President McCormick to write to his directors: "One of the advantages of building a new foundry organization will be that we will not have such a large percentage of Poles. It does not have a good effect to have so large a percentage of one class of men."[11] After World War I the Industrial Relations Department of International Harvester compiled regular reports on the nationality and race of its employees.[12]

The policy pursued by International Harvester during this period was to leave racial hiring policies to the superintendents of the different plants. However, the central management carefully monitored the proportion of black workers in the plants and cautioned the superintendents if black employment reached a certain level. The various plants of International Harvester followed one of two patterns. Some excluded blacks altogether. The others adopted a quota system, generally at about the 20 percent level.[13] The quota system appears to have been the product of two considerations. One was the desire to tap this pool of labor in a tight labor market. The other was the fear of ethnic solidarity.

The postwar labor shortage produced a sharp turnaround in the trend of hiring more minority labor. In this situation, International Harvester management reluctantly decided to increase the hiring of minorities rather than raising their labor costs by competing with other manufacturers for labor.[14] By 1923 the level of black labor at the central McCormick Works stood at 18 percent and at the McCormick Twine Mill, at 20 percent.[15] By 1929 it had risen to over 27 percent at the Twine Mill. Some plants, however, still employed no blacks.

The Wisconsin Steel plant of International Harvester provided an interesting variation on this situation. The policy of Wisconsin Steel was to hire no blacks at all. Confronted with the labor shortage, its solution was to hire Chicanos or Mexicans. In pursuit of this effort they recruited Chicano labor from as far away as

Table 1
Percentage of Mexicans Employed
at Wisconsin Steel, 1920s

Year	Percentage of Mexicans
1921	0.3
1922	0.6
1923	14.2
1924	14.8
1925	19.7
1926	21.8
1927	21.0
1928	19.5

Source: Paul Taylor, *Mexican Labor in the United States: Chicago and the Calumet Region* (Berkeley: University of California Press, 1932), table 3.

Kansas City and Texas.[16] The figures for "Mexican" employment at Wisconsin Steel during the 1920s are shown in Table 1.

The depression of the 1930s and the labor surplus that it brought with it, produced a sharp turnaround in the trend of hiring more minority labor. Now minority workers were laid off at a greater rate than white workers, and the percentages of minority workers declined. At the McCormick Works the proportion of black workers dropped from 18 percent in 1923 to 10.3 percent in 1940. At the Tractor Works it declined from 9 percent in 1923 to 6.5 percent in 1940. The McCormick Twine Mill saw a drop from 27.5 percent in 1929 to 18 percent in 1940.[17]

With the labor shortages of World War II, the situation was turned around once again. Federal antidiscriminatory and fair employment practices legislation combined with the labor shortage to end the complete exclusion of black workers that still existed at many International Harvester plants. In 1940 blacks constituted 4.5 percent of all workers employed in International Harvester plants. By 1944 the number had risen to 11.6 percent. In 1950 it was 12.8 percent, in 1960 9.3 percent, and in 1970 11 percent.[18] In 1974 it was 11.3 percent.[19] Thus, it would appear that there has been little change in the overall level of black employment since the end of World War II. One factor that has contributed to the stagnation in the level of black employment has been the recent trend of closing plants in the large urban centers such as Chicago and opening others in suburban and outlying areas.

There has continued to exist considerable variation in the levels of black employment at the different plants. The highest levels were reached at the McCormick Twine Mill before its closing in 1953. This plant, traditionally operated by female labor, reached a peak in 1957 of 75.6 percent in its employment of blacks. The McCormick Works, which closed in 1961, had a work force of 28.7 percent blacks in 1960.[20]

One of the most striking aspects of black employment at International Harvester has been its relative concentration in certain types of work and certain occupational levels. The two work sectors in which black employment was initially concentrated were the foundries, or metal-casting shops, and the twine mills. The foundries were the places with the most arduous working conditions. The twine mills were areas of low-wage employment, almost entirely female. In 1924, for example, black employment at the Tractor Works foundry was 35 percent and in the McCormick foundry, 29 percent. In the twine mills it was 24 percent.[21]

The typical minority employee was hired at the level of laborer, or unskilled worker, and there seems to have been a definite conception on the part of management as to what type of work minorities were suitable for. A special report on minority employment was initiated by President McCormick in 1925. Some of the representative quotes are: "In some instances the Negro is held to be suitable for semi-skilled work . . . Steel mills are more satisfied with Mexicans for common and semi-skilled labor . . . The Mexicans at the steel mills are developing into semi-skilled tradesmen but none are employed in mechanical or electrical trades."[22]

Paul Taylor presents figures (see Table 2) for two large steel plants in the Chicago area in 1928, and, while the figures are not specifically for International Harvester, they are probably indicative of the general pattern in the steel plants of the area.

Table 2
Race of Employees at Two Chicago-Area Steel Plants, 1928

	All employees		Mexican employees		Black employees	
	Number	Percentage	Number	Percentage	Number	Percentage
Skilled	8,101	36.7	38	1.8	128	4.7
Semiskilled	5,704	25.9	397	19.1	438	16.1
Unskilled	8,256	37.4	1,646	79.1	2,150	79.2
Total	22,061	100.0	2,081	100.0	2,716	100.0

Source: Paul Taylor, *Mexican Labor in the United States: Chicago and the Calumet Region* (Berkeley: University of California Press, 1932), p. 157. Data for Gary works and South works, Illinois Steel Company.

Of interest in this data is not only the sharp difference between minority occupational patterns and overall patterns but also the very similar patterns for Chicano and black workers.

A more recent study of the farm equipment and construction machinery industries in the United States indicates that these patterns persist in modified form today. According to Ozanne, "In plants visited by the author or by other Industrial Research Unit personnel (and these were larger companies), it was found generally the Negro craftsmen tended to be concentrated in the foundries in such crafts as molders and coremakers, rather than being broadly distributed throughout the plant."[23]

A review of occupational statistics presented in the same study reveals the following patterns for five large companies (not specified by name) in the farm equipment and construction machinery industries. In 1970, 35.5 percent of these companies' employees were classified as white collar (all non-blue-collar categories), although only 8.9 percent of the companies' black employees fell into this classification. Of the 8.9 percent, the overwhelming majority were located in the lowest white-collar category, that of office and clerical workers. At the highest level, that of officials and managers, only 0.9 percent of the black employees could be found, compared with 8.2 percent of all employees. Some 11.5 percent of the black employees were classified as craftsmen (skilled workers), 60 percent as operatives (semiskilled), 14.4 percent as laborers, and 5.2 percent as service workers. Black employees were overrepresented in proportion to their overall numbers in the bottom three categories and under-represented in all of the higher categories.[24] Several factors are also noted in the study that make these figures even bleaker. Thus, Ozanne states, "the designation 'craftsmen' covers such a broad category of jobs that it conceals the fact that the Negro penetration into truly skilled trades has been almost negligible. Furthermore, the future for this category is not bright because of the almost universal failure to enroll a sufficient number of Negroes in the apprenticeships."[25] Furthermore, "within the operatives classification, we observed a definite tendency for blacks to be overconcentrated at the lower ranges."[26]

At the white-collar level, the same study notes that blacks have been almost completely excluded from sales positions, and that "in the offices Negro employment is generally only tokenism.

Table 3
Occupational Categories of Blacks at International Harvester, 1974

Officials and managers	2.3%
Professionals	1.3
Technicians	1.8
Sales workers	0.9
Office and clerical	6.0
Craftsmen	8.3
Operatives	16.3
Laborers	29.3
Service workers	21.3

Firms in communities of high Negro population have failed to do much better in the proportion of Negroes hired for their offices than firms in communities of low Negro population. This probably indicates that until recently the main offices actually have been neglected in the firms' equal opportunity policy."[27]

In 1974, according to International Harvester's figures, blacks were represented in the various occupational categories in the manner presented in Table 3.[28]

In evaluating these figures and the marginal improvement they seem to represent over earlier periods, particularly in the craftsmen category, Ozanne's comments cited above should be kept in mind. The changing nature of the occupational structure is also relevant in this connection:

> The statistics constitute snapshot pictures of an occupational structure in a continual state of change. The pattern of change is one in which, generally speaking, new and expanding job categories appear at the higher status, more desirable end of the occupational spectrum pushing the older, stable, or declining categories downward toward lower status, less desirable position in the hierarchy. At the same time, the least desirable occupations become obsolete and disappear. Traditionally, this change in the job structure has been accompanied by the movement of whites into the expanding categories leaving the older, stable, and declining jobs vacant for blacks. Thus, blacks are always gaining access to new jobs, but their long-run position *relative* to whites does not change.[29]

On the matter of differential pay rates (different pay for the same work), there appears to be little evidence. From the information presented by Taylor for Mexican workers in the Chicago of the 1920s, it seems that such practices existed but do not appear to have been a major factor in the employment of minority labor.[30]

Another aspect of minority employment in the Chicago of the 1920s is touched upon in a comment by an employer from a large foundry: "We now have a good labor market, so we can replace the Mexicans with more desirable labor."[31]

Up to now the discussion has been concerned with the main International Harvester plants in the Midwest. Harvester's plants in the South deserve special comment. The three plants that have been studied are the Louisville Works, producer of tractors since 1946; the Memphis Works, where mechanical cottonpickers and other farm implements have been made since 1948; and the Evansville Works, which has manufactured refrigerators since 1946. The Louisville plant began with 4.2 percent black workers, employed 14.1 percent in 1950, reached a peak of 20.9 percent in 1955, and declined to 11.9 percent in 1960, the last year for which published figures are available.[32] The Evansville plant had 4.4 percent black workers in 1946 and 8.2 percent in 1950.[33] The Memphis plant started with 12.2 percent black workers in 1947 and had reached a level of 23.2 percent in 1949.[34] In 1968 their percentage of black employees was still at essentially that same level.[35]

A study of these three companies covering the late 1940s and early 1950s showed a sharp pattern of black concentration at certain occupational levels and in certain types of work. The basic pattern was that blacks were greatly overconcentrated in unskilled labor and greatly underrepresented in skilled and white-collar occupations. At the Louisville Works, for example, in 1951 black day-work production workers consisted of 54.8 percent unskilled and 2.8 percent skilled workers. Whites in the same category were 25.9 percent unskilled workers and 29.5 percent skilled.[36] The same author divided the production process into three stages and found that blacks were concentrated in the first stage, consisting of primary fabrication of parts from raw materials. Whites were more evenly distributed throughout the three stages, with the second stage being the finishing and assembling of parts and the third stage the inspection, packing, and shipping.[37] Blacks were almost totally excluded from clerical, technical, and managerial employment.[38] The author concluded on the basis of his study that International Harvester's officially stated policy of equal employment opportunity would soon produce significant occupational advancement for blacks. And yet a study based on 1969 data described the situation in the Memphis plant in the following terms:

> . . . the plant is still characterized by lily-white and overwhelmingly black departments. Of the roughly 300 men in the truly skilled trades, there was but one Negro, an electrician who was on layoff in January 1969 because he had only 50 days seniority in the electrical department. In welding, in 1969, there were roughly 3 Negroes out of 100, none of them with substantial seniority. In the machine department there were only 6 Negro machine operators out of 75 operators and inspectors, the most senior Negro having only six months' seniority. Among 279 foremen, 3 were Negro, 2 of them appointed in 1967, and the first in 1965. There were no Negro apprentices. Of 450 workers in the foundry, approximately 325 were Negroes, concentrated as usual in the hottest places, the forge shop and pouring the molten metal.[39]

John Hope's study gives us some insight into the origins of this situation in the 1940s and early 1950s. Hope stresses the opposition of white labor to the advancement of blacks, and he repeatedly states that management pursued an equal opportunity policy. However, management's role in this regard consisted primarily of placing some black workers in semiskilled positions. During the first few years of existence of the southern plants there was no union representation, and management had a relatively free hand in its placement policies. According to Hope, Harvester management made no effort to place blacks in skilled positions, and, as we have seen, there was virtually no black representation at the white-collar level.[40] Hope also mentions that there was a universally recognized taboo against appointing blacks to positions where they would be supervising white workers.[41] It was equally forbidden for blacks to "bump" or displace a white worker from a job, regardless of seniority or qualifications.[42] Any black tempted to file a grievance on the basis of discrimination was brought under intense pressure from union and company officials as well as fellow workers on the basis that it would be detrimental to good race relations.[43]

One of the most interesting aspects of the southern International Harvester plants was the use made of the public school system to maintain the pattern of black concentration. Vocational courses were made available to white students which would prepare them to enter the skilled trades at Harvester and other industrial plants. Vocational courses available to black students did not prepare them to enter such trades. In addition the schools conducted an adult evening Apprenticeship Training Program. These programs were run by the schools together with Joint Apprenticeship Committees composed of an equal number of representatives from the unions and from the major employers. The program was coordinated by a representative of the U.S. Bureau of Apprenticeship Training.[44] The result was an arrangement where the companies, the unions, the local schools, and the federal government combined to ensure that black workers were excluded from the training which could gain them entry to skilled occupations.

There is little evidence of the role of minority labor in cushioning white unemployment in the Southern plants. Ozanne, however, notes that

> when layoffs came in 1960 there were more in the assembly and foundry than in the tool room and maintenance. Thus, black layoffs were proportionately greater than white. This occurred at Memphis and Louisville even though the blacks had equal seniority

with the whites. In certain older Harvester plants which had been lily-white before World War II the disproportionate decline of black employment was caused by the lesser seniority of blacks.[45]

Another setting in which we can examine the uses of minority labor at International Harvester is provided by the company's Solar Division, located in San Diego. While time-series data for minority employment are not available here, an examination of Solar can provide us with a look at the contemporary situation in one Harvester plant.

Solar began as an aircraft company during the 1920s and became part of International Harvester in 1960. Since the 1960s its main product has been industrial gas turbines, a line which is currently prospering. Solar employs some three thousand workers in two San Diego plants, and has gross sales of over $100 million. In 1973 minority workers were 13.2 percent of the Solar work force. In the San Diego area as a whole, minorities represented 17.8 percent of the labor force, with approximately 12 percent being Chicano, 4 percent black, and 2 percent other minorities.

Table 4
Job Categories of Minorities at Solar, 1973

Officials and managers	2.8%
Professionals	4.3
Technicians	8.5
Office and clerical	12.6
Craftsmen	11.1
Operatives	23.0
Laborers	46.5
Service workers	54.8

As in other Harvester plants, the most obvious minority work pattern is that of concentration in some occupational categories and underrepresentation in others. In 1973 minorities at Solar were represented in the broad occupational categories used by the census in the manner presented in Table 4.[46]

In line with Ozanne's comments cited above, we find that minority workers are concentrated at the bottom within each of the categories as well. Thus, if the service component is divided into its two constituents, we find that only four of the twenty-one guards are minorities, while fully nineteen of the twenty-one custodians are minority workers. Likewise, five of the eight minority workers listed as officials and managers are foremen.

Looking only at the overall pattern, however, it is clear that the Solar minority work force is overrepresented in those occupations listed below the skilled workers and substantially underrepresented at occupational levels above office and clerical. Of all the occupational categories, the two largest by far are those of operatives and professionals. There is a relatively small number of laborers.

Judging from a variety of evidence, Solar management attaches little importance to changing this pattern of concentration and underrepresentation. For example, in 1966 Solar was visited by employment specialists from the Department of the Navy to audit Solar's compliance with equal opportunity laws and decrees (Solar has important military contracts). The Navy inspectors made a series of recommendations, which were listed along with suggestions by the Solar EEO (Equal Employment Opportunity) coordinator, at that time a regular member of the management team. The document reads, in part:

> RECOMMENDATION: Explore the possibility of setting up a "field employment office" in some minority populated areas ("poverty pockets") of town, to be staffed one or two days a week by an employment representative with authority to hire in the field.
>
> SUGGESTED ACTION: Do not implement. Any benefit to the company is questionable and the expense would probably not be justified. . . .
>
> RECOMMENDATION: Organize a training program or series of meetings for front-line supervisors and their employees to instill EEO principles firmly in them. Also, make it clear that any individual who does not firmly support EEO should seek employment elsewhere.
>
> SUGGESTED ACTION: Do not implement. A training program would be far too expensive and difficult to organize, and we feel this is hardly an appropriate subject for a formalized training program. . . .

Solar had also been under pressure to develop a Minority Skills Inventory in order to identify promotable minority workers. In 1970 the director of industrial relations wrote a memo indicating that he felt such a skills inventory should be developed and suggesting a procedure. He went on to say:

> Recognizing that this Skills Inventory will not be too useful, disclosure of its existence should be kept to a minimum, on a need to know basis. Expense should also be kept to a minimum. Since we are talking about 472 presently employed minorities plus all the new minority employees this will be a long, tedious process. I believe that once a format and official guidelines are developed the

O.F.C.C. (Office of Federal Contract Compliance) will be satisfied as long as we press forward. We should, however, all sing the same tune and have several examples of use and success for the Skills Inventory. . . .

Solar, along with all companies which are contractors with the federal government, is required to file an Affirmative Action Plan. This Affirmative Action Plan must describe patterns of minority employment within the company, identify any "underutilization" of minorities, locate barriers to fuller utilization within the company, and propose goals and mechanisms for eliminating any existing patterns of discrimination and underutilization. While Solar's Affirmative Action Plans have been approved every year by the federal agency charged with review of the plans, an examination of the plans for 1973 and 1974 shows that they are woefully inadequate. Solar's plans make no attempt to locate barriers to equal opportunity within the company, and they set no long-range goals for overcoming existing underutilization. Their analysis of underutilization, the most basic element of the plans, is full of inaccuracies and misleading use of statistics. Short-range (one-year) goals are the only ones that are set, contrary to the provisions of federal law, and these are so lacking in ambition as to call into serious question the company's desire to correct the existing patterns of concentration and underrepresentation. As an example, the goals in the 1973 plan call for adding one minority employee in the category of officials and managers, three minority professionals, and one minority technician. These three categories of employment combined totaled over twelve hundred employees at Solar in 1973. Yet even these insignificant goals were not achieved. In 1974 Solar had the same number of minorities in these three categories as it had in 1973. The 1974 plan made no mention of the fact that the 1973 goals had not been achieved, and proceeded blithely to set other goals.

The responsibility for enforcing equal opportunity and affirmative action within a company is supposed to rest upon a high-level official expressly appointed to that function. In 1973 Solar hired a young black employee and designated him its EEO coordinator, a position which carried little power. The EEO coordinator took his position seriously and began to try to revive the Minority Skills Inventory and implement other aspects of the Affirmative Action Plan. Within a couple of months he had been fired. The reason given for his termination was that he refused to supply his superiors in the Industrial Relations Department with the names of minority employees who had raised complaints about the company in private meetings held at employees' homes during nonworking hours.

The responsibility for reviewing Solar's Affirmative Action Plans and for general monitoring of its minority employment patterns is delegated by the Office of Federal Contract Compliance (OFCC) to the Department of Defense. The failure of the government to take action in this case to correct obvious patterns of unequal opportunity is only a reflection of a virtually universal pattern. As Ozanne states in his review of black employment in the farm equipment industry:

> In spite of the efforts of OFCC to establish concrete standards for employment integration, the judgment of "in compliance" or "non-compliance" is, to a great extent, a subjective one. The decision is made especially difficult because of the possible dire consequences of the only overt response provided for a ruling of "non-compliance," i.e., the denial or cancellation of a government contract which may put a plant out of business and/or prevent or hinder the government from obtaining necessary armaments or other materials.[47]

Thus, it appears that there will be little remedial action forthcoming from the government to change the patterns of minority employment that are so deeply entrenched at Solar and other branches of International Harvester.

Conclusion

From this review of minority employment practices, what can we conclude about the existence of colonial labor at International Harvester?

On the first aspect, that of concentration, there is strong and convincing evidence. It is clear that in the present, as in the past, minority workers have in fact disproportionately filled the least desirable jobs in the industry. It is also clear that in many, if not all, instances this has been a matter of conscious policy. Management has had definite ideas about what type of work was "suitable" for minorities, and it has consciously excluded them from other types of work. In the case of the South, we noted the manipulation of the educational system for the purpose of maintaining this state of affairs. While there is variation regionally and over time, the patterns remain strong everywhere. Furthermore, the lack of commitment to affirmative action can lead only to the assumption that management today is satisfied with the present arrangements. In this connection it is well to note that International Harvester has often been lauded as a leader and a "pioneer" in developing equal employment opportunities.[48] In general, then, we can say that the pattern of occupational concentration and exclusion or underrepresentation is an important aspect of colonial labor, at least in this particular company.

On the aspect of wage differentials there is little direct evidence. Wage differentials appear to have had some significance but not to have been a primary factor. One study at a southern plant argues for the existence of wage differentials, but it fails to separate out the effect of occupational concentration.[49] Interviews with Solar minority employees have failed to turn up wage discrimination as a complaint. It appears that unionization has largely eliminated racial wage differentials as a significant element in large and modern industrial plants. This is not necessarily the case for other types of industries.

Some evidence does exist for the use of minority labor as a buffer group. As noted above, severe labor surpluses such as that of the 1930s resulted in the disproportionate laying off of minority workers. Ozanne, cited above, describes how layoffs in some Harvester plants in 1960 disproportionately affected blacks, but he sees this as a side effect of blacks' concentration in certain types of jobs and of having lower seniority. In the same study Ozanne presents data for five large firms (unspecified) in the farm equipment and construction machinery industries during a period of layoffs from 1968 to 1970. According to him, in three of these five firms black blue-collar workers (but not white-collar workers) suffered substantially more job losses than whites, and did better in only one case. Here again he attributes the pattern to lack of seniority among the black workers.[50] In the case of Solar, a mild decline in employment in 1973 did not result in minority workers being laid off disproportionately. What would happen in the case of more severe dislocations remains to be seen.

The use of minority labor as an industrial reserve army is the fourth aspect of colonial labor. There is no question that minorities have been used as a pool of labor to be drawn upon in times of labor shortage. Minorities performed this function during the 1920s when minority hiring was clearly seen as an alternative to bidding up the price of labor. World War II provides a second clear example of a minority reserve force being put to use. While it is not thus difficult to cite historical examples of minority labor being used in this manner, it is more difficult to determine whether management simply took advantage of an existing situation or whether it has consciously contributed to its perpetuation. The existence of a pool of available surplus labor, of course, is something that cannot be determined by the managers of a single company. It is in large part a consequence of the overall level of employment, which is in turn affected by federal government policies and the general state of the economy. While the corporations can have their effect on this through their influence on government policy, this would require a different type of study to determine. However, corporate management can have a direct effect on the existence of a *minority* industrial reserve army through the adoption of a buffer-type policy. The disproportionate laying off of minority workers in times of labor constriction would help ensure a pool of such workers to be drawn upon when next needed. It also reduces the seniority of minority workers and makes them more vulnerable to layoffs. Excluding minorities from non-blue-collar and higher status jobs would also have this effect in that it would increase the number of minority unemployed and also concentrate minorities in those jobs which are most subject to layoffs. Thus, there is an interaction among the various aspects of colonial labor that may well result in the perpetuation of a minority industrial reserve army.

The final aspect of colonial labor has to do with the use of minority labor to divide workers, and there is good evidence on this point as well. International Harvester has been shown to be a highly ethnicity-conscious employer going back to the nineteenth century. While there is no recent direct evidence on this, it is difficult to think of a reason for International Harvester to abandon a practice which it has learned from over a century of labor-management relations. In this connection we can note that the very process of concentrating minority workers in certain types of occupations effectively produces divisions in the working class, in that it gives nonminority workers a seeming stake in perpetuating the colonial framework. This motivation could, in fact, be plausibly argued as an explanation for the early pattern followed in Harvester's southern plants of hiring black workers into semiskilled positions. The explanation advanced by Hope is that management was committed to the advancement of the black worker. The alternative, less benign, explanation would be that Harvester management wished to make use of black labor, but to do so in a way that would perpetuate the pattern of concentration in lower-status jobs and at the same time build in tension between the white and black workers. Such an explanation would be consistent with the adherence of Harvester managers to the principle of colonial labor that has been documented in other instances.

Thus, there appears to be substantial evidence for the existence of a colonial labor pattern at International Harvester. The subordinate position of minorities is institutionalized and historically persistent, there are important interests that are involved, and a considerable amount of conscious effort appears to have been exerted to create and maintain this situation. The degree of rationality and deliberateness is important here, as it is a factor which is generally underestimated even by radical theorists. As Reich, Gordon, and Edwards put it with regard to labor-market segmentation: "These efforts were 'conscious' in the following sense. Capitalists faced immediate problems and events and devised strategies to meet them. Successful strategies survived and were copied."[51] In addition, such groupings as the Special Conference Committee must provide useful forums for the exchange of information on labor policies for America's large, class-conscious firms.

While there have been modifications in the overall patterns under the impact of unionization and wartime labor shortages, there have also been important continuities. The pattern at International Harvester is probably fairly typical of large industrial firms, but considerable research is needed before a clear picture emerges of the uses of minority labor in the American economy as a whole. Such an understanding will provide a vital element for our conception of the sources of minority inequality in the United States today.

Notes

1. Robert Blauner, *Racial Oppression in America* (New York: Harper & Row, 1972), p. 23.
2. Harold Baron, "The Demand for Black Labor: Historical Notes on the Political Economy of Racism," *Radical America* (March-April 1971): 34.
3. Ibid., p. 36.
4. Tomás Almaguer, "Historical Notes on Chicano Oppression: The Dialectics of Racial and Class Domination in North America," *Aztlán* (Spring-Fall 1974): 41. Almaguer, in turn, draws upon an unpublished lecture given by Robert Allen.
5. Baron, "Demand for Black Labor," p. 36.
6. Donald Harris, "The Black Ghetto as 'Internal Colony': A Theoretical Critique and Alternative Formulation," *The Review of Black Political Economy* (Summer 1972): 26–27.
7. William Tabb, "Capitalism, Colonialsm, and Racism," *The Review of Radical Political Economics* (Summer 1971): 99.
8. Robert Ozanne, *The Negro in the Farm Equipment and Construction*

Machinery Industries, The Racial Policies of American Industry, Report no. 26 (Philadelphia: University of Pennsylvania, 1972), p. 13.

9. Robert Ozanne, *A Century of Labor-Management Relations at McCormick and International Harvester* (Madison: University of Wisconsin Press, 1967), pp. 157ff.
10. Ibid., p. 184.
11. Ozanne, *A Century of Labor-Management Relations,* p. 107.
12. Ibid., p. 184.
13. Ibid.
14. Robert Ozanne, *Wages in Practice and Theory: McCormick and International Harvester, 1860-1960* (Madison: University of Wisconsin Press, 1968).
15. Ozanne, *The Negro in the Farm Equipment and Construction Machinery Industries,* p. 22; and *A Century of Labor-Management Relations,* p. 185.
16. Paul Taylor, *Mexican Labor in the United States: Chicago and the Calumet Region* (Berkeley: University of California Press, 1932), p. 37; Ozanne, *A Century of Labor-Management Relations,* p. 185.
17. Ozanne, *The Negro in the Farm Equipment and Construction Machinery Industries,* p. 22; and *A Century of Labor-Management Relations,* pp. 185 and 192.
18. Ozanne, *A Century of Labor-Management Relations,* p. 192; and *The Negro in the Farm Equipment and Construction Machinery Industries,* p. 84.
19. 1974 EEO-1 Report for International Harvester, filed with the office of Federal Contract Compliance, U.S. Department of Labor.
20. Ozanne, *A Century of Labor-Management Relations,* p. 192.
21. Ibid., p. 185.
22. Ibid., p. 187.
23. Ozanne, *The Negro in the Farm Equipment and Construction Machinery Industries,* p. 62.
24. Ibid., p. 52.
25. Ibid., p. 53.
26. Ibid., p. 64.
27. Ibid., p. 60.
28. 1974 EEO-1 Report, International Harvester.
29. Peter Doeringer and Michael Piore, "Equal Employment Opportunity in Boston," *Industrial Relations* (May 1970): 329.
30. Taylor, *Mexican Labor in the United States,* pp. 78–79.
31. Ibid., p. 92.
32. Ozanne, *A Century of Labor-Management Relations,* p. 192.
33. John Hope, "Negro Employment in 3 Southern Plants of International Harvester Company," in *Selected Studies of Negro Employment in the South,* NPA Committee of the South, (Washington, D.C.: National Planning Association, 1955), p. 35.
34. Ozanne, *A Century of Labor-Management Relations,* p. 192.
35. Ozanne, *The Negro in the Farm Equipment and Construction Machinery Industries,* p. 84.
36. Hope, "Negro Employment," p. 43.

37. Ibid., p. 47.
38. Ibid., p. 132.
39. Ozanne, *The Negro in the Farm Equipment and Construction Machinery Industries,* pp. 84–85.
40. Hope, "Negro Employment," pp. 63–64.
41. Ibid., p. 110.
42. Ibid., p. 113.
43. Ibid., p. 124.
44. Ibid., pp. 32–33.
45. Ozanne, *The Negro in the Farm Equipment and Construction Machinery Industries,* p. 36.
46. This and other information for Solar is from sources in the author's possession.
47. Ozanne, *The Negro in the Farm Equipment and Construction Machinery Industries,* p. 106.
48. Ibid., pp. 36–37.
49. Robert Weintraub, "Employment Integration and Racial Wage Differences in a Southern Plant," *Industrial and Labor Relations Review* (January 1959): 214–26.
50. Ozanne, *The Negro in the Farm Equipment and Construction Machinery Industries,* pp. 92–93.
51. Michael Reich, David Gordon, and Richard Edwards, "A Theory of Labor Market Segmentation," *The American Economic Review* (May 1963): 361n.

Immigrant Workers and Class Struggles in Advanced Capitalism: The Western European Experience

Manuel Castells

Since the great social upheaval of May 1968 in France, class struggles in Western Europe seem to have re-entered a period of progressive development, both through a strengthening of trade-union and traditional practices and through the appearance of new issues and the mobilization of new social strata around these issues. Thus, the "old mole" is far from dormant, and its under-ground workings lead sometimes to explosions of mass rage and sometimes to the consolidation of new bases of protest and opposition to the system.

Among these new developments, the issue of immigration and the mobilization of migrants are particularly prominent. As the major trump card in capitalist expansion, and as the bogey scape-goat of the bourgeoisie always ready to feed the fires of xenophobia and racism, as a pretext for a reluctantly renewed charity, as a myth in mobilizing the European left, and as a source of confusion for trade unions and left-wing parties, immigrant workers constitute both in the reality of their daily oppression and in their potential for social revolt one of the most important and least-known stakes in the newly emerging class struggles of advanced capitalism.

In view of the complexity of the subject, the mass of fragmentary information, and the scarcity of adequate economic and statistical data, any analysis of immigrant workers must start by carefully defining its objectives. The problematic we take as a starting point conditions all our efforts at interpretation and provides a frame-work which organizes our approach to this reality. Our aim here is not to expose the scandal of the material conditions under which these workers live and work nor to justify their presence in order to increase the tolerance of the indigenous population toward them. Our point of departure is rather the fact of the growing importance of immigrant workers in the wage-earning working population of every country in Western Europe and the increase in political struggles and protest movements concerning them. For us the question is therefore to ask what specific effect is

Reprinted from *Politics & Society* 5, no. 1. (1975), with permission of the publishers. Copyright © 1975 by *Politics & Society*.

produced by immigrant workers on a class structure, and on the politics of the class struggle which result. In answering such a question, we will at the same time be able to describe the class content of the struggles of immigrant workers themselves and thereby start to assess their political practices.[. . .]

We shall start by recalling the fundamental structural tendencies of monopoly capitalism in Western Europe in order to locate the phenomenon of immigration within this specific social and economic logic. We will then draw out the implications for the class structure and for the trade-union and political parties which tend to flow from it. Finally we shall see how these different contradictions are articulated in the concrete history of newly emerging class struggles by referring more specifically to immigrant workers' movements in France. Our analysis remains at a fairly high level of generality, and the small amount of statistical data used is illustrative rather than demonstrative in purpose.[1] In fact a rigorous study of this subject within the problematic of the class struggle has yet to be undertaken. Thus, the present paper does not claim to be the endpoint of research within this perspective but, rather a point of departure. It is thus necessary to pose theoretically rigorous and historically concrete questions in order to obtain, by stages, answers which, instead of provoking pity for the lot of immigrant workers, will provide them with elements capable of clarifying their practice.[2]

Uneven Development and the Internationalization of the Labor Force

At first glance migratory movements may be analyzed as simply the result of two laws of the capitalist mode of production: *the submission of the worker* to the organization of the means of production dictated by capital (and, hence, to its spatial concentration in areas regarded as most profitable) and the *uneven development* between sectors and regions, and between countries, in accordance with intercapitalist competition and the political relationships between the major blocs under bourgeois hegemony historically constituted in the various social formations.

Seen this way, migratory movements have existed throughout the period of capitalist development, and rural exodus and the decline of regions whose productive structure has been weakened in favor of the most advanced capitalist forms are basic features of the social structure which constitutes monopoly capitalism.

Furthermore, one can even say that a veritable whirlpool of geographical and occupational mobility is inevitable to the extent that capital can only develop by continually decomposing those sectors which are backward compared with the most profitable forms. This frees an even larger labor force, whose members lose their existing jobs and move into new posts created in the most advanced sectors, a movement which is far from automatic and which necessitates increasingly costly retraining.

This uneven development does not, of course, derive from disparities in the distribution of natural resources but from the logic of capital and the division of labor it commands according to the imperatives of the rate of profit. Thus, for example, the French steel industry will close down its iron mines in Lorraine and leave the area to establish itself by the sea (Dunkerque, Fos) where it will use imported iron ore from Mauritania and Brazil.[3] Furthermore, in certain cases a political logic (dependent on the general interest of capital) rather than an immediately economic logic is at the source of uneven regional development. Thus, for example, the dichotomy between the highly developed north of Italy and the poverty-stricken Mezzogiorno derives from the particular forms taken by the political bargain underlying the constitution of the dominant class bloc in Italy as a whole: the banking and industrial bourgeoisie of the north accepts the maintenance of the social status quo in the south in order not to overturn the southern class structure which permits the domination of the traditional landed oligarchy. In exchange, the latter accepts bourgeois hegemony at the level of the state and guarantees the labor reservoir which has always been at the base of Italian capitalist growth.[4]

This same mechanism operates at the international level, where labor concentration is determined by the growth of capital. For a long period before World War II the advanced capitalist countries made sporadic use of labor from their colonies and from the backward European countries (Italy, Spain, Poland, etc.). In 1936 there were proportionately more foreigners in France than in 1972 (2,198,000 compared with a little under 4,000,000), and even at the time of the 1929 crisis 7 percent of the French population were foreigners.

A brief analysis of the countries importing and exporting labor is illuminating on this point: the lower a country's level of development (e.g., as measured by per capita GNP), the higher the level of emigration, and vice versa.

At first sight, then, emigration/immigration is simply a product of the uneven development inherent in the capitalist mode of production which affects the labor force. It must be noted, however, that this is not the same as viewing migration simply as the product of a succession of economic conditions, and hence as capable of being absorbed into jobs created by economic growth within each country. On the contrary, uneven development is a structural tendency of the mode of production, and the gaps between firms, sectors, trusts, regions, or countries tend to increase rather than diminish. For example, in recent years, despite having the highest growth rate in Western Europe, Spain has had a regularly increasing level of emigration, with small movements around this trend caused much more by recessions in the countries receiving immigrants than by any decline in requests to emigrate. Similarly, there are over two million Italian workers in other European countries despite Italy's high growth rate and production level. The reasons for such a permanent emigrant labor force are clear from the point of view of the sending country: decomposition of backward productive structures—especially in agriculture; structural unemployment in certain sectors; and the much higher nominal and real wages available in the advanced capitalist countries.

But though differences in levels of development explain the causes of emigration, immigration into the advanced countries is governed by much more deep-seated reasons, which cannot be reduced simply to the manpower needs of the economy. If they were the cause, immigration would be a conjunctural phenomena (and highly sensitive to the least sign of economic recession). While it is true that the employment situation is immediately reflected in increases and decreases in the level of immigration (thus, for example, the economic recession in Germany in 1967 resulted in the departure of a large number of immigrants), it is also the case that the long-term trend is continued growth in immigrant labor, which in 1972 represented at least 10 percent of the working population in the advanced capitalist countries of Western Europe (the Common Market countries, Austria, Norway, Sweden, and Switzerland). It might be argued that this trend is due precisely to the continuous economic growth of these countries, but this is completely tautological, since immigrant labor is in fact one of the motors of this growth, rather than simply a result.[5]

Two facts seem to be particularly significant in this respect: first, the size of the immigrant labor force in the most productive sectors (especially in industry) and immigrant labor's position in the working population as a whole make it impossible to regard immigration as a conjunctural phenomenon, even if one were to assume that it resulted simply from a superabundant supply of labor.

Thus, in 1972 there were 2,345,200 foreign workers in Germany, representing 10.8 percent of all wage earners. They constituted 25 percent of workers in the building industry and 80 percent in certain sectors of public works, but were also strongly represented in the metallurgical industry (11 percent of all wage earners). In France, according to official statistics, there were 1,800,000 immigrant workers on January 1, 1973 (8 percent of the working population)—a figure which appears to be an underestimate, since it takes little account of clandestine work. In building and public works they represent 27 percent of all workers (but this often rises to 90 percent on building sites in the Paris region), in metal industries 17 percent, and in extractive industry 16 percent. There are 530,000 immigrant workers in the automobile industry, of whom 200,000 are in the Paris region, i.e., 46 percent of all semiskilled workers, work on assembly lines. In Switzerland, according to official figures for 1968, there were 817,000 immigrant workers, representing 29.8 percent of the working population, but with a high concentration in the building, machine-tool, and hotel industries. Almost 40 percent of workers in Swiss factories are foreigners, and when one considers solely directly productive work, they already constitute a clear majority. In Belgium the 220,000 foreign workers employed in 1971 represented 7.2 percent of the working population and were particularly concentrated in the mining, building, and metallurgic industries, and this despite a marked recession in the Walloon region, which led to measures to restrict immigration. In the Netherlands the figure of 125,000 employed persons in 1972 (3.2 percent of the working population) is lower than elsewhere primarily because of trade-union opposition to immigration. In Denmark the same phenomenon is found, foreign workers numbering only 30,000 in 1972. In Great Britain the 1,780,000 immigrant workers in 1971 represented 7.3 percent of the working population in the building and machine-tool industries, commerce, and service industries. Immigrant labor is thus a fundamental element in the economic structure of European capitalism and not simply an extra source of labor in conditions of rapid growth.

But there is a second fact which is particularly disturbing: namely, the appearance over the long term (1950-1970) of a parallel increase between unemployment and immigration in most of the countries, with the *possible* exception of Germany, where, for the most part, full employment seems to have been effectively achieved. A detailed analysis of changes in the levels of unemployment, immigration, and productivity by country, sector, and type of firm would be necessary in order to verify this tendency. However, certain indications may be obtained by examining the figures for unemployment and immigration in France and the interrelation of changes in them. A combination of two phenomena is apparent: in the short term, for each year, there is a correspondence between the increase in unemployment and the decline in immigration. But in the long term, *there is a tendency for both phenomena to increase together.* This is all the more significant in that the immigration statistics refer only to official entries (a smaller figure) which most closely follow changes in economic conditions.

In other countries we find the following trends:

—In Belgium and in the Netherlands unemployment is *stable* and immigration rises moderately. (So in fact unemployment and immigration *coexist.*)

—In Germany unemployment is stable at a low level; at the same time, immigration rises at a high rate. So immigration is not produced by a full-employment situation in the labor market but by *selective full employment.*

—In Switzerland and Luxembourg a real full-employment labor market exists for native workers, with an increasingly strong percentage of immigrants (29.8 percent of the labor force in Switzerland and 27.8 percent in Luxembourg). In these countries we could analyze immigration as a matter of labor supply. But even here this interpretation must be linked to an explanation in terms of the specific characteristics of the immigrant labor force.

—In Britain a stable immigrant labor force coexists with an increasingly high rate of unemployment. In fact there is no complementary and opposite evolution of the two phenomena, as liberal economic theory would expect. The explanation must be in the terms of the structural position of immigrant workers in British industry.

The case of Great Britain is extremely revealing in this respect, because the permanent settlement of a large proportion of the immigrant labor force has been accompanied by a gradual increase in unemployment (up to 3 percent in 1972) and by a considerable increase in the level of *emigration* by Britons, especially those with high skill, to the United States. Thus, there is no manpower shortage but rather a reclassification of the characteristics required to carry out certain jobs.

We thus want to argue that immigration is not a conjunctural phenomenon linked to the manpower needs of expanding economies but a structural tendency characteristic of the current phase of monopoly capitalism. This structural tendency is supported by the discrepancies and disequilibria resulting from uneven development, but it is explained primarily by the internal dynamic of advanced capitalist societies. While uneven development explains why people emigrate, it does not explain why capital is ready to provide jobs for migrant workers in the advanced countries, occasionally even in conditions of unemployment. Neither does it explain why the dominant classes introduce a social and political element (immigrant labor) whose presence contradicts their ideology and necessitates more complex mechanisms of social control. In other words, the extent of immigration and the strategic role of immigration in the European economy have to be explained, not in terms of the technical demands of production, but by the specific interests of capital in a particular phase of its development.

Crisis of Capitalism, Countertendencies of Economic Policy, and Structural Role of Immigration

What are the current requirements of capital? And how are they translated into manpower policy, especially as regards immigrant labor?

In order to answer these questions we must introduce some elements of Marxist economic theory concerning the contradictory development of the capitalist mode of production. The basic structural contradiction demonstrated by Marx in volume 3 of *Capital* concerned the *tendency for the rate of profit to fall,* as a result of the increase in the organic composition of capital made inevitable by competition among capitalists, monopolistic concentration, and technical progress. If we consider only living labor, the labor force, as creating value, and hence surplus value, and profit as deriving from it, given the increase in the organic composition of capital, then the rate of profit must fall, since the variable capital used to pay the labor force grows more slowly than total capital (constant capital plus variable capital), and thus the source of value becomes proportionately smaller in relation to the mass of capital engaged in production. At the level of the system as a whole and in the long term, there is a tendency for the rate of profit to fall (even if the quantity of surplus value increases) and hence for the system to move toward crisis to the extent that capital stops investing as investment ceases to be profitable.

However, even though certain studies suggest the validity of this analysis in past periods,[6] the tendencies identified are no more than *tendencies,* i.e., can be partly counteracted in the historical practice of capital by the more or less deliberate introduction of countertendencies through economic policy.[7] One of the main examples of such action is the devalorization, or "putting to bed," of part of social capital, for which a lower or even nil rate of profit will be accepted, by placing it in the charge of the state. Moreover, this kind of action is combined with various subsidies and assistance from the state to the major private economic groups, drawing on collective resources, and thus removing a share from wages for purposes of accumulation. It may also be noted that state intervention extends to all fields, following the well-known Keynesian model, acting as regulator in every situation and *attempting* to establish a program for monopoly capital.

Beyond the measures involving capital itself, the basic countertendency introduced into the system is an increase in the rate of surplus value, i.e., the quantity of surplus value produced by a given variable capital. This increase is obtained in two complementary ways: by higher *productivity* through technical progress (which increases the excess labor in relation to the labor necessary to reproduce the labor force) and by the *reinforcement of exploitation* in intensity, in extensiveness, or a reduction of the mass of variable capital necessary for a certain quantity of surplus value.

Thus, the first question to be examined is this: *what is the relationship between the massive use of migrant labor and the countertendency to the tendency of the rate of profit to fall, especially with regard to the reinforcement of exploitation?*

There are other basic contradictions in the current phase of capitalism which, while related to the first, have relatively autonomous effects. On the one hand, there is the cyclical character of capitalist expansion with periodic recessions due to overaccumulation. Although the cyclical nature of crisis was concealed during a long expansionary period, since 1967 Europe has again become used to the idea of sudden fluctuations in economic activity as a part of the functioning of the system. In order to avoid the disequilibrating effect of these fluctuations, due to the chain reactions they cause in the economy, advanced capitalism has set up a number of anticyclical mechanisms, one of the most important of which is precisely immigrant labor.

Finally, the excess of capitals seeking investment opportunities and the creation of a mass of floating capitals in the advanced economies, on the one hand, and the necessity for ever-faster growth inherent in monopoly capital, on the other, are the source of the *structural inflation* characteristic of capitalism today. We advance the hypothesis that immigration has a specific role as a basic deflationary factor in controlling these critical effects of inflation. While statistics and economics give little guidance on this subject, a number of suggestions are possible.

If we can determine the role of immigrant labor in the management of these key problems of advanced capitalism, we shall have simultaneously established its place in the structural contradictions and in the social interests underlying different immigration policies and underlying the protests of the workers themselves.

Immigration and the Reinforcement of Capitalist Exploitation

In order to increase the degree of exploitation and raise the rate of surplus value, capital makes use of two methods, usually in combination: (1) paying a proportionately smaller value for the reproduction of the labor force, (2) increasing the duration and intensity of work. We have stated that in both cases immigrant labor represents a decisive trump card for capital. Let us now examine this in more detail.

As far as the first point is concerned, immigrant labor displays the following characteristics:

1. It is the part of the labor force which receives the lowest wages.

2. It is the part whose health conditions are best, contrary to widespread opinion. This is so for two very simple reasons: immigrants are generally young and in the prime of their working life and very rigorous health examinations ensure that immigrants who are not in good health are quickly replaced. This means that though the health of immigrants as individuals is more severely affected than that of nationals, as a group immigrants are more healthy, since only the young and healthy are retained . . . and only for as long as they remain in that condition.

3. It is the part of the labor force which works in the worst safety and health conditions, thereby permitting considerable savings in the organization of work, reducing still further the costs of reproduction.

4. When considered from the point of view of capital as a whole, rather than from that of the individual capitalist, one of the essential effects of immigration is to enable considerable savings to be made in the costs of social reproduction of the labor force as a whole, thereby raising correspondingly the overall average rate of profit. This occurs by means of three main mechanisms:

First, by recruiting immigrants primarily from among the young and productive, capital finds it possible to avoid paying the costs of "rearing" the worker and the maintenance costs after his/her working life has ended. According to an OECD estimate, these costs amount to $10,000 per worker, which implies a figure for the free human capital represented by immigrants in Europe of about $50 million.

Second, given the restrictive measures governing immigration and the conditions in which immigrants live and work, the majority are unmarried or "forced" bachelors, and the costs of reproduction of families are not borne by capital, which thereby saves on the cost of collective facilities, public housing, schools, hospital beds, welfare benefits, and so on. The savings are all the more significant in that outlays on such facilities are not profitable, since demand for them has to be subsidized.

Third, the conditions of reproduction of the immigrants themselves as well as of the families who succeed in accompanying them are clearly below the average standards of indigenous workers. Their housing conditions are particularly bad.[8] Not only does social capital not bear these costs but also the "sleep merchants" profit from the discrimination, creating a parallel housing market for immigrants, which even becomes profitable provided legality is set aside and summary methods are used to maintain order in the hostels, furnished rooms, or slums.[9]

This is why, to mention but two examples, 32 percent of immigrants in Germany live in temporary dwellings, according to official statistics, while 98 percent of shantytown dwellers in France are immigrants.

The effect of immigrant workers on wage levels concerns not only their own wages but also those of wage earners as a whole, since the possibility of appealing to the manpower of the dependent capitalist countries acts as a veritable world *reserve army* on the working class of the advanced capitalist countries. One cannot infer from this a conflict between the interests of the working class and those of immigrant workers, for once in the same boat together they can only get out of the vicious circle of their exploitation by joining together in opposition to capital. It remains true, *as a tendency,* that the very possibility of recourse to immigration causes a relative lowering of wages, thus contributing to the structural countertendency which helps delay the fall in the rate of profit.

Finally, turning to the intensity of their exploitation, on average immigrant workers work much longer hours than do nationals, occupy the worst jobs, and are subjected to the fastest speeds (to the extent that they work on assembly lines and are paid by piecework). The much higher rate of work accidents among immigrants is indicative both of their work conditions and of the speeds they are obliged to maintain.

All these empirically indisputable factors are, however, too obvious; acceptance of them is too automatic and even hides a sort of unconscious racist preconception. *Why should immigrant labor accept what, for the indigenous working class, has become unacceptable?* Because they are naturally submissive? Because of their extreme need? Even accepting the notion that the poverty experienced in their own countries makes immigrant workers willing to tolerate any and all conditions on their arrival, the problem is why this acceptance persists and, especially, why it is possible to treat them as individual wage earners, whereas the relationship of the indigenous working class with capital is established collectively, through the labor movement. This is the key to answering the question. Though working conditions, wage levels, and social benefits have improved, and though European workers have bettered their living conditions, this has not come about through the goodwill of capital but through the new sociopolitical conditions which flow from the balance of power between the classes created by the labor movement. In other words, *the utility of immigrant labor to capital derives primarily from the fact that it can act toward it as though the labor movement did not exist,* thereby moving the class struggle back several decades. A twenty-first-century capital and a nineteenth-century proletariat—such is the dream of monopoly capital in order to overcome its crisis. How does this happen? Not because of any presumed submissiveness of immigrants, whose many struggles in recent years have shown a degree of combativeness, however sporadic and limited. Rather their legal-political status as foreigners and their political-ideological isolation lead to the basic point: *their limited capacity for organization and struggle and very great vulnerability to repression.*[10] Their status as foreigners deprives immigrants of political rights and also, in practice, of their rights as trade unionists. Their participation in class struggles, their level of organization under these conditions is thus restricted to a vanguard, which is cut off from the mass of immigrants and is often regarded with suspicion by the indigenous labor movement. It is all the more easily repressed. Moreover, since the permanence of immigrant workers in each country is only relative, and their degree of subjective identification weaker, the workers' interest in participating in current struggles is limited, and generally concentrated in outbursts linked to their concrete living and working conditions.

Moreover, the racism and xenophobia diffused by the dominant ideology accentuate the cleavages derived from national cultural particularities[11] and determine the ideological isolation of immigrants. They are thus separated from their class and placed in a balance of power so unfavorable that often they fluctuate between an acceptance of the conditions of capital and pure individual or collective revolt. This cuts them off still more from the labor movement, in a sort of vicious circle which tends to reproduce the fragmentation and dislocation of the working class in advanced capitalism.

This brings us to the first result of our analysis, which should be underlined. Banal though it may be, some crucial implications for immigrant struggles follow from it: the advantage of immigrant labor for capital stems precisely from the specificity of their inferior position in the class struggle, which derives from the legal-political status of immigrants. From the *point of view of capital* this status can be modified in minor ways, but not transformed, because it is the source of the basic structural role of immigration. Thus, the basic contradiction concerning immigrants is one which opposes them not directly to capital but to the state apparatus of capital and to the political status given to them in its institutions. This has the following consequences:

1. The position of immigrants in the class struggle is very specific compared with the rest of the labor movement.

2. The contradiction in which they occupy the dominated role is a basic contradiction of capitalism.

3. The contradiction is immediately political insofar as it relates directly to the state apparatus.

4. Given a basic, directly political, and very specific contradiction, reinforced in the ideological sphere by their cultural particularities and the xenophobic tones of the dominant ideology, immigrants find themselves in an extremely unfavorable balance of power which tends to reproduce their separation from the rest of the labor movement.

The circle is not completely closed, as we shall see, since immigrants' membership in the working class determines an objective basis of interests common to *workers as a whole*. And from this basis, a unified labor movement *can be constructed* on the basis of a working class which, though objectively fragmented, is not split.

This analysis also sheds light on a common argument about the causes of immigration, which we have deliberately left aside in our discussion so as to be able to provide the answer once it was known. This is the idea that immigrants are necessary to carry out the arduous jobs rejected by the indigenous population. In fact, this is only a half-truth. While it is certain that immigrants do carry out the most arduous, the worst-paid, and the least-skilled jobs, it does not follow from this that these jobs, though necessary, have been given up by other workers. Such jobs are not given up because they are "dirty" and "soul-destroying" (since the jobs taken instead can hardly be said to be "fulfilling") but because they are less well paid. Whenever arduous work is relatively well paid (e.g., miners), nationals in particular are found doing it. It remains true, however, that these jobs are badly paid and are most arduous, but *in relation to what standard?* To the historical standard of the balance of power established by the labor movement in each country, to what would be unacceptable to a working class which had the necessary strength to impose better working conditions and higher wage levels? In brief, then, *immigrant workers do not exist because there are "arduous and badly paid" jobs to be done but, rather, arduous and badly paid jobs exist because immigrant workers are present or can be sent for to do them.*

The building industry, for example, has remained largely small scale in character because the employment of immigrants has made small fragmented capitals profitable without recourse to industrialized building methods. If immigrant labor were to disappear, *depending on the balance of power of the labor movement,* the building industry would be reconverted and modernized. But this is no more than a pious wish, because such a situation would considerably reduce the rate of profit, thus precipitating an economic crisis. This is why capital cannot do without the "arduous jobs" or the immigrant workers who do them. This is the "invisible structure" of the determination of capital of which one sees only the effects, sometimes combined with premature interpretations.

We now need to examine whether the political-ideological specificity of immigrants in the class struggle is also the basic feature which enables them to play a crucial role in the anticyclical and anti-inflationary policies of monopoly capital.

Economic Fluctuations, Inflation, Immigration

In spite of the systematic intervention of the state apparatus, in spite of the control mechanisms set up, the capitalist economy still undergoes cyclical fluctuations. They are of a new type insofar as the acceleration of technical progress, on the one hand, and the internationalization of capital, on the other, have introduced distortions into the regularity of the cycles, while magnifying the effects of recessionary periods.

In this perspective immigrant workers are one of the basic elements preventing recessions from turning into crises. Instead of accepting the reality of unemployment, advanced capitalist economies have regulated themselves with immigrant labor, from temporarily limiting immigration (as in Belgium in 1971 and Germany in 1972) to imposing new restrictive legislation (Switzerland, England, France) to simply expelling—in a more or less disguised fashion—part of the immigrant labor force. Thus, the 1967 recession in Germany resulted in a very large reduction in the number of foreign residents, thereby exporting a considerable fraction of the total unemployment. There were still 459,000 unemployed in 1967 in Germany, and 353,000 in 1968, who naturally received unemployment benefits. It has been calculated that the expulsion of foreign workers enabled savings of over DM1,000 million in unemployment benefits alone.[12]

This general trend, which has also been observed in France, is often interpreted in the banal terms of the supply and demand of jobs. Its significance lies precisely in the ease with which one can be rid of this labor, due to its inferior legal-political status. This again reveals the basic role of the status of foreigner from the point of view of the functioning of the capitalist economy.

Something more specific is also involved, which requires closer analysis. The crises of capitalism today are not classical crises caused by overproduction but crises produced primarily by inflation, which is itself the result of capital surpluses and financial movements linked to the activities of multinational firms, among other things.[13] What characterizes these crises is precisely the *combination of inflation and recession,* or "stagflation," as it has become known. The mechanism is quite simple: inflation results not from the play of supply and demand but from structural features of the current phase of capitalism, which cannot be discussed in detail here.[14] These mean that a rise in product prices is not counteracted by a fall in demand, since prices are determined by the cost of the capital invested, itself subject to inflationary pressures through financial mechanisms. Now and then prices will surge ahead of what demand can bear, thus causing relative overproduction, which leads to a recession. This further reduces the level of effective demand but without bringing about a proportionate fall in prices, unless a dangerous fall in the average rate of profit is acceptable. Under these conditions what are the characteristics of the ideal "worker-consumer" in order to counteract these periodic crises?

1. They must be very productive in the expansionary phase.

2. They must be excludable without difficulty in the recessionary phase when there is a danger of overproduction.

3. They must consume little, in order to reduce inflationary tensions in expansionary periods and especially to cushion the decline in demand in recessionary periods. This is possible since their disappearance as wage earners (and hence of their wage as purchasing power) has little effect on the overall level of effective demand. In this way productive capacity can be reduced with little change in effective demand, thereby avoiding the chain of events which can follow from applying brakes to growth. In this way fluctuations can be prevented from turning into crises.

The central role of immigrant labor as a regulator for capitalist crises is too often ignored, hidden by interpretations phrased in terms of the economic situation (adjustment of supply and demand) without attention to the determinants of these adjustments or discrepancies. Two conditions must be met in order for immigrant labor to play this role: (a) the status of foreigner, which is weak in political and ideological terms, must be maintained; (b) the immigration of families must be limited as much as possible and, at most, be restricted to a narrow and higher section of immigrants, whose ideological integration acts as an adequate guarantee.

These, then, are the reasons for the current orientation of immigration policies in all the European countries toward the so-called German solution: immigration limited to "unmarried" workers, rigorously controlled, for a limited period and with a high rate of turnover, in return for an improvement in material living conditions for the limited time during which the immigrants' services are provided. The British Immigration Act, the new Swiss measures, and, most of all, the Fontanet-Marcellin circular in France all point in this direction.

It must be mentioned, in passing, that from the point of view of a purely economic logic of capital the same aims (raising of the rate of profit by excess exploitation, countercyclical control) could be achieved by productive investments in the countries from which immigrants come—provided of course that a similar balance of power could be imposed on the workers there, i.e., through police states. Such an approach can be found in various schemes drawn up by large European, and especially French, business. However, in the short term it is unlikely that a policy of this type will emerge, since it ignores two basic features of immigration: its position in the various fractions of capital and its fragmenting, and hence weakening, effect on the working class.

This means, in turn, that such a tendency could only emerge once three conditions are met: the final unification of capital around monopolies; the incorporation of the labor movement so that it ceased to constitute a great danger for capital, which would thus no longer need to weaken it; finally, and most important, a strong development of immigrant struggles, which threaten the social equilibrium constructed at their expense. This latter development is already taking place in Switzerland, while it appears far off in France; Germany is an intermediate case.

The question, however, is significant in that it enables us to establish the limits of a purely economic analysis based on the logic of capital. We must now turn to an analysis of the relationship of immigrants to existing social classes.

Immigration, Social Classes, and Class Fractions

Immigrants are not just foreigners. The vast majority are foreign workers (98 percent in France), i.e., (1) *workers*, (2) *foreigners*. As soon as either of these two features, which define both their class situation and their specificity as a class fraction, is forgotten, one ceases to be able to understand the significance of immigrants for capital and, beyond that, for the transformation of society.

The specific class situation of foreign workers has to be related to the class struggle and existing class interests in order to uncover current alliances and contradictions and hence to deduce appropriate tactics and strategy, given the specific aims of these classes and fractions.

Thus, although the general interests of advanced capitalism concerning immigration may be those we have indicated, they are varied and specific for each fraction of capital, and in particular they diverge according to whether we are dealing with monopoly capital or capital invested in industries or sectors with lower rates of profit or smaller quantities of surplus value. For big capital the primary aim is to preserve the basic characteristics of the immigrant labor force, while stabilizing it in its production phase, e.g., by providing minimal material conditions for its reproduction (stabilizing the labor force but not, as a rule, the individual worker). Hence, big capital desires the "regularization" of immigration provided that this does not go too far and cause outbursts of trouble or interfere with the maintenance of the labor force. Thus, for example, measures concerning housing may be taken (France), the consultation of immigrant representatives by local authorities may be proposed (Belgium), or certain social security measures taken (Germany), always of course in a totally inadequate and fragmented way.[15] Big firms may even agree to job security for a small elite group of immigrants, thus offering a carrot to the "good immigrant" to improve one's job. More concretely: for big capital the basic concern is to avoid political and trade-union rights for immigrant workers, and hence to lessen their capacity to engage in struggle. Thus, its policy of control and minor modification concerning immigration, sometimes paternalistic in the economic sphere, always repressive (dissuasive) in the political sphere.

Conversely, for many small and medium-sized firms (especially in the building, textile, and service industries) the immigrant labor force is crucial to their *day-to-day survival* because of the excess exploitation that they can carry out given the lack of rights and of organization of these workers. For these firms immigrants are a source of the excess profit necessary to compensate for their below average rate of profit. They thus violate bourgeois social legality by hiring *clandestine* immigrants, in order to exploit the immigrant illegally, avoid paying social security contributions, and impose subhuman working conditions on them. In the case of small and medium firms, then, extreme violation of legal rights is added to the legal and controlled violations, regularized over the long term, demanded by large capital. This is why France, the most backward of the receiving countries, and the one with the highest proportion of small and medium-sized firms, tolerated without complaint up to 1972 a level of clandestine immigration which at that time represented almost 80 percent of all entries. (One must not use terms such as "small" or "large" capital but refer to the organic composition and dynamism of capital. Some large monopolies in the building industry also exploit clandestine immigrants.) For these firms any improvement in the living conditions of immigrants would be unacceptable, since it would affect their necessary excess profits. This argument applies *a fortiori* to speculative capital which profits from the destitute condition of immigrants in order to create a new source of accumulation ("sleep merchants" and others). The two fractions of capital, however, agree on one basic point: the structural need for the systematic political repression of immigrants, and the complete elimination of immigrants' ability to defend themselves. Having obtained satisfaction on this basic point, large capital can afford to fall back on "humanitarian" arguments when immigrant struggles oblige it to retreat, whereas for backward firms the excess exploitation of immigrants is a matter of life and death. These differences must be borne in mind in order to understand the variety of capitalist immigration policies. But this fragmentation of interests of capital presupposes a basic agreement on the maintenance of immigrants in a position of social and political "apartheid."

The *objective* political weakness of immigrant workers is not only an important countertendency used by capital to avert the impact of its own contradictions, but it is also a major trump card for the bourgeoisie in its struggle against the working class. The very presence of immigrant workers constitutes a permanent source of fragmentation within the working class, both inside and outside the firm. While immigrant and indigenous workers share the same historic interests and some immediate interests, they diverge on other immediate interests, e.g., working and housing conditions and, in particular, freedom of association, a basic issue for immigrants but superfluous for indigenous workers.

This fragmentation is a permanent and objective obstacle to the struggle and organization of *all* workers, since it places a substantial fraction of them in an inferior position, making participation in the struggle much more difficult and dangerous for them. This is too often forgotten, impressed as we are by the violence and audacity of certain immigrant struggles. On the rare occasions when such struggles do take place, they do so in spite of the initial disadvantages and considerable risks of repression incurred by the immigrants involved. This explains why only a small minority of immigrants takes part in these struggles and why they only develop at the price of very heavy sacrifices, a fact which clearly distinguishes such struggles from those of the rest of the labor movement. For immigrants, then, every struggle puts their embryonic organization in danger. This fragile stake had been overcome by the labor movement in advanced capitalism. The fragmentation of the working class represented by a permanent fraction of immigrant workers is, thus, a basic factor in maintaining immigration as a unified interest of the dominant classes.

This is all the more true since this split does not rest solely on the inferior political status of immigrants, but also on the racist and xenophobic reactions of the bourgeoisie.[16] The success of Powell and the National Front in England, the very large popular vote for the xenophobic bill known as the "Schwarzenbach initiative" in Switzerland, the wave of racist assassinations (especially in Marseilles) in autumn 1973 are symptoms of the ultimate weapon for dividing the working class: racism. These reactions occur even within the working class, not only among the indigenous population against immigrants but also in the opposite direction.

This objective and subjective split between indigenous and immigrant workers is often reinforced by the corporatism and blindness of trade unions, which, under the pretext of defending the jobs of nationals, fail to understand the real strategy of capitalism in this matter. They collaborate, in fact or in intention, with big capital in its policy of regularizing and controlling (ultimately with police help) immigration. Trade unions are sometimes afraid to counteract the xenophobic attitudes of part of the labor force (under the influence of the dominant ideology) and end up reinforcing the situation which they themselves denounce, or give lip service to denouncing. However, it is obvious that trade unions cannot be considered as a unit and that their attitudes will depend partly on their general orientation to the class struggle and partly on the pressure which immigrants are able to exercise on them. Thus, in France trade unions attempt immediately to work toward working class unity,[17] whereas in Switzerland they collaborate with the bourgeoisie. But trade unions no longer have a free hand in this respect, since they increasingly have to take account of the weight of immigrants among their membership. This is perhaps the key to the whole problem, since indigenous trade unions are often reinforced in their attitudes by the suspicion and antiunionism of many immigrants (due not to excessive consciousness, but to a lack of consciousness!) in a sort of vicious circle which risks reproducing the fragmentation of the working class with catastrophic consequences for the labor movement in advanced capitalism.

This vicious circle can only be broken by the common discovery by immigrant and indigenous workers of their basic identity of interests, an identity which must not be interpreted solely in terms of a distant historical destiny but in relation to the present conditions of the class struggle. Immigrants will never succeed in imposing their basic demand (equal rights) without a generalized battle supported by the labor and democratic movement as a whole. Indigenous workers must avoid at all costs a rupture in the working class which could lead to a major defeat which would strengthen, perhaps decisively, the balance of power in favor of the bourgeoisie.

This discovery of a concrete community of class interests can only occur through common struggles against capital. And these common struggles will come about through the participation of immigrants and indigenous workers in each other's specific struggles. In other words, the dynamic of social relations, while determined by the class structure, is organized in terms of the historically specific development of the practices of the struggle.

This is the subject to which we shall now turn, with special reference to the particularly rich example of France, before drawing some more general conclusions about the role of immigrants in the class struggle.

Immigrant Workers and Class Struggles: The French Example

The resurgence of social struggles in France since 1968 has had a profound effect on immigrant workers. For some time, though they were publicly defined as a "social problem," there were not, strictly speaking, any specific separate struggles of immigrant workers. Up to 1972 there were two basically different types of action concerning immigrant workers—on the one hand, an ideological exposure of the "scandal" of immigrant conditions, led primarily by the left-wing movement in its usual role as revealer of contradictions rather than as a political force; on the other, a series of working-class protest struggles in factories with high proportions of immigrant workers which indicated the concrete potential for mobilizing this stratum of workers. It may be noted that the most important struggles ("Grosteel" at Le Bourget, "Penarroya" at Lyon, both in 1972) were protest struggles led by trade unions, especially the CFDT, even though the style of action was quite innovative (primarily because of the severity of the struggles in the face of the intransigence of the employers, which were finally overcome). The struggles by semiskilled workers at Renault-Billancourt and at Renault-Flins, where there was a high degree of immigrant participation, allowed a new form of working-class struggle to develop outside trade-union channels because of a certain degree of Maoist penetration among the immigrants, concurrently with powerful trade-union action. What characterizes this set of struggles, however, is that they were working-class struggles involving immigrants but in no case advancing demands specific to immigrants. To this extent the incorrect initial social base persists, and the mass of immigrants remains cut off from the struggle of the labor movement, at the same time as the trade unions rarely go beyond the level of pious wishes with regard to demands for equal rights for all workers. But with the entry into force on September 18, 1972, of new regulations regarding immigration (the Fontanet-Marcellin circular) things started to change. These regulations represented a true offensive by large capital to regularize the field of immigration, giving prime emphasis to the repressive and police features of immigration control. The main measures in the circular can be summarized as follows:

1. No immigrant worker will be able to work or live in France without passing through the legal channels of the Office National d'Immigration. Illegal immigrants will no longer be able to regularize their position (up till then 80 percent of immigrants were clandestine).

2. Work and residence permits will be linked and granted for the same period. The length of this period will be determined by the work contract, which means that the right of an immigrant worker to stay in France will depend on the goodwill of the employer.

3. Before the issue of a residence permit, an immigrant worker must have a "decent dwelling." But since the causes of the housing crisis are not being touched, this measure may be regarded as a pious wish. In reality, it has a very great but different significance, since the description "decent" will depend on the judgment of the police. It thus introduces an arbitrary element into the granting of residence.

4. Finally, in order to deal with all aspects of the administration of immigrants together, the dossiers will be brought together into a single file in the care of the local police station, which will thus be able to carry out repressive operations at leisure.

This set of measures is justified, according to the circular, by the need to "regularize" immigration. In fact it is a regularization which reflects very closely the interests of big capital. It represents (a) the hegemony of monopoly capital over backward capitalism, in the field of immigration policy; (b) a drastic attempt to nip in the bud the rudimentary immigrant workers' movement, which was starting to develop out of several working-class struggles.

The circular thus has two features: the capitalist rationalization of immigration and the political repression of immigrants. Initially, labor unions saw only the first feature and were thus not terribly opposed to it (especially the CGT), since they agreed it was necessary to regularize immigration in order to avoid the worst abuses. But they were not aware of the economic impossibility of such a regularization. At the same time they underestimated the importance of the feature of the circular concerning the establishment of arbitrary employer and police power over immigrants as a whole (except for those entering under special agreements: Algerians, black Africans, EEC nationals).

On the other hand, it quickly became evident to immigrants from their everyday experience that something basic had changed. The police headquarters and local police stations stepped up their administrative checks, and deportations began. The measures

taken were carefully thought out and selective, the first to be hit
were Arab workers (mainly Tunisians and Moroccans, unpro-
tected by any special status), whose political-legal isolation is
well known, given the widespread anti-Arab racism among the
indigenous population. In the face of this intimidation, immigrant
workers mobilized in disorder, to a large extent spontaneously.
Two tendencies soon appeared within this movement. One tendency started from the specificity of immigrant workers, organizing
them into a "Defense Committee for Immigrants' Rights to Live
and Work" (CDVTI), on the fringe of the trade-union movement,
and had as a central plank the demand for a guaranteed legal
status which would eliminate the arbitrary powers of police and
employers and guarantee the presence of immigrants in the
country under satisfactory conditions, even while accepting the
inferior status of immigrant and the regularization of immigration.
The other tendency preached the class unity of all workers
and demanded equal rights through a common struggle by
workers of all nationalities, organized, for example, into "French-
Immigrant Unitary Committees" (CUFI). Both tendencies were
instigated by revolutionary groups, although the CUFI also
contained trade-union militants. The trade unions, for their part,
demanded the repeal of the circular without, however, launching
any major battles on this subject. As deportations increased,
semispontaneous actions were set off. The demands of the CUFI
were too ambitious for an immigrant movement to use from the
outset: they could only be imposed through trade-union action
within firms, and the trade unions had difficulty because of the
unresponsiveness of French workers. On the other hand, the
"defense of human rights" line of the CDVTI, which was specific
to immigrants, gained the support of many of those who were
primarily demanding not to be deported, as well as support from
prominent liberal and charitable figures (e.g., the Church played a
major role). As a form of struggle the CDVTI chose *hunger strikes*
by those threatened with deportation, the first of which was
launched in Valence at Christmas 1972. Following the success of
this first strike (the position of those involved was regularized
"because of the date"), a veritable wave of hunger strikes by
clandestine immigrants shook the whole of France. Supported by
public opinion and with a very high level of mobilization of
extreme left militants, almost all of the hunger strikes brought
success to the participants, but (a) the circular was not withdrawn,
(b) *in particular*, no mass movement was organized, since the
strikes mostly involved the persons directly affected, and (c) unity
with the labor movement was only at the level of declarations.

Parallel to this, the CUFI *gave support* to these initiatives and spent most of its time organizing neighborhood committees containing immigrants of various nationalities and French political militants. It succeeded in achieving national *coordination* between the almost one hundred local committees which sprang up semi-spontaneously throughout France.

As soon as the deportation campaign came to an end, so did the hunger strikes, thus showing their highly defensive and individual character. Nothing changed at the general level, and these struggles did not lead to the creation of any social force.

Immigrant working-class struggles, however, linking labor demands and demands specific to immigrants appeared during the same period (spring 1973) within certain factories, led primarily by the left wing of the CFDT and by independent groups of immigrants. A new strike at Renault, the Margoline's strike at Nanterre, the strike of Spanish women workers in the "Claude-St. Cyr" clothes firm were tough, exemplary, and victorious battles, which started to link together working-class and immigrant struggles through the *simultaneous* support of labor unions and nationally organized, independent immigrant organizations (Association of Moroccans in France, Co-ordination of Spanish Workers in the Paris Region, and later the Arab Workers Movement, etc.).

May 1, 1973, was an "Immigrants May 1," which saw a procession including thousands of immigrant workers, both inside and outside the trade-union contingents, linking their specific demands to those of the working class as a whole. And the trade unions were again taking up immigrants' demands.

This created a new balance of power. The government reacted with both integration and repression. On the one hand, the circular was made more "flexible" (for example, by giving a three-months' grace period after the expiration of a contract to enable a new job to be found), and it was suspended for four months in order to regularize the position of clandestine workers (which was not in fact done). But, on the other hand, the main provisions remained unchanged, and deportation orders were served *for political reasons* on the leaders of the new immigrant movement which had developed on the fringes of the trade-union movement. Finally, and most important of all, a racist campaign developed (officially disapproved of by the government), which included mass racist demonstrations in Marseilles and a wave of assassinations of Arabs, whose authors were never traced. This activity reached such a pitch that Algeria suspended emigration to France. The trial of strength between the immigrant movement and capital, which requires a certain status for immigrants, has started. It will be long and hard. All the more since the immigrant movement is starting to escape its isolation and gradually to find its place again in the trade-union movement through a reciprocal discovery of common class interests through common struggles.[18]

This said, a basic problem has been posed, without yet having really emerged in the practice of the immigrant-worker movement: insofar as the class struggle does not stop at protest struggle but is basically pulled together at the political level, what is the relation between immigrants' struggles and the political struggle between classes?

Immigrant Struggles, Working-Class Struggles, and Political Struggle Between Classes

We know[19] that no class struggle *of any consequence* takes place without raising the question of power and hence seeking the destruction-transformation of the state apparatus, the instrument by which the interests of the dominant classes as a whole are realized. Class struggles are thus concentrated within the political struggle between classes, which has as its objective the capture of power and, then, the transformation of social relationships by ending the exploitation of people by people.

In the case of immigrant workers' struggles the question immediately arises: which states are involved? Which capture of power is being referred to, that in the sending country or that in the receiving country? This question is by no means irrelevant, particularly if we bear in mind the whole series of ultrainternationalist interpretations. These argue from the facts of immigration and the internationalization of capital and advocate an international revolution, that is, they deny the possibility of any revolutionary process which operates at less than a European scale, at the very least. According to this view, one should speak of a single international working class, since an international proletariat is not only a goal but a reality already present in the relations of production.

Nothing could be further from the truth.

To speak in this way has meaning only in the context of an exclusively trade-union and economistic strategy. Certainly, it is necessary for trade unions primarily concerned with obtaining the best possible negotiating conditions to develop an international trade-union federation in opposition to the international grouping of employers. But to do no more than this is to forget that the interests of the working class are realized *politically*, that the political process concerns the state, and that the state has forms and patterns of change specific to each nation created by the bourgeoisie. Each state represents a particular system of interests and alliances, and it oppresses in a specific way a section of workers which is relatively united by history and mode of life. The confrontation of each state requires a separate strategy to develop class alliances and class struggle at the political level. It is obvious that there is a Holy Alliance of international capital. But the idea of an international struggle is no more than an idea. Today there is no united world proletariat confronting a single opponent. The unity of the proletariat will be built in the struggle, through the convergence of interests uncovered in the practices of the struggle. Given the uneven development of the class struggle in relation to each state, each proletariat must necessarily develop its own strategy. To talk of an international working class "on the Common Market level" is either an ideological position, expressing a desire without helping concretely to bring it about, or an economistic position which identifies the context of negotiations with the Europe of big capital. In neither case is it a political position connected with the strategy of classes engaged in a struggle for power.

To which revolutionary processes, then, does the class fraction immigrant workers belong? In relation to which political struggle are they defined? In our view, immigrant workers as a class fraction are defined within the class struggle of the receiving country. Nevertheless, as a labor movement, they have a twofold definition, since *within each country there is a multinational working class which corresponds to a multinational labor movement* and which is doubly linked: as a multinational entity it is directed *politically* towards the struggle whose goal is the state apparatus in the receiving country; and as a national component of such an entity it is part of the labor movement in the sending country, since, in practice, it continues to retain a close relation with the struggles in the sending country.

Such an analysis raises the problem of whether this multinational labor movement should not have a corresponding multinational political leadership. But such a measure would contradict the class alliances necessary in the revolutionary process in each country, insofar as classes other than the working class are not multinational. This is a real "contradiction within the people." But before it can be resolved politically from the point of view of the proletariat, there must first be unity of the multinational proletariat today fragmented within each country. The frequent preference for welding class alliances at the cost of the unity of the proletariat implies an acceptance from the outset of the submission of working-class interests to those of the intermediate strata. This, then, is an attempt to explain the strange passivity of the labor movement toward its immigrant fraction. The persistence of this fragmentation may be both a basic reason for the political weakness of the labor movement and the result of a strategy of alliances engendered by the interests of other classes. The link between immigrant workers and the political class struggle is thus both close and problematic.

Notes

1. For reasons of space a number of statistical tables in the original article have been excluded here. [Eds.]
2. This paper does not attempt to synthesize all the data available on immigration but simply to put forward certain ideas. The best work available on the subject, Stephen Castles and Godula Kosack, *Immigrant Workers and Class Structure in Western Europe* (London: Oxford University Press, 1973) collects together the basic data and also includes a select bibliography of material relating to a number of countries. Periodical information on the subject of immigration is available in the OECD *Bulletins* (Sopemi-Service) and in the journal *Hommes et migrations.*
3. M. Castells and F. Godard, *Monopolville* (Paris: Mouton, 1974).
4. Centre de Coorinamento Campano, "Sulle recenti tendenze dello sviluppo capitalistico in Campania," mimeographed, 1972.
5. Charles Kindleberger, *Europe's Postwar Growth: The Role of Labor Supply* (Cambridge, Mass.: Harvard University Press, 1967).
6. See the works of Boccara.
7. French Communist party, *Le capitalisme monopoliste d'état,* 2 vols. (Paris: Editions Sociales, 1971).
8. See *Le logement des migrants* (Droit et Liberté, 1975) and the bibliography of German and English works in Castles and Kosack, *Immigrant Workers.*
9. See P. and J. Calame, *Les travailleurs étrangers en France* (Paris: Les Editions Ouvrières, 1972).
10. See Andre Gorz, "Immigrant Labour," *New Left Review* (May 1970).
11. See the journal *Hommes et migrations* ("documents" series) and Clifford S. Hill, *How Prejudiced is Britain?* (London: Panther Books, 1967).
12. M.D., "Les effets économiques de la migration sur les pays d'accueil: tentative de bilan," *Economie et humanisme* (July-August 1971).
13. Charles Levinson, *Capital, Inflation and the Multinationals* (London: George Allen and Unwin, 1971).
14. J. L. Dallemagne, *L'inflation capitaliste* (Paris: Maspero, 1972).
15. See *Espaces et sociétés,* no. 4 (1971).

16. Uli Windisch, "Travailleurs immigrés et xenophobie: le cas de la Suisse," *Espaces et sociétés*, no. 4 (1971).

17. Leon Gani, *Syndicats et travailleurs immigrés* (Paris: Editions Sociales, 1972).

18. Francoise Pinet, *Travailleurs immigrés dans la lutte de classes* (Paris: Cerf, 1973).

19. Nicos Poulantzas, *Pouvoir politique et classes sociales* (Paris: Maspero, 1968; English translation, London: New Left Books, 1973).

Contract Labor in U.S. Agriculture:
The West Indian Cane Cutters in Florida

Josh DeWind, Tom Seidl, and Janet Shenk

U.S. agriculture is today a multibillion-dollar industry, increasingly dominated by large corporations and conglomerates through direct investments, vertical integration, or contract farming. Yet growers have perpetuated the myth of "family farming" to argue that agriculture cannot absorb the same labor costs as industry. They have fought successfully to exclude farmworkers from most protective legislation and in particular from collective-bargaining laws.

As a result, the average income of farmworkers is less than $3,000 a year. Farmworkers are four times as likely to die from job-related accidents as the average American workers, and their life expectancy is only forty-nine years.[1]

Traditionally, agricultural jobs have been filled only by the most desperate workers. Increasingly these workers are foreign, many of whom are working illegally. Because of the growers' dependence on cheap foreign labor, no other sector of capital is more concerned about the government's current plans to curb "illegal" immigration. The farm lobby is mobilized. In state legislatures throughout the country bills to levy fines on the employers of "illegals" contain specific exemptions for growers and ranchers. And in presenting his new immigration proposals to Congress, President Carter added the reassurance that steps would be taken to provide foreign workers where needed.

Growers can take heart in many of the provisions of Carter's immigration bills. A prime asset of aliens, in the eyes of capital, is their vulnerability to intimidation and, ultimately, to deportation. Under Carter's plan, immigrant workers who entered the country on or before January 1, 1977, would be granted temporary resident status for five years. They would be given no guarantees against deportation at the end of that period, however, and the criteria for deciding who stays and who leaves in 1982 could well include whether a worker participated in political or union activities. Furthermore, the incentives for shedding "illegality" by registering with the Immigration and Naturalization Service

Reprinted by permission of the North American Congress on Latin America (Box 57, Cathedral Station, New York, N.Y. 10025) from the *NACLA Report of the Americas* 11, no. 8 (November-December 1977): 5-17.

(INS) are exceedingly weak: "Why should they choose to increase their future risk of deportation—when deportation five years from now might mean a permanent one-way trip to Mexico—by coming out of hiding and surrendering themselves to the INS?"[2]

Immigrant workers will continue to constitute an underclass of workers in the United States, underpaid and difficult to organize. But growers are concerned that the immediate and long-term supply of such workers will be limited by Carter's plan to beef up the border patrols. Likewise, the Mexican government trembles at the possible political effects of closing off the immigration valve.

An Alternative to Illegality

Several options are being explored to counteract any negative effects of Carter's proposals on employers that rely heavily on foreign labor and on countries that export labor to the United States. One such option, mentioned with increasing frequency these days, is the expansion of an already existing program. Under Section H-2 of the Immigration and Nationality Act of 1952 (also known as PL 414), foreign workers may be issued temporary visas to work in U.S. agriculture when domestic workers are unavailable.

Approximately twenty thousand foreign agricultural workers enter the country each year under the H-2 program of temporary visas. The great majority are West Indians, employed in the sugar harvests of Florida and the fruit harvests of the eastern states. Five to six thousand Canadians are employed in the logging industry of New England, and several hundred workers of various nationalities work as sheepherders in the western states. A pre-arranged contract between the immigrant worker and a particular U.S. employer is a requirement of the program.

While H-2 workers have been employed in every region of the United States, East Coast growers have been the program's main beneficiaries. Today, they are demanding its expansion, while western growers look on with envy and anticipation. The Mexican goverment has intimated that a temporary-worker program would meet with its eager approval. And President Carter has instructed the secretary of labor to conduct a comprehensive review of labor needs in agriculture, with an eye toward temporary work programs and the H-2 program in particular.[3]

The H-2 program is not the only means by which the U.S.

government has attempted to institutionalize the legal use of foreign labor in agriculture and regulate illegal immigration. Hundreds of thousands of Mexican "wetbacks" became legal *braceros* in the 1940s under a system of government-to-government contracts. The *bracero* program was terminated in 1964 because of pressure from progressive sectors. Today, the Carter administration says it in no way contemplates a resumption of "bracero-type programs."[4] Yet in many respects, the H-2 program provides many of the same mechanisms for providing growers with a cheap supply of labor. Government-to-government contracts have been replaced by government-to-grower contracts which provide few protections for foreign workers, keep wages low for foreign and domestic workers, and inhibit unionization.

A Captive Labor Force

Despite the growing trend toward mechanization in U.S. agriculture, which is in part a response to unionization efforts in the fields, many of the major East Coast crops still remain highly labor-intensive. Automatic cane cutters sink in the mud and uproot the stalks. The slightest abrasion of shade tobacco leaves, inevitable with mechanical harvesting, makes them unusable as wrappers for fine cigars. Tree shakers can "pick" a whole tree of apples in a moment, but bruise the fruit. Mechanization has been largely reserved for crops that are processed into applesauce, canned tomatoes, and the like.

Unable to reduce their dependency on a sizable work force, eastern growers have gone to great lengths to procure a supply of cheap and steady labor, to keep it unorganized and tightly controlled.

Government-to-grower contracting of foreign labor offers the growers a number of distinct advantages over the domestic labor alternatives. First and foremost, the growers have the upper hand in negotiating the contracts. In the Caribbean high unemployment, political unrest, and slow economic growth compromise the ability of these governments to negotiate contracts that can adequately protect the worker. Although the worker signs the contract upon employment, that worker has no say whatsoever in its terms.

A second advantage is that growers can preselect their work force and hire only the most able, youthful, and productive. Workers with political or union backgrounds can be conveniently bypassed. Recruiting agents of the U.S. Sugar Corporation in Florida described a recruiting trip to Jamaica:

> We'll run through 800 men a day. . . . Three tables are set up representing three stages of processing. At the first table we simply look at a man as a physical specimen and try to eliminate those with obvious physical defects. At the second table, we're trying to test intelligence and see if the man can understand English as we speak it by asking simple questions. The third table is where we attempt to find out about the man's work background. We also check our black book to see if a man has been breached (i.e., sent home for violating the contract). . . . The final stage of pre-selection is the check by the Jamaican authorities of police records.[5]

Once these workers are airlifted to the mainland, growers need only supply housing for single males—crude dormitory buildings with limited sanitary, cooking, and eating facilities.

Finally, the contract program offers the growers an inordinate degree of control over the work force in the fields. Workers are contracted to a specific employer, an individual grower, or growers' association. Protests over living conditions, meals, wages, piece rates, or benefits can mean dismissal—tantamount to deportation. And organizing, the ultimate sin, means asking to be deported. No wonder growers refer to West Indians as an ideal labor force, combining "docility and obedience" with high productivity.

Growers are enchanted with the contract-labor system for the reasons cited above. But these reasons are not the argument they use to request foreign workers from the INS. In theory, only the "unavailability" of domestic workers can open the door to contract workers from abroad. Also, in theory, the wages and working conditions of domestic workers are protected from the adverse effects that may result from the importation of foreign workers. Inherent in the practice of this program, however, is a very different story.

Under the Immigration and Nationality Act (PL 414), final authority for deciding whether foreign workers should be admitted rests with the attorney general, "after consultation with appropriate agencies of Government upon petition of the importing employer." The INS then has the responsibility of administering the act, with the Department of Labor acting as the appropriate consultative agency.

Before any H-2 visas are granted, current INS regulations require that the Department of Labor certify that no qualified persons already in the country are available and that wages and living conditions of workers similarly employed in the United States will not be adversely affected.

To prove that domestic workers are unavailable, growers must file a job offer with the state employment service for as many workers as they require and offer wages that are equal to or above the minimum wage rate set for foreign workers. The job offer is then circulated to all fifty states and U.S. territories by the U.S. Employment Service. The Wagner-Peyser Act of 1933 set up this interstate clearance system to match workers from one state to jobs in another. In 1951 the system was extended to Puerto Rico, Guam, and the Virgin Islands. Growers must prove that no workers are available from any of these sources.

What's required on paper is rarely done in practice, however. Critics of the contract program say that growers rarely make a serious effort to recruit domestic workers, and often reject them in favor of contract labor. If a recent case in Texas is any indication, the government seems inclined to blink an eye now and then. Melon and onion growers in the Presidio Valley of Texas requested certification for Mexican workers to harvest their 1977 crops. The Department of Labor refused to certify a labor shortage. But an intense lobbying campaign by growers, culminating in a personal visit to the president from Texas Congressman Richard C. White, led to a presidential directive to approve the request. Some two hundred fifty domestic workers who had already contracted with these growers were told they were no longer needed.

Examples of maneuvers to hire foreign over domestic workers abound. But the question remains: with high unemployment rates throughout the East, and higher rates in Puerto Rico; with five thousand workers lining up in Detroit to answer an ad for fifty openings, how can growers argue that domestic workers are not available for agriculture? The answer is that domestic workers are not available in sufficient numbers because wage levels have been kept too low to attract them.

"Adverse Effect Wage Rates"

Since 1962 the Department of Labor has set a minimum hourly wage rate for each state that employs foreign agricultural workers on the H-2 program. As indicated by its name, this "adverse effect wage rate" is supposed to protect the jobs and wages of domestic farmworkers by setting a wage floor for agriculture. In other words, before employers can hire foreign workers, they must first offer domestic workers the adverse effect wage rate, and only if an insufficient number apply can the remaining job openings be filled by foreign workers.

On the surface this arrangement sounds quite reasonable. Yet a closer look reveals that the adverse effect wage rate acts not as a *minimum* wage level, but rather as a *ceiling* on wages offered to all workers in agriculture. Growers never have to raise their wage offer above this rate in order to attract a labor force. In 1977, for example, the average adverse effect wage rate for ten eastern states was $2.74 an hour. If there are no takers at this rate, growers get the green light to apply for a virtually inexhaustible supply of foreign workers. The undesirability of agricultural jobs thus becomes self-perpetuating.

Furthermore the ceiling set by the adverse effect wage rate has been historically *depressed* by the use of foreign contract labor, as well as other factors such as the lack of unionization in the fields.

The first adverse effect wage rates were established as a response to growing criticism of the *bracero* program and its effect on domestic workers. They were based on the prevailing wage rate in states employing Mexican *braceros* in 1962. That growers imported *braceros* precisely to avoid paying higher wages to domestic workers is hardly a disputed fact. In a 1961 speech President Kennedy cited the program's drawbacks, even as he signed a bill to extend it: "Studies of the operation of the Mexican labor program have clearly established that it is adversely affecting the wages, working conditions, and employment possibilities of our own agricultural workers."[6]

In other words, adverse effect wage rates in 1977 are based on prevailing wages that have been depressed by decades of importing foreign labor at substandard wages. If one combines the wage factor with all the nonwage advantages of hiring foreign contract labor, the fate of domestic farmworkers is sealed. For inherent in the concept of contract labor is the growers' ability to exert a degree of control over the labor force that virtually no other system affords.

The following part of the article examines the conditions of thousands of West Indian contract workers already employed in U.S. harvests.

A clear understanding of the West Indian program and other programs to supply farm labor to the East Coast (e.g., that devised by the Commonwealth Government of Puerto Rico) is needed now, before expansion plans proceed. For any program that attempts to maintain the second-class citizen status of foreign

Table 1
Peak Number of West Indian Agricultural Workers
by State, 1960-1976

	Total	Conn.	Fla.	Maine	Md.	Mass.	Mich.	N.H.	N.J.	N.Y.	Vt.	Va.	W. Va.	Other
1960	13,629	1,533	8,997	—	17	—	281	32	674	300	—	102	—	1,693
1961	13,773	1,567	9,663	—	16	—	172	33	875	310	—	261	—	876
1962	15,471	1,565	11,668	—	20	—	144	29	693	456	—	369	—	527
1963	15,937	1,628	12,727	—	8	—	218	39	451	299	—	564	—	3
1964	16,841	1,845	13,020	—	8	—	211	21	629	300	—	804	—	3
1965	15,265	777	13,099	—	7	—	1	—	577	247	30	524	—	3
1966	10,135	50	8,762	—	—	25	—	17	—	647	60	374	200	—
1967	11,401	89	9,056	—	—	56	—	150	—	910	147	665	328	—
1968	10,602	96	8,711	—	—	80	—	52	—	802	145	440	276	—
1969	10,909	89	8,230	—	—	140	—	60	—	1,044	124	756	466	—
1970	11,887	303	9,319	1	—	88	—	22	—	944	165	638	407	—
1971	12,244	92	9,050	40	—	188	—	210	—	1,105	234	492	833	—
1972	11,425	86	8,276	51	—	218	—	238	—	1,154	237	720	443	2
1973	12,837	103	8,639	105	182	286	—	309	—	1,595	213	887	515	3
1974	12,582	104	8,224	176	124	334	—	289	—	1,788	323	759	458	3
1975	12,813	93	8,427	206	184	345	—	228	—	1,570	303	927	526	4
1976	10,958	76	8,052	224	—	305	—	269	—	996	233	473	326	4

Source: British West Indies Central Labor Organization.

workers in the United States provides employers with the means to divide workers.

In August 1977 Secretary of Labor Ray Marshall addressed the United Farm Workers Convention. He was questioned about plans to expand the H-2 program in agriculture. He answered by saying, "Well, I don't think it would be terribly much greater than it is now, which is 18,000 . . . 25,000. I'd be surprised if it's more than 100,000."[7]

West Indians in Florida

Every year thousands of West Indian contract workers fly on chartered jets from Kingston, Jamaica, to mainland Florida. They travel late at night to be greeted at the airport by the Meranda Company of Miami, whose business it is to arrange the flights, house the arriving workers, and finally disperse them by commercial buses to the farms, fields, and orchards of the eastern United States.

These workers come primarily from Jamaica and to a lesser extent from other West Indian islands, such as St. Lucia and St. Kitts. They come from rural areas, where some of them own small plots, ply rural trades such as fishing, carpentry, and mechanics, or tend small stores. Others are jobless, since unemployment in Jamaica chronically hovers around 25 percent or higher. Unable to get by on what they earn at home, and lacking access to welfare or social security programs, these workers have little choice but to become migrant workers.

West Indians have been employed in almost every region of the United States during the past thirty-five years. They have picked cherries in Washington and Wisconsin, tended shade tobacco in the Connecticut Valley, picked apples from Virginia to New Hampshire, cut sugarcane and harvested citrus and winter vegetables in Florida, and picked peas in California.[8] In 1977 they were employed only in the Florida cane fields and the apple orchards of Appalachia and New England. Nevertheless, the number of workers annually entering the country has remained steady for the last fifteen years, ranging from ten thousand to fifteen thousand per year.

West Indians are no longer the emergency supplemental work force that the U.S. government first imported during World War II. Rather, they have become a regular part of the farm labor force of the United States. Fred Sikes, of the U.S. Sugar Corporation in Florida, described the origins of the contract program as it now exists:

> In the summer of 1947, we—that is the nationwide group of agricultural employers using off-shore labor—learned that the War and Food Administration was closing down. We were concerned that even though the war was over we would not be able to find sufficient American labor to harvest the crops. So we began to explore ways to continue the program on a private basis. . . . Exploring the situation further, we found that extreme unemployment problems existed throughout the Caribbean and that Jamaica, where unemployment was particularly severe, was interested in seeing the off-shore farm labor program continued.[9]

These growers succeeded in signing government-to-grower contracts for Jamaican and other West Indian workers.

We turn now to the role of West Indians in harvesting Florida's sugarcane, the conditions they endure, and the effect of their employment on domestic workers. Our analysis of the program's present operations serves as a warning of the perils awaiting farmworkers. The temporary-foreign-contract labor program, as it is currently run, provides growers with unique powers of control over farmworkers, and they use them freely at the expense of foreign and domestic workers alike.

Over one-third of all the sugarcane in the United States is grown in Florida, making it the largest cane-producing state in the union. Most of Florida's sugarcane is grown in the rich "muck" soil near Belle Glade, which became arable in the late 1940s when the Army Corps of Engineers constructed an extensive canal system and drained the swamps around Lake Okeechobee.

The recovered lands were first used to grow sugarcane after the U.S. government imposed an economic blockade on Cuba and stopped the importation of Cuban sugar. Sugarcane is now grown on 450 square miles of the southern part of the state, with an annual yield of about 10 million tons.[10] In recent years most of this cane has been harvested by eight thousand to ten thousand West Indian contract workers.

In the cane fields workers confront a virtually impenetrable jungle. The variety of cane grown in Florida tends to be very tall (twelve to fourteen feet) and exceptionally thick. Because of their height and weight, many stalks are bent over to the ground, with leaves and stalks intertwined. To remove the leaves, which have no sugar content, the fields are burned before they are cut. The burning also helps to drive out insects and other pests. Growers tell workers not to kill the snakes, however, because the snakes eat the rats.

Cutting cane is hard, dangerous, and dirty work. Swinging two-foot, razor-sharp knives, the workers must bend to cut the stalks off at the ground, gather the stalks into the cut pile, and trim off the tops. To protect themselves from the knives, workers wear awkward foot, shin, and hand guards, made of metal and reminiscent of medieval armor. Despite the guards, cutting accidents—often meaning the loss of a finger or toe—are common.

By the end of the day cane cutters are covered with sticky, black ash and cane fiber that cause the skin and scalp to itch. For protection they must wear hats and long-sleeved shirts—despite the humid, eighty-degree weather. A cooling breeze is only partly welcome, however, since it blows the fine soil and ash into dark clouds that invade the workers' eyes and mouths. Even under these conditions the companies demand that a worker cut a ton of trimmed cane every hour.

Few domestic farmworkers cut sugarcane. The problem is not so much that domestic workers are reluctant to take on such dirty and dangerous work, as the growers claim, but rather that they refuse to be driven at the required pace for such low pay. As a result the growers discourage them from applying for the jobs.

"The real reason the growers don't want us," said one North American who was refused employment, "is that they can pay those wetbacks [sic] less and they dog them around. Those Jamaicans don't stop cutting; they run all day. If they stop running, they are sent back to the islands. The growers know they can't dog Americans around like that."[11] In large measure, the ability of the growers to "dog" the West Indians is derived from the nature of the contract-labor system, and the specific character of the West Indian contract.

The West Indian workers have no say in negotiating the contracts they work under for one to nine months each year. From the beginning, the program has been controlled by government officials and growers who write the contracts to serve their own interests. In annual negotiations the West Indian governments are represented by the British West Indies Central Labor Organization (BWICLO) and the growers by associations organized on the basis of crops and regions.

The policies of BWICLO reflect the goal of the Jamaican and other participating West Indian governments: to promote labor emigration as a means of neutralizing social and political tensions which result from unemployment. That BWICLO functions to serve this end is determined by the organization's directorate, the Central Labor Board, composed of high-ranking government officials: the Jamaican secretary of labor, undersecretary of finance, and solicitor general, the Barbadian secretary of labor, and the prime minister of St. Lucia. The only board member representing labor is the head of the National Workers' Union of Jamaica, but the union is closely linked to the party of the current prime minister and can be depended upon to represent the government's policies. BWICLO maintains liaison officers in the United States to negotiate and enforce the labor contracts. In both functions, we shall see, the liaison officers are led to compromise the economic needs of the workers in order to ensure the possibility of employment in the United States.

In their negotiations to contract West Indian cane-cutters, the sugarcane growers are represented by two associations: the Florida Sugar Producers Association and the Florida Fruit and Vegetable Association, which together represent a dozen companies which hire foreign contract workers. Three of these companies, the U.S. Sugar Company, the Okeelanta Sugar Division of the Gulf & Western Food Products Company, and the Sugar Cane Growers Cooperative of Florida, hire about two-thirds of the contract workers. Not all the companies which hire West Indians are as large as these, but the smaller companies are dominated by the giant sugar milling and refining companies that purchase their cane. Regardless of their size, the labor needs of the cane-growing companies are equally well served by the contracts.

The Contract

The labor contracts stipulate the obligations of the workers, the growers, and BWICLO. The major requirements placed on the workers are so vague that they allow growers a free hand in their interpretation. Each worker must "diligently and faithfully perform the duties of an agricultural worker," which in this case is to cut sugarcane. They must also "obey and comply with all the rules and regulations of the employer." These rules must be approved by BWICLO, but the only specific limitation put on them in the contract is that the workers cannot be forced to work for more than eight hours a day for six days a week—what the contract defines as full-time work.

The obligations of the employers take up seven times more fine print than do those of the workers. In the end, however, they do not require as much. Growers must pay the workers' round-trip transportation from the islands. Presumably to ensure that the workers do not take advantage of the free ride and skip off, the growers are allowed to deduct the transportation costs from the workers' wages during the first half of the employment period. During the second half they must repay the workers.

Once the workers are in Florida, the growers are obliged to provide them with free housing. The growers must also supply the same medical care and compensation for work-related injuries and diseases that are required for domestic workers by state laws. If a worker dies, the company is supposed to provide a "suitable burial" or pay to have the body shipped home.

How much the growers must pay a worker for "diligently and faithfully" fulfilling his obligations is laid out in complicated clauses which establish an hourly wage rate, a minimum number of hours of work, and wage deductions. In sum, the growers must pay the workers the hourly or piece rates which prevail for similar workers in the region. The hourly wage rate is the adverse effect wage rate set by the Department of Labor. Piece rates are not stipulated in the contract, however, and this omission, as we shall see, provides the growers with the means to avoid paying what the contract requires. By the time the contract expires, growers must have provided full-time work at these wages for at least 75 percent of the contract period.

Before a worker receives his biweekly pay the following deductions are made: 3 percent of his wages are given to BWICLO to buy the workers life insurance or to pay for "expenses reasonably incurred on behalf of the worker in any emergency," a clause which gives BWICLO discretion over large sums of the workers' earnings. Another 18 percent is given to BWICLO as forced savings to be sent home to the workers' dependents. Up to $150 of these savings, however, can be kept in escrow to pay off any outstanding debts if the worker's contract is canceled. Finally, the growers are allowed to deduct the cost of meals. In total, about one-third of a worker's earnings is deducted from his pay check before he receives it.

Although BWICLO liaison officers are supposed to enforce the contract and look out for workers' interests on the mainland, none of these duties is written into the contract. The contract does not create any grievance procedure for the workers to follow if their rights are abused, and BWICLO is not required to take any remedial action on the workers' behalf. These omissions become crucial in light of a contract provision that gives the growers the right to terminate a worker's contract virtually at will.

If either the grower or BWICLO decides that a worker is "unwilling to work in accordance with the terms of this agreement or determines that the worker has committed an act of misconduct or indiscipline," then the grower can terminate the contract immediately and repatriate the worker at the worker's expense.

Minimum hourly wages for cane-cutting have risen from $1.15 in 1964 to $3.23 in 1977. To counter the increasing cost of labor, growers have made sure that workers produce more for their money.

Contract cane cutters are paid piece rates, according to how many rows or fractions of rows they cut per day. The standard row of cane in Florida is a quarter mile long, and one row corresponds to the average worker's daily "task."

Tasks are assigned to each worker every morning by the lead man, who also tells the workers how much the company will pay. Task payments often vary from field to field and even from row to row, depending on the estimated number of tons per row. How willingly the workers accept the task price is determined by factors which affect the difficulty of cutting quickly, such as the thickness and tangle of the stalks and how closely they are planted together. Outside rows, or "Charlie Franks," are usually the most tangled and difficult to cut.

Historically, piece rates have been used by employers to speed up the work process and maximize the output of each worker. In the case of contract workers, piece rates are especially effective when combined with a minimum work quota that every worker must achieve or be sent home.

Domestic workers in industries paying piece rates constantly bargain over the rate and frequently strike because of it. For contract workers that option has rarely worked. In the mid-1960s West Indian workers struck in protest over low task rates on the average of once a month. The field reports of the BWICLO officers describe how protests were typically "resolved":

> . . . Fifteen men were sent home for agitating and inciting others to strike.
> . . . The men returned to work the following day after five men were removed.
> . . . Since repatriation of one worker who was deemed the ring leader, work has progressed smoothly.[12]

The growers' methods have definitely been effective. According to a U.S. Department of Agriculture study of the sugar industry, 2.4 labor hours were required to required to produce a ton of Florida sugarcane in 1963. A decade later, workers took only 1.6 hours to harvest a ton, an increase in productivity of 30 percent.[13]

Overworked and Under-recorded

According to federal regulations, cane cutters paid at a piece rate must earn at least the equivalent of the minimum hourly wage as stipulated in the contract. A Department of Labor investigation found, however, that 65 percent of the workers were paid even less. The growers tried to hide this fact by systematically misrecording the number of hours cane cutters worked.

Timekeepers in the field typically recorded starting time only after the last worker had been assigned a row; they marked half an hour for lunch even when workers took short lunches to earn more; they recorded a worker's quitting time as the last time they saw him in the fields, or, in order to "simplify records," just rounded quitting time down to the last hour.

The Atlantic Sugar Association was not so creative. According to investigators, "The daily hours of work appear to have been simply reduced by whatever amount of time was needed to show daily minimum wage compliance."

Overall it was discovered that during the 1973-1974 harvest, workers, who for their part were whipping themselves to make every minute count, were being shortchanged by at least one and a half hours a day, or 20 percent of their earnings.[14]

Fearing that a strict enforcement of the contract might detract from the contract program's appeal, BWICLO and other West Indian officials do little or nothing to make sure that the few legal rights contract workers do have are respected. This situation is illustrated by BWICLO's ineffectiveness in correcting growers' disregard for the safety of their employees.

For years cane companies illegally transported cutters to and from the fields in trucks with standing room only. Before the 1973 harvest began, the Department of Labor ordered growers to provide trucks with fixed seating for each worker as required by law. Gulf & Western chose to ignore the directive. One of its trucks, overcrowded and top heavy with standing passengers, went off the side of a road. Thirty-six workers were hospitalized with broken bones, bruises, and lacerations from flying cane knives.

BWICLO took no effective action. Three weeks later another Gulf & Western truck skidded off the road and rolled over. All 86 passengers were injured and hospitalized, and one died. Gulf & Western was fined $1,800 by the U.S. Department of Labor.[15]

Shortly after the accidents Jamaica's ambassador to the United States visited the Florida camps. When asked about the growers' trucking practices, he replied: "Yes, it's a problem. But if a man came to me and asked my personal opinion of what he should do—the choice is not working—I think I would have to tell him: Risk the truck."

The ambassador took a similar position with regard to wages:

> Cutting cane is hard work . . . worth more than $2.15 an hour. I know I would not cut cane for $100 an hour. . . . But we fight for increased wages for our workers every year, and maybe we will get up to $5 an hour. But, then maybe Americans will want to cut cane and the Jamaicans will not be allowed to come anymore. So then the program ends.[16]

Unionization: It's Not in the Contract

> *If the supervisor sees us talking to a white man,*
> *we get sent home.*
> *We complain about the food here,*
> *we get sent home.*
> *We say we want more money for the cane,*
> *we get sent home.*
> *Anything we do the supervisor don't like,*
> *we get sent home.*

Growers never hesitate to use the power of repatriation, granted by the contract, or to remind workers that they have it. As a result, strikes by contract workers have been consistently smashed, and strike leaders, or "village lawyers" as the growers call them, have been quickly removed from the scene. In one season alone, 600 out of the 5,200 cane cutters employed by the Florida Sugar Producers Association were sent home for "breach of contract."[17] These breached workers are then "u-listed," which means that their chances of returning to the United States on contract are permanently blocked.

This control over the work force—an inherent feature of the contract system—has also been a barrier to unity between foreign agricultural workers and domestic farmworkers. West Indian contract workers have either been used as scab labor, or punished by deportation for their support of farmworker struggles. Two examples tell both these stories.

In 1972 the United Farm Workers were organizing sugar workers at the Talisman Sugar Corporation in South Bay, Florida. Talisman both grows sugar and operates one of the largest mills in the nation. Some hundred and fifty truck drivers at the mill went out on strike for union representation by the International

Association of Machinists and Aerospace Workers. When the company fired the striking workers, the UFW set up picket lines. One UFW supporter, Nan Freeman, was killed on the picket line by a truck.

Ultimately the strike was lost. Workers claimed that the company maintained production during the strike by using contract workers from Jamaica. The company admitted that Jamaicans had been employed but said they were U.S. residents.[18]

The UFW was convinced, however, that the contract program would have to be stopped before organizing efforts could succeed among sugar workers in the state of Florida. The union brought, and lost, a suit before a U.S. District Court judge, asking for a restraining order against the importation of foreign laborers to harvest cane. Eliseo Medina, in charge of the UFW in Florida at the time, argued to no avail that growers were keeping conditions so bad that North Americans would not apply for the jobs. "It's a classic example," he said, "of the poor people of one country being used against the poor of another."[19]

A different scenario developed at the Moore Haven Sugar House in 1976. Workers at the mill and refinery, owned by the Glades County Sugar Growers Cooperative, went out on strike over company efforts to revise the seniority system to avoid promoting black and latino workers into predominantly white departments.

At the time the Growers Cooperative employed some five hundred to six hundred West Indian contract workers. These workers supported the strike—and every single one of them was promptly repatriated.[20]

The debilitating effect the Jamaican contract program exerts on unionization efforts and direct struggles for better working conditions resides in two factors: the inherent powerlessness of a deportable worker and the chronically depressed economy of Jamaica, which makes its government beholden to such a program in the first place.

Of these, deportation is the real club, evident in the remark of Fred Sikes of the U.S. Sugar Corporation: "If I had a remedy comparable to breaching an unsatisfactory worker—which is allowed under the West Indian contract—that I could apply to the American worker, then he might work better too."

Notes

1. U.S. Senate, Committee on Labor and Public Welfare, Subcommittee on Migratory Labor, "Migrant and Seasonal Farmworker Powerlessness," July 1970.
2. Wayne A. Cornelius, "Undocumented Immigration: A Critique of the Carter Administration's Policy Proposals," *Migration Today* 5, no. 4 (October 1977): 8.
3. Office of the White House Press Secretary, "Undocumented Alien Fact Sheet: Summary of the President's Proposals" (mimeographed, August 4, 1977), p. 6.
4. Ibid.
5. Peter Kramer, *The Offshores: A Study of Foreign Farm Labor in Florida* (St. Petersburg, Fla.: Community Action Fund, 1966), p. 35.
6. Richard B. Craig, *The Bracero Program: Interest Groups and Foreign Policy* (Austin: University of Texas Press, 1971), p. 173.
7. Secretary of Labor Ray Marshall, Speech to the United Farm Workers Union Convention, Fresno, California, August 27, 1977.
8. NACLA interview with Harold Edwards, Chief Liaison Officer of the British West Indies Central Labor Organization (BWICLO), September 1977.
9. Kramer, *The Offshores*, p. 3.
10. U.S. Department of Agriculture, Economic Research Service, *The Sugar Industry's Structure, Pricing and Performance*, Agricultural Economic Report no. 364 (1977), p. 95.
11. Philip Shabecoff, "Florida Cane Cutters: Alien, Poor, Afraid," *New York Times*, March 12, 1973.
12. Kramer, *The Offshores*, p. 50.
13. U.S. Department of Agriculture, Economic Research Service, *Sugar Policy Options for the United States*, Agricultural Economic Report no. 351 (1977), pp. 33–34.
14. U.S. Department of Labor, "Wage Survey for 1973-74 South Florida Sugar Harvest," reprinted in *Oversight Hearings on Department of Labor Certification of the Use of Offshore Labor*, House of Representatives, Committee on Education and Labor, Subcommittee on Agricultural Labor, 94th Congress, March 20, 1975 (Washington, D.C.: Government Printing Office, 1975), pp. 209–53.
15. *Palm Beach Post*, December 18, 1973, January 8, 1973; Barry Marshall, "Conventional Wisdoms in Florida Agriculture," in *Florida's Farmworker . . . Toward a Responsible Public Policy* (Tallahassee, Fla.: Institute for Social Policy Studies, 1977), p. 30.
16. *Palm Beach Post*, January 24, 1974.
17. Kramer, *The Offshores*, p. 51.
18. *Miami Herald*, February 24, 1972.
19. *Miami Herald*, September 24, 30, 1972; *New York Times*, September 24, October 10, 1972, March 12, 1973.
20. Marti Kastner and I. C. Van Buskirk, "In South Florida Sugar Workers Strike," *Guardian*, March 24, 1976.

Part 5

Contemporary Struggles

Several of the protests described in part 1 of this volume concerned workers, new to the industrial process, who sought to avoid entering the system of industrial production by desertion, absenteeism, or communal revolt. Ultimately, however, as Marx foresaw, the capitalist mode of production decomposes previous modes of production and gradually makes survival outside its net impossible. The protests considered in this section, taking place over half a century later than those previously analyzed, show that "within system" struggles are all that can feasibly be considered by Third-World workers. Of course these struggles comprise a wide range of different activities: the struggle for legal rights and a basic living wage; the struggle to transcend immediate wage grievances and identify a class enemy; the struggle for survival among particularly repressed fractions of the workers, like women; the struggle, finally, to establish class organizations and to secure political representation. All these ongoing struggles are illustrated in one form or another by the articles in part 5. As a matter of convenience, we have taken "contemporary" to mean any study that is based on evidence from the late 1960s onward. It is always a temptation to include work on more immediate and dramatic events—for example, as this manuscript is being prepared, massive trials of strength between workers and their governments are being fought out in Tunisia and Peru. But we have resisted the temptation in order to ensure that the section comprises more "in-depth," rather than journalistic, articles, which are concerned with a theoretical and practical discussion of the present forms of working-class consciousness and struggle in the Third World.

The strike events described in the Durban article would not in some ways be remarkable—except that they took place in South Africa and the participants were African workers whose rights to organize, bargain, and join trade unions are severely curtailed, where they are not totally forbidden by the draconian laws of the white South African government. It is perhaps opportune to record that the members of the Institute of Industrial Education who wrote this article included Rick Turner, a young white Marxist, who was assassinated, presumably by right-wing vigilantes, on January 7, 1978. He was an important figure in the creation of a workers' benefit society which sought to coordinate the strikes in Durban described below. The workers' movement had the character of a "rolling" strike, with strikers from one plant raising the consciousness, and allaying the fears, of the next group along the line of factories. The strikes were concentrated in *the notorious Frame Group of textile plants, but soon spread to a wide variety of workers—Indian and African, municipal and private—right down to the grave diggers, market porters, and abattoir workers. Together with the Soweto riots, the Durban strikes opened up the most significant African challenge to the system of apartheid seen in recent times. At the same time one should be careful to note that some workers could, at first, still be mystified by the intervention of a paramount chief and that most workers ultimately settled for a modest wage raise, even though the political capacity of the local municipal administration was at its most fragile.*

Our second African article comes from Nigeria, Africa's most populous country and at present in the midst of an industrial boom triggered by the federal government's massive oil revenues. Though Peace's investigaton concerns the proletariat of an industrial estate established before the present industrial expansion, his description of the growth and form in which class consciousness and class action developed is of considerable contemporary interest. He starts with what is perhaps a too flat assertion that because they are members of a propertyless, contractual labor force, Nigerian proletarians are no different from their British or American counterparts. The differences he sees are in the expression of consciousness. The precipitant for the series of strikes Peace describes was the conclusions of a government wage commission in 1970, which argued that there was "intolerable suffering at or near the bottom of the wage and salary levels," while there were simultaneous "manifestations of affluence and wasteful expenditure." The commission's recommendations acted as a trigger to workers in the industrial estate, who demanded that a cost-of-living allowance be awarded across the board to all workers. In the course of their struggles workers, not without a sense of bitterness, saw that the accession to power of a national bourgeoisie had not changed their lot. Witness this worker interviewed by Peace: "The European managers have refused to give us the £2 owed to us, and the big men help them in this matter. Some of them used to be poor men, laborers, as we are now. But now that they are at the top, they are Ogas ('chiefs'), and our conditions are the same as ever."

Helen Safa also probes the dimensions and character of class consciousness, this time in relation to working-class women in Puerto Rico. The struggle to find themselves as women and as workers involves combating class oppression at the work place and sexual subordination at home. Certain conventional characterizations of Third-World women—for instance, that they spend much of their time at home in submissive service to their husbands—are decisively rebutted. Much of the cheap labor power which fueled "Operation Bootstrap" (the U.S.-sponsored thrust towards industrialization) was provided by women. Nearly half of the women surveyed in San Juan had worked, while increasing numbers had become the principal breadwinners and heads of households. Such women showed high levels of class consciousness. Safa also points to the contradictory nature of the family in the Puerto Rican social formation. On the one hand, it becomes a source of additional repression for the woman (where "Marianismo," the ideal of the long-suffering Virgin Mary, acts to mediate class awareness). On the other hand, the family provides a rallying point, a form of solidarity and refuge against capitalist exploitation outside. The struggle of the shantytown women is a struggle for survival and dignity, and, the author argues, these women have a strong class awareness of oppression within the family and in the wider society. The movement beyond this level of awareness—toward identifying the source of class oppression and evolving strategies to do something about it—must, she feels, await the recognition and acceptance of the special place of the women's struggle in Marxist theory and in practice.

Our final section concerns the organizational and political struggles of copper miners in Chile before and during the Allende regime. In some ways the internal, closed character of the mine gave the company— initially under Guggenheim's management—the capacity to act almost as a sovereign entity. Socialist politicians were denied the right to address the workers; and the company systematically violated workers' rights, while, even under Allende, the local labor inspector, who was meant to enforce the labor code, was little more than a puppet for the company. The primary struggle of the workers was thus for the rights of unionization and representation. But Zapata's examination of the political attitudes of the miners of Chuquicamata also provides an exceptional insight into their electoral choices and behavior. Because the electoral boundaries coincided exactly with the district where the miners lived, it proved possible for the author to consider the results of some thirteen elections—presidential, municipal, congressional, and union. Though the results are complicated and show important shifts between the competing political parties at different times and in response to different events, the underlying trend is clear: an electoral drift toward centrist or even right-wing parties. This the Unidad Popular failed to understand and consistently and falsely characterized the miners as the vanguard, or most conscious sector, of the working class. In effect, the author's conclusions provide a salutary warning to the left-wing politicians who may be prone to mistake instrumental and limited support for unqualified political sympathy. At the same time Zapata does not seek to reduce the workers' consciousness to electoral politics or to mere "economism." Yes, the miners were oriented to their unions and not, fundamentally, toward political parties, but this did not mean that they were disinterested or politically inactive. As Zapata succinctly puts it: "Unionism is their form of politics."

The Durban Strikes: South Africa 1973

Institute for Industrial Education

A Brief History of the Strikes

The wave of strikes began at the Coronation Brick and Tile Company, a brickworks in a minor industrial area on the northern outskirts of Durban. Here the entire African work force, nearly two thousand workers, went on strike on the morning of January 9, 1973. Their demand was for an increase in the minimum cash wage from 8.97 Rand to 20 Rand per week. Before long this demand escalated to 30 Rand per week.[. . .] Workers on the Number 1 plant report that the strike began when they were awakened at 3:00 A.M. by a group of their fellows and were told to gather at the main football stadium instead of reporting for work. An informal deputation went from this main plant to outlying depots in the neighboring suburb of Avoca and persuaded the workers there to join with the main body at the stadium. A high-spirited and positive response marked this early phase of the strike. Not one man from the main plant ignored the call to strike; workers from the Avoca plants marched to the stadium in two long columns, with a rather stirring disregard for the heavy traffic and legal restrictions. When they finally surged through the stadium gates, they were chanting "Filumuntu ufesadikiza," meaning "Man is dead but his spirit still lives." [. . .]
The initial reaction of the management was to blame the whole thing on "agitators" and "intimidation." These themes were embodied in a notice put out to the workers by the Coronation management on the day before the strike. It essentially made the following points: (1) that the talk of a strike on the following day was the work of communist agitators; (2) that loyal workers who routinely came to work would be protected from intimidation; (3) that the ringleaders would be severely punished. The notice was angrily rejected by the workers. One of them went so far as to claim, "We would not have gone on strike if this notice had not called us 'Communists.'"[1] The immediate consequence of the clause concerning ringleaders was that workers who had proved themselves, in the course of the strike, to be reasonably articulate and confident were reluctant to coalesce into a readily identifiable

Extracted from *The Durban Strikes* (Durban: Institute of Industrial Education, 1973).

group. Nor were they prepared to assume an ongoing individual prominence. The Coronation notice exemplified a management stance that could be described as threatening. It is within that context that one needs to assess subsequent claims by management and others that African workers, especially in a strike situation, were inchoate and impossible to negotiate with. Despite the "ringleaders will be punished" notice of January 8, the acting general manager of Coronation declared himself, on the evening of the ninth, neither willing nor able "to negotiate with 1,500 workers on a football field,"[2] and insisted that the workers elect a committee. One worker responded: "Our terms are quite clear. We don't need a committee. We need thirty Rand a week." In short, the fear of victimization by employers appears to have been a more pronounced feature of the strike than the much publicized "fear of intimidation."[. . .] It was finally the intervention of a traditional Zulu figure, Paramount Chief Goodwill Zwelithini, which broke the deadlock of the first day of the strike. In an hour-long talk the chief appealed to the workers to return to work and undertook to negotiate with management on their behalf.

The paramount chief's proposals did not elicit a very enthusiastic response from the two thousand workers then gathered on the field. A central reason for this might have been that a decision on their wages would only be made the following Wednesday, one week hence. They felt, as one worker said, that "You cannot extinguish fire by words, but by action," and feared that if they agreed to return before a settlement was reached, the initiative would be lost. The chief's proposals were accepted only after his representative, Prince Sithela Zulu, reminded the workers "that if they could not trust in the Chief's word, this would 'lower the dignity.'"[3][. . .] On Sunday, the fourteenth, an eleven-man wage delegation was elected by the workers. It was headed by Nathaniel Zulu, who had emerged as a prominent spokesman during the strike, despite the possibility of victimization. There were, however, no reports of meetings between management and the full committee. The committee leader was apparantly called to the office of the acting general manager early on Monday, but other members of the committee and the workers in general remained unaware of this move. One presumes, therefore, that workers enjoyed rather limited representation in any bargaining process that did occur. The Coronation management, then, although seriously affected by the strike itself, appears to have acted fairly autonomously in the revision of wage rates.

Nonetheless, the worker body in general indicated its resistance and determination by rejecting the company's first offer, on the Tuesday afternoon, of a 1.50 Rand per week increase. On the next day a second offer of a 2.07 Rand increase (bringing the minimum to 11.50 Rand per week) was grudgingly assented to.

Tight security arrangements accompanied this second offer. The workers were kept isolated on a plant basis and company officials moved from one plant to the next, making their offer. This tactic was obviously designed to prevent the likelihood of another mass rejection on the football field. The officials were escorted by a considerable force of police in land rovers and riot trucks. Although all plants accepted the offer, it was clear that extensive dissatisfaction with the new rates remained.

Although the Coronation workers themselves were relatively isolated in the company compounds, the strike was widely reported in the local press. Banner headlines were accompanied by photographs of the workers massed on the football field, or marching down the road carrying a red flag—for traffic control, rather than as a sign of political allegiance. This strike, with its relatively successful outcome, must have influenced the later events.

Even before it had been resolved, several minor strikes had broken out elsewhere. The first of these was an apparently brief and unsuccessful stoppage at the transport firm of A.J. Keeler on January 10, the morning after the Coronation strike began. This strike was triggered by what the workers considered to be a derisory pay offer of an increase of fifty South African cents per week. The manager blamed the strike on agitators, and the workers were back within forty-five minutes. On the following day a more sustained strike began at the small tea-packing firm of T.W. Beckett and Co. Here about one hundred fifty workers went on strike, demanding an increase of three Rand per week. The management reacted by calling in the police and dismissing all those who refused to return to work. There were no negotiations. According to one of the workers, "We were given ten minutes to make a decision."[4] About one hundred workers decided not to return to work. However, the following Tuesday the management let it be known that they would consider reinstating the dismissed workers, although still at the old pay levels. The managing director issued a press statement in which he said that his company tried to provide good labor conditions and that it had had no inkling that anything was amiss: "I believe that our wages are competitive by prevailing Durban standards, and although we are governed by a wage determination which is three years old, our minimum starting wage is ten Rand compared with the 8.50 Rand stipulated."[5] Most of the workers nevertheless remained out, and finally, on January 25, two weeks after the strike had begun, the firm announced a three Rand per week increase for all workers. Most of the workers were reinstated, but, according to the company, "We took this opportunity to weed out what we considered bad material."

In this dispute it seems to have been the Department of Labour which encouraged the firm to take an initial hard line. According to a press report, it was on the department's advice that the strikers were paid off in the first place.[6] The divisional inspector, G. Jackson, pointed out that the workers could be prosecuted for having deserted their employment.[7] However, in the event, no such action was taken.

While the Beckett strike was in progress, African ships' painters at several firms, including J.H. Akitt and Co. and James Brown and Hamer had also gone on strike. These workers were earning 2.60 Rand per day but claimed that they often only worked three days a week, and so needed an increase of ninety cents in their daily wage. These workers stayed out for several days, but it was not reported whether they finally received an increase. One or more of the companies involved considered the possibility of replacing them with convict labor in order to complete urgent contracts. A spokesman for James Brown and Hamer said, "I don't know who mooted this idea first, but it is worth looking into. We would otherwise have to get white workers, who use sprays— but this work is difficult in windy conditions. It is worth looking into the idea of using convict labour—they are used by the Railways to clean the harbour area."[8] Fortunately for all concerned this idea was taken no further.

Although at this stage there were still only scattered strikes, even these were considered a sufficiently remarkable phenomenon in South Africa to occasion a wide range of comment. Both the Afrikaans Sunday newspaper *Rapport* and the SABC called for improvements in black wages. A number of prominent black and white trade unionists predicted further unrest. Chief Buthelezi attacked low wages and called for full trade-union rights for African workers. He strongly criticized employers who met strikes with dismissals: "Firing people in these circumstances points to the insecurity of black people in general. This kind of insecurity is dangerous because blacks might ultimately ask themselves what have we to lose."[9]

The police also commented on the strikes, and in particular on the allegations that they were the work of agitators. On January 18 the Natal security police head, Colonel Steenkamp, said, "So far we have no evidence to indicate that there is anything organised."[10]

Three days later the *Sunday Express* claimed that senior police officers "had not ruled out" the possibility of overseas involvement in the strikes but also quoted a further denial from Colonel Steenkamp that there was any evidence of organization.

The last of the minor strikes began on Monday, January 22. Two hundred African convoy drivers employed by the Pinetown firm of Motorvia went on strike and organized a picket. They were demanding an increase to forty Rand per week. Management and workers put out conflicting statements about their current wages. Managers claimed that the wage varied between twenty and twenty-five Rand per week, but some of the drivers claimed that they were only guaranteed fifteen Rand per week, and sometimes did not even earn that. The management called in the police, and on the following morning dismissed two hundred and fifty workers after they had refused the first offer made by the company. A further offer was made. The workers remained on the premises through that Tuesday and Wednesday. They made a new demand for a guaranteed fifteen Rand per week and a minimum of five Rand per convoy driven. They also elected a five-man delegation, who lodged a complaint about the firm with the Pinetown Bantu Administration Department. Desultory negotiations continued via the *indunas* (African foremen), and the managers once more threatened to dismiss the already dismissed workers if they did not accept the last pay offer. Many of the workers agreed to return to work, but nearly one hundred were dismissed on the twenty-fifth.

It was on Thursday, January 25, that what had been a trickle of strike action began to turn into a wave when a series of large factories in the Pinetown-New Germany industrial complex were closed down by strikes. The move began at the Frametex textile factory in New Germany, where, according to trade-union officials, there had long been dissatisfaction with wages and conditions. At 8:00 A.M. that morning the workers left their machines and gathered in an open yard in the factory. They were invited by loudspeaker to elect a negotiating committee and return to work pending a settlement. They laughed at this, and refused. Their demand was for twenty Rand per week, in comparison with the five to nine Rand per week that they claimed they were getting at the time. As in most other cases, management and workers made contradictory claims about current wage levels, but it is clear that these workers were receiving particularly low wages. By the following day, Friday, the strike had spread to all the other Frame Group factories in the area and affected about six thousand African workers, as well as many Indian workers.

The workers were offered a small cost-of-living increase but rejected the offer. On Monday there was a mass meeting at which a further offer of increases, ranging from 1.75 to three Rand was made. The workers accepted this and returned to work. Meanwhile, however, the strike had spread to workers at two other large Frame factories, including Natal Canvas and Rubber in Durban itself, and also to several other factories in Pinetown and New Germany.[. . .]

On the thirty-first, work stopped at another major Frame factory, Consolidated Textile Mills (CTM), in the south Durban industrial area of Jacobs-Mobeni. The Department of Labour's Bantu labor officer, Mr. J. Skene, appealed to the workers to return to work. Their negotiating committee was also asked to get them back to work while negotiations were in progress but refused to do so. They sang "Nkosi Sikelele i Afrika," and were finally locked out and sent home, but not before they had encouraged workers at the neighboring Consolidated Fine Spinners and Weavers and Consolidated Woolwashing and Processing Mills (CWPM) to join them. A number of smaller firms also came out on the same day, and as the strike spread even further on Thursday, February 1, the day of the rumored transport boycott, the press gave up the attempt to give detailed coverage of each strike. The *Natal Mercury* printed a list of twenty-nine firms which had been affected by strikes during the month of January.

By this time the strike wave was the major daily news story in nearly all South African newspapers, and it was evident that it could develop into a major confrontation.[. . .] Throughout the first two weeks of February strikes were breaking out and ending all over Durban. On Monday, the fifth, the most tense and dramatic period began when three thousand African workers employed by the Durban Corporation stopped work, affecting road and drain works, the cleaning department, and the electricity department. They were demanding a ten Rand per week increase on an average wage of thirteen Rand. This strike spread rapidly to other corporation departments, involving sixteen thousand workers despite an offer of a two Rand increase made by the corporation on Tuesday morning. In some departments Indian and African workers work in separate gangs, while in other departments they work together, under white overseers. In both cases many Indian workers joined the strike, while others, according to the corporation, were sent home for fear of "intimidation." Although their wage scales are not necessarily the same as those of their African fellow workers, they all get very low wages. In some types of industry, Indian workers do have the right to strike under certain circumstances, but this is not the case in the municipal service. This is classified as an essential service and as such is excluded from those provisions of the Industrial Conciliation Act which permit strikes. This means that both African and Indian workers were acting with equal illegality.

The corporation strike inevitably had the most dramatic impact on the life of the city. Rubbish began to pile up, the grave diggers were on strike, and by Wednesday the market porters were no longer handling goods. The abbatoir also stopped work, and it became clear that the supply of all perishable foods was threatened. White volunteer "black-legs" were also at work in the market, unloading eighty railway truckloads of fresh produce. According to a press report, "Durban's Mayor, accompanied by a number of city Councillors, made an on-the-spot inspection. Also on the scene was a truckload of policemen in camouflage uniforms, swinging batons in one hand and bags of fruit in the other. Striking African workers looked on in amazement as the volunteer workforce turned the market into a scene from My Fair Lady with singing and jokes. Market agencies supplied the volunteer force with beers for their efforts." Meanwhile the corporation was asking the state to provide special services to bring essential food supplies to the city if the stike situation worsened.

By Wednesday there were an estimated thirty thousand workers on strike, including the sixteen thousand municipal workers. It seemed possible that the movement might develop into a general strike of all workers in Durban, and strikes were also beginning to occur in other parts of Natal, such as Pietermaritzburg and Port Shepstone. The possibility of violence also seemed to be increasing. Many bands of municipal workers marched through the streets near the city center, and there were eyewitness reports of minor cases of intimidation. One group stopped a refuse-removal truck and chased the African workers on it. Crowds are also reported to have threatened to burn down the city engineer's labor office if the African clerks there did not stop working. Helicopters were used over the city, apparently to monitor the progress of marching workers. A contingent of riot police in camouflage dress had been flown in from Pretoria on the previous day and were patrolling the industrial areas. Although the police had been on hand at most of the strikes, they had as yet taken no action. On Tuesday the officer in charge, Brigadier T.M. Bisschoff, told a reporter: "The police have nothing whatsoever against people demanding higher wages—provided they do not break the law." He listed four possible offenses: striking; holding a public meeting without a permit; carrying dangerous weapons; and creating a disturbance. However, it was clear that the police did not intend to take any action against strikers, but would confine themselves to attempting to prevent the other offenses. Brigadier Bisschoff also stressed that instructions had been given to use force only if absolutely necessary, and then only the minimum force necessary.[. . .]

Nevertheless, the situation was still explosive. The municipal workers had refused a 15 percent pay increase. The number of individual factories affected was still increasing, and most of the textile workers were still on strike. In the case of the textile workers, there had been a greater degree of coordination than usual, partly because there is one major employer in the industry and partly because this was the only major series of strikes in which a registered (i.e., non-African) trade union intervened to try to resolve the issue. The first mass meeting of striking textile workers had taken place at the Textile Workers' Industrial Union (TWIU) headquarters on the previous Saturday afternoon, February 3. A meeting of three hundred African and Indian workers, representing nearly all the strikers, formulated a joint demand for a five Rand per week increase. One worker told the meeting, "Although I make blankets for Mr. Philip Frame, I can't afford to buy blankets for my children." Another elderly worker claimed, "We are here today because we have tried to meet our employer, but he doesn't want to talk to us." This was confirmed by Mrs. Harriet Bolton, secretary of the TWIU, who said, "He is content just to sit tight and stare the workers out—with tacit government consent. The African workers want to negotiate with him, but he refuses to meet them. Then he refused to see me when I asked for talks."[11]

By Wednesday many of the textile workers had been out for seven days. A new meeting at Bolton Hall, attended by eight hundred workers, reaffirmed the call for five Rand, and one speaker who suggested that they should be willing to accept less was shouted down. But the meeting coincided with a meeting of the Industrial Council for the Textile Industry, at which it became clear that the Frame Group was not willing to increase its initial offer of approximately two Rand. After discussing this further, the mass meeting finally agreed to return to work on the following day.

At the same time the corporation workers were given an ultimatum either to accept a two Rand across-the-board increase or be dismissed. On Thursday nearly all the municipal workers also returned to work, and by Friday it was clear that the strike wave had broken. There were still many minor strikes in progress, particularly in the furniture industry, which were associated with the fact that a new industrial council agreement was being negotiated at the time. Scattered strikes continued into the following week. In March there were a total of fourteen strikes in Natal, involving some six thousand African workers, and strikes continued into 1974 at what would previously have been an unprecedented rate.

Strikes in the Textile Industry

The above account gives the sequence of events but does not give any clear idea as to how individual strikes proceeded. Although the main demand was always for improved wages, there were also frequent complaints about working conditions, fringe benefits, and employment practices. These need to be looked at in some detail. We have mentioned employer reactions briefly, but these also need to be more carefully analyzed. We therefore decided to undertake a more thorough investigation of the strikes in one particular industry. We chose the textile industry for two main reasons. First, the strikes in this industry were of a relatively long duration and played an important part in spreading the strike wave. Second, this was the only industry in which the registered trade union played any role in trying to settle the strikes. Officials of the TWIU were present at most of the key happenings and were able to provide us with much information. The account which follows is based almost entirely on lengthy interviews with these officials. Unless otherwise specified, all the incidents mentioned were reported by them. Of course it is probable that their perceptions of the events differ significantly from management's perceptions, and the reader should bear this in mind. Nevertheless two of the officials are also trained social scientists and are, we think, reliable observers. We also interviewed managers from four textile factories, who cooperated with us fully. These interviews dealt with more general aspects of the situation and are included in our general analysis of employer attitudes.[. . .]

The textile industry in Natal, as elsewhere, is divided into two labor-relations systems: the controlled sector covered by an industrial council which was established before World War II and which has a developed industrial-relations system; and the cotton sector, which is newly established and in which no wage-regulating measure existed at the time of the strikes. It is this sector in particular which has low wages, high labor turnover, and which lacks any communications system between workers and management. Before the Durban strikes took place, the Textile Workers Industrial Union (which represents Indian and Coloured workers) had its members largely in the blanket sector, although its organizer and research officer had recruited members in the cotton sector. Wages in the textile industry are approximately 20 percent lower than those in manufacturing as a whole. The depressed state of wages in the textile industry was particularly acute in Natal, where large sections of the industry were untouched by the trade union.[. . .]

In both sections of the industry in Natal there was very little wage drift at all. Although it is usually argued that the basic wage for weavers, in particular, is of little relevance as it is augmented by bonuses, overtime, and night-shift allowance, it is not difficult to conclude that real wages in the blanket section were in a state of decline. The relative importance of added earnings from bonuses in fact may operate against an actual increase in earnings, as the workers claim that the bonus systems are adjusted downward with every increase in basic wages so as to reduce the final earnings. In this way whatever the increase negotiated by the union, the management could then adjust the production bonus rates accordingly to keep final earnings static.

Worker-management relations were at a low ebb before the February strikes. There are three elements which have to be considered: (1) interworker relationships within each plant; (2) management-worker relations; and (3) union-management relations and the industrial-relations system.

Interworker Relations

Although it is clear that all workers have distinct differences with management, which can be most fruitfully analyzed in class terms, it is also true that racial differences generate tension and that racial attitudes cause division within the working class.

Apparently after the 1949 race riots in Durban, in which tension between the Indian and African communities exploded, the Frame Group decided to employ more African workers. This, at least, is the way the Indian workers see it. The Frame Group provided large-scale employment at low wages and African workers were seen to replace Indian workers at a rapid rate. The high turnover in the textile industry generally, and in the Frame Group in particular, led to African workers, and especially African women, taking a leading role in production. From the laboring jobs,

African workers soon took over virtually all spinning jobs, and then the large proportion of weaving jobs. Indian workers, in this situation, were likely to see African workers undercutting their standards and would try to use the union to enforce conditions which would limit the degree of African participation in the textile industry. Indian workers were, however, so divided among themselves into different factions, and workers spent so much of their time fighting among themselves, and even engaging in court action against union leaders, that the union was unable to fulfill its potential for maintaining "labor standards." Obviously this situation, which lasted until shortly before the last negotiation for a new agreement in 1972, prevented any effective worker action. At this time the total membership of the Natal branch of the Textile Workers Industrial Union was three hundred, and a minority of Indian workers in each plant belonged to the union. A concerted drive shortly before the agreement came into operation brought in about one hundred more members.

One further type of interworker tension is that existing between male and female workers of whatever race. An award made by the Industrial Tribunal before the agreement which expired in 1972 laid down a 20 percent lower wage for women workers. The difference in wages between men and women could be a source of dissension among workers.[. . .]

Management-Worker Relations

According to union officials, workers in the Frame Group have always disliked and even hated their managers. Workers had very little respect for any managers, despite the usual situation among any labor force where workers are highly perceptive in their appraisal of the individual qualities of particular managers. The hostility which existed between workers and management did not necessarily lead to a consistently militant policy on the part of leading workers and the union, but rather toward a pathetic grievance complex, with workers reciting endlessly how this was the worst management they had ever come across. The hopelessness and helplessness of the workers, so evident to an outsider, were really indications of bottled-up hatred. This "it can't be helped" attitude toward affairs inside the factory also led to indifference about the administration of the union, a subject which came to a head toward the end of 1972.

Union-Management Relations

Management had been openly contemptuous of the union following a lengthy period of mismanagement and maladministration and an open loss of confidence by the members in the union's key personnel.

Wages in the heavy section of the industry are laid down by an Industrial Council on which there is equal representation from union and management. A regional council for each province exists. All matters relating to the problems of workers in Natal should be aired in the regional council. According to TWIU officials, this rarely happened in practice. They complain that meetings of the regional council were few and far between, and conciliation in the spirit of the Industrial Conciliation Act was very difficult, with a secretary of the Industrial Council taking the view that disputes could only exist over matters prescribed in the agreement.[. . .] The union had been seen by workers and management as peripheral to the real determination of wages and working conditions in the plants. Union leadership was seen as discredited by management. In matters of real conflict the union had been totally ignored by management in attempting to settle disputes.

Negotiations

In July 1972 the textile union negotiated with the National Association of Textile Manufacturers for a new agreement. These negotiations were seen by the workers as a way of restoring their lost earning power, and the demands which were made by the union, even in its weak state, reflected the aspirations of the textile workers, who had participated in the formation of demands to a greater extent than in previous negotiations.

The union made the following demands: (1) a 60 percent increase over three years; (2) an increase in bonus rates; (3) three weeks' paid holidays; (4) all public holidays to be paid holidays; (5) an increase in overtime rates from time and a third to time and a half; (6) a forty-two-hour week; (7) a holiday bonus; and (8) the removal of wage discrimination against women.

The employers offered, in response, a 20 percent wage increase for laborers, 15 percent for qualified spinners, and 10 percent for qualified weavers, to be spread over three years. Employers also proposed that women should be paid 25 percent less than men instead of the prevailing 20 percent.

Negotiations between the trade-union delegates to the Industrial Council and the Textile Manufacturers Association broke down, and the dispute was referred to the minister of labor to appoint an arbitrator.[. . .] Following the breakdown of negotiations, all parties in the Industrial Council were confused about whether the minister of labor should have been approached to appoint an arbitrator. It was feared that an agreement dictated by the tribunal would have the same status as a wage-board determination and so would displace the Industrial Council. Eventually the matter was considered by the Industrial Tribunal on June 21, 1972. The employers made it quite clear that, in their view, if the Industrial Tribunal made a ruling in terms of the Industrial Conciliation Act, the Industrial Council would then have no reason for continued existence. This threat was a primary reason for the union's calling off the arbitration.

The wage increases originally offered by the employers were eventually accepted by the union and written into the new agreement, although the workers were bitterly disappointed that the arbitration was not pursued. The cautious optimism that prevailed before the arbitration ("Once they see how bad things are, they will have to give us a good increase") disintegrated. The atmosphere of bitterness and disillusion laid the basis for the conflict in February 1973.[. . .] The cotton workers came out on strike on Thursday, January 25, 1973, starting in the massive Frametex plant. Then followed the other cotton mills adjacent to Frametex in quick succession: Seltex, Nortex, Pinetex, and Natal Knitting Mills on the following day, Friday.

On Friday morning at Consolidated Woolwashing and Processing Mills (CWPM) in Pinetown, where the large bulk of the workers are women rag sorters, an organizer and Mrs. Bolton, secretary of the Natal branch of the Textile Workers' Industrial Union, addressed the workers on the necessity of making their demands known through the union and, if possible, then negotiating through the union. By this time it was hoped the atmosphere of labor unrest might have awakened management to the necessity for change and that union recognition might be secured at the same time. The plant manager refused to discuss the issues when approached and said he was too busy.

A letter outlining some of the workers' grievances was then written to the firm and the Industrial Council. In the letter the following demands of the workers were conveyed to the management: (1) an immediate increase of one Rand per week; (2) the introduction of an adequate long-service bonus; (3) a drastic reduction in the qualifying period for rag sorters; (4) an end to clocking out to see the doctor; (5) that the doctor come at a definite time each day; (6) that the practice of women workers having to see the manager before being able to see the doctor be stopped; (7) that the workers not be forced to report to the factory when sick; (8) that the practice of workers being punished by being laid off without being fired be stopped; (9) that notice pay be paid for workers who were dismissed; (10) that the workers be provided with adequate notice of overtime; (11) that the clock cards of workers not be taken from the factory and kept at the residence of the manager; (12) that the company ensure that proper transport be provided for workers; (13) that the workers' consent for being searched be required; (14) that the workers be allowed to leave the factory immediately after clocking out; (15) that the practice of keeping workers standing outside the factory if they were slightly late be stopped.

On Friday evening two senior officials of the TWIU left for a labor conference in Cape Town, leaving the affairs of the union in the hands of a recently appointed organizer. On Monday, January 29, 1973, there was not one Frame factory in operation in Natal. Consolidated Woolwashing and Processing Mills came out on strike as expected. The union organizer tried to negotiate with management, but this offer was refused, and the workers remained outside. The secretary of the Industrial Council had received the letter from the union but decided that since the agreement had not been violated by the management no "dispute" existed, and therefore the Industrial Council would have nothing to do with the issue. At the cotton mills in Pinetown the strikes continued, although in this case increases of between 1.75 Rand and 2.50 Rand a week were offered to the workers. By now there were about eight thousand textile workers on strike.

On Wednesday, January 31, the officials of the TWIU were at the factories. At CWPM the workers were milling around outside. The Indian and African women were grouped together on one side of the gate, and the African and Indian men grouped separately on the other. The TWIU officials spoke to their members about the possibility of workers returning to work and about the degree of unity behind the demands. Shortly before the usual opening time (6:45 A.M.), the gate of the factory was opened, and the workers were addressed by a new manager, who offered wage increases. He told the workers that the company would employ those workers who accepted the offer, and the others would be fired. The women workers made for the gate, and the men followed. At CWPM the strike was over. During this scene the union officials were completely ignored.

On Tuesday, January 30, the Consolidated Textile Mill plant (CTM) in Jacobs, the headquarters of the Frame Group, had come out on strike. The workers demanded up to thirty Rand a week. In this case the union was caught by surprise, and the new organizer had to make rapid contact with the TWIU shop stewards to find out the feelings of the workers. By this time he realized that an emergency situation existed in the textile industry and telephoned the officials of the Natal branch to return from Cape Town.

At CTM the strikers were in an angry mood. On Tuesday, January 30, the police had been called and had staged a show of strength. Despite all attempts to reach the Frame management, communications between the union officials and management were negligible. Since the secretary of the Industrial Council had refused to accept that a dispute existed, the machinery for arbitration could not be used.

The main complaint of the workers was the low level of wages in the Frame Group in comparison with the wages paid by firms in the surrounding area. The workers stressed, in particular, the rapid rise in the cost of living and gave specific examples, particularly of increased transport costs. Apart from their grievances in connection with lower wages, the weavers complained that they were being exploited by the piece-rate system in the plant, which was changed arbitrarily by the management. They felt that they had not really had an increase for decades, as the increase in basic wages was always offset by adjustments in the piece-rate system. Another grievance was that they were required to arrive much earlier than the starting time so that they could oil the looms and get the yarn for the day's production. If a worker was slightly late, they maintained, the loom was allocated to another worker, and the first was told to go home, even if there was some legitimate reason for being late. It was also said that the yarn supplied for the production of blankets was inferior and that with frequent stoppages it was impossible to make sufficient blankets to benefit from piece rates. A more general discontent was connected with the sick-benefit society. Membership in this society was a condition of service, and each week, irrespective of earnings during that week, deductions were made from the wages of the workers. When the workers wished to see the doctor, they had to clock out and lose time-wages, and then stand in long queues for medical attention. Numerous complaints about this system by the union had not changed the system, the workers said. It was alleged that by setting up the sick-benefit society the company avoided paying the full two weeks' sick pay required in section 21A of the Factories Act.

The union continued to press for some response from management, but without success. Mr. Frame was in Rhodesia, and the managers in charge refused to make any decision in his absence. On Thursday, February 1, however, the company made a press statement offering increased wages on condition the workers returned to work. Increases of one to two and a half Rand were offered to the workers, differing according to length of service and grade of work. The spinners and laborers were offered the higher increases. The workers rejected these wage proposals. A meeting of all textile workers was held at Bolton Hall, the new headquarters of the TWIU on that Thursday, and the wage proposals were rejected decisively. It was resolved to continue the strike.

Management then agreed to bring forward an Industrial Council meeting scheduled for Wednesday, February 7, and the TWIU hoped that at this meeting management would increase its wage offer and agree to a revision of the agreement, which was already irrelevant in Natal, in the light of wage increases offered by the employers. The Industrial Council meeting had, however, been called to consider the exemptions requested by the Frame Group for their mills in Harrismith and East London which would allow the firm to pay wages considerably lower than the recently negotiated national increase because the mills were situated in "border areas." The discussion about this and other matters dragged on, while the officials were aware that a meeting of workers scheduled for noon would be awaiting their return. When eventually the "current situation" was reached in the meeting, management was obdurate. No further offers could be made above those already made, management said.

At a mass meeting at Bolton Hall the union explained the position. The workers were not impressed: they attacked the agreement, which had held them down to low wages and made their rejection of the wage offer explicit. "The cost of living has gone so high I cannot afford to buy the blankets I make," said one worker. "We are not children, we are not on strike. We are asking for the managers to listen to our problems, then we will go back to work," said another worker. Finally, however, the workers had to face the fact that they were experiencing problems maintaining unity. On this, the seventh day of the strike, some workers were beginning to express their fear of losing their jobs. By this time also, some of the thrust of mass action in Durban had been blunted by other workers returning to work. After a long discussion the general secretary of the TWIU was asked to ring the Frame Group management to see whether there had been any change in their offer. After telling the management how obdurate the workers were in demanding increases above the offer of the managers, the general secretary was offered a further slight concession: one-day strike pay would be paid by the Frame Group if the workers returned to work on the following day, and no workers would be fired. With these two points, he returned to the meeting and advised the workers to return to work. A rather dispirited, but not defeated, group of textile workers eventually accepted that they would have to go back to work because it would be difficult to maintain unity much longer.[. . .]

Results

In some firms the workers went back without any concrete gains, but in most they won wage increases, usually of between 1.50 to 2.50 Rand per week. In many firms where there were no strikes, wages were also increased to avoid possible trouble. These increases usually applied across the board to all African, Indian, and Coloured workers, whether they had struck or not. It is clear, from the few cases in which details are available, that the workers had a wide range of grievances apart from low wages, but it is much more difficult to know whether these have also been remedied. Some of these grievances relate to easily removable points of friction, but many others are intimately related to the problem of controlling the work force, and probably remain unsolved. For the workers the other main achievement of the strike is less tangible but perhaps even more important: it is a sense of solidarity and potential power.

Notes

1. *Daily News* (Durban), January 9, 1973.
2. *Natal Mercury* (Durban), January 11, 1973.
3. Ibid.
4. *Rand Daily Mail* (Johannesburg), January 12, 1973.
5. Ibid., January 16, 1973.
6. Ibid., January 25, 1973.
7. Ibid., January 13, 1973.
8. *Daily News* (Durban), January 16, 1973.
9. *Sunday Times* (Johannesburg), January 14, 1973.
10. *Natal Mercury* (Durban), January 16, 1973.
11. *Sunday Tribune* (Durban), January 4, 1973.

Industrial Protest in Nigeria

Adrian Peace

Introduction

Despite the lack of detailed empirical studies of industrial workers in sub-Saharan Africa, commentaries on new forms of social stratification have attempted to place the industrial labor force in its appropriate position vis-à-vis other socioeconomic groups. Such commentaries have tended to be impressionistic, but together they testify to the economic, social, and political significance of this highly strategic population of wage earners in predominantly agrarian societies.[1]

Several accounts have rightly noted that African industrial workers have failed to develop a sustained organizational base and concerted strategies with which to increase their share of scarce resources, although they are far better placed to do so than other groups.[2]

Industrial plants are generally concentrated in a few urban centers, facilitating recognition of, and cooperation in support of, shared economic interests. Industrial employment creams off the educated and ambitious rural youth who provide potential leaders and cadres for the labor movement. Under colonial rule, a national system of wage negotiation was developed, and this came to be applied to both the public and private sectors, thus linking the welfare of all wage earners to the modus operandi of the political class. Furthermore, feelings of relative deprivation are heightened in the urban areas since the ruling elites are urban dwellers par excellence and flagrantly display their material wealth.[3]

The most important factors of all in promoting a political consciousness among workers are the clear division of labor in the industrial system and the workers' distinctive relationship to the mode of production. The division between those who own the

Reprinted from E. de Kadt and G. Williams, eds., *Sociology and Development* (London: Tavistock Publications, 1974), pp.141-67, with permission of the author and publisher. The author thanks Peter Lloyd and Gavin Williams, whose detailed criticisms have always proved invaluable at all stages of his research. The research upon which this article was based was financed by a grant made by the Social Science Research Council (UK).

means of production and those who merely sell their labor power is unparalleled in other areas of African economic life. In Marxist terms, the Nigerian industrial worker is a proletarian. As a member of a propertyless, contractual labor force the worker's class situation is, in this respect, essentially the same as that of British or American counterparts. Workers' situations contrast sharply with those of farmers and entrepreneurs, the two largest occupational categories in Nigeria today.

The central problem is not then the existence (or otherwise) of these new economic class relationships, but the extent to which they form the basis for expressions of class consciousness—social action that acknowledges common economic interests among those who share the same relationship to the mode of production, and takes account of the behavior of other social classes to whose interests their own are fundamentally opposed.

Many reasons have been given for the failure of wage earners in developing countries like Nigeria to organize themselves into powerful labor movements. During the colonial period, industrial workers were alleged to be "target workers," whose lack of "commitment" to industrial employment was held to stand in the way of the articulation of class interests. Today the virtual opposite is being promoted. Wage earners are held to constitute a "labor aristocracy" enjoying the inheritance of colonial rule and with vested interests in the status quo.[4] On the structural level, tribal organization not only serves as the basis of urban social relationships but is also said to carry over into class institutions and proves divisive within the trade-union movement.[5] On the cultural level, elements of the value systems of the open-mobility system characteristic of certain traditional African societies are said to continue to operate in the new urban-industrial context, preventing the emergence of a distinct lower-class consciousness.[6]

The cumulative effect of these and other distinctive factors is held to make gradual and sustained mobilization of class consciousness exceptionally difficult. Industrial action is likely to take the form of spontaneous, disorganized protests directed against particular injustices and deprivations, which can be broken by a show of force or slight political maneuver.[7]

Such interpretations are numerous and cannot be fully considered here. Suffice it to say that their applicability to workers and unions at Ikeja, the subject of this paper, is marginal. What these interpretations share is a common failure to ask what workers actually *do* and what interpretations they put on their actions. Here I will examine the development of a particular conflict situation in order to examine the structure of class relationships and to show how the workers' actions can be interpreted as expressions of class consciousness.

The Ikeja Industrial Estate
and the Development of Industrial Relations

The Ikeja Industrial Estate is situated some ten miles north of Lagos. On the estate some fifty factories provide employment for roughly twenty thousand workers, predominantly Yoruba from the Western State, but with some from the Midwest and the Eastern states. Expatriate influence is much in evidence, and the casual observer notes immediately the names of well-known European companies. The range of goods is wide: building materials, textiles, paints, rubber products, beer, cocoa, pharmaceuticals, enamelware, and footwear, to mention the most important.

The estate was developed in the late 1950s and early 1960s by the regional government at Ibadan when Ikeja fell within the Western Region. Since indigenous businessmen at that time lacked the finances to establish capital-intensive plants on the scale anticipated by the Western Region government, expatriate capital and technology have dominated the estate from the very beginning. On the eve of independence, such major colonialist firms as the United Africa Company were undergoing substantial restructuring, including the change from imperialist traffic, based on the export of primary produce and consumption goods, to manufacturing and industrial enterprise. The heaviest capital investment thus comes from companies based in the advanced industrial societies of the Western world.[8]

The government's role has been essentially promotional of the intensive utilization of capital, plant, and technical expertise, attempting to minimize difficulties and costs of an internal politico-economic nature, especially those relating to cheap wage labor.

The federal government has also done little to regulate industrial-relations procedure. The major determinant of formally constituted bargaining procedures between managements and workers has been the capital-intensive technology imported from advanced industrial societies. The costs of building new factory shells and developing, importing, and installing modern machinery were exceptionally high and, as in the case of the first United Africa Company firms, involved the transfer of substantial capital resources from long-established areas of profit accumulation. Factories operating immediately after independence were test cases for the new imperialism, and future investment would be greatly inhibited by low profit returns due to loss of production through perpetual labor disputes. Expatriate managers have therefore had considerable incentive to promote house unions within their factories and to formalize their relationships with workers.

On the other side, encouraged by relatively high wages and good conditions of service, employees from precisely those sectors of the wage-earning economy in which colonial rulers had promoted industrial relations on the British model (such as the Railway Corporation or the Ports Authority) were the first to organize their less experienced co-workers. An added feature was the established tradition of paternalism among expatriate managers reared in the major companies of the colonial era, a paternalism that today contrasts all the more strongly with nonpaternalistic exploitation by Lebanese, Indian, and Syrian companies. The latter are small-scale plants, with a low technological base, for the assembly of electrical equipment and the like. Workers can be trained within the space of a few days to maximum output levels. Those who attempt to form unions are often replaced at will by docile "applicants" ever available in Lagos and prepared to accept the lowest wages and worst working conditions without protest.

Ultimately, however, the strength of unionism depends on the nature of the labor force. Migration to the metropolitan area from Yorubaland and beyond is a highly selective process drawing on the young, educated population of the towns and villages. Factories generally recruit workers in their late teens and twenties with primary six or modern school education. At this stage their education is complete but limited. The shop-floor worker, with little chance of promotion to highly skilled or supervisory work on high wages, sees such employment as a means to accumulating sufficient capital for the critical transition to the role of entrepreneur.

We can briefly conceptualize the cognitive map of the young factory worker in the following terms. On the one hand, the factory situation provides regular employment and steady income, part of which the worker can save. But, essentially, it is a *closed*-mobility system. Well-paid white-collar and supervisory posts are out of the worker's reach, for these are the preserve of those with qualifications and training gained before entering industrial employment. Improvements in economic standing are achieved by negotiated wage increases or by moving to a new firm offering slightly higher wages. Workers need the union to act as a bargaining force in order to shorten their time as wage earners, to stave off rampant inflation in the urban center, and thus keep their rate of saving steady.

On the other hand, a combination of experience in the established Yoruba township and the new environment of the Lagos suburb, Ikeja or Agege townships, points to the *open* mobility of the entrepreneur, the independent. The low economic return from farming leads to an increased awareness in the established towns of the economic rewards and high status accruing to the trader, transporter, or businessman. And in the new urban situation, too, such impressions are reinforced by workers' day-to-day experiences in centers such as Agege township adjacent to the Ikeja Estate, where wealth, prestige, and local political influence are the preserve of the uneducated and semiliterate transporter, trader, garage owner, and general provisions store owner. It is the successful independent, not the industrial manager or civil servant, alongside whom the wage earner lives and establishes interpersonal relationships, who is the key reference point in the cognitive map of the industrial employee, and is the one with whom the worker can most clearly identify.

The most important consequence of this instrumental approach to industrial employment is high attachment to trade unions where they exist. The success or otherwise of the union determines the individual's chances of achieving the virtually universal goal of entrepreneurship beyond the confines of the factory. This is increasingly marked where low wages and the rocketing cost of living force workers to stay in wage-earning employment considerably longer than they initially anticipate on first migrating to the new urban-industrial context. Notwithstanding the almost universal desire to leave the factory, voluntary resignation rates are very low, and the labor force at Ikeja is becoming increasingly stabilized.

Thus, where unions do exist in the large factories at Ikeja, even though they are limited to individual companies, workers are vitally concerned about the success of negotiations with management and firm in supporting their leaders. Workers have arrived at an accommodation with the existing productive relationships and the structured inequalities arising therefrom.[9]

Strike action and lockouts are employed infrequently, although they are regarded as legitimate tactics when other channels have broken down. But where the formal negotiating procedure is broken on one or both sides, then the value system, which legitimates those procedures, is itself under attack and may be in danger of rejection. Implicitly, if not explicitly, such a rejection of established procedures illustrates dissatisfaction with the degree of social inequality in society at large.

The Immediate Political Background:
The Adebo Commission and the Roots of Conflict

With the end of the civil war in January 1970, the Federal Military Government (FMG) turned its attention to economic and social problems exacerbated by the extended war effort. In particular, inflation was causing acute concern in some areas. In July 1970 the government responded to the situation by establishing the Salaries and Wages Review Commission, under the distinguished chairmanship of Chief Simeon Adebo. Its terms of reference limited it formally to the review of public-sector incomes,[10] but the recommendations of previous commissions had invariably been followed by private companies.

The setting up of the Adebo Commission raised the workers' hopes of economic improvement for a number of reasons. Chief Adebo and other members of the commission, unlike many prominent ex-politicians still in powerful positions, had not compromised their reputations in such a way as to detract from the objective and apolitical spirit their roles demanded. Their concern for thorough investigation and amenability to all shades of opinion quickly became apparent. Parallels were quickly drawn between the Adebo Commission and the Morgan Commission of 1964, which had not only recommended substantial wage increases but, in its minority reports, had been severely critical of the increasing gap between the rich and the poor and of the failure of the political class to throw off the huge wage differentials of the colonial era.[11] The censorious tone of the commission, and the minimum wage levels proposed, had thrown the civilian government into such confusion that, by refusing to publish the report, a fourteen-day general strike had been precipitated, which paralyzed the whole country.[12] Certainly at Ikeja the general strike contributed substantially to the demand by workers for formal recognition of their right to form trade unions.

Only a handful of union leaders at Ikeja attempted to make a direct contribution to the commission's inquiries, and did so through the United Committee of Central Labour Organizations (UCCLO). The customary shortcomings of "national" leaders of the labor movement were, however, quickly made as manifest as ever. In a lengthy memorandum to the Adebo Commission, UCCLO members calculated the minimum living wage of the average worker with a wife and child as being £116 5s. 8d. per month![13] Although they cut this to an "irreducible" £48. 10s., their stand was generally dismissed as attractive but preposterous. UCCLO's principal contribution was the call for an interim award, which caught the popular imagination. The commission again demonstrated its sensitivity to public opinion, cut short its tour of the twelve states, and presented its first report to the FMG in Lagos.

The principal recommendation of the first report (several were planned) was an interim award of 1s. 7d. per day for daily-paid workers and £2 per month for wage and salary earners.[14] This cost-of-living allowance *(cola)* applied to all workers earning less than £500 per annum; those earning between £500 and £524 would receive increments to raise them to £524. All awards were to be backdated to April 1, 1970, nine months in all. The award was thus relevant to the vast majority of Ikeja workers, since most received between £10 and £25 per month. Only a very small minority of highly skilled technicians and experienced administrative employees fell outside the upper limits stipulated in the report.

The *cola* award was given specifically in recognition of the prevailing inflationary situation. As Adebo expressed it in the report: "In the circumstances, the award we feel able to recommend at this time is aimed only at relieving *intolerable suffering at or near the bottom of* the wage and salary levels" (emphasis theirs). As such it would be taken into account when the more general award to be given later was recommended.

On the general economic situation, the effects of the civil war, and the sacrifices which this had required, Adebo commented:

> Such sacrifice would be easiest to bear, however, if it was seen to fall equitably on all sections of the population such that the least sacrifice was made by those in the lowest income group. From some of the representations made to us, it is clear not only that there is intolerable suffering at the bottom of the income scale because of the rise in the cost of living, but also *that suffering is made even more intolerable by manifestations of affluence and wasteful expenditure which cannot be explained on the basis of visible and legitimate means of income.* (Emphasis theirs)

The immediate public response to the first report, which was exceptionally well publicized throughout the mass media, was favorable indeed. Further improvements were promised for the future, and Ikeja workers could look forward to nine months backdated pay—almost two weeks wages for those just within the maximum limit of the award, around two months for those on the lowest income levels.

Clearly, the commission planned to ameliorate conditions within the existing structure rather than suggest radical changes to the structure itself. Its strategy was one of accommodation at the national level in the same way that the organization of industrial relations at Ikeja has sought to promote accommodation at the local level. Only five days after the award was announced, circumstances changed drastically.

Following a meeting with the Nigerian Employers' Consultative Association (NECA), an organization dominated by the major expatriate concerns in industry and manufacturing, Chief Enahoro, the federal commissioner for labor and a long-prominent member of the political class, announced a significant qualification to the quite universal recommendations made by Adebo himself. NECA had argued that some of its members had made substantial wage increases since 1964; they could not be expected to pay the same increments now as companies that had paid none at all over the past six years, when minimum wage rates had last been laid down. In recognition of this "injustice" Enahoro announced that where companies in the private sector had made wage adjustments since 1964 *on the basis of the cost of living,* which were equal to, or in excess of, the *cola* award, such companies did not have to pay the Adebo allowance; where increases had been made but were less than the allowance, companies were expected to make up the balance; where there had been no such increase in wages, the full *cola* had to be paid.

Among Ikeja workers a general uncertainty prevailed on the subject of Enahoro's qualification. Details of management–house-union negotiations were rarely known. But one worker, sitting in an Agege bar with friends the same evening, expressed a widely held view: "Why is everyone surprised at what happened? This is the government at work and Enahoro used to be a politician for many years, and you know what that means. Nothing goes for nothing in Nigeria!"

While Lebanese, Indian, and Chinese companies at Ikeja paying the minimum wage rates had to agree to pay *cola* immediately, in several European companies managements and unions were faced with the onus of establishing the influence of the cost of living in up to six years of joint negotiation. This was exceptionally difficult, for management often bargained on the basis of one set of considerations (e.g., the introduction of new job classifications and re-allocation of the labor force), while the union bargained on others (from the cost of living to making daily-paid workers permanent).

Two weeks passed. Managements in different factories exchanged ideas between themselves and NECA on their possible stands, and union leaders conferred on future strategy—especially in the light of Decree 53, which, with the country in a state of emergency, forbade strike action or incitement to strike. Having covered the roots of the conflict, I turn to the sequence of events in two particular companies.

A Case Study of Conflict in a Textile Company

Shortly after Enahoro's statement, J.O., the house-union president, met the factory's personnel manager, who simply told him that management had not yet made a decision on the payment of *cola*. Despite repeated efforts, no clearer response was forthcoming, and so after some two and a half weeks, the union executive called a meeting in a local hotel. In a company of over three thousand workers divided between three shifts, comprehensive communication with the workers was difficult; general meetings were called when necessary. The core leadership was exceptionally popular, having ousted a corrupt and inefficient executive two years previously and won two substantial all-round increments. J.O. was known at Ikeja as a dedicated and steadfast president, a well-earned reputation.

Although only about two hundred workers attended the meeting, a lively debate was engaged. J.O., after filling in the background, complained that management was dragging its feet over a decision, aided by government procrastination. He had called a meeting because "the executive is only the voice of the workers." He wished to prepare for the management's decision. He felt that he had been correct to follow established procedure, despite management's tardiness. Now he was looking for a mandate from the workers to continue in this vein but, as always when he had been in power, he would take directions from the workers themselves.

Eight workers in all rose from the floor to congratulate J.O. on his "reasoned" approach. Management was always loathe to pay out money, said one worker, but J.O. had won increases for all workers nevertheless, and had not sold them out. If he felt that this was the right course, then he should continue. Other workers voiced much the same opinion. However, as the meeting drew to a close, M.L. stood up. He was a man well known for speaking his mind at such meetings, despite his limited English, the language of such formal meetings. He himself, he said, felt more direct action was required "to push the management forward and give us *cola*." Some workers in his section wanted to strike, but there were too many like himself who respected J.O. highly. "Every worker in this company follows you alone, and even if you walk out of the compound and leave just the big men (i.e., the management) there, we will follow immediately. Government and management are out to cheat the workers every time so we must stand behind our leaders." After shouts of approval, the meeting closed.

It was clear from this, and other scattered informal meetings, that the established negotiation procedure was generally favored. But although J.O. received the mandate he sought, the limitations on such negotiations were becoming clear. J.O. privately admitted that he had expected the issue of more direct action to come up, but the possibility of government informers (a legacy of colonial rule) at the meeting had limited his public pronunciation on the issue. Now he felt that workers were satisfied with his position, and during the next four days he made several representations to the management but met with the same response. Workers became increasingly impatient, but the established framework continued to hold.

On the fourth day after the meeting, a Thursday, as workers on the morning shift arrived, they saw police on guard outside the sheet-metal factory opposite. It quickly became common knowledge that there, on the previous evening, management had announced its refusal to pay *cola*. During the night shift there had been a complete sitdown strike until the police cleared the factory of workers. As the morning shift in the textile company got under way, workers in the dye house ceased work. They walked around the factory and encouraged others to down tools. Workers gradually drifted into the open factory compound and assembled there in small groups.

At this point, the unpopular personnel manager in charge of negotiations over *cola* arrived. As he left his car, he was abused and beaten up by a group of young workers. Several elderly employees and security men intervened, but as other managers entered the factory compound, they too were subjected to threats, and a decision was made to call the police. Before their appearance, J.O. entered and made a short speech. Workers could now return to their sections, he said, "for now the management know we mean business and will listen to the executive with well-opened ears." Production began again as members of the executive counseled patience.

But as the afternoon shift crossed with the morning contingent, several hundred workers stood around discussing the morning's events. J.O. again addressed the workers and allowed a senior manager to speak as the police entered the compound. Scarcely had he pointed out that management were still engaged in discussion with the Ministry of Labour than a chant of "No work, pay us *cola* now" started. At this, police armed with clubs and dogs began to clear the compound. Several workers were beaten, while the majority fled through the main gate or climbed over the compound perimeter. After discussions with police, the management declared a lockout for that day. As workers arrived at the factory the same evening and the following morning, to hear of the latest developments from the union leaders, fighting broke out with police as they tried to disperse the peaceful crowds of several hundred workers and observers.

The following morning J.O., members of his own executive, and leaders from other companies in which similar protests had occurred were called to the office of the commissioner of police in Lagos. He read to them Decree 53, indicating that under this he could imprison them for leading strike action. The leaders protested. The disputes were not of their creation. Indeed they had done all they could to prevent such disturbances, but the workers would not listen. He pointed out that, nevertheless, unless they brought the workers back into the factories, they would be prosecuted under the decree.

In itself, the threat had marginal impact. But when the union leaders returned to the textile factory, they effected a compromise with the management. Their respective cases would be submitted to the commissioner for labor, and management would accept his decision as final. Having studied the previous agreements, management anticipated that it would have to pay. This, however, should not be regarded as a guarantee: only the commissioner's judgment would be accepted. J.O. accepted this and decided to bring the workers back to the factory the same evening. The following day was payday, so the workers should be amenable to his instruction. In addition, during the course of the meeting, management had suggested that the executive had lost the respect of its followers and had allowed anarchy to prevail, a taunt which, although inaccurate, struck home.

As the night-shift workers assembled to hear of the union's progress, J.O. was present to address them. He felt confident now, he said, that the award would be paid because "workers have shown their power to the management." It was only a question of time: workers should enter the factory and resume production. This was quietly received, and there was general compliance. At this point, a management representative called J.O. aside. When he returned to the platform, he put the management's request that each worker should sign a guarantee against damaging company property.

Immediately after this was announced to the three hundred or so workers present, they began to shout "No work, all go home!" and many workers rushed away. A majority remained, but when K.L., a popular worker, pointed out that such a demand insulted not only the workers but the union too—"If the union says production should begin then that by itself should be enough for the managers"—everyone dispersed homeward.

Despite the fact that the following morning, Saturday, was payday, only a handful of workers arrived, and, after receiving their pay, were sent home. The vast majority of workers had evidently decided to stay at home over the weekend. J.O. had been unable to announce a general meeting before the Friday night meeting had dispersed, and, as a result, only sixty workers arrived on Sunday. J.O. pointed out that success was now in sight, for workers and union leaders had cooperated well throughout. Though management was "certain" to pay *cola*, they were cunning, especially when near defeat. The only way in which workers could avoid termination for going on strike was to follow the letter of the law.

Several workers exhorted the assembly to follow J.O. But K.L. brought the meeting to a close by pointing out that now, following the workers' major contribution, their protest had reached the point at which the expertise of the executive around the bargaining table *had* to be brought once again into play: "We are all on the point of success. . . . The management will surely have to pay us all *cola* for we have all done a good job."

On the Monday morning no demand for workers' signatures was forthcoming from the management. Although the shift was incomplete, production started. Within two days the full labor complement had returned, and four days later the management agreed to pay *cola* to all the workers, albeit without approval from the Ministry of Labour.

This completes the account of events in the one company in which I have concentrated on the changing balance of power between the union, the management, and the workers.[15][. . .]

Class Relationships and Class Consciousness

Quite obviously, the essential outcome of events described here was that the Ikeja workers gained through their collective action the Adebo award which a combination of management and government had attempted to deny them. But considering the manner in which the government took away with one hand that which had been given by the other, some form of protest appeared fairly inevitable. This being the case, can one legitimately term the action described here as an expression of class consciousness, which, as Lloyd points out "[implies] consciousness of the special interests of the class and activity directed towards preserving these interests"?[16]

Objectively, this was certainly so. The Adebo award was applicable to all wage earners in the public and private sectors, indicating them to be a special case; the Enahoro qualification then singled out workers within the private sector, defining their special interests even more clearly. Again, strike action originated on the shop floor among those workers on the lowest wage rates in their respective companies and with most to gain by taking a stand. But to what extent did the workers themselves see their action in these terms?

The most immediate judgments centered on the £2 award, but as the following comment shows, behind this specific issue lay a number of other grievances:

> This is our right, the £2 per month increase and we shall fight for it to the end. What does the government think it can do to us, the workers and the other poor people? . . . We have paid new taxes, we have paid NPF[17] and in the war we paid extra taxes to fight the Biafrans. Then there are all the duties to the government on imports so that the costs go up again. The war has ended, but how would we know when there has been no improvement for us? (A young unmarried worker from Ibadan, aged 25 and earning about £15 per month)

At one level, then, the protest was set against the background of the civil war and the manner in which the lower strata had borne its brunt, a fact recognized by Adebo himself. At another level, both the *cola* payment and postwar conditions were viewed in the context of economic and social inequalities rooted in the colonial experience but ingrained and cultivated throughout the period of independence:

> All the prices are going up and we can do nothing. . . . Let us say this man is a director, you are a manager, and I am a worker. We all go to the same market and our wives buy side by side. But the manager and the director, they do not feel anything at all. They have free houses and cars and their children go to good schools paid for by their companies. But I, the worker, I have scarcely enough money to pay my bus fare. From my house on Lagos Island near Tinabu is 3s. each day. A bottle of palm wine or two is 2s. and

chop from the petty trader here 2s. Then there is the rent for my one room which is £5 10s. each month. . . . And the manager and director have their big fine houses *free!* All we want is £2! (A junior supervisor earning £27 per month, aged 35 with five children)

And with a somewhat different emphasis on the present, workers viewed the *cola* issue as a clear illustration of the manner in which members of the political class, the managerial class, and other elites conspired to retain their monopoly of material rewards in Nigerian society, coming to terms among themselves to exploit the masses further:

> These big guns in Lagos, they are not interested in what happened to us, the laborers. The European managers have refused to give us the £2 owed to us, and the big men help them in this matter. Some of them used to be poor men, laborers, as we are now. But now they are at the top, they are *ogas* ("chiefs" or "big men") [and] our conditions are the same as ever. . . . What does this £2 mean to a top government officer or an Ikeja manager? Some of them go out for the night with their wives and spend £50, £100, even £500 on a ceremony. We want only this £2, a miserable sum, and we workers have the power and strength in our hands. (Newly employed worker, aged 19, one wife and child; salary—£9. 16s. per month)

In sum then, not only were workers acting in protection of quite specific economic interests, which they share by virtue of their common class situation, they also were taking advantage of the relative ease of mobilization allowed by such class experience to protest against a diversity of the exploitative economic and political processes to which the masses as a whole were subjected. Such processes, described in these and other comments made at the time, are not limited in application to the industrial order. They are manifest in the oppressive conditions facing the urban poor in general. This was not a protest by industrial workers solely against their position within the industrial system as such, but was against the prevailing inequalities within Nigerian society at large. The great majority of the urban masses have little possibility for such structured opposition: they look to the wage earners to provide the leadership in protest movements, and of this the wage earners themselves are acutely aware.

Where, beneath the veneer of social calm, the underlying resentment against the extent of inegalitarianism was as extensive as it certainly was at this time, then the protest even within this limited setting assumed the proportions of a minor insurrection against the prevailing order.

But, notwithstanding undercurrents of hostility and the fact that this was a crisis situation, there was little in the way of expressions by workers that indicates a vision of an alternative order radically different from the one prevailing at the time. On the contrary, most workers interpreted their action as a *variant on the normal processes of accommodation to the social order* which, during periods of social calm, were expressed through the channel of peaceful bargaining between unions and managements around the negotiating table. Far from being the condition of anarchy that many managers considered to obtain during this period, not only was this a highly structured conflict situation, it also was one that encouraged leaders and workers to adhere further to peaceful negotiation within their respective companies. Workers' own interpretations of the conflict in which they were involved and of subsequent developments give support to this view.

Essentially, the strategy developed by the workers at this time was viewed as a *complement* to the established procedure rather than a rejection of it, and one induced by the decree operative at that time forbidding strike action or incitement to strike. This is illustrated by the comment of one textile worker on the afternoon of the first strike action:

> What use for us if the executive were in jail because they had called for a go-slow or even a strike to get our rights? Our leaders are good leaders. We know that because of our achievements. If they had not done well in the past we would surely have removed them by now! We, the workers, we have made the protest, and we can see that the General Manager and his men are on the run. These managers, they are all so frightened at what we have done that they must give in soon. And yet our leaders remain quite free. When the manager comes to his bargaining table, they can be there to take over the whole business again. Then they can easily get the award written down, for they have experience of such things where people like myself do not.

Certainly I would not suggest that all workers expressed the nature of their relationship with union leaders so precisely. But this comment does illustrate the acknowledgment that, faced with Decree 53, elected representatives, who look after workers' well-being from day to day, had unavoidable restrictions at that time on the way in which they performed their duties. The expertise for which they had been elected had been eliminated from the rules of the game during this critical period. But it could be drawn upon later when "the management has been brought to its knees"—a common expression at this time.

Following the management's capitulation, union leaders did

indeed employ their expertise in this fashion. It is such a close congruity of interests between union leaders and workers that indicated the major source of strength of house unions at Ikeja. In everyday affairs, the working relationship between leaders and followers is an integral element in accounting for house unions gaining wage increments and improved conditions of employment. Local union leaders and shop-floor employees see their national spokesman to be as remote and self-interested as members of the political class. Where successful industrial action occurs at the local level, then workers' attachment to their democratically elected leaders is all the more heightened. So too is their short-term interest in supporting those institutional arrangements which indicate a general acknowledgment of the overall reward system generated by the present distribution of ownership of the means of industrial production. We can see this in the subsequent denouement to the Adebo affair.

Despite the furor surrounding the government's handling of the first Adebo report, hopes of further improvements for wage earners were high. But the recommendations of the second and final report presented seven months later were disappointing indeed.[18] Far from narrowing the gap between rich and poor, the recommendations widened it substantially. General wage and salary increments were awarded across the board on a sliding scale. Workers earning less than £200 per annum were to receive an increment of £36, £24 of which they had already received as *cola*. For the lowest-paid workers this meant a £1 per month increase. In the upper echelons, however, those with salaries between £2,000 and £2,500 were to receive increments of £240, while those with £2,500-plus were awarded a £300-per-year increase! This was an apparently incredible reversal of policy from a concern with "the intolerable suffering at or near the bottom of the wage and salary levels" to a cosseting of the "aristocracy" of public and private employment.

The predominant interpretations made by workers were that the government had either pressured Adebo to severely curtail his recommendations or subsequently tampered with the report: "The government top men have altered the report so they will get more money"; "our bosses have bribed the government officials so that Adebo cannot give the workers more pay"; "even though Adebo helped us before, it is always the big guns who win in the end."

If, as I have argued, the handling of the first award provided a focus around which crystallized many of the undercurrents of resentment against the prevailing social structure, one might have anticipated that the final award would provide yet another catalyst for collective action. In fact no such action was forthcoming, nor even realistically contemplated by workers or union leaders.

This is to be accounted for by reference to the views workers held on the consequences of their earlier strike action. Workers in the companies affected calculated the prospects for future collective bargaining in the light of the demonstration of unity and strength of purpose which had been so manifest throughout the critical two-week period. Neither workers nor leaders were aware of the external influences I have described here, knowing little of the important interest divisions between managements and government.

In their view, managements had capitulated because of the threat to production they had caused by withdrawing their labor power. Faced with the possibility of some violence from overeager workers but with the certainty of enormous loss of profits in their capital-intensive plants, managements had been forced to capitulate.

Leaders and workers were, then, increasingly optimistic of the opportunities available to take advantage of their earlier demonstration of strength in the face of government's and management's rejection of their rights. Following the second report, one union leader commented: "Our annual negotiation comes up in a month's time. Whatever increase I demand, the management will have to consider it very seriously. Now, in the light of the trouble *cola* caused them, they know precisely where [union] executives and workers stand."

A protest movement against the "adulteration" of the report, which many workers believed to have occurred, could have been no more than a political demonstration against the injustices of the Nigerian elite. By continuing to work as normal, in effect, the Ikeja wage earners *were* engaged in social action on class lines. They were taking account of their relationship to representatives of other social classes with interests opposed to their own, and rationally calculating the avenues available to them for future economic improvement in collective terms.

An explanation of the solidarity of the lower class within the industrial system can be attempted by describing the structure of relationships between leaders and followers within *that system*. Within the context of a neocolonial society, however, where ownership of the means of industrial production is in the hands of those outside the society itself, such a clear-cut parameter cannot be drawn. The social anthropologist, examining the nature of class relationships at the microlevel can only point to the consequences of the domination of imperialist capitalist interests over such underdeveloped economies and the effects that such domination has for the articulation of internal class conflicts.[19]

At Ikeja certain such effects were paradoxical in the extreme. Ikeja managers were faced with an unresolvable conflict of interests as intermediaries within a neocolonial situation. Either they could look to the interests of the international financiers whom they represent or act to buttress the incumbents of state office. They could not, in this situation, do both. In the event, they decided in favor of the former, and in doing so, they not only had to pay out the award, which their employees considered their right anyway, but they also created a situation that encouraged the workers to become further aware of their collective strength by virtue of their relationship to the means of production.

Such managers were, not surprisingly, extremely critical of the government's handling of the Adebo affair. They resented further the manner in which the government stood aside from the conflict, providing only a nominal display of physical force. This, too, perhaps is to be explained by the inherent conflicts in the processes of neocolonialism.

As noted at the outset, the capital-intensive nature of expatriate industry and the profits derived from industrial enterprise place a premium on industrial peace rather than on rigid adherence to minimum wage rates. However, relatively generous wage and salary increments by expatriate enterprise to safeguard sound union-management relationships not only can be passed on through price increases but also prove extremely embarrassing to the largest employer of wage labor, namely the government itself. It is the government above all other employers that has vested interests in keeping wages at the absolute minimum.

But the government has difficulty in objecting to wage increases within private enterprise. These are usually justified on the basis of the rising cost of living and increased productivity. The first is (as in the case of the Adebo Commission) acknowledged by the government; the second is the raison d'être for allowing expatriate enterprise to operate in the first place. In the light of the large differentials in wages and salaries between the private and the public sector, open resentment to the fact that "the country's manufacturers . . . remain a perpetual appendage of foreign industrial complexes"[20] is on the increase. Possibly, then, it becomes necessary for the government to take advantage of confrontations between expatriate industrial managers and their workers in order to demonstrate where power really lies and what the most preferable balance of competing interests is from the point of view of the indigenous political class.

Such realignments within the power structure of Nigerian society are essential to ensuring sociopolitical stability within the wider arena. Periodic reassessments of the distribution of wealth and power between the competing elites must not be allowed to upset the even more fragile balance between the elites and the masses. In the case of the Adebo affair we have some illustration of how this can be achieved.

Labor leaders and workers emerged from this conflict with a heightened sense of accommodation to the existing social order and an increased awareness of their ability to make certain economic gains within that framework. In doing so they were perhaps making the same point that Marx did over a century ago, that even members of the labor movement require to develop and sustain a comprehensive and politically sophisticated level of organization before the possibility of implementing an entirely different framework emerges.

A Perspective Summary

In this paper I have not regarded the existence of class relationships in Nigeria as problematic. In that one has, at Ikeja, a clear division between those who own and those who control the means of production on the one hand and those who contribute to the production process by selling their labor power on the other, then class relationships can be said to exist in that system.

Here I have concentrated on the *form* that such class relationships take, the interpretation of events by those involved in conflict situations, and the congruity or conflict of interests between those in dominant and subordinate positions within only the industrial sector of the economy.

Nevertheless, the existence of social classes even in the African industrial context has been frequently denied. Sociologists and ideologues have arrived at essentially the same conclusions, albeit by different routes. In an early study, *The Third World* (1967), Worsley, writing with a distinctly Marxist perspective, comments of the wage earners: "These are not, then, modern industrial workers at all. They are people only beginning to transform themselves into permanent city dwellers, learning the habits of industrial and urban society, struggling to piece together a new identity and community out of the kaleidoscopic fragments of their lives."[21]

Having failed to establish the existence of a proletarian consciousness, Worsley turns to the peasantry as a "potentially revolutionary force," "potentially" because: "Other social classes, to put it simply, are either not there or are only in the process of formation, or if they do exist, are impeded by a variety of factors from developing their own institutional ideological identity."[22]

Such equivocal statements as this (and Worsley's is one among many) are obviously unsatisfactory. At the most elementary level if they are not industrial workers, what then are they? But there are two major criticisms which can be directed at generalizations attempted in this fashion.

First, there is a failure to acknowledge that the very nature of uneven economic development of malintegrated neocolonial societies allows the existence of highly developed class relationships on the basis of one mode of production, but only marginally structured ones on the basis of another—and this within the same national polity.

Second, in the African context, class continues to be looked upon as a "thing," with a set of attributes according to the possession of which it qualifies, or does not qualify, for the appropriate label. An indication of this is the manner in which the wage-earning force, the urban masses, the peasantry, and so on, are presented as discrete categories with distinctive qualities; on this basis, and usually without examination of a single conflict situation, the existence of social classes has often been denied. But the analysis of class in the African context, as in any other, must proceed through the analysis of social relationships and social action, and the crucial class relationships are those determined by the mode of production.[23]

Within the limits of this paper I have accordingly tried to avoid these pitfalls in two ways. First, I have taken the major arena in which social action takes place as the system of relationships based on the industrial mode of production, regarding this as conceptually expedient in providing a natural set of parameters within which the conflicts and contradictions inherent in that mode of production are most clearly displayed. Where economic development is exceptionally uneven and competing and complementary modes of production diverse (as is usual in a neocolonial economy), such a strategy is not only heuristically valuable but analytically essential in keeping attention focused on the specific mode of production around which class relationships are structured.

Second, I have taken as my subject a conflict situation in which class interests are most clearly demonstrated by individuals and groups acting in protection of such interests and with reference to the behavior, actual and anticipated, of class members whose interests they perceive as being essentially opposed to their own. A conflict situation is a convenient issue, for it is at such times that what Weber calls the "naked class situation" is most transparently exposed.[24] But class relationships are the essence of ongoing politicoeconomic processes. The experience of direct class conflict, sporadic and ephemeral as it is, has important implications for the dialectical realignments of class relationships. And an integral part of explaining such consequences is an appreciation of the interpretations that class members themselves place on the conflicts in which they are involved.

Notes

1. See P. C. Lloyd, *Africa in Social Change* (Harmondsworth, Eng.: Penguin Books, 1967); P. C. Lloyd, *Classes, Crises, and Coups* (London: MacGibben and Kee, 1971); P. Worsley, *The Third World* (London: Weidenfeld, 1967); and S. Andreski, *The African Predicament* (London: Michael Joseph, 1968).

2. For an account of the Lagos labor force in historical perspective, see R. Cohen and A. Hughes, "Towards the Emergence of a Nigerian Working Class: The Social Identity of the Lagos Labour Force, 1897-1939," Occasional Paper, ser. D, no. 7 (Birmingham, Eng.: Faculty of Commerce and Social Science, University of Birmingham, 1971). On the success or otherwise of African workers in raising real wages, see P. Kilby, "Industrial Relations and Wage Determination: Failure of the Anglo-Saxon Model," *Journal of Developing Areas* 1 (1967): 489–520; J. Weeks, "A Comment on Peter Kilby: Industrial Relations and Wage Determination," *Journal of Developing Areas* 3 (1968): 7–17; J. Weeks, "Further Comments on the Kilby/Weeks Debate: An Empirical Rejoinder," *Journal of Developing Areas* 5 (1971): 164–74; and R. Cohen, "Further Comment on the Kilby/Weeks Debate," *Journal of Developing Areas* 5 (1971): 155–64.

3. See J. Weeks, "Wage Policy and the Colonial Legacy—A Comparative Study," *Journal of Modern African Studies* 9, no.3 (1971): 361–87; and P. C. Lloyd, ed., *The New Elites of Tropical Africa* (London: Oxford University Press, 1966).

4. See G. Arrighi and J. Saul, "Socialism and Economic Development in Tropical Africa," *Journal of Modern African Studies* 6, no. 2 (1968): 141–70; and G. Arrighi, "International Corporations, Labor Aristocracies and Economic Development in Tropical Africa," in *Imperialism and Underdevelopment: A Reader,* ed. R. I. Rhodes (New York: Monthly Review Press, 1970).

5. See R. Scott, *The Development of Trade Unions in Uganda* (Nairobi: East African Publishing House, 1966); and T. H. Yesufu, *An Introduction to Industrial Relations in Nigeria* (London: Oxford University Press, 1962). For a critique of Scott, see R. D. Grillo, "The Tribal Factor in

an East African Trade Union," in *Tradition and Transition in East Africa,* ed. P. H. Gulliver (London: Routledge & Kegan Paul, 1969). Cf. also A. L. Epstein, *Politics in an Urban African Community* (Manchester: Manchester University Press, 1958).

6. Lloyd, *Africa in Social Change.*
7. See, for example, A. Zolberg, *Creative Political Order* (Chicago: Rand McNally, 1966), p. 72; and I. O. Davies, *African Trade Unions* (Harmondsworth, Eng.: Penguin Books, 1966), pp. 125–26.
8. P. Kilby, *Industrialization in an Open Economy: Nigeria 1945-1966* (London: Cambridge University Press, 1969).
9. F. Parkin, *Class, Inequality and Political Order* (London: MacGibben and Kee, 1971), p. 91.
10. Adebo Report, *Second and Final Report of the Salaries and Wages Commission* (Lagos: Federal Ministry of Information, 1971).
11. Morgan Report, *Report of the Commission on the Review of Wages, Salaries and Conditions of Service of Junior Employees of the Federation and in Private Establishments* (Lagos: Federal Government of Nigeria, 1964).
12. R. Melson, "Nigerian Politics and the General Strike of 1964," in *Protest and Power in Black Africa,* ed. R. I. Rotberg and A. Mazrui (London: Oxford University Press, 1970).
13. United Committee of Central Labour Organisations, *Equitable Demand for Economic Growth and National Prosperity* (Ibadan: Government Printer, 1970).
14. Adebo Report, *First Report of the Wages and Salaries Review Commission* (Lagos: Federal Ministry of Information, 1971).
15. Another case study, describing the conflict in a beer company, has been deleted here for reasons of space. [Eds.]
16. Lloyd, ed., *The New Elites, p. 57.*
17. National Provident Fund Contributions.
18. Adebo Report, *Second and Final Report.*
19. The complementary nature of different levels of analysis required to build up a composite picture of such a complex subject as neocolonialism is well stated by Frank. See A. G. Frank, *Capitalism and Underdevelopment in Latin America* (New York: Monthly Review Press, 1969). I have sought to show how the processes of interaction at the micro level, determined in their general outlines by the macrolevel neocolonial relations, dialectically develop a self-conscious labor movement, a development of considerable significance for the internal class structure.
20. Nigeria, *Second National Development Plan, 1970-1974* (Lagos: Federal Ministry of Information, 1970), p. 143.
21. Worsley, *The Third World,* pp. 160–61.
22. Ibid, p. 163.
23. To be fair, Worsley does admit to the need to see class as "a *relationship* not a thing" (ibid., p. 163), but this is little more than an acknowledgment of the problem rather than an attempt to come to grips with it.

24. Weber is in fact discussing the much broader position when he uses this phrase. H. H. Gerth and C. W. Mills, eds., *From Max Weber: Essays in Sociology* (London: Routledge & Kegan Paul, 1967), p. 194.

Class Consciousness among Working-Class Women in Latin America: A Case Study in Puerto Rico

Helen Icken Safa

Conventional Marxist analysis of class consciousness in advanced capitalist or dependent underdeveloped societies has concentrated upon men and their participation in the labor force as primary factors. Women have generally been regarded as a secondary labor reserve, primarily responsible for "unproductive" domestic labor, and therefore not crucial to the development of proletarian consciousness in either developing or underdeveloped societies.

Recently this downgrading of female labor and participation in class struggle has been seriously criticized, particularly by writers with a feminine perspective.[1] These writers point out that woman's increasing participation in the urban labor force in both advanced industrial and Third-World societies is overlooked, while her role in peasant agricultural production has generally been ignored. There has also been a failure to recognize woman's domestic role in maintaining and reproducing the labor force as essential to the stability of the capitalist system.[2] The wages earned by male workers in effect also subsidize the unpaid labor of the housewives, which is automatically devalued because it is outside the money economy. However, as Benston notes, while woman's domestic labor may not produce exchange value, that is, wages, it does have use value that is consumed within the family.[3]

The distinction between exchange value and use value, Benston notes,[4] occurs primarily with the advent of capitalism, which takes commodity production outside of the home and into the factory and marketplace. In preindustrial peasant economies women worked alongside men as an integral family unit in agricultural production. Boserup's analysis[5] of woman's role in economic development in Third-World countries supports Engels' notion that woman's status declined with the advent of class society, industrial capitalism, and the sharp distinction between the private world of the family and the public world of work. Women were no longer partners with men in a joint economic enterprise, but dependent upon a man's wages for their family's survival.

Thus, under capitalism household labor remains in the pre-market stage.[6] Even if housework can be considered useful labor, it still leaves the woman dependent upon the man and isolates her from other women and men, since housework is carried out independently within each private household. Dependency upon the male and isolation from other workers, particularly women, are crucial factors inhibiting the development of class consciousness in women of all class sectors.

Engels felt that women's entry into the labor force would raise women's consciousness and status. However, while wage work outside the home may bring the woman more independence and freedom, it has also created a dual burden for most women, who are still held responsible for the care of the home and children. Several studies suggest that this dual burden may lead to severe stress and alienation, particularly among working-class women, who cannot afford to hire outside domestic help.[7] Thus, even when women work, they are *incompletely proletarianized*. They tend to regard their family roles as primary, and to see their jobs as another way of aiding their families.

In this paper it will be argued that because of the centrality of women's family roles, particularly in Latin America, they cannot be ignored in the formation of female class consciousness. Class consciousness in women, it will be shown, involves not only oppression in the work place, as members of the working class, but also sexual subordination in the home, resulting from a strongly patriarchal family structure. Sexual subordination affects women at all levels of society, but elite women are endowed with certain privileges, accruing from their class position, which make their sexual subordination less visible and onerous. Sexual subordination in Latin America is also masked by a female mystique, often called Marianismo, by which the ideal female role is compared with that of the Virgin Mary, long suffering but never complaining, sheltered and protected from evil worldly influences.[8] This ideal continues operative among working-class women and is used to justify class, as well as sexual, oppression.[9] However, working-class women enjoy none of the privileges of elite class position and thus are forced to bear the dual burden of sexual subordination at home and class oppression outside.

Women themselves clearly are not a class, but members of another class, depending on their socioeconomic position in society. All too often, the class position of women is defined, not by women themselves, even when they are working, but by their husbands or fathers, whose status they then assume. While this is another clear reflection of women's dependency on men, it does not mean that women cannot acquire class consciousness independently. It does suggest that the process by which women acquire class consciousness will be different and more difficult than it is for men.

Participation in the labor force may be a sufficient condition for the formation of class consciousness in men, but I would argue it is not sufficient for women, who suffer from sexual subordination as well as class oppression. Class consciousness is here defined as a cumulative process by which women (1) recognize that they are exploited and oppressed, (2) recognize the source of their exploitation and oppression, and (3) are willing and able to organize and mobilize in their own class interests. We thus distinguish between what Leggett, basing himself on Marx, has termed the cognitive and evaluative aspect of class consciousness. According to Leggett, "the cognitive aspect refers to whether workers utilize class terms, identify with this class, and display an awareness of the allocation of wealth within the community or society. The evaluative aspect refers to the extent to which workers think in terms of class struggle in order to achieve class goals."[10] Thus, only through class struggle is full consciousness achieved.

While this paper is limited to an analysis of class consciousness among working-class women in Latin America, it has obvious implications for working-class women in any capitalist society. Class consciousness always takes place within a particular cultural setting, so it is necessary to explore both specific cultural features as well as class factors in the formation of class consciousness. In this paper, the data are drawn largely from my own study of shantytown families in San Juan, Puerto Rico, including a broad survey sample conducted in 1959 and an intensive restudy of selected shantytown families in 1969, after their relocation to various parts of the San Juan Metropolitan Area. Since the data were not collected for the purpose of examining class consciousness, we have had to reinterpret much of the data in an attempt to shed light on this subject. We have also tried to suggest some of the changes taking place in women's family and occupational roles during this critical time period in Puerto Rican history, and their impact on class consciousness, particularly in the younger generation.

Operation Bootstrap and Female Employment

In the early 1940s Puerto Rico embarked upon an ambitious development program, popularly known as Operation Bootstrap, designed to transform the island from a stagnant rural economy, dependent largely on the export of sugarcane to American markets, to an industrialized society with higher standards of living through more employment, higher wages, better health, housing, education, and other social welfare measures.

The results of Operation Bootstrap are shown in the shift from agricultural to nonagricultural employment, particularly in manufacturing, trade, and services. After 1952 industry became the dominant mode of economic activity on the island, with manufacturing generating $999 million of net income in 1971.[11] Economic growth and high government expenditures for public health, housing, education, and so on have brought improved standards of living with sharp declines in mortality rates, illiteracy, and other indices of social well-being. However, increased employment has been unable to absorb dramatic population increases (resulting from improved living standards), with the result that unemployment has continued to hover around 12 percent. With the recent recession, felt much more acutely in Puerto Rico, unemployment has increased dramatically.

Industrialization and economic growth in Puerto Rico have resulted in increasing participation of women in the labor force.[12] In 1970 women constituted 27.1 percent of the total labor force, up from 22 percent in 1962, an increase due totally to non-agricultural employment.[13] This difference would appear to be due to the fact that, at least in this early phase of industrialization in Puerto Rico, which emphasized light manufacturing, women were employed at a rate nearly equal to that of men. Thus, in 1970 women constituted 48.6 percent, or nearly half, of the labor force in manufacturing.[14] They also constituted 44.8 percent of the persons employed in public administration and 47.2 percent of those in service jobs,[15] two other fast-growing employment sectors.

Women provided a cheap labor force for the start of industrialization in Puerto Rico. In the industries established through the Office of Economic Development, the salary differential was as high as 30.3 percent in industries where women predominated as compared with those employing mostly men.[16] This reflected the fact that women are concentrated in the manufacture of nondurable goods, such as textiles, clothing, leather goods, and tobacco, where pay is considerably lower than in durable goods, such as metal, stone, or glass products, where men predominate.[17] The average salary for all women working full time in 1970 was $3,006, compared with $3,382 for men. However, women were also concentrated in the lower-paid jobs, with 42.2 percent receiving less than $2,000 a year (compared with 26.7 percent of the men).[18]

The recent concentration upon heavy, capital-intensive industry in Puerto Rico as well as in other developing areas also threatens female employment. In these capital-intensive industries, labor tends to be reduced to a minimum and to be highly skilled, favoring the creation of a labor aristocracy in which men predominate. Recent case studies of three large petrochemical industries in Puerto Rico reveal a total absence of women in the production line and a very meager representation at official and managerial levels.[19]

Female Occupational Roles in the Shantytown

In the survey conducted in 1959 in Los Peloteros, a shantytown in the heart of the San Juan Metropolitan Area, 22 percent of the women were currently employed, while an additional 45 percent had been previously employed. Thus, the great majority of women in the shantytown have worked at some point in their lives, which completely contradicts the Latin American ideal of *la mujer en su casa* ("the woman in her home"). This ideal is also being questioned by women of the elite, who are seeking professional and other prestige forms of employment in increasing numbers. It was never practiced among women of the working class, who both in the rural and urban areas were always forced to work to add to the family income.

Paulita, now a young mother of seven children, recalls how she came to San Juan as a child together with her mother, two sisters, and a brother. Her mother worked as a domestic, and only one child could live with her; the others lived in foster homes. Speaking of the difficulties women faced at that time, Paulita notes:

> At that time women who had a problem, who had left their husbands, the majority became prostitutes *(paganas)*, right? Because they had no choice. If they were very young, they didn't want them working in families because they fell in love with the husband. And since they couldn't find work, those women went to sin because they didn't have any schooling.

Many women in Los Peloteros continued to work as domestic servants, or in other service occupations, while the most fortunate were employed in factories, considered the most desirable occupation. The salary differential is substantial, with factory workers in 1970 earning an average annual income of $2,571, compared with $874 for domestic servants.[20] In addition, domestic service is considered very demeaning and places the woman in a completely dependent patron-client relationship, in which it is difficult to develop any class consciousness or collective solidarity.[21] The domestic servant is one of the chief instruments by which elite women maintain their privileged status in capitalist society. She is as isolated as the housewife and more exploited.

Though job opportunities for women in the working class have been concentrated in low-paid, unskilled jobs, the rapid expansion of occupational opportunities in the last two decades has created in women a near universal desire for upward mobility. Most working-class women are optimistic about the future for themselves and other women; they feel it is each individual's responsibility to progress as much as possible. Lydia, one of our younger informants who has been particularly successful, compares herself with other girls in the shantytown where she grew up and notes:

> In general terms we had the same opportunities. . . . That is, we came from poor homes and at home we had more or less the same education in the moral and material sense. Nevertheless, many of them today are married, they have no further preparation. I even know of some girls who would like, if they could, to return and start their life over again. . . . The desire to excel *(superarse)* has not been as great in them as in others. The desire to excel of each individual, it doesn't matter where he is or where he lives, that helps a great deal to enable him to move forward.

This drive toward upward mobility has tended to mitigate the development of class consciousness among working-class women, since the emphasis is on individual initiative and competition rather than on collective class solidarity.

Expanding occupational opportunities have also placed a new value on education for women. Among the adult generation surveyed in the shantytown in 1959, despite generally low educational levels, women fared even worse than men: 22.3 percent of the women had never gone to school at all, and 39.4 percent had never gone beyond the fourth grade.[22] Most of these women were migrants who had grown up in the rural area, where, at that time, there were few schools beyond the fourth grade. Now, however, as jobs and educational opportunities for women have increased in the urban area, the value of education for girls has been recognized, and among the adolescent generation in the shantytown, the educational level of girls is on a par with that of boys.[23]

Flor reflects the new ideology of equality of opportunity for the sexes when she states: "Women can do everything as well as men. They can become presidents, they can become everything, they can rise to all men's jobs. Today there is no longer any difference between men and women." Flor gained much of her drive and initiative from her mother, Raquel, who managed to raise a family of eight children on the sale of *cañita,* or illegal rum. Flor's father was a chronic alcoholic who often beat his wife and children, and even turned in his wife to the police out of sheer resentment over her economic independence. Even when he worked, most of his salary went for drink for himself and his friends.

Women such as Raquel, who cannot rely on a husband to support them, are often forced to become the principal bread-winners for their families. In 1970, 47.6 percent of divorced women worked, compared with 22 percent of married women living with their husbands.[24] Men who are separated from their wives cannot be relied upon for child support and often migrate to the mainland to avoid family responsibilities. Welfare payments are generally too low for families to survive on, though they have increased substantially since the original study was conducted in 1959. At that time, for example, Carmen, a young widow with five small children, received $50 a month from public welfare, which she supplemented with part-time work as a laundress. Now she receives $82 a month for herself and one minor child, in addition to what the oldest children give her. Welfare, however, creates another form of dependency, not on the husband, but on the state. Thus, it is another factor inhibiting the development of class consciousness, particularly important in advanced capitalist societies, where welfare policies are more developed. Puerto Rico certainly has a more elaborate welfare program than most Latin American countries, and it is heavily subsidized by the U.S. federal government.

The growing number of female-based households among the working class in Latin America is an extremely important development for the formation of class consciousness among women. Women who are heads of households are more prone to develop a stronger commitment to their work role because they become the principal breadwinners for the family.[25] They cannot afford to regard their work roles as temporary or secondary, as do most of the married women in the shantytown. This lack of commitment to a work role plays a crucial role in the absence of class consciousness among women in the shantytown, since women never identify with their work role nor stay on one job long enough to develop a relationship with their peers. Thus, in the survey conducted in 1959, the great majority of women in the shantytown who had worked never saw their fellow employees after work nor participated in union activities. The reason is clear: women must rush home after work to care for children and other household chores, whereas men are free to join their friends, and, as the survey demonstrated, often meet their best friends through work. Women in the shantytown tend to work sporadically, as the need arises, for which such menial occupations as domestic service and other service jobs are ideally suited.

Women who are the sole support of their families are more likely to develop class consciousness than women who are still primarily dependent on men to support them. However, as a study of female textile workers in Mexico demonstrated, the pressure of family responsibilities and the fear of losing their jobs may also prevent these women from expressing open dissatisfaction with the long hours, low pay, and miserable working conditions.[26] Thus, female-based household heads are still restrained by the other factors we have outlined in this section which hamper the development of class consciousness among Latin American working-class women generally, such as the concentration in unskilled labor, the role of welfare, and the burden of family and household responsibilities. Although younger women have growing confidence in their ability to find work and to compete with men for better jobs, their family roles remain central, as will be shown in the next section.

Family Roles and Sexual Subordination

In order to understand the impact of the family on the class consciousness of women in Latin America, it is necessary to analyze the structure of the shantytown household and the sharp segregation of conjugal roles. The man's authority is based largely on his role as economic provider, which is weakened by factors such as the high rate of unemployment, poor wages, low skill and educational levels, and minimal possibilities for upward mobility. Even the traditional kinship and religious roles which may confer status on men in primitive or peasant societies are taken from them in an urban-industrial society. The woman's domestic role, on the other hand, is left relatively intact. She has primary responsibility for the care of the home and children and derives her authority from her close relationship with her children and female kin. The strong emotional bond between a woman, her children, and her female kin group results in a pronounced matrifocal emphasis in shantytown families.

Matrifocality, as used here, is not limited to families where the woman assumes the actual role as head of household, but is also found in families with a stable male head, where his role is marginal to the primary sphere of mother-child relationships. Though half of the households sampled in Los Peloteros were of the nuclear family type, household composition becomes more complex among older women who had been married twenty years or more; among these women there is a larger percentage of extended families and households headed by females, reflecting not only the greater life expectancy of women but also the increasing autonomy of women as they grow older. One-fourth of the women sampled report being married in consensual union, which often tends to be more unstable than civil or church marriages; more than half of these women have been married more than once.

Two-thirds of the adult women sampled were first married between the ages of fifteen and nineteen, a tendency which does not appear to be on the decline in the younger generation, except among the most upwardly mobile. Several of the daughters of our informants, born and raised in the urban area, have entered into marriage or consensual union at fourteen or fifteen, usually conceiving a child within the first year. They have little knowledge of the world outside the home and pass from dependence on their parents to dependence on their husbands. Clearly this is another factor inhibiting the development of class consciousness in working-class women.

Many girls marry young in order to escape the confinement of a parental home, only to face worse tyranny with their husbands. A woman may not be able to leave the house without her husband's permission, and generally confines her social life to family gatherings and informal visits with neighbors. Husbands and wives seldom go out together except as a family. She is required to wait on her husband, to have supper ready when he arrives from work, and to take care of all the housework and the children without his help. A common pattern is for the husband to give his wife a weekly allowance for household expenses, and she may not know, beyond this, how much money he makes or spends on himself. Many men prohibit their wives from working, even when they could use the extra income, because it casts doubt on their own ability as provider and gives the women too much independence.

Even the limited authority women enjoy in the domestic sphere is not translatable into social power or position in the larger society.[27] In the shantytown there is a sharp division between the

public world of work and the private world of the family, and men
try so far as possible to confine their wives to the latter. The man
acts as spokesman for his family in all dealings with the outside
world: on barrio committees, in the local housing cooperative, in
political parties, for example, the membership is almost exclusively
male. Responsibility for social control in the shantytown also rests
largely with the man. For example, men may attempt to end a
fight between neighbors or tell a drunkard to do his drinking
elsewhere, while women are hesitant to intervene in nonfamily
affairs. This lack of experience and authority in the public sphere
also limits the development of class consciousness in women.

Economic instability is the most frequent cause of marital
breakdown. There is no strong conjugal bond in the shantytown
household to hold a man and wife together in the face of economic
adversity. There is no investment in property, no status position
to uphold, no deep emotional tie. The younger generation of
women are less likely to accept the abuse their mothers stood for,
including beatings, infidelity, and lack of financial support. Flor,
Raquel's daughter, recalls how her father used to enter their
house in the middle of the night in a drunken rage and begin to
beat them all and chase them from the house. She said she would
not stand for the same behavior from her husband: "En absoluto
y si me pega yo no lo voy a soportar ni que me pege ni una sola
vez. Aquí en esta época tantas formas que hay de resolver los
problemas, que no me ponga ni un dedito encima." ("Absolutely,
and if he hits me, I won't stand for it, not even once. Here at this
time there are so many ways of solving problems, that he doesn't
lay a finger on me.") The younger generation of working-class
women clearly feel they have greater legal support and protection
from male abuse. Nearly all our respondents, male and female,
felt that women today enjoy more freedom and independence
than previously.

Nevertheless, the abuse suffered by many women at the hands
of their husbands makes them feel far more oppressed by men
and marriage than by their class position. Nearly three-fourths of
the women interviewed in 1959 felt that most marriages are
unhappy and blamed this largely on the man and his vices. It is
hard for women to realize that men may be taking out their
frustration and hostility toward tedious, unrewarding jobs and
lives on women and their children, who are the working-class
man's only subordinates. What women feel most directly is man as
the oppressor, and therefore much of their own hostility is
directed against men rather than against the class system. This
deflection of discontent onto men also limits the development of
class consciousness, since the issue becomes individual liberation

from men, rather than class struggle with men to overcome mutual exploitation.

Marital problems are handled in highly individualized ways, and women seldom confront their husbands openly with their dissatisfaction. Instead of protest, women attempt to manipulate men into doing what they want, and into believing that men are the real boss in the household while the women are quietly running things.[28] Much of the public deference to male authority is based on this premise. This manipulative strategy is very similar to that employed by both men and women to all persons in higher authority, to employers, government officials, doctors, storekeepers, and so on. "Obedezco pero no cumplo" ("I obey, but I do not comply") is an old Puerto Rican *jíbaro* ("peasant") saying. In the attempt to avoid open conflict, manipulation employs a highly individualistic mode of gaining the advantage over one's adversary. It emphasizes the subordinate nature of the client vis-à-vis the dominant patron by stressing the client's helplessness and dependency, and the need for the patron's (husband's) protection and guidance. This is seen most clearly during pregnancy, when women bear living proof of their husband's virility, but also make demands on their husbands which would be totally rejected at another time. These demands, known in Puerto Rico as *entojos*, are usually in the form of cravings for special food or drink, which if denied, according to folk belief, might harm the unborn fetus. Thus, even when pregnant, the woman is not representing her own interest, but the child's.

The way in which patron-client relationships limit the development of class consciousness and collective solidarity among the Latin American proletariat generally is widely recognized.[29] Patron-client relationships promote the development of dyadic, vertical relationships which hinder the formation of horizontal and collective peer-group relationships necessary to class consciousness. However, as Nash has pointed out,[30] the way in which these mechanisms of dependency permeate the entire social structure, including the family, helps to explain how these mechanisms are perpetuated from generation to generation. Women learn to be dependent at an early age and to use manipulative strategy with men. This mitigates the possibility of collective solidarity among women, who see each household as a private battleground.

Sources of Female Solidarity and Status

Despite these divisive tendencies, however, there is far more female solidarity in the shantytown than in middle-class neighborhoods characterized by isolated nuclear families. Much of the solidarity is expressed through the kin group which, despite the norm of bilaterality, tends to be mediated through women. Children generally maintain close contact with their parents after marriage, and the mother-daughter tie is particularly strong. The first child is often born in the grandmother's home and retains a close tie to her throughout life. For example, one of our younger informants has repeatedly returned home when her children were born so that the grandmother could take care of her children while she was in the hospital and help her during her convalescence. She also leaves her children with her (adopted) mother daily while she and her husband work.

There is also extensive mutual aid among families in the shantytown, particularly the women. They borrow from each other, including not only cups of sugar or electric irons but even water and electricity or the use of a refrigerator. They also share in childrearing. In the evening children may gather in a neighbor's house to watch television. If they are hungry, they are fed. Neighbors will rush to comfort crying children or try to entice them out of a temper tantrum with a bright new penny or a *lindbergh* (flavored ice cube). At the same time they do not hesitate to scold a naughty child or ask a neighbor's child to run an errand for them. In this way shantytown families avoid the intense and often strained relationships of the isolated nuclear family, where the woman has none of these sources of aid or friendship. In this sense the domestic role of the woman in the Puerto Rican shantytown is less isolating or alienating than that of the middle-class housewife. It may also be less tedious and exploitative than the occupational role of many shantytown men.

On the contrary, most women in the shantytown, working or not, would argue that their primary rewards lie within the domestic sphere of their children and family. A woman feels that her own validation and status as a woman rests with her children, for whom she feels primary responsibility. One woman who could not bear children of her own adopted three of her brother's children (after he was imprisoned for killing his wife for adultery). Several women whose husbands had died or left them continued to have children with other men. Sometimes it led to a stable relationship with the man, but more often it did not. Though clearly they were being exploited by these men, these women knew no other means of gaining self-identity or social recognition. The ideal role of wife and mother is for them still paramount.

The domestic role of the women in the shantytown can be compared with that of the black woman under slavery. Angela Davis has argued:

It was only in domestic life—away from the eyes and whip of the overseer—that the slaves could attempt to assert the modicum of freedom they still retained. . . . In the infinite anguish of ministering to the needs of the men and children around her (who were not necessarily members of her immediate family), she was performing the *only* labor of the slave community which could not be directly and immediately claimed by the oppressor. . . . She was therefore essential to the *survival* of the community.[31]

The woman in the shantytown, by being the mainstay of the family and the wider kin group, also provides this function for the oppressed urban proletariat. Though men and women are alienated in their work roles, they have a domestic sphere to which they can retreat and which capitalism has as yet been unable to destroy. Though the family has been destroyed as an economically productive unit, social relationships within the family and between neighbors and kin remain highly viable. This is particularly important to the working class, which has no other source of status and identity and which is subjected to extreme exploitation in its relationships with other classes in the metropolis, which are governed by status and market relationships.[32]

The nature of family and interpersonal relationships in the shantytown can be compared with those in public housing, a planned community created by the government to house the urban poor. In public housing the cohesion, built up over many years in the shantytown, breaks down; mutual aid is weakened, and families become more suspicious of each other. Housing management begins to intervene in the internal affairs of the family, checking on income, furnishings, household composition, and other private matters, and the family no longer provides the refuge it could in the shantytown. The public-housing family is alienated, not only because of its low socioeconomic status, which it shares with the shantytown family, but also because family and community life have been disrupted by agencies of the state. Public and private domains are blurred as the government begins to control the personal lives of public-housing residents.

Conclusions

Sexual subordination must be taken into account along with class oppression in assessing the potentialities for the development of class consciousness among working-class women in Latin America. The traditional subordination of the woman in the patriarchal family, found at all class levels in Latin American society, limits the woman's autonomy, freedom, and self-confidence. It restricts her to a narrow domestic sphere, where, however, she has been able to maintain considerable authority vis-à-vis the children and where extended kin and neighborly relations have prevented the alienation experienced by the woman in the isolated nuclear family.

Calls for the dissolution of the family and an end to childbearing as a liability are clearly no solution. We cannot simply dismiss the family as a reactionary instrument of capitalist society, particularly in the working class, where it fulfills so important a function as being the last refuge from capitalist exploitation. Were the family to be weakened, as is already happening in some working-class sectors of Puerto Rico, women would become as alienated as most men, who already are marginal to the domestic sphere and totally exposed to exploitative relationships on the job and in other public sectors.

I am not arguing for a reinstitution of the bourgeois nuclear family, which has proved extremely alienating and isolating to women. Unfortunately, many working-class families, as they move out of the shantytown and into middle-class *urbanizaciones*, are already following this pattern and acquiring the competitive, individualistic, and consumer-oriented values that often accompany upward mobility in a capitalist society. Nor am I arguing against the entry of more women into the labor force, though I agree with Vogel[33] and others that as long as women constitute primarily a source of cheap labor for capitalism, as is abundantly evident in Latin America today, they are not promoting their own liberation or class consciousness. Rather I am arguing that women's family roles be considered a potential source of revolutionary strength in the working class, rather than simply as a brake on the process of proletarianization.

Dalla Costa[34] and others suggest that women be paid for domestic work, which would end their dependence on men and give housework exchange value. However, it might also give the state (which would probably be required to pay) the means to control the woman's domestic labor the way capitalism now controls all exchange value. Welfare payments for female-based households have certainly led to greater control and merely shifted the dependency of women from their husbands to the state. Payment of women for domestic labor would redistribute income, as Benston suggests,[35] but would not necessarily lead to greater class consciousness.

Any movement for mobilization or class consciousness must take advantage of the natural basis of solidarity which already exists in the community. In the shantytown we have identified a strong sense of solidarity among female kin and neighbors expressed through mutual aid and close friendship. These ties could be strengthened through public support and channeled into cooperative day-care centers, health centers, and food-distribution centers, like those in Chile created under the government of the late Salvador Allende. This would be one way to break through the isolation of the nuclear family and to stimulate the development of more *communal* forms of child care and other household tasks, which could serve as the basis for the creation of a socialist society.

At this point we may say that shantytown women have not passed beyond the very initial stages of class consciousness—that is, they may feel a sense of oppression, both within the family and within the larger society, but they are very unclear as to the source of this oppression or how to deal with it. To use Leggett's terminology, they have not passed beyond the cognitive stage of class consciousness and are far from collectively representing their interests in the larger society.

However, it is clear that shantytown women share a greater sense of sexual subordination than of class oppression. It is men who abuse them, who fail to support them, and who confine them to the home and burden them with family responsibilities. As long as working-class women see their primary opponents as men and as long as men regard them as subordinates in the class struggle, then there is little hope for a shared struggle against common exploitation.

According to Pico,[36] working-class women did demonstrate greater class consciousness in the earlier stages of industrialization in Puerto Rico. Pico has shown how, prior to 1930, working-class women, employed chiefly in tobacco, home needlework, canning, and other early manufacturing industries, were active in the union movement as well as the Socialist party. The relative decline of these industries and the resulting dispersion of the female labor force into service as well as other marginal jobs apparently helped deflect this growth in class consciousness, as did the demise and eventual incorporation of the Socialist party into the reformist Popular party. The leadership of the women's movement was then taken over by petty-bourgeois women, who found a growing source of employment in public education and who were chiefly interested in legal and social equality, i.e., woman's suffrage and more education for women. Though pretending to speak for all women (as in the United States), the women's suffragette movement promoted primarily the class interests of elite women, to the point where illiterate women were initially denied the vote. The historic class split in the women's movement, both in the United States and in Puerto Rico, points to the virtual impossibility of building a woman's movement across class lines. Historically, as well as in the present, the class interests of elite and working-class women are too diverse, and this cannot overcome a common sense of sexual subordination.

The primary obstacles to the development of class consciousness among working-class women in Latin America lie in the strict sexual division of labor, at home and on the job, their subordination within a patriarchal family structure, and their restriction to the private sphere of domestic labor. No simple solution will eradicate all of these obstacles. Rather, any attempt to develop class consciousness among working-class women must attack all three areas where women are subordinate: work, the family, and the community. It must not only promote entry of women into the labor force but also end the sexual division of labor, which keeps women in poorly paid, low-status jobs and forces them to take on the dual burden of domestic responsibilities and employment. It must make men share in household responsibilities and socialize housework by creating public institutions which lighten the domestic role, such as free day-care centers, laundromats, and communal eating places, with "take-home" foods. It must also encourage women to take a greater role in community affairs, on barrio committees, and in political parties so that their needs and interests as women will also be represented.

Viewing class consciousness from a feminist perspective permits one to question whether the narrow focus on work roles is even appropriate for men in the Latin American working class. As the marginal labor force in the cities grows larger, due to capital-intensive industrialization and continued rural-urban migration, it also becomes harder for men to find stable employment or to identify with their work role. Unskilled men find jobs when and where they can and have no particular occupation. Under these circumstances, it also becomes difficult to develop class consciousness among men in the work place, and it may become necessary to explore men's family and community roles as an alternative.[37] We have seen that in the Puerto Rican shantytown some men participate actively in barrio committees, in political parties, and other community activities. In Chile the *campamentos* served as an important basis for the development of political activity and consciousness. The community may serve as a more appropriate locale than the factory for the development of class consciousness in the Latin American working class.

The analysis of class consciousness among working-class women in Latin America points up the need to revise traditional Marxist theory in the light of new conditions in Third-World as well as advanced capitalist societies. We cannot wait for all women to enter the labor force while jobs in the low-income sector are diminishing, nor can we expect women to carry the dual burden of family and job responsibilities any longer. Their class interests as women clearly rest both in promoting greater job opportunities for women at all class levels and in eliminating patriarchal family structures and sexual ideologies which relegate women to an inferior and dependent role. Such changes are unlikely to come about, in capitalist or socialist society, until working-class women themselves unite and demand attention to their needs within the larger society. As Rowbotham has written:

> The predicament of working-class women is the most potentially subversive to capitalism because it spans production and repro-duction, class exploitation and sex oppression. The movement of working-class women is thus essential for the emergence of socialist feminism because the necessary connections are forced upon women who are working-class when they take action.... They need each other, they need the support of male workers, and their fight at work connects immediately to their situation at home. Their organization and militancy is vital not only for women's liberation but for the whole socialist and working-class movement.[38]

Notes

1. E.g., Louise Lamphere, "Women's Work, Alienation and Class Consciousness" (paper presented at 72nd annual meeting of the American Anthropological Association, New Orleans, 1973); Eleanor Burke Leacock, ed., *The Origin of the Family, Private Property and the State*, by Friedrich Engels, with introduction by Leacock (New York: International Publishers, 1972); Lise Vogel, "The Earthly Family," *Radical America* 7, nos. 4-5 (July-October 1973): 9–50.
2. Isabel Larguia and John Dumoulin, "Toward a Science of Women's Liberation," *Women in Struggle* (NACLA, 1972).
3. Margaret Benston, "The Political Economy of Women's Liberation," *Monthly Review* 21, no. 4 (September 1969): 15.
4. Ibid., pp. 15–16.
5. Esther Boserup, *Woman's Role in Economic Development* (New York: St. Martin's Press, 1970).
6. Benston, "Political Economy of Women's Liberation," p. 15.
7. E.g., Lamphere, "Women's Work"; Virve Piho, "Life and Labor of the Female Textile Worker in Mexico City" (1973), in *Women Cross-Culturally: Change and Challenge*, ed. R. Rohrlich-Leavitt (The Hague:

Mouton, 1976); Rhona Rapoport and Robert Rapoport, *Dual Career Families* (Middlesex, Eng.: Penguin Books, 1971).

8. Cf. Evelyn P. Stevens, "Machismo and Marianismo," *Society* 10, no. 6 (September-October 1973): 57–63.

9. Cf. Jorge Gissi Bustos, "Mitologia sobre la mujer" (paper presented at SSRC Conference on Feminine Perspectives in Social Science Research in Latin America, Buenos Aires, 1974).

10. John Leggett, *Class, Race and Labor: Working Class Consciousness in Detroit* (New York: Oxford University Press, 1967), p. 39.

11. Informe Estadístico al Gobernador (Oficina del Gobernador, Junta de Planificación, Estado Libre Asociado de Puerto Rico, 1971), Table 8.

12. Although the number of women workers has increased steadily in this century, the percentage of all women fourteen years and over who are actually employed has declined from 26.1 percent in 1930 to 22.9 percent in 1970—Isabel Pico, "Apuntes preliminares para el estudio de la mujer puertorriqueña y su participación en las luchas sociales de principios del siglo XX" (paper presented at SSRC Conference on Feminine Perspectives in Social Science Research in Latin America, Buenos Aires, 1974). The percentage of men employed decreased even more dramatically, from 81.0 percent in 1930 to 54.7 percent in 1970 (ibid.). These decreases would appear to be due to factors such as overall population increase, increased life expectancy, and most importantly out-migration, particularly for men and women of working age.

13. Comisión de Derechos Civiles, "La igualdad de derechos y oportunidades de la mujer puertorriqueña" (Estado Libre Asociado de Puerto Rico, San Juan, 1972), p. 132.

14. Ibid., p. 133.

15. Ibid.

16. Ibid., pp. 138–39.

17. Ibid., p. 136.

18. Isabel Pico and Marcia Quintero, "Datos básicos de la mujer en la fuerza trabajadora en Puerto Rico" (Appendix to Pico, "Mujer puertorriquena"), p. 5.

19. Isabel Pico, "The Quest for Race, Sex, and Ethnic Equality in Puerto Rico" (paper presented at meeting of Latin American Studies Association, San Francisco, 1974), p. 4.

20. Pico and Quintero, "Datos básicos," p. 6.

21. Margo L. Smith, "Domestic Service as a Channel of Upward Mobility for the Lower Class Woman: The Lima Case," in *Female and Male in Latin America,* ed. A. Pescatello (Pittsburgh: University of Pittsburgh Press, 1973).

22. Helen Icken Safa, *The Urban Poor of Puerto Rico: A Study in Development and Inequality* (New York: Holt, Rinehart and Winston, 1974), p. 23.

23. Ibid.

24. Pico and Quintero, "Datos básicos," p. 1.

25. Cf. Piho, "Female Textile Worker."

26. Ibid.
27. Cf. Karen Sacks, "Engels Revisited," in *Woman, Culture, and Society,* ed. M. Rosaldo and L. Lamphere (Stanford, Calif.: Stanford University Press, 1974), p. 219.
28. Cf. Stevens, "Machismo and Marianismo."
29. Cf. Sidney Mintz, "Caribbean Nationhood in Anthropological Perspective," in *Caribbean Integration,* ed. S. Lewis and T. C. Mathews (Institute of Caribbean Studies, University of Puerto Rico, 1967).
30. June Nash, "Dependency and the Failure of Feedback: The Case of Bolivian Mining Communities," mimeographed, n.d., p. 23.
31. Angela Davis, "Reflections on the Black Women's Role in the Community of Slaves," *Black Scholar* 3, no. 4 (December 1971): 6–7.
32. Cf. Safa, *Urban Poor of Puerto Rico,* pp. 6–8.
33. Vogel, "The Earthly Family," p. 2.
34. Mariarosa Dalla Costa, "Women and the Subversion of the Community," *Radical America* 6, no. 1 (January-February 1972): 67–102.
35. Benston, "Political Economy of Women's Liberation," p. 23.
36. Pico, "Mujer puertorriquena."
37. Cf. Leggett, *Class, Race and Labor,* pp. 6–7.
38. Sheila Rowbotham, *Woman's Consciousness and Man's World* (Middlesex, Eng.: Penguin Books, 1973), p. 124.

Trade-Union Action and Political Behavior of the Chilean Miners of Chuquicamata

Francisco S. Zapata

The Chuquicamata Copper Mine

Chuquicamata[1] is located in the north of Chile, two hundred kilometers east of the port of Antofagasta. The deposit is 2,895 meters high in the arid and mountainous northern Atacama desert. Copper was mined at Chuquicamata as far back as 1536: Diego de Almagro, the Spanish conqueror of Chile, used copper horseshoes for his horses when he returned to Cuzco in Peru after his Chilean expedition. From 1560 to 1879 work was continued at the mine by Spaniards and Bolivians. At the time Chuquicamata was located in Bolivian territory. After the War of the Pacific (1879-1884), Chilean sovereignty was extended to this region, and the systematic exploitation of the mine became a real possibility when, in 1910, Albert Burrage, an American lawyer, heard about its enormous potential. The mine had been described to him as a very large deposit which, because the copper was in the form of an oxide, could not be worked with traditional technology using reduction and fusion of the ore. Burrage had studied a procedure for obtaining copper from this kind of deposit, using limestone as a precipitating agent. Because it seemed possible that the Chuquicamata copper ore could be treated in such a way, he sent an engineer to Chile to verify this. Burrage's representative immediately bought two extremely important mining concessions that were already being worked, and later he bought others. At this time Chuquicamata was worked by many small mine owners, and the amphitheater that is evident today did not exist. Burrage's procedure was extensively put to the test, and his systematic method of treating the Chuquicamata ore earned him the credit for having explored the possibility of exploiting the mine in its entirety, rather than concentrating only on high-content ore. Because the financial outlays necessary to make his method industrially viable were beyond his means, he invited the participation of Guggenheim, who in 1911, after a period of negotiation,

---

Originally published in French in *Sociologie du travail* (Paris), no. 3 (1975). This version, with some additions and changes by the author, was translated from the French by the author and Selina Cohen.

bought Burrage's concessions. At the beginning of 1912 Guggenheim, who also had large investments in Chilean nitrate, just a few miles from Chuquicamata, founded the Chile Exploration Company (CHILEX). Systematic exploration began in 1912 under Guggenheim's direction, and plans were made for large-scale exploitation of the mine. Copper production started in May 1915 and was continued under Guggenheim management until February 1923, when the Anaconda Copper Mining Corporation took control.[2]

The initial objective was to produce ten thousand tons of copper oxides a day, which would enable the company to sell one hundred million pounds of refined copper a year. Production capacity went up to 490 million pounds in 1941 due to new investments made in 1925, 1927, and after. In 1942 the American government asked for production to be increased to 540 million pounds. This was to be attained by working 335 days a year and by creating three shifts, seven days a week. During the war it was found that this level of production could not be maintained if only copper oxides were mined. From 1948 on, investments were made in new installations for treating sulphurous copper. In this way, what is now known as the *Planta de Súlfuros* came into being. These new installations, comprising a concentrator, several reverberatory ovens and converters, as well as a power plant, involved an investment of $30 million, which was incurred between 1948 and 1952, the year in which the plant began operations. From the viewpoint of the Chilean economy, the construction of these new facilities at Chuquicamata was significant, since other important investments were being made at the same time, especially in the steel industry (operations began at Huachipato in 1950), in hydroelectric power plants, and in petroleum production. Thus, by the beginning of the fifties, Chile had acquired the two most important mainstays for its economic development.

At Chuquicamata investment did not stop there. During the period of the Christian Democrat government (1964-1970), when what is known as the "Chileanization" of copper mines took place, a new refinery was built, and productivity was increased through small but useful changes in the production process. The power-generation capacity of the Tocopilla thermoelectric plant was also expanded. Meanwhile, commitments made by companies such as Anaconda and Kennecott before the "Chileanization" process began, and which were partly designed to postpone nationalization, were not honored. This meant that when, through Allende, the Unidad Popular coalition took power in 1970, many planned investments had not come to fruition. During the two-year period (July 1971-September 1973) in which responsibility for production at Chuquicamata was in the hands of Chilean officials, certain important projects, such as the exploration of the El Abra deposit near Chuquicamata, were initiated. By the time that Allende was deposed in 1973 a search for financial backing to exploit El Abra was already under way.

Production increased from 150,995 metric tons in 1940 to 262,996 metric tons in 1970, and earnings from the sale of that production rose from $37.9 million in 1940 to $361.8 million in 1970. During that same period employment rose from 7,406 to 10,250 workers, with a long period between 1950 and 1960 in which employment at the mine was lower than 5,500 workers. This period coincided with the outlawing of the Communist party, which was used by the company as an excuse to legitimate massive lay-offs of suspected militants and sympathizers.

Chile and Chuquicamata

Despite strict controls exerted by CHILEX on relations between its workers and the outside world, the Chuquicamata miners were not immune to the play of historical forces in Chile. Workers had connections with the national labor movement, and political participation was intense. CHILEX retaliated by preventing even presidential candidates from entering the company compound, where both production and housing were located. Pedro Aguirre Cerda, who had been denied the right to address workers in Chuquicamata when he was a candidate for the Popular Front coalition in 1938, refused to visit the mine. Salvador Allende, who had been a member of his party at that time, told this to Chuquicamata workers in March 1973 on an occasion when he donated the director's house to the trade unions. However, in spite of this and of the activities of the company's special police, Luis Emilio Recabarren, in his attempt between 1918 and 1920 to organize workers, gained the support of political organizations and trade unions alike. A small locality near the mine but outside its borders, called Punta de Rieles, gained a certain amount of notoriety for being the place where Recabarren organized his meetings. Recabarren tried to get the mine to respect Chilean sovereignty over its territory by writing letters to the manager asking why El socialista, a newspaper that he published in Tocopilla, could not be distributed in the mine. He mentioned Woodrow Wilson's liberal policies in the United States and asked why they were not practiced in Chuquicamata.

Working and living conditions among Chuquicamata miners at that time can be indicated from the eyewitness accounts of authors such as Ricardo Latcham.[3] Latcham and others indicate the closed character of the mine, the dangerous conditions under which production took place, the widespread practice of espionage. In particular they mention the existence of organized groups of spies who infiltrated the housing complexes, labor-union meetings, and even the production facilities and work teams. These witnesses refer to CHILEX's refusal to apply labor legislation approved by Parliament in 1924, particularly with respect to child labor. Latcham (who was an employee of the housing department at the time) drew attention to poor housing and sanitary conditions as well as to practices such as the "warm bed," whereby beds were used twenty-four hours a day by miners who worked in different posts and in different shifts.

The features that determine the political behavior of Chuquicamata miners have historical roots that need explication. Ever since the beginning of the mine in 1915 and even before trade unions were organized, the miners have expressed their grievances. Petitions were frequently presented to management without any legal protection, while political campaigns were organized on the site. Only in 1930-1931 were unions legally established, following the passing of the Labor Code. Chuquicamata workers belonged to two unions: the blue-collar union (*sindicato industrial*) and the white-collar union (*sindicato profesional*). Initially the unions fought for better working conditions and better salaries and also defended the right to present petitions (*pliegos de peticiones*). They asked for special protection for labor leaders so that they could work without fear of dismissal for their activities. A union manifesto distributed in 1938, and written by labor leader José Diaz Iturrieta, is explicit in this regard. When popular political organizations such as the Communist and Socialist parties gained strength around 1935 (the Socialist party was created in 1933, and the Communist party moved toward an alliance with it from early 1935), the unions were able to consolidate their position in relation to management.

The left received massive support from the miners during this period. When Pedro Aguirre Cerda won the presidential elections in 1938, 77.8 percent of the votes in the mine were cast in his favor. Miners progressively gained more bargaining strength (especially after the creation of the Confederation of Copper Workers in 1951), and this enabled them to obtain a series of social and monetary advantages denied to the rest of the Chilean working class. Meanwhile, in the mines, and in Chuquicamata in particular, general social conditions were not very different from those prevailing in the rest of the country: housing, education, and health facilities were far from satisfactory. It was only when the structural relationship between CHILEX and the Chilean government was reformulated between 1955 and the advent of "Chileanization," that any real changes in these conditions, especially in housing, took place. In any case, it is clear that differences in wages and social benefits between miners and the rest of the Chilean working class do not alter the structural position in which miners are located.

The union is the only vehicle available to the miners through which they can express their grievances. It represents the only legitimate channel through which miners can expose their problems. For this reason the unions have a very high level of legitimacy, which also extends to the position the labor movement occupies in the Chilean political system. Unlike in many other Latin American countries, pressure from workers is tolerated without too many constraints. Consequently, although the company exerts its control over union activities at the local level, it has to accept miners' petitions when the pressure is sufficiently strong, as well as the possibility of state intervention in labor relations at the plant level. Naturally this has a bearing on those factors that relate the labor movement to the power structure in the country. As a rule labor unions are inextricably bound to the national movement and have to be taken into account when political decisions are made with respect to labor. They can, on occasion, even change the balance of power. In fact this was clearly demonstrated in numerous situations, especially during the Allende period. The Christian Democrat labor leaders linked their action at the local level to the offensive that their party was building up at the national level.

Age, Length of Service, Wages, and Salaries

Before going on to analyze the political behavior of Chuquicamata miners in detail, it is first necessary to make some comments on the structural characteristics of the labor force.

Differences between blue- and white-collar workers that exist both in the mine and in the rest of the country are particularly significant in the Chilean case. Here, the separation between these two categories has unique characteristics because the distinction does not coincide, as it does elsewhere in the world, with manual or nonmanual categories of work. As a matter of fact, in order to conform to social security legislation, a distinction between manual and nonmanual categories was formulated, but it progressively lost its significance when subsequent decrees gave certain blue-collar workers, such as electricians, mechanics, and so on, the right to receive white-collar benefits while keeping the same job. The erosion of this distinction had certain practical consequences from the unions' point of view. White-collar unions, which traditionally represented administrative personnel, began to receive blue-collar members into their ranks, and consequently unions became involved with aspects of production and with specific manual jobs in the production system. This radically changed the character of white-collar unions in two important respects: (a) it modified the overall ratio of manual to nonmanual workers within the company, and (b) it caused a drop in the number of blue-collar union affiliates, thus altering the balance of power between the two unions.

Chuquicamata provides a good opportunity for observing the differences between the two categories of workers. In Tables 1, 2, and 3 these differences are shown in terms of age, length of service, and the structure of wages and salaries. In addition, there are more salary earners between the ages of thirty and forty-four than there are aged forty-four years and over. These data correspond to those existing at the national level—at least for the 1960 National Population Census. The age-structure figures for Chuquicamata bear a direct relationship to the length of service of the same population. Here we can observe that blue-collar

Table 1
Age of Blue- and White-Collar Workers in Chuquicamata, 1973
(In percentages)

Age	Blue collar (wage earners)	White collar (salary earners)	Total
Under 30 years	44	18	31
30-44 years	43	54	48
Over 44 years	13	28	21
	100	100	100

Table 2
Length of Service of Blue- and White-Collar Workers in Chuquicamata, 1973
(In percentages)

Length of Service	Blue collar	White collar	Total
0-5 years	59.7	33.0	46.6
6-10	20.8	30.6	25.6
11-15	8.3	14.0	11.1
16-20	5.9	10.8	8.3
21-25	2.2	5.0	3.6
26-30	2.0	4.2	3.1
Over 30 years	1.1	2.4	1.7
	100.0	100.0	100.0

Table 3
Composition of Earnings of Blue- and White-Collar Workers in
Chuquicamata, 1973
(Percentage of total earnings)

Source of earnings	Blue collar	White collar
Base salary	43	41
Overtime	16	20
Incentive pay	21	20
Family allowances	20	19
	100	100

workers (wage earners) have a shorter length of service record than do white-collar workers (salary earners). However, from this we should not adduce that a short length-of-service record is a specific characteristic of blue-collar workers, since these figures are low for all workers at the mine, implying a high rate of turnover at Chuquicamata. More than half of the personnel have worked there for less than five years, and more detailed data show that 76 percent of the workers began to work in the mine after

1970. Chuquicamata is therefore generally considered as a temporary work place, especially by blue-collar workers. Finally, we observe in Table 3 that the difference in salaries between white- and blue-collar workers is in fact very small, the only real disparity being in overtime payments. Overtime is mainly worked by blue-collar workers with white-collar status and by those engaged in maintenance work (e.g., mechanics, electricians, etc.).

The Political History of the Mine

As a rule, political sociology recognizes the specific norms of workers' political behavior as resulting from both their homogeneity in status and the presence of a worker culture or subculture that tend to create common orientations among the working classes. Labor organizations and the ideological influence of trade unions and popular political parties reinforce these shared orientations among the working-class sectors of society. There is evidence to suggest that in those Latin American countries where a parliamentary democracy operates, there is a positive correlation between the strength of the trade-union movement and the strength of popular political parties. These general considerations go some way toward explaining the political and electoral behavior of the Chuquicamata miners as well as the wider political orientations of the Chilean working class. This is of particular interest since it has a direct bearing on the relationship between a concrete working-class group, the miners, and the national labor movement.

The Chilean labor movement was just beginning to become organized when the mine first began operations, but it was in the nearby nitrate mines (150 km to the west) that the labor movement really came into its own through the activities of its leader, Luis Emilio Recabarren (1879-1924). Recabarren traveled from one nitrate mine to the other, founding newspapers, developing contacts among workers in Chacabuco, Alemania, Baquedamo, and Caracoles, arranging meetings in the *pampa* ("desert") and organizing strikes. In this manner, organizations such as the *mancomunales* were set up to counteract the capitalist associations: the parallel development of labor with capitalist organizations has been one of the principal causes of the strength of labor in Chile. Elias Lafferte, leader of the Chilean Communist party, wrote in his memoirs and in other documents of the close contact between these working centers in the 1910-1920 period during which many associations were founded.[4] The existence of the Chilean railroad network in the north of the country greatly facilitated these contacts. By the time Chuquicamata started production in 1915, the nitrate workers had already established their unions and centers for ideological training in Antofagasta, Tocopilla, and Iquique. At a national level the Federación Obrera de Chile (FOCh) had already obtained legal recognition, and the Partido Obrero Socialista, a dissident faction of the Partido Democrático, had already been founded at Iquique.[5] Early organizational work in the nitrate mines as well as in the ports and transport companies paid off at Chuquicamata, where, according to some witnesses, violent demonstrations took place, which manifested themselves in particular as protests against accidents and nonpayment for certain types of work. Recabarren was also associated with these activities in the early twenties. However, at Chuquicamata itself a union was not organized until after the official labor legislation was passed in 1924, which meant that all previous action taken by workers had been unlawful.

During the presidential elections of 1920 the organized working class put its strength behind the populist candidate, Alessandri. Alessandri's candidacy led to numerous discussions and polemics: some argued that Recabarren should have been the candidate, but Recabarren himself supported the idea of giving the labor vote to Alessandri. Nevertheless, despite his unwillingness to act as the labor candidate, he still obtained some votes in the elections.

The period from 1920 to 1938 is characterized by a series of parallel developments: the working class became integrated into a legal apparatus and at the same time into a political system and its institutions. Its modest vote was to play an increasingly important role in the political structure and at the end of the period would be instrumental in the election of the Popular Front. The support that the FOCh gave to the Popular Front and the existence of white-collar labor unions and of other middle-class organizations contributed toward the formation of a political base for the left, which was beginning to make itself felt in Chile.

During the thirties, at the time when unions were being formed at the mine, workers became conscious of national political problems. The meetings organized by Aguirre Cerda in Punta de Rieles (the small town just outside Chuquicamata) were attended by the miners, who had to violate prohibitions about leaving company premises at night in order to get there. During this period the management was particularly repressive with the *Guardia Especial* (its private police force) present everywhere—at trade-union meetings, in private homes, in working places, and so on.

Since there is no real labor history of the mine or sufficient information of electoral behavior, an analysis of the miners' political behavior at this time must necessarily be rather sketchy. However, on the basis of fragmentary data and a rather superficial examination of the company's archives, it is possible to say that worker-management relations at Chuquicamata have never been peaceful. Despite the existence of the Labor Code (instituted in 1931), any organization of labor conflict was forestalled by the company's systematic violation of workers' rights. As the author was able to observe,[6] even during the period of the Unidad Popular administration, the local labor inspector was nothing more than a mere appendage of the company. Perhaps it is in the nature of labor relations that there should be an element of hostility that blocks any possibility of agreement between labor representatives and management. The asymmetry which exists among the parties with respect to their relative power is responsible for this situation. Nevertheless, certain structural conditions, such as geographic isolation, the omnipotent power of the company, as well as the importance of the company as a key industry for the country's development, all contribute to the consolidation of this situation.

Table 4 shows some electoral results specific to the mine. In Chuquicamata it is easy to identify the miners' political orientations because the whole population lives in the district, and there are very few people there (some shop owners, public employees) who do not work in the mine. In addition, even after some miners moved to the nearby town of Calama (the government built houses there after the "Chileanization" process started in 1969), electoral cards were not changed, so these miners continued to cast their vote at the mine. As a result, Chuquicamata electoral results closely reflect the miners' political thinking.

From the data in Table 4 we can see a clear, though as yet small, decline in the miners' vote for the left. In the 1967 elections and in subsequent presidential elections, the left recuperated lost ground, though the decline reasserted itself in later years. The left's comeback in 1967 can be explained by events at El Salvador in 1966 when there was a confrontation between mine workers and the Chilean army in which many people died. This incident was followed by an important offensive by the left in all the mining centers (El Teniente, El Salvador, and Chuquicamata) led by the Confederation of Copper Workers (CTC). The popularity of the left candidate as well as the polarization of forces into two or three camps can explain the better results obtained by the left in the presidential elections. Table 4 also shows a correlation

Table 4
Elections at Chuquicamata from 1938 to 1973

Year	Type of election	Leftist parties	Percentage of votes for left	Number of voters (if available)
1938	Presidential	PR+PS+other	77.4	2,201
1947	Municipal	PC	68.0	—
1958	Presidential	PR+PC+PS	51.1	—
1960	Municipal	PC+PS	40.6	—
1961	Congressional	PC+PS	56.3	—
1963	Municipal	PC+PS	42.3	—
1964	Presidential	PR+PC+PS	44.7	—
1965	Congressional	PC+PS	51.3	—
1967	Municipal	PC+PS	53.8	—
1969	Congressional	PC+PS	24.3	5,563
1970	Presidential	PR+PC+PS	43.5	6,540
1972	Union (CUT)	PC+PS	30.5	4,617
1973	Local Chuquicamata union election	PC+PS+ PR+MAPU	26.3	6,519

Note: For adequate understanding of the above table it is necessary to take into account the following:

1. The pronounced loss of votes by the PC-PS alliance in 1969 was due to the division of the PS and the birth of Union Socialista Popular, which attracted most Chuquicamata votes. This situation also influenced local union election results in 1973.

2. Voting results for presidential elections in 1958, 1964, and 1970 only identify male votes: women's votes have been excluded because women are not significantly represented in the mine's employment. In other tables we include the women's vote to show differences in voting patterns between the mine and the nearby town of Calama.

Leftist parties: MAPU—Movement of Unitary Action; PC—Communist party; PR—Radical party; PS—Socialist party.

between parliamentary and municipal election results which demonstrates the overall strength of the left. This fact is confirmed by the labor-union election results (representing the professional vote) in which candidates demonstrated their solidarity with labor. Here again, electoral behavior can be seen to reflect national trends. From this we can deduce that there is no disparity between votes for different types of elections—the municipal, parliamentary, congressional, and union vote being equally politicized.

In the 1970 presidential election Chuquicamata miners (i.e., those who voted for Allende in Table 4) gave a narrow advantage to the popular parties' candidate who represented the national labor movement. Here, the miners' votes were distributed in almost equal part between Allende and the right-wing conservative candidate. If we examine the votes obtained by the popular parties in the parliamentary elections of 1969, we find that Allende did not exceed the total PC (Communist party), PS (Socialist party), PR (Radical party), and USOPO (Union Socialista Popular)[7] vote at this election, i.e., 65 percent of the male vote in Chuquicamata. Consequently, part of the popular parties' vote went to either the conservative right-wing candidate or to the Christian Democrat candidate, which is significant for the direction votes took at the mine.

A fundamental feature of both the presidential election results and the political behavior of the miners is the significant presence of USOPO and the support obtained by this splinter party in Chuquicamata during the 1967-1973 period. Indeed, it is interesting to note the extent of USOPO's influence. A dissident faction of the Socialist party of Chile which reflected the influence of important personalities such as Ampuero, Silvia Ulloa, and the labor leader Oscar Nuñez, USOPO was also a political force in its own right, and Chuquicamata was one of its main bastions. Out of a total of 29,123 votes cast nationally for the party during the 1971 municipal elections, 7,899 were from the Antofagasta province, and of these 4,826 were from Chuquicamata—i.e., over 60 percent of the USOPO votes in Antofagasta came from the mine. Another feature of USOPO's electoral results was that it was supported equally by men and women. Its popularity went beyond the traditional barriers that usually differentiate the male from the female vote in Chile. (This phenomenon occurred not only in Chuquicamata but also in the coal mines of the south of Chile.) This however does not pertain to the Socialist and Communist parties or to the vote obtained by Allende in 1970. USOPO's success, we feel, derives from the particular strategy followed by this party in the mine, and in particular with respect to labor-union matters.

Between 1958 and 1973 the presence of socialist labor leaders became important in the mine. When the split in the PS took place in 1969, from which USOPO originated, most of the socialist labor leadership followed USOPO. In the union elections of 1970 USOPO gained control over the mine's unions by placing three

Table 5
Presidential Elections in 1970 at Chuquicamata and Calama, by Sex
(In percentages)

Candidates	Men		Women		Total	
	Chuqui	Calama	Chuqui	Calama	Chuqui	Calama
Tomic (CD)	14.5	15.9	15.5	20.0	14.9	17.8
Alessandri (PN)	41.1	31.0	51.5	39.3	45.3	34.8
Allende (UP)	43.5	51.9	31.6	38.9	38.7	45.9
Null and void	0.9	1.2	1.4	1.8	1.1	1.5
Total	100.0	100.0	100.0	100.0	100.0	100.0
No. of voters	6,540	7,752	4,440	6,615	10,980	14,367

Table 6
Congressional Elections in 1969 at Chuquicamata and Calama, by Political Party and Sex
(In percentages)

Political party	Men		Women		Total	
	Chuqui	Calama	Chuqui	Calama	Chuqui	Calama
Communist party (PC)	14.3	24.4	9.8	16.7	12.6	20.9
Socialist party (PS)	10.0	9.3	7.9	8.0	9.2	8.7
Radical party (PR)	25.5	19.5	27.7	20.3	26.0	19.8
Union Socialista Popular (USOPO)	26.6	13.8	26.9	11.5	26.8	12.8
Padena	0.7	2.1	0.7	2.5	0.7	2.3
Christian Democrat (CD)	14.6	19.4	17.3	29.4	15.6	23.9
National Party (PN)	5.8	6.1	7.0	6.5	6.2	6.4
Null and void	3.0	5.4	2.7	5.1	2.9	5.2
Total	100.5	100.0	100.0	100.0	100.0	100.0
No. of voters	5,563	6,115	3,364	5,502	8,927	11,167

members in the industrial (blue-collar) union and two members in the professional (white- and blue-collar) union. In addition, two more of USOPO's leaders were elected in Antofagasta and Tocopilla. There is no doubt that election results both at the union level and at the parliamentary or presidential level reflect the strength and political influence of USOPO among the miners. We turn now to the question of how USOPO gained its popularity and influence.

In general terms we can say that USOPO's success derives from the economic tactics that it employed in the mine. In comparison with other mines Chuquicamata has had a very large number of wildcat strikes. In 1971 there were thirty-seven strikes, in 1972, ninety-two. There are many reasons for this: erratic behavior by some labor leaders trying to increase their power through demagogic petitions; grievances over hours of work, overtime, refusal to perform certain tasks, job classifications, problems over changing rooms, security, clothes, and so on; and finally the inability of the company to effectively implement the provisions of the collective contract and to put into practice the new wage structure and job definitions.

Yet although these reasons go some way toward providing an explanation for the wildcat strikes, wider motives are frequently at play, and the labor leadership's decisions to call these strikes are often contingent upon local, provincial, or national political considerations. This is not surprising in view of the close relationship that exists between political and trade-union elections. Through generating strikes and stoppages, the labor leadership can maintain control over its membership and thus use it as a lever for implementing its own political aims, which are often far removed from the work place. In Chuquicamata strikes and wildcat strikes are used as means of gaining political control over the workers.

During the 1971-1973 period, trade-union action in Chuquicamata must be seen in relation to USOPO's political hegemony and the important influence of the Christian Democrats (CD): both parties were working in the same direction against the Unidad Popular (UP) management of the mine.[8] Within the unions the UP was weak—it had only one member among the ten leaders of the mine's two unions. In addition, USOPO and the Christian Democrats formed an alliance to oppose any kind of compromise with the UP, either at the management or the political level. This weakness of the left was clearly demonstrated during the national CUT (National Confederation of Chilean Workers) leadership election of May 1972. During the preceding month of April, fifteen strikes were staged in the mine over irrelevant grievances to demonstrate the strength of the USOPO-CD alliance against any possible support the miners might give to the CUT. This strategy was again applied before the local union elections of February 1973 and again before the parliamentary elections of March 1973. The USOPO and the CD leadership therefore used strike action to pursue a national political objective, which in this case was to oppose Allende's government.

The situation was changed, however, by the local union elections of February 1973, in which Unidad Popular and the Christian Democrats jointly displaced USOPO as the dominant political force in the mine. Unidad Popular gained control over the industrial (blue-collar) union and the Christian Democrats over the professional (white- and blue-collar) union. From now on the two unions were no longer able to work together in the same way they had when USOPO and the Christian Democrats formed an alliance against Unidad Popular. February 1973 marked the end of such partnerships. In critical moments, such as the strike in solidarity with the El Teniente miners (April-June 1973), the two unions adopted different strategies. In this case, the industrial union managed to keep its members working, whereas, on the contrary, the professional union persuaded its members to participate in the solidarity strike. In addition, the relation of forces among the various political parties in the mine began to more closely approximate the national pattern than it had before the elections. If before the elections the mine had politically distinctive features due to the presence of USOPO, these had disappeared by February 1973. There had been a shift from a situation where Unidad Popular was in confrontation with both USOPO and the Christian Democrats to the one that existed in the country as a whole, where the main confrontation was between Unidad Popular and the Christian Democrats. This was borne out during the parliamentary elections of March 1973, during the course of which USOPO again lost its hold over the Chuquicamata miners (see Table 7 below).

These factors are important in order to understand the shift in the miners' vote. The fluctuations indicated above demonstrate a rationality in the miners' behavior which is as evident in their relations with the unions on a local level as it is in their relations with the labor movement on a national level.

In fact, the type of relations that exist in the mine between the labor leadership and its base, and the perceptions that the rank and file has of its leaders, are better analyzed in terms of patron-client relations than in terms of relations between a social class and

Table 7
Local Union Election Results at Chuquicamata
by Political Party and Type of Union, 1973

	Blue-collar union		White-collar union	
Political party	Votes	%	Votes	%
Unidad Popular (UP)	1,026	37.2	683	28.2
USOPO	739	26.8	300	12.4
Christian Democrats (CD)	824	30.0	1,080	44.6
National Party (PN)	165	6.0	356	14.8
Total	2,754	100.0	2,419	100.0

its leadership. However, to view trade-union action in Chuquica-mata as entirely economistic would be too formal a characterization of events. Even when USOPO was in control of the workers' representation, at a time when worker orientations were particu-larly clearly demonstrated at the mine, its action was directed more toward the political system than toward direct, nonmediated defense of workers' interests. This tie with the political system may well have served to defend the workers' interests, but this was of secondary importance, USOPO's main objective being to maintain the viability of the party.

This type of labor action does not always lead to a coherent policy: workers are used for the purposes of party politics, and they move further and further away from the possibility of class action. Rather than unifying the workers and integrating them into a mass organization (such as the Chilean labor movement), USOPO's rather particularistic interests tended to work against a class strategy by alienating the workers from the national labor movement. When USOPO was removed from the political arena, a new combination of political forces came into play at Chuqui-camata. The miners then divided their loyalties between the Christian Democrats and Unidad Popular and gave very little support to the other political tendencies or to the independent groups. In addition, the increasing preference of the miners for the right, revealed during the 1970 presidential elections and to a lesser degree in the trade-union and parliamentary elections of 1973, casts doubt on the validity of the assumption held by

Unidad Popular that the miners were the conscious sector of the Chilean working class. Although it is not totally false to interpret the miners' behavior as revolutionary in the light of earlier historical events, what was happening in 1970-1973 did not produce any evidence whatsoever to support the UP's belief that the miners were the vanguard of the Chilean working class.

The shifting of the miners' vote toward a polarization between the Christian Democrats and the left revealed a complete transformation of their political orientations. This reinforces the thesis that refutes the miners' radicalism. In fact the patron-client character of labor action which was demonstrated during the period of USOPO influence is not limited to that contingency, but has very much deeper roots. It is possible, as the solidarity strike with the miners of El Teniente has shown, that the union factor in the political behavior of the miners clearly overdetermines the ideological factor that was made so central to the historical analysis provided at the beginning of this paper.

Trade-Union Action and Political Behavior

Throughout this article reference has been made to the specific experience of Chuquicamata and to the political behavior of its miners. This experience can now be placed in a wider context to provide a more general analysis. Chuquicamata lends itself well to analysis within the framework of the industrial-relations theory of company towns first formulated by Kerr and Siegel in 1954:[9] industrial towns produce their own particular brand of labor relations. In addition, Chuquicamata is important in the context of the economic situation in Latin America as a whole insofar as it is a raw-material-producing center, and raw materials contribute substantially to the hard currency necessary for importing consumer and capital goods from industrialized nations. In Bolivia, Chile, Peru, and Venezuela the percentage of mineral exports in relation to total exports by these countries in 1972 were 73.2 percent, 81.1 percent, 64.8 percent, and 99.2 percent, respectively. And finally, Chuquicamata should also be analyzed within the framework of those theories pertaining to the upper strata of the working class, sometimes unjustly termed the "labor aristocracy": these theories examine the ways in which these workers differ from those located in the less important economic sectors. An attempt will be made to formulate some conclusions with regard to Chuquicamata in relation to these three theories.

Essential features will be isolated, but they will not necessarily be linked to any one of the theories.

First, one can argue that the political behavior of the miners can be explained in terms of their strong bargaining power. This is derived from the geographical isolation of the centers within which raw-material-producing industries, such as copper in Chile, invariably operate. Work stoppages, strikes, and conflicts all lower productivity, which can cause considerable losses in production and consequently in the level of exports. The miners are conscious of the bargaining power that this brings them. Their degree of consciousness is shown by the intensity of the conflict, and this often leads to a belief in the radicalism of the miners. At the most elementary level they utilize the key position they hold in the country's economy to ameliorate their economic and social situation, and they do this through frequent and intense recourse to their bargaining strength. Nevertheless, it should not be forgotten that if the miners have this power against the mine owner, the latter, in turn, is strategically located in relation to the government of the country. What this means is that what the owner withholds or concedes to the workers is for the most part decided upon in collusion with the government. Thus, the whole political system is affected by the system of labor relations at the mine. Conflicts in the company town are immediately felt at a governmental level.

On the other hand, some authors hold the view that the miners' political activities have ideological foundations which explain the high level of their class consciousness, the violence of labor conflicts, their close relationship with leftist parties, and so forth.[10] In other words, the political action of miners accurately reflects their political radicalism. From the analysis presented here, the hypothesis of ideologically determined political radicalism is at the very least ambiguous when the recent development of labor and political attitudes among the miners of Chuquicamata is taken into account. As a matter of fact, we observe a progressive transfer of the support previously given by the miners to the left toward the parties of the center, such as the Christian Democrats, or to the right, such as the National Party. The miners appeared to support the left while it was in opposition. When it was in power, they no longer used it as a political lever for their union action, despite the political autonomy maintained by the labor movement during the period of the Unidad Popular government. From this we can infer the proposition that the miners' political radicalism is not of an ideological nature but is instead connected to a search for political support for simple bread-and-butter issues. The miners look for political support wherever they can find it and are willing to act as the clientele of whatever political party is prepared to offer it to them. These considerations should be borne in mind when observing the particular relationships which existed between the miners and the political parties at Chuquicamata during the various periods of their history. Although adequate enough for explaining electoral data, this proposition cannot be applied to an analysis of certain other manifestations, such as the strike in solidarity with the El Teniente miners that was set in motion by the white-collar workers at Chuquicamata. Solidarity between workers of different companies cannot be explained solely by economic motives. This is essentially a political manifestation. In the case of the El Teniente solidarity strike, one last possible explanation remains. This unites the political and economistic character of the miners' action and links it to a fundamental component of the relations of production in company towns: the labor union.

As a matter of fact, the strike at Chuquicamata in solidarity with the El Teniente workers expresses the preoccupation of the miners who supported the Christian Democrats in the union elections of February 1973. These workers were concerned about the survival of the union structure which they perceived as the principal means for the defense of their interests. The process of direct worker participation in the management of state enterprises, as well as the political circumstances in Chile during the first few months of 1973, led the miners to believe that the very existence of the union was threatened. Workers, especially those that were not committed to the left, thought that participation and the strike at El Teniente were signs of this menace. Even ignoring the political differences that existed among the workers (there were not many militants of the Christian Democratic party at Chuquicamata), the defense of the union became the decisive factor in determining the workers' political behavior. The workers' bargaining strength and the action of the political parties contributed toward the defense of their union, but the workers also accomplished this task by their own radicalism in defense of the victories they had gained. The token support that workers gave, at the level of their federal union organizations, to the nationalization of Mineria del Cobre (see note 1) was dictated by considerations for the position of their union. The violent confrontations that erupted between miners and police during the solidarity strike also confirm this explanation and reinforce the proposition that the miners are essentially union-oriented. These orientations clearly dominate ideological or purely trade-unionist considerations. For the miners, unionism *is* their form of politics. This is not necessarily the same thing as "trade unionism" or "economism." It goes beyond economism because it implies a political affiliation which can naturally change and which binds the miners to the political system. Their demands and grievances provide the workers with an opportunity to define their place in the political system and in the power structure of society. It is within the framework of the union, the organization created by the workers in order to express their grievances, that the miners formulate their political interests.

Notes

1. In Chile copper production is organized at three levels: the Gran Mineria del Cobre (GMC), the Pequeña Mineria, and the Mediana Mineria. The Gran Mineria del Cobre exports everything it produces, the second provides copper for national manufacturing industries, while the Mediana Mineria also exports most of its production. In 1970 the GMC exported copper worth over $700 million. Its production originated in five principal mines: Chuquicamata, El Salvador-Potrerillos, El Teniente, Exotica, and Andina. These mines employ about twenty-five thousand workers, who represent less than 1 percent of Chile's working population and 25 percent of the active mining population, which also contains workers in iron ore, gold, and other metallic and nonmetallic minerals. The organization of production of the GMC is separated from the Pequeña and Mediana Mineria. The GMC is owned by the National Copper Corporation (CODELCO), while the Mediana and Pequeña Mineria are controlled by the Empresa Nacional de Mineria (ENAMI). When nationalization of the GMC took place in 1971, CODELCO continued to play an important role in production aspects but had to enter into the labor-relations aspect, which, until then, had not been under its jurisdiction.

2. See B. A. Kennedy et al., "A Case Study of Slope Stability at the Chuquicamata Mine, Chile," *Society of Mining Engineers, Transactions* 250 (March 1971); also *Mining Engineering*, December 1952, where a series of articles retrace the technical history of Chuquicamata; other technical data appear in *Mining Engineering*, January 1955, December 1960, and November 1969.

3. See Ricardo Latcham, *Chuquicamata, estado yanki, vision de la montaña roja* (Santiago: Ed. Nascimento, 1928). Also, Eulogio Gutiérrez and Marcial Figueroa, *Chuquicamata, su grandeza y sus dolores* (Santiago, 1920).

4. See Elias Lafferte, *Vida de un comunista* (Santiago: Ed. Quimantu, 1972).

5. For a discussion of these bodies and of other early Chilean labor organizations, see the chapter by Alan Angell in part 1 of this book. [Eds.]

6. The author was a sociologist at the mine during the Allende government. He was put in charge of labor relations at the request of David Silberman, general manager of the Compañía de Cobre Chuquicamata, who disappeared in October 1974.

7. USOPO originated from the division of the Socialist Party of Chile in 1967.

8. The program of Unidad Popular, led by Salvador Allende, was signed in Santiago in 1969 by the PS, PC, PR, MAPU, the Social Democrat Party, and Independent Popular Action. When UP is referred to in the text, it refers to this alliance of left-wing parties. [Eds.]

9. See Clark Kerr and Abraham Siegel, "Inter-industry Propensity to Strike," in *Collective Bargaining*, ed. A. Flanders (London: Penguin Books, 1966). Other literature on miners and company towns includes Dirk Krujit and Menno Vellinga, "La politique économique des enclaves minières au Pérou," *Tiers monde* (Paris), October-December 1977; Heraclio Bonilla, *El Minero de los Andes* (Lima: Instituto de Estudios Peruanos, 1976); René Zavaleta, *El proletariado minero en Bolivia* (manuscript presented to the Seminar on Labor and Economic Development in Latin America, Bariloche, Argentina, 1974); Lawrence Whitehead, *El comportamiento político de los trabajadores mineros: un enfoque comparativo* (manuscript, CEPLAN, Santiago, Chile, 1973).

10. On El Teniente miners see James Petras and Maurice Zeitlin, "Miners and Agrarian Radicalism," *American Sociological Review*, August 1967. Also James Petras and Maurice Zeitlin, "En torno a la situación política Chilena: huelga en El Teniente," *Mensaje* (Santiago), June 1973 (reproduced by *El Trimestre Económico* [Mexico], no. 160).

Further Reading

General

Bates, R. H. "Approaches to the Study of Unions and Development." *Industrial Relations* 9, no. 4 (1970): 365–78.

Berg, E. "Some Problems in the Analysis of Urban Proletarian Politics in the Third World." *Comparative Urban Research* 3, no. 3 (1975-1976): 46–60.

Friedland, W. H. *Unions and Industrial Relations in Underdeveloped Countries*. Ithaca: New York School of Industrial and Labor Relations, 1964.

Galenson, W., ed. *Comparative Labor Movements*. Englewood Cliffs, N.J.: Prentice-Hall, 1953.

———. *Labor and Economic Development*. New York: John Wiley & Sons, 1959.

———. *Labor in Developing Countries*. Berkeley and Los Angeles: University of California Press, 1963.

Ghosh, S. *Trade Unionism in the Underdeveloped Countries*. Calcutta: Bookland Private, 1960.

Gutkind, P. C. W. *Urban Anthropology: Perspectives on "Third World" Urbanization and Urbanism*. Assen, The Netherlands: Van Gorcum, 1974.

Hyman, R. *Marxism and the Sociology of Trade Unionism*. London: Pluto Press, 1971.

Jolly, R.; De Kadt, E.; Singer, H.; and Wilson, F., eds. *Third World Employment Problems and Strategy*. London: Penguin Books, 1973.

Kassalow, E. M. *National Labor Movements in the Post-War World*. Evanston, Ill.: Northwestern University Press, 1963.

Kerr, C.; Dunlop, J. T.; Harbison, F.; and Myers, C. A. *Industrialism and Industrial Man*. Cambridge, Mass.: Harvard University Press, 1960.

London University. *Collected Seminar Papers on Labour Unions and Political Organizations*. Institute of Commonwealth Studies Paper, no. 3. London: London University, Institute of Commonwealth Studies, 1967.

Marquand, H. A., ed. *Organized Labor in Four Continents*. London and New York: Longmans, Green and Co., 1939.

Millen, B. H. *The Political Role of Labor in Developing Countries*. Washington: Brookings Institution, 1963.

Moore, W. E. *Industrialization and Labor*. Ithaca, N.Y.: Cornell University Press, 1951.

Roberts, B. C. "Labor Relations in Overseas Territories." *Political Quarterly* 28 (1957): 390–404.

———. *Labor in the Tropical Countries of the Commonwealth*. Durham, N.C.: Duke University Press, 1964.

Ross, A. M., ed. *Industrial Relations and Economic Development.* London: Macmillan, 1966.

Sandbrook, R. "The Working Class in the Future of the Third World." *World Politics* 15, no. 3 (1973): 448–78.

Sufrin, S. C. *Unions in Emerging Societies: Frustrations and Politics.* Syracuse, N.Y.: Syracuse University Press, 1964.

Waterman, P. "Workers in the Third World." *Monthly Review* 29 (September 1977): 50–64.

Africa

Ainslie, R. *Masters and Serfs: Farm Labour in South Africa.* London: International Defence and Aid Fund, 1973.

Allen, C. "Unions, Incomes and Development." In *Developmental Trends in Kenya,* pp.61–92. Edinburgh: University of Edinburgh, Centre of African Studies, 1972.

Allen, V. L. "The Meaning of the Working Class in Africa." *Journal of Modern African Studies* 10, no. 2 (1972): 169–88.

Amsden, A. H. *International Firms and Labour in Kenya: 1945-1970.* London: Frank Cass & Co., 1971.

Ananaba, W. *The Trade Union Movement in Nigeria.* London: C. Hurst & Co., 1969.

Arrighi, G. and Saul, J. S. *Essays on the Political Economy of Africa.* New York: Monthly Review Press, 1973.

Bates, R. H. *Unions, Parties and Political Development: A Study of Mineworkers in Zambia.* New Haven: Yale University Press, 1971.

Beling, W. A. *Modernization and African Labor: A Tunisian Case Study.* New York: Praeger, 1965.

———, ed. *The Role of Labor in African Nation-Building.* New York: Praeger, 1968.

Berg, E. J. and Butler, J. "Trade Unions." In *Political Parties and National Integration in Tropical Africa,* edited by J. S. Coleman and E. G. Rosberg. Berkeley and Los Angeles: University of California Press, 1964.

Bissman, K. "Industrial Workers in East Africa." *International Journal of Comparative Sociology* 10, nos. 1/2 (1969): 22–30.

Braverman, R. E. "The African Working Class: Recent Changes, New Prospects." *The African Communist* 59 (fourth quarter 1974): 48–60.

Burawoy, M. "The Colour of Class on the Copper Mines: From African Advancement to Zambianization." *Zambian Papers* 7 (1972).

Clarke, D. G. "African Workers and Union Formation in Rhodesia." *South African Labour Bulletin* 1, no. 9 (1975): 1–65.

———. *Contract Workers and Underdevelopment in Rhodesia.* Gwelo, Rhodesia: Mambo Press, 1974.

Clayton, A. and Savage, D. C. *Government and Labour in Kenya 1895-1963.* London: Frank Cass & Co., 1975.

Cohen, R. *Labour and Politics in Nigeria.* London: Heinemann, 1974.

———. "From Peasants to Workers." In *The Political Economy of Contemporary Africa,* edited by P. C. W. Gutkind and I. Wallerstein. Beverly Hills: Sage Publications, 1976.

Cohen, R. and Hughes, A. *Towards the Emergence of a Nigerian Working Class: The Social Identity of the Lagos Labour Force, 1897-1939.* Occasional Paper, series D, no. 7, Faculty of Commerce and Social Science. Birmingham: University of Birmingham, 1971.

Cohen, R. and Michael, D. "The Revolutionary Potential of an African Lumpenproletariat: A Sceptical View." *Bulletin - Institute of Development Studies* 5, nos. 2/3 (1973): 31–41.

Conway, H. E. "Labour Protest Activity in Sierra Leone during the Early Part of the 20th Century." *Labour History* 15 (November 1968): 49–63.

Davies, I. *African Trade Unions.* Harmondsworth, Eng.: Penguin Books, 1966.

Davis, J. M. *Modern Industry and the African.* London: Frank Cass & Co., 1967.

Elkan, W. *Migrants and Proletarians.* London: Oxford University Press, 1960.

Epstein, A. C. *Politics in an Urban African Community.* Manchester: Manchester University Press, 1958.

Fawzi, S. *The Labour Movement in the Sudan 1946-55.* London: Oxford University Press, 1957.

Frank, G. "Bibliography on the Development of Trade Unions in Africa South of the Sahara." *Genève-Afrique* 13, no. 1 (1974): 101–18 and no. 2 (1974): 98–117.

Friedland, W. H. "Paradoxes of African Trade Unionism, Organizational Chaos and Political Potential." *Africa Report* 10, no. 6 (1965): 6–13.

———. *Unions, Labor and Industrial Relations in Africa: An Annotated Bibliography.* Ithaca, N.Y.: Cornell University Press, 1965.

———. *Vuta Kamba: The Development of Trade Unions in Tanganyika.* Stanford, Calif.: Hoover Institute Press, 1969.

———. "African Trade Union Studies: Analysis of Two Decades." Paper read at the African Studies Association, November 8-11, 1972, in Philadelphia.

Geiss, I. *Gewerkschaften in Afrika.* Bonn: Friedrich Ebert Stiftung, 1965.

Gordon, R. J. *Mines, Masters and Migrants: Life in a Namibian Mine Compound.* Johannesburg: Ravan Press, 1977.

Greenstreet, M. "Labour Conditions in the Gold Coast During the 1930s with Particular Reference to Migrant Labour and the Mines." *The Economic Bulletin of Ghana* 2, no. 2 (1972).

———. "Labour Relations in the Gold Coast with Special Reference to the Ariston Strike." *The Economic Bulletin of Ghana* 2, no. 3 (1972): 30–39.

Grillo, R. D. *African Railwaymen: Solidarity and Opposition in an East African Labour Force.* Cambridge: Cambridge University Press, 1973.

Gutkind, P. C. W. *The Emergent African Urban Proletariat.* Occasional Paper Series, no. 8, Centre for Developing Area Studies. Montreal: McGill University, 1974.

Handley, W. "The Labour Movement in Egypt." *Middle East Journal* (July 1949): 277–92.

Harbison, F. H. and Ibrahim, I. A. "Some Labor Problems of Industrialization in Egypt." *Annals of the American Academy of Political and Social Science* 305: 114–234.

Harris, P. *Black Industrial Workers in Rhodesia.* Gwelo, Rhodesia: Mamba Press, 1974.

————. "Industrial Workers in Rhodesia, 1946-1972." *Journal of Southern African Studies* 1, no. 2 (1975): 139–61.

Heisler, H. "A Class of Target-Proletarians." *Journal of Asian and African Studies* 5, no. 3 (1970): 161–75.

Henderson, I. "Early African Leadership: The Copperbelt Disturbances of 1935 and 1940." *Journal of Southern African Studies* 2, no. 1 (October 1975): 83–97.

Hermassi, A. "Sociologie du milieu docker." *Revue tunisienne des sciences sociales* 7 (1966): 153–79.

International Labor Office. *African Labor Survey.* Geneva: International Labor Office, 1958.

Ivanov, Y. "Labor Migration and the Rise of a Working Class in Tropical Africa." Paper presented at the third session of the International Congress of Africanists, Moscow, 1973.

Johns, S. W. "Trade Union, Political Pressure Group or Mass Movement? The Industrial and Commercial Workers Union of Africa." In *Protest and Power in Black Africa,* edited by R. I. Rotberg and A. A. Mazrui. New York: Oxford University Press, 1970.

Kadalie, C. *My Life and the ICU.* London: Frank Cass & Co., 1970.

Kane-Berman, J. *Contract Labour in South West Africa.* Johannesburg: South African Institute of Race Relations, 1972. Mimeographed.

Kapferer, B. *Strategy and Transaction in an African Factory: African Workers and Indian Management in a Zambian Town.* Manchester: Manchester University Press, 1972.

Kirkwood, M. "The Defy Dispute: Questions of Solidarity." *South African Labour Bulletin* 2, no. 1 (May-June 1975).

Krizsán, L. "Aspects of an Analysis of the Labor Structure of the Nigerian Working Class." *Studies in Developing Countries.* Budapest: Center for Afro-Asian Research, Hungarian Academy of Sciences, 1970.

Levy, L. "African Trade Unionism in South Africa." *Africa South in Exile* 5, no. 3 (April-June 1961): 32–43.

Lomas, P. K. "African Trade Unionism in the Copperbelt of Northern Rhodesia." *South African Journal of Economics* 26, no. 9 (June 1958): 110–12.

Lynd, G. E. [pseud.] *The Politics of African Trade Unionism.* New York: Praeger, 1968.

Mackenzie, J. M. "African Labour in the Chartered Company Period." *The Rhodesian Journal of Economics* 1 (1970): 43–58.

Malapo, N. and Ngotyana, B. "African Workers and the National Struggle." *The African Communist* 44 (1971): 56–64.

Mapolu, H. "The Organization and Participation of Workers in Tanzania." *African Review* 2, no. 3: 381–417.

Melson, R. "Nigerian Politics and the General Strike of 1964." In *Protest and Power in Black Africa,* edited by R. I. Rotberg and A. A. Mazrui. New York: Oxford University Press, 1970.

Meynaud, J. and Salah Bey, A. *Trade Unionism in Africa.* London: Methuen, 1967.

Mhlongo, S. "Black Workers' Strikes in South Africa." *New Left Review* 83 (1974): 41–49.

Mihyo, P. "The Struggle for Workers' Control in Tanzania." *Review of African Political Economy* 4 (November 1975): 62–84.

Minces, J. "Autogestion et lutte de classe en Algérie." *Temps modernes* 229 (June 1965): 2204–31.

Mitchell, J. C. "Occupational Prestige and Social Status among Urban Africans in Northern Rhodesia." *Africa* 29 (1959): 22–40.

Newbury, C. "Historical Aspects of Manpower and Migration in Africa South of the Sahara." In *Colonialism in Africa.* Vol. 4, *The Economics of Imperialism,* edited by L. H. Gann and P. Duignan. Cambridge: Cambridge University Press, 1975.

Norman, J. *Labor and Politics in Libya and Arab Africa.* New York: Beskman Associates, 1965.

November, A. *L'évolution du mouvement syndical en Afrique occidental.* Paris: Editions Mouton, 1965.

Ogionwo, W. "The Alienated Nigerian Worker: A Test of the Generalisation Theory." *Nigerian Journal of Economic and Social Studies* 13, no. 3 (1972): 267–84.

O'Meara, D. "The 1946 African Mine Workers' Strike and the Political Economy of South Africa." *The Journal of Commonwealth and Comparative Politics* 13, no. 2 (1975): 146–73.

Orde-Browne, G. St. J. *The African Labourer.* London: Frank Cass & Co., 1967.

Oyemakinde, W. "The Nigerian General Strike of 1964." *Geneve-Afrique* 13, no. 1 (1974): 53–71.

Peil, M. *The Ghanaian Factory Worker: Industrial Man in Africa.* Cambridge: Cambridge University Press, 1972.

Pfefferman, G. *Industrial Labor in Senegal.* New York: Praeger, 1968.

Phimister, Z. R. "The Shamva Mine Strike of 1927." *Rhodesian History* 2 (1971): 65–88.

Présence Africaine. *Le travail en Afrique Noire.* Paris: Editions du Seuil, 1952.

Richardson, P. "Coolies and Landlords: The North Randfontein Chinese Miners' Strike of 1905." *Journal of Southern African Studies* 2, no. 2 (April 1976): 151–77.

Rimmer, D. "The New Industrial Relations in Ghana." *Industrial and Labor Relations Review* 14, no. 1 (January 1961): 206–26.

Roberts, B. C. and de Bellecombe, L. G. *Collective Bargaining in African Countries.* London: Macmillan, 1967.

Roux, E. *Time Longer than Rope.* London: Gollancz, 1949.

Sandbrook, R. *Proletarians and African Capitalism: The Kenyan Case 1960-1972.* Cambridge: Cambridge University Press, 1975.

———. "Patrons, Clients and Unions: The Labour Movement and Political Conflict in Kenya." *Journal of Commonwealth Political Studies* 10, no. 1 (1972): 3–27.

Sandbrook, R. and Cohen, R., eds. *The Development of an African Working Class: Studies in Class Formation and Action.* London: Longmans, 1975.

Scott, R. *The Development of Trade Unions in Uganda.* Nairobi: East African Publishing House, 1966.

Simons, H. J. and R. E. *Class and Colour in South Africa 1850-1950.* Harmondsworth, Eng.: Penguin Books, 1969.

Singh, M. *A History of Kenya's Trade Union Movement to 1952.* Nairobi: East Africa Publishing House, 1969.

Smock, D. R. *Conflict and Control in an African Union.* Stanford: Hoover Institute Press, 1969.

Thomas, R. W. "Forced Labor in British West Africa: The Case of the Northern Territories of the Gold Coast, 1906-27." *Journal of African History* 14, no. 1 (1973): 79–103.

Trachtman, L. N. "The Labor Movement of Ghana: A Study in Political Unionism." *Economic Development and Cultural Change* 10, no. 2 (1962): 183–200.

Van Onselen, C. *Chibaro: African Mine Labour in Southern Rhodesia 1900-1933.* London: Pluto Press, 1976.

———. "The 1912 Wankie Colliery Strike." *Journal of African History* 15, no. 2 (1974): 275–89.

Walker, I. L. and Weinbren, B. *2000 Casualties: A History of the Trade Unions and the Labour Movement in the Union of South Africa.* Johannesburg: South African Trade Union Council, 1961.

Warmington, W. A. *A West African Trade Union.* London: Oxford University Press, 1960.

Waterman, P. "Toward an Understanding of African Trade Unionism." *Présence africaine* 76 (1970): 96–112.

———. "The Labor Aristocracy in Africa: Introduction to a Debate." *Development and Change* 6, no. 3 (July 1975): 57–73.

Wickins, P. C. "The One Big Union Movement Among Black Workers in South Africa." *International Journal of African Historical Studies* 7, no. 3 (1975): 391–416.

Wilson, F. *Labour in the South African Gold Mines, 1911-1969.* Cambridge: Cambridge University Press, 1972.

———. *Migrant Labour in South Africa.* Johannesburg: South African Council of Churches and SPRO-CAS, 1972.

Latin America and the Caribbean

Adams, R. N. "Rural Labor." In *Continuity and Change in Latin America*, edited by J. J. Johnson. Stanford: Stanford University Press, 1964.

Alba, V. *Historia del movimiento obrero en América Latina*. Mexico City: Libreros Mexicanos Unidos, 1964.

———. *Politics and the Labor Movement in Latin America*. Stanford: Stanford University Press, 1969.

Alejandro, C. D. *Essays on the Economic History of the Argentine Republic*. New Haven: Yale University Press, 1970.

Alexander, R. J. *Labour Movements in Latin America*. London: Fabian Publications, 1947.

———. *Labor Relations in Argentina, Brazil and Chile*. New York: McGraw-Hill, 1962.

———. *Organized Labor in Latin America*. New York: Free Press, 1965.

Almeida, A. M. and Lowy, M. "Union Structure and Labor Organization in the Recent History of Brazil." *Latin American Perspectives* 3, no. 1 (Winter 1976): 98–119.

American Institute for Marxist Studies. *A Bibliography of the History of the Latin American Labor and Trade Union Movements, as of 1967*. Bibliographical Series 1. New York: American Institute for Marxist Studies, 1967.

Anguiano, A. *El estado y la política obrera del cardenismo*. Mexico: Editorial Era, 1974.

Antezana, E. L. *El movimiento obrero boliviano (1935-1943)*. 1966.

Aparicio, A. L. *El movimiento obrero en México*. Mexico: Editorial Jus, 1952.

Araiza, L. *Historia de la casa del obrero mundial*. Mexico: n.p., 1963.

———. *Historia del movimiento obrero mexicano*. 4 vols. Mexico City, 1964.

Arcos, J. *El sindicalismo en América Latina*. Bogotá: FERES, 1964.

Arismendi, R. *Uruguay y América Latina en los años setenta: experiencias y balance de una revolución*. Montevideo: Pueblos Unidos, 1973.

Aronson, R. L. "Labor Commitment among Jamaican Bauxite Workers." *Social and Economic Studies* 10 (1961): 156–82.

Autores, V. *Vida, obra, y trascendencia de Sebastian Marotta: juicio, semblanzas, y anecdotaria de un precursor del sindicalismo*. Buenos Aires: n.p., 1971.

Baily, S. L. *Labor, Nationalism, and Politics in Argentina*. New Brunswick, N.J.: Rutgers University Press, 1967.

Barrera, M. *El sindicato industrial como instrumento de lucha de la clase obrera chilena*. Santiago: Universidad de Chile, 1971.

Barría Serón, J.I. *Los movimientos sociales de Chile desde 1910 hasta 1926*. Santiago, 1960.

———. *Trajectoria y estructura del movimiento sindical chileno, 1946-1962*. Santiago: INSORA, 1963.

———. *Breve historia del sindicalismo chileno*. Santiago, 1967.

———. *Las relaciones colectivas del trabajo en Chile*. Santiago, 1967.

————. *Historia de la CUT*. Santiago, 1971.

Basurto, J. *El desarrollo del proletario industrial*. Mexico: Instituto de Investigaciones Sociales, Universidad Nacional Autónoma de México, 1975.

Bauer, A. "Chilean Rural Labor in the 19th Century." *American Historical Review* 76, no. 4 (1971): 1059–83.

Bayer, B. and Spalding, H., Jr., eds. "NACLA's Bibliography on Latin America." *NACLA's Latin America and Empire Report* 7, no. 3 (1973): 2–40.

Bishop, E. W. "The Guatemala Labor Movement 1944-1959." Ph.D. diss., University of Wisconsin, 1959.

Blanksten, G. *Peron's Argentina*. Chicago: University of Chicago Press, 1953.

Blum, A. A. and Thompson, M. "Unions and White-Collar Workers in Mexico." *Industrial and Labor Relations Review* 26 (1972): 646–59.

Bodenheimer, S. J. "The AFL-CIO in Latin America: The Dominican Republic: A Case Study." *Viet Report* 3, no. 4 (September-October 1967): 19–28.

Bonilla, F. "The Urban Worker." In *Continuity and Change in Latin America*, edited by J. J. Johnson. Stanford: Stanford University Press, 1964.

Bourricaud, F. "Syndicalism et politique: le cas péruvien." *Sociologie du travail* 3, no. 4 (October-December 1961): 33–49.

Brunori, P. G. "El sindicalismo y la reforma agraria." *Económica* (Bogota) 2, no. 4 (1964): 50–56.

Burnett, B. and Poblette Troncoso, M. *The Rise of the Latin American Labor Movement*. New Haven: College and University Press, 1962.

Bush, A. C. *Organized Labor in Guatemala, 1944-1949: A Case Study of an Adolescent Labor Movement in an Underdeveloped Country*. New York: Colgate University Press, 1950.

Byars, R. "Culture, Politics and the Urban Factory Worker in Brazil: The Case of Ze Mora." In *Latin American Modernization Problems*, edited by R. E. Scott. Urbana: University of Illinois Press, 1973.

Callelo, H.; Murmis, M.; and Martin, J. "Un sindicalismo de tradición artesanal." In *Estructuras sindiçales*, edited by T. DiTella. Buenos Aires, 1969.

Cárdenas, G. H. *Historia Argentina: curso básico de capacitación sindical: Sindicato de Luz y Fuerza*. Buenos Aires, 1966.

Cardoso, F. H. "Proletariado e mundança social en São Paulo." *Sociologica* (March 1960): 3–11.

Carr, B. *El movimiento obrero y la política en México, 1910-1929*. 2 vols. Mexico City, 1976.

Carri, R. *Sindicatos y poder en la Argentina*. Buenos Aires, 1967.

Casaretto, M. S. *Historia del movimiento obrero argentino*. 2 vols. Buenos Aires, 1945-1946.

Chaplin, D. "Industrial Labor Recruitment in Peru." *América Latina* 9, no. 4 (October-December 1966): 22–46.

———. "Blue Collar Workers in Peru." *International Journal of Comparative Sociology* 10 (1969): 31–45.

———. *The Peruvian Industrial Labor Force*. Princeton: Princeton University Press, 1967.

Chase, A. *A History of Trade Unionism in Guyana, 1900-1961*. Georgetown, Guyana: Demerara, New Guyana Co., 1968.

Chilcote, R. H. *The Brazilian Communist Party: Conflict and Integration: 1922-1972*. New York: Oxford University Press, 1974.

Chilcote, R. H. and Edelstein, J. C., eds. *Latin America: The Struggle with Dependency and Beyond*. Cambridge, Mass.: Schenkman Publishing Co., 1974.

Cockcroft, J. D.; Frank, A. G.; and Johnson, D. L. *Dependence and Under-development in Latin America's Political Economy*. New York: Anchor Books, 1972.

Comitas, L. and Lowenthal, D., eds. *Work and Family Life: West Indian Perspectives*. New York: Anchor Books, 1973.

Cone, C. A. "Perceptions of Occupations in a Newly Industrializing Region of Mexico." *Human Organization* 32, no. 2 (1973): 143–51.

Corradi, J.; Nash, J.; and Spalding, H. A., Jr., eds. *Ideology and Social Change in Latin America*. New York: Gordon and Breach, 1977.

Corten, A. "Valor de la fuerza de trabajo y formas de proletarización." *Revista Latina Americana de sociologica* (1974): 45–65.

Daniel, G. T. "Labor and Nationalism in the British Caribbean." *Annals of the American Academy of Political and Social Science* 310 (1957): 162–71.

de Jesús, C. M. *Child of the Dark: The Diary of Caroline Maria de Jesús*. New York: Dillon, 1962.

Delich, F. J. *Crisis y protesta social: Córdoba, mayo de 1969*. Córdoba: Ediciones Signos, 1970.

D'Espirary Laline, C. and Zylberberg, J. "Une variable oubliée de la problématique agraire: le prolétariat urbain (le cas du Chili)." *Civilisations* 23/24, nos. 1/2 (1973-74): 51–64.

Díaz Santana, A. "The Role of Haitian Braceros in Dominican Sugar Production." *Latin American Perspectives* 3, no. 1 (Winter 1976): 120–32.

di Tella, T. *El sistema político argentino y la clase obrera*. Buenos Aires: EUDEBA, 1964.

———. "The Working Class in Politics." In *Latin America and the Caribbean: A Handbook*, edited by C. Veliz. London: Anthony Blond, 1968.

Durruty, C. *Clase obrera y peronismo*. Córdoba: Ediciones Pasado y Presente, 1969.

Erickson, K. P. "Corporatism and Labor in Development." In *Contemporary Brazil: Issues in Economic and Political Development*, edited by H. J. Rosenbaum and W. G. Tyler. New York: Praeger, 1972.

——— et al. "Research on the Urban Working Class and Organized Labor in Argentina, Brazil and Chile: What Is Left to Be Done?" *Latin American Research Review* 9, no. 2 (Summer 1974): 115–42.

———— and Peppe, P. V. "Dependent Capitalist Development, US Foreign Policy, and Repression of the Working Class in Chile and Brazil." *Latin American Perspectives* 3, no. 1 (Winter 1976): 19–44.

Fernandez, A. *El movimiento obrero en la Argentina*. Buenos Aires, 1935-1937.

Fluharty, V. *Dance of the Millions: Military Rule and the Social Revolution in Colombia 1930-56*. Pittsburgh: University of Pittsburgh Press, 1957.

Frucht, R. "A Caribbean Social Type: Neither 'Peasant' nor 'Proletarian.'" *Social and Economic Studies* 13, no. 3 (1967).

Fuentes Díaz, V. "Desarrollo y evolución del movimiento obrero." *Ciencias políticas y sociales* 17 (July-September 1959).

Gale, R. P. "Industrial Development and the Blue-Collar Worker in Argentina." *International Journal of Comparative Sociology* 10 (1969): 117–50.

García, A. "Los sindicatos en el esquema de la revolución nacional." *Trimestre económico* (October-December 1966): 597–629.

Germani, G. "Inquiry into the Social Effects of Urbanization in a Working-Class Sector of Greater Buenos Aires." In *Urbanization in Latin America*, edited by D. M. Hauser. New York: Columbia University Press, 1961.

Godio, J. *El movimiento obrero y la questión nacional: Argentina: inmigrantes asalariados y lucha de clases, 1880-1910*. La Plata, 1972.

Grobart, F. "The Cuban Working Class Movement from 1925-1933." *Science and Society* 29, no. 1 (Spring 1975): 73–103.

Gurrieri, A. "Consideraciones sobre los sindicatos chilenos." *Aportes* (June 1969): 77–114.

Gutierrez, L. "Recopilación bibliográfica y de fuentes para el estudio de la historia y situación achial de la clase obrera argentina." *Documento de trabajo* 63. Buenos Aires: Instituto Torcuato Di Tella.

Harding, T. "The Politics of Labor and Dependency in Brazil: An Historical Approach." *International Socialist Review* 33, no. 7 (July-August 1973): 13.

Harrod, J. *Trade Union Foreign Policy: A Study of British and American Trade Union Activities in Jamaica*. New York: Doubleday, 1972.

Hoyt, E. E. "The Indian Laborer on the Guatemalan Coffee Fincas." *Inter-American Economic Affairs* 9, no. 1 (1955): 33–46.

Iparraquirre, H. and Pianetto, O. *La organización de la clase obrera en Córdoba, 1870-1895*. Córdoba, 1968.

Iscaro, R. *Origen y desarrollo del movimiento sindical argentino*. Buenos Aires: Editorial Anteo, 1958.

Jayawardena, C. *Conflict and Solidarity in a Guianese Plantation*. London: Athlone Press, 1963.

Jobet, J. C. *Recabarren: los origenes del movimiento obrero y del socialismo chileno*. Santiago, 1955.

Johnson, D. L. "Industrialization, Social Mobility and Class Formation in Chile." *Studies in Comparative International Development* 3, no. 7: 121–51.

Jonas, S. "Trade Union Imperialism in the Dominican Republic." *NACLA's Latin America and Empire Report* 9 (April 1975): 13–30.

Kahl, J. A. "Three Types of Mexican Industrial Workers." In *Workers and Managers in Latin America,* edited by S. M. Davis and L. W. Goodman. London: D. C. Heath & Co., 1972.

Kantor, H. *The Ideology and Program of the Peruvian Aprista Movement.* Berkeley: University of California Press, 1952.

Kuhn, G. C. "Liberian Contract Labor in Panama, 1887-1897." *Liberian Studies Journal* 6, no. 1 (1975): 43–52.

Landsberger, H. A. "The Labor Elite: Is It Revolutionary?" In *Elites in Latin America,* edited by S. M. Lipset and A. Solari. New York: Oxford University Press, 1967.

Landsberger, H. S.; Barrera, M.; and Toro, A. "The Chilean Labor Union Leader: A Preliminary Report on His Background and Attitudes." *Industrial and Labor Review* 19, no. 3: 399–420.

Lehmann, D. "The Agrarian Working Class." In *Latin America and the Caribbean: A Handbook,* edited by C. Veliz. London: Anthony Blond, 1968.

Lengerman, P. M. "Working Class Values in Trinidad and Tobago." *Social and Economic Studies* 20, no. 2 (1971): 151–63.

Lopes, J. R. B. "Aspects of the Adjustment of Rural Migrants to Urban-Industrial Conditions in São Paulo, Brazil." In *Urbanization in Latin America,* edited by P. M. Hauser. New York: UNESCO, 1961.

———. "O ajustamento do trabalhador a industria: Mobilidade social e motivacão." In *Mobilidade e trabalho,* edited by B. Hutchinson. São Paulo, 1960.

Lopez, A. *Historia del movimiento social y la clase obrera argentina.* Buenos Aires, 1971.

Losovsky, A. *El movimiento sindical latino americano.* Montevideo: Rumbos Nuevos, 1929.

Lowy, M. "Structure de la conscience de classe ouvrière du Brésil." *Cahiers internationals de sociologie* 49 (1970): 133–42.

Marcilio, M. L. "Industrialisation et mouvement ouvrier à São Paulo au début du XXe siècle." *Le mouvement social* 53 (1965): 112–29.

Marín, G. R. *El mercado del trabajo.* Mexico: Fondo de Cultura Económica, 1954.

———. "El movimiento obrero." In *México: cincuenta años de revolución.* Vol. 2, *La vida social.* Mexico: Fondo de Cultura Económica, 1961.

Marotta, S. *El movimiento sindical argentino, su génesis y desarrollo.* 2 vols. Buenos Aires: Ediciones "Lacio," 1960-1961.

Martínez, H. *La hacienda capana.* Serie monográfica, no. 2. Plan nacional de integración de la población indígena. Lima, 1962.

Martínez-Alier, J. "Peasants and Labourers in Southern Spain, Cuba and Highland Peru." *Journal of Peasant Studies* 1, no. 2 (1974): 133–63.

Martins, I. "Proletariado e inequietação rural." *Revista brasiliense* 42 (1962).

Máspero, E. "Trade Unionism as an Instrument of Latin American

Revolution." In *Latin American Radicalism*, ed. I. L. Horowitz, J. de Castro, and J. Gerassi. New York: Random House, 1969.

Massari, R. "Le 'Cordobazo.'" *Sociologie du travail* 4 (1975): 403–19.

Mejía-Valera, J. and Briones, G. *El obrero industrial*. Instituto de Investigaciones Sociológicas. Lima: Universidad Nacional Mayor de San Marcos, 1964.

Mesa-Lago, C. "Unpaid Labor in Socialist Cuba." In *Workers and Managers in Latin America*, edited by S. M. Davis and L. W. Goodman. London: D. C. Heath & Co., 1972.

Métraux, A. "Cooperative Labor Groups in Haiti." In *Peoples and Cultures of the Caribbean*, edited by M. M. Horowitz. New York: The Natural History Press, 1971.

Meyers, F. "Party, Government and the Labour Movement in Mexico: Two Case Studies." In *Industrial Relations and Economic Development*, edited by A. M. Ross. London: Macmillan, 1966.

Mintz, S. W. "Labor and Sugar in Puerto Rico and in Jamaica 1800-1850." *Comparative Studies in Society and History* 1, no. 3 (1959): 273–81.

———. *Worker in the Cane: A Puerto-Rican Life History*. New Haven: Yale University Press, 1960.

Nash, M. "Machine Age Maya: The Industrialization of a Guatemalan Community." *Memoir of the American Anthropological Association* 87 (1958).

North American Congress on Latin America. *Argentina in the Hour of the Furnaces*. New York: NACLA, 1975.

———. "Hit and Run: US Runaway Shops on the Mexican Border." *Latin America and Empire Report* 9 (July-August 1975).

Orde Browne, G. St. J. *Labour Conditions in the West Indies*. Cmd. 6070. London: His Majesty's Stationery Office, 1938.

Page, C. A. "Communism and the Labor Movements of Latin America." *Virginia Quarterly Review* 31 (Summer 1955): 373–82.

Payne, J. L. *Labor and Politics in Peru: The System of Political Bargaining*. New Haven: Yale University Press, 1965.

Peppe, P. V. and Spalding, H. A., Jr. "Research on the Urban Working Class and Organized Labor in Argentina, Brazil, and Chile: What Is Left to Be Done?" *Latin American Research Review* 9, no. 2 (Summer 1974): 123–25.

Pérez-Stable, M. "Whither the Cuban Working Class?" *Latin American Perspectives* 2, no. 4 (Supplement 1975): 60–77.

Perlman, J. E. *The Myth of Marginality: Urban Poverty and Politics in Rio de Janeiro*. Berkeley and Los Angeles: University of California Press, 1976.

Petras, J. "Reflections on the Chilean Experience: The Petit Bourgeoisie and the Working Class." *Socialist Revolution* 4, no. 1 (1974): 39–57.

———. "Chile: Nationalization, Socio-Economic Change and Popular Participation." *Studies in Comparative International Development* 8, no. 1 (1973): 24–51.

——— and Zeitlin, M. *El radicalismo político de la clase trabajadora chilena*. Buenos Aires: Centro Editorial de América Latina, 1969.

Pintos, F. R. *Historia del movimiento obrero del Uruguay.* Montevideo, 1960.

Poblete Troncoso, M. *Condiciones de vida y de trabajo de la población indígena del Perú.* Geneva, 1938.

Quijano, A. "Imperialism and the Working Class in Latin America." *Latin American Perspectives* 3, no. 1 (Winter 1976): 15–18.

Radosh, R. *American Labor and United States Foreign Policy.* New York: Random House, 1969.

Rama, C. *Mouvements ouvriers et socialistes: L'Amérique latine: 1492-1936.* Paris: Editions ouvrières, 1959.

Ramirez Necochea, H. *Historia del movimiento obrero en Chile.* Santiago: Austral, 1956.

Retinger, J. H. *Morones of Mexico.* London: Labour Publishing Co., 1926.

Roberts, B. R. *Organizing Strangers: Poor Families in Guatemala City.* Austin: University of Texas Press, 1973.

Rodrigues, L. M. *Conflito industrial e sindicalismo no Brasil.* São Paulo: Difusão Européia do Livro, 1966.

Rohrlich-Leavitt, R., ed. *Women Cross-Culturally: Change and Challenge.* The Hague: Mouton Publishers, 1975. Articles by Silvestrini-Pacheco, Nash, and Piho.

Romualdi, S. *Presidents and Peons: Recollections of a Labor Ambassador in Latin America.* New York: Funk & Wagnells, 1968.

Rottenberg, S. "Labor Relations in an Underdeveloped Economy." *Economic Development and Cultural Change* 1 (1952-1953): 250–60.

Ruiz, R. E. *Labor and the Ambivalent Revolutionaries: Mexico, 1911-1923.* Baltimore: Johns Hopkins University Press, 1976.

Safa, H. I. *The Urban Poor of Puerto Rico: A Study in Development and Inequality.* New York: Holt, Rinehart and Winston, 1974.

Salazar, R. *La CTM, su historia, su significado.* Mexico: Ediciones T.C. Modelo, 1956.

——. *La casa del obrero mundial.* Mexico: Costa-Amic, 1963.

Senen Gonzales, S. *El sindicalismo después de Perón.* Buenos Aires: Editorial Galerna, 1971.

Silva-Michelena, J. A.; Bonilla, F.; and Cotler, J. "La investigación sociológica y la formulación de políticas." *América Latina* 8, no. 2 (1965): 3–47.

Silverman, B. "Labor Ideology and Economic Development in the Peronist Epoch." *Studies in Comparative International Development* 3, no. 4 (1968-1969): 243–58.

Simão, A. "O voto operario em São Paulo." *Anais do primeiro congresso brasileiro de sociologia* (1954): 201–14.

——. *Sindicato e estado.* São Paulo: Dominus, 1966.

Slotkin, J. S. *From Field to Factory: New Industrial Employees.* Glencoe, Ill., The Free Press, 1966.

Smith, M. C. "Domestic Service as a Channel of Upward Mobility for the Lower Class Woman: The Lima Case." In *Female and Male in Latin America,* edited by A. Pescatello. Pittsburgh: University of Pittsburgh Press, 1973.

Smith, M. G. "Patterns of Rural Labor." In *Work and Family Life: West Indian Perspectives,* edited by L. Comitas and D. Lowenthal. New York: Anchor Books, 1973.

Solomonoff, J. N. *Ideologiás del movimiento obrero y conflicto social de la organización nacional hasta la Primera Guerra Mundial.* Buenos Aires: Editorial Proyección, 1971.

Spalding, H. A., Jr. *La clase trabajadora argentina: documentos para su historia, 1890-1912.* Buenos Aires: Editorial Galerna, 1970.

------. "The Parameters of Labor in Hispanic America." *Science and Society* 36, no. 2 (1972): 202–16.

------. "Recent Labor Studies: Old Assumptions and New Approaches." *Latin American Research Review* 10 (Summer 1975).

------. *Organized Labor in Latin America: Historical Case Studies of Urban Workers in Dependent Societies.* New York: Harper & Row, Harper Torchbooks, 1977.

Stavenhagen, R., ed. *Agrarian Problems and Peasant Movements in Latin America.* Garden City, N.Y.: Doubleday & Co., 1970.

Stephan, A., ed. *Authoritarian Brazil: Origins, Policies and Futures.* New Haven: Yale University Press, 1973.

Steward, J. H., ed. *The People of Puerto Rico.* Urbana, Ill.: University of Illinois Press, 1956.

Stone, C. "Social Class and Partisan Attitudes in Urban Jamaica." *Social and Economic Studies* 21, no. 1 (March 1972): 1–29.

Sturmthal, A. *La tragedia del movimiento obrero.* Mexico: Fondo de Cultura Económica, 1945.

Torre, J. C. "Sindicatos y clase obrera en la Argentina post-peronista." *Revista latinoamericana de sociológia* (March 1968): 108–14.

------. "Workers' Struggle and Consciousness." *Latin American Perspectives* 1 (Fall 1974): 73–81.

Touraine, A. "Industrialisation et conscience ouvrière à São Paulo." *Sociologie du travail* 4 (October-December 1961): 77–95.

------. "Social Mobility, Class Relations and Nationalism in Latin America." *Studies in Comparative International Development* 1, no. 3 (1965).

Touraine, A. and Pecaut, D. "Working Class Consciousness and Economic Development in Latin America." In *Masses in Latin America,* edited by I. L. Horowitz. New York: Oxford University Press, 1970.

Touraine, A. and Raguzzi, O. *Ouvriers d'origine agricole.* Paris: Editions du Seuil, 1961.

Trejo Delarbe, R. T. "The Mexican Labor Movement: 1917-1975." *Latin American Perspectives* 3, no. 1 (Winter 1976): 133–53.

Turner, J. K. *Barbarous Mexico.* Austin, Tex., 1969. Reprint of Chicago: C. H. Kerr & Co., 1911.

Urbina, A. T. and Barrera, T., eds. *Ley federal del trabajo, reformada y adicionada.* Mexico City: Editorial Porrúa, 1965.

Urrutia, M. *The Development of the Colombian Labor Movement.* New Haven: Yale University Press, 1969.

Valdes, V. M. *The Labor Relations of the Chilean Copper Industry.* Santiago, 1968.

Varela, P. C. "Situação dos trabalhadores." *Revista civilização brasileira* 1, nos. 9/10 (1966).

Vianna, F. J. de O. *Direito de trabalho democracia social.* Rio de Janeiro: José Olimpio Editores, 1951.

Weffort, F. C. "State and Mass in Brazil." *Studies in Comparative International Development* 2, no. 12 (1966).

————. *Participação e conflito industrial: Contagem e Osasco, 1968.* São Paulo: CEBRAP, 1972.

Whyte, W. F. "Culture, Industrial Relations and Economic Development: The Case of Peru." *Industrial and Labor Relations Review* 16 (July 1963): 583–94.

Winn, P. "Loosening the Chains: Labor and the Chilean Revolutionary Process, 1970-1973." *Latin American Perspectives* 3, no. 1 (Winter 1976): 70–84.

Yepes Zuloaga, H. "El movimiento sindical colombiano." *Estudios de derecho* 18, no. 55 (1959).

Zapata, F. "The Chilean Labor Movement under Salvador Allende, 1970-1973." Mimeographed. Centro de Estudios Sociológicos, El Colegio de México, 1974.

Zeitlin, M. *Revolutionary Politics and the Cuban Working Class.* Princeton: Princeton University Press, 1967.

Zeitlin, M. and Petras, J. "Agrarian Radicalism in Chile." *British Journal of Sociology* 19 (September 1968): 254–70.

————. "Miners and Agrarian Radicalism." *American Sociological Review* 32 (1967): 578–86.

————. "The Working Class Vote in Chile: Christian Democracy versus Marxism." *British Journal of Sociology* (March 1970): 16–29.

Zimbalist, A. and Petras, J. "Workers' Control in Chile during Allende's Presidency." *Comparative Urban Research* 3, no. 3 (1975/76): 21–30.

Asia

Agarwala, A. N., ed. *Indian Labour Problems.* London: A. Probsthain, 1947.

Alavi, H. "Peasants and Revolution." *The Socialist Register 1965* (New York and London, 1966), pp. 241–77.

All-India TUC. "Five Glorious Days." New Delhi: AITUC-New Delhi, 1961.

Awberry, S. S. and Dalley, F. W. *Labour and Trade Union Organization in the Federation of Malaya and Singapore.* London: His Majesty's Stationery Office, 1948.

Bardhan, P. "Green Revolution and Agricultural Laborers." *Economic and Political Weekly* 5 (July 1970): 1239–46.

————. "Green Revolution and Agricultural Laborers: A Correction." *Economic and Political Weekly* 5 (November 1970): 1861.

Béteille, A. *Caste, Class and Power: Changing Patterns of Stratification in a Tanjore Village.* Berkeley and Los Angeles: University of California Press, 1965.

Bettelheim, C. *India Independent.* New York: Monthly Review Press, 1968.

Blackton, C. S. "The Action Phase of the 1915 Riots" [Ceylon]. *Journal of Asian Studies* 29, no. 2 (February 1970): 235–54.

Chakravarty, P. *Strikes and Morale in Industry.* Calcutta: Eastern Law House, 1969.

Chamanlal, D. *Coolie: The Story of Labour and Capital in India.* Lahore, Pakistan: Oriental Publishing House.

Chou Tse-tung. *The May Fourth Movement: Intellectual Revolution in Modern China.* Cambridge, Mass.: Harvard University Press, 1960.

Dandekar, M. and Rath, N. "Poverty in India. I: Dimensions and Trends." *Economic and Political Weekly,* January 2, 1971, pp. 25–48.

Das, R. K. *The Labor Movement in India.* Berlin: Walter de Gruyter & Co., 1923.

Deole, C. S. "The Bombay Strikes." *Journal of the Indian Economic Society* 2, no. 4 (December 1919): 193–202.

Desai, M. H. *A Righteous Struggle.* Ahmedabad, India: Navajivan Publishing House, 1951.

Doctor, K. and Gallis, H. "Modern Sector Employment in Asian Countries: Some Empirical Estimates." *International Labor Review* 90, no. 6 (1964): 544–68.

Dumont, R. *La révolution dans les campagnes chinoises.* Paris: Editions du Seuil, 1957.

Dutt, R. P. *India Today.* London: Victor Gollancz, 1940.

Employers Federation of India. *The General Strike in the Bombay Cotton Mill Industry.* Bombay, 1940.

Feuerwerkar, A. *China's Early Industrialization: Shang Hsuan-huai (1844-1916) and Mandarin Enterprise.* Cambridge, Mass.: Harvard University Press, 1958.

GEPEI Section Extrême-Orient. *Mouvements migratoires et population urbaine en Chine (1953-1957).* Paris, March 1966.

Gough, K. and Sharma, H. P., eds. *Imperialism and Revolution in South Asia.* New York: Monthly Review Press, 1973.

Graia, S. "The Jeepneys of Manila." *Traffic Quarterly* 26, no. 4 (1972): 465–83.

Hutchinson, L. *Conspiracy at Meerut.* London: George Allen & Unwin, 1935.

James, R. C. "Trade Union Democracy: Indian Textiles." *The Western Political Quarterly* 11, no. 3 (September 1958): 563–73.

———. "Politics and Trade Unions in India." *Far Eastern Survey* 27 (1958): 41–45.

Jayawardena, V. K. *The Rise of the Labor Movement in Ceylon.* Durham, N.C.: Duke University Press, 1972.

Kannappan, S. "The Tata Steel Strike: Some Dilemmas of Industrial Relations in a Developing Economy." *The Journal of Political Economy* 67 (1959): 489–505.

Karnik, V. B. *Indian Trade Unions: A Survey.* Bombay: P.C. Maraktala & Sons Private, 1966.

———. *Strikes in India.* New Delhi: Allied Publishers Private, 1967.

Kennedy, V. D. "The Role of the Unions in the Plant in India." *Proceedings of Industrial Relations Research Association.* Madison, Wis., 1956.

———. "The Conceptual and Legislative Framework of Labor Relations in India." *Industrial and Labor Relations Review* 11 (July 1958): 487–505.

Kulkarni, P. D. "Textile Trade Unionism in Bombay." *The Indian Journal of Social Work* 7 (December 1946): 224–38.

Laksman, P. O. *Congress and Labour Movement in India.* Allahabad, India: Economic and Political Research Department, 1947.

Lambert, R. D. "Labor in India." *Economic Development and Cultural Change* 8 (January 1960): 206–13.

———. *Workers, Factories and Social Change in India.* Princeton: Princeton University Press, 1963.

Levine, S. B. "Labor Patterns and Trends." *Annals of the American Academy of Political and Social Science* 308 (1956): 102–12.

McGee, T. G. *Hawkers in Hong Kong: A Study of Planning and Policy in a Third World City.* Hong Kong: University of Hong Kong Press, 1973.

Mahmud, K. *Trade Unionism in Pakistan.* Lahore, Pakistan: Punjab University Press, 1958.

Mao Tse-tung. "Report on an Investigation of the Peasant Movement in Hunan." *Selected Works of Mao Tse-tung.* Vol. 1. Peking: Foreign Language Press, 1967.

Mathur, A. S. and J. S. *Trade Union Movement in India.* Allahabad, India: Chaitanya, 1957.

Morris, M. D. "Caste and Evolution of the Industrial Workforce in India." *Proceedings of the American Philosophical Society* 104, no. 2 (April 1960): 124–33.

———. "Trade Unions and the State." In *Leadership and Political Institution in India,* edited by R. L. Park and I. Tinker. Princeton: Princeton University Press, 1959.

———. "Labor Discipline, Trade Unions and the State in India." *Journal of Political Economy* 4, no. 63 (August 1955): 293–308.

———. "Order and Disorder in the Labor Force: The Jamshedpur Crisis of 1958." *Economic Weekly* 10 (November 1958): 1387–95.

———. *The Emergence of an Industrial Labor Force in India: A Study of the Bombay Cotton Mills 1854-1947.* Berkeley and Los Angeles: University of California Press, 1965.

Mukhtar, A. *Trade Unionism and Labour Disputes in India.* London: Longmans, Green & Co, 1935.

Myers, C. A. *Labor Problems in the Industrialization of India.* Cambridge, Mass.: Harvard University Press, 1958.

Nanda, G. L. "Labour Unrest in India." *Indian Journal of Economics* 3 (January 1921): 460–80.

Nichoff, A. "Factory Workers in India." *Publications in Anthropology* 5. Milwaukee: Milwaukee Public Museum, 1959.

Ornati, O. A. *Jobs and Workers in India.* Ithaca: Cornell University Press, 1955.

―――. "Problems of Indian Trade Unionism." *Annals of the American Academy of Political and Social Science* 310 (1957): 151–61.

Parmer, J. N. "Trade Unions in Malaya." *Annals of the American Academy of Political and Social Science* 310 (1957): 142–50.

Patel, S. J. *Agricultural Labourers in Modern India and Pakistan.* Bombay: Current Book House, 1952.

Pillai, P. P., ed. *Labour in S.E. Asia: A Symposium.* New Delhi: Indian Council of World Affairs, 1947.

Pradhu, P. "Social Effects of Urbanization on Industrial Workers in Bombay." *Sociological Bulletin* 5, no. 2 (1956): 127–43.

Punekar, S. D. *Trade Unionism in India.* Bombay, 1948.

Punekar, S. D. and Madhuri, S. *Trade Union Leadership in India.* Bombay: Lalvani Publishing House, 1967.

Rahman, M. A. "Organised Labour and Politics in Pakistan." *Labour Unions and Political Organisations* 3 (January-May 1967): 102–21.

Raman, N. P. *Political Involvement of India's Trade Unions.* London: Asia Publishing House, 1967.

Ramanujam, G. "Strikes and Lockouts in Industrial Relations." *The Indian Worker,* August 15, 1955.

Rao, B. S. *The Industrial Worker in India.* London: George Allen & Unwin, 1939.

Rao, V. K. R. V. *Agricultural Labour in India.* Bombay: Asia Publishing House, 1962.

Roberts, H. S. and Brissenden, P. F., eds. *The Challenge of Industrial Relations in the Pacific-Asian Countries.* Honolulu: East-West Center Press, 1965.

Ruikar, M. "Women in Trade Unions." *Indian Journal of Social Work* 13 (March 1953): 250–56.

Shah, S. A., ed. *Towards National Liberation: Essays on the Political Economy of India.* Montreal, 1973.

Sharma, B. R. "The Indian Industrial Worker." *International Journal of Comparative Sociology* 10 (1969): 161–77.

Sharma, G. K. *Labour Movement in India.* Delhi: Universal Publishers, 1963.

Snow, E. *Red Star Over China.* New York: Grove Press, 1968.

Soares, J. F. "The Port Workers Union, Rangoon." *International Transport Workers Journal* (June 1955).

Soekarno, A. *Marhaen and Proletarian.* Ithaca, N.Y.: Dept. of Far Eastern Studies, Cornell University, 1960.

Suyin, H. *The Morning Deluge.* Vol.1, *1893-1935;* Vol.2, *1935-1949.* St. Albans, Eng.: Panther Books, 1976.

Tawney, R. H. *Land and Labour in China.* London: G. Allen & Unwin, 1932; New York: Octagon Books, 1964.

Tedjasuknana, I. *The Political Character of the Indonesian Trade Union Movement.* Ithaca, N.Y.: Cornell University Press, 1958.

Thompson, V. *Labor Problems in South East Asia.* New Haven: Yale University Press, 1947.

Thorner, D. and A. *Land and Labour in India.* Bombay and New York: Asia Publishing House, 1962.

Totten, G. O. "Labor and Agrarian Disputes in Japan Following World War I." Part 2. *Economic Development and Cultural Change* 9, no. 1 (1960): 187–212.

Weiner, M. *The Politics of Scarcity.* Chicago: University of Chicago Press, 1962.

Wertheim, W. F. "The Integration of Town and Countryside in China." *Culture et developpément* 6, no. 4 (1974): 723–36.

White, L. T. "Shanghai's Contract Proletariat." *Comparative Urban Research* 3, no. 3 (1975/76): 31–39.

Third-World Workers and Advanced Capitalism

Agnoli, J. *Die Gastarbeiter und die Reservarmee in Spätkapitalismus.* Makriallen zum Projektbereich, "Ausländische Arbeiter," N 3/1. Katholische Deutsche Studenten Einigung. Mimeographed. N.d.

Allaya, M. *Les migrations internationales: des travailleurs du bassin Méditerraneén et la croissance économique.* Montpelier, 1974.

Allen, S. "Race and Economy: Some Aspects of the Position of Non-Indigenous Labor." *Race* 13, no. 2 (1971): 170–74.

———. *New Minorities, Old Conflicts: Asian and West Indian Migrants in Britain.* New York: Random House, 1972.

———. "Race and Ethnicity in Class Formation: A Comparison of Asian and West Indian Workers." In *The Social Analyses of Class Structure*, edited by F. Parkin. London: Tavistock, 1974.

Augarde, J. "La migration algérienne." *Hommes et migrations etudes* 116 (1970).

Bacci, M.L., ed. *The Demographic and Social Pattern of Emigration from Southern European Countries.* Florence, 1972.

Bagley, C. *Social Structure and Prejudice in Five English Boroughs.* Special Series. London: Institute of Race Relations, 1970.

Belloula, T. *Les Algériens en France.* Algiers: Editions Nationales Algériennes, 1965.

Bendifallah, S. *L'immigration algérienne et droit français.* Paris, 1974.

Bennoune, M. "Maghrebin Migrant Workers in France." *Race and Class* 17, no. 1 (1975): 39–56.

Berger, J. and Mohr, J. *A Seventh Man: The Story of a Migrant Worker in Europe.* Harmondsworth, Eng.: Penguin Books, 1975.

Bingemer, K. et al. *Leben als Gastarbeiter.* Opladen: Westdeutscher Verlag, 1970.

Blauner, R. *Racial Oppression in America*. New York: Harper & Row, 1972.

Böhning, W. R. *The Migration of Workers in the United Kingdom and the European Community*. London: Oxford University Press, 1972.

Bonilla, F. and Girling, R., eds. *Structures of Dependency*. Stanford: Stanford Institute of Political Science, 1973.

Calame, P. and J. *Les travailleurs étrangers en France*. Paris: Les Editions Ouvrières, 1972.

Cambridge, A. X. "Loughborough: Black Workers and Trade Unions." *The Black Liberator* 2, no. 3 (1973): 70–79.

Campbell-Platt, K. *Workers in Britain from Selected Foreign Countries*. London: Runnymede Trust.

Capdevielle, J. and Mouriaux, R. "Conflit social et immigration: le cas de la Cellophane." *Projet* 22 (February 1968).

Castles, S. and Kosack, G. *Immigrant Workers and Class Structure in Western Europe*. London: Oxford University Press, 1973.

Churches' Committee on Migrant Workers in Western Europe. *Relations between Migration and Development: Guidelines Emerging from the St. Polten Conference*. 1970.

———. *Migrant Workers in Europe: Illegal Migration; Women Migrants; The Impact of the World Energy Crisis*. Geneva, 1974.

Cinanni, P. *Emigrazione e imperialismo*. Rome: Editori Riuniti, 1968.

Collard, D. "Immigration and Discrimination: Some Economic Aspects." *Economic Issues in Immigration*. London: Institute of Economic Affairs, 1970.

Comarond, P. de and Duchet, C., eds. *Racisme et société*. Paris: Maspero, 1969.

Daniel, W. W. *Racial Discrimination in England*. Harmondsworth, Eng.: Penguin Books, 1968.

Davison, R. B. *Commonwealth Immigrants*. London: Oxford University Press for Institute of Race Relations, 1964.

Deakin, N.; Cohen, B.; and McNeal, J. *Colour, Citizenship and British Society*. London: Panther, 1970.

Descloitres, R. *The Foreign Worker*. Paris: OECD, 1967.

Diarra, S. "Les travailleurs africains noirs en France." *Bulletin de l'IFAN*. T.30, sér.B., no. 3, 1968.

Edmond-Smith, J. "West Indian Workers in France." *New Community* 1, no. 5 (1972-1973): 444–50; 2, no. 3: 74–79; 2, no. 4: 306–14.

Foot, P. *Immigration and Race in British Politics*. Harmondsworth, Eng.: Penguin Books, 1965.

Gani, L. *Syndicats et travailleurs immigrés*. Paris: Editions Sociales, 1972.

Ghys, J. "Moslem Workers in France." *Migration News* 5 (September-October 1965): 6–10.

Gorz, A. "Immigrant Labour." *New Left Review* 61 (May 1970): 28–31.

Gorz, A. and Gavi, P. "La Bataille d'Ivry." *Les temps modernes* 26 (March 1970): 1388–1416.

Granotier, B. *Les travailleurs immigrés en France*. Paris, 1970.

Hepple, B. *Race, Jobs and the Law in Britain*. London: Allen Lane and Penguin, 1968.

Hermet, G. *Les Espagnols en France*. Paris: Les Editions Ouvrières, 1967.

Hoffman, N. "Global Social Aspects of Relationships Between Trade Unions and Migrant Workers." *Migration Today* 11 (1968).

Homze, E. L. *Foreign Labor in Nazi Germany*. Princeton: Princeton University Press, 1967.

Houte, H. van and Melgert, W. *Foreigners in Our Community*. Amsterdam: Keesing, 1972.

Issac, J. *British Post-War Migration*. Cambridge: Cambridge University Press, 1964.

Jackson, J. A. *The Irish in Britain*. London: Routledge & Kegan Paul, 1963.

———, ed. *Migration*. Cambridge: Cambridge University Press, 1969.

Jerrome, D. "Ibos in London: A Case Study in Social Accommodation." *New Community* 3, nos. 1/2 (1974): 79–86.

Jones, K. and Smith, A. D. *The Economic Impact of Commonwealth Immigration*. Cambridge: Cambridge University Press, 1970.

Kammrad, H. *Gastarbeiter Report*. Munich: R. Piper & Co. Verlag, 1971.

Kindleberger, C. P. *Europe's Postwar Growth: The Role of Labor Supply*. Cambridge, Mass.: Harvard University Press, 1967.

Kirkham, P. "Asian Women on Strike." *Women's Voice* 4 (1973): 11–12.

Klaasen, L. H. and Drew, P. *Migration Policy in Europe*. Lexington, Mass.: Lexington Books, 1973.

Klee, E., ed. *Gastarbeiter: Analysen und Berichte*. Frankfurt am Main: Suhrkamp, 1972.

Kosack, G. "Migrant Women: The Move to Western Europe: A Step Towards Emancipation?" *Race and Class* 17 (Spring 1976): 369–79.

Ligue Marxiste Révolutionnaire. *Capitalisme suisse et travailleurs étrangers*. Lausanne: Ligue Marxiste Révolutionnaire, 1970.

Lyon, M. "Ethnicity and Gujarati Indians in Britain." *New Community* 2, no. 1: 72–73.

Manvel, H. *Spanish-Speaking Children of the South West*. Austin: University of Texas Press, 1965.

Massenet, M. "Les travailleurs étrangers en France: un renfort nécessaire ou une source de conflit." *Hommes et migrations documents* 793 (September 1970).

Moore, R. "Immigrant Workers in Europe: A Spectre of New Slavery." *Patterns of Prejudice* 7, no. 4 (1973): 1–5.

N'Dongo, S. *La "co-opération" franco-africaine*. Paris, 1972.

Nikolinakos, M. *Politische Okonomie der Gastarbeiterfrage*. Hamburg: Rowalt Gmbh, 1973.

———. "Notes Towards a General Theory of Migration in Late Capitalism." *Race and Class* 17, no. 1 (Summer 1975): 5–17.

Ozanne, R. *A Century of Labor-Management Relations at McCormick and International Harvester*. Madison: University of Wisconsin Press, 1967.

Paine, S. *Exporting Workers: The Turkish Case*. Cambridge: Cambridge University Press, 1974.

Patterson, S. *Immigrants in Industry*. London: Oxford University Press for Institute of Race Relations, 1968.

Peach, C. *West Indian Migration to Britain.* London: Oxford University Press for Institute of Race Relations, 1968.

Pinet, F. *Travailleurs immigrés dans la lutte de classes.* Paris: Cerf, 1973.

Power, J. and Hardman, A. *Western Europe's Migrant Workers.* Minority Rights Group Report, no. 28. London, 1976.

Redford, A. *Labour Migration in England, 1800-50.* Manchester: Manchester University Press, 1926.

Rose, E. J. B. *Colour and Citizenship.* London: Oxford University Press for Institute of Race Relations, 1969.

Rüstow. "Gastarbeiter - Gewinn oder Belastung für unsere Volkswirtschaft." *Beinefte der Konjunkfurpolitik, Heft 13: Probleme der ausländischen Arbeitskräfte in der Bundesrepublik.* Berlin: Duncker und Humbolt, 1966.

Schechtmann, J. B. *Postwar Population Transfers in Europe 1945-55.* Philadelphia: University of Pennsylvania Press, 1962.

Smith, D. J. "The Nature of White Workers' Resistance." *New Society* 28 (1974): 696–99.

Stephen, D. and MacDonald, J. *The Invisible Immigrants.* London: Runnymede Trust, 1972.

Stirn, H., ed. *Ausländische Arbeiter im Betrieb.* Frechen/Köln: Bartmann Verlag, 1964.

Taylor, P. *Mexican Labor in the United States: Chicago and the Calumet Region.* Berkeley and Los Angeles: University of California Press, 1932.

Union Générale des Travailleurs Sénégalais en France. *Le livre des travailleurs africains en France.* Paris: UGTSF, 1970.

Ward, A. "European Capitalism's Reserve Army." *Monthly Review* 27, no. 6 (November 1975).

Wolstenholme, G. E. W., ed. *Immigration: Medical and Social Aspects.* London: J. A. Churchill, 1966.

Windisch, U. "Travailleurs immigrés et xenophobie: le cas de la Suisse." *Espaces et Societies* 4 (1971).

Wright, P. L. *The Coloured Worker in British Industry.* London: Oxford University Press, 1968.

Zubaida, S., ed. *Race and Racialism.* London: Tavistock Publications, 1970.

Not Elsewhere Classified

Form, W. H. "Occupational and Social Integration of Automobile Workers in Four Countries: A Comparative Study." *International Journal of Comparative Sociology* 10 (1969): 95–116.

Gordon, L. and Friedman, L. "Peculiarities in the Composition and Structure of the Working Class in the Economically Underdeveloped Countries of Asia and Africa: The Example of India and UAR." In *The Third World in Soviet Perspective,* edited by T. Thornton. Princeton: Princeton University Press, 1964.

Huizer, G. "How Peasants Became Revolutionaries: Some Cases from Latin America and Southeast Asia." *Development and Change* 6, no. 3 (1975): 27–56.

Jamieson, S. "Native Indians and the Trade Union Movement in British Columbia." *Human Organization* 20 (Winter 1961-1962): 219–25.

Kester, G. "Workers' Participation by Surprise." *Development and Change* 5, no. 3: 68–83.

Martínez-Alier, J. *Labourers and Landowners in Southern Spain.* London: George Allen & Unwin, 1971.

Newbury, C. "Colour Bar and Labour Conflict on the New Guinea Goldfields: 1935-1941." *The Australian Journal of Politics and History* 21, no. 3 (1975): 25–39.

Wipper, A. "A Comparative Study of Nascent Unionism in French West Africa and the Philippines." *Economic Development and Cultural Change* 13, no. 1: 20–55.

Journals Specializing in Migration to Western Europe

Die Volkswirtschaft/La vie économique. Bern. Monthly.

Droit et liberté. Paris. Monthly review of the Mouvement contre la Racisme, l'Antisémitisme et pour la Paix (MRAP).

France-Algérie. Paris. Monthly bulletin of the Association France-Algérie.

Hommes et migrations documents. Paris. Bimonthly. Etudes Sociales Nord Africaines (ESNA).

Hommes et migrations études. Paris. Quarterly. ESNA.

L'Algérien en Europe. Paris. Quarterly. Organ of Emigration Algérienne.

Migration News; Migrations; Menschen unterwegs. Geneva. Quarterlies. International Catholic Migration Commission (ICMC).

Migration Today. Geneva. Biannual. World Council of Churches.

Race; Race and Class. London. Quarterlies. Institute of Race Relations.

Race Today. London. Monthly. Institute of Race Relations.

Vivre en France. Paris. Quarterly review of Amicale pour L'Enseignement des Etrangers.

Wirtschaft und Statistik. Wiesbaden. Monthly.